KERBALĀ AND BEYOND

Yasin T. al-Jibouri

اللهم آرزقنا شفاعة الحسين

AuthorHouse™
1663 Liberty Drive
Bloomington, IN 47403
www.authorhouse.com
Phone: 1-800-839-8640

First published by AuthorHouse   8/26/2011

ISBN: 978-1-4634-2074-1 (sc)
ISBN: 978-1-4634-2070-3 (hc)
ISBN: 978-1-4670-2613-0 (e)

Library of Congress Control Number: 2011910041

Printed in the United States of America

اللهم صلِ على محمـد وآل محمد

السلام على الشيب الخضيب، السلام على الخد التريب

السلام على البدن السليب ، السلام على الثغر المقروع بالقضيب

السلام على الرأس المرفوع، السلام على الاجسام العارية في الفلوات

السلام على المرمل بالدماء، السلام على المهتوك الخباء

السلام على خامس أصحاب الكساء، السلام على غريب الغرباء

السلام على شهيد الشهداء، السلام على قتيل الأدعياء

السلام على ساكن كربلاء، السلام على من بكته ملائكة السماء
و رحمة الله و بركاته

O Allāh! Bless Muhammed and the progeny of Muhammed

Peace with the blood-drenched gray hair. Peace with the dust-covered cheek. Peace with the marauded body. Peace with the mouth beaten with the iron bar. Peace with the head raised [atop a spear]. Peace with the bodies exposed in the plains. Peace with the one covered with blood. Peace with the one whose privacy was violated. Peace with the fifth of the Fellows of the Covering Sheet. Peace with the stranger of all strangers. Peace with the martyr of all martyrs. Peace with the one killed by the *da'is*. Peace with the one who resides in Kerbalā. Peace with the one mourned by the angels of the heavens. Peace with you, O Father of Abdullāh…

TABLE OF CONTENTS

اللهم صلي على محمد و آل محمد

اللهم آرزقنا شفاعة الحسين

TREE LAMENTS AND BLEEDS ON *ĀSHŪRA*

In Qazween city, Iran there is an old tree which for so long has been wailing and lamenting the martyrdom of Imām Hussain (ع). Its branches bleed warm blood on the 10th Muharram, i.e. Āshūra, when the Imām was martyred, and it keeps doing so till the 11th night of Muharram. The faithful residing in Qazween and surrounding areas gather there and commemorate Āshūra.

■ الشجرة الدامية قبيل الفجر حيث يبدأ لونها يميل إلى الحمرة

Bleeding tree shortly before dawn when its color starts changing to red

■ آثار الدم الحسيني على الشجرة المعجزة بعد شروق الشمس

Marks of Hussaini blood visibly appear on the miracle tree after sunrise

The faithful take blood specimens to show others

In the Name of Allāh, the most Gracious, the most Merciful

PREFACE

This is the U.S. edition of the third of nine books written so far by Yasin T. al-Jibouri, and hopefully the reader will eventually read the others as well. The first was *Fast of the Month of Ramadan: Philosphy and Ahkam*, and the second was his best book yet titled *Allāh: the Concept of God in Islam*. Since the reader is most likely interested in knowing who the author is, we would like to state the following:

Al-Jibouri was born on August 14, 1946 in Baghdad, Iraq, and he lived most of his life in the holy city of al-Kādhimiyya (Kādhimain). In 1969, he graduated from the College of Arts, Baghdad University, where he majored in English which he taught at a high school in Babylon (Hilla) then at a vocational institute in al-Ahsa, Saudi Arabia, from which he flew in 1972 to the United States in order to pursue his Graduate degree which he earned in 1978. In the Winter of 1973, he founded the Islamic Society of Georgia, Inc. and started in January of 1974 editing and publishing its newsletter *Islamic Affairs* which evolved from a four-page newsletter to a twelve-page bulletin, becoming at the time the most widely circulated Shī'a (Shī'ite) publication in the United States with readers in all 50 U.S. States and in 67 countries world-wide.

In 1975, al-Jibouri received instructions to facilitate the entry to the United States of the very first representative of the then Grand Ayatullah Abul-Qasim al-Khoei, may Allāh reward him, in North America, namely Shaikh Muhammed Sarwar of Quetta, Pakistan.

Due to the author's sponsorship through his organization, the Islamic Society of Georgia, Inc., Shaikh Sarwar did, indeed, arrive at the U.S. on January 25, 1976; a few days later, the Shaikh became al-Jibouri's roommate in a very poor section of Atlanta, Georgia. A few months later, the Shaikh moved from Atlanta to New York where there has been a much larger Shī'a population.

Al-Jibouri not only writes his books, he often designs their covers as well. He developed a passion for computers, hardware and software, and in March of 1988, he obtained a Certificate with honours from N.R.I. of Washington, D.C., in microcomputers and microprocessors and later added to it three more Certificates in electronics and programming, including advanced programming. Putting that knowledge together, he wrote more than a hundred dBASE programs in order to accommodate his extensive and sophisticated mailing list and those of others, proving that we all ought to put modern technology at the service of Islam, Muslims and all mankind.

The author has edited and revised three English translations of the Holy Qur'ān by: 1) S.V. Mir Ahmed Ali, 2) A. Yusuf Ali, and 3) M.H. Shakir. He also edited *Nahjul-Balāgha* نهج البلاغة by Imām Ali ibn Abu Talib (ع) (published in New York, U.S.A., its 9th Edition is dated 2009; Library of Congress Catalog Number 2005900698; British Library Cataloguing in Publication Data; ISBN: Paperback 978-1-879402-34-8, ISBN: Casebound 978-1-879402-35-5). He also edited several newsletters and magazines, including *Middle East Business Magazine* of which he became Senior Editor. Among the other books which he edited are: *Socio-Economic Justice with Particular Reference to Nahjul-Balāgha* by Dr. S.M. Waseem, and *A Biography of Leaders of Islam* by Sayyid Ali Naqi Naqwi, English translation by Dr. Sayyid Nazir Hassan Zaidi, and *Your Kalima and the Savior* by Wajahat Hussain. He also edited 14 pamphlets for the youths titled *The Fourteen Infallibles* which were published in Beirut, Lebanon, in 1419 A.H./1998 A.D. and which were originally written by M.N. Sultan. They are very professionally produced pamphlets that employ pictorial narratives and an easy and flowing style, and they ought to be in the possession of each and every Muslim fāmily raising children and caring for the youths.

Al-Jibouri is the first person ever to translate works of the martyred economist imām Muhammad Bāqir al-Sadr such as:

1) *Contemporary Man and the Social Problem* الإنسان المعاصر و المشكلة الاجتماعية,
2) *A General Outlook at Rituals* نظرة عامة في العبادات,
3) *The General Bases of Banking in the Muslim Society* الاسس العامة للبنك في المجتمع الاسلامي, and
4) *What Do You Know About Islamic Economics?* ماذا تعرف عن الاقتصاد الاسلامي؟

The Author has also translated five other books where his name as the Translator was omitted for selfish reasons; these are: 1) *Best Month, Best Night*; 2) *The Book of Istikhara*; 3)*Weapon of the Prophets*; 4) *Miracles of the Holy Qur'ān* and 5) *The Great Names of Allāh.*

So far, the list of the books which he has written includes the following titles arranged chronologically according to their completion but not necessarily the date of publication: 1) *Memoirs of a Shī'a Missionary in America: Two Decades of Da'wah* (his auto-biography which details his experience in Islamic work in the U.S.), 2) *Fast of the Month of Ramadan: Philosophy and Ahkam*, 3) *Mary and Jesus in Islam*, 4) *Allāh: the Concept of God in Islam*, 5) *Muhammed: Prophet and Messenger of Allāh*, 6) *The Ninety-Nine Attributes of Allāh*, 7) *Kerbalā' and Beyond* (this book), 8) *Ghadīr Khumm: Where Islam was Perfected*, and 9) *Dictionary of Islamic Terms* (in three Volumes); the first Volume of this dictionary is about to go to the press, and the Glossary at the end of this book is excerpted from it.

The author translated 2 books by the famous religious authority the late Grand Ayatollah Muhammed al-Shirazi: 1) *Canon: A Glimpse at the Islamic Law*, and 2) *The Pathway to an Islamic Revival*. He has recently translated the following titles; the ISBN numbers for some of these books are available with the author who can be contacted via Facebook, Scribd, Linked-in and other professional Internet platforms:

1. *Kashf al-Reeba an Ahkam al-Gheeba* كشف الريبة عن أحكام الغيبة (removing doubt from gheeba [backbiting] rulings) by the First Martyr, Sheikh Taqi ad-Din Ibrahim son of Ali al-`Āmili,

2. *Pretension and Conceit* الرياء و العجب by Sayyid Ahmad al-Fahri,

3. *Uswat al-Ārifeen* أسوة العارفين by Mahmoud al-Badri,

4. *Amicable Companionship* العشرة بالمعروف: *Marriage and Divorce, Obligations, Rights and Mannerisms* by Sayyid Mahdi al-Ameen under the auspices of the main U.S. representative office of Iraq's highest religious authority, namely Grand Ayatollah Sayyid Ali al-Seestani, in Dearborn, Michigan,

5. *Khums* الخمس for the main U.S. representative office of Iraq's highest religious authority, al-Seestani, in Dearborn, Michigan,

6. *Al-Siraj* السراج: *The Lantern on the path to Allāh Almighty* by Shaikh Husain ibn Ali ibn Sādiq al-Bahrāni and

6. *Heart Comforter at the time of the loss of children and loved ones* مسكن الفؤاد في فقد الأحبة و الأولاد By Zayn al-Din Ali ibn Ahmad al-Jab'i al-Āmili.

Al-Jibouri also completed the translation of مرشد المغترب "Expatriate Guide" by His Holiness Grand Ayatollah Sayyid Muhammed-Saeed al-Hakim. His next project includes the translation of the four volumes of الالهيات, lectures of mentor/professor Jaafar al-Subhani written by Shaikh Hassan Muhammed Makki al-Āmili.

Al-Jibouri is a well known translator, and he is the very first person ever to translate the works of Martyr Muhammed Bāqir as-Sadr, the greatest economist, philosopher, author and political figure in the modern history of Iraq, such as: *A General Outlook at Rituals* (which was published in 1979), *Contemporary Man and the Social Problem* (which was published in 1980), *The General Bases of Banking in the Muslim Society* (which was published in Maryland, U.S.A., in 1981), and *What Do You Know About Islamic Economics?* which was published by the Imāmia Center of Lanham, Maryland, U.S.A., in the month of Ramadan 1410 A.H./April 1990

A.D. When Imām Muhammed Bāqir as-Sadr was martyred in 1980,, al-Jibouri shifted his attention to politics, putting out several pamphlets, circulars, letters to the news media and two newsletters, *Islamic Revival, Rafidain News, Al-Muqatiloon* and *Al-Intifada*. *Islamic Revival* was dedicated to the Islamic liberation movements throughout the Muslim world in general and in Iraq in particular.

Al-Jibouri twice published his translation titled *A General Outlook at Rituals* here in the U.S., getting their latest registered with the Library of Congress of Washington, D.C. He also translated and/or published many other titles; among them are: *A Biography of Muhammed Bāqir as-Sadr, The Form of Islamic Government and Wilayat al-Faqeeh, About the World Political Situation from a Muslim's Viewpoint*, and *Our Faith*. The latter work is written by Sayyid Muhammed Hussain al-Jalali, a famous scholar, researcher, critic and theologian presently living in Chicago, Illinois.

Other works which the author of this book has translated are: *A Biography of Imām ar-Ridha* (by the late Shaikh Muhammed Jawad Fadlallāh; this book was published in the United Kingdom, *Al-Murāja'āt: A Shii-Sunni Dialogue* (by Sharafud-Deen Sadr ad-Deen al-Musawi; this book was published in Beirut, Lebanon, in 1415 A.H./1995 A.D. It had previously been translated and published under the title *The Right Path*). It later was published by Ansāriyan first in 2001 then in 2005. Its fourth edition was reprinted in 2008 and is presently receiving world-wide circulation through the marketing of international booksellers in the United States and Europe. He also translated *Shī'as are the Ahl as-Sunnah* الشيعة هم أهل السنة (by Dr. Muhammed at-Tijani as-Samawi; this book was published in New York by Vantage Press and is available for sale on the Internet from both Amazon Books and Barnes and Noble, and its ISBN number is: 0-533-12055-1. The reader is strongly urged to get his/her own copy of it; its first copies were sold "like hot cakes;" therefore, Vantage Press had to reprint it a number of times till the present, and it is being marketed world-wide), and *Maqtal al-Hussain* (ع) مقتل الحسين by the late Abd ar-Razzaq al-Muqarram, which is the major reference utilized for writing this book. *Maqtal al-Hussain*, in turn was primarily based on a book by the same title written by the great Sunni writer al-Zamakhshari about whom the reader will come to know later in this book, *Insha-Allāh* (God willing).

Al-Jibouri has also written numerous essays and articles dealing with various themes. Most of them were published in more than one publication, whereas he circulated the others on his own throughout the U.S. and abroad. Several of his articles were published in *Islamic Monitor*, a fairly short-lived top quality magazine (lived for less than 3 years) which used to be published in Washington, D.C. Among such articles carried the following headings: "An Interview with Professor Fazlallah Reza" (once chancellor of the University of Tehran, Ambassador at Paris to the United Nation's UNESCO and Ambassador of the Islamic Republic of Iran to Canada), "Violation of Women's Rights in Saudi Arabia," "Bahrain: A Shameful Human Rights Record," "The Drug Epidemic," and many others. Some of his political writings appeared in *Echo of Islam*. His other writings also appeared in *Mahjubah* magazine, in *Jafari Observer* magazine of Bombay, India, and elsewhere.

Yasin T. al-Jibouri is discussed in detail by Prof. Larry Poston in his book *Islamic Dawah in the West: Muslim Missionary Activity and the Dynamics of Conversion to Islam* (New York, United States, and Oxford, United Kingdom: Oxford University Press, 1992; ISBN No. 0-19-507227-8). One of the essays, which he wrote and widely circulated at his own expense despite his acute financial hardship, is an extensive, thorough and exhaustive research rebutting Samuel P. Huntington's famous article "The Clash of Civilizations?" which appeared in *Foreign Affairs* magazine in the Summer of 1993. His rebuttal is actually a laborious research which consumed two weeks of his time, effort and many sleepless nights; it is dated October 26, 1993. He plans to post it on his Scribd web site in the near future, *Insha-Allāh*.

Thanks are due to Sr. Zeinab Donati for her effort to prepare this book's manuscript for publication. Her suggestions and input have been invaluable, and may she be richly rewarded on behalf of all those who will benefit from this book. Efforts of Sr. Zainab Tahir al-Bayati in setting Arabic type of some poems eulogizing Imām al-Hussain (ع) are also greatly appreciated. Some of these poems have

13

been copied and pasted from Internet sites, while others were extracted from other sources, scanned then incorporated into this text. It is hoped that in the future, those who love the Imām (ع) will exert an effort to typeset these poems in a better way and earn rewards from the Almighty with Whom Imām al-Hussain (ع) surely enjoys a special status. May the Almighty assist all of us and keep our feet firm on His Right Path, *Assirāt al-Mustaqeem*, *Allāhomma Āameen*.

PROLOGUE

ETERNAL STRUGGLE BETWEEN RIGHT AND WRONG

This is a tale of an ongoing struggle between right and wrong, truth and falsehood, piety and impiety, worldliness and spirituality. Such struggles take place in our life each and every day on different scales. Other religions, too, have immortalized the struggle between right and wrong: the struggle of Rama against Ravana, the contest between Moses, peace be with him, and Pharaoh, the challenge of Abraham, peace be with him, to Nimrud, the contest of Jesus Christ, peace be with him, against Herod... All these are examples of the contest, the struggle, the ongoing war, between right and wrong, truth and falsehood. Falsehood appears to the eyes of most people as being very strong, armed with material power. It has the authority of the ruling government, of the veto at the "U.N. Security Council," of the awe of military might, the carriers and the cruise missiles, the satellites and the spy planes, the lackeys and the stooges, the silver and the gold, and the numerical superiority... Its ostentatious grandeur and splendor cannot be denied, nor can its glittering crowns, thrones studded with gems, palaces and dazzling swords... And the truth! The humble truth! The meek and weak truth! It appears helpless, handicapped, powerless... But the truth possesses the vigor of faith, the reliance on the Almighty, and the precious asset of spiritual power. These armaments of the truth are so powerful, they smash the head of falsehood, reducing its splendor and grandeur to dust. Truth, in the end, triumphs, achieving success so splendidly that the world is awe-stricken... Such is the epic of heroism recorded on the pages of history not with the ink of the writers but with the blood of the martyrs. Such is each and every epic of heroism... Such is the epic of martyrdom of Imām al-Hussain (ع).

In the Name of Allāh, the Most Gracious, the Most Merciful

INTRODUCTION

This book contains a brief yet documented narrative of an incident that took place in Kerbalā', Iraq, in 61 A.H. (After Hijra, or Hegira)/680 A.D. It has stamped the history of the Muslim nation ever since, and it will continue to do so till the reappearance of the Awaited One, the Mahdi from among the offspring of Prophet Muhammed (ص). It refers to a revolution against tyranny and oppression led by Imām al-Hussain (ع) son of Imām Ali ibn [son of] Abū [father of] Talib (ع) and grandson of Prophet Muhammed (ص). The confrontation left a lone male survivor from Imām al-Hussain's camp: Imām al-Hussain's son Ali, titled "as-Sajjād," the one who quite often prostrates to Allāh, and also "Zain al-Ābidīn," the best of worshippers of Allāh. He later became the fourth in the series of the Twelve Infallible Imāms (ع). His offspring migrated to north Africa where they founded the Fatimide caliphate that lasted from 296 - 566 A.H./909 - 1171 A.D. Having conquered Egypt in 358 A.H./969 A.D., they built Cairo in order to make it their capital and founded in the next year the al-Azhar mosque and university. The latter was founded by caliph "al-Muizz li Deenillah," Abū Tameem Maadd ibn al-Mansur who was born in 319 A.H./931 A.D. and died in 365 A.H./975 A.D.; he ruled from 341 A.H./953 A.D. till his death.

The bloody confrontation between Hussain's tiny group of family members and supports and the huge army raised according to orders issued by the ruler of his time, namely Yazid "son" of Mu'awiyah , which is referred to in history books as the Taff Battle, started on the first day of Muharram, 61 A.H./October 4, 680 A.D. and ended ten

16

days later with the barbaric killing of Imām al-Hussain (ع) and all males with him—with the exception of his ailing son referred to above, namely Ali—, including his infant Abdullāh, who was six months old and who was shot with an arrow in the neck. Imām al-Hussain (ع) was pleading to those folks to give Abdullāh some water to drink. Imām al-Hussain (ع) and his small band were not permitted to the end to have access to the water of the Euphrates that lied a short distance from their camp. This reveals the extent of cruelty of those who fought Imām al-Hussain (ع) and his small band of supporters, the brave defender of principles and the reformer of the nation that he was, the man whom the Prophet on many occasions praised and honoured as one of the Masters of the Youths of Paradise, the other Master being his older brother Hassan (ع). Imām al-Hussain's body was trampled under the hoofs of the soldiers' horses and his head was cut off, placed on top of a spear and paraded before his women and children, who were all tied and chained as captives and conveyed in the most cruel manner the entire distance from Kerbalā', as the Taff area came to be called, to Damascus, Syria, seat of the Umayyad tyrant Yazid "son" of Mu'awiyah ibn Abū Sufyan. The heads of the other heroes who fought on Imām al-Hussain's side were also cut off and paraded in the same manner as trophies although Islam does not permit the mutilation of anyone's body, be he a Muslim or a non-Muslim. Little did those killers care to know about Islam, and the same can be said about those who refrain from condemning them and who, thus, share in the burden of sins those killers shall bear on the Day of Judgment.

The primary sources of this book are: *Maqtal al-Hussain* by Abdul-Razzaq al-Musawi al-Muqarram, and *Tarikh al-Umam wal Muluk* by Abū Ja'far Muhammed ibn Jarar at-Tabari (better known as *Tarikh at-Tabari*). Several secondary references, in Arabic and English, have been consulted and are cited in elaborate footnotes.

It is hoped that this book will open the eyes of new Muslim converts in the West in general and here in the U.S. in particular so that they may see the other side of the coin. Most of them were not taught Islamic history because, in most likelihood, it would indict their mentors. It is also hoped that such converts will realize the pitfalls of little knowledge which is surely a dangerous thing.

There is a story behind every book. This one is no exception. As of the date of writing this Introduction (Shawwal 1419 A.H./February 1999), Northern Virginia Muslims who love and revere Imām Hussain (ع) do not have a place of their own where they can assemble to commemorate the Kerbalā' tragedy, the greatest of all; therefore, they have to meet here and there, mostly at homes and apartments of their brethren who can accommodate them. The most prominent of such dedicated brethren have been: Hamzah ash-Shawwaf (nicknamed Abū Muhammed-Ali), Abdul-Muhsin as-Sa'igh (Abū Abdul-Aziz), and Ahmed al-Haddad (Abū Abdullāh). These brethren have always opened their homes and hearts to all those who cherish the memory of Imām Hussain (ع) and of all other Imāms belonging to the Prophet's Progeny, "Ahl al-Bayt," peace and blessings of Allāh be upon all of them. During the past commemoration (Muharram 1419/May 1998), an Azari brother named Salashour who runs a rug store tried his best to make us feel at home, permitting us to use the premises of his business for the first ten days of the month of Muharram. It was there and then that another very dedicated brother named Ja'far Madan suggested that I write a few pages in English about the martyrdom of Imām Hussain (ع) in order to circulate them on the Internet. Alhamdu-Lillah, both I and he did what we promised. Then Br. Madan asked me whether I would consider turning those few pages into a book for the American and European readers. We liked the idea. You see, a good word, a wise suggestion, is like a seed; if it finds the right soil, it will shoot roots and sprout, and soon a seed becomes a tree bearing fruit, and the fruit carry seeds that will eventually be sowed, and they, too, will set roots, sprout and bear fruit..., and so on. May the Almighty bless and reward our dear brother Ja'far Madan for his suggestion, and may He bless all other dedicated brethren like him. May He forever guide our steps to what He loves and prefers, *Allāhomma AAameen.*

As the Dedication suggests, the publication of this book has been made possible by the generosity of a number of such dedicated lovers of Imām al-Hussain (ع), and of his Ahl al-Bayt (ع), and who reside in metropolitan Washington, D.C., and elsewhere. The author apologizes if some of the photographs are not of good quality. May

18

the Almighty reward all those who brought this book to light and who circulate it and help others benefit from it with the very best of His rewards in the life of this world and in the hereafter, *Allāhomma Āmeen.*

PART I

HUSSAIN AND HIS FOES, MARTYRDOM

ABŪ SUFYAN

Abū Sufyan was a wealthy and influential man who belonged to the Banu Umayyah clan of the once pagan tribe of Quraish of Mecca, Hijaz, that fought the spread of Islam relentlessly during the time of the Prophet of Islam (ﷺ). He was contemporary to the Prophet of Islam (ﷺ) whom he fought vigorously. His date of birth is unknown, but he died in 31 A.H./652 A.D. "Abū Sufyan" is his *kunya*, surname; his name is Sakhr ibn Harb ibn Umayyah. He is father of Mu'awiyah and grandfather of Yazid.

Abū Sufyan led pagan Quraish in its many wars against Prophet Muhammed (ﷺ) and his small band of supporters, making alliances with other pagan tribes and with the Jews of Medīna against the new rising power of Islam. He kept leading one battle after another till the fall of Mecca to the Muslims in 630 A.D. It was then that he had to either accept the Islamic faith or face a sure death for all the mischief he had committed against the Muslims, so he preferred to live in hypocrisy as a "Muslim," though only in name, rather than accept death. He was the most cunning man in all of Arabia and one of its aristocrats and men of might and means. He saw Islam as the harbinger of the waning of his own personal power and prestige and those of his tribe, Quraish, not to mention the decline of his faith, paganism, and the pre-Islamic way of life to which he and his likes were very much accustomed, the life of promiscuity, lewdness and debauchery, with all the wine, women and wealth aristocrats like him very much enjoyed. His likes are present throughout the Islamic lands in our time and in every time and clime... This has always been so, and it shall unfortunately remain so...

MU'AWIYAH AND YAZID

Mu'awiyah son of Abū Sufyan was born out of wedlock in 602 A.D. during the *jahiliyya*, the time of ignorance, the period that preceded Islam. His mother, Maysun, was one of his father's slave-girls. Maysan had a sexual intercourse with one of Mu'awiyah's slaves and conceived Yazid by him. Mu'awiyah, in total disregard for Islamic or traditional Arab traditions, claimed Yazid as his son. A testimony to this fact is the well-documented tradition of the Prophet (ص) wherein he said, "The murderer of my [grand]son al-Hussain is a bastard." This tradition is quoted on p. 156, Vol. 1, of Kanz al-Ummal of al-Muttaqi al-Hindi. The stigma of being a bastard applies actually not only to Yazid but also to both Shimr ibn Thul-Jawshan and Ubaydullāh ibn Sa'd, the accomplices about whom the reader will read later; all of these men were born out of wedlock.

Mu'awiyah played a major role in distorting the Islamic creed by paying writers to tailor design "traditions" to serve his interests and support his deviated views. He installed  himself as ruler of Syria in 40 A.H./661 A.D. and ruled for twenty long years till his death at the age of seventy-eight. Shortly before his death, which took place in the month of Rajab of 60 A.H./May of 680 A.D., he managed to secure the oath of allegiance to his corrupt and immoral son Yazid as his successor. He did so by intimidation once and once by buying loyalty and favours, spending in the process huge sums of money that belonged to the Muslims. The weak-minded majority of the Muslims of his time swore allegiance to him. This proves that the majority does not necessarily have to be right. Imām al-Hussain (ع), together with a small band of devotees to the cause of truth, refused to bow their heads to the oppressive forces, hence this tale of heroism.

Mu'awiyah declared himself "caliph" in Syria when he was 59 years old and assumed authority by sheer force. He was not elected, nor was he requested to take charge. He did not hide this fact; rather, he bragged about it once when he addressed the Kufians saying, "O people of Kūfa! Do you think that I fought you in order that you may establish prayers or give zakat or perform the pilgrimage?! I know that you do pray, pay zakat and perform the pilgrimage. Indeed, I fought you in order to take command over you with contempt, and Allāh has given me that against your wishes. Rest assured that whoever killed any of us will himself be killed. And the treaty between us of amnesty is under my feet."[1]

Mu'awiyah's rule was terror in the whole Muslim land. Such terrorism was spread by many convoys sent to various regions. Historians have narrated saying that Muawiyh summoned Sufyan ibn 'Awf al-Ghamidi, one of the commanders of his army, and said to him, "This army is under your command. Proceed along the Euphrates River till you reach Heet. Any resistance you meet on your way should be crushed, and then you should proceed to invade Anbar. After that, penetrate deeply into Mada'in. O Sufyan! These invasions will frighten the Iraqis and please those who like us. Such campaigns will attract frightened people to our side. Kill whoever holds different views from ours; loot their villages and demolish their homes. Indeed, fighting them against their livelihood and taking their wealth away is similar to killing them but is more painful to their hearts."[2]

Another of his commanders, namely Bishr ibn Arta'ah, was summoned and ordered to proceed to Hijaz and Yemen with these instructions issued by Mu'awiyah: "Proceed to Medīna and expel its people. Meanwhile, people in your way, who are not from our camp, should be terrorized. When you enter Medīna, let it appear as if you are going to kill them. Make it appear that your aim is to exterminate

---

[1]Ibn Abul-Hadid, *Sharh Nahjul-Balagha* شرح نهج البلاغة, Vol. 16, p. 15.

[2]*Ibid.*, Vol. 2, p. 86.

them. Then pardon them. Terrorize the people around Mecca and Medīna and scatter them around."[1]

During Mu'awiyah's reign, basic human rights were denied, not simply violated. No one was free to express his views. Government spies were paid to terrorize the public, assisting the army and the police in sparing no opportunity to crush the people and to silence their dissent. There are some documents which reveal Mu'awiyah's instructions to his governors to do just that. For instance, the following letter was addressed to all judges: "Do not accept the testimony of Ali's followers (Shī'as) or of his descendants in (your) courts." Another letter stated: "If you have evidence that someone likes Ali and his fāmily, omit his name from the recipients of rations stipulated from the *zakat* funds." Another letter said, "Punish whoever is suspected of following Ali and demolish his house."[2] Such was the situation during the government of Mu'awiyah, Yazid's infamous father. Historians who were recording these waves of terror described them as unprecedented in history. People were so frightened, they did not mind being called atheists, thieves, etc., but not followers of Imām Ali ibn Abū Talib (ع), Prophet Muhammed's right hand, confidant and son-in-law.

Another aspect of the government of Mu'awiyah was the racist discrimination between Arabs and non-Arabs. Although they were supposed to have embraced Islam which tolerates no racism in its teachings, non-Arabs were forced to pay *khiraj* and *jizya* taxes that are levied from non-Muslims living under the protection of Muslims and enjoying certain privileges, including the exemption from the military service. A non-Arab soldier fighting in the state's army used to receive bare subsistence from the rations. Once, a dispute flared up between an Arab and a non-Arab and both were brought to court. The judge, namely Abdullāh ibn amir, heard the non-Arab saying to his Arab opponent, "May Allāh not permit people of your kind (i.e. Arabs) to multiply." The Arab answered him by saying, "O Allāh! I

---

[1]*Ibid.*

[2]*Ibid.*

invoke You to multiply their (non-Arabs') population among us!" People present there and then were bewildered to hear such a plea, so they asked him, "How do you pray for this man's people to multiply while he prays for yours to be diminished?!" The Arab opponent said, "Yes, indeed, I do so! They clean our streets and make shoes for our animals, and they weave our clothes!"

Imām al-Hussain's older brother, Imām al-Hassan (ع), was elected in Medīna on the 21st of the month of Ramadan, 40 A.H./January 28, 661 A.D. as the caliph, but his caliphate did not last long due to the terrorism promoted by Mu'awiyah who either intimidated, killed, or bribed the most distinguished men upon whom Imām al-Hassan (ع) depended to run the affairs of the government. Finally, Mu'awiyah pushed Imām al-Hassan (ع) out of power after signing a treaty with him the terms of which were, indeed, honourable and fair, had they only been implemented. Finding his men too weak or too reluctant to fight Mu'awiyah, Imām al-Hassan (ع) had no alternative except to sign the said treaty with a man whom he knew very well to be the most hypocritical of all and the most untrustworthy. Since there are too many ignorant folks who dare to blaspheme and cast doubt about the integrity of Imām al-Hassan (ع), we have to review the terms of that treaty and leave the reader to draw his own conclusion; those terms, in brief, were:

1) **Mu'awiyah shall rule according to the Holy Qur'ān and the Sunnah of the Prophet (ص) in the territories under his control.**
2) **Mu'awiyah shall have no right to nominate his successor.**
3) **All people in Syria, Iraq, Hizaj and Yemen shall lead their lives safely and securely.**
4) **The lives and properties of the followers (Shī'as) of Imām Ali ibn Abū Talib (ع), wherever they may be, shall remain safe and secure.**
5) **Mu'awiyah shall not try, openly or secretly, to harm or to kill Imām al-Hassan (ع) son of Imām Ali ibn Abū Talib (ع), his brother Imām al-Hussain (ع), or any other member of the family of the Prophet (ص), nor shall they be threatened or terrorized.**
6) **The abusive language, the cursing of Imām Ali (ع) during**

Mu'awiyah had ordered all Imāms who led congregational prayers not to descend from their pulpits before cursing Ali (ع), a practice which they labeled as "Sunnah." It is documented that one such Imām forgot once to curse Ali (ع), whereupon people shouted at him that he had violated the Sunnah. Those who prayed at home and who forgot to curse Ali (ع) after their prayers felt obligated to repeat them, being convinced that such cursing was an integral part of the compulsory prayers without which they would not be accepted by Allāh... Such abominable blasphemy continued from the year when Othman was killed, that is, 35 A.H./656 A.D. till it was terminated by orders of the only righteous Umayyad caliph, namely Omer ibn Abdul-Aziz, one year after his becoming caliph, that is, in 100 A.H./718 A.D., for a total of 62 years. Historians say that the public actually did not stop cursing Ali (ع) even then but continued to do so for at least 18 more years, extending the total to 80 years... Omer ibn Abdul-Aziz was killed in 101 A.H./719 A.D. after having ruled for only two years and five months because he was fair and just and, most importantly, because he was sympathetic to the Prophet's family (Ahl al-Bayt); peace and blessings of Allāh be with him.

Shortly after concluding the said treaty, Mu'awiyah lured Imām al-Hassan's wife, Juda daughter of al-Ash'ath ibn Qays, into poisoning her husband with the promise that he would marry her off to his son and heir apparent Yazid. Juda killed her husband who died on Safar 28, 50 A.H./March 30, 670 A.D. She was cursed by the Almighty with an embarrassing ailment for which nobody could find any cure. Mu'awiyah, as expected, did not fulfill his promise.

Having succeeded in getting Imām al-Hassan (ع), Imām al-Hussain's older brother, killed, Mu'awiyah sent letters to one of his Umayyad relatives, namely Marwan ibn al-Hakam, a cousin of Othman ibn Affan and bearer of his seal, a seal which he used quite often for his own gains and even without the knowledge of the aging caliph, instructing him to obtain the oath of allegiance for his son Yazid as his (Mu'awiyah's) successor. By the way, the Umayyads succeeded in making this same Marwan caliph in 64 A.H./683 A.D., and his government lasted for seventeen months till it ended in 65 A.H./684-85 A.D. when he died at the age of 63 and was buried in Damascus. Marwan, accordingly, delivered a speech following the prayers and concluded it by saying, "The commander of the faithful (meaning Mu'awiyah) is of the view that he chooses his son Yazid to succeed him as your ruler following in the footsteps of Abū Bakr and Omer ibn al-Khattab..." He was at that moment interrupted by Abdul-Rahman son of first caliph Abū Bakr. "Nay!," Abdul-Rahman ibn Abū Bakr shouted, "You mean in the footsteps of Kisra (Khosro, emperor of Persia) and Caesar (emperor of Rome)! Neither Abū Bakr nor Omer appointed their sons or relatives as their successors...!"

In 51 A.H./671 A.D., Mu'awiyah performed the pilgrimage then went to Medīna where he called to his presence Abdullāh son of second caliph Omer ibn al-Khattab. His father, Omer , succeeded Abū Bakr as the caliph in 13 A.H./634 A.D.; he remained caliph for ten years till he was killed by a Persian slave in the month of Thul-Hijja, 23 A.H./November 644 A.D. He was succeeded by Othman ibn Affan who ruled for eleven years (till 35 A.H./656 A.D.). Mu'awiyah said to Abdullāh ibn Omer, "O son of Omer ! You used to tell me that you never liked to sleep one night without knowing who your Imām (here the word means "ruler") is, and I warn you against spreading the seeds of dissension among the Muslims or corrupting their views." Abdullāh praised Allāh then said, "There were other caliphs before you who had sons who were not inferior to yours, yet they did not decide to do what you have decided to do regarding your son. Rather, they let the Muslims make their own choice. You warn me against dissension, and I am not an advocate of dissension. I am just one of the Muslims, and if they are unanimous regarding an issue, I will then add my voice to theirs." Having said so, Abdullāh left. Then Muhammed, son of first caliph Abū Bakr, referred to above, was presented before Mu'awiyah. The latter started his rhetoric but Abdul-Rahman interrupted him by saying, "All you want to say is that you wish we obey your son after obeying Allāh, and this, by Allāh, we will never do. And, by Allāh, we shall settle this issue by mutual consultation among the Muslims; otherwise, we will treat you as you were treated at the dawn of

Islam...!" Then he, too, stood up and left.

Yazid son of Mu'awiyah was born in 17 A.H./645 A.D. and inherited his father's post in 60 A.H./680 A.D. He ruled for only three years and one month then died in mid-Rab'iul-Awwal of 64 A.H./December 14, 683 A.D. at the young age of 38. He was a playboy, a drunkard, and a man who used to enjoy seeing animals fight. He used to play with animals. Monkeys were dressed in gold-embroidered multi-colored clothes and trained to dance for him, and he had salaried "officials" to look after his animal collection. Such collection included monkeys and race dogs. He was fond of gambling and wine drinking, and he demonstrated disrespect towards the Mosque of the Prophet (ﺹ) and towards the Ka'ba itself, causing very serious damages to its structure as the reader will come to know in a later part of this book. He forced women to take their veils off and killed thousands of innocent people and encouraged the rape of women, girls, and children during the uprisings that took place in Hijaz, particularly in the Harra incident, details of which will follow. In short, Yazid did not have one iota of respect for Islamic tenets or moral ethics. Strange enough, there are some ignorant Muslims who sing his praise, justify and defend his barbaric conduct...

This much gives the reader an idea about what type of persons Abū Sufyan, Mu'awiyah, and Yazid were. Now let us review the brief biography of their opponents.

ALI, HUSSAIN'S FATHER

Imām al-Hussain's father, Ali (ﻉ), needs no introduction, but for the benefit of those who do not know much about him, we would like to state the following:

Ali was born in May of 600 A.D. inside the Ka'ba, the holiest of all holy places in Islam, the cubic symbol of "Allāh's House" in Mecca, Hijaz, northern part of today's Saudi Arabia, the only country in the world named after its ruling dynasty! No other human being was ever born in the holiest of holies besides him. Ali (ﻉ) was raised and cared for by his cousin Muhammed (ﺹ), the Messenger of Allāh, who wished to return the favor Ali's father had done him when he was a child. You see, when Muhammed (ﷺ) was orphaned, Ali's father, Abū Talib, took him in his custody and raised him, so Muhammed (ﷺ) wanted to return the favor especially after seeing how Abū Talib's trade business was not doing well in his old age. Muhammed (ﷺ)'s upbringing of Ali (ع) polished the lad's personality and prepared him to play a major role in the dissemination of the Islamic creed. He was the first male to believe in Muhammed (ﷺ) and to offer prayers with him. The second was another young man who was also raised and cared for by Muhammed (ﷺ), namely Zaid ibn Harithah who later commanded the army of the Muslims during the Battle of Mu'ta of 629 A.D., and so did his son Usamah in 632 A.D., both proving their military ability, insight and wisdom. The third to embrace the Islamic faith was Muhammed's longtime friend Abū Bakr.

When pagan Meccans wanted to assassinate Muhammed (ﷺ) in 622 A.D., Ali (ع) slept in his (Muhammed's) bed, offering his life as a sacrifice to save his, while the Prophet succeeded in leaving his house safely even under the nose of the infidels, having recited the first eight verses of Sūrat Yasin (Chapter 36 of the Holy Qur'ān) and thrown a handful of dust before their eyes. They could not see him leave. Muhammed (ﷺ) safely reached Quba, a suburb of Medīna where he camped and waited for Ali (ع) to rejoin him. He did not want to enter Medīna triumphantly without Ali (ع). After a few days, Ali (ع) walked all alone the entire distance from Mecca to Medīna, about 250 Arabian miles, arriving there with swollen and lacerated feet, bleeding and fatigued.

Ali (ع) defended Islam in the Battle of Badr (624 A.D.) and married Fātima, the Prophet's only surviving offspring, in the same year. He also fought in the Battle of Uhud in the next year, in the Battle of Moat (Khandaq) in 627 A.D., in the Battle of Khayber (against the Jews of Medīna) in 628 A.D., and took part in the Conquest of Mecca in 630 A.D. He also fought in the Battle of Hunain in the same year. On Thul-Hijjah 18, 10 A.H., corresponding to March 19, 632 A.D., and according to divine orders which Muhammed (ﷺ) had received from his Lord in the form of Qur'ānic verse No. 67 of Sūrat al-Ma'ida (Chapter 5), the Prophet of Islam delivered a speech at a place between Mecca and Medīna known as Ghadīr Khumm in the Juhfa valley wherein he enumerated some of Ali's merits and informed the huge crowd of an estimated 132,000 pilgrims who had accompanied him during his last pilgrimage, the Farewell Pilgrimage, that just as they had accepted him as the Prophet, they were bound to accept Ali (ع) as "Ameerul-Mu'mineen," Commander of the Faithful, title of one who rules the Muslims as the supreme political leader and, at the same time, as the highest religious authority. Details of and references to this historic event are recorded, with the entire original Arabic text (23 pages) of the Prophet's historic sermon, are in my book titled *Ghadīr Khumm: Where Islam was Perfected.*

Because of the numerous battles in which Ali (ع) participated and the number of those whom he killed, he was not popular with those who considered blood relations more important than earning the Pleasure of the Almighty; therefore, only a few months after that date did some people promote Abū Bakr, a wealthy Meccan and a very successful businessman, to the post of "Ameerul-Mu'mineen." This took place in 11 A.H./632 A.D. He ruled for two years and a half, dying on a Tuesday, 13 A.H./634 A.D. at the age of 63... They promoted Abū Bakr to be "Ameerul-Mo'minnen" instead of Ali (ع), forgetting or pretending to forget what they had heard from and pledged to the Prophet (ص) only two months and nine days ago at Ghadīr Khumm. This took place immediately after the Prophet's demise on Safar 28, 11 A.H./May 28, 632 A.D. (By the way, like all lunar Hijri years, the solar calendar year 632 of the Christian Era coincided with both the 10th and the 11th Hijri years.)

Imām Ali (ع) did not receive any significant recognition during the reign of the first three caliphs, and even his wife's property, Fadak, was confiscated; thus, his family was deprived of a good source of income. Abū Bakr ordered the confiscation in 632 A.D. The only just and fair Umayyad ruler, namely the last one, Omer ibn Abdul-Aziz, returned Fadak to Fātima's offspring in 718 A.D., 86 years after its confiscation with profound apologies. When Ali (ع) was elected as caliph in 36 A.H./657 A.D., tribalism and racism were as rampant as they used to be during the pre-Islamic era. Islam's teachings were either forgotten or distorted. In Syria, Mu'awiyah ibn Abū Sufyan had declared himself "caliph" and was buying people's conscience and loyalty. He was, once more, raising one army after another to fight Ali (ع) just as his father Abū Sufyan had raised one army after another to fight Muhammed (ص), causing tens of thousands of Muslims to be killed in the process. Most of Ali's time was spent in defending law and order; he hardly had time to rest and to improve the conditions which he knew were in need of improvement because of the injustices of past regimes that did not protect the Islamic creed from liars and fabricators of traditions, indirectly assisting in the distortion of the Sunnah.

Caliph Ali (ع) had to fight the Battle of Jamal (Camel), which broke out at the end of Rab'i II 36 A.H./June 28, 632 A.D., the forces of dissent which had been herded and led by Aisha daughter of the same Abū Bakr mentioned above and one of the Prophet's wives. She was then nineteen years old and was riding a huge camel named Askar, hence the name of the battle: Harb al-Jamal, battle of the camel. She kept urging her men to fight Ali (ع) and his men. It was the first time that Muslims killed Muslims, and such killing has been going on ever since. Look at Afghanistan, Algeria, Iraq and Iran (during the 1980s when more than a million Muslim lives were lost), and remember the civil wars in Lebanon, Somalia, Yemen, and elsewhere... History repeats itself. Those who do not learn from the mistakes of past generations are doomed, condemned and destined to repeat them, rest assured. Aisha accused Ali (ع) of having collaborated with those who had killed her Umayyad relative Othman ibn Affan who became caliph in 24 A.H./645 A.D. and ruled till he was killed in 35 A.H./656 A.D. when he was 89. Ali (ع), in fact, had sent both of his sons, Imām al-Hassan (ع) and Imām al-Hussain (ع) (the latter being the hero of this brief report), to defend Othman who was placed by the angry protesters under virtual house arrest and his mansion was twice subjected to a siege. Water and food supplies were blocked from reaching him. Ali (ع) used to get water and food smuggled to Othman's mansion during the night passed on from one person to another from one flat rooftop to another till they reached Othman's mansion. The public outrage stemmed from Othman's mismanagement of public funds and preference of his own relatives over all others for top government jobs even when such relatives were not fit at all to occupy any government post. He himself lived in luxury unseen before, getting mansions built for him and for his wife, and silk clothes and exotic perfumes were being imported especially for him and for her. His wife, Na'ila daughter of al-Qarafisah, used to wear so much jewelry that people could hear the jingle from a distance! Such should not be the conduct of successors of Prophets. While defending Othman, Imām al-Hassan (ع) received a wound on his forehead. But the huge number of the angry crowd finally assaulted Othman's mansion and dealt him blows with their swords, killing him instantly. It was the first time Muslims killed their caliph. Na'ila tried to defend her husband with her bare hands, getting four of her fingers cut off. She sent those fingers together with the copy of the Holy Qur'ān which Othman was reciting when he was killed and which was stained with his blood to Mu'awiyah in Damascus to use them to excite people and to urge them to seek revenge for Othman's murder.

Aisha, ironically, was one of those who had urged the Muslims to kill Othman, making her historic statement which we would like to quote here in its original Arabic text verbatim: أقتلوا نعثلا فقد كفر "Uqtulu Na'thalan faqad kafar," that is, "Kill Na'thal, for he has committed apostasy." Na'thal was a contemporary Jew famous for his untidy and too long beard; hence, Aisha was comparing Othman with a Jew. She, in fact, was trying to get either Talhah ibn Ubaydullāh, her cousin who aspired to marry her after the demise of the Prophet (ص), something which Islam prohibited, or az-Zubair ibn al-Awwam, son of her older sister Asma' daughter of Abū Bakr, become caliph instead of Ali (ع). Az-Zubair ibn al-Awwam did, in fact, succeed in declaring himself as the caliph after rebelling against the Umayyads as the reader will come to know in the chapter dealing with the Harra incident. Aisha disliked Ali (ع) very much despite all the praise lavished on him by her husband, the Messenger of Allāh (ع), and although he did not do anything to warrant such an attitude.

There is no room here to detail all the grievances the Muslims raised against their caliph, Othman, in addition to the above, for these would fill an entire volume, and books have, in fact, been already written about this subject. One such book is titled الفتنة الكبرى Al-Fitnatul-Kubra (the greatest dissension) by the renown Egyptian scholar Dr. Taha Hussain (winner of a Nobel prize for literature) and published in Cairo, Egypt, a book which the author may have modelled after at-Tabari's book bearing the exact title and dealing with the same theme. One of the best references written about the Battle of the Camel is al-Mas'ūdi's famous book مروج الذهب *Muraj at-Thahab*. Ali (ع) won the battle; 13,000 men from aisha's camp and 5,000 from Ali's were killed, according to p. 177, Vol. 5, of *Muraj at-Thahab*. The heaviest casualty was the loss of thousands who knew the entire text of the Holy Qur'ān by heart and whose knowledge, during that critical time, was crucial. The Prophet of Islam has said: موت العالم موت العالم "Mawt al-aalim mawt al-aalam," that is, "The death of a scholar spells the death of the world." What is the world without scholars? It is darkness without light, trees without fruit, river without water... Islam very much encourages scholarship and reveres scholars, writers, intellectuals, researchers, scientists, etc.

After the Battle of Camel, Ali (ع) had to fight the Battle of Siffeen (40 A.H./661 A.D.) against the army of Mu'awiyah ibn Abū Sufyan, Yazid's father. Shortly after that, and in the same year, and to be exact on the 19th of the month of Ramadan, 40 A.H./January 29, 661 A.D., Ali (ع) was killed by Ibn Muljim al-Muradi, one of the Kharijites, those who were fed-up with certain Muslim caliphs and with some of the latter's un-Islamic practices. These Kharijites had been crushed by Ali (ع) in the Battle of Nahrawan, which started on Safar 6, 38 A.H./July 17, 658 A.D., but their remnants scattered thereafter throughout the Islamic lands. When he was killed, Ali (ع) was leading the morning prayers at Kūfa's grand mosque. Ali (ع) was the embodiment of everything Islam stands for. Even his name, Ali (ع), is derived from "Al-Aliyy," one of the Amighty's ninety-nine Attributes known as Asma' Allāh al-Husna, Allāh's most beautiful names. Scholars of tafsir, exegesis of the Holy Qur'ān, have identified numerous Qur'ānic verses praising Ali (ع) and his family, his Ahl al-Bayt أهل البيت. The most widely known of such verses is No. 33 of Chapter 33 of the Holy Qur'ān (Ayat at-Tathir, Sūrat al-Ahzab).

This much should suffice the reader to form an idea about Imām al-Hussain's father, so let us now discuss the hero of our story.

> قال رسول الله (ص): "حسين مني و أنا من حسين؛ أحب
> الله من أحب حسينا"

The Messenger of Allāh (ص) has said, "Hussain is of me, and I

> السَّلام عَلَى الْحُسَيْنِ ، وَعَلَى عَلِيِّ بْنِ الْحُسَيْنِ ، وَعَلَى أَوْلادِ الْحُسَيْنِ وَعَلَى أَصْحابِ
> الْحُسَينِ

**Peace with al-Hussain, with Ali son of al-Hussain, with the
offspring of al-Hussain and with the companions of al-Hussain**

IMĀM HUSSAIN SON OF IMĀM ALI (ع)

Imām al-Hussain (ع), the Master of Martyrs and the hero of this
brief history review, was the greatest spiritual leader of his time in
the entire world of Islam. He was an Imām, the brother of an Imām,
and the son of an Imām. None in history ever enjoyed such merits.
All religious authorities admitted his moral, spiritual and religious
superiority over everyone else. They admitted that if there was an
individual fit for the spiritual and religious vicegerency of the Holy
prophet of Islam (ع), Imām al-Hussain (ع) was the person best suited
for it. Imām al-Hussain (ع) was born in Medīna on the 15th of the
month of Ramadan, 3 A.H./March 1, 625 A.D. and was named " al-
Hussain" which means "Junior al-Hassan," since his older brother is
named " al-Hassan." Ali (ع) chose to name both his sons after
Shabar and Shubayr, sons of prophet Aaron, older brother of Prophet
Moses, peace be with both of them. Even during his childhood,
Imām al-Hussain (ع) was known for his brilliance, piety, and lofty
upbringing. His grandfather, the Prophet of Islam, surrounded him
with his affection and taught him a great deal, making him the
custodian of Allāh's knowledge, and so did Imām al-Hussain's
mother, Fātima (ع), the Head of all the Women of the World, and so
did his father Imām Ali (ع) whom the Prophet (ص) took as a
"brother" when he joined the Ansār and the Muhajirun with the bond
of brotherhood following his historic migration from Mecca to
Medīna. The Prophet (ص), who never uttered a word out of
favoritism or in response to an emotional outburst, called Imām al-
Hussain (ع) and his older brother Imām al-Hassan (ع) "Masters of
the Youths of Paradise;" all the residents of Paradise are young.

Imām al-Hussain's life and status in the Islamic history are formidable. Fātima (ع), his mother, was the dearest daughter of her father (ص). At-Tirmithi cited Usamah ibn Zaid ibn Harithah (referred to above) saying that the Prophet (ص) had said, "The dearest member of my family to me is Fātima." She was declared by the Prophet as the Head of all the Women of the world. She and her husband were members of the family who were distinguished for their qualities and services to Islam. They are role models for all Muslim men and women. Their role was an extension of the Prophet's role in leading the great cultural transformation from the darkness of an infidel culture to the light of Islam, the beacon of guidance and the guarantor of happiness in this life and in the one to come.

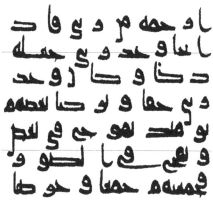

Page of the Holy Qur'ān handwritten by Imām al-Hussain (ع)

Historians recorded the birth of Imām al-Hussain (ع) as an exciting event for the Muslims of Medīna and especially for the Prophet of Allāh (ع). The Muslims congratulated each other for the new child whom the Prophet considered as his own son. The Prophet once declared, "Hussain is of me, and I am of Hussain. O Allāh! Be pleased with whoever pleases al-Hussain!" This testimony was not accidental, nor was it the result of emotional expressions. This declaration came from a responsible wise leader, the Prophet of Allāh, who would never commit a mistake during the performance of his Prophetic mission. It is easy to understand the first part of this weighty statement: " al-Hussain is of me," for surely Imām al-Hussain (ع) was of the Prophet's own lineage through his daughter Fātima.(ع). But what about the other half, that of "and I am of al-Hussain"? How could the grandfather be of his grandson? If you consider this statement in the light of the role Imām al-Hussain (ع) played in Islam's history, you will understand what the Prophet meant. He simply meant to say, "And my Message is to be continued through al-Hussain's martyrdom." The Prophet, in this statement, was delivering an important message and foretelling people of who would act as the fountainheads of Islamic guidance and who would guard his divine message in the future. Emotions and sentiments are not loose in a Muslim's life but are controlled by Islamic concepts and principles. There is always a criterion for "like" and "dislike" which evolves from the deeply rooted Islamic concepts. Although Abū Lahab was an uncle of the Prophet (ص), his infidelity made him cursed till the Day of Judgment. The same applied to another uncle, Abū Jahal. The Prophet of Allāh made another statement which leaves no doubt about Imām Imām al-Hassan's and Imām al-Hussain's roles. As indicated above, he (ع) said, " al-Hassan and al-Hussain are the masters of the youths of Paradise." This was presented as a credential to the Muslim nation so that it would uphold their leadership.

At a certain time, the Muslims in Medīna realized and appreciated the Islamic message's glory and sweet tasting fruits, so they intended to reward the Prophet (ص) for his efforts in guiding them out of the darkness of jahiliyya and into the light of Islam. The gift they presented to the Prophet (ص) was some gold which they had collected. The Prophet's answer came not from him personally but, rather, from his Lord on his behalf in the text of the following Qur'ānic verses which were revealed during this very incident:

Say (O Muhammed !): "No reward do I ask you for this (conveying of the Message) except that you be kind to those of my kin." (Qur'ān, 23:42)

Muhammed Jawad Maghniyyah, author of تفسير الكاشف _Tafsir al-Kashif_[1], narrates saying that when this verse was revealed, people asked the Prophet (ص), "O Messenger of Allāh! Who are these of your kin for whom respect is made obligatory on us by this verse?" The Prophet (ص) answered, "They are Ali, Fātima, and their two sons." However, this did not imply disrespect for other members of

---

[1]The fourth edition of this famous 7-volume _tafsīr_ adorns our library and it was published in Beirut, Lebanon, in Thul-Qi'da 1410 A.H./June 1990 A.D. by Dar al-Ilm lil Malayeen (P.O. Box 1085, Beirut, Lebanon).

his kinsfolk or companions. Looking objectively at the message of this verse, it will indicate to you, first of all, reluctance to accept material rewards. If a reward is not suitable, it cannot, and it must not, be accepted. Hence, the verse was enjoining respect for specific people, not because they are only the Prophet's relatives. But the real reason behind this respect was to safeguard the Islamic message. The role these holy personalities played in the Islamic history required such respect in order to enable them to perform their duties.

Al-Hakim quoted Au Sa'd al-Khudri saying that the Prophet (ص) once said, "One who dislikes us, we Ahl al-Bayt [ع] (family of Prophet Muhammed [ص]), Allāh shall hurl him into the fire of Hell." This implies that those who dislike the Islamic conduct and way of life as personified by these individuals, through their exemplary conduct, shall receive the Almighty's condemnation and shall taste of His torment.

Jābir ibn Abdullāh al-Ansāri[1], a maternal relative and one of the greatest of all companions of Prophet Muhammed (ص), narrated once saying that in a speech delivered immediately following the performance of his last pilgrimage, the Farewell Pilgrimage referred to above, the Prophet (ص) said, "O people! I am leaving among you the Book of Allāh and my Itrat (Progeny) for your guidance. So long as you hold fast to them both (at the same time), surely you will never stray." This tradition was narrated not only by Jābir but also by at least twenty other eyewitnesses who heard it in person and who participated in that same pilgrimage, and their statements are recorded in numerous references. Such statements were transmitted by chains of trusted narrators of hadīth. In his renown book Sahīh,

---

[1]Jābir ibn Abdullāh al-Ansāri is a maternal relative and one of the greatest *sahabis* of Prophet Muhammed (ص), a first-class traditionist and a most zealous supporter of Imām Ali ibn Abū Talib (ع). When the Prophet (ص) migrated from Mecca to Medīna in 622 A.D., he was hosted by Jābir for one week. According to *Al-Isti'ab*, Jābir died at the age of 94 in 74 A.H./693 A.D. (some say in 77 and others in 78 A.H./696 or 697 A.D. respectively), and his funeral prayers were led by Aban ibn Othman, then governor of Medīna. He was the very last to die from among the Prophet's closest companions.

Muslim cites some of them. In another tradition transmitted by Abū Tharr al-Ghifāri, the Prophet (ص) is quoted as saying, "O people! Let my family act among you like the head of the body, and like the eyes of the head among you." These traditions are impressive in many respects. First, they were narrated by different sources of different inclinations; this adds to their credibility. Second, the same content indicates their consistency, underscoring their authenticity.

Imām al-Hussain (ع) was one member of the family of the Prophet (ص). He was brought up in the Prophetic guidance where he received the direct attention of the Prophet (ص). The ideal atmosphere where he had grown up with his grandfather, father, mother, and elder brother, was the highest level ever attained. Thus, he acquired wisdom and learned generosity, bravery, piety while attaining the highest knowledge. He occupied outstanding posts during his father's caliphate. During the terror and corruption which swept the Muslim world at the hands of the Umayyad dynasty that ruled the Islamic world (from 661 - 750 A.D.) with an iron fist, he was the sole hope of the Muslims to restore the Islamic laws and to thus bring them prosperity, peace, and happiness in both worlds.

Having seen how his older brother Imām al-Hassan (ع) was betrayed by his friends and poisoned by his foes, Imām al-Hussain (ع) remained in seclusion from the public for ten years, feeling helpless against the tide of Umayyad corruption and tyranny. Gradually, people realized that none could save them from such tyranny except Imām al-Hussain (ع) himself, so they kept appealing to him to lead them against the Umayyads, and he kept ignoring their pleas due to his knowledge that he could not rely on them to remain steadfast on the battlefield against Mu'awiyah's mighty Syrian army, being convinced that they would betray him just as they had betrayed his older brother and his father. They did exactly so as you will see...

Most of the pleas came from the people of Kūfa, Iraq, mostly Shī'as who were subjected to untold atrocities by Kūfa's then governor (appointed on behalf of the central Umayyad government in Damascus) Muhammed ibn al-Ash'ath and the top men who supported him and his Umayyad superiors, namely Shurayh, Kūfa's judge, a typical preacher of the rulers, by the rulers, and for the rulers, a man who was issuing verdicts according not to the teachings of the Holy Qur'ān and the Sunnah but to please the Umayyads who were paying his salary and showering him and his likes with gifts from time to time, and Omer ibn Sa'd. The letters those Kufians sent to Imām al-Hussain (ع) numbered ten to twelve thousand, and many of them threatened Imām al-Hussain (ع) of questioning him before the Almighty on the Day of Judgment as to: "Why did you not respond to the people who sought your assistance to put an end to tyranny and oppression?" Imām al-Hussain (ع) had to oblige despite all the odds against him. He, in fact, knew fully well that he was marching to his death, having already been informed of his martyrdom in the land of Kerbalā' by none other than his holy grandfather who even named his killer. He was informed of his women and children taken captive and of the time and day when he would be martyred. Everything was already decreed, and Imām al-Hussain (ع) had no choice except to fulfil a decree by sacrificing himself and all the dear ones with him for the sake of Islam. We only wish here to unveil the startling aspects of the revolution's message which is often neglected in its traditional commemoration.

Confronting all the details of this momentous event, we have to answer many pressing questions such as: Why did this revolution

take place? What were its implications and procedures? And what were its conclusive results? The answers may provide a guiding light so that we may form our conclusions. The following account is based on the most popular and trustworthy authorities on the subject.

To understand Imām al-Hussain's personality and the collective culture of the society, a summary of Islam's view of life is necessary.

ISLAM'S MESSAGE TO HUMANITY
Islam is a way of life. It gives reasons and sets a purpose for living.

38

We were not placed on earth by accident or without a purpose. Everything in life has a purpose; every being has a role to play; every inanimate object serves an end. Islam elevates the spirit while satisfying the material needs...

Islam considers man as God's vicegerent on earth. This status is a lofty and weighty one, but it is also critical: the requirements must be met, the conditions must be satisfied; the mission must be accomplished. Thus, man is in an envied position and, consequently, his acts and norms of conduct are expected to conform with the high level he is to occupy.

The Islamic concepts and laws are inseparable parts of the Islamic ideology; milk is inseparable from water. They make up the practical expression of Islam in society and in life as a whole. These concepts and laws are essentially to harmonize people's relationships with each other, with other beings, with nature and the environment and, above all, with the Creator.

The basic Islamic outlook of this life is one of an introductory course; the real life is the one to come, not this one. This worldly life is a prelude to another eternal one; therefore, this world is a preparatory stage for people in order to attain the spiritual level which permits them to enter Paradise. It is a microcosm of the real eternal macrocosm. The other side of the picture is the horror of Hell for people who misuse or abuse the power placed at their disposal. Hence, success and failure are not measured by the known criteria of this world, by, say, materialistic supremacy, wealth and power. The Islamic criteria differ from the materialistic ones; they account for the life hereafter; they take into consideration the next phase of our existence. Death is not the end of everything; it is the beginning of real life. To die is to wake up from a brief dream. To please Allāh is the sublime goal which surpasses all other wishes and desires, or so should it be. This by no account means that we should neglect acquiring materialistic supremacy, wealth and riches, by legitimate means; it only means that we must put such supremacy, or such wealth, in its rightful place: to serve man and to please Allāh. What a noble concept! It is with pleasing Allāh and with His support that Muslims seek materialistic supremacy. Alas! The Muslims now do not have any materialistic supremacy at all. Their natural resources are being sold for less than it costs to produce them; their countries are supermarkets for goods manufactured by those who despise them and look down upon them; their leaders can hardly agree on one common cause, and their nations have no say about who should rule them and who should not, and they are robbed of their freedom of expression, worship, and movement. Turkey, for example, used to be the center of the Islamic world and the source of its pride and glory. Now its ruling juntas, supported by non-Muslim and anti-Islamic "superpowers," by Zionists and imperialists, are fighting Islam with all their might and means. The same can be said about the rulers of many other countries who are Muslims only in name. The Muslims are now prisoners in their own homes. They are the underdogs of the world. Gone are the days of their supremacy and glory and shall never return unless and until they regret and return to their creed and practice it as it should be.

ORIGINS OF DEVIATION

How did Mu'awiyah ascend to the post of ruler of the Muslims, and how did he dare to claim succession to the Prophet (ص), the irreligious, liar, cheating, cunning and conniving man that he was? What happened to the Muslim world? Why was it silent at seeing the assumption of power by an ignoble person like Yazid? Indeed, it is astonishing to witness the indifference and irresponsibility demonstrated by the vast majority of Muslims. One is tempted to say that such indifference is present even in our own time. Our time, in fact, can best be described as the neo-*jahiliyya*. There are already too many Yazids but no al-Hussain to come to the rescue. Islamic values and ideals were as if totally alien to the society. What happened to the dynamic forces that had awakened the world and shaken it like never before? The Prophet's voice had not yet died away regarding the responsibility of the Muslims. He once said, "One who sees a cruel governor violating Allāh's laws, breaking His covenant, acting in contrast to the tradition of the Prophet, committing mischief and intruding upon peoples' rights, without trying to change that governor through his action, or speech,

Allāh will then reserve a suitable place for him in Hell."

We all may wonder about the causes of deviation which led to this deplorable state of affairs. We know for sure that Islam is a perfect and practical religion, a complete way of life. Islam, no doubt, assured us of guiding us to a secure and prosperous life. The question of deficiency in the Islamic message, however, if there is such deficiency at all, or in the way it was conducted by the Prophet (ص), has no place here. The only possible shortcomings, therefore, are confined to the subsequent status of the Muslims, to their way of handling their affairs, and to their conformity to the Islamic laws besides the "natural" obstacles encountered in the sequence of events. Following is the major cause that contributed to the deplorable status quo of the Muslims of the time and is still contributing to that of our own and will continue to do so till the end of time.

FALSIFICATION OF *HADĪTH* AND DISTORTION OF THE *SUNNA*

The worst mischief upon which Mu'awiyah embarked was the fabrication of hadīth, traditions detailing what the Prophet of Islam (ع) said or did. Hadīth is one of the two sources of Islam's legislative system, the Shari'a. Selecting Imām Ali (ع) as his lifetime's adversary, Mu'awiyah soon found out that his cause was hopeless. Ali's merits were very well recognized by every Muslim while Mu'awiyah's family and dismal conduct were the objects of their contempt. Mu'awiyah's past record was dark and shameful whereas that of Ali (ع) was glorious and shining, full of heroism in defense of Islam.

In order to sustain his campaign and raise the status of his likes, Mu'awiyah had to attract the remnant of some companions of the Prophet (ص) whose characters were known as weak and who had a genuine interest in this world and in its vanishing riches. He employed them to fabricate traditions custom-designed to his own tailoring. This trend of fabricating hadīth constituted a grave danger to the integrity of the Islamic tenets. Hadīth is second in importance to the Holy Qur'ān. It was very important to ward off such a danger. To expose such a trend to the Muslims at large was very vital, pivotal, of the highest priority. It would be accomplished by exposing and disgracing those who embarked upon committing and nurturing such a terrible mischief. Imām al-Hussain's revolution broke out in order to undertake this very task.

Let us now review a few samples of fabricated traditions[1].

Abū Hurayra is supposed to have quoted the Prophet (ص) as saying, "Allāh has trusted three persons for His revelation: Myself, Gabriel and Mu'awiyah." We wonder what Allāh was doing for the revelation when Mu'awiyah was in the camp of the infidels. This quotation is cited by Ibn Asakir, Ibn Uday, Muhammed ibn Aa'ith, Muhammed ibn Abd al-Samarqandi, Muhammed ibn Mubarak al-Suri and al-Khateeb al-Baghdadi who all quote Abū Hurayra saying, "سمعت رسول الله يقول: ان الله انتمن على وحيه ثلاثة أنا و جبرائيل و معاوية." Imagine! He even puts his name before that of arch-angel Gabriel! *Astaghfirullāh!*

According to al-Khateeb al-Baghdadi, Abū Hurayra claimed, " ناول النبي معاوية سهما فقال: خذ هذا السهم حتى تلقاني به في الجنة!" The Prophet (ص) gave Mu'awiyah an arrow then said to him, "Take this arrow until we meet in Paradise." What a lucky arrow to enter Paradise! Let us stop here to discuss this man, Abū Hurayra, who may have had the lion's share in distorting the Prophet's Sunnah especially when we come to know that he was quoted by a host of *tabi'in* who in turn are quoted by hundreds others who in turn are quoted by thousands others..., and so on and so forth. This is why his name is in the forefront of narrators of *hadīth*.

There is no agreement about what Abū Hurayra's name was, nor

---

[1]For more information about this man, Abū Hurayra, refer to *Shī'as are the Ahl as-Sunnah*, a book written in Arabic by Dr. Muhammed at-Tijani as-Samawi and translated into English by myself. It is available for sale from Vantage Press, Inc., 516 West 34th Street, New York, N.Y. 10001, or you may order it through the Internet's worldwide web: www.amazon.com. Its title in the said web is "Shī'as are the Ahl as-Sunnah."

when he was born or when he died. He is said as having died in 59 A.H./678 A.D., and some say that his name was Abdul-Rahman ibn Sakhr al-Azdi, while others say it was Umair ibn amir ibn Abd Thish-Shari ibn Taraf. But it is agreed upon that he belonged to the Yemenite tribe of Daws ibn Adnan and that his mother's name was Umaima daughter of Safeeh ibn al-Harith ibn Shabi ibn Abū Sa'd; she, too, belonged to the Daws tribe. It is said that the Prophet (ص) nicknamed him "Abū Hurayra" after a kitten to which he was attached. He accepted Islam in 7 A.H./628-9 A.D. immediately after the Battle of Khaybar, and he was then more than thirty years old. He was one of those indigent Muslims who had no house to live in, so they were lodged at the Suffa, a row of rooms adjacent to the Prophet's mosque at Medīna. These residents used to receive the charity doled out to them by other Muslims. He used to see the Prophet (ص) mostly when it was time to eat. He missed most of the battles in defense of Islam waged after that date although he was young and healthy and capable of serving in the army.

What is the meaning of his title "Abū Hurayra", man of the kitten? Ibn Qutaybah al-Dainuri quotes Abū Hurayra on p. 93 of his book titled *Al-Ma'arif* المعارف as saying, "... و كنيت بأبي هريرة بهرة صغيرة كنت ألعب بها "... And I was called 'Abū Hurayra' because of a small kitten I used to play with." In his *Tabaqat* book, Ibn Sa'd quotes Abū Hurayra as saying, " كنت أرعى غنما و كانت لي هرة صغيرة فكنت اذا كان الليل وضعتها في شجرة فاذا أصبحت أخذتها فلعبت بها فكنوني أبا هريرة" "I used to tend to a herd, and I had a small kitten. When it was night time, I would place her on a tree. When it was morning, I would take her and play with her, so I was called 'Abū Hurayra' [man of the small kitten]."

The time Abū Hurayra spent in the company of the Prophet (ص), that is to say, on and off, is by the most generous estimates three years, yet this man narrated more traditions of the Prophet (ص) than anyone else in history. The total number of "traditions" which he attributed to the Prophet (ص) reached the astronomical figure of 5,374 of which only 326 are quoted by al-Bukhari, the most famous compiler of hadīth, and who endorses no more than 93 of them! Muslim, another compiler of hadīth, endorses only 89 of Abū Hurayray's alleged ahadīth. These facts and figures are stated in the famous classic reference titled Siyar Alam an-Nubala' by at-Thahbi.

Compare this unrealistic figure of 5,374 "traditions" attributed to the Prophet (ص) and compiled during less than three years with the 586 traditions compiled by Ali ibn Abū Talib (ع), the Prophet's cousin and son-in-law who was raised by the Prophet (ص) since his birth in 600 A.D. and who followed the Prophet (ص) like his shadow for 32 years. Compare it with the figure of 142 traditions narrated by Abū Bakr, one of the closest companions and a longtime friend of the Prophet (ص) and one of the earliest to embrace Islam. Compare it with the figure of 537 traditions narrated by the second caliph Omer ibn al-Khattab and with the 146 traditions narrated by Othman ibn Affan, keeping in mind that all these men knew how to read and write whereas Abū Hurayra was illiterate; he could neither read nor write...

The Umayyads found in Abū Hurayra the right man to fabricate as many "traditions" as they needed to support their un-Islamic practices and then attribute them to the Prophet (ص), hence the existence of such a huge number of traditions filling the books of the Sunnah. And the Umayyads rewarded Abū Hurayra very generously. When he came from Yemen to Hijaz, Abū Hurayra had only one single piece of striped cloth to cover his private parts. When Mu'awiyah employed Abū Hurayra to work in the factories producing custom-designed "traditions," he rewarded him by appointing him as the governor of Medīna. He also married him off to a lady of prestige for whom Abū Hurayra used to work as a servant and built him al-Aqeeq mansion. Who was that lady?

She was Bisra daughter of Ghazwan ibn Jābir ibn Wahab of Banu Mazin, sister of Prince Utbah ibn Ghazwan, an ally of Banu Abd Shams, the man who was appointed by Omer ibn al-Khattab as governor of Basra. Utbah ibn Ghazwan was a famous *sahabi* and a hero of Islam, and he died during the time of Omer ibn al-Khattab. The Umayyads married Abū Hurayra off to Utbah's sister, Bisra, a number of years after the death of her famous brother. He used to work for Bisra as a servant. Ibn Hajar al-Asqalani mentions Bisra in the first setion of his famous work *Al-Isaba fi Akhbar al-Sahāba* and says the following about Bisra, " و كانت قد استأجرته في العهد النبوي ثم تزوجها بعد ذلك لما كان مروان يستخلفه في امرة المدينة على عهد معاوية " She used to let him work for her during the time of the Prophet, then he

44

Night view of the Prophet's Mosque in Medīna, Saudi Arabia

married her after that when Marwan [ibn al-Hakam] used to let him be in charge of Medīna during the time of Mu'awiyah." In his *Tabaqat*, Ibn Sa'd quotes Abū Hurayra as saying the following about his wife, Bisra, " ...أكريت نفسي من ابنة غزوان على طعام بطني و عقبة رجلي فكانت تكلفني أن أركب قائما، و أورد حافيا، فلما كان بعد ذلك زوجنيها الله فكلفتها أن **تركب قائمة و أن تورد حافية!!** "I placed myself at the service of the daughter of Ghazwan in exchange for food for my stomach and for something to wear on my feet... She used to order me to ride while serving her and to approach her barefoot to serve her. After that, Allāh made her my wife, so I ordered her to ride as she served me and to approach me barefoot!!" Thus, Abū Hurayra "got even" with the unfortunate lady!

Abū Hurayra found himself during the Umayyads' reign of terror and oppression a man of wealth and influence, owning slaves and having servants. Prior to that, Omer ibn al-Khattab appointed him as governor of Bahrain for about two years during which Abū Hurayra amassed a huge wealth, so much so that people complained about him to Omer who called him to account for it. Finding his excuse too

45

petty to accept, Omer deposed him. Omer also questioned him about the unrealistically abundant traditions which he was attributing to the Prophet (ص), hitting him with his cane and reprimanding him for forging traditions and even threatening to expel him from the Muslim lands. All these details and more can be reviewed in famous references such as: Ar-Riyad an-Nadira الرياض النضرة by at-Tabari, in Vol. 4 of the original Arabic text of al-Bukhari's *Sahīh*, where the author quotes Abū Hurayra talking about himself, in Abū Hurayra by the Egyptian scholar Mahmoud Abū Rayyah, in سير أعلام النبلاء *Siyar Alam an-Nubala'* by at-Thahbi, in شرح نهج البلاغة *Sharh Nahjul-Balāgha* by Ibn Abul-Hadad, in البداية و النهاية *Al-Bidaya wal Nihaya* by Ibn Katheer, in طبقات الفقهاء *Tabaqat al-Fuqaha* by Ibn Sa'd (also famous as Tabaqat Ibn Sa'd), in تأريخ الأمم و الملوك *Tarikh al-Umam wal Muluk* by at-Tabari, in تاريخ الخلفاء *Tarikh al-Khulafa* by as-Sayyuti, in فتح الباري *Fath al-Bari* by Ibn Hajar al-Asqalani, in المستدرك *Al-Mustadrak* by al-Hakim, and in numerous other references. Yet some Muslims label Abū Hurayra as "Islam's narrator," propagating for his fabrications without first studying them in the light of the Qur'ān and going as far as invoking the Almighty to be pleased with him....

Abdullāh ibn Omer (ibn al-Khattab), too, claimed that the Prophet said, "You will see greed after me and things with which you will disagree." People, he went on, asked, "O Messenger of Allāh! What do you order us to do then?" The Prophet, Abdullāh continued, said, "Give the governor what is his and plead to Allāh for yours." Islam, true Islam, never condones toleration of unjust rulers. Another fabricated tradition is also by Abdullāh ibn Omer who quoted the Prophet (ص) saying, "Put up with whatever conduct you do not like of your rulers because if you abandon the جماعة Jama'a (group) even the distance of one foot and then die, you will die as unbelievers." Surely many despots ruling the Muslim world nowadays can appreciate such "traditions" and will not hesitate to publicize for them and be generous to those who promote them; they would give them generous salaries and build them mansions... Such fabricated "traditions" are not only in total contrast with the Qur'ān and the Sunnah as well as with other verified traditions, they invite the Muslims to be the slaves of their rulers. This is exactly what Mu'awiyah wanted, and this is exactly what so-called "Muslim" rulers like him want in our day and time... Unfortunately for the Muslims and fortunately for their enemies, there are quite a few "Muslim" rulers like this Mu'awiyah. This is why there is poverty, ignorance, dictatorship, injustice, oppression and subjugation to the enemies of Islam throughout the Muslim world nowadays.

YAZID APPOINTED AS SUPREME RULER

Yazid's grandfather, Abū Sufyan, advised and managed the infidel's campaigns against Islam till the conquest of Mecca, as stated above. His wife Hind (mother of Mu'awiyah and grandmother of Yazid) tried to chew the liver of Hamzah, uncle of the Prophet (ص), because of her burning hatred and cannibalism. Mu'awiyah, too, was an active opponent of Islam. Indeed, Abū Sufyan's family was performing the strategic, financial and morale boosting in the infidel's campaign against the Muslims for many years. Their efforts, wealth and diplomacy formed a great obstacle in the way of spreading Islam.

Time had lapsed and Mecca was suddenly besieged with the considerably large forces of the Muslims. The unbelievers in Mecca were stunned at seeing the Muslim fighters who had caught them by surprise, thanks to the shrewd military tactics of the Prophet (ص). Thus, the infidels, including Abū Sufyan, had no choice except to abandon their arrogance and to accept Allāh's sovereignty, or so did most of them pretend. Mu'awiyah was then 28 years old. Having seen how his father "accepted" Islam, though reluctantly, he fled for Bahrain where he wrote his father a very nasty letter reprimanding him for his "conversion." It is not clear when Mu'awiyah brought himself to profess adherence to the Islamic creed. During this incident, i.e. the fall of Mecca to the Muslims, which was accomplished on a Friday, the 20th of the month of Ramadan, 8 A.H., corresponding to January 14, 630 A.D., less than two years before the Prophet's demise, historians recorded some peculiar stories about Abū Sufyan's family; however, there is one thing certain: They accepted Islam unwillingly, and they were treated in a special way on that account. For instance, they were given more than their share of the treasury in order to gain their hearts and win them over to Islam. But whether this generosity had any effect in producing any change at all in their attitude is quite another story.

47

Indeed, subsequent events revealed the fact that no change at all had taken place in their way of thinking.

Clock Tower overlooking the Ka'ba Haram, Mecca, Saudi Arabia

Yazid was brought up in such a family whose atmosphere was electrified with emotions of its dead who fought Islam and who were killed mostly during Islam's first major battle, that of Badr which broke out on a Friday, the 17th of the month of Ramadan, 2 A.H., corresponding to March 16, 624 A.D. and to which the Holy Qur'ān refers in 8:5-11. Seventy prominent pagan Quraishites were killed in it, half of them at the hands of Imām al-Hussain's father Ali ibn Abū Talib (ع). That, by the way, was Ali's first battle; he was 24 years old. Among the Umayyads who were killed in it were: Utbah, father-in-law of Yazid's father Mu'awiyah, Utbah's son al-Walid ibn al-Mugharah (father of the famous military leader Khalid ibn al-Walid), and Shaybah, Utbah's brother. Al-Walid ibn al-Mugharah is cursed in the Holy Qur'ān in 74:11-30 (Sūrat al-Muddaththir). Utbah is father of Hind, mother of Yazid, who tried to chew the liver of Hamzah, Prophet Muhammed (ص)'s dear uncle and valiant defender of Islam. Add to this the fact that such family witnessed how those who had killed their kinsfolk received full honour, recognition, and respect by the entire community, not to mention the wasted wealth, the injured pride, and the loss of privileges which they used to enjoy during the pre-Islamic period known as the *jahiliyya*. Yet Yazid himself had some unique characteristics in the negative and adverse sense of the word in addition to what we recorded above. He was known as a playboy; he is on record as the first person ever to compose pornographic poetry. He described each and every part of his aunt's body for sensual excitement, doing so without being reprimanded by his father or mother or anyone else. Historians record his being seen drunk in public, his committing adultery, and his leading quite a corrupt life, a life which did not last for long, thank Allāh. In one of his poetic verses, Yazid stated, "The family of Hashim (the Prophet's clansmen) staged a play to get a kingdom. Actually, there was neither news from Allāh (*wahi*) received nor a revelation."

Mu'awiyah was not ruling as an individual but was representing a way of thinking which differed in nature from everything Islam stands for. However, he was not satisfied to leave the ruling stage without making sure that it was properly looked after. His pragmatic and materialistic mind drove him to prepare for the crowning of his son, Yazid, as his successor. Mu'awiyah had made many pledges not to install Yazid when he saw the conditions at the time not conducive to such a plan because Muslims were still politically conscious and desired to see the restoration of the Islamic laws and values. Mu'awiyah, hence, had a difficult job at hand before leaving this world. He, in fact, tried his best to buy the allegiance for his son from his army's commanders, tribal chiefs and chieftains, and entire tribes as well as men of distinction and influence, spending huge sums of money in the process. But his efforts did not succeed with

Night view of the shrine of Ma'suma daughter of Imām ar-Ridha (ع) in Qum, Iran

everyone. One of his failed attempts was when he wrote Imām al-Hussain (ع) soliciting his endorsement for his appointment of Yazid as the heir apparent to the throne. Imām al-Hussain's answer was a scathing criticism of all what Mu'awiyah and Yazid had committed. Mu'awiyah, therefore, forewarned his son Yazid to beware of Imām al-Hussain (ع).

 Yazid eventually succeeded his father Mu'awiyah as the ruler. Yazid now spared no means to secure the submission for his unholy practices, oppression and aggression, from everyone. He knew very well that in reality, he had no legitimate right whatsoever to make claims or to issue demands. On the contrary, he was guilty of having committed many illegal and sacrilegious deeds for which he should have been killed, had there anyone powerful enough to implement the Islamic code of justice.

Once in charge, Yazid took his father's advice regarding Imām al-Hussain (ع) seriously. He wrote the then governor of Medīna, al-Walid ibn Utbah, ordering him to secure the oath of allegiance to him as the new ruler from everyone in general and from Imām al-Hussain (ع), Abdullāh ibn Omer (son of second caliph Omer ibn al-Khattab), and Abdullāh ibn az-Zubair in particular, being the most prominent personalities. Yazid in an unmistakable language ordered al-Walid to secure such an oath for him by force if necessary, and that if Imām al-Hussain (ع) refused, he should behead him and send his severed head to him in Damascus. But al-Walid's efforts were fruitless. Imām al-Hussain's reply was exact and direct; said he, "Ameer (Governor)! I belong to the Ahl al-Bayt (family) of the Prophet. Allāh has consigned to and charged us with the Imāmate (spiritual and political leadership of the Muslims). Angels pay us visits. Yazid is a wicked sinner, a depraved reprobate, a wanton drunkard, a man who sheds blood unjustly, and a man who openly defies Allāh's commandments. A man like me will never yield his allegiance to a person like him."

THE NOBLE MOTIVES BEHIND IMĀM HUSSAIN'S REVOLUTION

Such motives were numerous. Some of them stemmed from the grievances of the general public, while others were ideological in nature and noble in objective. They may be summed up as follows:

1) The most urgent need was to stop the attempts to distort the Islamic concepts and code of conduct, particularly the falsification of hadīth as discussed above. This was of the utmost significance; it preoccupied the minds of responsible Muslims at the time. Such fabrication was quite rampant, epidemic in nature, festered by the funds available for those who rushed to please the Umayyads with their pens, those who did not hesitate to sell their religion for a trifling. Such fabrication was poisonous in effect, and it affected the lives of all Muslims, and it still does. It was giving the Umayyads a free hand to do whatever they desired of unfair and unethical policies in dealing with their subjects. The mask of religion with which they used to hide their un-Islamic conduct was quite dangerous. In the long run, such danger

would eventually change the pristine concepts introduced by Islam and substitute them with anything but Islam. Stripping such a mask and exposing the true picture of the Umayyads was the most urgent task of a revolutionary like Imām al-Hussain (ع).

1) The Umayyads considered the Islamic world as their own real estate property. The zakat and other Islamic taxes were levied, but nobody knew where the funds went. Large gifts were doled out from the state treasury (called in Islam bayt al-mal) to governors, government officials, tribal chiefs, army commanders, and officers who surpassed others in their cruelty and oppression... Large sums of money were spent on activities which Islam prohibits: racing, gambling, wines, slave women to entertain the high class and the people in power, etc.

2) The State's structure was built on un-Islamic premises. Quraish was born to rule; non-Arabs were second-class citizens who formed the base of the society's pyramid. That was the general social picture of the Islamic world under the Umayyad's rule. Anyone who dared to express an opinion which did not agree with that of the Umayyads had to be placed under house arrest if not altogether eliminated. His property would then be confiscated and his life would be at stake. He would live in fear for the rest of his miserable life. Nowadays, there are millions of Muslims who live under such conditions. You see, the Umayyads are not dead; they are very much alive and well...

The majority of Muslims were left on the brink of starvation while the ruling clique enjoyed the social and material privileges. It very much is like what one sees happening nowadays in many Muslim countries. Let us face it; most Muslims are nowadays the laughing stocks of the world; انا لله و انا اليه راجعون *Inna Lillah wa Inna Ilayhi Rajioon* (We belong to Allāh, and to Him shall we return).

4) The Muslims had apparently become accustomed to the un-Islamic rule of the Umayyads as time passed by. Their resistance

Interior gate to the shrine of Imām al-Hussain (ع)

gradually slackened, and some people began adjusting to the new realities. The revolutionary spirit of Islam began to disappear little by little from the Muslims' lives and thoughts. A new stimulant to their souls was necessary in order to bring life back to their misled souls and to restore the Islamic conduct and way of life to the society.

THE REVOLUTION'S PROCESS

Having refused to swear the oath of allegiance to Yazid, Imām al-Hussain (ع) realized that his stay in Medīna was becoming impossible, unsafe; therefore, he decided to bid farewell to it. Bidding his people and friends to get ready for the journey, he went at night to the tomb of his grandfather Prophet Muhammed (ص). Approaching the grave, he greeted him then said, "Assalamo Alaikom, O Messenger of Allāh! I am the son of the beloved portion of your heart Fātima. Grandfather! You yourself had bequeathed to our Umma (nation) urging them to look after me and to take care of me, but they have neglected doing so and quite forgotten all of that."

He spent the entire night at the tomb occupied in prayer the entire period, returning after daybreak. He did the same in the following night. One of his prayers in that second night was:

Allāh! This is the resting-place of Your beloved Prophet Muhammed (ص) and I am his grandson. You know well the present situation in which I am, and You know what is in the innermost of my heart. I invoke You, Lord, to keep me by the grace of this holy place firmly steadfast in my pursuit of whatever meets Your Pleasure and the Pleasure of Your Prophet.

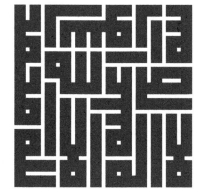

At-Tabari, Abū Mikhnaf and many other historians record saying that Imām al-Hussain (ع) saw his grandfather the Prophet (ص) in his vision at the end of that same second night calling unto him thus:

Come to me, O Hussain! Come to me going by and passing through the torturous stage of martyrdom and claim the right position reserved for you. The Lord, Allāh, will resurrect me, your parents, your elder brother (al-Hassan) and yourself at the same time and gather us all at the same place on the Day of Judgment.

Umm Salamah, the virtuous wife of Prophet Muhammed (ص), hurried to Imām al-Hussain (ع) as soon as she heard that he intended to depart from Medīna. She said to him, "Son! How will I be able to bear your journey to Iraq? I have heard your grandfather (the Prophet [ص]) saying, My son al-Hussain will be murdered on a tract of land people will call Kerbalā'.'" "By Allāh, mother," Imām al-Hussain (ع) answered, adding, "I know all that. I also know on what day I will be murdered, and the name of the man who will murder me. I know, too, the people who will inter my dead body and the members of my Ahl al-Bayt and friends who will meet their martyrdom along with me. If you desire, I will show you the exact spot of my grave." On Rajab 28, 60 A.D./May 7, 680 A.D., Imām al-Hussain (ع) left Medīna for good accompanied by 21 male children in addition to the ladies.

HUSSAIN IN MECCA
When Yazid came to know that al-Walid had allowed Imām al-Hussain (ع) and Abdullāh ibn az-Zubair to leave Medīna for Mecca

without taking their oath of allegiance to him, he became very angry and immediately deposed al-Walid from his post and appointed Amr ibn Sa'd in his place. Amr, in turn, appointed Omer ibn az-Zubair as his chief executive officer. Omer began to harass and intimidate the supporters of Abdullāh ibn az-Zubair. The Imām (ع) understood that those were scaring tactics meant to convey the message that he would be next to harass and intimidate; therefore, he felt that it was not safe for him to stay even in Mecca. There, Imām al-Hussain (ع) received thousands of letters, mostly from the people of Kūfa, pleading to him to rescue them from the Umayyads' tyranny.

According to the renown writer al-Balathiri, Imām al-Hussain (ع) received as many as six hundred letters in one day and a total of twelve thousands, all requesting the same. Among those who wrote him were these renown Kufians some of whom betrayed him then fought him: Shabth ibn Rab'i, Hijar ibn Abjar, Yazid ibn al-Harith, Izrah ibn Qays, Amr ibn al-Hajjaj, and Muhammed ibn Omayr ibn Utarid. First, Imām al-Hussain (ع) did not respond to any of these letters, then he wrote one

letter which he entrusted to Hani ibn Hani as-Subayi and Sa'd ibn Abdullāh al-Hanafi wherein he said, *"In the Name of Allāh, the Most Benevolent, the Most Merciful.* Hani and Sa'd brought me your letters, and they are the last to deliver such letters to me. I understand what you narrate, and the gist of most of your letters is: "We have no Imām; so, come to us, perhaps Allāh will gather us with you on the path of guidance and righteousness." I have sent you my brother and cousin and the confidant of my Ahl al-Bayt and ordered him to write me with regard to your conditions, views and intentions. So, if he writes me saying that your view is united with that of those of distinction and wisdom from among you and in agreement with what your messengers and letters state, I shall, by the Will of Allāh, come to you very soon. By my life, an Imām is one who acts upon the Book [of Allāh] and implements justice and follows the path of righteousness; he dedicates himself to follow Allāh's Commandments, and peace be with you."

He handed his letter to his cousin Muslim ibn Aqeel saying, "I am dispatching you to the people of Kūfa, and Allāh shall deal with you as He pleases. I wish that I and you should be in the company of the martyrs; so, proceed with Allāh's blessing and help. Once you get there, stay with the most trustworthy of its people."

Muslim left Mecca on the fifteenth of the month of Ramadan, corresponding to June 22, 680 A.D., via the Mecca-Medīna highway. He reached Medīna and went to the Mosque of the Prophet (ص), then he bade his family farewell after having hired two road guides from the tribe of Qays. One night the road guides were lost, and they became extremely thirsty, and it was very hot. They said to Muslim (ع) once they recognized some road marks, "Take yonder road and follow it, perhaps you will be saved." He, therefore, left them, following their advice. Both road guides died of thirst. He could not carry them because they were about to pass away. What those road guides had actually seen was not the road itself but some landmarks leading thereto. The distance between them and water was not known, and they were unable to ride on their own, nor could they ride with someone else. Had Muslim (ع) stayed with them, he, too, would have perished. The most urgent matter was to preserve precious lives and to continue the march till water could be reached, hence his decision to abandon them where they were. Muslim and those serving him barely survived till they reached the highway and the water source where they rested for a short while.

Muslim sent a letter to Imām al-Hussain (ع) with a messenger whom he hired from those who settled near that water source. He told him about the death of the road guides, about the hardship he underwent, and that he was staying at a narrow passage at Batn al-Khabt awaiting his instructions. The messenger met Imām al-Hussain (ع) at Mecca and delivered the letter to him. Al-Imām al-Hussain (ع) wrote him back ordering him to continue his march to Kūfa without any delay. Having read the letter, Muslim immediately resumed his trip and passed by a watering place belonging to the tribe of Tay. He Alighted there then departed. He saw a man shooting and killing a deer, so he took it as a sign of good omen: the killing of his foe. On the twenty-fifth of Shawwal, 60 A.H./July 27, 680 A.D., Muslim ibn Aqeel entered Kūfa and stayed with al-Mukhtar ibn Abū Ubayd ath-Thaqafiwho was highly respected among his people, a generous man, a man of ambition and daring, one well experienced and determined, and a formidable opponent of the enemies of Ahl al-Bayt, peace be with them. He was a man of great discretion especially with regard to the rules of the battle and the means of subduing the foe. He kept company with the Progeny of the most holy Prophet (ص), so he benefitted from their ethics and virtuous morals, and he sought their advice publicly and privately.

MUSLIM SWEARS OATH OF ALLEGIANCE FOR HUSSAIN

The Shī'as of Kūfa came in groups to meet Muslim as he stayed at al-Mukhtar's house, pledging to him their obedience. This increased his happiness and elation. When he read to them Imām al-Hussain's letter, Abis ibn Shibeeb ash-Shakiri stood and said, "I do not speak on behalf of the people, nor do I know what they conceal in their hearts, nor do I deceive you in their regard. By Allāh! I can tell you what I personally have decided to do. By Allāh! I shall respond to your call, and I shall fight your enemy. I shall defend you with my sword till I meet Allāh desiring nothing except what He has in store for me." Habib ibn Muzahir said, "You have briefly stated your intention, and by Allāh, the One and only Allāh, I feel exactly as you do." Sa'd ibn Abdullāh al-Hanafi made a similar statement. Other Shī'as came to swear the oath of allegiance to him till his *diwan* counted as many as eighteen thousand men. Some historians say that they were as many as twenty five thousand men. According to ash-Sha'bi, however, the number of those who swore allegiance to him reached forty thousand. It was then that Muslim wrote Imām al-Hussain (ع) a letter which he handed to Abis ibn Shibeeb ash-Shakiri informing him of the consensus among the people of Kūfa to obey him and to wait for his arrival. In it, he said, "A scout does not lie to his people. Eighteen thousand Kufians have already come to me; so, hurry and come here as soon as this letter reaches you." That was twenty-seven days before Muslim's martyrdom. The Kufians, too, added to it their own letter wherein they stated the following: "Hurry and come to us, O son of the Messenger of Allāh! A hundred thousand swords are in Kūfa on your side; so, do not tarry."

This angered a group of the Umayyads with vested interests. Among them were Omer bin Sa'd, son of the renown Sa'd ibn Abū Waqqas, Abdullāh ibn Muslim ibn Rabi'ah al-Hadrami, and Imarah ibn Uqbah ibn Abū Mueet. They wrote Yazid warning him of the arrival of Muslim ibn Aqeel and the rallying of the people of Kūfa behind him, adding that an-Numan ibn Basheer, governor of Kūfa, was not strong enough to stand in his [Aqeel's] way. Yazid deposed an-Numan ibn Basheer and appointed Ubaydullāh ibn Ziyad in his place. The new governor was a man very well known for his ruthfulness. Yazid ordered Ubaydullāh ibn Ziyad to rush to Kūfa in the company of Muslim ibn Omer al-Bahili, al-Munthir ibn al-Jarad, and Abdullāh ibn al-Harith ibn Nawfal escorted by five hundred soldiers whom he hand-picked from among the people of Basra. Ibn Ziyad rushed to Kūfa, paying no attention to anyone who fell off his horse due to exhaustion even if he were one of his own closest friends. For example, when Shurayk ibn al-A'war fell on the way, and even when Abdullāh ibn al-Harith fell, thinking that Ibn Ziyad would slow down for their sake, Ibn Ziyad paid no attention to them, fearing that Imām al-Hussain (ع) might reach Kūfa before him. Whenever he passed by a checkpoint, its guards thought that he was Imām al-Hussain (ع), so they said, "Welcome, O son of the Messenger of Allāh!" He remained silent till he reached Kūfa via the Najaf highway. When he arrived, people welcomed him and said in one voice: "Welcome, O son of the Messenger of Allāh!" This only intensified his outrage. He continued his march till he reached the governor's mansion. An-Numan did not open the gate for him, and he spoke to him from the mansion's roof-top. Said he, "I shall not return the trust to you, O son of the Messenger of Allāh!" Ibn Ziyad said to him, "Open the gate, for your night has extended too long!" A man heard his voice and recognized him. He, therefore, said to the people, "He is Ibn Ziyad, by the Lord of the Ka'ba!" They, therefore, opened the gate for him then dispersed, going back home.

In the morning, Ibn Ziyad gathered people at the grand mosque. There, he delivered a speech warning them against mutiny and promising them generous rewards for conforming. Said he, "Anyone found to be sheltering one of those who scheme against the authority of the commander of the faithful [meaning Yazid] and who does not hand him over will be crucified on the door of his own house."

When Muslim ibn Aqeel came to know about Ibn Ziyad's speech and his explicit threats and having come to know about people's conditions, he feared being assassinated. He, therefore, left al-Mukhtar's house after the dark and went to the house of Hani ibn Urwah al-Mathhaji who was a very zealous Shī'a. He was also one of Kūfa's dignitaries, one of its *qaris* of the Holy Qur'ān, and the shaikh and chief of the Banu Murad. He could easily raise four thousand troops fully armed and eight thousand cavaliers. If he includes his tribe's allies from Kindah, the number would swell to thirty thousand. He was one of the closest friends of the Commander of the Faithful Imām Ali ibn Abū Talib (ع) on whose side he fought in all his three battles. He had seen and was honored by being a companion of the Prophet (ص). When he was later killed in defense of Imām al-Hussain (ع), he was more than ninety years old. Muslim ibn Aqeel stayed at the house of Shareek ibn Abdullāh al-A'war al-Harithi al-Hamadani al-Basri, one of the main supporters of the Commander of the Faithful, peace be with him, in Basra. He had participated in the Battle of Siffeen and fought side by side with the great *sahabi* Ammar ibn Yasir. Due to his distinction and prominence, Ubaydullāh ibn Ziyad appointed him as Governor of Kerman on behalf of Mu'awiyah. He used to be in contact with and in the company of Hani ibn Urwah.

The Shī'as kept meeting Muslim ibn Aqeel secretly at Hani's house without attracting the attention of Ibn Ziyad, admonishing each other to keep it to themselves. Ibn Ziyad, therefore, could not know where Muslim was. He called Maqil, his slave, to meet him. He gave him three thousand [dinars] and ordered him to meet the Shī'as and to tell them that he was a Syrian slave of Thul-Kila and that Allāh blessed him with loving Ahl al-Bayt of His Messenger (ع), that it came to his knowledge that one of the members of Ahl al-Bayt (ع) had come to that country, and that he had with him some money which he wanted to deliver to him. Maqil entered the grand mosque and saw Muslim ibn Awsajah al-Asadi offering his prayers. Having seen him finish his prayers, he came close to him and made the above claim to him. Muslim ibn Awsajah prayed Allāh to grant that man goodness and success. He then accompanied him to the place where Muslim ibn Aqeel was hiding. The spy delivered the money to Muslim and swore the oath of allegiance to him. The money was handed over to Abū Thumamah as-Saidi who was a far-sighted and a brave Shī'a dignitary appointed by Muslim to receive the funds and to buy thereby weapons. That man kept meeting Muslim every day. No secrets were kept from him, so he kept gathering intelligence and getting it to Ibn Ziyad in the evening.

HANI IBN URWAH

When the matter became clear to Ibn Ziyad, who by now knew that Muslim was hiding at the house of Hani ibn Urwah, he had Asma' ibn Kharijah, Muhammed ibn al-Ash'ath and Amr ibn al-Hajjaj brought to him. He asked them why Hani had not been coming lately to visit him at his governor's mansion. They told him that it was due to his sickness, but he was not convinced especially since his informers had already told him that Hani used to sit at the door of his house every evening. These same men rode to Hani and asked him to meet the sultan, for "He cannot stand you staying away from him," they said, pressuring him till he yielded. Hani, therefore, rode his mule and went. As soon as Ibn Ziyad saw him, he said, "His feet, the feet of the treacherous one, have brought him to you." Then he turned to his judge Shurayh and cited verses about judges who rush to please their tyrannical rulers who appoint them in their positions rather than implement Islam's legislative system, the Sharaa. Ibn Ziyad turned to Hani and said, "You brought Aqeel's son to your house and gathered weapons for him, did you not?" Hani denied, and when their argument intensified, Ibn Ziyad ordered Maqil to be brought to him. Hani, hence, understood that that man was actually Ibn Ziyad's spy, so he said to Ibn Ziyad, "Your father had done me great favors, and I now wish to reward him. Why do you not listen to my good advice and safely depart for Syria with your family and wealth? Someone who is more worthy than you and your friend [meaning Yazid] of taking charge has come here." Ibn Ziyad said, "And under the foam is the pure sour cream."

Ibn Ziyad then said to him, "By Allāh! You will not stay out of my

60

sight before you bring him to me." Hani said, "By Allāh! Had he been under my foot, I would not have lifted it!" Ibn Ziyad then spoke rudely to him and even threatened to kill him. Hani, therefore, said, "In that case, there will be plenty of swords around you," thinking that the tribesmen of Murad would protect him from Ibn Ziyad who then pulled Hani's braids, hitting his face with his sword, breaking his nose and scattering the flesh from his cheeks and forehead on his beard. He then jailed him at his mansion.

Amr ibn al-Hajjaj heard that Hani had been killed. Hani's wife Raw'a, who is well known as the mother of Yahya son of Hani, was the sister of Amr ibn al-Hajjaj. The latter, therefore, rode with a multitude from the tribe of Mathhaj, and they all surrounded the mansion. When Ibn Ziyad came to know about it, he ordered Shurayh, the judge, to see Hani and then to tell those horsemen that Hani was still alive. Shurayh narrates saying, "When Hani saw me, he said in a loud voice, O Muslims! Should ten persons enter here, you must come to my rescue!' Had Hameed ibn Abū Bakr al-Ahmari, the policeman, not been with me, I would have conveyed his message, but I had to simply say instead that Hani was still alive. Amr ibn al-Hajjaj then praised Allāh and went back accompanied by the other men."

MUSLIM'S UPRISING
When Muslim came to know about what had happened to Hani, he feared being assassinated; therefore, he rushed to rise before the time he had set with the people. He ordered Abdullāh ibn Hazim to call upon his men, who had then filled the houses surrounding him, to gather together. Four thousand men assembled. They were shouting Badr's call which was: "O Supported One! Annihilate them!"

Ubaydullāh ibn Amr ibn Aziz al-Kindi was placed in command of the Kindah and Rabi'ah quarters. "March ahead of me," said Muslim, "in command of the cavalry." Muslim ibn Awsajah al-Asadi was placed in command of Mathhaj and Banu Asad. "Take charge of the infantry," Muslim ordered him. Abū Thumamah as-Saidi was placed in charge of Tameem and Hamadan, whereas al-Abbas ibn Jadah al-Jadli was given the command of the Medīna troops.

They marched towards the governor's mansion. Ibn Ziyad fortified himself inside it, locking all its gates. He could not resist because there were only thirty policemen with him and twenty of his close men and slaves. But the substance from which the people of Kūfa were made was treachery; so, their standards kept disappearing till no more than three hundred men remained out of the original four thousand. Al-Ahnaf ibn Qays described them as a whore who demanded a different man every day.

When those inside the mansion called upon the people of Kūfa saying, "O Kufians! Fear Allāh and do not expose yourselves to Syrian cavaliers whose might you have already tasted and whom you have already tested on the battlefield," the remaining three hundred dispersed, so much so that a man would come to his son, brother, or cousin and tell him to go home, and a wife would cling to her husband till he returned home.

Muslim offered the evening prayers at the [grand Kūfa] mosque accompanied by only thirty men. Then, when he went to Kindah's quarters, only three men accompanied him. He hardly proceeded for a short while before finding himself without anyone at all to show him the way. He alighted from his horse and cautiously traversed Kūfa's alleys not knowing where to go.

When people abandoned Muslim, their noise died down, and Ibn Ziyad could not hear the voice of any of their men. Ibn Ziyad ordered his bodyguards to inspect the mosque's courtyard to see whether there were any men lying in ambush. They, therefore, kept lowering their lanterns down its walls and lighting reeds then lowering them down with ropes till they reached the mosque's courtyard. They could not see anyone, so they informed Ibn Ziyad who ordered his caller to call people to assemble at the mosque. When they filled the mosque, he ascended the pulpit and said, "Aqeel's son has caused the dissension and disunity with which you all are familiar; so, there is no security henceforth to any man in whose house we find him. Anyone who captures him and brings him to us will be paid his blood money. O servants of Allāh! Fear Allāh and safeguard your obedience and oath of allegiance, and do not expose yourselves to peril."

Then he ordered al-Haseen ibn Tameem, chief of his police force, to search homes and highways, warning him that he would kill Muslim should he succeed in escaping from Kūfa.

Al-Haseen stationed his guards at highway crossroads and pursued the dignitaries who had supported Muslim, arresting Abdul-Ala ibn Yazid al-Kalbi and Imarah ibn Salkhab al-Azdi. He threw them in jail then killed them. Then he jailed a group of prominent leaders as a safeguarding measure against what they might do. Among them were al-Asbagh ibn Nubatah and al-Harith al-A'war al-Hamadani.

AL-MUKHTAR JAILED

When Muslim marched out, al-Mukhtar was at a village called Khatwaniyya. He came accompanied by his supporters raising a green standard while Abdullāh ibn al-Harith was raising a red one. Having planted his standard at the door of Amr ibn Hareeth's house, he said, "I want to stop Amr." It became obvious to them that both Muslim and Hani had been killed, and it was suggested to them that they would feel more secure in the company of Amr ibn Hareeth, and so they did. Ibn Hareeth testified that they had both avoided Muslim ibn Aqeel... Ibn Ziyad ordered them jailed after having reviled al-Mukhtar and hit his face with a lance, gouging one of his eyes. They remained in prison till Imām al-Hussain, peace be with him, was martyred.

Ibn Ziyad ordered Muhammed ibn al-Ash'ath, Shabth ibn Rab'i, al-Qaqa ibn Shawr at-Thuhli, Hijar ibn Abjar, Shimr Thul-Jawshan, and Amr ibn Hareeth to surrender and to discourage people from rebelling. A number of men who were controlled by fear responded positively to his call in addition to others who coveted rich rewards and were thus deceived, whereas those whose conscience was pure went underground, waiting for an opportunity to launch an attack on the camp of falsehood.

MUSLIM AT THE HOUSE OF TAW'A

Ibn Aqeel's feet took him to the quarters of Banu Jiblah who belonged to the tribe of Kindah. He stood at the door of a house of a freed bondmaid named Tawa who had a number of sons. She used to be the bondmaid of al-Ash'ath ibn Qays who freed her. Aseed al-Hadrami married her, and she gave birth to his son Bilal who was in the crowd when his mother was standing at the door waiting for him. Muslim requested her to give him some water, which she did. He then requested her to host him, telling her that he was a stranger in that land without a family or a tribe, and that he belonged to a family capable of intercession on the Day of Judgment, and that his name was Muslim ibn Aqeel. She took him to a room which was not the same one where her son used to sleep, and she served him some food. Her son was surprised to see her entering that room quite often, so he asked her about it. She refused to answer his question except after obtaining an oath from him to keep the matter to himself.

But in the morning he informed Ibn Ziyad of where Muslim had been hiding. Ibn Ziyad dispatched al-Ash'ath accompanied by seventy men who belonged to the Qays tribe in order to arrest him. Upon hearing the horses' hoofs ploughing the ground, Muslim realized that he was being pursued, so he hurried to finish a supplication which he was reciting following the morning prayers. Then he put on his battle gear and said to his hostess Tawa: "You have carried out your share of righteousness, and you have secured your share of the intercession of the Messenger of Allāh. Yesterday, I saw my uncle the Commander of the Faithful in a vision telling me that I was going to join him the next day."

He came out to face them raising his unsheathed sword as they assaulted the house, succeeding in repelling their attack. They repeated their attack, and again he repelled them, killing as many as forty-one of their men, and he was so strong that he would take hold of one man then hurl him on the rooftop.

Ibn al-Ash'ath sent a messenger to Ibn Ziyad requesting additional enforcements. The messenger came back to him carrying the latter's blame of his incompetence. He, therefore, sent him this message: "Do you think that you sent me to one of Kūfa's shopkeepers, or to a Nabatean from Heera?! Rather, you sent me to one of the swords of [Prophet] Muhammed ibn Abdullāh !" Ibn Ziyad then assisted him with additional soldiers.

Fighting intensified. Muslim and Bakeer ibn Hamran al-Ahmari exchanged blows. Bakeer struck Muslim on the mouth, cutting his upper lip, wounding the lower and breaking two of his lower teeth. Muslim fiercely struck him with one blow on his head and another on his shoulder muscle, almost splitting his stomach, killing him instantly.

Then they attacked him from the house's rooftop, hurling rocks at him. They kept burning reed bales then throwing them at him. He attacked them in the alley. His wounds were numerous; he bled extensively, so he supported his body on the side of the house. It was then that they assaulted him with arrows and stones. "Why do you hurl stones at me," he asked them, "as non-believers are stoned, the member of the household of the pure Prophet that I am? Do you not have any respect for the Messenger of Allāh with regard to one of his own descendants?" Ibn al-Ash'ath said to him, "Please do not get yourself killed while you are in my custody." Muslim asked him, "Shall I then be captured so long as I have some strength in me? No, by Allāh! This shall never be." Then he attacked Ibn al-Ash'ath who fled away before him. They attacked him from all directions. Thirst had taken its toll on him. A man stabbed him from the back, so he fell on the ground and was arrested.

Another account says that they dug a hole for him which they covered then fled before him, thus luring him to fall into it, then they arrested him. When they took his sword away from him, he wept. Amr ibn Ubaydullāh as-Salami was surprised to see him weep. A man without his weapon is helpless, defenseless and vulnerable.

MUSLIM MEETS IBN ZIYAD

Muslim ibn Aqeel was brought to Ibn Ziyad. At the entrance of the mansion he saw an urn containing cooled water. He asked to drink of it. Muslim ibn Amr al-Bahili said to him, "You shall not taste one drop of it till you taste of the *hameem* in the fire of hell." Muslim asked him, "Who are you?" He said, "I am one who knew the truth which you rejected, and who remained faithful to his imām as you betrayed him." Muslim ibn Aqeel said to him, "May your mother lose you! How hard-hearted and rude you are! You, son of Bahilah,

65

are more worthy of tasting of the *hameem* (hell)." Having said so, he sat down, supporting his back on the mansion's wall.

Imarah ibn Uqbah ibn Abū [son of] Mu'eet sent a slave named Qays to give him water. Whenever Muslim was about to drink of it, the cup became full of his blood. In his third attempt to drink, the cup became full of his blood and both his front teeth fell in it, so he abandoned it saying, "Had it been prescribed in destiny for me to drink it, I would have drunk it."

Ibn Ziyad's guard came out to escort Muslim. Having entered Ibn Ziyad's room, Muslim did not greet him. The guard asked Muslim, "Why did you not greet the *ameer* (ruler)?" "Shut your mouth," said Muslim, "he is not my *ameer*." It is also said that he said to Ibn Ziyad, "Peace be upon whoever followed the right guidance, feared the consequences in the hereafter, and obeyed the Exalted King," so Ibn Ziyad laughed and said, "Whether you greet or not, you shall be killed." Muslim said, "If you kill me, someone worse than you had already killed someone much better than me. Besides, you shall never abandon committing murders, setting a bad example, thinking ill of others, or being mean; having the upper hand will be the doing of anyone else but you."

Ibn Ziyad said, "You disobeyed your imām, divided the Muslims, and sowed the seeds of dissension." Muslim said, "You have uttered falsehood. Rather, those who divided the Muslims are Mu'awiyah and his son Yazid. The seeds of dissension were sown by your father, and I wish Allāh will grant me to be martyred at the hand of the worst of His creation."

Then Muslim asked permission to convey his will to some of his people. He was granted permission, so he looked at those present there and saw Omer ibn Sa'd. "There is kinship between me and you," said he to him, "and I need a favor of you which you should oblige, and it is a secret between us." But he refused to listen to it, whereupon Ibn Ziyad said to him, "Do not hesitate to tend to your cousin's need." Omer stood with Muslim in a way that enabled Ibn Ziyad to see them both. Muslim conveyed his desire to him to sell his sword and shield and pay a debt in the amount of six hundred

66

dirhams which he had borrowed since entering Kūfa, to ask Ibn Ziyad to give him his corpse to bury it, and to write al-Hussain to tell him what had happened to him. Omer ibn Sa'd stood up and walked to Ibn Ziyad to reveal the secret with which he had just been entrusted by Muslim! Ibn Ziyad said to Muslim, "A trustworthy person never betrays you, but you have placed your trust in a treacherous person."

Then Ibn Ziyad turned again to Muslim and said, "O son of Aqeel! You came to a united people and disunited them." Muslim said, "No, indeed, I did not come to do that, but the people of this country claimed that your father killed their best men, shed their blood, and did what Kisra and Caesar do, so we came to them in order to enjoin justice, and to invite all to accept the judgment of the Book [of Allāh]." Ibn Ziyad said, "What do you have to do with all of that? Have we not been dealing with them with equity?" Muslim said, "Allāh knows that you are not telling the truth. You, in fact, kill when angry, out of enmity, and for mere suspicion." Ibn Ziyad then verbally abused him and abused Ali, Aqeel, and al-Hussain, whereupon Muslim said, "You and your father are more worthy of being thus abused; so, issue whatever decree you wish, you enemy of Allāh!"

It was then that Ibn Ziyad ordered a Syrian to go to the top of the mansion and to behead Muslim and throw both the head and the body to the ground. The Syrian took Muslim to the flat rooftop of the mansion as the latter kept repeating, "*Subhan-Allāh! La ilaha illa-Allāh! Allāhu Akbar!*" He also kept repeating, "O Allāh! Judge between us and the people who deceived, betrayed and lied to us," then he faced Medīna and saluted Imām al-Hussain (ﻉ).

The Syrian struck Muslim's neck with his sword and threw his head and body to the ground and hurried down; he was very, very much startled. Ibn Ziyad asked him what was wrong with him. "The moment I killed him," said he, "I saw a black man with an extremely ugly face standing beside me biting his finger, so I was frightened." "Perhaps you lost your mind for a moment," said Ibn Ziyad.

Hani was taken to an area of the market place where sheep are sold;

his arms were tied. He kept saying, "O Mathhaj! Any man from Mathhaj to help me this day?! O Mathhaj! Where has Mathhaj gone away from me?!" Having seen that there was none to respond to him, he somehow managed to get one of his arms out of the ropes and said, "Is there anyone who would hand me a stick, a knife, a rock, or even a bone so that a man may be able to defend himself?" Guards attacked him and tied him again. He was ordered to stretch his neck so that they might strike it with their swords. "I am not going to give it away to you so generously. I shall not assist you at the cost of my own life." A Turkish slave named Rasheed owned by Ubaydullāh ibn Ziyad struck him with his sword, but he missed. Hani said, "To Allāh is my return! O Allāh! To Your Mercy do I come and to Your Pleasure!" Rasheed hit him again and killed him. This same slave was killed by Abdul-Rahman ibn al-Haseen al-Muradi after having seen him at the Khazar (Caspian Sea, also the Basque Sea, Tabarestan Sea, and Baku Sea, *bahr baku* in Arabic, an area where Islam reached in the early 9th century A.D.) in the company of Ubaydullāh.

Ibn Ziyad ordered the corpses of both Muslim and Hani to be tied with ropes from their feet and dragged in the market places. Then he crucified them upside-down at the garbage collection site then sent their severed heads to Yazid who displayed them at one of the streets of Damascus.

He, Ubaydullāh Ibn Ziyad, wrote Yazid saying,

"Praise to Allāh Who affected justice on behalf of the commander of the faithful and sufficed him for having to deal with his foes. I would like to inform the commander of the faithful, may Allāh bless him, that Muslim ibn Aqeel had sought refuge at the house of Hani ibn Urwah al-Muradi, that I assigned spies for them and let men infiltrate their assemblies and plotted against them till I forced them out. Allāh gave me the upper hand over them, so I killed them and sent you both of their heads with Hani ibn Abū Hayya al-Wadii al-Hamadani and az-Zubair ibn al-Arwah at-Tameemi who both are from among those who listen to and obey us; so, let the commander of the faithful ask them whatever he pleases, for there is knowledge with them, and there is truth, understanding, and piety. And peace be with you."

Yazid wrote Ibn Ziyad saying,

"You do not cease to be the source of my delight. You have behaved with strictness and assaulted with courage, maintaining your composure. You have done very well and testified to the correctness of my good impression of you. I invited your messengers and asked them and confided in them, and I found their views and merits just as you indicated; so, take good care of them. It has also come to my knowledge that al-Hussain ibn Ali has marched towards Iraq. You should, therefore, set up observation posts, prepare with arms, be cautious for mere suspicion. Kill anyone whom you suspect (of dissent). Your tenure is put to the test by this al-Hussain rather than by anyone else, so is your country and your own self as governor. The outcome will determine whether you will be freed or whether you will return to slavery; so, you have to either fight him or arrest and transport him to me."

Let us now leave Kūfa and its Kufian men of treachery and to al-Hussain in Mecca where he was performing the rites of the pilgrimage. As he was thus engaged, Yazid dispatched thirty men disguised as pilgrims with strict instructions to assassinate him. Commenting on this attempt to assassinate him, al-Hussain said, "Even if I were to bury myself in some hideout, they are sure to hunt me out and to try to force me to swear the oath of allegiance to Yazid. And if I refused, they would kill me and would not spare me without inflicting upon me the same torture as the Jews had done to Jesus." There were unsuccessful attempts to prevent him from leaving Mecca.

Imām al-Hussain (ع) did not mask his intentions and determination to fight the Umayyad regime of corruption. The speeches he delivered at Mecca were consistent with those he made elsewhere. So does his will which he wrote and entrusted to his brother Muhammed ibn al-Hanafiyya who stayed in Medīna when al-Hussain (ع) left it first for Mecca then for Kerbalā', Iraq. This said will was, in fact, a formal declaration of his holy revolution. He, peace be with him and upon his Ahl al-Bayt, wrote saying, "I am not campaigning because I am unwilling to accept righteousness, nor do I intend to do mischief or suppress people. Indeed, I have decided to seek to reform my grandfather's nation. I want to enjoin what is right and to forbid what is wrong. If people accept my call for righteousness, Allāh is the Master of the righteous people. Those who reject my call, I shall remain steadfast till Allāh passes His judgment; surely Allāh is the best of judges."

Imām al-Hussain's statements were aiming directly at stripping the "religious" mask behind which the Umayyads were hiding as they ruled the Muslim masses. He was introducing himself to people and explaining his message to the nation. In fact, the very personality of Imām al-Hussain (ع) and his religious devotion and impeccable character were all beyond question or doubt. No wonder, then, that he shouldered such a tremendous task, one which many distinguished personalities were not able to shoulder or even to raise a finger and point at the oppressors.

Let us now follow the Imām on his journey to martyrdom and eternal bliss.

Imām al-Hussain (ع) left Mecca on Thul-Hijja 8, 60 A.H./September 12, 680 A.D. accompanied by his family members, slaves and Shī'as from among the people of Hijaz, Basra, and Kūfa who joined him when he was in Mecca. According to p. 91 of *Nafas al-Mahmum* by Shaikh Abbas al-Qummi, he gave each one of them ten dinars and a camel to carry his luggage.

The places (including water places and caravans' temporary tent lodges), cities and towns by which Imām al-Hussain (ع) passed on his way to Taff area, where the famous Taff Battle took place, were: as-Sifah, That Irq, al-Hajir, al-Khuzaymiyya, Zarood, at-Thalabiyya, ash-Shuqooq, Zubala, al-Aqaba, Sharif, al-Bayda, ar-Ruhayma, al-Qadisiyya, al-Uthayb, and Qasr Muqatil. At as-Sifah, Imām al-Hussain (ع) met the famous poet al-Farazdaq ibn Ghalib and asked him about the people whom he had left behind, since al-Farazdaq had come from the opposite direction and had been in Kūfa. Al-Farazdaq, as we are told on p. 218, Vol. 6, of at-Tabari's *Tarikh*, said, "Their hearts are with you; the swords are with Banu

Umayyah, and Destiny descends from the heavens."

QASR MUQATIL

When the Imām reached Qasr Muqatil, a place not far from Kūfa, he found it like a beehive, full of men and horses with rows of pitched-up tents spread all over, far and wide. Ibn Ziyad had sent a detachment of 1,000 troops (very brave ones!) under the command of Hurr ibn Yazid ar-Riyahi to divert the Imām and his small band to a particular site chosen for them, and not to permit them to go anywhere except to Kūfa. At that time, when the Imām reached there, Hurr's army had become thirsty. Its water supply had been fully exhausted, and no water could be seen around for miles. On becoming aware of this, the Imām at once ordered his men to serve water to the thirsty enemy army and to their horses as well. When the time of noon prayers approached, the Imām admonished Hurr's army to give up fighting on the side of tyranny and falsehood adding, "But if you disapprove of us, and are willfully ignoring our claim and reneging from your pledge to support us, a proxy pledge that you expressed in your letters and through your messengers, well, in that case, it does not matter, for I am quite prepared to go back (where I had come from)." But orders had already been issued to Hurr to take the Imām in his custody. The Imām asked Hurr, "Why have you come here at all?" "In obedience to my imām (meaning Ubaydullāh ibn Ziyad, the governor)," answered Hurr. In obeying your imām," responded Imām al-Hussain (ع), "you have committed a great sin against Allāh," adding after a short while, "You have lost your all, ruined your life here as well as your life hereafter. You have kindled the fire of hell for your own self and kept it ready for you to be hurled therein on the Day of Judgment. As for your imām, Allāh has explicitly said in the Holy Qur'ān, And We made them imāms inviting them to the fire, and on the Day of Judgment, no help shall they find. In this world We made a curse to follow them, and on the Day of Judgment, they will be among the loathed and the despised' (Qur'ān, 28:41-42)."

Later on, another order to Hurr came from Ubaydullāh ibn Ziyad to confine the Imām and his companions to a water land waste at a distance of about 9 - 10 miles from Kūfa off the bank of the Euphrates river. This area, known as at-Taff, later came to be called

71

"Kerbalā'." It is there that the historical battle which stamped and is still stamping the Islamic history and the conduct of all Muslims, took place. As a matter of fact, this battle was already predicted in the Old Testament in the following verse in Jeremiah 46:10:

... For this is the day of the Lord Allāh of hosts, a day of vengeance, that He may avenge him of his adversaries, and the sword shall devour, and it shall be satiated and made drunk with their blood, for the Lord Allāh of hosts has a sacrifice in the north country by the river Euphrates.

In his famous book titled الصواعق المحرقة *As-Sawaiq al-Muhriqa* ("the burning thunderbolts), Ibn Hajar al-Asqalani writes saying that when the Imām came to that place, he took a handful of its soil and, having smelt it, he declared, "By Allāh! This is the land of *karb* (affliction) and *bala'* (trial and tribulation)! Here the ladies of my *haram* will be taken prisoners! Here my children will be butchered and our men will be slain! Here Ahl al-Bayt of the Prophet (ص) will be subjected to indignities! Here my beard will be stained with the blood of my head! And here our graves will be dug."

Historians contemporary to the Imām related that after coming to Kerbalā', the Imām purchased that lot from its owners for 60,000 dinars, although it was only four miles square, so that it would be the site of his and his family's and relatives' graves.

THE KUFIAN HOSTS

Different accounts of he full number of al-Hussain's camp range from seventy-two to a hundred fighters..., but how many were al-Hussain's foes?! Omer ibn Sa'd was dispatched to Kerbalā' to fight the Imām with 6,000 strong. Then Shabth ibn Rab'i went there to take charge of the largest fighting force of 24,000 men. The commanders' names and the numbers of their troops are here provided for the kind reader:

1. Omer ibn Sa'd	6,000
2. Shabth ibn Rab'i	24,000
3. Urwah ibn Qais	4,000
4. Sinan ibn Anas	4,000

5. Haseen ibn Nameer	9,000
6. Shimr ibn Thul-Jawshan	4,000
7. Mazar ibn Ruhaynah	3,000
8. Yazid ibn Rikab	2,000
9. Najr ibn KharShī'ah	2,000
10. Muhammed ibn al-Ash'ath	1,000
11. Abdullāh ibn Haseen	1,000
12. Khawli ibn Yazid al-Asbahi	1,000
13. Bakr ibn Kasab ibn Talhah	3,000
14. Hijr ibn Abjar	1,000
15. Hurr ibn Yazid ar-Riyahi	3,000

TOTAL: 68,000

The reader can notice that some of these commanders had already written al-Hussain (ع) inviting him to go to Kūfa so that they would support him in putting an end to the tyranny of the Umayyads. The details of how those men changed heart and the amounts of money they received are too lengthy to include in this brief account.

EFFORTS TO SECURE WATER

The access to water was cut off on the seventh day of Muharram and, before the evening of the eighth, the young, the children, and the women grew extremely restless, being overcome by the pangs of thirst. On the morning of the eighth, al-Abbas son of Ali ibn Abū Talib, al-Hussain's brother, who was appointed by al-Hussain (ع) as commander-in-chief of the tiny force, began digging wells assisted by all loyal companions and kinsmen of the Imām. They succeeded in boring a well, but stones were found instead of water. They soon dug another, but no water was found in it. The Imām then requested his brother al-Abbas to go to fetch water from the Euphrates. Al-Abbas took thirty cavaliers and twenty footmen and twenty large-size empty water-bags. After a fierce battle at the river's bank, they succeeded in fetching water. Although they themselves were extremely thirsty, they refused to drink before the others. Al-Abbas, hence, was given the title of "Saqqah," the water-bearer, ever since.

When Omer ibn Sa'd came to know about this incident, he reinforced the detachment sent to guard the Euphrates against al-Hussain's people having access to the water. The total force guarding the water now reached 800...! Ubaydullāh ibn Ziyad himself sent a letter to Omer ibn Sa'd telling him that, "It is necessary to take more precautions so that they (al-Hussain's folks) may not be able to obtain a drop of water."

CONDITIONAL RESPITE GRANTED

Imām al-Hussain (ع) knew that war was unavoidable, so he asked his foes to put off the fighting for one night since, he said, he wanted to spend it praying to Allāh. It was grudgingly granted. On the other hand, the misery of the prevailing conditions at al-Hussain's camp due to the shortage of water caused by the water supply being intercepted could not be imagined. The only survivor of that tragedy, namely al-Hussain's ailing son Ali, said later on about their suffering, "We, all in all, were twenty children, and we were very thirsty and crying for water, gasping with thirst." It is also noteworthy that this same survivor's offspring and supporters later on established the Fatimide ruling dynasty in north Africa with its capital first at Qairawan, Tunisia, then at Cairo, Egypt. The Fatimide caliph al-Muizz li Deenillah founded Cairo and built its renown al-Azhar mosque and university.

ANOTHER CONFRONTATION AT WATERING PLACE

Burayr al-Hamadani, a loyal companion of Imām al-Hussain (ع), tried to fetch water, igniting a fierce battle at the river's bank. He and only three brave warriors had to face the entire 800-strong regiment guarding the watering place. The battle cries reached al-Hussain's camp, whereupon the Imām ordered a rescue mission. Water was miraculously brought in a single water-skin. All the children rushed to it, frantically trying to quench their thirst therewith. Crowding around it, some were pressing it to them, others falling upon it till, alas, suddenly the mouth of the water-skin flung open by the children's crowding upon it and all the water flowed out on the dusty floor. All the children loudly cried and lamented saying, "O Burayr! All the water you have brought us is gone!"

FIRM RESOLUTION

In the eve of the ninth of Muharram, Imām al-Hussain (ع) gathered all his companions together and said to them, "Whoever remains with me will be killed tomorrow; so, consider this opportunity as Allāh-sent and take advantage of the darkness and go home to your villages." He then extinguished the light so that those who wanted to go away might not be too embarrassed when seen by others. al-Hussain's loyal companions burst out in inconsolable weeping and distressfully said to him, "Mawla (master)! Do not thus shame us before the Messenger of Allāh, before Ali and Fātima! With what face will we present ourselves to them on the Day of Judgment? Were we to desert you, may the wild beasts of the jungle tear us to pieces."

Having said so, the faithful companions drew their swords out of their scabbards. Then they threw the scabbards in the fire of a ditch dug to protect the tents of the ladies. Holding their naked swords, they offered humble supplications to the Almighty beseeching Him thus: "O Lord of the creation! We are passing through the sea of trouble and sorrow in obedience to Your Prophet (ص) and in defense of the religion. You are the Sustainer of our honor and reputation. You are our Lord and Master. Grant us the strength of will and the spirit of enduring patience and perseverance so that we may remain firm and give our all in Your Path."

LOVE AND DEVOTION

Al-Qasim son of Imām al-Hassan son of Ali ibn Abū Talib, nephew of Imām al-Hussain (ع), was a 13-year old lad. He sought audience with the Imām in order to inquire whether his name was on the list of martyrs. "Your name," answered al-Hussain (ع), "is also included in the list of martyrs. You will be killed, and so will my suckling baby Ali al-Asghar (Junior)." After a short while, the Imām continued saying, "I, too, will be killed, but Allāh will continue my lineage. How would the cruel oppressors succeed in putting an end to his [Ali Zain al-Ābidīn's] life when eight Imāms are to be born as his offspring?"

In a tent sat Umm Kulthum, sister of al-Abbas, watching her brother polishing his weapons. She wore a woe-begone face, and tears kept trickling down her cheeks. Suddenly al-Abbas happened to look up. Seeing her tears, he inquired, "Honoured sister, why are you weeping?" "How could I help doing so," she replied, adding, "since I am an unlucky childless woman? Tomorrow, all the ladies will offer the lives of their sons for the Imām, whom shall I offer, having no son of my own?" Tears trickling down his cheeks, al-Abbas said, "Sister! From now on, I am your slave, and tomorrow you offer me, your slave, as a sacrifice for the Imām." Who else, dear reader, would call himself a slave of his sister besides al-Abbas? Such are the Ahl al-Bayt, and such are their manners.

ASHURA

The author of النشأتين صلاح *Salah an-Nash'atayn* records saying that the tragic and historical battle culminated on a Friday, the tenth of Muharram, 61 A.H., corresponding to October 13, 680 A.D., a day known in Islamic history as Ashura. Imām al-Hussain (ع) delivered two sermons to the misled souls that surrounded him from all directions, trying to bring them back to their senses, but it was to no avail.

ثمَّ دعا براحلته فركبها ، و نادى بصوت عال يسمعه جلّهم : أيّها النّاس اسمعوا قَولي ، ولا تعجلوا حتّى أعظكم بما هو حقٌّ لكم عليَّ ، وحتّى أعتذر إليكم من مَقدمي عليكم ، فإن قبلتم عذري وصدقتم قَولي وأعطيتموني النّصف من أنفسكم ، كنتم بذلك أسعد ، ولم يكن لكم عليَّ سبيل . وإنْ لَم تقبلوا مِنّي العذر ولَم تعطوا النّصف من أنفسكم ، فأجمعوا أمركم و شركاءكم ثمَّ لا يكن أمركم عليكم غمّة . ثمَّ اقضوا إليَّ ولا تنظرون . إنّ وليّيَ الله الذي نزل الكتاب وهو يتولّى الصالحين. فلمّا سمعنَ النّساء هذا منه صحنَ وبكينَ وارتفعت أصواتهنَّ ، فأرسل إليهنَّ أخاه العبّاس وابنه عليّاً الأكبر وقال لهما : (سكّتاهنَّ فلعمري ليكثر بكاؤهنَّ. ولمّا سكتنَ ، حمد الله وأثنى عليه وصلّى على محمّد وعلى الملائكة والأنبياء وقال في ذلك ما لا يحصى ذكره ولَم يُسمع متكلّم قبله ولا بعده أبلغ منه في

منطقه ، ثمّ قال : عباد الله ، اتقوا الله وكونوا من الدنيا على حذر ؛ فإنّ الدنيا لَو بقيت على أحد أو بقي عليها أحد لكانت الأنبياء أحقّ بالبقاء وأولى بالرضا وأرضى بالقضاء ، غير أنّ الله خلق الدنيا للفناء ، فجديدها بالٍ ونعيمها مضمحل وسرورها مكفهر ، والمنزل تلعة والدار قلعة ، فتزوّدوا فإنّ خير الزاد التقوى ، واتقوا الله لعلّكم تفلحون . أيّها النّاس إنّ الله تعالى خلق الدنيا فجعلها دار فناء وزوال متصرفة بأهلها حالاً بعد حال ، فالمغرور من غرّته والشقي من فتنته ، فلا تغرّنكم هذه الدنيا ، فإنّها تقطع رجاء من ركن إليها وتُخيّب طمع من طمع فيها . وأراكم قد اجتمعتم على أمر قد أسخطتم الله فيه عليكم وأعرض بوجهه الكريم عنكم وأحلّ بكم نقمته ، فنعمَ الربّ ربّنا وبئس العبيد أنتم ؛ أقررتم بالطاعة وآمنتم بالرسول محمّد (ص) ، ثمّ إنّكم زحفتم إلى ذريّته وعترته تريدون قتلهم ، لقد استحوذ عليكم الشيطان فأنساكم ذكر الله العظيم ، فتبّاً لكم ولِما تريدون . إنّا لله وإنّا إليه راجعون هؤلاء قوم كفروا بعد إيمانهم فبُعداً للقوم الظالمين .أيّها النّاس أنسبوني مَن أنا ثمّ ارجعوا إلى أنفسكم وعاتبوها وانظروا هل يحلّ لكم قتلي وانتهاك حرمتي ؟ ألستُ ابن بنت نبيّكم وابن وصيّه وابن عمّه وأول المؤمنين بالله والمصدّق لرسوله بما جاء من عند ربّه ؟ أوَ ليس حمزة سيّد الشهداء عمّ أبي ؟ أوَ ليس جعفر الطيّار عمّي ، أوَ لَم يبلغكم قول رسول الله لي ولأخي : هذان سيّدا شباب أهل الجنّة ؟ فإنْ صدّقتموني بما أقول وهو الحقّ ـ والله ما تعمدتُ الكذب منذ علمت أنّ الله يمقت عليه أهله ويضرّ به من اختلفه . وإنْ كذبتموني فإنّ فيكم مَن إنْ سألتموه عن ذلك أخبركم ، سلوا جابر بن عبد الله الأنصاري ، وأبا سعيد الخدري ، وسهل بن سعد الساعدي ، وزيد بن أرقم ، وأنس بن مالك يخبروكم أنّهم سمعوا هذه المقالة من رسول الله لي ولأخي ، أما في هذا حاجز لكم عن سفك دمي ؟! فقال الشمر : هو يعبد الله على حرف إنْ كان يدري ما يقول. فقال له حبيب بن مظاهر : والله إنّي أراك تعبد الله على سبعين حرفاً ، وأنا أشهد أنّك صادق ما تدري ما يقول ، قد طبع الله على قلبك . ثمّ قال الحسين (ع) :فإنْ كنتم في شكّ من هذا القول ، أفتشكّون أنّي ابن بنت نبيّكم ، فوالله ما بين المشرق والمغرب ابن بنت نبي غيري فيكم ولا في غيركم ، ويحكم اتطلبوني بقتيل منكم قتلته ؟! أو مال لكم استهلكته ؟! أو بقصاص جراحة ؟ !، فأخذوا لا يكلّمونه ! فنادى : يا شبث بن ربعي ، ويا حَجّار بن أبجر ، ويا قيس بن الأشعث ، ويا زيد بن الحارث: ألم تكتبوا إليَّ أنْ اقدم قد أينعت الثمار واخضرّ الجناب ، وإنّما تقدم على جند لك مجنّدة ؟ فقالوا: لَم نفعل . قال : سبحان الله ! بلى والله لقد فعلتم .ثمّ قال : أيّها النّاس ، إذا كرهتموني فدعوني أنصرف عنكم إلى مأمن من الأرض .فقال له قيس بن الأشعث : أولا تنزل على حكم بني عمّك ؟ فإنّهم لَن يروك إلاّ ما تُحبّ ولَن يصل إليك منهم مكروه . فقال الحسين عليه السّلام : أنت أخو أخيك ، أتريد أن يطلبك بنو هاشم أكثر من دم مسلم بن عقيل ؟ لا والله لا أعطيكم بيدي إعطاء الذليل ولا أفرّ فرار العبيد ، عباد الله إنّي عذتُ بربّي وربّكم أنْ ترجمون ، أعوذ بربّي وربّكم من كلّ متكبّر لا يؤمن بيوم الحساب .(ثمّ أناخ وأمر عقبة بن سمعان فعقلها .

The dumb and stonehearted rogues were not affected by al-Hussain's eloquent sermons. He asked them, "Am I not your Prophet's grandson? Am I not the son of the Commander of the

Faithful, cousin of the Prophet and the first male to believe in the divine message of Allāh? Is not Hamzah, the head of the martyrs, my father's uncle? Is not the martyr Ja'far at-Tayyar my uncle? Did the Prophet not reach your ears with words spoken in reference to me and to my elder brother (al-Hassan), saying, These (al-Hassan and al-Hussain (ع) are the masters of the youths of Paradise'?"

The renown historian at-Tabari and all other historians unanimously record that when al-Hussain (ع) proceeded so far in his sermon, the audience was moved against their wish, so much so that tears began to flow from the eyes of friends and foes alike. It was only al-Hurr, however, who was truly moved to the extent of stirring to action. Slowly did he walk as he kept saying, "Allāh! I turn to You in repentance from the depth of my heart, so do forgive me and forgive my sinful misconduct towards the Prophet's beloved Ahl al-Bayt." Approaching the Imām with eyes streaming with tears, with his shield turned the other way and his spear turned upside-down, he knelt down and kept crawling on his knees till he reached the Imām and fell on his feet kissing them, begging for his forgiveness. Al-Hussain (ع) accepted his apologies and prayed for him. Meanwhile, al-Hurr's defection alarmed Omer ibn Sa'd, the commander-in-chief of the enemies of al-Hussain (ع) and of Allāh. He was afraid such defection might encourage other commanders of his army to do likewise. Calling his slave, who was bearing the standard, he put an arrow on the string of his bow and discharged it at al-Hussain (ع), signaling the beginning of the battle. Martyrs fell one after another, recording epics of heroism unlike any others in the entire history of the human race. Their names and deeds of heroism are recorded on the pages of history for all generations to come.

خطبة الحسين (ع) الثانية

ثمّ إنّ الحسين (ع) ركب فرسه ، وأخذ مصحفاً ونشره على رأسه ، ووقف بإزاء القوم وقال : (يا قوم ، إنّ بيني وبينكم كتاب الله وسنّة جدّي رسول الله (ص) . ثمّ استشهدهم عن نفسه المقدّسة وما عليه من سيف النّبي (ص) ولامته وعمامته فأجابوه بالتصديق . فسألهم عمّا أخذهم على قتله ؟ قالوا : طاعةً للأمير عبيد الله بن زياد ، فقال عليه السّلام :)(تبّاً لكم أيّتها الجماعة و ترحاً ، أحين استصرختمونا والهين فأصرخناكم موجفين ، سللتم علينا سيفاً لنا في أيمانكم وحششتم علينا ناراً اقتدحناها على عدوّنا وعدوّكم ، فأصبحتم إلباً لأعدائكم على أوليائكم ، بغير عدل أفشوه فيكم ولا أمل أصبح لكم فيهم .

78

فهلاً ـ لكم الويلات ! ـ تركتمونا والسّيف مشيم والجأش طامن والرأي لما يستحصف ، ولكنْ أسرعتم إليها كطيرة الدبا وتداعيتم عليها كتهافت الفراش ، ثمَ نقضتموها ، فسحقاً لكم يا عبيد الأمة وشذاذ الأحزاب ونبذة الكتاب ومحرّفي الكلم وعصبة الإثم ونفثة الشيطان ومطفئيّ السّنَن ! ويحكم أهؤلاء تعضدون وعنّا تتخاذلون ! أجل والله غدر فيكم قديم وشجت عليه أصولكم وتأزّرت فروعكم فكنتم أخبث ثمرة ، شجى للناظر وأكلة للغاصب ! ألا وإنّ الدعيّ بن الدعيّ قد ركز بين اثنتَين ؛ بين السّلة والذّلّة ، وهيهات منّا الذّلّة ، يأبي الله لنا ذلك ورسوله والمؤمنون وحجور طابت وطهرت وأنوف حميّة ونفوس أبيّةً ، من أن نؤثر طاعة اللئام من مصارع الكرام ، ألا وإنّي زاحف بهذه الأسرة على قلّة العدد وخذلان النّاصر .(ثمَ أنشد أبيات فروة بن مُسيك المرادي. أما والله ، لا تلبثون بعدها إلّا كريثما يركب الفرس ، حتّى تدور بكم دور الرحى وتقلق بكم قلق المحور ، عهدِ عَهَده إليَّ أبي عن جدّي رسول الله ، فاجمعوا أمركم وشركاءكم ، ثمَ لا يكن أمركم عليكم غُمّة ثمَ اقضوا إليَّ ولا تنظرون ، إنّي توكّلت على الله ربّي وربّكم ، ما من دابّة إلّا هو آخذ بناصيتها إنَّ ربّي على صراط المستقيم .2)ثمَ رفع يدَيه نحو السّماء وقال :)(اللهمَ ، احبس عنهم قطر السّماء ، وابعث عليهم سنين كسنيّ يوسف ، وسلّط عليهم غلام ثقيف يسقيهم كأساً مصبرة ، فإنّهم كذبونا وخذلونا ، وأنت ربّنا عليك توكّلنا وإليك المصير .3) والله لا يدع أحداً منهم إلّا انتقم لي منه ، قتلةً بقتلة وضربةً بضربة ، وإنّه لينتصر لي ولأهل بيتي وأشياعي .

THE FIRST LADY MARTYR

Wahab ibn Abū Wahab, a Christian, and his wife, also a Christian, were married only a fortnight ago. Having witnessed what went on between al-Hussain (ع) and his foes, they sympathized with al-Hussain (ع) and embraced the Islamic creed at his hands. The words of the Imām's sermons penetrated their hearts and found an echo. Wahab's mother, still Christian, said to her son, "I will not be pleased with you till you give your life away for the sake of al-Hussain (ع)." Wahab charged at the enemies of Allāh like a lion, and when a man from Kūfa severed his right arm, he transferred the sword to the left and went on fighting as if nothing at all had happened. Soon his left arm, too, was lopped off by a single stroke of a sword, and the hero fell to the ground. His wife watched the whole scene. She pleaded to the Imām thus as she darted towards his enemies, "O Imām! Please do not ask me to go back! I prefer to die fighting rather than to fall captive in the hands of Banu Umayyah!" The Imām tried to dissuade her, explaining to her that fighting is not mandated on women, but at seeing her husband martyred, she ran to him and, putting his lifeless head in her lap, she began to wipe it with her clothes. Soon a slave of Shimr ibn Thul-Jawshan put an end to her life while she was thus engaged; may the Almighty shower

His blessings on her. It is unanimously agreed on by the historians that she was the first lady martyred on that day. Wahab's mother was very happy. She said, "Allāh! Thank You for saving my honour through my son's martyrdom before the Imām." Then the old Christian lady turned to the Kufians and said, "You wicked people! I bear witness that the Christians in their churches and the Zoroastrians in their fire houses are better people than you!" Saying so, she seized a stout candle (or, according to other accounts, a tent post) in her hand and fell upon the enemies, sending two of them to hell. The Imām sent two of his companions to bring her back. When she stood before him, he said to her, "O bondmaid of Allāh! Women are not allowed to go to war. Sit down; I assure you that you and your son will be with my grandfather in Paradise." Another martyr to be mentioned here, who was also Christian, is John, a slave of the great *sahabi* Abū Tharr al-Ghifāri, may Allāh be pleased with both of them. He had been for many years in the service of Abū Tharr, and although he was a very old man (according to some accounts, he was 90 years old), he fought al-Hussain's enemies till he was martyred.

AL-ABBAS IS MARTYRED

The story of the martyrdom of al-Abbas is a very sad one. Unfortunately, there is no room here to provide you with all its details due to the lack of space; therefore, we have to summarize it to you in a few words. Al-Abbas ventured to bring water to the wailing thirsty children. He individually had to face the eight hundred soldiers guarding the bank of the Euphrates against al-Hussain (ﻉ) and his small band having access to it. He was al-Hussain's standard-bearer. Both his arms were severed, one after the other,

and arrows made his body look like a porcupine. One of those arrows penetrated his right eye... When al-Hussain (ﻉ) saw his brother fall like that, he wept profusely as he said, "Now I have become spineless..." When al-Hussain (ع) tried to carry him to his camp, al-Abbas pleaded to him not to do so since he could not stand hearing the cries of the thirsty children especially since he had promised to bring them some water. He hated to go back to them empty-handed. Al-Hussain (ع), therefore, honoured his last wish; al-Abbas breathed his last as his brother al-Hussain (ع) was holding to him...

MARTYRDOM OF THE IMĀM

The Imām was also very courageous, so much so that he had already been called "the lion of Banu Hashim." He had participated in the wars waged by his father, the Commander of the Faithful Ali ibn Abū Talib (ع), in defense of the creed against the hypocrites led by the Umayyads and against the Kharijites, proving his military ability and mastership of the art of war. Had the Muslims of today mastered this art, and had they been able to make their own weapons rather than import them from others, they would not have been forced to sell their God-given natural resources, especially oil, dirt cheap to those who do not wish them any good. Had the rulers of the Muslim world learned how to get along with each other, they would have cooperated with each other for their own common good. Had the Muslims of the world implemented the commandments of their creed as strictly as they are supposed to, no unjust or tyrannical ruler would have ever ruled them... I think that such rulers, the likes of Yazid, are the main cause of the pathetic situation wherein the Muslims of the world find themselves at the present time, yet these rulers derive their strength from the weakness of their subjects; so, one problem is connected to the other...

Narrators of this incident record saying that there was hardly any place in al-Hussain's body that escaped a sword stroke or an arrow, and the same can be said about his horse as-Sahab which used to belong to Prophet Muhammed (ص) who, shortly before breathing his last, gave it to his right hand, cousin, and son-in-law Ali ibn Abū Talib (ع). Al-Hussain's older brother, Imām al-Hassan (ع), inherited it; after his martyrdom, it became the property of Imām al-Hussain (ع). Having become too feeble to fight, he stood to rest. It was then that a man threw a stone at him, hitting his forehead and causing his blood to run down his face. He took his shirt to wipe his blood from his eyes just as another man shot him with a three-pronged arrow which pierced his chest and settled in his heart. He instantly said, "In the Name of Allāh, through Allāh, and on the creed of the Messenger of Allāh [do I die]." Raising his head to the heavens, he said, "Lord! You know that they are killing a man besides whom there is no other son of Your Prophet's daughter." As soon as he took the arrow out of his back, blood gushed forth like a drain pipe. He placed his hand on his wound and once his hand was filled with blood, he threw it above saying, "Make what has happened to me easy for me; it is being witnessed by Allāh." Not a single drop of that blood fell on the ground. Then he put it back a second time, and it was again filled with blood. This time he rubbed it on his face and beard as he said, "Thus shall I appear when I meet my Lord and my grandfather the Messenger of Allāh (ﻉ), drenched in my blood. It is then that I shall say: O grandfather! So-and-so killed me.'"

Bleeding soon sapped his strength, so he sat down on the ground, feeling his head being too heavy. Malik ibn an-Nisr noticed his condition, so he taunted him then dealt him a stroke with his sword on the head. Al-Hussain (ﻉ) was wearing a burnoose which soon became full of blood. Al-Hussain (ﻉ) said, "May you never be able to eat or drink with your right hand, and may Allāh gather you among the oppressors." Having said so, the dying Imām threw his burnoose away and put on a turban on top of his capuche cap.

Hani ibn Thabeet al-Hadrami has said, "I was standing with nine other men when al-Hussain (ﻉ) was killed. It was then that I looked and saw one of the children from al-Hussain's family wearing a robe and a shirt, and he was wearing two ear-rings. He held a post from those buildings and stood startled looking right and left. A man came running. Having come close to that child, the man leaned from his horse and killed that child with his horse. When he was shamed for thus killing a helpless child, he revealed his last name..."

That child was Muhammed ibn Abū Sa'd ibn Aqeel ibn Abū Talib. His mother, dazed, stunned, and speechless, kept looking at him as the incident unfolded before her very eyes...

The enemies of Allāh waited for a short while then returned to al-

Hussain (ع) whom they surrounded as he sat on the ground unable to stand. Abdullāh son of Imām al-Hassan (ع), grandson of the Prophet (ص), who was eleven years old, looked and saw how his uncle was being surrounded by those people, so he came running towards him. Zainab, al-Hussain's revered sister, wanted to restrain him but he managed to evade her and to reach his uncle. Bahr ibn Ka'b lowered his head to strike al-Hussain (ع), so the child shouted, "O son of the corrupt woman, are you going to strike my uncle?" The man dealt a blow from his sword which the child received with his hand, cutting it off. The child cried in agony, "O uncle!" Then he fell in the lap of al-Hussain (ع) who hugged him and said, "O son of my brother! Be patient with regard to what has befallen us, and consider it as goodness, for Allāh, the most Exalted, will make you join your righteous ancestors." Then he raised his hands and supplicated saying, "O Allāh! Let them enjoy themselves for some time then divide them and make them into parties, and do not let their rulers ever be pleased with them, for they invited us to support us, then they turned their backs to us and fought us."

Harmalah ibn Kahil shot the child with an arrow, killing him as he sat in his uncle's lap.

Al-Hussain (ع) remained lying on the ground for some time. Had those rogues wished to kill him, they could have done so, but each tribe relied on the other to do what it hated to do itself. Ash-Shimr shouted, "What are you standing like that for?! What do you expect the man to do since your arrows and spears have wounded him so heavily? Attack him!" Zarah ibn Shareek struck him on his left shoulder with his sword while al-Haseen shot him with an arrow which penetrated his mouth; another man struck him on the shoulder. Sinan ibn Anas stabbed him in his collar bone area of the chest then shot him with an arrow in the neck. Salih ibn Wahab stabbed him in the side...

قال هلال بن نافع: كنت واقفاً نحو الحسين وهو يجود بنفسه ، فوالله ما رأيت قتيلاً قطّ مضمّخاً بدمه أحسن منه وجهاً ولا أنور ، ولقد شغلني نور وجهه عن الفكرة في قتله . فاستقى في هذه الحال ماء فأبوا ان يسقوه . وقال له رجل : لا تذوق الماء حتّى ترد الحامية فتشرب من حميمها . فقال عليه السّلام) :(أنا أرد الحامية ؟! وإنّما أرد على جدّي رسول الله وأسكن معه في داره في مقعد صدق عند مليك مقتدر وأشكو إليه ما

83

ارتكبتم منّي وفعلتم بي) .فغضبوا بأجمعهم حتّى كأنّ الله لَم يجعل في قلب أحدهم من الرحمة شيئاً .

Hilal ibn Nafi` has said, "I was standing in front of al-Hussain (ع) as he was drawing his last breath. Never did I ever see anyone whose face looked better or more glowing as he was stained with his own blood! In fact, the light emanating from his face distracted me altogether from the thought of killing him! As he was in such a condition, he asked for some water to drink, but they refused to give him any."

A man said to him, "You shall not taste of water till you reach hell from whose hot boiling water shall you drink." He, peace be with him said, "Am I the one who will reach it? Rather, I will reach my grandfather the Messenger of Allāh (ع) and reside with him in his abode of truth near an Omnipotent King, and I shall complain to him about what crimes you committed against me and what you have done to me." They all became very angry. It is as if Allāh did not leave an iota of compassion in their hearts. When his condition worsened, al-Hussain (ع) raised his eyes to the heavens and said,

"O Allāh! Sublime You are, Great of Might, Omnipotent, Independent of all creation, greatly Proud, Capable of doing whatever You please, Forthcoming in mercy, True of Promise, Inclusive of Blessings, Clement, Near to those who invoke Him, Subduing His creation, Receptive to Repentance, Able, Overpowering, Appreciative when thanked, Remembering those who remember Him! Thee do I call upon out of my want, and Thee do I seek out of need! From Thee do I seek help when in fear and cry when depressed! Thine help do I seek in my weakness, and upon Thee do I rely! O Allāh! Judge between us and our people, for they deceived and betrayed us. They were treacherous to us, and they killed us although we are the *Itrat* of Your Prophet and the offspring of the one You love: Muhammed (ص) whom You chose for Your Message and entrusted with the revelation. Do find an ease for our affair and an exit, O most Merciful of all merciful ones! Grant me patience to bear Your destiny, O Lord! There is no Allāh but You! O Helper of those who seek help! I have no Allāh besides You, nor do I adore anyone but You! Grant me to persevere as I face Your

84

decree, O Helper of the helpless, O Eternal One Who knows no end, O One Who brings the dead back to life, O One Who rewards every soul as it earned, do judge between me and them; surely You are the best of judges."

HUSSAIN'S HORSE

Al-Hussain's horse came circling around him, rubbing his head on his blood. It was then that Ibn Sa'd shouted, "The horse! Get the horse, for it is one of the horses of the Messenger of Allāh!" Horsemen surrounded that horse which kept kicking with its front legs, killing forty riders and ten horses. Ibn Sa'd then said, "Leave him and let us see what he does." Once he felt secure, the horse went back to al-Hussain (ع) to rub his head on the Imām's blood as he sniffed him. He was neighing very loudly. Imām Abū Ja'far al-Bāqir (ع) used to say that that horse was repeating these words: "Retribution! Retribution against a nation that killed the son of its Prophet's daughter!" The horse then went to the camp neighing likewise. When the women saw the horse without its rider and its saddle twisted, they went out, their hair spread out, beating their cheeks, their faces uncovered, screaming and wailing, feeling the humiliation after enjoying prestige, going in the direction of the place where al-Hussain (ع) had been killed.

Umm Kulthum, Zainab the wise, cried out, "O Muhammed! O father! O Ali! O Ja'far! O Hamzah! Here is al-Hussain in the open slain in Kerbalā'!" Then Zainab said, "I wish the heavens had fallen upon the earth! I wish the mountains had crushed the valley!" She was near al-Hussain (ع) when Omer ibn Sa'd came close to her flanked by some of his men. Al-Hussain (ع) was drawing his last breath. She cried out, "O Omer ! Should Abū Abdullāh be killed as you look on?!" He turned his face away. His tears were flooding his beard. She said, "Woe unto you! Is there any Muslim man among you?" None answered her. Then Omer Ibn Sa'd shouted at people, "Alight and put him to rest!" Ash-Shimr was the first to do so. He kicked the Imām with his foot then sat on his chest and took hold of his holy beard. He dealt him twelve sword strokes. He then severed his sacred head...

AL-HUSSAIN MARAUDED

Those folks now took to maurauding the Imām: Ishāq ibn Hawayh took his shirt. Al-Akhnas ibn Murthid ibn Alqamah al-Hadrami took his turban. Al-Aswad ibn Khalid took his sandals. Jamee ibn al-Khalq al-Awdi, and some say a man from Tameem named al-Aswad ibn Hanzalah, took his sword.

Bajdal came. He saw the Imām (ع) wearing a ring covered with his blood. He cut his finger off and took the ring... Qays ibn al-Ash'ath took his velvet on which he since then used to sit, so he came to be called "Qays Qateefa." Qateefa is Arabic for velvet. His worn out garment was taken by Jaoonah ibn Hawiyyah al-Hadrami. His bow and outer garments were taken by ar-Raheel ibn Khaythamah al-Ju'fi and Hani ibn Shabeeb al-Hadrami and Jarar Ibn Mas'ūd al-Hadrami. A man among them wanted to take his underpants after all his other clothes had been taken away by others. This man said, "I wanted to take it off, but he had put his right hand on it which I could not lift; therefore, I severed his right hand... He then put his left hand on it which I also could not lift, so I severed it, too, and I was about to bare him and take it off when I heard a rumbling like that of an earthquake, so I became frightened. I left him and fell into a swoon, a slumber. While I was unconscious, I saw the Prophet, Ali, Fātima, and al-Hassan, in a vision. Fātima was saying, O son! They killed you! May Allāh kill them!' He said to her, O mother! This sleeping man has severed my hands!' She then invoked Allāh's curse on me saying, May Allāh cut your hands and legs, and may He blind you and hurl you into the fire!' Indeed, I am now blind. My hands and legs have already been amputated, and nothing remains from her curse except the fire."

اللهم آرزقنا شفاعة الحسين

PART II

A SUMMARY OF
POST-MARTYRDOM EVENTS

When al-Hussain (ع) was martyred, people fell upon his luggage and belongings looting everything they could find in his tents[1], then they set the tents to fire. People raced to rob the ladies of the Messenger of Allāh (ع). Daughters of Fātima az-Zahrā' (ع) tearfully ran away, their hair uncovered[2]. Scarves were snatched, rings were pulled out of fingers, ear-rings were taken out, and so were ankle-rings[3]. A man took both ear-rings belonging to Umm Kulthum, riddling her ears in the process[4]. Another approached Fātima daughter of al-Hussain (ع), taking her ankle-rings out. He was weeping as he committed his foul deed. "What is the matter with you?," she asked him. "How can I help weeping," he answered, "since I am looting the daughter of the Messenger of Allāh?" She asked him to leave her alone. He said, "I am afraid if I do not take it, someone else will."[5]

---

[1]Ibn al-Atheer, *At-Tarikh al-Kāmil*, Vol. 4, p. 32.

[2]at-Tabari, *Tarikh*, Vol. 6, p. 260.

[3]Ibn Nama, *Muthir al-Ahzan*, p. 40.

[4]Muhammed Jawad Shubbar, *Al-Dam'a as-Sakiba*, p. 348.

[5]as-Sadūq, *Aamali*, p. 99, *majlis* 31. at-Thahbi, *Siyar Alam an-Nubala'*, Vol. 3, p. 204.

Another man was seen driving the women with the butt of his spear, having robbed them of their coverings and jewelry as they sought refuge with one another. He was seen by the same Fātima. Having realized that she had seen him, he went towards her, and she fled away. He threw his spear at her; she fell headlong and fainted. When she recovered, she saw her aunt, Umm Kulthum, sitting at her head crying.[1]

A woman from the clan of Bakr ibn Wa'il, who was accompanied by her husband, saw the daughters of the Messenger of Allāh (ﷺ) in such a condition, so she cried out, "O offspring of Bakr ibn Wa'il! Do you permit the daughters of the Messenger of Allāh (ﷺ) to be robbed like that? There is no judgment except Allāh's! O how the Messenger of Allāh (ﷺ) should be avenged!" Her husband brought her back to his conveyance[2].

The rogues reached Ali son of al-Hussain (ﷺ) who was sick on his bed unable to stand up[3]. Some were saying, "Do not let any of them, young or old, alive." Others were saying, "Do not be rash in your

---

[1]Mawla Hussain ibn Mawla Muhammed al-Jammi (known as the virtuous man of Jamm) *Riyad al-Masa'ib fil Mawaiz wal Tawarikh wal Siyar wal Masa'ib*, p. 341. al-Qazwini, *Tazallum az-Zahra'*, p. 130.

[2]Ibn Tawoos, namely Sayyid Ali ibn Musa ibn Ja'far, *Al-Luhuf fi Qatla at-Tufuf*, p. 74. Ibn Nama, *Muthir al-Ahzan*, p. 41.

[3]Reference to the sickness of Ali son of al-Hussain, as-Sajjād (ﷺ) is referred to by at-Tabari on p. 260, Vol. 6, of his *Tarikh*. It is also mentioned by Ibn al-Atheer on p. 33, Vol. 4, of his book *At-Tarikh al-Kāmil*, by Ibn Katheer on p. 188, Vol. 8, of his book *Al-Bidaya*, by al-Yafii on p. 133, Vol. 1, of his book *Mir'at al-Jinan*, by Shaikh al-Mufid in his book *Kitab Al-Irshad*, by Ibn Shahr Ashub on p. 225, Vol. 2, of his book *Manaqib*, by at-Tibrisi on p. 148 of his book *I'lam al-Wara bi A'lam al-Huda*, by Muhammed ibn Ahmed ibn Ali an-Nishapuri on p. 162 of his book *Rawdat al-Waizeen*, and by al-Mas'udi on p. 140 of his book *Ithbat al-Wasiyya*.

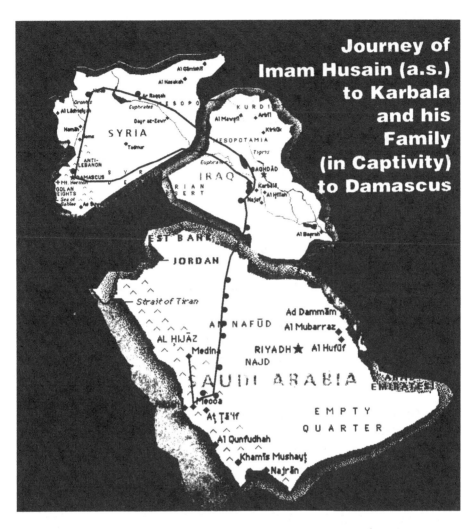

Journey of Imam Husain (a.s.) to Karbala and his Family (in Captivity) to Damascus

judgment till we consult the governor Amr ibn Sa'd."[1] Ash-Shimr unsheathed his sword with the intention to kill Ali. Hameed ibn Muslim said to him, "Glory to Allāh! Do you really kill children?! He is only a sick lad!"[2] He said, "Ibn Ziyad ordered all al-Hussain's sons killed." Ibn Sa'd went to extremes to stop him[3] especially after

---

[1] al-Qazwini, *Tazallum az-Zahra'*, p. 132.

[2] at-Tabari, *Tarikh*, Vol. 6, p. 260.

[3] Shaikh Abbas al-Qummi, *Nafas al-Mahmum*.

having heard the wise lady Zainab daughter of the Commander of the Faithful (ع) saying, "You will not kill him before killing me first;" so, they left him alone[1].

Ibn Sa'd himself came to the ladies who burst in tears upon seeing him. He ordered the men to stay away from them. Those men had already taken all the ornaments those ladies had had and never returned any of them back. He assigned to a group of men the task of protecting them, then he returned to his tent.

THE STEED
Ibn Sa'd shouted, "Who volunteers to make sure that the chest and the back of al-Hussain (ع) are run over by the horses?" Ten men stood up.[2] Those miscreant "volunteers" were: Ishāq ibn Hawiyyah, al-Ahbash ibn Murshid ibn Alqamah ibn Salamah al-Hadrami, Hakeem ibn at-Tufayl as-Sinbisi, Amr ibn Sabeeh as-Saydawi, Raja' ibn Munqith al-Abdi, Salim ibn Khaythamah al-Ju'fi, Salih ibn Wahab al-Ju'fi, Wakhit ibn Ghanim, Hani ibn Thabeet al-Hadrami, and Aseed ibn Malik. They rode their horses and trampled upon the body of the fragrant flower of the Messenger of Allāh...

Ibn Ziyad ordered liberal awards to be given to them[3]. Al-Bayruni has said that they did to al-Hussain (ع) what no other nation had ever done to their most evil ones: killing with the sword or the spear, with stone throwing, and with horse trampling[4]. Some of those horses reached Egypt were their shoes were pulled out and fixed on doors as means of seeking blessings. This became a custom among them,

---

[1]al-Qarmani, *Tarikh*, p. 108.

[2]at-Tabari, *Tarikh*, Vol. 6, p. 161. Ibn al-Atheer, *At-Tarikh al-Kāmil*, Vol. 4, p. 33. al-Mas'udi, *Muraj at-Thahab*, Vol. 2, p. 91. al-Maqrazi, *Khutat*, Vol. 2, p. 288. Ibn Katheer, *Al-Bidaya*, Vol. 8, p. 189. al-Khamees, *Tarikh*, Vol. 3, p. 333. Shaikh al-Mufid, *Al-Irshad*. at-Tibrisi, *I'lam al-Wara bi A'lam al-Huda*, p. 888. Muhammed ibn Ahmed ibn Ali an-Nishapuri, *Rawdat al-Wa'izeen*, p. 662. Ibn Shahr Ashub, *Al-Manaqib*, Vol. 2, p. 224.

[3]Ibn Tawoos *Al-Luhuf*, p. 75. Ibn Nama, *Muthir al-Ahzan*, p. 41.

[4]*Al-Aathar al-Baqiya*, p. 329.

so much so that many of them started making the like of those shoes and hanging them over the doors of their houses.[1]

THE SEVERED HEADS

Ibn Sa'd ordered the heads to be severed from their bodies. They were distributed to various tribes that used them as means to seek favor with Ibn Ziyad. The Kindah tribe took thirteen brought by their envoy Qays ibn al-Ash'ath. The Hawazin tribe brought twelve with their "man" Shimr ibn Thul-Jawshan. The Tameem tribe brought seventeen; the Banu Asad tribe brought sixteen; the Mathhaj tribe brought seven, and the other tribes brought the rest[2]. The tribe to which al-Hurr ar-Riyahi belonged refused to cut anyone's head or to let their horses trample on the Imām's body[3].

On the tenth day, Ibn Sa'd had already entrusted the head of Imām al-Hussain (ع) to Khawli ibn Yazid al-Asbahi and Hameed ibn Muslim al-Azdi. He entrusted the heads of the Imām's family members and those of his companions to ash-Shimr, Qays ibn al-Ash'ath and Amr ibn al-Hajjaj[4]. Khawli's house was one farasang from Kūfa. He hid the head from his Ansari wife whom he knew to be loyal to Ahl al-Bayt, peace be with them. But when she saw a light emanating from the bakery oven [where it was hidden], she was terrified. When she came closer, she heard the voices of al-Hussain's women mourning al-Hussain (ع) in the most somber way. She mentioned this to her husband then went out crying[5]. Since then, she

---

[1]al-Karakchi, *Kitab at-Taajjub*, p. 46.

[2]Ibn Tawoos *Al-Luhuf*, p. 81. Al-Ayni, *Umdat al-Qari fi Sharh al-Bukhari*, Vol. 7, p. 656, where the name of Urwah ibn Qays is included among them.

[3]Al-Hajj Shaikh Muhammed Baqir ibn Mawla Hassan al-Qa'ini al-Birjandi as-Safi, *Al-Kibrit al-Ahmar fi Shar'iat Ahl al-Minbar*.

[4]Shaikh al-Mufid, *Al-Irshad*.

[5]Muhammed an-Nishapuri, *Rawdat ash-Shuhada'*. On p. 190, Vol. 8, Ibn Katheer says that his wife saw the light emanating from underneath the lid and stretching to the heavens as white birds kept hovering around it. He

never used any kohl nor any perfume out of her grief for al-Hussain (ع). She was called Ayoof[1].

In the morning, Khawli took the head to the governor's mansion. By then, Ibn Ziyad had returned from his camp at an-Nakheela. Khawli put the head in front of Ibn Ziyad as he recited these poetic verses:

إنّي قتلت السيّد المحجّبا   إمـلأ ركابي فضّة أو ذهبا

قـتلت خير الناس أُمّاً وأبا   وخيرهم من يذكرون النسبا

فساء ابن زياد قوله أمام الجمع فقال له : إذا علمت إنّه كذلك فلِمَ قتلته ؟ والله لا نلت نّي شيئاً.

Fill my stirrup with silver or with gold:
I killed the master of every honor told,
Their best when they mention descent.
I killed the best of people, son of the best parent.

But these words, spoken in front of everyone, were met by Ibn Ziyad with outrage. "Since you knew that he was that honorable," said Ibn Ziyad, "why did you then take part in killing him? By Allāh, you will receive nothing from me at all."[2]

---

adds saying that his other wife, Nuwar daughter of Malik, said to him, "Have you brought the head of the son of the Messenger of Allah, peace of Allah and His blessings upon him and his family, here?! I shall never share a bed with you henceforth." She separated from him.

[1]al-Balathiri, *Ansab al-Ashraf*, Vol. 5, p. 238.

[2]According to p. 133, Vol. 1, of al-Yafi'i's book *Mir'at al-Jinan*, Ibn Ziyad was very angry with him, so he killed him, but the author does not identify the name of the head bearer. On p. 213, Vol. 2, of *Al-Iqd al-Farid fi Marifat al-Qira'a wal Tajwad* of Sayyid Muhammed Ridha ibn Abul-Qasim ibn FathAllah ibn Nejm ad-Din al-Hussaini al-Kamali al-Asterbadi al-Hilli (died in 1346 A.H./1927 A.D.), the head bearer is identified as Khawli ibn Yazid al-Asbahi who was killed by Ibn Ziyad. Historians contend among themselves about who had brought the head and who had said the above verses. According to Ibn Jarir at-Tabari, who indicates so on p. 261, Vol. 6, of his *Tarikh*, and Ibn al-Atheer who states so on p. 33, Vol. 4, of his book *At-Tarikh al-Kāmil*, the poet was Sinan ibn Anas who

LEAVING KERBALĀ

When Ibn Sa'd sent the heads to Kūfa, he remained with the army till noon on the eleventh day [of Muharram]. He gathered those killed from his army and performed the funeral prayers for them then buried them, leaving the corpses of the Master of the Youths of Paradise (ع) and those of his Ahl al-Bayt (ع) and companions unwashed, unshrouded, and unburied[1], exposed to the wind and to the wild beasts of the desert.

After the time of *zawal*, Ibn Sa'd left for Kūfa with the women, the children, the bondmaids, and the surviving family members of al-Hussain's companions. They included twenty women[2] whom they

recited them to Omer ibn Sa'd. On p. 144 of *Tathkirat al-Khawass* of Ibn al-Jawzi, the grandson, Omer said to him, "You are insane! Had Ibn Ziyad heard you, he would have killed you!" On p. 193, Vol. 1, of ash-Sharishi's *Maqamat*, the author says that the poet recited them to Ibn Ziyad. According to al-Irbili's *Kashf al-Ghumma* and al-Khawarizmi's p. 40, Vol. 2, of *Maqtal al-Hussain (ع)*, Bishr ibn Malik recited them to Ibn Ziyad. On p. 76 of Ibn Talhah's *Matalib as-Saool*, there is the addition of "... and whoever says his prayers in both Qiblas," whereupon Ibn Ziyad became very angry with him and had him beheaded. On p. 437 of *Riyad al-Musa'ib*, it is stated that ash-Shimr is the one who recited these verses. Since you know that ash-Shimr is al-Hussain's killer according to the text of the *ziyarat* of the sacred area and according to a host of historians, you likewise know that he must be the one who recited them. It is very unlikely that he kills him and lets someone else take the head and use it to seek favor with Ibn Ziyad. We have mentioned the story from Khawli only to follow in the footsteps of those who wrote about the Imām's martyrdom.

[1]al-Khawarizmi, *Maqtal al-Hussain (ع)*, Vol. 2, p. 39.

[2]Shaikh Abbas al-Qummi, *Nafas al-Mahmum*, p. 204. On p. 234, Vol. 2, of an-Nawari's book *Mustadrak al-Wasa'il* (first edition), both Shaikh al-Mufid and Sayyid Ibn Tawoos cite Imām as-Sadiq (ع) saying that he, peace be with him, had prayed two *rek'ats* at al-Qā'im, a place on the highway leading to al-Ghari (Najaf), then said, "Here was the head of my grandfather al-Hussain (ع) placed when they went to Kerbala' then carried it to Ubaydullah ibn Ziyad." Then the Imām (ع) recited a supplication to be recited following the prayer saying, "This place is called al-Hananah."

mounted on camels without saddles just as was the custom then with Turks or Romans taken captive although they belonged to the best of all prophets (ع). With them was as-Sajjād Ali ibn al-Hussain (ع) who was twenty-three years old[1]. He was placed on a lean camel without a saddle, and he was worn out by sickness[2]. His son [the later Imām] al-Bāqir[3], who was two years and a few months old[4], accompanied him. Among the children of Imām al-Hassan (ع) taken captive were: Zaid, Amr, and al-Hassan II. The latter was captured after he had killed seventeen men. He received eighteen wounds, and his right arm had been cut off. Asma' ibn Kharijah al-Fizari intervened to get him freed because his mother was also Fizari, so Ibn Sa'd left her husband take him[5]. With them was Uqbah ibn Saman, a slave of ar-Rubab, al-Hussain's wife. When Ibn Ziyad came to know that that man was ar-Rubab's slave, he released him. Ibn Ziyad was informed that al-Muraqqa' ibn Thumamah al-Asadi had scattered his arrows around then fled to his tribe where he sought and received protection, he ordered him to be banished to az-Zara[6].

---

[1]Mis'ab az-Zubairi, *Nasab Quraish*, p. 58.

[2]Ibn Tawoos, *Al-Iqbal*, p. 54.

[3]Muhammed Hassan ash-Shaban Kurdi al-Qazwini, *Riyad al-Ahzan*, p. 49. al-Mas'udi, *Ithbat al-Wasiyya*, p. 143.

[4]al-Mas'udi, *Ithbat al-Wasiyya*, p. 143 (Najaf edition). According to p. 203, Vol. 1, of Abul-Fida''s *Tarikh*, Vol. 1, p. 203, he was three years old.

[5]al-Majlisi, *Bihār al-Anwār*, Vol. 10, in the chapter discussing the offspring of Imām al-Hassan (ع). According to p. 28 of *Isaf ar-Raghibeen*, commenting on a footnote in *Nar al-Absar*, and also according to p. 8 of *Al-Luhuf* by Ibn Tawoos, he treated him at Kufa, and when he healed, he transported him to Medīna.

[6]at-Tabari, *Tarikh*, Vol. 6, p. 261. Ibn al-Atheer, *At-Tarikh al-Kāmil*, Vol. 4, p. 33. According to p. 367, Vol. 4, of Yaqut al-Hamawi's *Mu'jam al-Buldan*, az-Zara is a village in Bahrain, and there is another in West Tripoli as well as another in the upper Delta of the Nile. According to p. 692, Vol. 2, of al-Bikri's book *Al-Mu'jam mimma Istajam'*, it is a place in the Bahrain area where wars waged by an-Nu'man ibn al-Munthir, who was nicknamed al-Gharoor (the conceited one), battled al-Aswaris. It also

The ladies pleaded to him thus: "For the love of Allāh! Please take us to those killed." When they saw how they had lost their limbs, how the spears had drank of their blood, and how the horses had trampled upon them, they screamed and beat their faces in anguish[1].

Zainab cried out,

يا محمّداه ! هذا حسين بالعراء ، مرمّل بالدماء ، مقطّع الأعضاء ، وبناتك سبايا ، وذريّتك مقتّلة . فأبكت كلّ عدو وصديق

"O Muhammed! Here is al-Hussain in the desert covered with blood,

---

is a city in Persia where a duel took place between al-Bara' ibn Malik and the city's satrap, al-Bara' killed the latter and cut his hand off. He took his belt and both his bracelets the value of which was thirty thousand dinars. Omer ibn al-Khattab took the *khums* of the loot, and that was the first time in the history of Islam that a loot was taxed by 1/5 and delivered to the caliph (whereas it was/is supposed to be given to the Prophet's descendants according to the injunctions of the Holy Qur'an). On p. 10, Vol. 4, of his book *At-Tarikh al-Kāmil*, Ibn al-Atheer says that Ibn Ziyad threatened to banish the people of Kufa [who refused to fight al-Hussain (ع)] to Oman's Zara. Also on p. 86, Vol. 8, where the events of the year 321 A.H./933 A.D. are discussed, it is stated that Ali ibn Yaleeq ordered Mu'awiyah and his son Yazid to be cursed from the pulpits in Baghdad, whereupon the Sunnis were outraged. There, al-Barbahari, a Hanbalite, used to stir trouble; he ran away from Ali ibn Yaleeq. The latter captured al-Barbahari's followers and shipped them in a boat to Oman. It appears from the latter account that Zara is a place in Oman. On p. 256 of al-Dainuri's book *Al-Akhbar at-Tiwal*, Ibn Ziyad banished al-Muraqqa to az-Zabada where the latter stayed till Yazid's death and Ibn Ziyad's flight to Syria. Al-Muraqqa, therefore, left it and went back to Kufa. On p. 9, Vol. 8, of *Nashwar al-Muhadara wa Akhbar al-Muthakara* by at-Tanakhi, the judge, namely Muhsin ibn Ali ibn Muhammed Abul-Fahm (329 - 384 A.H./941 - 994 A.D.), it is stated that Muhammed al-Muhallabi banished Muhammed ibn al-Hassan ibn Abdul-Aziz al-Hashimi to Oman in a boat because of something he had done which angered him.

[1]Ibn Nama, *Muthir al-Ahzan*, p. 41. Ibn Tawoos, *Al-Luhuf*, p. 74. Al-Khawarizmi, *Maqtal al-Hussain (ع)*, Vol. 2, p. 39. At-Turayhi, *Maqtal al-Hussain (ع)*, p. 332.

his limbs cut off! Here are your daughters taken captive and your offspring slaughtered!" These words caused friends and foes alike to weep[1], even the horses' tears ran on their hooves[2]. Then she put her hands under his sacred body and lifted it as she supplicated saying, "O Lord! Do accept this sacrifice from us[3]."

Sukayna[4] hugged the body of her father al-Hussain (ع) and kept telling him how she had heard him saying,

---

[1] al-Maqrazi, *Khutat*, Vol. 2, p. 280. According to the authors of both *Maqtal al-Hussain (ع)* and *Al-Luhuf*, the mourning was even on a much larger scale.

[2] al-Khawarizmi, *Maqtal al-Hussain (ع)*, Vol. 2, p. 39. Shaikh LutfAllah ibn al-Mawla Muhammed Jawad as-Safi al-Gulpaigani, *Al-Muntakhab al-Athar fi Akhbar al-Imām at-Thani Ashar* (usually referred to as simply *Al-Muntakhab*), p. 332.

[3] al-Birjandi as-Safi, *Al-Kibrit al-Ahmar*, Vol. 3, p. 13, citing *At-Tiraz al-Muthahhab*.

[4] According to p. 163, Vol. 1, of an-Nawawi's *Tahthib al-Asma'*, p. 58, Vol. 1, of Shaikh Muhammed Ali ibn Ghanim al-Qatari al-Biladi al-Bahrani's book *Al-Kawakib al-Durriyya*, p. 160 of ash-Shiblinji's *Nar al-Absar*, and Ibn Khallikan's *Wafiyyat al-Ayan*, where the author details her biography, Sukayna daughter of al-Hussain (ع) died on a Thursday, Rabi' I 5, 117 A.H./April 8, 735 A.D. According to Abul-Hassan al-Amri's book *Al-Mujdi* and to at-Tibrisi's book *Alam al-Wara bi Alam al-Huda*, p. 127, where the biographies of the offspring of Imām al-Hassan (ع) are discussed, and also according to p. 163, Vol. 12, of Abul-Faraj al-Isfahani's book *Al-Aghani*, she married her cousin Abdullāh ibn al-Hassan ibn Ali ibn Abū Talib (ع) who was killed during the Battle of at-Taff. She did not bear any children by him. But the author *I'lam al-Wara bi A'lam al-Huda*, namely at-Tibrisi, says that he was killed before marrying her, and that during the Battle of at-Taff, she was a little more than ten years old, and that she was born before the the death [martyrdom] of her uncle Imām al-Hassan (ع). The statement in her honor made by the Master of Martyrs (ع), "Sukayna is overcome by deep contemplation upon Allah," as is recorded by as-Sabban in his book *Isaf ar-Raghibeen*, clearly outlines for us the status his daughter occupied in the sacred canons of Islam's *Shari'a*.

شيعتي ما أَنْ شربتم عَذْبَ ماء فاذكروني
أو سمعتم بغريب او شهيد فاندبوني

O my Shī'as! Whenever of water you drink
Never from mentioning my name should you shrink.
And whenever you are a stranger on a sojourn
Or see a martyr, me should you remember and mourn. [1]

Only a number of them could collectively remove her from his
corpse, forcefully dragging her away. [2]

When Ali ibn al-Hussain (ع) looked at his slaughtered family, he felt
greatly grieved and worried. When his sister Zainab al-Kubra read
his face, she felt upset on his account and took to consoling him and
admonishing him to be patient although even the mountains could
not match him in his patience and fortitude. Among what she said to
him is the following:

ما لي أراك تجود بنفسك يا بقيّة جدّي وأبي وإخوتي؟ فوالله إنّ هذا لعهد من الله إلى جدّك
وأبيك ، ولقد أخذ الله ميثاق أناس لا تعرفهم فراعنة هذه الأرض ، وهم معروفون في أهل
السّماوات ، إنّهم يجمعون هذه الأعضاء المقطّعة والجسوم المضرّجة ، فيوارونها
وينصبون بهذا الطفّ علماً لقبر أبيك سيّد الشهداء لا يُدرس أثره ولا يُمحى رسمه على
كرور الليالي والأيّام ، وليجتهدنّ أئمّة الكفر وأشياع الضلال في محوه وتطميسه ، فلا
يزداد أثره إلاّ علوّاً.

"Why do I see you pleading for death, O the legacy of my
grandfather, of my father and brothers? By Allāh, this is something
which Allāh had divulged to your grandfather (ع) and to your father
(ع). Allāh took a covenant from people whom you do not know, the
mighty ones on this land, and who are known to the people of the
heavens, that they would gather these severed parts and wounded
corpses and bury them, then shall they set up on this Taff a banner

---

[1] These verses are recorded on p. 376 of the Indian edition of *Misbah al-Kaf'ami*.

[2] al-Qazwini, *Tazallum az-Zahra'*, p. 135.

for the grave of your father, the Master of Martyrs (ع), the traces of which shall never be obliterated, nor shall it ever be wiped out so long as there is day and night. And the leaders of apostasy and the promoters of misguidance shall try their best to obliterate and efface it, yet it shall get more and more lofty instead."[1]

Zajr ibn Qays came to them and shouted at them to leave as he kept whipping them. Others surrounded them and mounted them on camel humps.[2]

Zainab the wise rode her own she-camel. She recollected the days of lofty honor and inviolable prestige, guarded by fierce and honorable lions of Abdul-Muttalib's offspring. And she used to always be surrounded by servants who would not enter without her permission.

AT KŪFA

When the daughters of the Commander of the Faithful (ع) entered Kūfa, the city's residents gathered to see them, so Umm Kulthum shouted at them, "O people of Kūfa! Do not you have any sense of shame before Allāh and His Messenger so you look at the ladies of the Prophet?"[3]

One of Kūfa's women came to them and saw their condition for which even a most bitter enemy would feel sorry. She asked them what captives they were, and she was told: "We are captives belonging to the Progeny of Muhammed."[4] The people of Kūfa kept doling out dates, walnuts and bread to the children, whereupon Umm

---

[1]Shaikh Abul-Qasim Ja'far ibn Muhammed ibn Ja'far ibn Musa ibn Qawlawayh al-Qummi (died in 367 A.H./977 A.D.), *Kāmil az-Ziyarat*, p. 361, chapter 88, virtues of Kerbala' and merits of viziting the grave site of al-Hussain (ع).

[2]Radiyy ad-Din ibn Nabi al-Qazwini (died in 1134 A.H./1722 A.D.), *Tazallum az-Zahra'*, p. 177.

[3]Muhammed Jawad Shubbar, *Al-Dam'ah as-Sakibah*, p. 364.

[4]Ibn Nama, p. 84. *Al-Luhuf*, p. 81.

Kulthum, that is, Zainab al-Kubra, shouted at them that they were prohibited from accepting charity. She threw away what had been given to the children[1]. A poet once composed these lines addressing Imām Ali ibn Abū Talib (ع):

O father of Hassan!
She overlooks and in the slumber she delights,
But only with her hand can Zainab now cover her face.
O father of Hassan!
Does this sight you please:
Each of your women chained, uncovered the face,
While Banu Harb's women in their chambers veiled with grace?
Does your side on the bed find comfort and ease,
While your daughters on the camels to Syria are brought?
Are you pleased when your wise ladies are exposed?
With lashes they are whipped when they cry, having no rest..
To the east they are once taken by the mean gangs, the worst,
And once towards the land of shame are taken, to the west.
None to protect them as they cross every plain,
None heeds their complaints when they complain.
Their voices were lost and their hearts squeezed,
Their breath by grief is almost snatched away
Amazed am I about one who thinks of fate
And wonders and upon it does he contemplate:
A fornicator leisurely turns about on his throne,
As al-Hussain on the ground is left, unburied, alone,
And his head is on a lance openly carried,
And with the crown is crowned the son of a whore.
For three days did Hussain stay unburied or more.
One's body is to cruel elements is left exposed
As the other covers his with silk and with gold.[2]

---

[1] ar-Rashti al-Ha'iri, *Asrar ash-Shahada*, p. 477. Al-Qazwini, *Tazallum az-Zahra'*, p. 150.

[2] Excerpted from a poem in praise of al-Hussain (as) by Shaikh Hassoon al-Hilli who died in 1305 A.H./1888 A.D. as we are told on p. 155, Vol. 2, of *Shuara' al-Hilla*.

ZAINAB'S SPEECH

The daughter of the Commander of the Faithful (ع) explained to people Ibn Ziyad's villainy and meanness in a speech which she delivered to them. When she signaled to them to calm down, they did. They stood speechless and motionless, and even the bells of their animals stopped ringing. It was then that she, calm and composed and with courage reminiscent of that of her father Haider (ع) addressed them saying,

يقول الراوي : لمّا أومأت زينب ابنة علي (ع) إلى النّاس ، فسكنت الأنفاس والأجراس ، فعندها اندفعت بخطابها مع طمأنينة نفس وثبات جأش ، وشجاعة حيدريّة ، فقالت صلوات الله عليها: الحمد لله والصلاة على أبي محمّد وآله الطيّبين الأخيار .

أمّا بعد ، يا أهل الكوفة ، يا أهل الختل والغدر ، أتبكون ؟! فلا رقأت الدمعة ، ولا هدأت الرنّة ، إنّما مثلكم كمثّل التي نقضت غزلها من بعد قوّة أنكاثاً ، تتّخذون أيمانكم دخلاً بينكم ، ألا وهل فيكم إلاّ الصلف النطف والعجب والكذب والشنف وملق الإماء، وغمز الأعداء؟! أو كمرعى على دمنة أو كقصّة على ملحودة، ألا بئس ما قدّمتْ لكم أنفسكم أنْ سخط الله عليكم ، وفي العذاب أنتم خالدون .

أتبكون وتنتحبون ؟! إي والله فابكوا كثيراً ، واضحكوا قليلاً ؛ فلقد ذهبتم بعارها وشنارها ، ولن ترحضوها بغسل بعدها أبداً ، وأنّى ترحضون قتّل سليل خاتم النبوّة ومعدن الرسالة ، ومدرة حجّتكم و منار محَجّتكم ، وملاذ خيرتكم ومفزع نازلتكم ، وسيّد شباب أهل الجنّة ، ألا ساء ما تزرون .

فتعساً و نكساً وبُعداً لكم وسحقاً ، فلقد خاب السّعي وتبّت الأيدي ، وخسرت الصفقة ، وبوّتم بغضب من الله ورسوله ، وضُربت عليكم الذّلّة والمسكنة .ويلكم يا أهل الكوفة ، أتدرون أيّ كبد لرسول الله فريتم ؟ وأيّ كريمة له أبرزتم ؟ وأيّ دم له سفكتم ؟ وأيّ حرمة له انتهكتم ؟ لقد جئتم شيئاً إدّاً ، تكاد السّموات يتفطّرن منه ، وتنشقّ الأرض ، وتخرّ الجبال هدّاً . ولقد أتيتم بها خرقاء شوهاء كطلاع الأرض وملء السّماء .

أفعجبتم أنْ مطرت السّماء دماً ولعذاب الآخرة أخزى وهم لا يُنصرون ، فلا يستخفنّكم المهل ، فإنّه لا يحفزه البدار ، ولا يخاف فوت الثار ، وإنّ ربّكم لَبِالمرصاد.

All Praise is due to Allāh. Peace and blessings be upon my father Muhammed (ص) and upon his good and righteous Progeny (ع). May the resounding [of this calamity] never stops. Your similitude is one who unspins what is already spun out of the desire to violate [a trust]. You make religion a source of your income... Is there anyone among you who is not a boaster of what he does not have, a charger of debauchery, a conceited liar, a man of grudge without any justification, one submissive like bondmaids, an instigator, a pasture of what is not wholesome, one who recites a story to someone who is buried? Truly bad is that which your souls have committed. You have reaped the Wrath of Allāh, remaining in the chastisement for eternity. Do you really cry and sob? By Allāh, you should then cry a great deal and laugh very little, for you have earned nothing but shame and infamy, and you shall never be able to wash it away, and how could you do so? The descendant of the Bearer of the Last Message (ﷺ), the very essence of the Message, the source of your security and the beacon of your guidance, the refuge of the righteous from among you, the one who saves you from calamity, the Master of the Youths of Paradise... is killed. O how horrible is the sin that you bear...! Miserable you are and renegades from the path of righteousness; may you be distanced and crushed. The effort is rendered futile, the toil is ruined, the deal is lost, and you earned nothing but Wrath from Allāh and His Messenger (ﷺ). You are doomed with servitude and humiliation. Woe unto you, O Kūfians (Kūfans)! Do you know whose heart you have burned, what a "feat" you have labored, what blood you have shed, and what sanctity you have violated? You have done a most monstrous deed, something for which the heavens are about to split asunder and so is the earth, and for which the mountains crumble. You have done something most uncanny, most defaced, as much as the fill of the earth and of the sky. Do you wonder why the sky rains blood? Surely the torment of the hereafter is a greater chastisement, and they shall not be helped. Let no respite elate you, for rushing does not speed it up, nor does it fear the loss of the opportunity for revenge. Your Lord is waiting in ambush for you.[1]

Imām as-Sajjād (ﷺ) said to her, "That is enough, O aunt, for you are, Praise to Allāh, a learned lady whom none taught, one who

---

[1] This speech is compiled from the writings of Shaikh at-Tusi in his *Aamali* as well as that of his son, from *Al-Luhuf*, Ibn Nama, Ibn Shahr Ashub, and from at-Tibrisi's book *Al-Ihtijaj*.

comprehends without being made to do so."[1]

FĀTIMA DELIVERS A SPEECH

Fātima, al-Hussain's daughter[2], delivered a speech wherein she said,

---

[1]at-Tibrisi, *Al-Ihtijaj*, p. 166 (Najaf's edition).

[2]Fatima daughter of al-Hussain (ع), peace be with him, was a great personality; she enjoyed a great status in the creed. Her father, the Master of Martyrs, testifies to this fact. When al-Hassan II approached him asking him for the hand of either of his two daughters, he, peace be with him, as we are told on p. 202 of *Nar al-Absar*, said to him, "I choose for you Fatima, for she, more than anyone else, is like my mother Fatima daughter of the Messenger of Allah (ع). As far as the creed is concerned, she stays awake all night long offering prayers, and the daytime she spends fasting. In beauty, she looks like the *huris* with large lovely eyes." On p. 442, Vol. 12, of Ibn Hajar's *Tahthib at-Tahthib*, she is said to have narrated *hadīth* from her father, brother Zain al-Ābidīn, aunt Zainab, Ibn Abbas, and Asma' daughter of Umays. Her sons Abdullāh, Ibrahim, al-Hussain (ع), and her daughter Umm Ja'far, offspring of al-Hassan II, quote her *hadīth*. Abul-Miqdam quotes her *hadīth* through his mother. Zuhayr ibn Mu'awiyah quotes her *hadīth* through his mother. On p. 425 of *Khulasat Tahtheeb al-Kamal*, it is stated that the authors of *sunan* books, including at-Tirmithi, Abū Dāwūd, and an-Nassa'i, have all quoted her *ahadīth*. So does the author of *Musnad Ali*. Ibn Majah al-Qazwini does likewise. Ibn Hajar al-Asqalani says, "She is mentioned in the book of funerals in Bukhari's *Sahīh*, and Ibn Haban holds her reliable, adding that she died in 110 A.H./729 A.D." So do both authors al-Yafii, on p. 234, Vol. 1, of his book *Mir'at al-Jinan*, and Ibn al-Imad on p. 39, Vol. 1, of his book *Shatharat*. Based on what Ibn Hajar says in his book *Tahthib at-Tahthib*, she must have lived for almost ninety years, placing her year of birth at about 30 A.H./651 A.D. Hence, she must have been almost thirty years old during the Battle of at-Taff. She died seven years before her sister Sukayna. On p. 35, Vol. 4, of Ibn al-Atheer's book *At-Tarikh al-Kāmil*, and also according to p. 267, Vol. 6, of at-Tabari's *Tarikh*, Fatima was older than her sister Sukayna. On p. 18 of *Tahqiq an-Nusra ila Maalim Dar al-Hijra* by Abū Bakr ibn Hussain ibn Omer al-Maraghi (d. 816 A.H./1414 A.D.), one of the signs of her lofty status with Allah is that when al-Walid ibn Abdul-Malik ordered to deposit the relics at the mosque, Fatima daughter of al-Hussain (ع) went out to al-Harra where she had a house built for her. Then she ordered a well to be dug up; a stone appeared in it, and she was informed of it. She made her ablution then

الحمد لله عدد الرمل والحصى ، وزنة العرش إلى الثرى ، أحمده وأؤمن به وأتوكّل عليه وأشهد أنْ لا إله إلاّ الله وحده لا شريك له وأنّ محمداً عبده ورسوله ، وأنّ أولاده ذُبحوا بشطّ الفرات ، من غير ذحل ولا ترات .

اللهمّ إنّي أعوذ بك أنْ أفتري عليك ، وأنْ أقول عليك خلاف ما أنزلت من أخذ العهود والوصيّة لعلي بن أبي طالب المغلوب حقّه ، المقتول من غير ذنب كما قُتل ولده بالأمس ، في بيت من بيوت الله تعالى ، فيه معشر مسلمة بألسنتهم ، تعساً لرؤوسهم ما دفعت عنه ضيماً في حياته ولا عند مماته ، حتّى قبضه الله تعالى إليه محمود النّقيبة طيّب العريكة ، معروف المناقب مشهور المذاهب ، لم تأخذه في الله سبحانه لَومة لائم ولا عذل عاذل ، هديته اللهمّ للإسلام صغيراً ، وحمدت مناقبه كبيراً ، ولم يزل ناصحاً لك ولرسولك ، زاهداً في الدنيا غير حريص عليها ، راغباً في الآخرة ، مجاهداً لك في سبيلك ، رضيته فاخترته وهديته إلى صراط مستقيم .

أمّا بعد، يا أهل الكوفة ، يا أهل المكر والغدر والخيلاء ، فإنّا أهل بيت ابتلانا الله بكم ، وابتلاكم بنا . فجعل بلاءنا حسناً ، وجعل علمه عندنا وفهمه لدنيا ، فنحن عَيبة علمه ، ووعاء فهمه وحكمته ، وحجّته على الأرض في بلاده لعباده ، أكرمنا الله بكرامته ، وفضّلنا بنبيّه محمّد (صلّى الله عليه وآله) على كثير ممّن خلق الله تفضيلاً ، فكذّبتمونا وكفرتمونا ، ورأيتم قتالنا حلالاً ، وأموالنا نهباً ، كأنّا أولاد ترك أو كابل ، كما قتلتم جدّنا بالأمس ، وسيوفكم تقطر من دمائنا أهل البيت لحقد متقدّم ، قرّت لذلك عيونكم ، وفرحت قلوبكم افتراءً على الله ومكراً مكرتم، والله خير الماكرين ، فلا تدعونّكم أنفسكم إلى الجذل بما أصبتم من دمائنا ، ونالت أيديكم من أموالنا ، فإنّ ما أصابنا من المصائب الجليلة ، والرزايا العظيمة في كتاب من قبل أن نبرأها ، إنّ ذلك على الله يسير ؛ لكيلا تأسوا على ما فاتكم ولا تفرحوا بما آتاكم ، والله لا يحبّ كل مختال فخور .

تبّاً لكم فانظروا اللعنة والعذاب ، فكأنّ قد حلّ بكم وتواترت من السّماء نقمات ، فيسحتكم بعذاب ويذيق بعضكم بأس بعض ، ثمّ تخلدون في العذاب الأليم يوم القيامة ؛ بما ظلمتمونا ، ألا لعنة الله على الظالمين .

ويلكم ! أتدرون أيّة يد طاعنتنا منكم ؟ وأيّة نفس نزعت إلى قتالنا ؟ أم بأيّة رجل مشيتم إلينا ؟ تبغون محاربتنا ، قست قلوبكم وغلظت أكبادكم وطبع الله على أفئدتكم ، وختم على سمعكم وبصركم وسوّل لكم الشيطان وأملى لكم ، وجعل على بصركم غشاوة فأنتم لا تهتدون .

---

sprinkled the leftover water on it. After that, it was not difficult at all to dig that well. People used to seek blessings through the use of its water, and they named it "Zamzam". On p. 474, Vol. 8, of Ibn Sa'd's *Tabaqat* (Sadir's edition), Fatima daughter of al-Hussain (ع) used to use knots on a string as her rosary beads.

تبّاً لكم يا أهل الكوفة ، أيّ ترات لرسول الله قِبَلَكم ، وذحول له لديكم ؟ بما عندتم بأخيه على بن أبي الطالب جدّي وبنيه وعترته الطيّبين الأخيار ، وافتخر بذلك مفتخركم:

| بسيوف هنديّة ورماح | نحن قتلنا عليّاً وبني علي |
| و نطحناهم فـأيّ نطاح | وسبينا نساءهم سبي ترك |

بفيك أيها القائل الكثكث والأثلب؛ افتخرت بقتل قوم زكّاهم الله وطهّرهم وأذهب عنهم الرجس، فأكضم وأقع كما أقعى أبوك فإنّما لكلّ امرىء ما اكتسب وما قَدّمت يداه .

حسدتمونا، ويلاً لكم، على ما فضّلنا الله تعالى ، ذلك فضل الله يؤتيه مَن يشاء والله ذوالفضل العظيم . ومَن لَم يجعل الله له نوراً فما له من نور .

فارتفعت الأصوات بالبكاء والنّحيب وقالوا : حسبكِ يا ابنة الطاهرين فقد حرقت قلوبنا وأنضجت نحورنا وأضرمت أجوافنا ، فسكتت .

"All Praise is due to Allāh, as much as the number of the sands and of the stones, as much as the Arsh weighs up to the ground. I praise Him, believe in Him and rely upon Him. And I testify that there is no Allāh other than Allāh, the One and Only Allāh, there is no partner with Him, and that Muhammed is His servant and Messenger, and that his offspring have been slaughtered by the Euphrates river neither on account of blood revenge nor out of dispute over inheritance. Lord! I seek refuge with You against telling a lie about You and against saying anything contrary to what You have revealed of taking many a covenant regarding the vice-regency of Ali ibn Abū Talib (ع), the man whose right is confiscated, who was killed without having committed a sin, just as his son was only yesterday killed, at one of the houses of Allāh, the most Exalted One, at the hand of those who give Islam nothing but lip service. Destruction may afflict their heads that did not ward off from him any injustice as long as he lived nor at his death, till Allāh Almighty took his soul to Him while his essence was praised, his dealing with others was commendable, his merits were well known, and his beliefs well admitted by everyone. Never did he ever accept anyone's blame nor the criticism of any critic in doing what is right. Lord! You guided him to Islam even when he was a child and praised his virtues when he grew up. Never did he ever cease enjoining others to follow Your Path and that of Your Messenger

(ع). He always paid no heed to the riches of this world. He always desired the hereafter, a man who carried out jihad for Your Cause. With him were You pleased, so You chose him and guided him to a Straight Path. O people of Kūfa! O people of treachery, of betrayal and conceit! We are members of a Household tried on your account by Allāh, afflicted by you. He made our dealing with you good, and He entrusted His knowledge to us, and He bestowed upon us its comprehension; so, we are the bastion of His knowledge, understanding and wisdom, and His Arguments on the earth which He created for the good of His servants! Allāh bestowed upon us His blessings and greatly honored us with His Prophet, peace and blessings of Allāh be upon him and his Progeny, favoring us over many of those whom He created. Yet you called us liars and apostates, and in your eyes you deemed killing us as lawful, and so is looting our possessions, as if we were the offspring of the Turks or of Kabul, just as you killed our grandfather in the past. Your swords drip with our blood, the blood of Ahl al-Bayt, out of past animosity. Thus have your eyes been cooled, and thus have your hearts been elated, telling lies about Allāh and out of evil plans which you hatched, while Allāh is the very best of planners. So do not be carried away with your excitement because of our blood which you have spilled or our wealth which you have snatched, for what has befallen us is truly a great tragedy and a momentous calamity "In a Book even before We created them; surely this is easy for Allāh, so that you may not be grieved because of what you missed nor feel happy because of what you acquired, and Allāh does not love anyone who is conceited, boastful" (57:23). May you be ruined! Expect to be cursed and to be tormented, for it seems as though it has already befallen you, and more and more signs of Wrath are on their way to you from the heavens till He makes you taste of the chastisement and make some of you taste of the might of others, then on the Day of Judgment shall you all remain for eternity in the painful torment on account of the injustice with which you have treated us; the curse of Allāh be upon the oppressors. Woe unto you! Do you know what hand you have stabbed, what soul found fighting us agreeable? Rather, by what feet did you walk towards us with the intention to fight us? Your hearts became hardened, and Allāh sealed your hearts, your hearing, and your vision, and Satan inspired to you and dictated, placing a veil over your eyes, so you can never be guided. Destruction is your lot, O people of Kūfa! What a legacy of the Prophet (ص) is standing before you, and what blood revenge will he seek from you on account of your enmity towards his brother Ali ibn Abū Talib (ع), my grandfather, and towards his good and righteous offspring, yet you even brag about it saying,

We killed Ali and Ali's sons,
With Indian swords and spears
And we placed their women in captivity
Like the Turks! We crushed them with severity.

May stones and pebbles fill your mouths! You brag about killing people whom Allāh chose and whom He purified with a perfect purification and from whom He kept away all abomination. Suppress it, then, and squat just as your fathers did, for each will get the rewards of what he earns and will be punished for what he committed. You envied us, woe unto you, for what Allāh, the most Exalted One, favored and preferred us. Such is Allāh's favor: He bestows His favors upon whomsoever He pleases, and surely with Allāh are great favors. For whoever Allāh does not make a *noor*, he shall have no light at all."

Voices were raised with weeping and wailing, and they said to her, "Enough, enough, O daughter of the pure ones, for you have burnt our hearts and necks," so she took to silence.

AS-SAJJĀD DELIVERS A SPEECH
Ali ibn al-Hussain (ع) was brought on a lean camel. Chains were placed on his neck, and he was handcuffed. Both sides of his neck were bleeding. He was repeating these verses:

O nation of evil, may your quarter never tastes of water!
O nation that never honored in our regard our Grandfather!
Should we and the Messenger of Allāh meet
On the Judgment Day, how would you then plead?
On bare beasts of burden have you
Transported us, as if we never put up a creed for you!

He signaled to people to be silent. Once they were silent, he praised

106

Allāh and glorified Him and saluted the Prophet (ص). Then he said,

أيّها النّاس ، مَن عرفني فقد عرفني ، ومَن لَم يعرفني فأنا علي بن الحسين بن علي بن أبي طالب ، أنا ابن من انتُهكت حرمته ، وسُلبت نعمته وانتهب ماله ، وسُبِي عياله ، أنا ابن المذبوح بشطّ الفرات من غير ذحل ولا تراث ، أنا ابن من قُتل صبراً ، وكفى بذلك فخراً .

أيّها النّاس، ناشدتكم الله هل تعلمون أنّكم كتبتم إلى أبي وخدعتموه وأعطيتموه من أنفسكم العهود والميثاق والبيعة ، وقاتلتموه ؟

فتبّاً لكم لما قدّمتم لأنفسكم ، وسوأة لرأيكم ، بأيّة عين تنظرون إلى رسول الله ؟ إذ يقول لكم : قتلتم عترتي ، وانتهكتم حرمتي ، فلستم من أمّتي .

فارتفعت الأصوات بالبكاء وقالوا : هلكتم وما تعلمون .

ثمّ قال عليه السّلام : (رحم الله امرءاً قبل نصيحتي ، وحفظ وصيّتي في الله وفي رسوله وأهل بيته ، فإنّ لنا في رسول الله أسوة حسنة.)

فقالوا بأجمعهم : نحن يابن رسول الله سامعون مطيعون حافظون لذمامك ، غير زاهدين فيك ، ولا راغبين عنك ، فمرنا بأمرك يرحمك الله ، فإنّا حرب لحربك ، وسِلم لسلمك ، نبرأ ممّن ظلمك وظلمنا .

فقال عليه السّلام: هيهات هيهات، أيّها الغدرة المكرة ، حيل بينكم وبين شهوات أنفسكم ، تريدون أن تأتوا إليَّ كما أتيتم إلى أبي من قبل ؟ كلّا وربّ الراقصات ، فإنّ الجرح لمّا يندمل ، قُتل أبي بالأمس وأهل بيته ، ولَم ينس ثكل رسول الله وثكل أبي وبني أبي ، إنّ وجده والله لبين لهاتي ومرارته بين حناجري وحلقي ، وغُصّته تجري في فراش صدري:

فبعين جبّار السّما لم يكتم	مـهلاً بـني حرب فما قد نـالنا
بالرسل يقدم حاسراً عن معصم	فكأنّني يوم الحساب بأحمد
وتركتم الأسياف تنطف من دمي	و يـقول ويلكم هتكتم حرمتي
أم أيَّ خـود سـقتُمُ في المغنم	تـدرون أيَّ دم أرقتم في الثرى
وحرائري تسبى كسبي الديلم	أمـن الـعدالة صونكم فتياتكم
و كبود أطفالي ظماء تضرم	والماء تورده يـعافير الفلا
رهطي لما ارتكبوا لذاك المعظم	تالله لـو ظفرت سراة الكفر في
طـعن الحناجر بعد حزّ الغلصم	يـا لـيت شعر محمّد ما فاتكم

O people! Whoever recognizes me knows me, and whoever does not, let me tell him that I am Ali son of al-Hussain (ع) ibn Ali ibn Abū Tālib (ع). I am the son of the man whose sanctity has been violated, whose wealth has been plundered, whose children have been seized. I am the son of the one who has been slaughtered by the Euphrates neither out of blood revenge nor on account of an inheritance. I am the son of the one killed in the worst manner. This suffices me to be proud. O people! I plead to you in the Name of Allāh: Do you not know that you wrote my father then deceived him? Did you not grant him your covenant, your promise, and your allegiance, then you fought him? May you be ruined for what you have committed against your own souls, and out of your corrupt views! Through what eyes will you look at the Messenger of Allāh (ع) when he says to you, "You killed my Progeny, violated my sanctity, so you do not belong to my nation"?

Loud cries rose, and they said to each other, "You have perished, yet you are not aware of it." Then he, peace be with him, said, "May Allāh have mercy on anyone who acts upon my advice, who safeguards my legacy with regard to Allāh, His Messenger (ع), and his Ahl al-Bayt (ع), for we have in the Messenger of Allāh (ع) a good example of conduct to emulate." They all said, "We, O son of the Messenger of Allāh, hear and we obey, and we shall safeguard your trust. We shall not turn away from you, nor shall we disobey you; so, order us, may Allāh have mercy on you, for we shall fight when you fight, and we shall seek asylum when you do so;  we dissociate ourselves from whoever oppressed you and dealt unjustly with you." He, peace be with him, said, "Far, far away it is from you to do so, O people of treachery and conniving! You are separated from what you desire. Do you want to come to me as you did to my father saying, No, by the Lord of all those [angels] that ascend and descend'?! The wound is yet to heal. My father was killed only yesterday, and so were his Ahl al-Bayt (ع), and the loss inflicted upon the Messenger of Allāh (ع), upon my father (ع), and upon my family is yet to be forgotten. Its pain, by Allāh, is between both of these [sides] and its bitterness is between my throat and palate. Its choke is resting in my very chest."[1]

THE BURIAL
Historians record saying that the Master of Martyrs (ع) set up a tent

---

[1]All these speeches are mentioned by Ibn Tawoos in his book *Al-Luhuf* and by Ibn Nama in his book *Muthir al-Ahzan*.

on the battlefield[1], ordering those killed from among his companions and Ahl al-Bayt (ع) to be carried to it. Whenever a fresh martyr was brought, he, peace be with him, would say, "You have been killed just as the prophets and the families of prophets are killed."[2] He did so to everyone with the exception of his brother al-Abbas, peace be with him, whom he left where he fell near the river bank of the Euphrates.

When Omer ibn Sa'd accompanied those whom he arrested of the custodians of the Message and left for Kūfa, he left behind those who were described by the Commander of the Faithful (ع) as the masters of martyrs in the life of this world and in the hereafter, an honor to which nobody ever preceded nor will anyone succeed them[3], lying on the sands incinerated by the sun and sought by the wild beasts of the desert.

Among them was the Master of the Youths of Paradise who was in a condition that would split the hardest of the stones, yet divine lights were emanating from his corpse, and sweet scents were surrounding him from all directions.

A man belonging to Banu Asad has narrated the following:

Once the army left, I came to the battlefield and saw light emanating from those corpses that were covered with blood and smelled sweet scents. I saw a terrifying lion walking between the amputated parts till he reached the embodiment of sanctity and the sacrifice of guidance. He rubbed himself on his blood and rubbed his body on his as he kept muttering and letting out a very strange sound. I was amazed. Never have I ever seen such a fierce lion abandon what

---

[1] at-Tabari, *Tarikh*, Vol. 6, p. 256. Ibn al-Atheer, *At-Tarikh al-Kāmil*, Vol. 4, p. 30. Al-Mufid, *Al-Irshad*.

[2] This is narrated on p. 211, Vol. 10, and p. 125, Vol. 13, of al-Majlisi's *Bihār al-Anwār* where an-Nu'mani's book *Al-Ghaiba* is cited.

[3] al-Qummi, *Kāmil az-Ziyarat*, p. 219.

would be for his likes nothing but a meal. I hid among the marshes and kept watching to see what else he would do. I was more amazed when midnight came. It was then that I saw candles with voices that filled the earth with painful cries and wailing.[1]

On the 13th day of Muharram, Zain al-Ābidīn (ع) came to bury his martyred father, peace be with him, since only an Imām buries another Imām.[2]

When as-Sajjād (ع) came to the place, he saw Banu Asad assembled around the slain not knowing what to do. They could not identify the corpses especially since their killers had separated the heads from the bodies. Had it been otherwise, they could have inquired about them with the families and the tribes of those slain. But he, peace be with him, informed them that it was his task to bury those pure bodies. He informed them of the names of the slain, identifying those who belonged to Banu Hashim from the rest. Crying and wailing rose, and tears filled the eyes of everyone present there and then. The ladies of Banu Asad loosened their hair in grief and beat their cheeks.

Imām Zain al-Ābidīn (ع) walked to his father's body, hugged it and wept loudly. Then he came to the grave-site and lifted a handful of its soil. A grave already dug appeared, and so did a pre-constructed shrine... He placed his hands under the Imām's back and said, "In the Name of Allāh, and according to the creed of the Messenger of Allāh. Allāh has said the truth, and so has His Messenger (ع). The will of Allāh be done; there is neither power nor might except in Allāh, the Great." Then he took it and went down without being assisted by anyone from among the Banu Asad to whom he said, "I have with me someone who will assist me." Once he laid it down in the grave, he put his cheek on his father's sacred neck and said, "Congratulations to the land that contains your pure body, for the world after you is dark whereas the hereafter in your light shall

---

[1]al-Bahrani, *Madeenat al-Ma'ajiz*, p. 263, chapter 127.

[2]al-Mas'udi, *Ithbat al-Wasiyya*, p. 173.

shine. As to the night, it is the harbinger of sleep, while grief remains forever, for Allāh shall choose for your Ahl al-Bayt (ع) your abode wherein you shall abide. From me to you is Salam, O son of the Messenger of Allāh, and the mercy of Allāh and His blessings."

On the grave he wrote: "This is the grave of al-Hussain son of Ali son of Abū Talib, the one whom they killed even as he was a thirsty stranger." Then he walked to the body of his uncle al-Abbas, peace be with him, and he saw him in a condition that had left the angels in the heavens' strata baffled and caused the *huris* to weep even as they were in the chambers of Paradise. He fell upon it kissing his sacred neck and saying, "May the world after you be obliterated, O moon of Banu Hashim, and peace from me to you, O martyr, and the mercy of Allāh and His blessings."

He dug a grave for him and took him down in it by himself just as he had done to the corpse of his martyred father (ع). He said to Banu Asad, "There is someone with me to help me."

Yes, he gave a piece of jewelry to Banu Asad as a token of appreciation for consoling him in burying the martyrs, and he assigned for them two places, ordering them to dig two pits in the first of which he buried those slain from Banu Hashim and in the second those slain from among the companions[1].

As regarding al-Hurr ar-Riyahi, his corpse was taken away by his tribe that buried it where it now stands. It is said that his mother was present then and there, and when she saw what was being done to the corpses, she carried her son's corpse somewhere else.[2]

---

[1]See *Al-Kibrit al-Ahmar fi Shara'it Ahl al-Minbar* الكبريت الأحمر في شريعة أهل المنبر by the narrator Shaikh Muhammed Baqir son of Mawla Hassan al-Qa'ini al-Birjandi as-Safi, *Asrar ash-Shahada* by Sayyid Kadhim ibn Qasim ar-Rashti al-Ha'iri (died in 1259 A.H./1843 A.D.), and *Al-Iyqad*.

[2]Al-Hajj Shaikh Muhammed Baqir al-Birjandi as-Safi, *Al-Kibrit al-Ahmar fi Shara'it Ahl al-Minbar*. On p. 344 of his book *Al-Anwar an-Nu'maniyya*, Sayyid al-Jaza'iri cites testimonials to this statement. He, for example, details how [sultan] Isma'eel as-Safawi [founder of the Safavid dynasty; he lived from 904 - 930 A.H./1499 - 1524 A.D. and ruled Iran from 907 - 930

The closest in proximity to the grave of al-Hussain (ع) from among the martyrs is his son Ali al-Akbar, peace be with him. In this regard, Imām as-Sādiq (ع) says to Hammad al-Basri, "The father of Abdullāh was killed a stranger away from home; he is mourned be whoever visits his grave-site, and whoever does not visit it grieves for him; whoever doe not see him is very depressed on account of being deprived of doing so, so he grieves; whoever sees the grave of his son at his feet in a desolate land, far away from his kinsfolk, invokes Allāh's mercy for him because of the fact that he was not supported when he called upon people to uphold righteousness, and because the renegades assisted one another against him till they killed him and did not have any respect for him, so much so that they exposed his corpse to the wild beasts and prohibited him from drinking of the water of the Euphrates of which the dogs drink. They disregarded their obligations in his respect towards the Messenger of Allāh (ع) who had enjoined them to be kind to him and to his Ahl al-Bayt (ع). He became abandoned in his grave, slain among his kinsfolk and Shī'as. In loneliness, being near his grave removes the pain of loneliness and so is his being distant from his grandfather (ع) and from the house which none could enter except those whose conviction of heart Allāh tested, and by those who recognize our rights. My father has told me that since he was killed, his place has never been empty of those who bless him from among the angels, the *jinns*, mankind, and even the wild beasts. Whoever visits it is envied and is rubbed for blessing, and looking at his grave is done in anticipation of earning goodness. Allāh boasts to the angels of those

---

A.H./1502 - 1524 A.D.] dug up the place, whereupon he saw the deceased as though he had just been killed; there was a bandage on his head. Once he untied it in person, blood started pouring out, and the bleeding did not stop till he tied it back again. He built a dome above the grave and assigned an attendant for it. So, when an-Nawari, in his book *Al-Lulu wal Marjan*, denies that he had been buried, he did not support his denial with any evidence at all. On p. 37, Vol. 1, of *Tuhfat al-Alim*, Sayyid Ja'far Bahr al-Ulum states that Hamid-Allah al-Mustawfi has indicated in his book *Nuzhat al-Quloob* saying that there is in Kerbala' the grave of al-Hurr [ar-Riyahi] which is visited by people. He is al-Hurr's grandson up to 18 generations back.

who visit it. As far as what such pilgrim receives from us, we invoke Allāh's mercy for him every morning and every evening. It has come to my knowledge that some Kūfians as well as others in Kūfa's outskirts pay it a visit in the eve of the middle of Shaban. They recite the Holy Qur'an; they narrate his story; they mourn him, and women eulogize him while others compose their own eulogies." Hammad said to the Imām (ع), "I have personally witnessed some of what you have described." The Imām, peace be with him, then said, "Praise to Allāh Who has made some people come to us, praise us, and mourn us, and praised is He for making our enemy shame them for doing so, threaten them, and describe what they do as ugly."[1]

AT THE GOVERNOR'S MANSION
Having returned from his camp at Nakheela, Ubaydullāh Ibn Ziyad went straight to his mansion[2]. The sacred head was brought to him, and it was then that the walls started bleeding[3] and a fire broke out from one part of the mansion and made its way to the place where Ibn Ziyad was sitting[4]. He fled away from it and entered one of the

---

[1] al-Qummi, *Kāmil az-Ziyar az-Ziyarat*, p. 325. at-Tibrisi, *Mazar al-Bihar*, p. 124, citing the previous reference.

[2] According to p. 142, Chapter 9, of at-Thaalibi's book *Lataif al-Maarif*, Abdul-Malik ibn Ameer al-Lakhmi has narrated saying, "I saw the head of al-Hussain (ع) ibn Ali ibn Abū Talib (ع) at the government mansion of Ubaydullah ibn Ziyad placed on a shield, and I saw the head of al-Mukhtar with Mis'ab ibn az-Zubair on another shield. I saw the head of Mis'ab in front of Abdul-Malik ibn Marwan on yet another shield! When I told Abdul-Malik [ibn Marwan ibn al-Hakam] about that, he regarded it as a bad omen and left the place." The same is narrated by as-Sayyati on p. 139 of his book *Tarikh al-Khulafa'*, and by Sibt ibn al-Jawzi on p. 148 of his book *Tathkirat al-Khawass* (Iranian edition) by Ibn al-Jawzi, the grandson..

[3] Ibn Asakir, *Tarikh*, Vol. 4, p. 329. Ibn Hajar al-Asqalani, *As-Sawa'iq al-Muhriqa*, p. 116. *Thakha'ir al-Uqba*, p. 145. Ibn Tawoos, *Al-Malahim*, p. 128 (first edition).

[4] Ibn al-Atheer, *At-Tarikh al-Kāmil*, Vol. 4, p. 103. Ibn Hajar al-Asqalani, *Mujma az-Zawa'id*, Vol. 9, p. 196. Al-Khawarizmi, *Maqtal al-Hussain (ع)*, Vol. 2, p. 87. At-Turayhi, *Al-Muntakhab*, p. 339 (Hayderi Press edition).

mansion's rooms. The head spoke out in a loud voice that was heard by Ibn Ziyad as well as by those who were present there and then. It said, "Where do you flee to? If fire does not catch you in the life of this world, it shall be your abode in the hereafter." The head did not stop speaking till the fire was out. Everyone at the mansion was stunned; nothing like this had ever taken place before[1]. Yet Ibn Ziyad was not admonished by an incident such as that, so he ordered the captives to be brought to him. The ladies of the Messenger of Allāh (ع) were brought to him, and they were in the most pathetic condition[2].

Al-Hussain's head was placed in front of him, so he kept hitting its mouth with a rod which he had in his hand for some time. Zaid ibn Arqam said, "Stop hitting these lips with your rod, for by Allāh, the One and Only Allāh, I saw the lips of the Messenger of Allāh (ع) kissing them," then he broke into tears. Ibn Ziyad said to him, "May Allāh cause you never to cease crying! By Allāh, had you not been an old man who lost his wits, I would have killed you." Zaid went out of the meeting place saying, "A slave is now a monarch ruling them, treating them as his property. O Arabs! Henceforth, you are the slaves! You have killed Fātima's son and granted authority to the son of Marjana who kills the best among you and permits the evil ones among you to be worshipped. You have accepted humiliation, so away with whoever accepts humiliation."[3]

Ibn Katheer, *Al-Bidaya*, Vol. 8, p. 286.

[1]*Sharh Qaseedat Abi Firas*, p. 149.

[2]Abul-Abbas Ahmed ibn Yusuf al-Qarmani, *Akhbar al-Duwal*, Vol. 1, p. 8.

[3]Ibn Hajar al-Asqalani, *As-Sawa'iq al-Muhriqa*, p. 118. At-Tabari, *Tarikh*, Vol. 6, p. 262. Ibn Katheer, *Al-Bidaya wal Nihaya*, Vol. 8, p. 190. Ibn Hajar al-Asqalani, *Mujma az-Zawa'id*, Vol. 9, p. 195. Ibn Asakir, *Tarikh*, Vol. 4, p. 340. These authors have expressed their disbelief of what he has said. The fact that he was blind does not necessarily render his statement inaccurate, for it is quite possible he had heard the same. Ibn Asakir's statement that Zaid was present then and there supports his.

Zainab daughter of the Commander of the Faithful (ع) kept a distance from the women as she remained disguised, but she could not disguise the prestige of being brought up in the lap of prophethood and in the glory of Imāmate, so she attracted Ibn Ziyad's attention. He inquired about her. He was told that she was Zainab, the wise lady, daughter of the Commander of the Faithful (ع). He wanted to tell her how rejoiced he was at what had happened. Said he, "Praise be to Allāh Who exposed you to shame, Who killed you and proved you liars." She, peace be with her, responded with: "Praise be to Allāh Who honored us by choosing Muhammed [from among us] as His Prophet and purified us with a perfect purification. Rather, only a debauchee is exposed to shame, and a sinner is proven to be a liar, and we are neither."

Ibn Ziyad asked her, "How have you seen what Allāh has done to your Ahl al-Bayt (ع)?" She, peace be with her, said, "I have seen Him treating them most beautifully. These are people to whom Allāh prescribed martyrdom, so they leaped from their beds welcoming it, and Allāh shall gather you and them, and you shall be questioned, and your opponents shall charge you[1]; so, you will then find out whose lot shall be the crack of hell, may your mother, O son of Marjana, lose you."[2]

This statement enraged Ibn Ziyad, and her words incinerated him with ire, especially since she said it before such a huge crowd. He, therefore, was about to kill her when Amr ibn Hareeth said to him, "She is only a woman; can she be held accountable for what she said? She cannot be blamed when she thus prattles."

Ibn Ziyad turned to her one more time and said, "Allāh has healed my heart by letting me seek revenge against your tyrant and against the rebels and mutineers from among his Ahl al-Bayt (ع)!" The wise lady calmed herself and said, "By my life! You have killed my

---

[1]at-Tabari, *Tarikh*, Vol. 6, p. 262.

[2]Ibn Tawoos *Al-Luhuf*, p. 90.

middle-aged protector, persecuted my family, cut off my branch and pulled out my roots; so, if all of this heals your heart, then you are indeed healed."[1]

He then turned to Ali ibn al-Hussain (ع) whom he asked what his name was. "I am Ali son of al-Hussain (ع)," came the answer. Ibn Ziyad asked Ali, "Did not Allāh kill Ali (ع)?" As-Sajjād (ع) answered, "I used to have an older brother[2] also named Ali whom people killed." Ibn Ziyad responded by repeating his statement that it was Allāh who had killed him. As-Sajjād, therefore, said, "Allāh takes the souls away at the time of their death; none dies except with Allāh's permission." Ibn Ziyad did not appreciate him thus responding to his statement rather than remaining silent, so he ordered him to be killed, but his aunt, the wise lady Zainab, put her arms around him and said, "O Ibn Ziyad! Suffices you what you have shed of our blood..., have you really spared anyone other than this?[3] If you want to kill him, kill me with him as well." As-Sajjād (ع) said [to Ibn Ziyad], "Do you not know that we are used to being killed, and that martyrdom is one of Allāh's blessings upon us?"[4]

---

[1]Ibn al-Atheer, *At-Tarikh al-Kāmil*, Vol. 4, p. 33. Al-Khawarizmi, *Maqtal al-Hussain (ع)*, Vol. 2, p. 42. At-Tabari, *Tarikh*, Vol. 6, p. 263. Al-Mufid, *Al-Irshad*. At-Tibrisi, *I'lam al-Wara bi A'lam al-Huda*, p. 141. According to p. 145, Vol. 3, of *Kāmil al-Mibrad* (1347 A.H./1735 A.D. edition), Zainab daughter of Ali ibn Abū Talib (ع), the eldest of those taken captive to Ibn Ziyad, was quite eloquent, driving her argument against the latter home. Ibn Ziyad, therefore, said to her, "If you achieved your objective behind your oratory, your father was an orator and a poet." She said to him, "What would women do with poetry?" Ibn Ziyad, in fact, used to stutter, and he had a lisp; his speech had a heavy Persian accent.

[2]Such is the statement of Muhammed ibn Jarir at-Tabari in his book *Al-Muntakhab* in a footnote on p. 89, Vol. 12, of his *Tarikh*. So does Abul Faraj al-Isfahani on p. 49 of the Iranian edition of his book *Maqatil at-Talibiyeen*, and al-Dimyari in his book *Hayat al-Hayawan*, as well as at-Turayhi's book *Al-Muntakhab*, p. 238 (Hayderi Press edition). It is also indicated on p. 58 of Mis'ab az-Zubayhi's book *Nasab Quraish*.

[3]at-Tabari, *Tarikh*, Vol. 6, p. 263.

[4]Ibn Tawoos *Al-Luhuf*, p. 91. Al-Khawarizmi, *Maqtal al-Hussain (ع)*, Vol.

Ibn Ziyad looked at both of them then said, "Leave him for her. Amazing is their tie of kinship; she wishes to be killed with him."[1]

Ar-Rubab, wife of Imām al-Hussain (ع), took the head and put it in her lap. She kissed it and composed poetry lines mourning

When it became clear to Ibn Ziyad that there were many people present who were voicing their resentment of what he had committed and how everyone was repeating what Zainab had said, he feared an uprising, so he ordered the police to jail the captives inside a house adjacent to the grand mosque[2]. Ibn Ziyad's doorman has said, "I was with them when he issued his order to jail them. I saw how the men and women assembled there weeping and beating their faces."[3] Zainab shouted at people saying, "Nobody should tend to us except either a bondmaid, a freed bondmaid, or *umm wuld* أم ولد[4], for they were taken captive just as we have been."[5] Only a female captive is familiar with the pain and humiliation of captivity; therefore, she would be sympathetic and would not rejoice nor enjoy seeing them in captivity. This is undeniable.

Ibn Ziyad again called them to his presence. When they were brought to him, their women saw al-Hussain's head in front of him with its divine rays ascending from its curves to the depth of the heavens. Ar-Rubab, al-Hussain's wife, could not check herself from falling upon it and composed more poetry eulogizing him.

2, p. 13.

[1]Ibn al-Atheer, Vol. 4, p. 34.

[2]Ibn Tawoos *Al-Luhuf*, p. 91. Al-Khawarizmi, *Maqtal al-Hussain (ع)*, Vol. 2, p. 43.

[3]Muhammed an-Nishapuri, *Rawdat al-Waizeen*, p. 163.

[4]"Freed mother of son" means a bondmaid who bears sons by her master and who is set free on that account but remains in his custody as his wife.

[5]Ibn Tawoos *Al-Luhuf*, p. 92. al-Bahrani, *Maqtal al-Awalim*, p. 130.

Hameed ibn Muslim has said, "Ibn Ziyad ordered to hold a congregational prayer service. They assembled at the grand mosque. Ibn Ziyad ascended the pulpit and said, All Praise is due to Allāh Who manifested the truth and elevated those who act according to it and Who granted victory to the commander of the faithful Yazid and to his party, and Who killed the liar and the son of the liar Hussain son of Ali and his Shī'as.'[1] Nobody among that crowd that had sunk in misguidance objected to such a preposterous statement except Abdullāh ibn Afeef al-Azdi and also one of the sons of Walibah al-Ghamidi who both stood up and said to him, O son of Marjana! The liar and the son of the liar is you and your father, and so is everyone who accepts your authority and his son! O son of Marjana! Do you really kill the offspring of the prophets and still talk about who is truthful and who is a liar?!'[2] Ibn Ziyad asked who the speaker was. Ibn Afeef answered by saying, I am the speaker, O enemy of Allāh! Do you really kill the righteous offspring from whom Allāh removed all abomination then claim that you are a follower of the Islamic creed?! Oh! Is there anyone to help?! Where are the sons of the Muhajirun and the Ansar to seek revenge against your tyrant, the one who and whose father were both cursed by Muhammed (ص), the Messenger of the Lord of the Worlds.' Ibn Ziyad's anger now intensified. He ordered him to be brought to him. The police grabbed him.[3] It was then that Ibn Afeef shouted the slogan (*nakhwa* نخوة) used by the Azdis which was: يا مبرور! *Ya Mabroor!*' This caused a large number of the Azdis present there to leap to his rescue and to forcibly free him from the police and take him safely home."

Abdul-Rahman ibn Makhnaf al-Azdi said to him, "Woe unto someone else other than you! You have surely condemned yourself and your tribe to destruction!"[4]

---

[1] Ibn al-Atheer, Vol. 1, p. 34.

[2] at-Tabari, *Tarikh*, Vol. 6, p. 263.

[3] Ibn Tawoos *Al-Luhuf*.

[4] at-Tabari, *Tarikh*, Vol. 6, p. 263.

Ibn Ziyad ordered Jandab ibn Abdullāh al-Azdi, who was an old man, to be brought to him. He said to him, "O enemy of Allāh! Did you not fight on Abū Turab's side during the Battle of Siffeen?" The old man answered, "Yes, and I love him and am proud of him, while I despise you and your father especially after you have killed the grandson of the Prophet (ص) and his companions and the members of his family without fearing the One and Only Allāh, the Great Avenger." Ibn Ziyad said, "You have less feeling of shame than that blind man, and I seek nearness to Allāh through shedding your blood." Jandab said, "In that case, Allāh shall never bring you closer to Him." Ibn Ziyad, on a second thought, feared the might of the man's Azd tribe, so he left him alone saying, "He is only an old man who has lost his mind and his wits." He released him.[1]

AL-MUKHTAR ATH-THAQAFI

At the same time when Ibn Ziyad ordered the captives to be brought to his meeting place, he also ordered al-Mukhtar son of Abū Ubayd ath-Thaqafito be brought to him, too. Al-Mukhtar had been in prison since the assassination of Muslim ibn Aqeel. When al-Mukhtar saw that horrific and most deplorable scene, he sighed loudly and an exchange of harsh words took place between him and Ibn Ziyad wherein the harshest words were al-Mukhtar's. Ibn Ziyad became burning with outrage and ordered him to be sent back to jail[2]. Some say that he whipped him, blinding one of his eyes.[3]

After the execution of Ibn Afeef, al-Mukhtar was released due to the interference of Abdullāh son of Omer ibn al-Khattab who asked Yazid to have him released. Yazid was the husband of al-Mukhtar's sister Safiyya daughter of Abū Ubayd at-Thaqafi. But Ibn Ziyad

---

[1]Ibn Nama, *Muthir al-Ahzan*, p. 51. Al-Khawarizmi, *Maqtal al-Hussain (ع)*, Vol. 2, p. 55.Muhammed Hassan ash-Shaban Kurdi al-Qazwini, *Riyad al-Ahzan*, p. 52.

[2]*Riyad al-Ahzan*, p. 52.

[3]Ibn Rustah, *Al-Alaq an-Nafisa*, p. 224.

postponed carrying out Yazid's order for three days. Having ordered the execution of Ibn Afeef, Ibn Ziyad delivered a speech wherein he abused the Commander of the Faithful (ع), causing al-Mukhtar to denounce and to taunt him to his face saying, "You are the liar, O enemy of Allāh and enemy of His Messenger! Rather, Praise to Allāh Who dignified al-Hussain (ع) and his army with Paradise and with forgiveness just as He humiliated Yazid and his army with the fire and with shame." Ibn Ziyad hurled an iron bar at him that fractured his forehead, then he ordered him to be sent back to jail, but people reminded him that Omer ibn Sa'd was the husband of his sister while another brother-in-law was none other than Abdullāh ibn Omer [ibn al-Khattab]. They reminded him of his lofty lineage, so he changed his mind of having him killed, yet he insisted on sending him back to prison. For the second time did Abdullāh ibn Omer write Yazid who in turn wrote Ubaydullāh ibn Ziyad ordering him to release the man[1].

Al-Mukhtar incessantly kept after that informing the Shī'as of the merits which he knew of the companions of the Commander of the Faithful (ع), of how he rose seeking revenge for al-Hussain (ع), and how he killed Ibn Ziyad and those who fought al-Hussain (ع).[2]

One incident he narrated was the following which he recollected about the time when he was in Ibn Ziyad's jail:

Abdullāh ibn al-Harith ibn Nawfal ibn Abdul-Muttalib and Maytham at-Tammar were two of his cell mates. Abdullāh ibn al-Harith asked for a piece of iron to remove the hair in certain parts of his body saying, "I do not feel secure against Ibn Ziyad killing me, and I do not want him to do so while there is unwanted hair on my body." Al-Mukhtar said to him, "By Allāh he shall not kill you, nor shall he kill

---

[1]al-Khawarizmi, *Maqtal al-Hussain (ع)*, Vol. 2, pp. 178-179. The author of *Riyad al-Ahzan,* namely Muhammed Hassan ash-Shaban Kurdi al-Qazwini, briefly narrates it on p. 58.

[2]al-Majlisi, *Bihār al-Anwār*, Vol. 10, p. 284, citing Ibn Nama's book *Akhth at-Thar.*

me, nor shall you face except very little hardship before you become the governor of Basra!" Maytham heard their dialogue, so he said to al-Mukhtar, "You yourself will rise seeking revenge for al-Hussain's blood, and you shall kill the same man who wants us to be killed, and you shall trample on his cheeks with your very foot."[1] This came to be exactly as these men had said. Abdullāh ibn al-Harith was released from jail after Yazid's death and became the governor of Basra. After only one year, al-Mukhtar rose seeking revenge against the killers of al-Hussain (ع), killing Ibn Ziyad, Harmalah ibn Kahil, Shimr ibn Thul-Jawshan and a large number of the Kūfians who had betrayed al-Hussain (ع). As Ibn Nama al-Hilli tells us, he [and his army] killed eighteen thousand Kūfians, then almost ten thousand[2] of them fled away from him and sought refuge with Mus'ab ibn az-Zubair. Among them was Shabth ibn Rab'i who reached him riding a mule whose ears and tail he had cut off and who was wearing a torn outer garment and shouting, "Help! Lead us to fight this debauchee who demolished our homes and killed our honorable men!"[3]

THE SACRED HEAD SPEAKS

Since his early childhood, the martyred grandson of the Prophet (ص) remained an ally of the Qur'an. Thus were both he and his brother (ع), for they were the legacy of the Messenger of Allāh and his vicegerents. The greatest Prophet (ص) had stated that they and the Holy Qur'an would never part from one another till they would meet him at the Pool of Kawthar. Al-Hussain (ع), therefore, never ceased reciting the Qur'an all his life as he taught and cultivated others, when he was at home or when travelling. Even during his stand in the Battle of Taff, although surrounded by his foes, he used the Qur'an to argue with them and to explain his point of view to them.

---

[1] Ibn Abul-Hadid, *Sharh Nahj al-Balagha*, Vol. 1, p. 210 (Egyptian edition). Al-Majlisi, *Bihār al-Anwār*, Vol. 10, p. 284. Al-Mufid, *Al-Irshad*.

[2] Abū Hanifah al-Dainuri, namely Ahmed ibn Dāwūd (died in 281 A.H./894 A.D.), *Al-Akhbar at-Tiwal*, p. 295.

[3] at-Tabari, *Tarikh*, Vol. 7, p. 146.

Thus was the son of the Messenger of Allāh (ﻉ) marching towards his sacred objective energetically, so much so that now his sacred head kept reciting the Qur'an even as it stood atop a spear, perhaps someone among the people would be illuminated with the light of the truth. But this lamp-post of guidance did not see except people whose comprehension was limited, whose hearts were sealed, and whose ears were deafened: "Allāh sealed their hearts and hearing, and over their vision there is a veil" (Qur'an, 2:7).

Zaid ibn Arqam has said, "I was sitting in my room when they passed by, and I heard the head reciting this verse: Or do you think that the fellows of the cave and the inscription were of Our wonderful signs?' (Qur'an, 18:9). My hair stood up, and I said, By Allāh, O son of the Messenger of Allāh! Your head is much more amazing!"[1]

When the severed head was placed at the money changers' section of the bazaar, there was a great deal of commotion and noise of the dealers and customers. The Master of Martyrs (ﻉ) wanted to attract the attention to him so that people would listen to his terse admonishment, so his severed head hawked quite loudly, thus turning all faces to it. Never did people hear a severed head hawking before the martyrdom of al-Hussain (ﻉ). It then recited Sūrat al-Kahf from its beginning till it reached the verse saying, "They were youths who believed in their Lord, and We increased their guidance" (Qur'an, 18:13), "... and do not (O Lord!) increase the unjust aught but error" (Qur'an, 71:24).

---

[1]al-Mufid, *Al-Irshad. Al-Khasa'is al-Kubra*, Vol. 2, p. 125. On p. 362, Vol. 1, of *Sharh Nahj al-Balagha*, Ibn Abul-Hadid says, "Zaid ibn Arqam was one of those who deviated from the line of the Commander of the Faithful Ali, peace be with him. He was reluctant to testify that the Commander of the Faithful (ﻉ) was appointed [by the Prophet] to take charge of the nation after him, so he (ﻉ) condemned him with blindness. He, indeed, became blind till his death. According to Ibn al-Atheer, who indicates so on p. 24, Vol. 4, of his book *At-Tarikh al-Kāmil*, Ibn Ziyad ordered the head of al-Hussain (ﻉ) to be paraded throughout Kufa. The same is stated by Ibn Katheer on p. 191, Vol. 8, of his book *Al-Bidaya*, and also by al-Maqrizi on p. 288, Vol. 2, of his *Khutat*.

The head was hung on a tree. People assembled around it looking at the dazzling light that emanated from it as it recited the verse saying, "And those who oppressed shall come to know what an end they shall meet" (Qur'an, 26:227)[1].

Hilal ibn Mu'awiyah has said, "I saw a man carrying the head of al-Hussain (ع) as it [the head] was saying, You separated between my head and my body, so may Allāh separate between your flesh and bones, and may He make you a Sign for those who stray from the Straight Path.' He, therefore, raised his whip and kept whipping the head till it ceased."[2]

Salamah ibn Kaheel heard the head reciting the following verse from the top of the spear where it had been placed: "Allāh shall suffice you for them, and He is the Hearing, the Knowing" (Qur'an, 2:137)[3].

Ibn Wakeedah says that he heard the head reciting Sūrat al-Kahf, so he was doubtful whether it was, indeed, the voice of the Imām (ع), whereupon he, peace be with him, stopped his recitation and turned to the man to say, "O son of Wakeedah! Do you not know that we, the Imāms, are living with our Lord receiving our sustenance?" He, therefore, decided to steal and bury the head. It was then that the glorious head spoke again to him saying, "O son of Wakeedah! There is no way to do that. Their shedding my blood is greater with Allāh than placing me on a spear; so, leave them alone, for they shall come to know when the collars are placed around their necks and when they are dragged with chains."[4] Al-Minhal ibn Amr has said, "I saw al-Hussain's head in Damascus atop a spear and in front of it

---

[1]Ibn Shahr Ashub, Vol. 2, p. 188.

[2]*Sharh Qasidat Abi Firas*, p. 148.

[3]*Asrar ash-Shahada*, p. 488.

[4]*Sharh Qasidat Abi Firas*, p. 148.

stood a man; the head was reciting Sūrat al-Kahf. When the recitation came to the verse saying, Or do you think that the fellows of the cave and the inscription were of Our wonderful signs?' (Qur'an, 18:9) , the head spoke in an articulate tongue saying, More wonderous than the fellows of the cave is killing me and thus transporting me.'"[1]

When Yazid ordered the killing of a messenger sent by the then Roman [Byzantine] emperor who resented what Yazid had committed, the head loudly articulated these words: La hawla wala quwwata illa billah! (There is no power nor might except in Allāh)."[2]

AL-ASHDAQ
Ibn Jarar at-Tabari, the renown historian, narrates the following:

"Ibn Ziyad wanted to send Abdul-Malik ibn al-Harith as-Salami to Medīna in order to inform Amr ibn Sa'd al-Ashdaq[3] of the killing of al-Hussain (ع), but he sought to be excused of such an undertaking, claiming to be sick. Al-Ashdaq refused to accept his excuse. Ibn Ziyad is described as very heavy-handed, nobody can tolerate his ire. He ordered the man to rush and to buy another she-camel if the one he was riding was not fast enough, and not to let anyone reach the destination before him. He, therefore, rushed to Medīna. A man from Quraish met him and asked him why he seemed to be in such a hurry. The answer rests with the governor,' was his answer. When

---

[1] as-Sayyati, *Al-Khasa'is*, Vol. 2, p. 127.

[2] al-Bahrani, *Maqtal al-Awalim*, p. 151.

[3] According to p. 240, Vol. 5, of Nar ad-Din Abul-Hassan, namely Ibn Hajar al-Haythami's book *Mujma az-Zawa'id wa Manba al-Fawa'id*, and also according to p. 141 of *As-Sawa'iq al-Muhriqa*, Abū Hurayra is quoted as saying, "I have heard the Messenger of Allah, peace of Allah be upon him and his progeny, saying, One of the tyrants of Banu Umayyah shall have a nosebleed on my pulpit, and his blood will flow thereupon.'" Amr ibn Sa'd did, indeed, have a nosebleed as he was on the pulpit of the Messenger of Allah (ع), staining it with his blood.

Ibn Sa'd was informed of al-Hussain (ع) having been killed, he was very happily excited and was subdued with elation. He ordered a caller to announce it in the city's alleys, and before long, the cries and the wailings coming from the Hashemite ladies mourning the Master of the Youths of Paradise (ع) were heard like never before. These cries reached all the way to the house of al-Ashdaq who laughed and quoted a verse of poetry composed by Amr ibn Ma'di-Karb. He maliciously added saying, "A wailing noise like the one we raised when Othman was killed."[1] Then he turned to the grave of the Messenger of Allāh (ع) and again maliciously said, "Now we have gotten even with you, Messenger of Allāh, for what you did to us during the Battle of Badr." A number of men from the Ansar rebuked him with shame for having made such a statement.[2]

He ascended the pulpit and said, "O people! It is a blow for a blow, and a crushing for a crushing! A sermon followed another! This is sound wisdom, so no nathr can do any good. He condemned us as we praised him, cut off his ties with us though we did not, just as it was his habit, and just as it was ours, but what else can we do to a man who drew his sword with the intention to kill us other than to put an end to the danger to which he exposed us?"

Abdullāh ibn as-Sa'ib stood up and said to him, "Had Fātima (ع) been alive, and had she seen al-Hussain's [severed] head, she would have wept for him." Amr ibn Sa'd rebuked him and said, "We are more worthy of Fātima than you: Her father was our uncle, her husband was our brother, his mother was our daughter. And had Fātima been alive, she would have cried but would not have blamed those who killed him in self-defense."[3]

Amr was very crude and uncouth, a man of legendary cruelty. He

---

[1] at-Tabari, *Tarikh*, Vol. 6, p. 368.

[2] Shaikh Abbas al-Qummi, *Nafas al-Mahmum*, p. 222. Ibn Abul-Hadid, *Sharh Nahjul Balagha*, Vol. 1, p. 361.

[3] al-Bahrani, *Maqtal al-Awalim*, p. 131.

ordered Amr ibn az-Zubair ibn al-Awwam[1], head of the police force, after al-Hussain (ع) had been killed, to demolish all the houses of Banu Hashim [the Prophet's clansmen]. He did, oppressing them beyond limits... He also demolished the home of Ibn Mutee and beat people with cruelty. They fled from him and went to join Abdullāh ibn az-Zubair[2]. The reason why he was called "al-Ashdaq" [one whose jaws are twisted to the right or to the left] is due to the fact that his jaws were twisted after having gone to extremes in taunting Imām Ali ibn Abū Talib (ع)[3]. Allāh, therefore, punished him [in this life before the hereafter] in the worst manner. He was carried to Abdul-Malik ibn Marwan chained; after he profusely remonstrated with the latter, he was ordered to be killed[4].

Escorted by a number of women from her kinsfolk, the daughter of Aqeel ibn Abū Talib went out to visit the grave of the Prophet (ص) where she threw herself on it, burst in tears then turned to the Muhajirun and the Ansar and came forth instantaneously with these verses:

What will you on the Judgment Day
To the Prophet stand and say?
Surely what you will hear will be true:
Those who betrayed his Progeny were you.
Were you present, or were you not there at all
And justice is combined in the Lord of all...?

---

[1]According to p. 23, Vol. 4, of al-Balathiri's book *Ansab al-Ashraf*, the mother of Amr ibn az-Zubair was Ama daughter of Khalid ibn Sa'd ibn al-as. Her father was in command of an army which Amr ibn Sa'd al-Ashdaq dispatched to Mecca to fight Abdullāh ibn az-Zubair. Abdullāh's army captured Amr ibn az-Zubair, so Abdullāh ordered everyone who had suffered an injustice at his hand to whip him. The whipping led to his death.

[2]Abul-Faraj al-Isfahani, *Al-Aghani*, Vol. 4, p. 155.

[3]al-Mirzabani, *Mu'jam ash-Shuara'*, p. 231.

[4]Abū Hilal al-'Askari, *Jamharat al-Amthal*, p. 9 (Indian edition).

You handed it over to those who are never fair
So your intercession with Allāh will go nowhere.
Though on the Taff Day absent was he,
Yet all the dead did your very eyes see.
You saw all those who did die,
So to Allāh you shall never come nigh.

All those present wept. There was no such weeping ever before[1]. Her sister Zainab kept mourning al-Hussain (ع) in the most somber manner.

ABDULLĀH IBN JA'FAR

Ibn Jarar at-Tabari has said that when the news of al-Hussain's martyrdom was announced, Abdullāh ibn Ja'far held a mourning majlis, so people came to him to offer their condolences. His slave Abul-Lislas[2] said to him, "This is what we got from al-Hussain (ع)!" He hurled his sandal at him as he said, "O son of the stinking woman! How dare you say something like that about al-Hussain (ع)?! By Allāh! Had I been with him, I would not have liked to part with him before being killed defending him. By Allāh! What consoles me is that both my sons were martyred in his defense together with my brother as well as my cousin who all stood firmly on his side." Then he turned to those in his presence and said, "Praise to Allāh! It surely is very heavy on my heart to see al-Hussain (ع) get killed, and that I could not defend him with my life, but both my sons have."[3]

THE CAPTIVES TAKEN TO SYRIA

Ibn Ziyad sent a messenger to Yazid to inform him that al-Hussain (ع) and those in his company were killed, that his children were in

---

[1]Shaikh at-Tusi, *Al-Amali*, p. 55. On p. 227, Vol. 2, of his book *Al-Manaqib*, Ibn Shahr Ashub says it was Asma' who had composed those verses.

[2]His name as stated on p. 194 of al-Irbili's book *Kashf al-Ghummah* was "Abul-Salasil," the man of the chains.

[3]at-Tabari, *Tarikh*, Vol. 6, p. 218.

Kūfa, and that he was waiting for his orders as to what to do with them. In his answer, Yazid ordered him to send them together with the severed heads to him[1].

Ubaydullāh wrote something, tied it to a rock then hurled it inside the prison where the family of Muhammed (ﺹ) was kept. In it he said, "Orders have been received from Yazid to take you to him on such-and-such a day. If you hear the *takbeer*, you should write your wills; otherwise, there is security." The post returned from Syria with the news that al-Hussain's family is being sent to Syria[2].

Ibn Ziyad ordered Zajr ibn Qays and Abū Burda ibn 'Awf al-Azdi as well as Tariq ibn Zabyan to head a band of Kūfians charged with carrying al-Hussain's severed head and of those killed with him to Yazid[3]. Another account says that Mujbir ibn Murrah ibn Khalid ibn Qanab ibn Omer ibn Qays ibn al-Harth ibn Malik ibn Ubaydullāh ibn Khuzaymah ibn Lu'ayy did so[4].

They were trailed by Ali ibn al-Hussain (ﻉ) with his hands tied to his neck in the company of his family[5] in a condition the sight of which

---

[1]Ibn Tawoos *Al-Luhuf*, pp. 95-97.

[2]at-Tabari, *Tarikh*, Vol. 6, p. 266. On p. 96, at-Tabari states that Abū Bukrah was given one week by Bishr ibn Arta'ah to go to Mu'awiyah. He went back from Syria on the seventh day. On p. 74 of his book *Muthir al-Ahzan*, Ibn Nama says that Amirah was dispatched by Abdullāh ibn Omer to Yazid in order to get him to release al-Mukhtar at-Thaqafi. Yazid wrote a letter in this regard to Ubaydullah ibn Ziyad. Amirah brought him the letter to Kufa, crossing the distance from Syria to Kufa in eleven days.

[3]*Ibid.*, Vol. 6, p. 264. Ibn al-Atheer, Vol. 4, p. 34. *Al-Bidaya*, Vol. 8, p. 191. Al-Khawarizmi. Al-Mufid, *Al-Irshad*. At-Tibrisi, *I'lam al-Wara bi A'lam al-Huda*, p. 149. Ibn Tawoos, *Al-Luhuf*, p. 97.

[4]Ibn al-Atheer (died in 630 A.H./1232 A.D.), *Al-Isaba fi Tamyeez as-Sahāba*, Vol. 3, p. 489, where Murrah's biography is discussed.

[5]at-Tabari, *Tarikh*, Vol. 6, p. 254. al-Maqrazi, *Khutat*, Vol. 2, p. 288.

128

would cause anyone's skin to shiver[1].

With them was Shimr ibn Thul-Jawshan, Mujfir ibn Thulabah al-a'idi[2], Shabth ibn Rab'i, Amr ibn al-Hajjas, in addition to other men. They were ordered to mount the heads on spears and to display them wherever they went[3]. They hurried till they caught up with them[4].

Ibn Lahee'ah is quoted as saying that he saw a man clinging to Ka'ba's curtains seeking refuge with his Lord and saying, "And I cannot see You doing that!" Ibn Lahee'ah took him aside and said to him, "You must be insane! Allāh is most Forgiving, most Merciful. Had your sins been as many as rain drops, He would still forgive you." He said to Ibn Lahee'ah, "Be informed that I was among those who carried al-Hussain's head to Syria. Whenever it was dark, we would put the head down, sit around it and drink wine. During one night, I and my fellows were guarding it when I saw lightning and creatures that surrounded the head. I was terrified and stunned and remained silent. I heard crying and wailing and someone saying, O Muhammed! Allāh ordered me to obey you; so, if you order me, I can cause an earthquake that will swallow these people just as it

---

[1]al-Qarmani, *Tarikh*, p. 108. Al-Yafii, *Mir'at al-Jinan*, Vol. 1, p. 134. In both references, it is stated that the daughters of Imām al-Hussain (ع) son of Ali ibn Abū Talib (ع) were taken into captivity, and Zain al-Ābidīn (ع) was with them, and that he was sick. They were driven as captives; may Allah be the Killer of those who did it. Only Ibn Taymiyyah differed from all other historians when he stated on p. 288 of his book *Minhaj al-I'tidal* saying that al-Hussain's women were taken to Medīna after he had been killed.

[2]On p. 165 of Ibn Hazm's book *Jamharat Ansab al-Arab*, it is stated that, "Among Banu aidah are: Mujfir ibn Murrah ibn Khalid ibn Aamir ibn Qaban ibn Amr ibn Qays ibn al-Harith ibn Malik ibn Ubayd ibn Khuzaymah ibn Lu'ayy, and he is the one who carried the head of al-Hussain (ع) son of Ali, peace be with both of them, to Syria."

[3]at-Turayhi, *Al-Muntakhab*, p. 339 (second edition).

[4]al-Mufid, *Al-Irshad*.

swallowed the people of Lot.' He said to him, O Gabriel! I shall call them to account on the Day of Judgment before my Lord, Glory to Him.' It was then that I screamed, O Messenger of Allāh! I plead to you for security!' He said to me, Be gone, for Allāh shall never forgive you.' So, do you still think that Allāh will forgive me?"[1]

At one stop on their journey, they put the purified head down; soon they saw an iron pen that came out of the wall and wrote the following in blood[2]:

Does a nation that killed al-Hussain really hope for a way
His grandfather will intercede for them on the Judgment Day?

But they were not admonished by such a miracle, and blindness hurled them into the very deepest of all pits; surely Allāh, the most Exalted One, is the best of judges.

One farasang before reaching their destination, they placed the head on a rock; a drop of blood fell from it on the rock. Every year, that drop would boil on Ashura, and people would assemble there around it and hold mourning commemorations in honor of al-Hussain (ع). A great deal of wailing would be around it. This continued to take

---

[1]Ibn Tawoos *Al-Luhuf*, p. 98.

[2]Ibn Hajar al-Asqalani, *Mujma az-Zawa'id*, Vol. 9, p. 199. As-Sayyati, *Al-Khasa'is*, Vol. 2, p. 127. Ibn Asakir, *Tarikh*, Vol. 4, p. 342. Ibn Hajar al-Asqalani, *As-Sawa'iq al-Muhriqa*, p. 116. *Al-Kawakib al-Durriyya* by al-Qatari al-Biladi al-Bahrani, Vol. 1, p. 57. Ash-Shabrawi, *Al-Ithaf bi Hubbil-Ashraf*, p. 23. On p. 98 of his book *Al-Luhuf*, Ibn Tawoos attributes this statement to *Tarikh Baghdad* by Ibn an-Najjar. On p. 108 of his *Tarikh*, al-Qarmani says, "They reached a monastery on the highway where they stayed for the afternoon. They found the said line written on one of its walls." On p. 285, Vol. 2, of his *Khutat*, al-Maqrazi says, "This was written in the past, and nobody knows who said it." On p. 53 of his book *Muthir al-Ahzan*, Ibn Nama says, "Three hundred years before the Prophetic mission, there was some digging in the land of the [Byzantine] Romans, and this line was found inscribed in the *Musnad* on a rock, and the *Musnad* is the language of the offspring of Seth."

place till Abdul-Malik ibn Marwan ascended the throne in 65 A.H./684 A.D.. He ordered that rock to be removed. It was never seen after that, but the spot where that rock stood became the site of a dome built in its honor which they called "an-Nuqta" (the drop)[1].

Near the town of Hamat and among its orchards stood a mosque called "Masjid al-Hussain (ع)." People there say that they escorted the rock and the head of al-Hussain (ع) that bled all the way to Damascus[2].

Near Aleppo there is a shrine known as "Masqat as-Saqt."[3] The

---

[1]Shaikh Abbas al-Qummi, *Nafas al-Mahmum*, p. 228. It is stated on p. 23, Vol. 3, of *Nahr at-Thahab fi Tarikh Halab* that, "When al-Hussain's head was brought with the captives, they reached a mountain to the west of Aleppo. One drop of blood fell from the sacred head above which a mausoleum called Mashhad an-Nuqta [mausoleum of the drop] was erected." On p. 280, Vol. 3, it cites Yahya ibn Abū Tay's *Tarikh* recounting the names of those who constructed and renovated it. On p. 66 of the book titled *Al-Isharat ila Marifat az-Ziyarat* by Abul- al-Hassan Ali ibn Abū Bakr al-Harawi (who died in 611 A.H./1215 A.D.), it states that, "In the town of Nasibin, there is a mausoleum called "Mashhad an-Nuqta", a reference to a drop from al-Hussain's head. Also, there is at Suq an-Nashshabin a place called Mashhad ar-Ras where the head was hung when the captives were brought to Syria."

[2]The mentor and revered *muhaddith* Shaikh Abbas al-Qummi says the following in his book *Nafas al-Mahmum*, "I saw that stone on my way to the pilgrimage, and I heard the servants talking about it."

[3]On p. 173, Vol. 3, of *Mu'jam al-Buldan*, and on p. 128 of *Khareedat al-Ajaib*, it is referred to as "Mashhad at-Tarh." On p. 278, Vol. 2, of *Nahr at-Thahab*, it is calle "Mashhad al-Dakka." Mashhad at-Tarh is located to the west of Aleppo. In the *Tarikh* of Ibn Abū Tay is cited saying that "Mashhad at-Tarh" was built in the year 351 A.H./962 A.D. according to the order of Sayf al-Dawlah. Other historians have said that one of al-Hussain's wives had miscarried in that place when al-Hussain's children and the severed heads were brought with them. There used to be a useful mineral in that area, but when its residents felt elated upon seeing the captives, Zainab invoked Allah's curse against them; therefore, that mineral lost its useful qualities. Then the author goes on to document the

reason why it was called so is that when the ladies of the Messenger of Allāh (ﷺ) were taken to that place, al-Hussain's wife had miscarried a son named Muhsin[1].

At some stops, the head was placed atop a spear next to a monk's monastery. During the night, the monk heard a great deal of *tasbeeh* and *tahleel*, and he saw a dazzling light emanating from it. He also heard a voice saying, "Peace be upon you, O father of Abdulah!" He was amazed and did not know what to make of it. In the morning, he asked people about that head and was told that it was the head of al-Hussain (ﷺ) ibn Ali ibn Abū Talib (ﷺ), son of Fātima (ﷺ) daughter of Prophet Muhammed (ﷺ). He said to them, "Woe unto you, people! True are the accounts that said that the heavens would rain blood." He asked their permission to kiss the head, but they refused till he paid them some money. He declared his *shahada* and embraced Islam through the blessing of the one who was beheaded just for supporting the divine call. When they left that place, they looked at the money the monk had given them and saw this verse inscribed on it: "And those who oppressed shall come to find how evil their end shall be" (Qur'an, 26:227)[2].

IN SYRIA
When they were near Damascus, Umm Kulthum sent a message to ash-Shimr asking him to let them enter the city from the least crowded highway, and to take the heads out so that people might be diverted by looking at them rather than looking at the women. He escorted them as they were in a condition from which skins shiver

---

history of its renovations.

[1]In the discussion of the subject of "Jawshan," on p. 173, Vol. 3, of his work *Mu'jam al-Buldan*, and also on p. 128 of *Khareedat al-Ajaib*, where reference to the Jawshan Mountain is made, it is stated that one of al-Hussain's family members taken captive asked some of those who worked there to give him bread and water. When they refused, he invoked Allah to curse them, thus condemning the labor of all laborers at that place to always be unprofitable.

[2]Ibn al-Jawzi, the grandson, *Tathkirat al-Khawass*, p. 150.

and senses quiver. Ash-Shimr instead ordered his men to take the captives for display before onlookers and to place the severed heads in their midst[1].

On the first day of Safar, they entered Damascus[2] and were stopped at the Clocks Gate[3]. People came out carrying drums and trumpets in excitement and jubilation. A man came close to Sukayna and asked her, "What captives are you all from?" She said, "We are captives belonging to the fāmily of Muhammed (ص)."[4]

Yazid was sitting at a surveillance outpost overlooking the mountain of Jerun. When he saw the captives with the heads planted atop the spears as their throng came close, a crow croaked; so he composed these lines:

---

[1]Ibn Tawoos *Al-Luhuf*, p. 99. Ibn Nama, *Muthir al-Ahzan*, p. 53. *Maqtal al-Awalim*, p. 145.

[2]Such is recorded on p. 331 of the offset edition of al-Bayrani's book *Al-Aathar al-Baqiya*, al-Bahai's book *At-Tarikh al-Kāmil*, p. 269 of *Musbah al-Kaf'ami*, and p. 15 of al-Fayd's book *Taqwim al-Muhsinin*. According to p. 266, Vol. 6, of at-Tabari's *Tarikh*, the time from their imprisonment till the post coming from Syria informing them of their arrival at Syria in the beginning of the month of Safar must have been a lengthy one except if birds had been used to carry such mail.

[3]According to p. 61, Vol. 2, of al-Khawarizmi's book *Maqtal al-Hussain (ع)*, they were brought to Damascus through Toma's Gate [Gate of St. Thomas]. This Gate, according to p. 109 of *Al-Maqasid*, was one of the ancient gates of Damascus. Abū Abdullāh Muhammed ibn Ali ibn Ibrahim, who is known as Ibn Shaddad and who died in 684 A.H./1286 A.D., says on p. 72, Vol. 3, of *Alaq al-Khateera*, "It was called the Clocks Gate because atop that gate there were clocks marking each hour of the day: small copper sparrows, a copper raven and a copper snake marked the timing: at the end of each hour, sparrows would come out, the raven would let a shriek out, and one (or more) stone would be dropped in the copper washbowl [making it sound]."

[4]as-Saduq, *Al-Aamali*, p. 100, *majlis* No. 31. Al-Khawarizmi, *Maqtal al-Hussain (ع)*, Vol. 2, p.60.

لما بدت تلك الحمول و أشرقت   تلك الرؤوس على شفا جيرون

نعب الغراب فقلت: قل أو لا تقل   فقد اقتضيت من الرسول ديوني

When those conveyances drew nigh
And the heads on the edge of Jerun,
The crow croaked so said I:
Say whatever you wish to say
Or say nothing at all,
From the Messenger have I today
What he <u>owed me</u> he did repay.[1]

It is due to these verses that Ibn al-Jawzi and Abū Ya'li, the judge, as well as at-Taftazani and Jalal as-Sayyuti permitted cursing Yazid and labelling him as *kafir*, apostate, unbeliever.[2]

Sahl ibn Sa'd as-Sa'idi came close to Sukayna daughter of al-Hussain (ع) and asked her, "Is there anything I can do for you?" She asked him to pay the man who was carrying the head some money and to ask him in return to stay away from the women so that people

---

[1]According to p. 161 of the offset Damascus edition of Ibn Hawqal's book *Sourat al-Ard*, there is none in the Islamic world better than it. It used to be a temple for the Sabaeans, then the Greeks used to worship in it, then the Jews as well as Pagan kings. The gate of this mosque is called Jayrun's Gate. It is over this gate that the head of John the Baptist (Yahya son of Zakariyya) was crucified. It was on this same Jayrun's Gate that the head of al-Hussain (ع) ibn Ali ibn Abū Talib (ع) was crucified in the same place where the head of John the Baptist was crucified. During the reign of al-Walid ibn Abdul-Malik, its walls were covered with marble. It seems that this is the same as the Umayyad Mosque.

[2]al-Ālusi, *Ruh al-Ma'ani*, Vol. 26, p. 73, where the verse "So do you wish, if you take charge... etc." is explained. The author says, "He meant, when he said, I have taken back from the Messenger (ع) what he owed me,' that he avenged the loss which he had suffered during the Battle of Badr at the hands of the Messenger of Allah when his grandfather Utbah, his uncle, and others were killed. This is nothing but obvious apostasy. Such was the similitude struck by Ibn az-Zubari before accepting Islam.

would be distracted by looking at the head instead of looking at the women. Sahl did so[1].

An elderly man came near as-Sajjād and said, "Praise be to Allāh Who annihilated you and Who granted the governor the upper hand over you!" At such a juncture, the Imām poured of his own kindness over that poor [ignorant] man who was brainwashed by falsehood in order to bring him closer to the truth and to show him the path of guidance. Such are the Ahl al-Bayt (ع): their light shines over those whom they know to be pure of heart and pure of essence and, as such, who are ready to receive guidance. He, peace be with him, asked the man, "Have you read the Qur'an, O *shaikh*?" The man answered as-Sajjād in the affirmative. "Have you read," continued as-Sajjād, "the verse saying, Say: I do not ask you for a reward for it [for conveying the Islamic Message to you] except that you treat my kinsfolk with kindness,' the verse saying, And give the [Prophet's] kinsfolk their due rights,' and the verse saying, And be informed that whatever you earn by way of booty, for Allāh belongs the fifth thereof and for the Messenger [of Allāh] and for the [Prophet's] kinsfolk'?" The man answered by saying, "Yes, I have read all of them." He (ع) then said, "We, by Allāh, are the kinsfolk referred to in all these verses." Then the Imām (ع) asked him whether he had read the verse saying, "Allāh only desires to remove all abomination from you, O Ahl al-Bayt, and purifies you with a perfect purification" (Qur'an, 33:33). "Yes" was the answer. As-Sajjād, peace be with him, said to him, "We are Ahl al-Bayt whom Allāh purified." "I ask you in the Name of Allāh," asked the man, "are you really them?" As-Sajjād, peace be with him, said, "By our grandfather the Messenger of Allāh, we are, without any doubt."

It was then that the elderly man fell on as-Sajjād's feet kissing them as he said, "I dissociate myself before Allāh from whoever killed you." He sought repentance of the Imām (ع) from whatever rude remarks he had earlier made. The encounter involving this elderly man reached Yazid who ordered him to be killed[2]...

---

[1]al-Bahrani, *Maqtal al-Awalim*, p. 145.

[2]Ibn Tawoos, *Al-Luhuf*, p. 100. According to p. 112, Vol. 4, of Ibn

Before being brought to Yazid's court, they were tied with ropes. The beginning of the rope was around the neck of Zain al-Ābidīn [Ali son of Imām al-Hussain (ﷺ), also called as-Sajjād, the one who prostrates to Allāh quite often], then around the necks of Zainab, Umm Kulthum, up to all the daughters of the Messenger of Allāh (ﷺ)... Whenever they slow down in their walking because of fatigue, they were whipped till they were brought face to face with Yazid who was then sitting on his throne. Ali ibn al-Hussain (ﷺ) asked him, "What do you think the reaction of the Messenger of Allāh (ﷺ) might have been had he seen us looking like this?" Everyone wept. Yazid ordered the ropes to be cut off.[1]

Katheer's *Tafsir*, p. 31, Vol. 25, of al-Ālusi's *Ruh al-Ma'ani*, and p. 61, Vol. 2, of al-Khawarizmi's book *Maqtal al-Hussain (ﷺ)*, as-Sajjād (ﷺ) had recited the verse invoking compassion (for the Prophet's family) to that old man who accepted it as a valid argument.

[1]al-Yafi'i, *Mir'at al-Jinan*, p. 341. On p. 35, Vol. 4, of his book *At-Tarikh al-Kāmil*, Ibn al-Atheer, as well as the author of *Muraj at-Thahab*, both indicate that when the head was brought to Yazid, the latter kept hitting it with a rod in his hand as he cited these verses by the poet al-Haseen ibn Humam:

> *Our people refused to be fair to us, so*
> *Swords in our hands bleeding did so,*
> *Splitting the heads of men who are to us dear*
> *Though they were to injustice and oppression more near.*

On p. 313, Vol. 2, of *Al-Iqd al-Farid*, where Yazid's reign is discussed, the author says, "When the head was placed in front of him, Yazid cited what al-Haseen ibn al-Hamam al-Mazni had said." He quoted the second verse [in the above English text, the last couple]. Ibn Hajar al-Haythami, on p. 198, Vol. 9, of his book *Mujma az-Zawa'id wa Manba al-Fawa'id*, quotes only the second verse. On p. 61, Vol. 2, of his book *Maqtal al-Hussain (ﷺ)*, al-Khawarizmi contents himself by simply saying that they stood on the steps of the mosque's gate. These verses are cited by al-Aamidi on p. 91 of his book *Al-Mu'talif wal-Mukhtalif*. Then he traces the lineage of the poet al-Haseen ibn Humam ibn Rabaah and cited three verses, including these couple, from a lengthy poem. On p. 151 of *Ash-Shi'r wash-Shu'ara'*, three verses are cited which include this couple. On p. 4 of *Al-Ashya wal*

They were lined up on the stairs leading to the gate leading to the [Umayyad Grand] mosque as was their custom with all captives, and the sacred head was placed in front of Yazid who kept looking at the captives and reciting poetry verses extolling his foul deed and demonstrating his elation. Then he turned to an-Nu'man ibn Basheer and said, "Praise to Allāh Who killed him [al-Hussain (ع)]." An-Nu'man said, "Commander of the faithful Mu'awiyah used to hate killing him." Yazid said, "That was before he rebelled. Had he rebelled against the commander of the faithful, he would have killed him."[1]

Yazid turned to as-Sajjād (ع) and asked him, "How did you, Ali, see what Allāh did to your father al-Hussain (ع)?" "I saw," answered as-Sajjād (ع), "What Allāh, the One and Only Allāh, the most Exalted One, had decreed before creating the heavens and the earth." Yazid consulted those around him as to what to do with as-Sajjād (ع), and they advised him to kill him. Imām as-Sajjād Zain al-Ābidīn (ع) said, "O Yazid! These men have advised you to do the opposite of what Pharaoh's courtiers had advised Pharaoh saying, Grant him and his brother a respite.' The *ad'iyaa* أدعياء (plural of *da'iy*, one who pretends to be Muslim) do not kill the prophets' sons and grandsons." This statement caused Yazid to lower his head and contemplate for a good while[2].

Among the dialogue that went on between both men is Yazid quoting this Qur'anic verse to Ali ibn al-Hussain (ع): "Whatever misfortune befalls you is due to what your hands commit" (Qur'an, 45:22). Ali ibn al-Hussain (ع) responded by saying, "This verse was not revealed in reference to us. What was revealed in reference to us

---

Nada'ir, where immortalized ancient poems and those composed during the time of *jahiliyya* are cited, only the second verse is quoted. On p. 120, Vol. 12, of the Sassi edition of Abul-Faraj al-Isfahani's voluminous book *Al-Aghani*, thirteen lines are quoted, including this couple.

[1]al-Khawarizmi, *Maqtal al-Hussain (ع)*, Vol. 2, p. 59.

[2]al-Mas'udi, *Ithbat al-Wasiyya*, p. 143 (Najafi edition).

was this verse: Whatever misfortune befalls the earth or your own selves is already in a Book even before we cause it to happen; this is easy for Allāh, so that you may not grieve about what you missed nor feel elated on account of what you receive' (Qur'an, 57:22)[1]. We do not grieve over what we missed nor feel elated on account of what we receive."[2] Yazid then cited the following verse by al-Fadl ibn al-Abbas ibn 'Utbah:

Wait, O cousins, wait, O masters, do not hurry!
Do not bring to surface what we did bury.[3]

As-Sajjād, peace be with him, sought permission to speak. "Yes," said Yazid, "provided you do not utter verbal attacks." He (ع) said, "I am now standing like one who ought not verbally attack anyone, but tell me: How do you think the Messenger of Allāh (ع) would have felt had he seen me looking like this?" Yazid ordered him to be untied.[4]

Yazid ordered the person who used to recite the Friday *khutba* (sermon) to ascend the pulpit and insult Ali and al-Hussain (ع), which he did. As-Sajjād (ع) shouted at him saying, "You have traded the pleasure of the creature for the Wrath of the Creator, so take your place in the fire [of hell]."[5]

---

[1] al-Kamali al-Istarbadi al-Hilli, *Al-Iqd al-Farid*, Vol. 2, p. 313. At-Tabari, *Tarikh*, Vol. 6, p. 267.

[2] Ali ibn Ibrahim, *Tafsir*, p. 603, where the Chapter of ash-Shura is discussed.

[3] ar-Raghib al-Isfahani, *Al-Muhadarat*, Vol. 1, p. 775, in a chapter about those who boast of antagonizing their kinsfolk. This is one of five verses by al-Fadl ibn al-Abbas ibn Utbah ibn Abū Lahab recorded by Abū Tammam in his book *Al-Hamasa*. Refer to p. 223, Vol. 1, of *Sharh at-Tabrizi*.

[4] Ibn Nama, *Muthir al-Ahzan*, p. 54.

[5] Shaikh Abbas al-Qummi, *Nafas al-Mahmum*, p. 242.

He asked Yazid saying, "Do you permit me to ascend this pulpit to deliver a speech that will please Allāh Almighty and that will bring good rewards for these folks?" Yazid refused, but people kept pleading to him to yield, yet he was still relentless. His son Mu'awiyah II said to him, "Permit him; what harm can his words cause?" Yazid said, "These are people who have inherited knowledge and oratory[1] and spoon-fed with knowledge[2]." They kept pressuring him till he agreed.

The Imām said,

ورد في كتاب فتوح ابن اعثم 5 / 247 ، ومقتل الخوارزمي 2 / 69 : إنّ يزيد أمر الخطيب أن يرقى المنبر ، ويثني على معاوية ويزيد ، وينال من الإمام علي والإمام الحسين ، فصعد الخطيب المنبر ، فحمد الله وأثنى عليه ، وأكثر الوقيعة في علي والحسين ، وأطنب في تقريض معاوية ويزيد ، فصاح به علي بن الحسين : "ويلك أيها الخاطب ، اشتريت رضا المخلوق بسخط الخالق ؟ فتبوأ مقعدك من النار". ثمّ قال : (يا يزيد ائذن لي حتى أصعد هذه الأعواد ، فأتكلم بكلمات فيهن لله رضا ، ولهؤلاء الجالسين أجر وثواب) ، فأبى يزيد ، فقال الناس : يا أمير المؤمنين ائذن له ليصعد ، فلعلنا نسمع منه شيئاً ، فقال لهم : إن صعد المنبر هذا ، لم ينزل إلا بفضيحتي ، وفضيحة آل أبي سفيان ، فقالوا : وما قدر ما يحسن هذا ؟ فقال : إنّه من أهل بيت قد زقوا العلم زقا . ولم يزالوا به حتى أذن له بالصعود ، فصعد المنبر ، فحمد الله وأثنى عليه ، وقال) : أيها الناس ، أعطينا ستاً ، وفضلنا بسبع : أعطينا العلم ، والحلم ، والسماحة والفصاحة ، والشجاعة ، والمحبة في قلوب المؤمنين ، وفضلنا بأن منا النبي المختار محمد (صلى الله عليه وآله) ، ومنا الصدّيق ، ومنا الطيار ، ومنا أسد الله وأسد الرسول ، ومنا سيدة نساء العالمين فاطمة البتول ، ومنا سبطا هذه الأمَّة ، وسيدا شباب أهل الجنة ، فمن عرفني فقد عرفني ، ومن لم يعرفني أنبأته بحسبي ونسبي : أنا ابن مكة ومنى ، أنا ابن زمزم والصفا ، أنا ابن من حمل الزكاة بأطراف الرداء ، أنا ابن خير من ائتزر وارتدى ، أنا ابن خير من انتعل واحتفى ، أنا ابن خير من طاف وسعى ، أنا ابن خير من حج ولبّى ، أنا ابن من حمل على البراق في الهواء ، أنا ابن من أسري به من المسجد الحرام إلى المسجد الأقصى ، فسبحان من أسرى ، أنا ابن من بلغ به جبرائيل إلى سدرة المنتهى ، أنا ابن من دنا فتدلى ، فكان قاب قوسين أو أدنى ، أنا ابن من صلّى بملائكة السماء ، أنا ابن من أوحى إليه الجليل ما أوحى ، أنا ابن محمد المصطفى ، أنا ابن من ضرب خراطيم الخلق ، حتى قالوا لا اله إلا الله ، أنا ابن من بايع البيعتين ، وصلّى القبلتين ، وقاتل ببدر وحنين ، ولم يكفر بالله طرفة عين ، يعسوب المسلمين ، وقاتل الناكثين والقاسطين

---

[1]*Kāmil al-Bahai.*

[2]al-Qazwini, *Riyad al-Ahzan*, p. 148.

والمارقين ، سمح سخي ، بهلول زكي ، ليث الحجاز ، وكبش العراق ، مكّي مدني ، أبطحي تهامي ، خيفي عقبي ، بدري أحدي ، شجري مهاجري ، أبو السبطين ، الحسن والحسين ، علي بن أبي طالب ، أنا ابن فاطمة الزهراء ، أنا ابن سيدة النساء ، أنا ابن بضعة الرسول).

قال : ولم يزل يقول : أنا أنا ، حتى ضج الناس بالبكاء والنحيب ، وخشي يزيد أن تكون فتنة ، فأمر المؤذّن يؤذّن ، فقطع عليه الكلام وسكت ، فلمّا قال المؤذّن : الله أكبر. قال علي بن الحسين : كبرت كبيراً لا يقاس ، ولا يدرك بالحواس ، ولا شيء أكبر من الله؛ فلمّا قال : أشهد أن لا اله إلا الله ، قال علي : (شهد بها شعري وبشري ، ولحمي ودمي ، ومخي وعظمي) ، فلمّا قال : أشهد أن محمداً رسول الله ، التفت علي من أعلا المنبر إلى يزيد ، وقال : (يا يزيد محمد هذا جدّي أم جدّك ؟ فإن زعمت أنه جدّك فقد كذبت ، وان قلت أنه جدّي ، فلم قتلت عترته ؟) .

قال : وفرغ المؤذّن من الأذان والإقامة ، فتقدّم يزيد ، وصلّى الظهر ، فلمّا فرغ من صلاته ، أمر بعلي بن الحسين ، وأخواته وعماته (رضوان الله عليهم) ، ففرغ لهم دار فنزلوها ، وأقاموا أياماً يبكون ، وينوحون على الحسين (عليه السلام). وبراءة الذمة...

All Praise is due to Allāh for Whom there is no beginning, the ever-Lasting for Whom there is no end, the First for Whom there is no starting point, the Last for Whom there is no ending point, the One Who remains after all beings no longer exist. He measured the nights and the days. He divided them into parts; so, Blessed is Allāh, the King, the all-Knowing... O people! We were granted six things and favored with seven: We were granted knowledge, clemency, leniency, fluency, courage, and love for us in the hearts of the believers. And we were favored by the fact that from among us came a Prophet, a Siddeeq, a Tayyar, a Lion of Allāh and of His Prophet (ص), and both Masters of the Youths of Paradise from among this nation. O people! Whoever recognizes me knows me, and whoever does not recognize me, let me tell him who I am and to what family I belong: O people! I am the son of Mecca and Mina; I am the son of Zamzam and as-Safa; I am the son of the one who carried the *rukn* on his mantle; I am the son of the best man who ever put on clothes and who ever made *tawaf* and *sa'i*, of whoever offered the hajj and pronounced the *talbiya*. I am the son of the one who was transported on the *buraq* and who was taken by Gabriel to *sidrat al-muntaha*, so he was near his Lord like the throw of a bow or closer still. I am the son of the one who led the angels of the heavens in the prayers. I am the son to whom the Mighty One revealed what He revealed. I am the son of the one who defended the Messenger of Allāh (ع) at Badr and Hunayn and never disbelieved in Allāh not even as much as the twinkling of an eye. I am the son of the best of the believers and of the heir of the prophets, of the leader of the Muslims and the noor of those who offer jihad and the killer of the renegades and those who deviated from the straight path and who scattered the *ahzab* and the most courageous one, the one with the firmest determination: such is the father of the grandsons of the Prophet (ص), al-Hassan and al-Hussain (ع), such is Ali ibn Abū Talib (ع). I am the son of Fātima az-Zahrā' (ع), the Head of all Women, the son of Khadija al-Kubra. I am the son of the one with whose blood the sand mixed. I am the son of the one who was slaughtered at Kerbalā'. I am the son of the one for whom the jinns wept in the dark and for whom the birds in the air cried.

Having said this much, people's cries filled the place, and Yazid feared dissension, so he ordered the *mu'aththin* to call the *athan* for the prayers. The latter shouted: Allāhu Akbar! The Imām (ع) said, Allāh is Greater, more Magnanimous, and more Kind than what I fear and of what I avoid." The prayer caller now shouted: *Ashhadu an la ilaha illa-Allāh!* He (ع) said, "Yes, I testify with everyone who testifies that there is no Allāh besides Him nor any other Lord." The caller shouted: *Ashahadu anna Muhammedan rasool-Allāh!* The Imām (ع) said to the prayer caller, "I ask you by Muhammed to stop here till I speak to this man," then he turned to Yazid and asked him, "Is this great Messenger of Allāh (ع) your grandfather or mine? If you say that he is yours, everyone present here as well as all other people will come to know that you are a liar, and if you say that he is mine, then why did you kill my father unjustly and oppressively and plundered his wealth and took his women captive? Woe unto you on the Day of Judgment when my grandfather will be your opponent."

Yazid yelled at the prayer caller to start the prayers immediately. A great deal of commotion now could be heard among the people. Some people prayed whereas others left.[1]

---

[1]Shaikh Abbas al-Qummi, *Nafas al-Mahmum*, p. 242. This lengthy sermon is quoted on p. 69, Vol. 2, of al-Khawarizmi's book *Maqtal al-Hussain (ع)*.

HUSSAIN'S SEVERED HEAD

Yazid ordered al-Hussain's head to be brought to him. He put it in a gold washbowl[1]. The women were behind him. Sukayna and Fātima stood and tried anxiously to steal a look at it as Yazid kept hiding it from them. When they did see it, they burst in tears[2]. He then permitted people to enter to see him[3]. Yazid took a rod and kept hitting al-Hussain's lips with it[4] saying, "A day for a day: this day is [in revenge] for Badr[5]." Then he cited these verses by al-Haseen ibn al-Humam:[6]

---

[1]al-Yafii, *Mir'at al-Jinan*, Vol. 1, p. 135.

[2]Ibn al-Atheer, *At-Tarikh al-Kāmil*, Vol. 4, p. 35. Al-Haythami, *Mujma az-Zawa'id*, Vol. 9, p. 195. Ibn as-Sabbagh, *Al-Fusool al-Muhimmah*, p. 205.

[3]Ibn al-Atheer, *At-Tarikh al-Kāmil*, Vol. 4, p. 35.

[4]at-Tabari, *Tarikh*, Vol. 6, p. 267. Ibn al-Atheer, *At-Tarikh al-Kāmil*, Vol. 4, p. 35. Ibn al-Jawzi, the grandson, *Tathkirat al-Khawass*, p. 148. Ibn Hajar al-Asqalani, *As-Sawa'iq al-Muhriqa*, p. 116. Ibn Muflih al-Hanbali, *Fiqh al-Hanabilah*, Vol. 3, p. 549. Ibn Hajar al-Asqalani, *Mujma' az-Zawa'id*, Vol. 9, p. 195. Ibn as-Sabbagh, *Al-Fusool al-Muhimma*, p. 205. Al-Maqrazi, *Khutat*, Vol. 3, p. 289. Ibn Katheer, *Al-Bidaya*, Vol. 8, p. 192. Ash-Shareeshi, *Sharh Maqamat al-Harari*, Vol. 1, p. 193, at the end of the 10th *maqam*. Muhammed Abul-Fadl and Ali Muhammed al-Bijawi, *Ayyam al-Arab fil Islam*, p. 435. Ibn Shahr Ashub, *Al-Manaqib*, Vol. 2, p. 225. According to p. 23 of *Al-Ithaf bi Hubbil-Ashraf*, Yazid kept hitting al-Hussain's front teeth, and so is stated by al-Bayruni on p. 331 of the offset edition of his book *Al-Aathaar al-Baqiya*.

[5]Ibn Shahr Ashub, *Al-Manaqib*, Vol. 2, p. 226.

[6]Ibn al-Atheer, *At-Tarikh al-Kāmil*, Vol. 4, p. 35. Ibn as-Sabbagh, *Al-Fusool al-Muhimma*, p. 205. The first line, according to p. 135, Vol. 1, of al-Yafii's *Mir'at al-Jinan*, is:

> *We took to patience, so patience proved to be our will*
> *Even as our swords kept severing hands and arms.*

It is narrated by Sibt ibn al-Jawzi on p. 148 of his book *Tathkirat al-Khawass* with some variation in its wording. A host of historians have

To be fair to us our folks never did dare,
So swords dripping with blood were to them fair;
We split the heads of men dear to us
For they severed their ties and did oppress.

Abū Barzah al-Aslami said, "I bear witness that I saw the Prophet
(ﷺ) kissing his lips and those of his brother al-Hassan (ع) and say to
them: You are the masters of the youths of Paradise; may Allāh fight
whoever fights you; may He curse him and prepare hell for him, and
what an evil refuge it is!'" Yazid became angry and ordered him to
be dragged out of his courtroom[1].

A [Christian] messenger sent by emperor Caesar was present there;
he said to Yazid, "We have in some islands the hoof of the donkey
upon which Jesus rode, and we make a pilgrimage to it every year
from all lands and offer nathr to it and hold it in as much regard as
you hold your sacred books; so, I bear witness that you are
wrongdoers."[2] This statement enraged Yazid who ordered him to be
killed. The messenger stood up, walked to the head, kissed it and
pronounced the kalima. At the moment when that messenger's head
was cut off, everyone heard a loud and fluent voice saying, *La hawla
wala quwwata illa billah!* (There is neither power nor might except
in Allāh).[3]

---

contented themselves by citing only the second verse. Among them is ash-
Shareeshi who does so on p. 193, Vol. 1, of his book *Sharh Maqamat al-
Harari*, so does al-Ālusi on p. 313, Vol. 2, of his book *Al-Iqd al-Farid*. So
does Ibn Katheer on p. 197, Vol. 8, of his book *Al-Bidaya*, the mentor
Shaikh al-Mufid in his book *Al-Irshad*, and so does Ibn Jarir at-Tabari on
p. 267, Vol. 6, of his *Tarikh*, adding that the verse was composed by al-
Haseen ibn al-Hamam al-Murri.

[1]Ibn Tawoos, *Al-Luhuf*, p. 102. The incident is abridged on p. 205 of *Al-
Fusool al-Muhimma*, on p. 267, Vol. 6, of at-Tabari's *Tarikh*, and on p. 26,
Vol. 2, of Ibn Shahr Ashub's book *Al-Manaqib*.

[2]Ibn Hajar al-Asqalani, *As-Sawa'iq al-Muhriqa*, p. 119.

[3]al-Bahrani, *Maqtal al-Awalim*, p. 151. Ibn Nama, *Muthir al-Ahzan*. On p.

143

The head was taken out of the court and hung for three days on the mansion's gate[1]. When Hind daughter of Amr ibn Suhayl, Yazid's wife, saw the head on her house's door[2] with divine light emanating from it, its blood still fresh and had not yet dried, and it was emitting a sweet fragrance[3], she entered Yazid's court without any veil crying, "The head of the daughter of the Messenger of Allāh (ﷺ) is on our door!" Yazid stood up, covered her and said, "Mourn him, O Hind, for he is the reason why Banu Hashim are grieving. [Ubaydullāh] Ibn Ziyad hastily killed him."[4]

Yazid ordered the heads to be hung on the gates and on the Umayyad Mosque, and his order was carried out[5].

Marwan [ibn al-Hakam] was very happy about al-Hussain (ﷺ) being killed, so he composed poetry lines and kept hitting al-Hussain's face with a rod.

A SYRIAN ENCOUNTERS FĀTIMA
Historians record that a Syrian looked at Fātima daughter of Ali (ﷺ)[6]

72, Vol. 2, of his book *Maqtal al-Hussain (ﷺ)*, al-Khawarizmi states the dialogue between the Christian and Yazid and how the first was killed, but he does not indicate that the most sacred head spoke.

[1]al-Maqrazi, *Al-Khutat*, Vol. 2, p. 289. *Al-Ithaf bi Hubbil-Ashraf*, p. 23. Al-Khawarizmi, *Maqtal al-Hussain (ﷺ)*, Vol. 2, p. 75. Ibn Katheer, *Al-Bidaya*, Vol. 8, p. 204. *Siyar Alam an-Nubala'*, Vol. 3, p. 216.

[2]al-Bahrani, *Maqtal al-Awalim*, p. 151. In the Introduction to this book, her father is introduced to the reader and so is her husband.

[3]al-Maqrazi, *Al-Khutat*, Vol. 2, p. 284.

[4]al-Khawarizmi, *Maqtal al-Hussain (ﷺ)*, Vol. 2, p. 74.

[5]Shaikh Abbas al-Qummi, *Nafas al-Mahmum*, p. 247.

[6]at-Tabari, *Tarikh*, Vol. 6. Ibn Katheer, *Al-Bidaya*, Vol. 8, p. 194. As-Saduq, *Al-Aamali*, p. 100, *majlis* 31. Both Ibn Nama, on p. 54 of his *Muthir al-Ahzan*, and al-Khawarizmi, on p. 62, Vol. 2, of his *Maqtal al-*

then asked Yazid to give her to him to serve him. This daughter of the Commander of the Faithful (ع) was terrified; she clung to her sister Zainab and said, "Serve him?! How could I do that?!" Zainab said to her, "Do not be concerned; this shall never happen at all." Hearing her, Yazid said, "It could if I would!" She said to him, "Not unless you renege from our religion." He answered her by saying, "Those who reneged from the religion are your father and your brother." Zainab said, "By Allāh's religion and the religion of my grandfather do I swear that it was through my father and brother that you and your father received guidance, had you been a Muslim at all." He said to her, "You lie, you enemy of Allāh!" She, peace be with her, toned down her language and said to him, "You are an emir over the destiny of people; you oppressively taunt and subdue others."[1] The same Syrian man repeated his plea to Yazid who now rebuked him and said, "May Allāh grant you a fate that will put an end to you!"[2]

ZAINAB DELIVERS ANOTHER SPEECH
Both Ibn Nama and Ibn Tawoos[3] say that Zainab daughter of Ali ibn Abū Talib[4] (ع) heard Yazid quoting the following verses by Ibn az-Zu'bari[5]:

Hussain (ع), say that she was Fatima daughter of al-Hussain (ع).

[1]Ibn al-Atheer, Vol. 4, p. 35.

[2]at-Tabari, *Tarikh*, Vol. 6, p. 265.

[3]This sermon is documented on p. 21 of *Balaghat an-Nisa* ' (Najafi edition), and on p. 64, Vol. 2, of al-Khawarizmi's book *Maqtal al-Hussain (ع)*.

[4]In his book *Maqtal al-Hussain (ع)*, al-Khawarizmi identifies her mother as Fatima (ع) daughter of the Messenger of Allah (ص).

[5]These verses are attributed by Ibn Tawoos to Ibn al-Zu'bari, as he so states on p. 102 of his book *Al-Luhuf*, but they are not all his. Al-Khawarizmi on p. 66, Vol. 2, of his book *Maqtal al-Hussain (ع)*, Ibn Abul-Hadid on p. 383, Vol. 3, of his book *Sharh Nahjul Balagha* (first Egyptian edition), and Ibn Hisham in his *Seerat*, where he discusses the Battle of

I wish my forefathers at Badr had witnessed
How the Khazraj are by the thorns annoyed,
They would have Glorified and Unified Allāh
Then they would make tahleel and say in elation:
"May your hands, O Yazid, never be paralyzed!"
We have killed the masters of their chiefs
And equated it with Badr, and it was so, indeed
Hashim played with the dominion so indeed,
No news came, nor was there a revelation revealed.
I do not belong to Khandaf if I do not
Seek revenge from Ahmed's children
For what he to us had done.

She reacted to these lines and said the following:

All Praise is due to Allāh, Lord of the Worlds. Allāh has blessed His
Messenger and all His Messenger's Progeny. Allāh, Glory to Him,
has said the truth when He said, "Then the end of those who
committed evil was that they disbelieved in Allāh's Signs and they
were ridiculing them." (Qur'an, 30:10) Do you, O Yazid, think that
when you blocked all the avenues before us, so we were driven as
captives, that we are light in the sight of Allāh and that you are
superior to us? Or is it because you enjoy with Him a great status, so
you look down at us and become arrogant, elated, when you see the
world submissive to you and things are done as you want them, and
when our authority and power became all yours? But wait! Have you
forgotten that Allāh has said, "Do not regard those who disbelieved
that We grant them good for themselves? We only give them a
respite so that they may increase their sins, and for them there is a
humiliating torment" (Qur'an, 3:178)? Is it fair, O son of *taleeqs*,
that you keep your free as well as slave women in their chambers
and at the same time drive the daughters of the Messenger of Allāh

---

Uhud, all state sixteen lines which do not include except the first and the
third lines mentioned by Ibn Tawoos. Al-Bayruni cites all of them on p.
331 of the offset edition of his book *Al-Aathaar al-Baqiya*, excluding the
fourth line.

146

(ع) as captives with their veils removed and faces exposed, taken by their enemies from one land to another, being viewed by those at watering places as well as those who man your forts, with their faces exposed to the looks of everyone near or distant, lowly or honorable, having none of their protectors with them nor any of their men? But what can be expected from one [descended from those] whose mouths chewed the livers of the purified ones and whose flesh grows out of the blood of the martyrs? How can it be expected that one who looks at us with grudge and animosity, with hatred and malice, would not hate us, we Ahl al-Bayt (ع)? Besides you, without feeling any guilt or weighing heavily what you say, you recite saying,

Then they would make tahleel *and say in elation:*
"May your hands, O Yazid, never be paralyzed!"

How dare you hit the lips of Abū Abdullāh (ع), the Master of the Youths of Paradise? But why should you not do so, since you stirred a wound that almost healed, and since all mercy is removed from your heart, having shed the blood of the offspring of Muhammed, peace and blessings of Allāh be upon him and his Progeny, and the stars on earth from among the family of Abdul-Muttalib? Then you cite your mentors as if you speak to them... Soon shall you be lodged with them, and soon shall you wish you were paralyzed and muted and never said what you said nor did what you did. O Allāh! Take what belongs to us out of his hands, seek revenge against all those who oppressed us, and let Your Wrath descend upon whoever shed our blood and killed our protectors! By Allāh! You have burnt only your own skin! You have cut only your own flesh! You shall come face to face with the Messenger of Allāh, peace of Allāh be upon him and his Progeny, bearing the burdens of the blood which you have shed, the blood of his offspring, and of his sanctities which you violated, the sanctities of his women, his kinsfolk, his flesh and blood, when Allāh gathers them together and seeks equity on their behalf. "And do not reckon those who are slain in the Way of Allāh as dead. Nay! They are living with their Lord, receiving their sustenance" (Qur'an, 3:169). Allāh suffices you as your Judge and Muhammed, peace and blessings of Allāh be upon him and his progeny, as your opponent, and Gabriel as your foe. All those who instigated you to do what you did and who put you in charge so that

147

you might play havoc with the lives of the Muslims, how evil the end of the oppressors is and which of you shall have the worst place and will be the least protected? Although calamities have forced me to speak to you, I nevertheless see you small in my eyes and find your verbal attacks monstrous, and I regard your rebuke too much to bear, but these eyes are tearful, and the chests are filled with depression. What is even more strange is that the honored Party of Allāh is being killed by the *taleeq* party of Satan. Such hands are dripping with our blood; such mouths are feeding on our flesh, while those sacred and pure corpses are offered as food to the wild beasts of the desert and are dirtied by the brutes. If you regard us as your booty, you shall soon find us as your opponents, that will be when you find nothing but what your hands had committed, and your Lord never treats His servants unjustly. To Allāh is my complaint, and upon Him do I rely. So scheme whatever you wish to scheme, and carry out your plots, and intensify your efforts, for by Allāh, you shall never be able to obliterate our mention, nor will you ever be able to kill our inspiration, nor will your shame ever be washed away. Your view shall be proven futile, your days numbered, and your wealth wasted on the Day when the caller calls out, "The curse of Allāh be upon the oppressors" (Qur'an, 11:18). All Praise is due to Allāh, Lord of the Worlds, Who sealed the life of our early ones with happiness and forgiveness, and that of our last with martyrdom and mercy. We plead to Allāh to complete His rewards for them and grant them an increase and make succession good for us; He is the most Merciful, the most Compassionate. Allāh suffices us, and how great He is!

Yazid responded to her speech by quoting a couplet of poetry demonstrating his excitement. This should not surprise anyone. Anyone who is familiar with Yazid and with his misguidance cannot be surprised at all to hear him asking with a full mouth the Syrian jackals around him: "Do you know where Fātima's son came from, and what prompted him to do what he did and to fall into the pitfalls of what he committed?" They answered in the negative. Said he, "He claims that his father is better than my father, that his mother Fātima (ع) daughter of the Messenger of Allāh (ع) is better than mine, that his grandfather (ع) is better than mine, and that he is more worthy than me of taking charge. As regarding his saying that his father is better than my father, my father had asked Allāh, the Great, the Sublime, to arbitrate between them, and people know best in whose favor He ruled. As regarding his saying that his mother is better than mine, by my life, Fātima (ع), daughter of the Messenger of Allāh (ع), is better than my mother. As regarding his saying that his grandfather (ع) is better than my grandfather, by my life, nobody who believes in Allāh and in the Last Day can find anyone among us equal to the Messenger of Allāh (ع). But he speaks with a little understanding of what he says and has not read the verse saying, Say: Lord! Owner of the domain! You grant authority to whomsoever You please, and you take the authority from whomsoever You please; You exalt whomsoever You please, and You abase whomsoever You please,' (Qur'an, 3:26) and he did not read the verse saying, Allāh grants His domain to whomsoever He pleases.' (Qur'an, 2:247)"[1].

AT THE HOUSE OF RUIN
The speech quoted above, which was delivered by Zainab, shook the very foundations of Yazid's court, and people started discussing with one another as to what extent they had been misled, and in what valley of abyss they had been hurled. Yazid had no choice except to get the women out of his court and to lodge them at a house of ruins which could not protect them against any heat or any cold. They remained there weeping and wailing, mourning al-Hussain (ع)[2] for three days[3].

---

[1] at-Tabari, *Tarikh*, Vol. 6, p. 266. Ibn Katheer, *Al-Bidaya*, Vol. 8, p. 195.

[2] Ibn Tawoos *Al-Luhuf*, p. 207. as-Saduq, *Al-Aamali*, p. 101, *majlis* 31.

[3] al-Khawarizmi, *Maqtal al-Hussain (ع)*, Vol. 2, p. 34. This shed, or say jail, as stated on p. 146, Vol. 4, of al-Yunini's *Mir'at az-Zaman*, where the events of the year 681 A.H./1283 A.D. are discussed. Says he, "On the eleventh night of the month of Ramadan, the felt market in Damascus caught fire and was burnt in its entirety, and the fire engulfed the Booksellers' Bridge, the fountain square, and the cloth market known as Saq AsAllah, as well as the watering area of Jayrun. The fire reached the Ajam street in the midst of Jayrun, scorching the wall of the Omeri Mosque adjacent to the jail were Zain al-Ābidīn (ع) had been imprisoned."

149

One evening as-Sajjād (ﷺ) went out for a walk. Al-Minhal ibn Omer met him and asked him, "How have you received the evening, O son of the Messenger of Allāh (ﷺ)?" "We have received the evening," the Imām (ﷺ) answered, "like the Israelites among the people of Pharaoh: they kill their sons and take their women captive. The Arabs brag before the non-Arabs saying that Muhammed (ﷺ) was one of them, while Quraish boasts before the rest of the Arabs of Muhammed (ﷺ) belonging to it. We, his Ahl al-Bayt (ﷺ), are now homeless; so, to Allāh do we belong, and to Him shall we all return."[1] Al-Minhal is quoted as saying, "While he was thus talking to me, a woman came out after him and said, Where are you going, O best of successors?' He left me and hurried back to her. I inquired about her, and I was told that she was his aunt Zainab (ﷺ)."[2]

BACK TO MEDĪNA

Yazid was very happy about killing al-Hussain (ﷺ) and those with him as well as the capture of the ladies who descended from the Messenger of Allāh, peace of Allāh be upon him and his progeny[3]. He was seen at his court looking very excited, being unaware of the fact that he was an atheist and an apostate as testified by his own citing of the poetry of az-Zu'bari quoted above to the extent that he denied that the Messenger of Allāh Muhammed (ﷺ) had ever received any revelation. But when he was rebuked by more and more people, it gradually appeared to him how he had failed and erred in what he had committed: a sin the like of which had never been committed by anyone who belongs to the Islamic creed. It was then that he realized the implication of Mu'awiyah's will to him wherein he said, "The people of Iraq shall not leave al-Hussain (ﷺ) till they pressure him to revolt. If he rebels against you, forgive him,

---

[1] Ibn Nama, *Muthir al-Ahzan*, p. 58. Al-Khawarizmi, *Maqtal al-Hussain (ﷺ)*, Vol. 2, p. 72.

[2] *Al-Anwar an-Numainiyya*, p. 340.

[3] as-Sayyati, *Tarikh al-Khulafa*, p. 139.

for he was begotten in sacred wombs, and he enjoys a lofty status."[1]

His closest courtiers, and even his family members and women, stayed away from him. He heard the statements uttered by the most sacred severed head when he ordered the messenger of the Roman emperor to be killed: *La hawla wala quwwata illa billāh!* (There is neither power nor might except in Allāh).[2]

Yazid's most abominable crime and extreme cruelty were now being discussed at every gathering, and such discussions were finding an echo throughout Damascus. Yazid at that juncture had no choice except to shift the blame to the shoulder of Ubaydullāh ibn Ziyad in order to distance the taunting from him, but what is already established cannot be removed.

When he feared dissension and repercussions, he rushed to get as-Sajjād and the children out of Syria and to send them back home. He carried out their wishes, ordering an-Nu'man ibn Basheer and a number of other men with him to escort them to Medīna and to treat them with kindness[3].

When they reached Iraq, they asked the road guide to take the highway leading to Kerbalā'. They reached the place where al-Hussain (ع) had been martyred. There, they found Jābir ibn Abdullāh al-Ansari accompanied by a group of Banu Hashim and some of the family members of the Messenger of Allāh (ص). They had all gone there to visit al-Hussain's grave. They met each other weeping and grieving, beating their cheeks. They stayed there mourning al-Hussain (ع)[4] for three days.[5]

---

[1]at-Tabari, *Tarikh*, Vol. 6, p. 180.

[2]al-Bahrani, *Maqtal al-Awalim*, p. 150.

[3]al-Mufid, *Al-Irshad*.

[4]Ibn Tawoos, *Al-Luhuf*, p. 112. Ibn Nama, *Muthir al-Ahzan*, p. 79 (old edition).

[5]Muhammed Hassan al-Qazwini, *Riyad al-Ahzan*, p. 157.

Jābir ibn Abdullāh al-Ansari stood at the grave and burst in tears then thrice called out al-Hussain's name, then he said, "Why a loved one does not answer one who loves him?" But soon he answered his own query by saying, "How can he answer while his cheeks are torn and his head is separated from his body? Yet I testify that you are the son of the Seal of Prophets (ع), the son of the master of the faithful (ع), the son of the inseparable ally of piety, the descendant of guidance, the fifth of the fellows of the kisa', the son of the master of *naqeebs*, the one who was brought up in the lap of the pious, that you were raised on the milk of iman, that you were weaned with Islam, so you were good when you were alive, and you are so when dead. But the hearts of the faithful are not pleased with parting with you, nor do they have any doubt about goodness being yours. So peace of Allāh be upon you and His Pleasure. And I bear witness that you treaded the same path treaded before you by your brother [prophet] Zakariyya (Zacharias)."

Having said so, Jābir turned his head around the grave as he said, "Assalamo Alaikom, O souls that abide at al-Hussain's courtyard! I bear witness that you upheld the prayers and paid the *zakat*, enjoined what is right and prohibited what is wrong, struggled against the atheists and adored Allāh till death overtook you. By the One Who sent Muhammed, peace of Allāh be upon him and his Progeny, as His Prophet sent with the truth, I testify that we have a share in what you have earned." Atiyyah al-'Awfi [his companion[1] who was leading him, since he, a maternal relative and one of the greatest sahabis of Prophet Muhammed (ص), as indicated above in a footnote, was by then a blind old man] asked him, "How so when we did not descend upon a valley nor ascend a mountain, nor did we strike with a sword, whereas the heads of these people have been severed from their bodies, their sons have been orphaned and their wives widowed?" Jābir answered: "I heard the Messenger of Allāh (ع) whom I very much love saying, One who loves a people will be lodged with them, and one who loves what some people do will have a share in [the rewards of] their deeds.' By the One Who sent

---

[1]Some accounts say that Atiyyah was his slave.

Muhammed (ص) as a Prophet with the truth, my intention and that of my companions is similar to that for which al-Hussain (ع) and his companions were all killed."[1]

THE SEVERED HEAD REJOINS BODY

Once Zain al-Ābidīn (ع) came to know of Yazid's consent, he asked him for the heads so that he could bury them. Yazid showed no hesitation to do so, ordering the heads, including those of Zain al-Ābidīn's family members, to be handed over to him. Zain al-Ābidīn reunited them with their respective bodies.

The list of writers of biographies who recorded his bringing the heads to Kerbalā' includes Shaikh Abbas al-Qummi, author of *Nafas al-Mahmum*, who discusses this issue on p. 253 of his book, and it is also discussed on p. 155 of *Riyad al-Ahzan* of Muhammed Hassan ash-Sha'ban Kurdi al-Qazwani.

As regarding al-Hussain's head, we read about it on p. 165 of al-Fattal's book *Rawdat al-Wa'izeen*, and on p. 85 of *Muthir al-Ahzan* by Ibn Nama al-Hilli. The latter reference is the one the Shī'as consider as the most accurate as stated on p. 112 of *Al-Luhuf* by Ibn Tawoos. On p. 151 of at-Tibrisi's book *I'lam al-Wara bi A'lam al-Huda*, as well as on p. 154 of *Maqtal al-'Awalim*, as is the case with both *Riyad al-Musa'ib* and *Bihār al-Anwār*, the same view is the most famous among scholars. On p. 200, Vol. 2, of his book titled *Al-Manaqib*, Ibn Shahr Ashub says, "In some of his letters, al-Murtada has stated that al-Hussain's head was reunited with its body in Kerbalā'." At-Tusi has said that that incident was the basis for *ziyarat al-arba'een*. The author of *Bihār al-Anwār* cites *Al-Udad al-Qawiyya* by the brother of allama al-Hilli. On p. 67 of his book *Aja'ib al-Makhlooqat*, al-Qazwani indicates that it was on the twentieth of Safar that al-Hussain's head was returned to its body. Ash-Shabrawi says, "The head was returned to the body after forty

---

[1] Abū Ja'far Muhammed ibn Abul-Qasim ibn Muhammed ibn Ali at-Tabari al-Āmili, *Bisharat al-Mustafa*, p. 89 (Hayderi Press edition). This author is one of the 5th century A.H./11th century A.D. scholars who were tutored by Shaikh at-Tusi's son.

days."[1] According to Ibn Hajar's book Sharh al-Bawsari's Hamziyya[2], forty days after his martyrdom, al-Hussain's head was returned [to its body]. Sabt ibn al-Jawzi has said, "It is most widely known that it [the head] was returned to Kerbalā' and buried with the body."[3] On p. 57, Vol. 1, of his book Al-Kawakib al-Durriyya, al-Qatari al-Biladi al-Bahrani records the consensus among Imāmite Shī'as that the head was returned to Kerbalā', and that this view was the one accepted by al-Qurtubi. He did not list his sources but attributed it to "some people of knowledge as well as eye witnesses," becoming evident to him that the head was, indeed, returned to Kerbalā'. Abul-Rayhan al-Bayruni states that it was on the twentieth of Safar that al-Hussain's head was reunited and buried with its body.[4]

Based on the above, any statements to the contrary should not be taken seriously especially those claiming that he was buried with his father (ع), a claim with which the scholars mentioned above are familiar and which they all discard. Their rejection of such a claim proves that it cannot be relied upon especially since its *isnad* is not complete and its narrators are not famous.

THE ARBA'EEN

It is customary to pay tribute to a deceased person forty days after his death by doing acts of righteousness on his behalf, by eulogizing him and enumerating his merits. This is done at organized gatherings in order to keep his memory alive just when people's minds start to forget about him and their hearts start to ignore him. Thus, he remains alive in people's minds.

---

[1]ash-Shabrawi, *Al-Ithaf bi Hubbil-Ashraf* الاتحاف بحب الأشراف, p. 12.

[2]"Hamziyya همزية" means a poem the rhyme of which ends with a *hamza* (ء).

[3]Ibn al-Jawzi, the grandson, *Tathkirat al-Khawass* تذكرة الخواص, p. 150.

[4]*Al-Athar al-Baqiya* الآثار الباقية, Vol. 1, p. 331.

Both Abū Tharr al-Ghifāri and Ibn Abbas[1] quote the Prophet (ص) saying, "The earth mourns the death of a believer for forty mornings."[2] Zurarah quotes Abū Abdullāh Imām as-Sādiq (ع) saying, "The sky wept over al-Hussain (ع) for forty mornings with blood, while the earth wept over him for forty mornings with blackness. The sun wept over him for forty mornings with an eclipse and with redness, whereas the angels wept over him for forty mornings. No woman among us ever dyed with henna, nor used any oil, nor any kohl nor cohabited with her husband till the head of Ubaydullāh ibn Ziyad was brought to us, and we are still grieving even after all of that."[3]

This is the basis of the ongoing custom of grieving for the deceased for forty days. On the 40th day, a special mourning ceremony is held at his grave-site attended by his relatives and friends. This custom is not confined to Muslims. Adherents of other creeds hold commemorative mourning ceremonies for their lost ones. Some gather at a church and conduct a special funeral prayer service. Jews renew their mourning service thirty days after one's death, nine months after one's death, and one year after one's death[4]. All of this is done in order to keep his memory alive and so that people may not forget his legacy and deeds if he is one of the great ones with merits and feats.

At any rate, a researcher does not find in the band described as reformers a man so well shrouded in feats of the most sublime meanings, one whose life, uprising, and the tragic way in which he was killed..., a divine call and lessons in reform, even social

---

[1]His full name is: Abdullāh ibn Abbas ibn Abdul-Muttalib, a cousin of the Prophet of Islam (ص). He is known as the Islamic nation's scholar. The traditions of the Prophet which he reported fill the Sahīh books. He died in Ta'if in 68 A.H./687 A.D. after having lost his eye-sight.

[2]al-Majlisi, *Bihār al-Anwār*, Vol. 2, p. 679.

[3]an-Nawari, *Mustadrak al-Wasa'il*, p. 215, chapter 94.

[4]*Nahr at-Thahab fi Tarikh Halab*, Vol. 1, pp. 63 and 267.

systems, ethics, and sacred morals..., other than the master of the youths of Paradise, the man who was martyred for his creed, for Islam, for harmony, the martyr for ethics and cultivation, namely al-Hussain (ع). He, more than anyone else, deserves to be remembered on various occasions. People ought to make a pilgrimage to his sacred grave-site on the anniversary of the passage of 40 days since the date of his martyrdom so that they may achieve such lofty objectives.

The reason why most people hold only the first such an anniversary is due to the fact that the merits of those men are limited and temporal, unlike those of the Master of Martyrs: his feats are endless, his virtues are countless. The study of his life and martyrdom keeps his memory alive, and so is the case whenever he is mentioned. To follow in his footsteps is needed by every generation. To hold an annual ceremony at his grave on the anniversary of his Arba'een brings his revolution back to memory. It also brings back to memory the cruelty committed by the Umayyads and their henchmen. No matter how hard an orator tries, or how well a poet presents his theme, new doors of virtue, which were closed before, will then be opened.

This is why it has been the custom of the Shī'as to bring back to memory on the Arba'een those events every year. The tradition wherein Imām al-Bāqir (ع) says that the heavens wept over al-Hussain (ع) for forty mornings, rising red and setting red[1], hints to such a public custom.

So is the case with a statement made once by Imām al-Hassan al-'Askari (ع) wherein he said, "There are five marks for a believer: his fifty-one *rek'at* prayers, *ziyarat al-arba'een*, his audible recitation of the *basmala*, his wearing his ring on the right hand, and his rubbing his forehead with the dust."[2]

---

[1]al-Qummi, *Kāmil az-Ziyarat* كامل الزيارات, p. 90, Chapter 28.

[2]This is narrated by Shaikh at-Tusi on p. 17, Vol. 3, of his *Tahthib* تهذيب, in a chapter discussing the merits of visiting the grave-site of Imām al-Hussain (ع). In it, he quotes Imām "Abū Muhammed" al-Hassan al-

Such a statement leads us to the ongoing public custom being discussed. Holding a mourning ceremony for the Master of Martyrs and holding meetings in his memory are all done by those who are loyal to him and who follow him. There is no doubt that those who follow his path are the believers who recognize him as their Imām; so, one of the marks highlighting their *iman*, as well as their loyalty to the master of the youths of Paradise, the one who was killed as he stood to defend the divine Message, is to be present on the Arba'een anniversary at his sacred grave in order to hold a mourning ceremony for him and remember the tragedies that had befallen him and his companions and Ahl al-Bayt (ع).

To twist the meaning of *ziyarat al-arba'een* by saying that it means visiting the grave-sites of forty believers is simply indicative of twisted minds, an attempt at distortion, one which good taste resents. Moreover, it is without any foundation. Had the goal been to visit forty believers, the Imām (ع) would have used the term "*ziyarat arba'een [mu'mineen]*." The original wording indicates that ziyarat al-arba'een is one of the conditions enumerated in the hadīth cited above saying that it is one of the marks of one's iman and an indication of his loyalty to the Twelve Imāms (ع).

All the Imāms who descended from the Prophet (ص) were the gates of salvation, the arks of mercy. Through them can a believer be distinguished from a non-believer. They all left this world after being killed as they stood to defend the divine Message, accepting the possibility of their being killed for the stand which they took in obedience to the Command of their Lord, Glory to Him, the One Who sent His *wahi* to their grandfather the Prophet (ص). Father of Muhammed, al-Hassan (ع) son of the Commander of the Faithful Ali (ع), has pointed out to this fact saying, "The mission which we undertake is assigned to Twelve Imāms (ع) each one of whom is either to be killed or poisoned."

'Askari, peace be with him. It is also narrated on p. 551 of the Indian edition of *Musbah al-Mutahajjid* مصباح المتهجد.

For all of these reasons, the Imāms from among the Prophet's Progeny (ع) found no alternative to attracting the attention to such a glorious revolution because it contains tragedies that would split the hardest of rocks. They knew that persistence in demonstrating the injustice dealt to al-Hussain (ع) would stir the emotions and attract the hearts of sympathizers. One who hears the tales of such horrible events will come to conclude that al-Hussain (ع) was a fair and just Imām who did not succumb to lowly things, that his Imāmate was inherited from his grandfather the Prophet (ص) and from his father the *wasi* (ع), that whoever opposes him deviates from the path of equity. Whoever absorbs the fact that right was on al-Hussain's side and on that of his infallible offspring would be embracing their method and following their path.

This is why the Imāms (ع) did not urge the holding of mourning ceremonies for the Arba'een anniversary of any of them, not even for that of the Prophet of Islam (ع), so that it alone would be the memory of his tragedy that would make a strong case for safeguarding the link with the creed. Turning attention to it is more effective in keeping the cause of the Infallible Ones dear to all those who discuss it: "Keep our cause alive, and discuss our cause."

The kind reader, anyway, can easily see why *ziyarat al-arba'een* is an indication of one's iman when he gets to know similar indications to which the *hadīth* has referred.

The first of such marks, namely the 51-*rek'at* prayers, legislated during the night of the Prophet's *mi'raj*, and which, through the Prophet's intercession, were reduced to only five during the day and the night, are: seventeen *rek'at* for the morning, the noon and the afternoon, the sunset and the evening, and the *nafl* prayers timed with them, in addition to night's *nafl* prayers: they all make up thirty-four: eight before the noon-time prayers, eight before the after-noon prayers, four after sunset prayers, and two after the evening prayers regarded as one, and two before the morning prayers, and finally eleven *rek'at* for the night's nafl prayers. Add to them the *shaf'* and *witr rek'at*, and you will come to a total of obligatory and optional prayers of fifty-one *rek'at*. This is applicable to the Shī'as only. Although they agree with the Shī'as with regard to the number of obligatory *rek'at*, the Sunnis differ when it comes to optional prayers. On p. 314, Vol. 1, of Ibn Humam al-Hanafi's book *Fath al-Qadeer*, they are: two *rek'at* before the *fajr* prayers, four before the noon prayers and two after that, four before the afternoon prayers, or just two *rek'at*, two more after the sunset prayers and four thereafter, or just two, making up twenty-three *rek'at*. They differ about the night's *nafl* prayers whether they ought to be eight, only two, or thirteen, or even more. Hence, the total of optional and compulsory *rek'at* will in no case be fifty-one; so, the fifty-one *rek'at* are relevant to Imāmite (Twelver) Shī'as only.

The second on the list of marks referred to in the said hadīth is the audible pronunciation of the *basmala*. Imāmites seek nearness to Allāh, the most Exalted One, by making it obligatory to pronounce it audibly in the audible prayers and voluntary in the inaudible ones, following the text of their Imāms (ع). In this regard, al-Fakhr ar-Razi says, "Shī'as are of the view that it is a Sunnah to audibly pronounce the *basmala* in the audible prayers as well as the inaudible ones, whereas the majority of faqihs differ from them. It is proven through tawatur that Ali ibn Abū Talib (ع) used to audibly pronounce the *basmala*. Anyone who follows Ali (ع) in as far as his creed is concerned will surely be on the right guidance by token of the *hadīth* saying, O Allāh! Let right be with Ali wherever he goes.'"[1] This statement of ar-Razi was not digested by Abul-Thana' al-Ālusi who followed it with his comment in which he said, "Had anyone acted upon all what they claim to be *mutawatir* (consecutively reported) from the Commander of the Faithful (ع), he will surely be an apostate; so, there is no alternative to believing in some and disbelieving in others. His claim that anyone who emulates Ali (ع) in as far as his creed is concerned will be on the right guidance of Islam is accepted without any discussion so long as we are sure that it is proven as having been said by Ali, peace be with him. Anything else besides that is steam."[2]

---

[1] *Mafatih al-Ghayb*, Vol. 1, p. 107.

[2] *Ruh al-Ma'ani*, Vol. 1, p. 47.

Shī'as are not harmed when al-Ālusi and others assault them especially since their feet are firm on the path of loyalty for the master of *wasis* (ع) to whom the Messenger of Allāh (ع) says, "O Ali! Nobody knows Allāh, the most Exalted One, (fully well) except I and you, and nobody knows me (full well) except Allāh and you, and nobody knows you (fully well) except Allāh and I."[1]

Sunnis have opted to do the opposite with regard to such a pronouncement. On p. 478, Vol. 1, of Ibn Qudamah's book *Al-Mughni*, and also on p. 204, Vol. 1, of *Badai' as-Sanai'* by al-Kasani, and also on p. 216, Vol. 1, of az-Zarqani's *Sharh* of Abul-Diya's *Mukhtasar* of Malik's *fiqh*, audible pronouncement is not a Sunnah in the prayers.

The third mark mentioned in the said hadīth, that is, wearing a ring in the right hand, is something practiced religiously by the Shī'as on account of the traditions they quote from their Imāms (ع). A multitude among the Sunnis disagrees with them. Ibn al-Hajjaj al-Maliki has said, "The Sunnah has recorded everything as abominable if handed by the left hand and everything *tahir* if handed by the right. In this sense, it is highly recommended to wear a ring in the left hand to be taken by the right one and then placed on the left."[2] Ibn Hajar narrates saying that Malik hated to wear a ring on his right hand, believing it should be worn on the left[3]. Shaikh Isma'eel al-Barusawi has said the following in *Iqd al-Durr*: "Originally, it was a Sunnah to wear a ring on the right hand, but since this is the distinguishing mark of the people of *bid'as*, innovations, and of injustice, it became a Sunnah in our time to place the ring on a finger on the left hand."[4]

---

[1]*Al-Muhtadir*, p. 165.

[2]*Al-Madkhal*, Vol. 1, p. 46, in a chapter dealing with the etiquette of entering mosques.

[3]*Al-Fatawa al-Fiqhiyya al-Kubra*, Vol. 1, p. 264, in a chapter dealing with what to wear.

[4]This is narrated by the authority Shaikh Abdul-Hussain Ahmed al-Amini an-Najafi in his 11-volume encyclopedia titled *Al-Ghadīr* quoting p. 142,

The fourth mark mentioned in the said *hadīth* is the placing of the forehead on dust [or dry soil]. Its message is to demonstrate that during the *sajda*, the forehead has to be placed on the ground. Sunnis

---

Vol. 4, of the exegesis titled *Ruh al-Bayan*. This is not the first issue wherein Sunnis practice the opposite of what the Shī'as practice. On p. 137, Vol. 1, of Abū Ishāq ash-Sharazi's book *Al-Muhaththab*, on p. 47, Vol. 1, of al-Ghazali's book *Al-Wajeeza*, on p. 25 of an-Nawawi's *Al-Minhaj* as well as on p. 560, Vol. 1, of its *Sharh* by Ibn Hajar titled *Tuhfat al-Muhtaj fi Sharh al-Minhaj*, on p. 248, Vol. 4, of al-Ayni's book *Umdat al-Qari fi Sharh al-Bukhari*, on p. 681, Vol. 1, of Ibn Muflih's book *Al-Furoo*, and on p. 505, Vol. 2, of Ibn Qudamah's book *Al-Mughni*, planing graves is looked upon as a mark of innovators. On p. 88, Vol. 1, of ash-Sharani's book *Rahmat al-Ummah bi Ikhtilaf al-A'immah*, a book written as a comment on the exegesis titled *Al-Mizan* by 'allama Tabatabai, the author states the following: "It is a Sunnah to plane graves. But since it became a distinguishing mark for the Rafidis, it is better to do contrariwise." Among other issues wherein Sunnis do the opposite of what the Shī'as do is blessing the Prophet (ﷺ) and his progeny (ع). Some of them suggest its elimination altogether. For example, az-Zamakhshari states the following comment after being tried to explain verse 56 of Sūrat al-Ahzab (Chapter 33 of the Holy Qur'an) in his book *Al-Kashshaf*: "It is *makrooh* to bless the Prophet (ﷺ) because it causes one to be charged with being a Rafidi, especially since he [the Prophet {ﷺ}] has said, Do not stand where you may be prone to being charged.'" The same theme exists on p. 135, Vol. 11, of Ibn Hajar's book *Fath al-Bari*, in "Kitab al-Da'awat" (book of supplications), where the author tries to answer the question: "Should one bless anyone else besides the Prophet (ﷺ)?" Says he, "There is a disagreement with regard to blessing anyone besides the prophets although there is a consensus that it is permissive to greet the Living One. Some say it is permissive in its absolute application, while others say it is conditional because it has become a distinguishing mark of the Rafidis." Even in the manner of dressing do some Sunnis want to distinguish themselves from others: On p. 13, Vol. 5, of az-Zarqani's book *Sharh al-Mawahib as-Saniyya*, it is stated that, "Some scholars used to loosen their tassels from the left front side, and I have never read any text that a tassel should be loosened from the right side except in a weak *hadīth* narrated by at-Tabrani. Now since this has become a distinguishing mark of the Imāmites, it ought to be abandoned in order to avoid looking like them." Imagine! Notice the prejudice and the narrow-mindedness!

do not place their forehead on the ground. Abū Haneefa, Malik, and Ahmed are reported as having authorized the prostrating on turban coils[1], or on a piece of garment[2] worn by the person performing the prayers or any piece of cloth. Hanafis have authorized placing it on the palms if one feels grudgingly that he has no other choice[3]. They also permit prostrating on wheat and barley, on a bed, on the back of another person standing in front of you who is also performing the same prayers![4]

The objective behind such a reference is that it is highly commendable, when one prostrates to thank Allāh, to rub his forehead on the dust as a symbol of humility and to shun arrogance. An examination of the original text will show any discreet person that it is equally commendable to rub both sides of the face on it.

Rubbing the cheeks exists when reference is made to *sajdat ash-Shukr*[5], something whereby prophet Moses son of Imran [Amram] (ع) deserved to be drawn closer to the Almighty whenever he addressed Him silently [during the *munajat*][6]. Nobody contradicted the Imāmites with regard to such rubbing, be it on the forehead or on the cheeks. Sunnis never bound themselves to rub their foreheads on dust when they perform their prayers or when they perform *sajdat ash-Shukr*. This is so despite the fact that an-Nakh'i, Malik, and Abū Haneefa have all disliked to perform *sajdat ash-Shukr*, although the

---

[1]ash-Sha'rani, *Al-Mizan*, Vol. 1, p. 138.

[2]al-Marghinani, *Al-Hidaya*, Vol. 1, p. 33.

[3]Abdul-Rahman al-Jazari, *Al-Fiqh ala al-Mathahib al-Arba'ah*, Vol. 1, p. 189.

[4]Ibn Najeem, *Al-Bahr ar-Ra'iq*, Vol. 1, p. 319.

[5]Shaikh al-Mufid, *Al-Kafi ala Hamish Mir'at al-Uqool*, Vol. 3, p. 129. As-Saduq, *Al-Faqih*, p. 69. Shaikh at-Tusi, *At-Tahthib*, Vol. 1, p. 266, in a chapter dealing with what ought to be recited following the prayers.

[6]Shaikh as-Saduq, *Al-Faqih*, p. 69.

Hanbalis observe it[1], and so do the Shafi'is[2] whenever they receive a divine blessing or whenever a sign of Allāh's wrath is removed from them.

IN MEDĪNA

As-Sajjād (ع) had no choice except to leave Kerbalā' and set forth to Medīna (which used to be called Yathrib during the pre-Islamic era) after having stayed there for three days. It was too much for him to see how his aunts and the other women, as well as the children, were all crying day and night while visiting one grave after another. Bashir ibn Hathlam has said, "When we came close to Medīna, Ali ibn al-Hussain (ع) alighted and tied his she-camel then set up a tent where he lodged the women. He said to me, O Bashir! May Allāh have mercy on your father! He was a poet. Can you compose any of it at all?' I said, Yes, O son of the Messenger of Allāh! I, too, am a poet.' He (ع) said, Then enter Medīna and mourn the martyrdom of Abū Abdullāh (ع).' So I rode my horse and entered Medīna. When I came near the Mosque of the Prophet, peace and blessings of Allāh be upon him and his progeny, I cried loudly and recited these verses:

قُتل الحسينُ فأدمعي مدرار   يا أهل يثربَ لا مُقَام لكم بها،

والرأس منـه على القناة يُدار   الجسم منـه بكربلاء مضرّج

O people of Yathrib! May you never stay therein!
Al-Hussain (ع) is killed, so my tears now rain,
His body is in Kerbalā covered with blood
While his head is on a spear displayed.

"Then I said, Here is Ali ibn al-Hussain (ع) accompanied by his aunts and sisters; they have all returned to you. I am his messenger to you to inform you of his place.' People went out in a hurry, including women who had never before left their chambers, all

---

[1]Ibn Qudamah, *Al-Mughni*, Vol. 1, p. 626. Ibn Muflih, *Al-Furoo'*, Vol. 1, p. 382.

[2]*Kitab al-Umm*, Vol. 1, p. 116. Al-Mazni, *Al-Mukhtasar*, Vol. 1, p. 90. Al-Ghazali, *Al-Wajeeza*, Vol. 1, p. 32.

weeping and wailing. All those in Medīna were in tears. Nobody had ever seen such crying and wailing. They surrounded Ali, Zain al-Ābidīn (ع), to offer him their condolences. He came out of the tent with a handkerchief in his hand with which he was wiping his tears. Behind him was one of his slaves carrying a chair in which the Imām (ع) later sat, being overcome by grief. The cries of the mourners were loud. Everyone was weeping and wailing. Ali signaled to people to calm down. Once they stopped crying, he, peace be with him said,

All Praise is due to Allāh, Lord of the Worlds, the Most Gracious, the Most Merciful, the King of the Day of Judgment, Creator of all creation Who is Exalted in the high heavens, Who is so near, He hears even the silent speech. We praise Him on the grave events, on time's tragedies, on the pain inflicted by such tragedies, on the crushing of calamities, on the greatness of our catastrophe, on our great, monstrous, magnanimous and afflicting hardships. O people! Allāh, the most Exalted One, Praise to Him, has tried us with great trials and tribulations, with a tremendous loss suffered by the religion of Islam. The father of Abdullāh, al-Hussain (ع) and his family have been killed, and his women and children taken captive. They displayed his head in every land from the top of a spear... Such is the catastrophe similar to which there is none at all. O people! Which men among you are happy after him, or which heart is not grieved on his account? Which eye among you withholds its tears and is too miser with its tears? The seven great heavens wept over his killing; the seas wept with their waves, and so did the heavens with their corners and the earth with its expanse; so did the trees with their branches and the fish in the depths of the seas. So did the angels who are close to their Lord. So did all those in the heavens. O people! Which heart is not grieved by his killing? Which heart does not yearn for him? Which hearing hears such a calamity that has befallen Islam without becoming deaf? O people! We have become homeless, exiles, outcasts, shunned, distanced from all countries as though we were the offspring of the Turks or of Kabul without having committed a crime, nor an abomination, nor afflicted a calamity on Islam! Never did we ever hear such thing from our fathers of old. This is something new. By Allāh! Had the Prophet (ص) required them to fight us just as he had required them to be

164

good to us, they would not have done to us any more than what they already have. So we belong to Allāh, and to Him is our return from this calamity, and what a great, painful, hard, cruel, and catastrophic calamity it is! To Allāh do we complain from what has happened to us, from the suffering we have endured, for He is the Omnipotent, the Vengeful.

السَّلام عَلَيْكَ يَا أبا عَبْدِ الله وَعلَى الأرواح الَّتِي حَلَّتْ بِفِنائِكَ ، وَأنَاخَت بِرَحْلِك، عَلَيْكَ مِنّي سَلامُ الله أبَداً مَا بَقِيتُ وَبَقِيَ اللَّيْلُ وَالنَّهارُ ، وَلا جَعَلَهُ اللهُ آخِرَ العَهْدِ مِنّي لِزِيَارتِكُمْ أهْلَ البَيتِ، السَّلام عَلَى الحُسَيْنِ ، وَعَلَى عَليّ بْنِ الحُسَيْنِ ، وَعَلَى أوْلادِ الحُسَيْنِ ، وَعَلَى أصْحابِ الحُسَيْنِ و رحمَة الله و بركاتِه.

Peace with you, O father of Abdullāh, and with the souls that landed in your courtyard! Allāh's Greeting to you from me forever, so long as there is night and day! May Allāh not make it the last time I greet you, O Ahl al-Bayt! Peace with al-Hussain, with Ali son of al-Hussain, with the offspring of al-Hussain, and with the companions of al-Hussain, the mercy of Allāh and His blessings.

"Sa'sa'ah ibn Sawhan al-Abdi, an invalid who could barely walk on his feet, stood up and apologized to the Imām (ع) for not rushing to help his family due to his handicap. He, peace be with him, responded to him by accepting his excuse, telling him that he thought well of him, thanked him and sought Allāh's mercy for his father. Then Zain al-Ābidīn (ع) entered Medīna accompanied by his family and children.[1]

Ibrahim ibn Talhah ibn Ubaydullāh came to the Imām (ع) and asked him, "Who won?" The Imām, peace be with him, answered, "When the time for prayers comes, and when the *athan* and *iqama* are called, you will know who the winner is."[2]

Zainab took both knobs of the mosque's door and cried out, "O grandfather! I mourn to you my brother al-Hussain (ع)!"

Sukayna cried out, "O grandfather! To you do I complain from what we have been through, for by Allāh, I never saw anyone more hard-hearted than Yazid, nor have I ever seen anyone, be he an apostate or a polytheist, more evil than him, more rough, or more cruel. He

---

[1] Ibn Tawoos, *Al-Luhuf*, p. 116.

[2] Shaikh at-Tusi, *Al-Aamali*, p. 66.

165

kept hitting my father's lips with his iron bar as he said, How did you find the battle, O al-Hussain (ع)?!'"[1]

The ladies who were born and grew up in the lap of Prophethood held a mourning ceremony for the Master of Martyrs (ع). They put on the most coarse of clothes; they shrouded themselves in black, and they kept weeping and wailing day and night as Imām as-Sajjād was cooking for them[2].

Once Imām Ja'far as-Sādiq (ع) said, "No lady who descended from Hashim used any dye, nor any oil, nor any kohl, for full five years; it was then that al-Mukhtar sent them the head of Ubaydullāh ibn Ziyad."[3]

As regarding ar-Rubab, she wept over [her husband] Abū Abdullāh (ع) till her eyes were no longer capable of producing any more tears. One of her bondmaids told her that using a particular type of herb was tear stimulant, so she ordered it to be prepared for her in order to induce her tears[4].

Ali Zain al-Ābidīn (ع), the only surviving son of Imām al-Hussain (ع), stayed aloof from the public in order to avoid being involved in their disputes with one another and in order to dedicate his entire time to worshipping Allāh and mourning his father. He kept weeping day and night. One of his slaves said to him, "I fear for you lest you should perish." He (ع) said to him, "I only convey my complaints and my grief to Allāh, and I know from Allāh what you all do not know. Jacob was a prophet from whom Allāh caused one of his sons to be separated. He had twelve sons, and he knew that his son

---

[1] al-Qazwini, *Riyad al-Ahzan*, p. 163.

[2] al-Barqi, *Mahasin*, Vol. 2, p. 420, in a chapter dealing with providing food for a mourning ceremony.

[3] *Mustadrak al-Wasa'il*, Vol. 2, p. 215, chapter 94.

[4] al-Majlisi, *Bihār al-Anwār*, Vol. 10, p. 235, citing *Al-Kafi* of Shaikh al-Mufid.

(Joseph) was still alive, yet he wept over him till he lost his eye sight. If you look at my father, my brothers, my uncles, and my friends, how they were slain all around me, tell me how can my grief ever end? Whenever I remember how Fātima's children were slaughtered, I cannot help crying. And whenever I look at my aunts and sisters, I remember how they were fleeing from one tent to another..."

To you, O Messenger of Allāh (ﷺ), is our complaint from the way whereby your nation treated your pure offspring, from the oppression and persecution to which they were subjected, and all Praise is due to Allāh, Lord of the Worlds.

عُذْراً، إِذَا انْقَطَعَ الكَـلامُ .. فَالـرُّوحُ يَقْتُـلُهـا الحَنِيـنْ..

وَأَنَـا الـمُكَـبَـلُ بِـالـهَـوى .. والـحُـبُّ قَيْدٌ لا يَـلِيـنْ..

هَيْهَـاتَ أَنْسَـى كَرْبَـلاءٍ .. وَأَنَـا بِـذِكْـرَاهـا سَجِيـنْ..

سَـأَظَـلُّ أَذْكُـرُ كَرْبَـلاءَ .. وَأَظَـلُّ أَهْـتِـفُ يَاحُسَيـنْ

اللهم أرزقنا شفاعة الحسين

PART III

THE REVOLUTION'S OUTCOME

What place does Imām al-Hussain's revolution occupy in Islamic history? Those who are not familiar with its motives "innocently" or ignorantly inquire about its results, outcomes, fruits, achievements, etc. Others have even questioned its wisdom, arguing that to challenge a mighty force like that of the Umayyads of the time was fatal, suicidal, futile.

The revolution's motives have already been discussed; therefore, a brief review of the changes brought about in its aftermath throughout the Muslim world is appropriate at this stage.

Murdering Imām al-Hussain (ع), grandson of the Messenger of Allāh (ع), produced great shock waves throughout the Islamic world due to its horrible nature, to the unprecedented cruelty with which he and his family members and companions were treated, to the fact that he and his family were forbidden from having access to water while dogs and pigs were drinking of it, to the fact that he and his family were recognized as the most prestigious people on the face of earth, securing the highest esteem and regard of the Muslims who still remembered some of the statements made by their Prophet (ص) in honor of al-Hassan and al-Hussain (ع) in particular and of Ahl al-Bayt (ع) in general. Muslims, as a result, loathed to associate themselves with his murderers or with anyone who had a hand in that massacre, in effect performing an act of civil disobedience of their rulers. Many of them openly cursed his murderers, for who can call himself a Muslim and who does not curse the murderer of his Prophet's family? Thus, the revolution achieved the task of unveiling the Umayyad's un-Islamic character to the general public,

168

leaving no doubt in anyone's mind about what kind of barbarians those Umayyads were.

The concepts which the Umayyads were promoting were now being questioned by everyone; they were for the first time being recognized for what they really were: a distortion of everything Islam stands for. This isolated the Umayyads and changed the public's attitude towards them and towards anything they said or did.

Imām al-Hussain's revolution set a living example as to what every Muslim should do in such situations. It had deeply penetrated people's hearts, producing a great pain and feeling of guilt at thus abandoning al-Hussain (ع) and leaving him to be slaughtered at the hands of Allāh's worst creatures without assisting him. Such feeling of shame grew greater and greater, transforming itself into sincere repentance and translating into open and massive popular revolutions against the Umayyads' regime of terror and, in the end, succeeding in putting an end to Yazid's authority and to that of his likes. Thus, al-Hussain's revolution prompted the public to shake the dust of neo-*jahiliyya* brought about by the Umayyads and to stir, in a dynamic movement, to action to demolish all its edifices and altars.

Now let us review some of these massive popular uprisings. Among the references the reader can review for more information are: at-Tabari's *Tarikh*, al-Mas'udi's *Muraj at-Thahab*, and Ibn Katheer's *Tarikh*.

The first of those revolutions took place in Mecca after the news of the barbaric way wherein Imām al-Hussain (ع) and his small band of supporters were butchered had reached the Meccans who started discussing them. It was led by Abdullāh bin az-Zubair and is known in history books as the Harra incident which, according to p. 374, Vol. 4, of the Arabic text of at-Tabari's *Tarikh* (the issue consulted by the writer is dated 1409 A.H./1989 A.D. and is published by al-A'lami Establishment for Publications, P.O. Box 7120, Beirut, Lebanon), broke out on a Wednesday, Thul-Hijja 28, 63 A.H./August 31, 683 A.D.

THE HARRA INCIDENT

This incident started on a Wednesday, Thul-Hijja 28, 63 A.H./August 31, 683 A.D. and was led by Abdullāh ibn az-Zubair. Let us stop here to introduce the reader to this man although he is too well known to any average student of Islamic history.

His full name is Abdullāh ibn az-Zubair ibn al-Awwam. His mother was Asma', the oldest daughter of caliph Abū Bakr and older sister of Aisha, the youngest wife of Prophet Muhammed (ﺹ). He was born in 1 A.H. and died in 73 A.H. (622 - 692 A.D.) and participated in the Muslim invasions of Persia, Egypt and North Africa and sided with his maternal aunt, Aisha, during the Battle of the Camel against Imām Ali ibn Abū Talib (ﻉ). He lived most of his life in Medīna and rebelled against the government of Yazid ibn Mu'awiyah and against Umayyad rulers of Hijaz, declaring himself caliph. He extended his influence to Iraq after the Battle of Marj Rahit till al-Hajjaj ibn Yousuf at-Thaqafi[1] succeeded in putting an end to his reign, executing him in the most ruthless way by nailing him to the Ka'ba..

---

[1]al-Hajjaj ibn Yusuf at-Thaqafi's cruelty and disrespect for Islamic tenets are matched only by those demonstrated by Yazid. His date of birth is unknown, but he died in 95 A.H./762 A.D. He was born at Ta'if, not far from Mecca, and was famous for his loyalty to the Umayyads. Marwan ibn al-Hakam, with whom the reader is already familiar, placed him in command of an army he raised to subject Hijaz to the Umayyads' control, rewarding him for his success by appointing him as governor of Mecca and Medīna to which he later added Ta'if and Iraq. He founded the city of Wasit (located in Iraq midway between Basra and Kufa), where he died, and expanded the territory under the Umayyads' control. He also crushed the Kharijites. He was proverbial in his ruthlessness and love for shedding blood. His passion for shedding blood can be understood from the way he was born. Having just been born, he refused to take his mother's breast. It is said that Satan appeared in human form and said that the newborn had to be given the blood of animals to drink and to be fed with insects for four days. His cruelty towards those whom he jailed was unheard of. His prisoners were fed with bread mixed with ashes. At the time of his death, may he be placed in the deepest depths of hell, he and his Umayyad mentors and their supporters, his prisoners numbered 33,000 men and women, 16,000 of whom were completely naked and left to sleep without any blanket or sheet covering whatsoever.

Abdullāh ibn az-Zubair delivered a sermon once wherein he strongly condemned those responsible for killing Imām al-Hussain (ﻉ), his family and friends, describing Yazid as a shameless drunkard, a man who preferred to listen to songs rather than to the recitation of the Holy Qur'ān, who preferred wine drinking over fasting and the company of his hunting party to any majlis where the Qur'ān is explained. Amr ibn Sa'd ibn al-as was then governor of Mecca, and he was quite ruthless in dealing with Abdullāh ibn az-Zubair, keeping him under constant surveillance, sending spies to his meeting places and constantly harassing him. When Yazid heard about Ibn az-Zubair's denunciations, he pledged to have him chained, so he dispatched some of his men with a silver chain, ordering them to tie Ibn az-Zubair with it. His deputies passed by Medīna on their way to Mecca and met with Marwan ibn al-Hakam who joined them in their effort to arrest Ibn az-Zubair, but the party failed in carrying out its mission, and more and more people pledged to assist Ibn az-Zubair against Yazid.

Having come to know of such failure, Yazid called to his presence ten men from among the most prominent supporters of his bloody regime, and there are always those who support bloody regimes in every time and clime. He ordered these ten men to meet with Ibn az-Zubair to dissuade him from rebelling. But they, too, failed in their attempt due to the public support Ibn az-Zubair was enjoying. Yazid now resorted to deposing Mecca's governor Amr ibn Sa'd and appointing al-Walid ibn Utbah in his place, prompting Ibn az-Zubair to write Yazid to describe his newly appointed governor as an idiot who never listened to advice nor enjoyed any wisdom. Yazid deposed al-Walid ibn Utbah and replaced him with Othman ibn Muhammed ibn Abū Sufyan, a young man who knew absolutely nothing about politics or diplomacy.

The first action the new governor undertook was dispatching a fact finding committee to Damascus to ascertain all the rumors about Yazid being a corrupt bastard, a man unfit to rule. Among the members of the mission were: Abdullāh ibn Hanzalah al-Ansāri[1],

---

[1]Abdullāh ibn Hanzalah belonged to the Ansar of the Aws tribe, and he

Abdullāh ibn Abū Amr al-Makhzumi, al-Munthir ibn az-Zubair, and a good number of the most prominent men of Hijaz. Yazid received them with open arms and showered them with money and presents, but when they returned, they cursed Yazid for his blasphemy and un-Islamic conduct and encouraged people to revolt against him, using the money they had received from him to finance the rebellion against him. While passing by Medīna, the residents heard the report of the members of this committee. They, therefore, deposed their governor, Othman ibn Muhammed, and elected Abdullāh ibn Hanzalah as their new governor.

When the Umayyads saw how the public turned against them, they sought refuge at the house of Marwan ibn al-Hakam, cousin of caliph Othman ibn Affan, where they were besieged. The siege was not lifted till those Umayyads solemnly swore not to take any measure against those who laid the siege against them and not to help Yazid in any way, a pledge which they did not keep, for Abū Sufyan, Mu'awiyah and Yazid were their mentors, and these men never honored a pledge.

When the rebellion reached such a point, Yazid realized that he had lost control over the people of Hijaz, and that only an army sent against them from Damascus would do the job. He, therefore, appointed a ruffian named Muslim ibn Uqbah al-Murri who was, at the time, quite advanced in age, to undertake such a task. Despite his age, Muslim agreed to shoulder the responsibility of quelling the rebellion. An army, hence, of twenty thousand strong set out from Damascus to quell the rebellion in Hijaz with clear orders from Yazid to "... invite the people to renounce their rebellion and to renew their pledge of loyalty [to Yazid]. Give them three days to consider doing so. If they persist in their defiance, let the soldiers have a free hand in the city for three days: Any money or weapons or food they lay their hands on is theirs. Once the three days are over, leave the people alone, and spare Ali son of al-Hussain (ﻉ),

---

was one of the most famous of the *tabi'een*, a man of legendary courage and fortitude. When the people of Medīna rebelled against Yazid, they chose him as their governor. He was killed during the Harra incident.

and admonish everyone to be good to him and show respect to him, for he did not join the rebellion," as at-Tabari tells us.

Yazid's troops first attacked Medīna then Mecca. In Medīna, according to al-Mas'udi and al-Daynari, they demolished homes, raped women, girls and even children, plundered anything and everything they found in their way, committing untold atrocities justified only by those who follow Yazid and who do not curse or condemn him, hence they shall receive their share of the Almighty's condemnation on the Day of Judgment and shall be lodged in hell in the company of Yazid and his likes. In his renown Tarikh, Ibn Katheer tells us that as many as seven hundred men who knew the text of the Holy Qur'ān by heart, including three close *sahabis* of the Prophet (ص), were killed in that incident which is referred to in the books of history as the Incident of the Harra, a reference to "Harrat Waqim" where Yazid's army first attacked. This place is named after a man belonging to the Amaliqa ("the giants") and is one of two Medīna suburbs bearing the same name: the eastern Harra, this same "Harrat Waqim," located on the eastern side of Medīna, and the western Harra, as we are told by Imām Shihabud-Deen Abū Abdullāh Yaqut ibn Abdullāh al-Hamawi ar-Rami al-Baghdadi, famous as Yaqut al-Hamawi, who describes several places each one of which is called "Harra," then he details Harrat Waqim and comments saying the following on pp. 287-288, Vol. 2, of his voluminous work *Mu'jam al-Buldan*:

It was at this Harra that the famous "Harra Incident" took place during the lifetime of Yazid son of Mu'awiyah in the year 63 A.H./683 A.D. The commander of the army, who had been appointed by Yazid, was Muslim ibn Uqbah al-Murri who, on account of his ugly action, was called "al-musrif" (the one who went to extremes in committing evil). He [Muslim] came to Harrat Waqim and the people of Medīna went out to fight him. He vanquished them, killing three thousand and five hundred men from among the *mawali*, one thousand and four hundred from among the Ansār, but some say one thousand and seven hundred, and one thousand and three hundred men from among Quraish. His hosts entered Medīna. They confiscated wealth, arrested some people and raped women. Eight hundred women became pregnant and gave birth, and the offspring were called "the offspring of the Harra." Then he brought prominent personalities to swear the oath of allegiance to Yazid ibn Mu'awiyah and to declare that they were slaves of Yazid ibn Mu'awiyah. Anyone who refused was killed.

The people of Medīna had re-dug the moat (*khandaq*) which had been dug during the Battle of the Moat, preparations for which started at the beginning of the month of Shawwal, 5 A.H. (the end of February, 627 A.D.), according to the orders of the Prophet (ص) and in response to a suggestion presented to him by the great *sahabi* Salman al-Farisi as they stood to defend themselves against a huge army raised by Abū Sufyan to fight them. They also tried to fortify their city with a bulwark.

Yazid's army succeeded in putting an end to the rebellion at a very high cost, but Abdullāh ibn az-Zubair survived unscathed. A number of highly respected *sahāba* and *tabi'een* as well as narrators of *hadīth* and Sunna were branded like animals as an additional insult.

WHAT HAPPENED IN MECCA?
Having finished with the people of Medīna, Muslim, the aging commander of Yazid's handpicked troops, marched to Mecca. On the way, he camped at a place called al-Mushallal. There, he felt that death was approaching him, so he called to his presence al-Haseen ibn Nameer as-Sukuni and said to him, "O son of the donkey's saddle! By Allāh, had I not felt that death was approaching me, I would never have given you command of this army. But the commander of the faithful (meaning Yazid) had put you second in command, and none can override his orders. Listen, therefore, carefully to my will, and do not listen to any man from Quraish at all. Do not stop the Syrians from slaughtering their foes, and do not stay for more than three days before putting an end to the reprobate Ibn az-Zubair." This is sated by at-Tabari on p. 381, Vol. 4, of the Arabic text of his famous voluminous *Tarikh* where he provides details of this incident. Muslim died and was buried there. Once the Syrian army left al-Mushallal, people dug up his grave, took his corpse out and hanged it on a palm tree. When the army came to know about this incident, a detachment was sent to investigate and to kill those suspected of hanging the corpse which was buried again

and soldiers were assigned to guard it at all times. These details and many more are stated on p. 251, Vol. 2, of al-Ya'qubi's *Tarikh*.

Catapults were installed around Mecca and in the vicinity of the Ka'ba, the holiest of holies in Islam. Fireballs were hurled and the Ka'ba was soon in flames... Its walls collapsed and were burnt, and its ceiling crumbled... According to pp. 71-72, Vol. 3, of al-Mas'udi's voluminous book *Muraj at-Thahab*, a thunderbolt hit the Syrian army on a Saturday, Rab'i I 27, 61 A.H./December 28, 680 A.D., only eleven days before Yazid's death, burning eleven of the attackers. Pleas to spare the Ka'ba went unheeded, and the fighting went beyond the three days' deadline put by Muslim. The fighting took place during the last days of the month of Muharram and continued through the entire month of Safar. When the news that Yazid had died reached Mecca, Ibn az-Zubair addressed the Syrians thus: "Your tyrant has just died; so, whoever among you wishes to join the people (in their rebellion) may do so or he may return to Syria." But the Syrians attacked him. The people of Mecca saw the extent of savagery of the Syrian army, so they collectively shielded Ibn az-Zubair and forced the army to retreat and to confine itself to its camp. Slowly the Syrians slipped out of their camp and joined the Umayyads in Mecca who sheltered them and transported them back to Syria in small groups, as we are told by at-Tabari who details these events on pp. 16-17, Vol. 7, of his *Tarikh*.

Abdullāh ibn az-Zubair declared himself as caliph and appointed a new governor for Mecca, and the people of Hijaz enjoyed a measure of self-rule till the year 72 A.H./692 A.D. when al-Hajjaj ibn Yousuf ath-Thaqafiwas ordered by the Umayyad "caliph" then, namely Abdul-Malik ibn Marwan, to bring the people of Hijaz back under his rule. It was in the month of Thul-Qida 72 A.H./March 692 A.D. that Mecca was attacked again (some of the war equipment used then included five catapults, predecessors of today's field artillery) and burnt again and its governor was deposed. A new governor loyal to the Umayyads was installed in his place, and he was a Syrian named Thu'labah who demonstrated utmost disregard and disrespect towards the Islamic tenets and towards the people of Hijaz while still claiming to be a Muslim!

Detailing the events of the year 73 A.H./692-93, at-Tabari, on p. 202, Vol. 7, of his *Tarikh*, narrates saying that when the Ka'ba was burnt, a dark cloud came from the direction of Jiddah roaring with lightning and thunder. It stood above the Ka'ba and poured its water on it and put the fire out. Then it went to the Abū Qubays mountain area where its lightning damaged one of the five catapults, killing four of the soldiers tending to it. Another lightning hit, killing forty other men. This incident is narrated by several other historians besides at-Tabari. It was not long before al-Hajjaj was able to arrest and behead Ibn az-Zubair whose severed head he sent to Damascus together with those of Abdullāh ibn Safwan, Imarah ibn Amr ibn Hazm and others. Those who carried the heads and displayed them on the way in Medīna were generously rewarded by Marwan ibn Abdul-Malik.

Not everyone supported the revolt led by Abdullāh ibn az-Zubair. The famous *sahabi* and cousin of the Prophet (ص), Ibn Abbās, that is, Abdullāh ibn Abbās ibn Abdul-Muttalib, was among those who did not support Ibn az-Zubair, considering him as an opportunist. When Imām Hussain (ع) was in Mecca immediately after his departure from Medīna, and when the Meccans expressed their support for him, Abdullāh ibn az-Zubair isolated himself and did not show any support for the Imām (ع), considering him as a competitor for his own bid to power. When the Imām (ع) left Mecca, Abdullāh ibn az-Zubair felt relieved. Ibn Abbās composed poetry depicting such an attitude of Abdullāh ibn az-Zubair. The reader is already acquainted with Ibn Abbās in a footnote above. Since Aisha could not get Ibn az-Zubair, son of her sister Asma' daughter of caliph Abū Bakr, to become the caliph following the murder of her cousin, caliph Othman ibn Affan, Ibn az-Zubair now tried on his own to acquire the caliphate for himself, and he met with success though for a short while.

Having come to know that Abdullāh ibn Abbās refused to swear the oath of allegiance to Ibn az-Zubair, Yazid wrote him saying,

It has come to my knowledge that the atheist son of az-Zubair invited you to swear the oath of allegiance to him and to be obedient to him so that you might support him in his wrongdoing and share in his sins, and that you refused and kept your distance from him because Allāh made you aware of our rights, we family members of the Prophet; so, may He grant you the rewards due to those who maintain their ties of kinship, those who are true to their promise. No matter what I forget, I shall never forget how you always remained in contact with us, and how good the reward you have received, the one due to those who obey and who are honored by being relatives of the Messenger of Allāh. Look, then, after your people, and look at those whom the son of az-Zubair enchants with his words and promises and pull them away from him, for they will listen to you more than they will to him; they would hear you more than they would hear that renegade atheist, and peace be with you.

Ibn Abbās wrote Yazid back saying,

"I received your letter wherein you mentioned Ibn az-Zubair's invitation to me to swear the oath of allegiance to him, and that I refused due to recognizing your right. If that is the case [as you claim], I desire nothing but being kind to you. But Allāh knows best what I intend to do. And you wrote me urging me to encourage people to rally behind you and to discourage them from supporting Ibn az-Zubair... Nay! Neither pleasure nor happiness is here for you; may your mouth be filled with stones, for you are the one whose view is weak when you listened to your own whims and desires, and it is you who is at fault and who shall perish! And you wrote me urging me to hurry and to join my ties of kinship. Withhold your own, man, for I shall withhold from you my affection and my support. By my life, you do not give us of what is in your hand except very little while withholding a lot; may your father lose you! Do you think that I will really forget how you killed al-Hussain (ع) and the youths of Banu Abdul-Muttalib, the lanterns that shone in the dark, the stars of guidance, the lamp-posts of piety, and how your horses trampled upon their bodies according to your command, so they were left unburied, drenched in their blood on the desert without any shrouds, nor were they buried, with the wind blowing on them and the wolves invading them, and the heinas assaulting them till Allāh sent them people who do not have shirk running through their veins and who shrouded and buried them...? From me and from them come supplications to Allāh to torment you! No matter what I forget, I shall never forget how you let loose on them the *da'iyy* (pretender of following Islam) and the son of the *da'iyy*, the one begotten by that promiscuous whore, the one whose lineage is distant, whose father and mother are mean, the one because of whose adoption did your father earn shame, sin, humiliation and abasement in the life of this world and in the hereafter. This is so because the Messenger of Allāh (ﷺ) said, "The son is begotten by wedlock, whereas for the prostitute there are stones." Your father claims that the son is out of wedlock, and it does not harm the prostitute, and he accepts him as his son just as he does his legitimate offspring! Your father killed the Sunnah with ignorance while deliberately bringing to life all misguidance. And no matter what I forget, I shall never forget how you chased al-Hussain (ﷺ) out of the sanctuary of the Messenger of Allāh [Medīna] to that of Allāh Almighty [Mecca], and how you dispatched men to kill him there. You kept trying till you caused him to leave Mecca and to go to Kūfa pursued by your horsemen, with your soldiers roaring at him like lions, O enemy of Allāh, of His Messenger (ﷺ), and of his Ahl al-Bayt (ﷺ)! Then you wrote Marjana's son ordering him to face al-Hussain (ﷺ) with his cavalry and infantry, with spears and swords. And you wrote him ordering him to be swift in attacking him and not to give him time to negotiate any settlement till you killed him and the youths of Banu Abdul-Muttalib who belong to Ahl al-Bayt (ﷺ) with him, those from whom Allāh removed all abomination and whom He purified with a perfect purification. Such are we, unlike your own uncouth fathers, the livers of donkeys! You knew fully well that he was most prominent in the past and most cherished in the present, had he only sought refuge in Mecca and permitted bloodshed in its sanctuary. But he sought reconciliation, and he asked you to go back to your senses, yet you went after the few who were in his company and desired to eradicate his Ahl al-Bayt (ﷺ) as if you were killing dynasties from Turkey or from Kabul! How do you conceive me as being friendly to you, and how dare you ask me to support you?! You have killed my own brothers, and your sword is dripping with my blood, and you are the one whom I seek for revenge. So if Allāh wills, you shall not be able to shed my blood, nor shall you be faster than me in seeking revenge so you would be more swift in killing us just as the prophets are killed, considering their blood equal to that of others. But the promise is with Allāh, and

178

Allāh suffices in supporting the wronged, and He seeks revenge for the oppressed. What is truly amazing is your own transporting the daughters of Abdul-Muttalib and their children to Syria. You see yourself as our vanquisher, and that you have the right to humiliate us, although through me and through them did Allāh bestow blessings upon you and upon your slave parents. By Allāh! You welcome the evening and the day in security indifferent to my wounds; so, let my own tongue wound you instead, and let my tying and untying not provoke you to argue. Allāh shall not give you a respite following your killing of the Progeny of the Messenger of Allāh (ﷺ) except for a very short while before He takes you like a Mighty One, and He shall not take you out of the life of this world except as an abased and dejected sinner; so, enjoy your days, may you lose your father, as you please, for what you have committed has surely made you abased in the sight of Allāh."[1]

Ibn Abbās never swore the oath of allegiance to the tyrant Yazid till his death.

Following the revolt of Abdullāh ibn az-Zubair, other revolts erupted throughout the Islamic lands. One of them was the Revolt of the Tawwabeen (the penitents) which broke out in Kūfa in 65 A.H./684-85 A.D., then the revolt in 66 A.H./686 A.D. which was led by al-Mukhtar who killed all those who had participated in killing al-Hussain (ﷺ). The Alawites (Alawids) followed with revolts of their own, including that of the great martyr Zaid ibn Ali and his son Yahya and finally the revolt of the Abbāsides who put an end to the Umayyads' rule for good.

---

[1]This text is compiled from the contents of p. 250, Vol. 7, of *Mujma az-Zawa'id* of Abū Bakr al-Haythami, p. 18, Vol. 4 (first edition), of al-Balathiri's book *Ansab al-Ashraf*, p. 77, Vol. 2, of al-Khawarizmi's great book *Maqtal al-Hussain (ﷺ)*, p. 50, Vol. 4, and of Ibn Katheer's book *At-Tarikh al-Kāmil*, where the events of the year 64 A.H./684 A.D. are detailed, an account which agrees with what is recorded in al-Mas'udi's book *Muraj at-Thahab*.

AL-HUSSAIN'S GRAVE

Anyone who is lucky enough to visit Imām Hussain's grave-site stands awe-stricken at the beauty of the magnificent shrine housing his tomb, a shrine which has been renovated time and over again all these centuries. It truly is a masterpiece of architecture, a jewel of art, and a pleasure to the eyes of the beholder. It also houses a grand center for theological studies. Yet many tyrants and fanatics tried to obliterate it and reduce it to rubble, while the Almighty has always been protecting it and getting it rebuilt and renovated. This is made partially possible through the generous donations of those who love the Imām (ع) and who seek nearness to Allāh by visiting the grave-site of one of His true servants, a man of honorable descent who

 sacrificed his life and family and everything he had for the sake of reawakening the Islamic world and getting it to refine Islam from the distortion introduced into it by the Umayyad tyrants and miscreants. Let us, therefore, stop here

for a minute to review the history of the attempts aiming at obliterating Imām Hussain's grave and identify them, call them and shame them, condemn them and condemn those who do not condemn them. What is truly amazing is that all those who attacked this shrine claim to be Muslims who follow the Sunnah of the Messenger of Allāh (ع)!

In 236 A.H./850-51 A.D., the Abbāside caliph al-Mutawakkil Billah aimed at demolishing the shrine and all its attachments by razing it to the ground and planting the area where it stands. He hoped to prohibit anyone from visiting it or visiting any places held by Shī'as as sacred, threatening their pilgrims with stiff penalties. During his reign, which lasted from 232 - 247 A.H. (847 - 861 A.D.), he issued

180

such orders four times. The first time such an attempt was made is dated 232 A.H./846 A.D. He was outraged because one of his singing concubines had gone to perform the pilgrimage to it during the month of Sha'ban of that year. The second attempt was four years later (in 236 A.H./850 A.D.). The third attempt took place in the next year, 237 A.H./850-51 A.D. The fourth attempt took place in 247 A.H./861 A.D., in the aftermath of which he himself was killed by his son, the later Abbāside caliph al-Muntasir, who was a pious and ascetic and sympathetic towards the family members (Ahl al-Bayt) of the Prophet (ﺹ). All these attempts were carried out, according to al-Mutawakkil's orders, by a Jew named Ebrahim (Abram) who was nicknamed Deezaj, the dumb donkey. Yet despite all these attempts, the shrine kept standing again and again due to the zeal of those who believed in the message for which Imām Hussain (ﻉ) sacrificed himself and all those who were dear and near to him.

Another demolition attempt was carried out by one Zabbah ibn Muhammed al-Asdi, a highway robber by profession, who, assisted by a number of Bedouin tribesmen, committed his foul act in 369 A.H./979-80 A.D. for which he was chased and punished by the Buwayhid ruler Izzud-Dawlah who put the shrine of Imām Hussain (ﻉ) in Kerbalā' and that of his father Imām Ali (ﻉ) in Najaf under his protection. This incident took place during the reign of the Abbāside ruler at-Ta'i Lillah.

In 407 A.H./1016 A.D., during the reign of the Abbāside ruler al-Qadir Billah, a mid-night fire engulfed the shrine, damaging the dome and the corridors. Some historians believe that it was not an accident but a deliberate sabotage. The said Abbāside ruler was siding with one Muslim sect against another, sowing the seeds of discord among various Islamic sects.

The most serious damage to the shrine was inflicted by the Wahhabis, followers of Muhammed ibn Abdul-Wahhab who invented an odd interpretation of Islam which does not respect the grave-sites of any holy person, including that of the Prophet of Islam

(ﺹ). Since the Wahhabis have proven to be the most antagonistic[1] towards the followers of Ahl al-Bayt (ﻉ), it is not out of place here to introduce the reader to their man, Muhammed ibn Abdul-Wahhab, while narrating the mischief he and his ignorant Bedouin zealots committed against the shrine of Imām Hussain (ﻉ) in Kerbalā' and that of his father, Imām Ali (ﻉ), in Najaf.

Muhammed ibn Abdul-Wahhab was born in 1115 A.H./1703 A.D. in the small town of Uyayna in Najd, the southern highland of Arabia's interior, and died in 1206 A.H./1791-92 A.D. He belonged to the tribe of Tamim. His father was a lawyer and a pious Muslim adhering to the Hanbalite sect founded by Imām Ahmed ibn Hanbal who, with the most rigid consistency, had advocated the principle of the exclusive validity of the *hadīth* as against the inclination among the older sects to make concessions to reason and commonsense, especially since Islam is the religion of commonsense. In Baghdad, Muhammed learned the jurisprudence of the Hanbali Sunni sect which remains to be predominant among the people of Najd and Hijaz: Whabbis constitute no more than 8% of the entire population of today's Saudi Arabia, the only country in the world named after its ruling clan. The reader has already come to know how much distortion exists in *hadīth* and can appreciate the danger of believing in each and every hadīth as though it were the inviolable and irrefutable gospel truth. He also studied jurisprudence at Mecca and Medīna where his mentors were admirers of Ibn Taymiyyah who, in the 7th Century A.H./the 14th Century A.D., had revived the teachings of Imām Ahmed ibn Hanbal. The founder of the sect, the last in the series of the four Sunni sects, namely Ahmed ibn Hanbal, was a theologian born in and died in Baghdad; the year of his birth is 164 A.H./780 A.D. and that of his death is 241 A.H./855 A.D.

Since his childhood, Muhammed ibn Abdul-Wahhab was influenced by the writings of Ibn Taymiyyah[2] and, therefore, looked askance at

---

[1]Such antagonism has proven to be bloody especially in India, Pakistan, Bangladesh and Afghanistan. Wahabbis also justify the killing of other Sunnis who do not subscribe to their beliefs as they have done in Iraq.

[2]Ibn Taymiyyah, mentor of Wahhabis and Takfiris, is Ahmed ibn Abdul-

many religious practices of the people of Najd (southern section of today's kingdom of the Wahhabi Al Saud clan). Such an influence convinced him that the dominant form of contemporary Islam, particularly among the Turks of his time, was permeated with abuses. He, therefore, sought to restore the original purity of the doctrine and of life in its restricted milieus. The facts that the Wahhabis are the minority of all Muslim minorities, and that the people of Najd and Hijaz are still predominantly Hanbalites who do not subscribe to Wahhabism by choice, prove that he did not achieve his objective and, most likely, such an objective will never be achieved despite all Saudi Arabia's petro-dollars and the abundance of those who solicit such dollars, the ruler-appointed preachers most of whom are Salafis.

Having joined his father, with whom he debated his personal views, Muhammed ibn Abdul-Wahhab caused a seriously violent confrontation to erupt from such an exchange of opposite views, for his father's views were consistent with mainstream Hanbali Muslim thought. He performed the pilgrimage for the first time, visiting Mecca and Medīna where he attended lectures on different branches of Islamic learning. His mentors included Abdullāh ibn Ibrahim ibn

---

Halim ibn Abdul-Salam ibn Abdullāh al-Khidr, "Taqiyy ad-Din ," "Abul-Abbās," a Hanbali scholar who was born in Harran (ancient Carrhae where Mudar Arabs lived, a town built by Harran brother of prophet Abraham [ع] from whom it derived its name), Iraq, in 661 A.H./1263 A.D. and died inside a Damascus, Syria, prison in 728 A.H./1328 A.D. He had his own radical and un-orthodox way of interpreting hadīth which was different from everyone else's, distinguishing him from all other scholars of jurisprudence. Those who adopt his views are called "Salafis," followers of the "salaf," the "pious" predecessors. He is on the record as the first person to disbelieve in intercession (shafaa). For more details, refer to the 463-page book titled Ibn Taymiyyah by Sa'ib Abdul-Hamid, published in Arabic in Qum, Islamic Republic of Iran, by the Ghadīr Center for Islamic Studies. There are many fanatical groups in India, Pakistan, Bangladesh and Afghanistan that adopt this "Salafi" ideology disseminated by government-sponsored Saudi mis-sionary activities and funded by petro-dollars.

Shrine of Imām Ali (ع) in Najaf, Iraq

Saif and Hayat as-Sindi, who both were admirers of Ibn Taymiyyah. They both rejected the principle of *taqlid* (imitation) which is commonly accepted by all four Sunni schools of jurisprudence as well as by Shī'a Muslims. These men's teachings had a great impact on Muhammed ibn Abdul-Wahhab who began to take a more aggressive attitude in preaching his views and, hence, he publicly expressed his denunciation of the sanctification of the holy precincts of the Prophet's shrine and of the shrines of any "saint." Then he went back home and decided to go to Basra, Iraq, on his way to Damascus, Syria. During his stay in Basra, he expressed the same views, whereupon its people kicked him out of the city. He almost died of thirst once, due to exhaustion and to the intensity of the heat in the desert, when he was on his way from Basra to the city of Zubair but was saved by a Zubairi man. Finding his provisions

184

insufficient to travel to Damascus, Muhammed had to change his travel plan and to go to the (Saudi) al-Ahsa (or al-Hasa) province then to Huraymala, one of the cities of Najd, to which his father and the entire family had to move because of the public's denunciation

Prophet's Mosque in Medīna, Saudi Arabia, at dusk

of young Muhammed's views, reaching it in 1139 A.H./1726-27 A.D. By then, Muhammed's good and pious father had lost his job as *qadi* (judge) on account of his son's radical preaching. The denunciation continued till his father's death in 1153 A.H./1740 A.D.

His father's death emboldened him to express his thoughts more freely and consolidate his movement. His preaching found an echo among some of the people of his town, and his fame started on the rise, so much so that he was welcomed by the ruler of his home town Uyayna, namely Othman ibn Muammar Al Hamad, who offered him protection and appointed him as his personal assistant. In order to cement his ties with Othman, Muhammed ibn Abdul-Wahhab married Jawhara, Othman's aunt. Othman ordered his townsmen to observe the Wahhabi teachings, and Muhammed now felt strong

185

enough to demolish the monument erected on the burial site of Zaid ibn al-Khattab. But the new alliance between Muhammed ibn Abdul-Wahhab and Othman ibn Muammar Al Hamad disturbed the scholars of Najd who complained against the first to the emir (provincial governor) of the al-Ahsa province. The emir wrote Othman reprimanding and warning him of dire consequences for encouraging Muhammed ibn Abdul-Wahhab to revolt against the established authority and creed. Finding himself in a precarious situation and his job in jeopardy, Othman dismissed Muhammed ibn Abdul-Wahhab from his service and asked him to leave the town.

In 1160 A.H./1746-47 A.D., having been expelled from Uyayna, Muhammed ibn Abdul-Wahhab sought refuge in Dar'iyya, only six hours away from Uyayna, at the invitation of its ruler, Muhammed ibn Saud[1], ancestor of the Al Saud dynasty now ruling Saudi Arabia. Muhammed ibn Saud lived in a fortified settlement as chief of the Unayza clan. Soon, an alliance was forged between both men, each promising the other glory, fame, and riches for his support. The people of that town lived at the time in utter destitution, and something was needed to bring them relief. Muhammed ibn Saud rejected any veneration of the Prophet (ص) or of other men of piety. It was there that Muhammed ibn Abdul-Wahhab stayed for more than two years. Both men felt that it was time to declare "jihad" against all those who rejected the new Wahhabi dogma, forming a small band of raiders mounted on horseback to invade various towns, kill and loot. The lives and property of all those who did not

---

[1] The correct pronunciation of "Saud" is Sa'ood," but we will stick to the commonly used spelling of this word.

دار السيدة خديجة التي كانت منزل النبي (ص) و
مولد فاطمة الزهرا (ع) الواقعة في سوق الصاغة
في مكة هدمتها الحكومة السعودية عام ١٤١٣ هـ .

House (left of photo) of Lady Khadija, Prophet's wife, before the Wahhabi minority rulers of Saudi Arabia demolished it in 1413 A.H./1993 A.D. This is where Fatima, Prophet's only daughter, was born and where Gabriel used to bring the Almighty's messages to the Prophet.

subscribe to the views of these two men were now in jeopardy for they were considered as guilty of being pagans fighting against whom is justified by the Qur'ān until they converted or extirpated. These raids extended far beyond Dar'iyya to include all of Najd and parts of Yemen, Hijaz, Syria and Iraq. In 1187 A.H./1773 A.D., the principality of Riyadh fell to them, marking a new era in the lucrative career of Muhammed ibn Abdul-Wahhab.

During a short period of time, the destitutes of Dar'iyya found themselves wearing sumptuous clothes, carrying weapons decorated with gold and silver, eating meat, and baking wheat bread; in short, they found their dreams come true, going from rags to riches, thanks to those raids which continued till Muhammed ibn Abdul-Wahhab died in 1206 A.H./1791-92 A.D., leaving his band to carry out more and more raids and his form of "Wahhabism" embraced by the Al Saud clansmen who eventually ascended to power, due to the support they received from the British who used them to undermine the last Islamic power, the Ottoman Sultanate. Al Saud became the sole rulers of Najd and Hijaz, promoting and publicizing for Wahhabism by any and all means, spending in the process funds which belong to the Muslim masses, not to them.

After the death of Muhammed ibn Abdul-Wahhab, his band of raiders, under the leadership of the Al Saud dynasty, pursued their campaigns in the pretext of disseminating Wahhabism. In the years that followed Muhammed ibn Abdul-Wahhab's death, the Wahhabis gradually became burdensome to their neighbors. They pursued their northward advance; therefore, the Pasha of Baghdad found himself compelled to take defensive measures against them, having heard about their ruthlessness and disregard for the lives of all non-Wahhabis. He, therefore, led an army of about seven thousand Turks and twice did his army of mostly Arabs attacked them in their richest and most fertile oasis, that of al-Ahsa, in 1212 A.H./1797 A.D. but did not move on their capital, Dar'iyya, at once, as he should have, laying a siege for a month to the citadel of al-Ahsa. When Muhammed ibn Saud himself advanced against the Pasha, the latter did not dare to attack him but concluded a six-year peace treaty with him, a treaty for which the Wahhabis later demonstrated their disregard. By then, they had already set their eyes on plundering the shrine of Imām Hussain (ع) and all the valuable relics it contained.

On the anniversary of the historic Ghadīr Khumm incident, that is, Thul-Hijja 18, 1216 A.H./April 21, 1801 A.D.[1], Prince Saud

---

[1]Other references consulted for this book indicate that the said attack was carried out on Thul-Hijja 14, 1215 A.H./April 28, 1801 A.D., but we are of the view that the above date is more accurate.

mobilized an army of twenty thousand strong and invaded the holy city of Kerbalā'. First they laid a siege of the city then entered the city and brutally massacred its defenders, visitors and inhabitants, looting, burning, demolishing and wreaking havoc ... The city [Kerbalā'] fell into their hands. The magnificent domed building over the grave of Hussain was destroyed and enormous booty dragged off.[1]

More than five thousand Muslims were slaughtered. Then the Saudi prince turned to the Kerbalā' shrine itself; he and his men pulled gold slabs out of their places, stole chandeliers and Persian rugs and historical relics, plundering anything of value. This tragedy is immortalized by eulogies composed by poets from Kerbalā' and elsewhere. And the Wahhabis did not leave Kerbalā' alone after this massacre; rather, they continued for the next twelve years invading it, killing and looting, taking advantage of the administrative weakness of the aging Ottoman Sultanate responsible for protecting it. During those twelve years, more and more Bedouin tribes joined them for a "piece of the action." In 1218 A.H./1803 A.D., during the time of hajj (pilgrimage), the Wahhabis, led by Abdul-Aziz Al Saud, attacked Mecca, which surrendered to them after putting up a brief resistance. They looted whatever possessions the pilgrims had had. The governor of Mecca, Sharif Ghalib, fled to Jiddah which was shortly thereafter besieged, and the leader of the Syrian pilgrim caravan, Abd-Allāh Pasha of Damascus, had to leave Mecca, too. On Rajab 19, 1218 A.H./November 4, 1803, Abdul-Aziz Al Saud paid with his life for what he had committed; he was killed in Dar'iyya. His son, Saud ibn Abdul-Aziz Al Saud, lifted the siege of Jiddah and had Sharif Ghalib sent back to Mecca as his vassal in exchange for Jiddah's customs revenue.

In 1220 A.H./1805 and 1221 A.H./1806 A.D., Mecca and Medīna fell to the Wahhabis[2] respectively. The Wahhabis unleashed their

---

[1]Carl Brockelmann, ed., *History of the Islamic Peoples* (London, 1980), p. 354.

[2]*Ibid.*

wrath on both holy cities, committing untold atrocities and razing the cemetery, where many relatives and *sahāba* (companions) of the Prophet (ﷺ) were buried, to the ground[1]. Having spread their control over Riyadh, Jiddah, Mecca and Medīna, all of today's Saudi Arabia became practically under their control.

The next major invasion of the holy city of Kerbalā' by the Wahhabis took place on the 9th of the holy month of Ramadan of 1225 A.H., corresponding to October 8, 1810 A.D. It was then that both Kerbalā' and Najaf (where the magnificent shrine of Imām Ali ibn Abū Talib (ع) is located) were besieged. Roads were blocked, pilgrims were looted then massacred, and the shrines were attacked and damaged. The details of this second invasion were recorded by an eyewitness: Sayyid Muhammed Jawad al-Āmili, author of the famous book of jurisprudence titled *Miftah al-Karama* which was completed shortly after midnight on the very first day when the siege was laid. The writer recorded how terrified he and the other residents of Kerbalā' felt at seeing their city receiving a major attack from the Wahhabis. A large number of pilgrims were killed. Their number varies from one account to another, and the most realistic figure seems to be the one provided by Sayyid Muhammed Jawad al-Āmili who puts it at one hundred and fifty.

The Wahhabis no longer attack and demolish Imām Hussain's shrine, but they have been relentlessly attacking the creed of those who venerate him through a flood of books written and printed world-wide. They fund their writing, publication and circulation. They sometimes distribute them free of charge during the annual

---

[1]The Wahhabis have carried out their campaigns against the burial grounds of the Prophet's family and companions well into the next century. For example, in 1343 A.H./1924 A.D., they demolished the grave-sites of many family members and companions (*sahāba*) of the Prophet (ﷺ) against the wish and despite the denunciation of the adherents of all other Muslim sects world-wide. And in 1413 A.H./1993, they also demolished the house of Khadija, wife of Prophet Muhammed (ﷺ), as well as the house where the Prophet (ﷺ) had been born, which stood approximately 50 meters northward from Khadija's house, turning both of them into public bathrooms...

pilgrimage season while prohibiting all pilgrims from carrying or distributing any literature at all... During recent years, they have been beheading Shī'ite scholars wherever they can find them, destroying Shī'ite shrines, such as the famous 'Askari Shrine in Samarra, Iraq, which was bombed and destroyed in February of 2006 and in June of 2007; it houses the remains of both Imām Ali al-Hadi and Hassan al-'Askari, peace be with them, who descended from the immediate family of the Prophet of Islam, peace and blessings of the Almighty be with him and his progeny. Many other Shī'ite mosques and Hussainiyyas were bombed by the Wahhabis and are still targets of their mischief, yet these rogues will never be able to destroy Shī'ite Islam till the Resurrection Day. They have plenty of money, so they send their filthy money to Iraq to get the Muslims to kill each other, the Shī'ite to kill the Sunni and vice versa, thus making Satan the happiest being on earth, for nothing pleases this damned creature more than seeing Muslims at each other's throats. Such is the desire of all the enemies of Islam and Muslims. Actually, due to the barbarism of these fundamentalist Wahhabis, more and more Muslims are getting to be curious about Shī'ite Islam, so they study it and many of them end up eventually switching their sect from Sunni to Shī'ite Islam. There is no harm in a Sunni becoming Shī'ite or in a Shī'ite becoming Sunni: Islam is one tree stalk having two major branches. After all, religions of the world have sects, and people change the sect they follow according to their personal convictions and satisfaction. It happens every day, and nobody fusses about it. Thus, the Wahhabis' mischief is actually having the opposite result of what these fundamentalist fanatics, who have ruined the reputation of Islam and Muslims world-wide, anticipate.

PERFORMING *ZIYARAT* TO HUSSAIN'S SHRINE

When you visit a dignitary of a special social or political status, you are expected to follow a protocol of etiquette which you may have to learn from a secretary or a protocol specialist. Muslims believe that the soul never dies; it only travels from one stage of life to another. The Holy Qur'ān tells us that we should not consider those who die in defending His cause as dead; they are living though we are not aware of it; here is the Qur'ānic proof: "And do not reckon those who are slain in the Way of Allāh as dead. Nay! They are living with their Lord, receiving their sustenance" (Qur'ān, 3:169). So, when you visit Hussain's sacred shrine or greet it from a distance, wherever you may be in Allāh's spacious earth, you have to observe certain basic principles of etiquette such as having ablution and wearing clean clothes. There are many statements you can recite, but we have chosen this one which is known as "ziyarat warith," visiting the heir, the one who inherited the message and the knowledge of his pious predecessors. We would like to quote it here for you in its original Arabic text, then I will *Insha-Allāh* translate it for you:

السَّلام عَلَيْكَ يَا أَبا عَبْد الله وَعَلَى الأرواح الَّتي حَلَّتْ بِفِنائِكَ ، وَأَنَاخَت بِرَحْلِك، عَلَيْكَ مِنِّي سَلامُ الله أَبَداً مَا بَقِيتُ وَبَقِيَ اللَّيْلُ وَالنَّهَارُ ، وَلا جَعَلَهُ اللهُ آخِرَ العَهْد مِنِّي لِزِيَارَتِكُمْ أَهْلَ البَيتِ.

السَّلام عَلَى الحُسَيْن ، وَعَلَى عَلِيِّ بْنِ الحُسَيْنِ ، وَعَلَى أَوْلاد الحُسَيْنِ ، وَعَلَى أصْحابِ الحُسَيْن و رحمة الله و بركاتِه. اللهم ارزقنا شفاعة الحسين.

اللهم آرزقنا شفاعة الحسين

زيارة الإمام الحسين (عليه السلام)

زيــارة وارث

السَّلامُ عَلَيكَ يا وارِثَ آدَمَ صِفوَةِ اللهِ السَّلامُ عَلَيكَ يا وارِثَ نوحٍ نَبِيِّ اللهِ السَّلامُ عَلَيكَ يا وارِثَ إِبراهيمَ خَليلِ اللهِ السَّلامُ عَلَيكَ يا وارِثَ موسى كَليمِ اللهِ السَّلامُ عَلَيكَ يا وارِثَ عيسى روحِ اللهِ السَّلامُ عَلَيكَ يا وارِثَ مُحَمَّدٍ حَبيبِ اللهِ السَّلامُ عَلَيكَ يا وارِثَ أَميرِ المُؤمِنينَ عَلَيهِ السَّلامُ السَّلامُ عَلَيكَ يا ابنَ مُحَمَّدٍ المُصطَفى السَّلامُ عَلَيكَ يا ابنَ عَلِيٍّ المُرتَضى السَّلامُ عَلَيكَ يا ابنَ فاطِمَةِ الزَّهراءِ السَّلامُ عَلَيكَ يا ابنَ خَديجَةَ الكُبرى السَّلامُ عَلَيكَ يا ثارَ اللهِ وَابنَ ثارِهِ وَالوِترَ المَوتورَ أَشهَدُ أَنَّكَ قَد أَقَمتَ الصَّلاةَ وَآتَيتَ الزَّكاةَ وَأَمَرتَ بِالمَعروفِ وَنَهَيتَ عَنِ المُنكَرِ وَأَطَعتَ اللهَ وَرَسولَهُ حَتّى أَتاكَ اليَقينُ فَلَعَنَ اللهُ أُمَّةً قَتَلَتكَ وَلَعَنَ اللهُ أُمَّةً ظَلَمَتكَ وَلَعَنَ اللهُ أُمَّةً سَمِعَت بِذلِكَ فَرَضِيَت بِهِ يا مَولايَ يا أَبا عَبدِ اللهِ أَشهَدُ أَنَّكَ كُنتَ نوراً فِي الأَصلابِ الشّامِخَةِ وَالأَرحامِ المُطَهَّرَةِ لَم تُنَجِّسكَ الجاهِلِيَّةُ بِأَنجاسِها وَلَم تُلبِسكَ مِن مُدلَهِمّاتِ ثِيابِها وَأَشهَدُ أَنَّكَ مِن دَعائِمِ الدّينِ وَأَركانِ المُؤمِنينَ وَأَشهَدُ أَنَّكَ الإِمامُ البَرُّ التَّقِيُّ الرَّضِيُّ الزَّكِيُّ الهادِي المَهدِيُّ وَأَشهَدُ أَنَّ الأَئِمَّةَ مِن وُلدِكَ كَلِمَةُ التَّقوى وَأَعلامُ الهُدى وَالعُروَةُ الوُثقى وَالحُجَّةُ عَلى أَهلِ الدُّنيا وَأَشهِدُ اللهَ وَمَلائِكَتَهُ وَأَنبِياءَهُ وَرُسُلَهُ أَنّي بِكُم

مُؤمِنٌ وبِآبائِكُم مُوقِنٌ بِشَرائِعِ دِينِي وَخَواتِيمِ عَمَلِي وَقَلْبِي لِقَلْبِكُم سِلْمٌ وَأمْرِي لِأمْرِكُم مُتّبِعٌ صَلَواتُ اللهِ عَلَيْكُم وَعَلى أزْواجِكُم وَعَلى أجْسادِكُم وَعَلى أجْسامِكُم وَعَلى شاهِدِكُم وَعَلى غائِبِكُم وَعَلى ظاهِرِكُم وَعَلى باطِنِكُم.

ثُمّ انكَبّ على القبر وقَبّله وقُل: بِأبِي أنْتَ وأُمّي يا ابْنَ رَسُولِ اللهِ بِأبِي أنْتَ وأُمّي يا أبا عَبْدِ اللهِ لَقَدْ عَظُمَتِ الرّزِيّةُ وَجَلّتِ المُصِيبةُ بِكَ عَلَيْنا وَعَلى جَمِيعِ أهْلِ السّماواتِ والأرضِ فَلَعَنَ اللهُ أُمّةً أسْرَجَتْ وألْجَمَتْ وَتَهَيّأتْ لِقِتالِكَ يا مَوْلايَ يا أبا عَبْدِ اللهِ قَصَدْتُ حَرَمَكَ وَأتَيْتُ إلى مَشْهَدِكَ أسْألُ اللهَ بِالشّأنِ الّذِي لَكَ عِنْدَهُ وَبِالمَحَلِّ الّذِي لَكَ لَدَيْهِ أنْ يُصَلّي عَلى مُحَمّدٍ وَآلِ مُحَمّدٍ وأنْ يَجْعَلَني مَعَكُم فِي الدُّنْيا والآخِرَةِ.

ثُمّ قُم فَصَلّ رَكعتين عند الرّأس إقرأ فيها ما أحببت فإذا فرغت من صلاتك فقُل:

اللّهُمّ إنّي صَلّيْتُ وَرَكَعتُ وَسَجَدْتُ لَكَ وَحْدَكَ لا شَرِيكَ لَكَ لِأنّ الصّلاةَ والرُّكُوعَ والسُّجُودَ لا تَكُونُ إلّا لَكَ لِأنّكَ أنْتَ اللهُ لا إلهَ إلا أنْتَ اللّهُمّ صَلّ على مُحَمّدٍ وَآلِ مُحَمّدٍ وأبْلِغْهُم عَني أفْضَلَ السّلامِ والتّحِيّةِ وَارْدُدْ عَلَيّ مِنْهُمُ السّلامَ اللّهُمّ وَهاتانِ الرّكْعَتانِ هَدِيّةٌ مِنّي إلى مَوْلايَ الحُسَينِ بنِ عَلِيٍّ عَلَيْهِما السّلامُ اللّهُمّ صَلّ عَلى مُحَمّدٍ وَعَلَيْهِ وَتَقَبّلْ مِنّي واجُرْنِي على ذَلِكَ بِأفْضَلِ أمَلِي وَرَجائي فِيكَ وَفِي وَلِيّكَ يا وَلِيَّ المُؤمِنِينَ.

السّلامُ عَلَيْكَ يَا أبا عَبْدِ اللهِ وَعَلى الأرواحِ الّتِي حَلّتْ بِفِنائِكَ، وأناخَتْ بِرَحْلِكَ، عَلَيْكُمْ مِنّي سَلامُ اللهِ أبَداً مَا بَقِيتُ وَبَقِيَ اللّيْلُ والنّهارُ، وَلا جَعَلَهُ اللهُ آخِرَ العَهْدِ مِنّي لِزِيارَتِكُمْ أهْلَ البَيتِ

194

TRANSLATION:

Assalamo Alaikum, O heir of Adam, the one chosen by Allāh (as His vicegerent on earth)! *Assalamo Alaikum*, O heir of Noah, the prophet of Allāh! *Assalamo Alaikum*, O heir of Abraham, the Friend of Allāh! *Assalamo Alaikum*, O heir of Moses who spoke to Allāh! *Assalamo Alaikum*, O heir of Jesus, the Spirit of Allāh! *Assalamo Alaikum*, O heir of Muhammed, the one loved by Allāh! *Assalamo Alaikum*, O heir of the Commander of the Faithful, peace be with him! *Assalamo Alaikum*, O son of Muhammed, the chosen one! *Assalamo Alaikum*, O son of Ali, the one with whom Allāh and His Messenger are pleased! Assalamo Alaikum, O son of Fatima az-Zahra! Assalamo Alaikum, O son of Khadija al-Kubra! *Assalamo Alaikum*, O revolutionary for the cause of Allāh and the son of a revolutionary for the cause of Allāh, the oppressed one who is yet to receive redress and the son of an oppressed one who has not been redressed! I testify that you upheld the prayers, paid the *zakat*, enjoined what is right, prohibited what is wrong, and obeyed Allāh and His Messenger till death overtook you; so, the curse of Allāh be on a people who killed you, and the curse of Allāh be on a people who oppressed you, and the curse of Allāh be on those who heard about you being oppressed and were pleased thereby! O master! O father of Abdullāh! I testify that you were a light in the lofty loins and purified wombs: the *jahiliyya* never polluted you nor spread its garments over you! And I further testify that you are among the pillars of the creed and the corner-stones of the believers! And I further testify that you are the Imām who is kind, pious, pure, guiding to righteousness and is rightly guided, and I testify that the Imāms from among your offspring are the embodiment of piety and the flag-poles of guidance, the strong niche and the argument against the people of the world! And I further implore Allāh, His angels, prophets and messenger, to testify that I believe in you, being convinced that you shall return according to the tenets of my faith and the conclusions of my deeds, and that my heart is at ease with whatever pleases you, and my will is subservient to yours! The blessings of Allāh be upon you, upon your souls, upon your bodies, upon your being, upon those present from among you and those absent, upon what you reveal and what you conceal.

Having thus saluted the Imām, you should kiss the tomb then say the following:

By my parents (do I swear), O son of the Messenger of Allāh, by my parents (do I swear), O father of Abdullāh, that the calamity is great and the catastrophe magnanimous, and it has afflicted us and all the residents of the heavens and the earth, so may the curse of Allāh be upon a people that gathered their forces to fight you, O master, O father of Abdullāh! I have come to your sacred site and desired to be at your shrine, pleading to Allāh by the status which you enjoy with Him to bless Muhammed and the progeny of Muhammed and to permit me to be with you in the life of this world and in the life hereafter

After that you should perform two prostrations (rek'at) at the Imām's head, and you may recite in them whatever *suras* (Qur'ānic chapters) you wish. Once you have finished your prayers, you should recite the following:

O Allāh! I have performed my prayers, and I have knelt and prostrated to You, and only to You, the One and Only God, there is no partner with You, for the prayers, the kneeling and the prostrating cannot be to anyone but to You, since You are Allāh, there is no god but You! O Allāh! I plead to You to bless Muhammed and the progeny of Muhammed and to convey the best of my Salam to them and the best of salutation and, O Lord, do convey their own greeting to me! O Allāh! These two rek'at are a gift from me to my master al-Hussain son of Ali, peace be with both of them! O Allāh! Bless Muhammed and bless him, and do accept it from me and reward me for it with the best of what I anticipate, and my hope rests upon You, and upon Your servant, O Master of the believers!

PART IV

HUSSAIN'S SUCCESSORS: NINE INFALLIBLE IMĀMS (ع)

The hero of Kerbalā', Imām Hussain (ع), was succeeded by nine sinless and infallible Imāms who led the Islamic nation and are still leading it to the Straight Path, the path of happiness in the life of this world and salvation in the life to come. Following is a brief account of these Imāms (ع)[1].

1) IMĀM ALI IBN AL-HUSSAIN ZAIN AL-ĀBIDĪN (ع)

Imām Hussain (ع) was succeeded as the nation's spiritual leader by his only surviving son Ali, nicknamed "Zain al-Ābidīn," the best of those who worship the Almighty, and also "as-Sajjād," the one who quite often prostrates to Allāh. Ali was born on the fifteenth of Jumada II, 38 A.H. (November 19, 658 A.D.) when his grandfather, Imām Ali ibn Abū Talib (ع), was administering the affairs of caliphate at Kūfa. Kerbalā' used to be a suburb of Kūfa, but it later expanded into a large city, due to the shrine built for Imām Hussain (ع), a shrine which many tyrants, including the fanatical Wahhabis of Saudi Arabia, attacked, looted, and tried unsuccessfully to

---

[1]In the writing of this chapter, I utilized one of the books which I edited: *Biographies of Leaders of Islam* by Sayyid Ali Naqi Naqwi, published in 1990 by Imām Hussain Foundation, P.O. Box 25-114, Beirut, Lebanon.

obliterate, and housing a prestigious theological center.

Ali's graceful personality was the combination of Arab and Persian nobility. On paternal side, he inherited the spiritual grace of the Prophet (ص), while through his mother, Shahr Banu, daughter of the last Persian emperor Yazdajerd, he inherited the dignity of the Persian royal dynasty. How did this great-grandson of the Prophet (ص) get to have a Persian princess as his mother?! In order to get the answer to this question, we have to review history going back to the time of the Prophet of Islam (ع).

In 595 A.D., young Muhammed (ص) visited Syria for the second time for a couple of months as a businessman trading on behalf of his wealthy relative Khadija whom he married in the same year. His first visit to Syria took place in 582 A.D. in the company of his uncle Abū Talib, great-grandfather of Imām Zain al-Ābidīn (ع). During this second visit, one of his observations was that a feud was brewing between the then mightiest nations on earth: the Romans and the Persians, each vying for hegemony over Arabia's fertile crescent. Indeed, such an observation was quite accurate, for after only a few years, a war broke out between these mightiest nations that ended with the Romans losing it, as the Holy Qur'ān tells us in Chapter 30 (The Romans), which was revealed in 7 A.H./615-16 A.D., only a few months after the fall of Jerusalem to the Persians, just to win in a successive one. Only four years prior to that date, the Persians had scored a sweeping victory over the Christians, spreading their control over Aleppo, Antioch[1], and even Damascus.

---

[1]The city of Antioch is situated on the banks of the river al-asi (Orontes). It was founded about 300 B.C. by Celeucus I (Nicator) who died in 280 B.C. Celeucus I was a general of Alexander the Great. Antioch is the city where the followers of Jesus Christ were called "Christians" (rather than Nazarines) for the first time. It is the seat of a Melchite, or Maronite, and a Jacobite patriarch. It fell to the Persians in 538 A.D., to the Arabs in 637 A.D. (16 A.H.), to the Byzantians from 969 - 1084 A.D. (358 - 477 A.H.), to Seljuk Turks in 1085 A.D. (478 A.H.), to the Crusaders in 1098 A.D. (491 A.H.), to Egyptian Mamlukes in 1268 A.D. (666 A.H.), and to Ottoman Turks in 1516 A.D. (922 A.H.). It was transferred to Syria by Western powers in 1920 (1339 A.H.) but restored to Turkey in 1939 A.D. (1358 A.H.). This is why the reader sometimes may see Antioch identified

The loss of Jerusalem, birthplace of Christ Jesus son of Mary (ع), was a heavy blow to the prestige of Christianity. Most Persians were then following Zoroastrianism, a creed introduced in the 6th century before Christ by Zoroaster (628-551 B.C.), also known as Zarathustra, whose adherents are described as worshippers of the "pyre," the holy fire. "Persia," hence, meant "the land of the worshippers of the pyre, the sacred fire." Modern day Iran used to be known as "Aryana," land of the Aryan nations and tribes. Some Persians had converted to Christianity as we know from Salman al-Farisi who was one such adherent till he fell in captivity, sold in Mecca and freed to be one of the most renown and cherished *sahabis* and narrators of hadīth in Islamic history, so much so that the Prophet of Islam (ع) said, "Salman is one of us, we Ahl al-Bayt (People of the Household of the Prophet)."

The war referred to above was between the then Byzantine (Eastern Roman) emperor Heraclius (575 - 641 A.D.) and the Persian king Khusrau (Khosrow) Parwiz (Parviz) or Chosroes II (d. 628 A.D.). It was one of many wars in which those mighty nations were embroiled and which continued for many centuries. Yet the hands of Divine Providence were already busy paving the path for Islam: the collision between both empires paved the way for the ultimate destruction of the ancient Persian empire and in Islam setting root in that important part of the world. Moreover, Muhammed's offspring came to marry ladies who were born and raised at Persian as well as Roman palaces. Imām Hussain ibn Ali ibn Abū Talib (ع), Muhammed's grandson and our Third Holy Imām and father of Imām Zain al-Ābidīn, married the daughter of the last Persian emperor Jazdagird (Yazdegerd) III son of Shahryar and grandson of this same Khusrau II. Jazdagerd ruled Persia from 632 - 651 A.D. and lost the Battle of Qadisiyya to the Muslim forces in 636, thus ending the rule of the Sassanians (Sassanids) for good. Having been defeated, he fled for Media in northwestern Iran, and from there to Merv[1], an ancient Central Asian city near modern day Mary in

---

as a Syrian town and some other times as Turkish! What a busy little town!

[1]Merv is an ancient city located in a large oasis of the Kara Kum desert, Turkmenistan (formerly part of the Soviet Union). During the Abbāside

Turkmenistan (until very recently one of the republics of the Soviet Union), where he was killed by a miller. The slain emperor left two daughters who, during their attempt to escape, following the murder of their father, were caught and sold as slaves. One of them, Shah-Zenan, ended up marrying our Third Holy Imām, al-Hussain ibn Ali ibn Abū Talib (ع); her sister, Mir-Warid (which means "prearl" in ancient Pahlavi Persian), married the renown scholar and acclaimed *muhaddith* (traditionist) Muhammed son of the first Muslim caliph Abū Bakr. Shah-Zenan was awarded a royal treatment and was given a new name in her own Persian mother tongue: Shahr Banu, which means "mistress of the ladies of the city." The marriage between her and Imām Hussain (ع) produced our Fourth Holy Imām Zain al-Ābidīn, or as-Sajjād, namely Ali ibn al-Hussain ibn Ali ibn Abū Talib (ع).

After the Battle of Qadisiyya (637 A.D.), Shahr Banu was brought in custody to Medīna. With the age-old racist attitude still alive, not too many Arabs would have expressed due respect to her. But it was the humane chivalry of Imām Ali ibn Abū Talib (ع) who paid full regard to this royal prisoner whom he married to his noble son Hussain (ع), as explained above. Imām Zain al-Ābidīn was, thus, the grandson of Imām Ali (ع) and the Persian emperor Jazdagird (Yazdegerd) III son of Shahryar, rendering him in high esteem by both Arab and Persian nations.

Imām Zain al-Ābidīn (ع) could not enjoy the love of his mother for a long time. She died soon after giving birth to him. At the age of two, his grandfather Imām Ali (ع) was also martyred. He was, thus, brought up and instructed by his father Imām Hussain (ع) and by his uncle Imām Hassan (ع). He was twelve when Imām Hassan (ع) died and the burdens of the Imāmate fell on Hussain's shoulders. The cunning of Mu'awiyah, the then Umayyad ruler of Syria, led to the tragedy of Kerbalā' during the reign of his son Yazid; therefore, youthful Zain al-Ābidīn watched the pace of the events which culminated in that terrible massacre. Imām Hussain (ع), who was

---

period, it served as the capital of ancient Persia and a thriving center of Islamic culture.

leading a peaceful life in Medīna, arranged the marriage of his son to Fatima daughter of Imām Hassan (ع), thus ensuring that the series of Imāmate would continue even in the face of coming events.

Upon his departure from Medīna to Mecca, then from Mecca to Kerbalā', Imām Hussain (ع) took his son Ali Zain al-Ābidīn, who was then twenty-two years old, with him. It cannot be ascertained whether Zain al-Ābidīn fell ill during the journey or after reaching Kerbalā. On the tenth of Muharram, 61 A.H./October 10, 680 A.D., he was too ill to move. As access to the Euphrates was blocked for three days and water was extremely scarce, the illness of Zain al-Ābidīn intensified. For the most part of that day, he lay unconscious and could not participate in the battle which was carried on by all the male members of his family. So when Imām Hussain (ع) bade his family farewell and went to the battlefield, he could not talk with his son Zain al-Ābidīn. Providence had perhaps destined Zain al-Ābidīn to be tested in another way when he was to lead his distressed family as prisoners.

Immediately after the martyrdom of Imām Hussain (ع), the ruthless enemies turned to his tents to burn and plunder, as the reader has already come to know. The overwhelming grief, the flames of burning tents, the tumult among the widowed ladies and orphans must have taken its toll on the sensitive Sajjād. Neither tongue nor pen could have described the psychological impact. But the son of Hussain (ع) maintained his composure and spiritual serenity. In spite of illness and crushing distress, he kept the grace of a true believer. Having said the night prayers on that fateful eve, he lay in prostration with his forehead on the ground and his tongue repeating these phrases all night long till dawn:

There is no deity but Allāh in all certainty;
There is no god but Allāh in truth and faith;
I bear witness to this in submission and humility.

Next day, Omer ibn Sa'd assembled all his slain soldiers, performed the funeral prayers for them and arranged for their burial, leaving the corpse of Imām Hussain (ع), Prophet Muhammed's grandson, and those of his faithful adherents uncovered, unshrouded, and unburied, simply lying on the ground. It was a most painful sight for Zain al-Ābidīn to pass through the site of the onslaught accompanied by the ladies, all being captives. He was shocked to realize that he could not bury his kith and kin due to his captivity.

Not less heart-rending might have been the event when this pillaged caravan was brought to the court of Ibn Ziyad, governor of Kūfa. As-Sajjād might have remembered that it was the same town where once his grandfather Imām Ali ibn Abū Talib (ع) ruled as caliph and the ladies of the household were the royalty. Ibn Ziyad now rejoiced over his victory as the Prophet's family was brought as captives.

From Kūfa these people were sent to Damascus. When their caravan entered the capital, it noticed how the bazaars were festively decorated and people were embracing each other, congratulating each other. The agony of humiliation suffered by Imām Hussain's helpless folk was immeasurable, yet Zain al-Ābidīn still stood and carried out Imām Hussain's mission of guiding the nation.

Having been released from confinement in Damascus, Zain al-Ābidīn went with his family to Medīna to lead a quiet life, but that city was now in revolt against Yazid's cruel regime. Political parties pressured Zain al-Ābidīn to join them, but he knew their unreliability; therefore, he declined to do so. So, when Yazid's army invaded Medīna, the invaders did not harass Zain al-Ābidīn's family.

Yet he was greatly shocked to see how for three days the invading host, led by Muslim ibn Uqbah, tied their horses at the Prophet's mosque, turning the sacred place into a filthy stable filled with horses' refuse, killing hundreds of innocent people and raping chaste women and children. It was too intolerable for the Imām who had to practice a great deal of control of his feelings. When different revolutionary parties rose to avenge Hussain's innocent blood, he wisely kept aloof from them. He deemed their uprisings as untimely, and he kept himself occupied in worship and preaching through excellent supplications, setting an example of forbearance and endurance.

Undoubtedly, Sulayman ibn Surad al-Khuza'i or al-Mukhtar ibn

'Ubaidah ath-Thaqafiavenged Imām Hussain's precious blood. Imām Zain al-Ābidīn (ع) had compassion for them; he prayed for al-Mukhtar's success and used to often inquire about those who were captured and executed. Certainly al-Mukhtar relieved the Imām's wounded heart by punishing the culprits. But the Imām was so cautious that his outward appearance gave the impression that he was indifferent, so much so that the cruel government could not suspect him of any subversion.

His whole lifespan was a time of trouble for the Prophet's family and for their supporters. A few years after Yazid's death, the ruthless Umayyad government put to death a large number of supporters of the Prophet's family at the hands of al-Hajjaj ibn Yousuf at-Thaqafi. It kept a constant surveillance over their activities and communications through its undercover agents. Under such circumstances, it was impossible for Imām Zain al-Ābidīn (ع) to propagate the Prophet's teachings or guide the public in the open, so he lived Islam and made his life an example for others to emulate.

After the tragedy of Kerbalā', the Imām lived 34 years under very odd circumstances. During that entire period, patience and fortitude were his main characteristics. Staying away from worldly pursuits, he kept himself busy by either worshipping his Lord or narrating the heart-rending events of Kerbalā', thus keeping its memories alive. He wept whenever he remembered his father and whenever he saw food or water, reflecting upon the thirst and hunger of his father, Imām Hussain (ع).

In spite of the quiet life Imām as-Sajjād (ع) was leading, the Umayyad government considered him a potential threat to the regime. Abd al-Malik ibn Marwan ordered the governor of Medīna to arrest him and take him into custody to Damascus. There, he remained confined for three days, but the Almighty Allāh and the spiritual influence of Imām as-Sajjād (ع) made Abd al-Malik ashamed of his cruel behaviour, so he ordered him to be released and sent back home.

It was characteristic of the Prophet's family, particularly the twelve Imāms (ع), to personify the excellence of the human perfections.

Imām as-Sajjād (ع) was a true copy of his ancestors. In both Kerbalā' and Kūfa, he demonstrated extreme patience and courage. In Medīna, he proved to be most forbearing and forgiving. Once, an insolent person spoke to Imām as-Sajjād (ع) in an abusive and taunting tone. The serene, high-spirited Imām replied saying, "May Allāh forgive me if you have told the truth or forgive you if you are wrong." The man was impressed by his noble conduct and lowered his head in shame as he said, "In reality, what I said was wrong." When another person tried to slander him, the Imām (ع) ignored him. The impudent fellow raised his voice saying, "It is you whom I meant." Imām as-Sajjād (ع), with an air of loftiness, replied, "And it is you whom I ignored." The Imām's reply echoed the Qur'ānic verse in which the Almighty asked the Prophet (ص) to "Hold to forgiveness; command what is right, but turn away from the ignorant" (Qur'ān, 7:199).

Hisham ibn Isma'eel behaved insolently towards Imām as-Sajjād (ع). Omer ibn Abd al-'Aziz, the only righteous Umayyad caliph, came to know about it and wrote Imām as-Sajjād (ع) saying that he had all intention to punish the rogue, but Imām as-Sajjād (ع) nobly replied, "I do not like that the man be harmed on my account."

Service of the nation and generosity to it were his outstanding traits. In the darkness of dreary nights, he used to carry flour and loaves of bread to the needy. Many of them did not know who the benefactor was because he always hid his face. It was only when Imām as-Sajjād (ع) died that those needy people came to know who he was. In addition to all these virtues, even opponents acknowledged his knowledge and admitted that none could match him in jurisprudence and religious sciences. Yet he told people that one should not boast about the nobility of his ancestors. Whenever he went to another town, he avoided revealing his name or illustrious lineage. When asked about the reason, he humbly said, "It is not fair for me to trace my lineage to the Holy Prophet (ص) since I do not have his virtues." His ocean of knowledge was sought by the most distinguished scholars and theologians of the time, and many rose to a lofty status after obtaining such knowledge from him. They came to him from all parts of Arabia, the Middle and Far Easts, and from Africa.

The list of individuals who benefitted from his knowledge and thus became scholars in their circles includes, according to Bihār al-Anwār of *'allama* Majlisi: Abū Hamzah at-Thumali, Thabit ibn Dinar, al-Qasim ibn Muhammed ibn Abū Bakr (grandson of first caliph Abū Bakr), Ali ibn Rafi', al-Dhahhak ibn Muzahim al-Khurasani, Hamid ibn Mūsa al-Kūfi, Abul-Fadl as-Sudair ibn Hakim as-Sairafi, Abdullāh al-Barqi, the poet al-Farazdaq[1], Furat ibn Ahnaf, Ayyub ibn al-Hassan, Abū Muhammed al-Qarshi as-Saddi, Tawoos ibn Kaisan al-Hamadani, Aban ibn Taghlib ibn Rabah, Qays ibn Rummana, Abū Khalid Wardan al-Kabuli (of Kabul, Afghanistan), Sa'd ibn al-Mūsayyab al-Makhzumi, Omer ibn Ali ibn al-Hussain and his brother Abdullāh, Jābir ibn Muhammed ibn Abū Bakr (another grandson of the first caliph), and many, many others. The most distinguished of his followers are these great persons: Jābir ibn Abdullāh al-Ansāri, Amir ibn Wa'ila al-Kinani, Sa'd ibn al-Mūsayyab ibn Hazan, and Sa'd ibn Jihan al-Kinani. Among the tabieen, the most distinguished were: Sa'd ibn Jubayr, Muhammed ibn Jubayr ibn Mutim, al-Qasim ibn 'Awf, Isma'eel ibn Abdullāh ibn Ja'far, Ibrahim ibn Muhammed ibn al-Hanafiyya and his brother al-Hassan, Habib ibn Abū Thabit, Abū Yahya al-Asadi, Abū Hazim al-Araj, Salamah ibn Dinar al-Madani, and many, many others. The most famous of those who narrated hadīth from him were: az-Zuhri,

---

[1]One of the greatest of all Arab poets, al-Farazdaq was born in Basra in about 641 A.D. and died in about 732 A.D. His real name is Hammam ibn Ghalib ibn Mujashi al-Darmi at-Tamimi. He was contemporary to another very famous poet, Jarir, with whom he had exchanged extensive literary criticism which lasted al his lifelong. Al-Farazdaq once praised Imām as-Sajjād with a poem considered as one of the best masterpieces of Arab poetry, and he did so in the presence of then caliph Hisham ibn Abdul-Malik who asked him why he did not compose one like it in his own praise. Al-Farazdaq said, "Had your grandfather been like his grandfather (ع), and had your father been like his father (ع), and had your mother been like his mother (ع), I would have done so." Hisham was so angry that he ordered him to be jailed at a place called Usfan, located between Mecca and Medīna, where he continued to compose poetry taunting and belittling Hisham who finally had to set him free, hoping he would leave him alone and stop the barrage of poems exposing him and his likes from among Banu Umayyah.

Sufyan ibn Uyainah, Nafi, al-Awzai, Muqatil, Muhammd ibn Ishāq, among others. Authors who quoted the traditions transmitted through him were: at-Tabari, Ibn al-Bay, Imām Ahmed ibn Hanbal, Ibn Batta, Abū Dāwūd, the authors of *Hilyat al-Awliya'*, *Asbab an-Nuzul*, *At-Targhib wat-Tarhib*, *Al-Fa'iq*, *Al-Mustafa*, and others. These were certainly not his contemporaries, yet they verified and recorded the traditions which he had narrated.

As regarding the great poet al-Farazdaq, to whom reference is made above, we would like to quote his masterpiece poem for the enjoyment of the Arabic-speaking readers. The poem praises Imām Zain al-Ābidīn in the most beautiful way, actually too beautiful to render into English or any other language:

رائعة الفرزدق .. في مدح الإمام زين العابدين بن الحسين بن علي

هذه قصيده للفرزدق يمدح بها الإمام زين العابدين بن الحسين بن علي رحمه الله وهي من أجمل مقال الفرزدق...... وسبب القصيده هو أن هشام بن عبد الملك حج، فحاول أن يلمس الحجر الأسود فلم يستطع من شدة الازدحام فوقف جانباً، وإذا بالإمام مقبلاً يريد لمس الحجر فانفرج له الناس ووقفوا جانباً تعظيماً له حتى لمس الحجر وقبله ومضى فعاد الناس الى ما كانوا عليه. فانزعج هشام وقال: من هذا؟ وصادف أن كان الفرزدق الشاعر واقفاً فأجابه هذا علي بن الحسين بن علي ثم أنشد فيه قصيدته المشهورة التي يقول فيها:

يا سائلي أين حلَّ الجود و الكرم؟	عندي بيان إذا طلا به قدموا
هذا الذي تعرف البطحاء وطئته	والبيت يعرفه والحلّ والحرمُ
هذا ابن خير عباد الله كُلُّهُم	هذا التقي النقي الطاهر العلمُ
هذا الذي أحمد المختار والده	صلى عليه إلهي ما جرى القلم
لو يعلم الركن من قد جاء يلثمه	لخرَّ يلثم منه ما وطئ القدم
هذا علي رسول الله والده	أمست بنور هداه تهتدي الأمم
هذا الذي عمه الطيار جعفر و ال	مقتول حمزة ليث حبه قسم
هذا ابن فاطمة إنْ كنت جاهله	بجده انبياء الله قد ختموا
الله فضله قدمًا و شرفه	جرى بذاك له في لوحه القلم
من جده دان فضل الأنبياء له	و فضل أمته دانت لها الأمم
وليس قولك منْ هذا؟ بضائره	العرب تعرف من انكرت والعجمُ
كلتا يديه غياثٌ عمَ نفعهما	يستوكفان و لا يعروهما عَدَمُ
سهل الخليقة لاتخشى بوادره	يزينه اثنان: حسنُ الخلقِ والشيمُ
لا يخلف الوعد ميمونا نقيبته	رحب الفناء أريب حين يعترم

206

حمّال اثقال اقوام اذا امتدحوا   حلو الشمائل تحلو عنده نعمُ

إن قال قال بما يهوي جميعهم   و إن تكلم يوما زانه الكلمُ

ما قال لا قطّ الا في تشهده   لولا التشهّد كانت لاءه نعمُ

عمّ البرية بالاحسان فانقشعت   عنها الغياهب و الاملاق و العدمُ

اذا رأته قريش قال قائلها   الى مكارم هذا ينتهي الكرمُ

يُغضي حياءً و يغضي من مهابته   فلا يكلّم الا حين يبتسمُ

بكفّه خيزرانُ ريحها عبق   من كف اروع في عرنينه شممُ

يكاد يمسكه عرفان راحته   ركن الحطيم اذا ما جاء يستلمُ

الله شرّفه قدماً و عظّمه   جرى بذاك له في لوحة ا لقلمُ

ايُّ الخلائق ليست في رقابهمُ   لأوّليّه هذا اوله نعمُ

من يشكر الله يشكر اوّليّه ذا   فالدين من بيت هذا ناله الامَمُ

ينمي الى ذروة الدين التي قصرت عنها الاكفّ و عن احراكها القدمُ

من جده دان فضل الانبياء له   و فضل امته دانت له الامَمُ

مشتقة من رسول الله نبعته   طابت مغارسه و الخيم و الشيمُ

ينشق نور الدجى عن نور غرته   كالشمس تنجاب عن اشراقها الظلمُ

من معشرٍ حبهم دينٌ و بغضهمُ   كفرٌ و قربهم منجى و معتصمُ

يستدفع السوء و البلوى بحبهم   و يستزاد به الإحسان و النعم

مقدّمٌ بعد ذكر الله ذكرهمُ   في كلّ بدءٍ و مختوم به الكلمُ

إن عدَّ اهل التقى كانوا ائمتهم   او قيلَ من خير اهل الارض؟ قيل هُم

لا يستطيع جوادٌ بعد جودهم   و لا يدانيهم قوم و إن كرموا

هم الغيوث اذا ما ازمة ازمت   والاسد اسدُ الشرى والبأس محتدم

أي القبائل ليست في رقابهم   لأولية هذا اوله نعمُ

من يعرف الله يعرف أولية ذا   فالدين من بيت هذا ناله الأمَمُ

بيوتهم في قريش يستضاء بها   في النائبات و عند الحكم إن حكموا

فجده من قريش في أرومتها   محمد و علي بعده علم

بدر له شاهد و الشعب من أحد   و الخندقان و يوم الفتح قد علموا

و خيبر و حنين يشهدا له   و في قريضة يوم صيلم قتم

مواطن قد علت في كل نائبة   على الصحابة لم أكتم كما كتموا

لاينقص العسر بسطأ من اكفّهم   سيّان ذلك إن اثروا وان عدموا

يستدفع الشرُّ و البلوى بحبّهم   و يستربُّ به و الاحسان والنعمُ

His chief attribute which earned him the titles of "Zain al-Ābidīn" and "Sayyid as-Sajidan" was his sincere worship of the Almighty. He was an eyewitness to the tragedy of Kerbalā', and the scenes of his near and dear ones being slaughtered were always fresh in his memory. Such depressing events naturally make any ordinary person indifferent to all other normal activities of everyday life, but they could not make Imām as-Sajjād (ع) relax his fear of Allāh. His complexion faded and his whole frame shook whenever the water for ablution was presented to him, or whenever he stood to say his prayers. When asked about the reason, he explained, "Can you at all imagine in Whose presence I am going to stand?! It is in the presence of the Lord of lords."

While putting on his pilgrimage garb, intending to utter "Labbayka Allāhomma Labbayk!" (I am answering Thy Call, O Lord!), colour disappeared from his face. His whole frame shook, so much so that those who saw him inquired what was wrong with him. Imām as-Sajjād (ع) said, "I tried to say *Labbayk!*' but I feared lest the Lord of the House calls out: No admittance for you.'" Tears flooded his eyes so excessively that he ultimately fainted. Whenever everyone else prostrated before the pomp of haughty Umayyad monarchy, it was Imām as-Sajjād (ع) who demonstrated how the King of kings should be worshipped.

His supplications were later compiled and named As-Sahifa as-Sajjādiyya, the book of as-Sajjād, which is dubbed "the Psalms of Muhammed's family." The reader who wishes to read some of its contents are referred to pp. 462 - 469 of my book titled *Allāh: The Concept of Allāh in Islam* (published by Ansāriyan Publications). I feel honored and humbled by the Almighty enabling me to translate such a precious text. It is only He Who enables His servants to do whatever good they do, whatever useful knowledge they acquire and disseminate; He, and only He, is the source of all goodness.

The reign of the antagonistic Umayyad rulers never permitted Imām Zain al-Ābidīn (ع) to deliver discourses and addresses as his grandfather Imām Ali (ع) did, nor to illustrate the creed as he had done. Later, Imām Muhammed al-Bāqir and Imām Ja'far as-Sādiq (ع), son and grandson of Imām as-Sajjād respectively, had the opportunity to fathom the depths of religious problems at study circles attended by inquisitive students. But, alas, such a favorable atmosphere was not available to Imām as-Sajjād (ع). He, therefore, adopted quite a different method which no worldly power could obstruct. He suspended all worldly contacts and took to hymns and prayers. The words of those prayers are a treasure-houses of theological mysteries and reflective of the relationship between the Creator and His creation. A collection of these hymns and prayers, known as *As-Sahifa al-Kāmila*, or *As-Sahifa as-Sajjādiyya*, has survived despite all the odds. In the pages of this collection, we can find what we cannot perhaps attain even from reading lengthy addresses and discourses presented in a similarly appealing manner, if such can be found at all.

The calm and peaceful life of the Imām could not be tolerated by the cruel Umayyad regime. The Syrian monarch al-Walid ibn Abdul-Malik had him poisoned, and the Imām died inside the Medīna jail on the 25th of Muharram, 95 A.H. (October 20, 713 A.D.). Imām Muhammed al-Bāqir (ع) conducted the burial ceremony, laying him to rest in the graveyard of Jannat al-Baqi' beside his uncle, Imām Hassan (ع). May the Almighty cut off the hands of the tyrants and those who support them wherever and whoever they may be...

2) IMĀM MUHAMMED AL-BĀQIR (ع)

He was named after his great grandfather Prophet Muhammed, peace be with him and his progeny, and he was called "al-Bāqir" which means "the splitter of knowledge". His father is Imām Zain al-Ābidīn (ع) and his mother is Fatima daughter of Imām Hassan (ع), the Prophet's grandson. His lineage, therefore, reaches the Prophet of Islam (ع) on both parents' sides. Imām Hussain (ع), the younger grandson of the Prophet, is his grandfather. He has the unique attribute of having inherited the qualities of Imām Ali ibn Abū Talib (ع) and Fatima daughter of the Prophet Muhammed (ص).

The Imām was born on Rajab 1, 57 A.H./May 10, 677 A.D., seven years after the martyrdom of Imām Hassan (ع), and he spent more than three years in the company of his grandfather Imām Hussain (ع). He was an eyewitness to the tragedy of Taff, and he was contemporary to his father Imām as-Sajjād (ع) during the entire period of his Imāmate. The Kerbalā tragedy was a troublesome and tumultuous period of time for the Prophet's offspring and their followers, supporters of Ahl al-Bayt (ع). Imām Ali's friends were always hunted, arrested, then hanged.

According to *Al-Irshād* of al-Mufid, *Al-Fusul al-Muhimma* of Ibn as-Sabbagh al-Maliki, Vol. 3 of al-Ya'qubi's *Tarikh* (history), and *Tathkirat al-Khawass* of Ibn al-Jawzi, the great *sahabi* Jābir ibn

Abdullāh al-Ansāri narrates saying, "The Messenger of Allāh, peace be with him and his progeny, said to me: You shall live long enough to meet one of the descendants of Hussain who shall be named Muhammed and who shall split the core of knowledge; so, convey my Salam to him'."

According to *Ikmal ad-Din wa Itmam an-Ni'ma*, and on p. 252 of Shaikh as-Sadūq's work, Jābir ibn Abdullāh al-Ansāri asked the Messenger of Allāh (ص) saying, "O Messenger of Allāh, who are the Imāms from the descendants of Ali ibn Abū Talib (ع)?" He (ع) answered: "Al-Hassan, al-Hussain, masters of the youths of Paradise, then the master of the forbearing of his time, Ali ibn al-Hussain, then al-Bāqir Muhammed ibn Ali, and, O Jābir! You shall live to see him! So when you do, convey my Salam to him."

Vol. 42, p. 25 of *Bihār al-Anwār*, and also both *I'lam al-Wara bi A'lam al-Huda* and *Kashf al-Ghumma fi Marrifat al-A'imma*, when Imām Ali ibn Abū Talib (ع) was on his death-bed, his will to his oldest son al-Hassan was: "O son! The Messenger of Allāh (ص) ordered me to give you my books and weapons just as he had ordered me to take his books and weapons and to tell you to pass them over to your brother Hussain before you die." Then he turned to Imām Hussain (ع) and said, "... and the Messenger of Allāh (ص) ordered that you (Imām Hussain) should pass them on to your son Muhammed ibn Ali and to convey to him Salam from the Messenger of Allāh and from me."

For three years, Imām al-Bāqir (ع) enjoyed the cherished love of his grandfather Imām Hussain (ع), and when he had to leave Medīna, al-Bāqir, too, was one of the family members who made the journey across the desert. Imām Hussain (ع) left for Kūfa and his journey terminated at Kerbalā'. Since the 7th of Muharram, when the Prophet's family was denied access to the water of the Euphrates, Imām al-Bāqir (ع) suffered from the pangs of thirst till the tragedy was over. Providence, however, intended to preserve the Imāmate by safeguarding his life, whereas even a baby like Imām Ali al-Asghar (ع) had already been killed by an enemy arrow.

Like his father Imām Zain al-Ābidīn (ع), Imām al-Bāqir (ع) could not physically participate in the battle. The 10th of Muharram, 61 A.H./ October 10, 680 A.D. brought its hideous events with Imām Hussain (ع) gathering the corpses of his slain warriors all day long, the women wailing, the children crying because of being extremely thirsty, startled and bewildered, then came the last farewell bidden by Imām Hussain (ع), the murder of his baby Ali al-Asghar, the return of Imām Hussain's horse to his master's tent without his master... Young al-Bāqir (ع) witnessed all these events. Al-Bāqir witnessed the tents being burnt, the children reeling in panic, the heartless enemy plundering, and the ladies of the Prophet's family being deprived even of their sheets and scarves. Who can possibly imagine how young Imām al-Bāqir (ع) felt, or what a permanent impression such scenes had left on his mind?

On the next day, Imām al-Bāqir (ع) witnessed the ladies of the Prophet's family being shackled with chains, hand-cuffed, then transported as captives by the enemy the entire distance from Kerbalā' to Kūfa, then to Damascus. Having been released, he witnessed their journey back to Medīna, again passing by Kerbalā'. The profoundly sad impressions could never have been erased from the memory of young Imām al-Bāqir (ع).

After Kerbalā', Imām Zain al-Ābidīn (ع) led a very calm life, staying aloof from the pursuits of this materialistic world. Secluded from the society, he spent his time either weeping as he reminisced on the agonies of his father Imām Hussain (ع), or worshipping the Almighty, while the heart of his son Imām al-Bāqir (ع) was being squeezed painfully as he watched helplessly. In this sad environment, Imām al-Bāqir (ع) grew up studying the manners of his saintly father and availing himself from his knowledge and noble conduct.

Imām al-Bāqir (ع) was in the full bloom of youth, ascending the heights of physical and spiritual perfection, when his revered father died. On his death-bed, Imām Zain al-Ābidīn (ع) handed over to Imām al-Bāqir (ع) a box containing books of religious sciences exclusively known to this illustrious Ahl al-Bayt (ع). Calling together all his offspring, he resigned them to the care of Imām al-Bāqir (ع), now named the fifth in the successive series of the successors of the holy Prophet. He was then 38 years old.

The Umayyad monarchy was heading towards its decline and decay. The cruelties inflicted on the Hashemites, especially the massacre at Kerbalā', had produced shock waves throughout the Muslim world. Yazid witnessed the aftermath of Kerbalā' and may have regretted his heinous sins. After a brief rule, he died in 64 A.H., and his son Mu'awiyah II succeeded him briefly then abdicated. The later Umayyad rulers, therefore, were fully aware of the consequences of the atrocities of their predecessors. The bloody battles waged by the Tawwaban movement, the penitents, led by Sulayman ibn Surd al-Khuza'i and later by al-Mukhtar, led to a powerful uprising against the Umayyads. Everyone now demanded to avenge the holy blood of Imām Hussain (ﻉ) and those who defended the Prophet's fāmily. That movement ruffled the peace of the ruling despots and shook the foundations of their government. The good result was that Imām Muhammed al-Bāqir (ﻉ) had the opportunity to free himself from the clutches of the tyrannical government. He had at that time better chances to peacefully guide the Muslim nation to the Right Path.

The Imāms, the Prophet's leading offspring, had rivers of knowledge in their bosoms which were blocked by the oppressing government and thus their waters could not moisten the lips of the thirsty. In the days of Imām al-Bāqir (ﻉ), when the grip of the oppressive government loosened a little bit, the confined river of knowledge gushed forth, irrigating the fields of faith-seeking hearts. Having displayed his great skill in solving tough religious problems, he was called al-Bāqir (discloser or splitter of hidden knowledge). The number of those who benefited from him and learned the teachings of Ahl al-Bayt (ﻉ) reached thousands of seekers of knowledge. Many others, belonging to different schools of thought such as Imām Zuhri, Imām Awzai, Attar ibn Jarih, or Hafiz ibn Ghiyath, the judge, who all are considered as outstanding traditionists of the Sunni sects, came to seek knowledge from him and are counted among his students.

Volume 3 of *Manaqib al Abi Talib* states that Abdullāh son of second caliph Omer ibn al-Khattab was asked once for the solution of a complex theological problem, and he could not provide one.

"Go to that young boy," Omer said to the person who raised the question, pointing to Imām al-Bāqir (ع), "Ask him and tell me what his answer will be." The inquirer approached Imām al-Bāqir (ع), obtained the answer, and went back to the son of Omer ibn al-Khattab to tell him what treasures of knowledge he had just acquired, and Abdullāh commented: "They are a family immersed in knowledge."

Al-Irshād by al-Mufid, in a chapter on the Imāmate of al-Bāqir (ع), and in *Hilyat al-Awliya'* and *Tathkirat al-Khawass* of Ibn al-Jawzi, the grandson, Abdullāh ibn Ata' al-Makki says, "I never saw scholars shrink as I saw them in the presence of Abū Ja'far Muhammed ibn Ali ibn Hussain. And I saw al-Hakam ibn 'Uyainah, despite his greatness, looking like a young boy before his teacher."

One of the testimonies to the excellence of his political thought is his advice to the renowned Umayyad caliph Omer ibn Abdul-Aziz in which he said, "I advise you to regard young Muslims as your sons, the adults as your brothers, and the elderly as your parents; therefore, be kind to your sons, stay in touch with your brothers, and be generous to your parents."

One of his students, Muhammed ibn Muslim, is quoted in Vol. 46, as saying, "Every time I faced a complex (theological) problem, I had to seek its solution from Abū [the father of] Ja'far, till I asked him about thirty thousand questions." One of his companions, Jābir ibn Yazid al-Ju;fi, may Allāh be pleased with him, said once, as quoted in the same references which also quotes *Al-Ikhtisas*, saying, "Abū Ja'far narrated to me as many as seventy thousand traditions." Advising Jābir ibn Yazid al-Ju'fi, he said, "I admonish you regarding five things: If you are wronged, do not commit wrongdoing to others; if your are betrayed, do not betray anyone; if you are called a liar, do not be furious; if you are praised, do not be jubilant; if you are criticized, do not fret and think of what is said in criticism: if you find in yourself what is criticized about you, then your falling down in the eyes of Allāh, when you are furious about the truth, is a much greater calamity than your falling down in the eyes of people. And if you are the opposite of what is said (in criticism) about you, then it is a merit you acquired without having to tire yourself in obtaining it."

The dissemination of religious and scientific knowledge of Ahl al-Bayt (ع) was achieved by Imām Muhammed al-Bāqir (ع). Out of the benefits gained from such a high-ranking mentor, the students wrote several books on various branches of knowledge. Here is a brief description of some of his disciples and their works which reflects the extent of Islamic learning imparted by the Imām:

1. Aban ibn Taghlib. He was the famous lexicographer and reciter of the Holy Qur'ān who wrote the work *Ghara'ib al-Qur'ān* غرائب القرآن, the first book explaining the intricate diction of the Holy Qur'ān. He died in 141 A.H./758 A.D.

2. Abū Ja'far Muhammed ibn al-Hassan ibn Abi Sarh ar-Rawasi, the famous scholar of recitation, syntax and exegesis. *Kitab al-Faisal* and *Ma'ani al-Qur'ān* are two among five books which he authored. He died in 101 A.H./720 A.D.

3. Abdullāh ibn Maimun, Abul-Aswad al-Du'ali. A biography of the Holy Prophet and another book expounding on Paradise and Hell are among his works. He died in 105 A.H./723 A.D.

4. Atiyyah ibn Sa'd al-'Awfi. He wrote an exegesis of the Holy Qur'ān in five volumes; he died in 111 A.H./729 A.D.

5. Isma'eel ibn Abd ar-Rahman as-Saddi al-Kabir (as-Saddi senior), the well-known author of Tafsir. He is frequently referred to by all Muslim writers of *tafsir* (exegesis) books as as-Saddi. He died in 127 A.H./745 A.D.

6. Jābir ibn Yazid al-Ju'fi. He committed to memory 50,000 (or 70,000 according to some biographers) traditions which he had heard from Imām al-Bāqir (ع). He is quoted in Muslim's Sahīh. He wrote several volumes on tradition, *tafsir* and jurisprudence. He died in 128 A.H./746 A.D.

7. Ammar ibn Mu'awiyah al-Wahni. A book on jurisprudence is his contribution. He died in 133 A.H./752 A.D.

214

8. Salim ibn Abi Hafsah (Abū Yousuf) al-Kūfi. He is the writer of a book on jurisprudence. He died in 137 A.H./754 A.D.

9. Abdul-Mu'min ibn Qasim (Abū Abdullāh) al-Ansāri. He is the writer of a book on jurisprudence. He died in 147 A.H./764 A.D.

10. Abū Hamzah at-Thumali. He wrote a book on *tafsir* (exegesis) of the Holy Qur'ān. *Kitab an-Nawadir* and *Kitab az-Zuhd* are among his works. He died in 150 A.H./767 A.D.

11. Zararah ibn Ayun, a high-ranking Shī'a scholar who wrote several books on tradition, jurisprudence and *kalam*. He died in 150 A.H./767 A.D.

12. Muhammed ibn Muslim. He was a great scholar who recorded 30,000 traditions which he learned from Imām al-Bāqir (ﻉ). He wrote many books, including the "Four hundred problems of *halal* and *haram*." He died in 150 A.H./767 A.D.

13. Yahya ibn Qasim (Abū Basīr) al-Asadi. He was a revered scholar who wrote *Kitab Manasik al-Hajj* and *Kitab Yawmun wa Lailah*. He died in 150 A.H./767 A.D.

14. Ishāq al-Qummi. He has a book on jurisprudence.

15. Isma'eel ibn Jābir al-Khashami al-Kūfi. He wrote many volumes on hadīth (tradition) and one on jurisprudence.

16. Isma'eel ibn Abdul-Khaliq. He was a high ranking jurist and had a book to his credit.

17. Bard al-Asqaf al-Azdi. He wrote on jurisprudence.

18. Al-Harith ibn al-Mughirah. He authored a book on the problems of jurisprudence.

19. Huthaifah ibn Mansūr al-Khuza'i. He had a book on jurisprudence.

20. Hassan ibn Sirri al-Katib. He wrote one book.

21. Hussain ibn Saur ibn Abi Fakhita, author of *Kitab an-Nawadir*.

22. Hussain ibn Muhammed 'Abidi al-Kūfi; he is author of one book.

23. Hussain ibn Mus'ab al-Bajali. He has a book to his credit.

24. Hammad ibn Abi Talha; he wrote one book.

25. Hamzah ibn Hamran ibn Ayun. He was nephew of Zurarah and author of one book.

These are quite a few scholars, traditionists and jurists who learned from Ahl al-Bayt (ع), mostly from Imām Muhammed al-Bāqir (ع), and safeguarded such knowledge by recording it in their books. Later, in the days of the Imām's son, namely Imām Ja'far as-Sādiq, hundreds of volumes were written—the sources from which such valuable collections of hadīth as *Al-Kāfi, Man la Yahdharuhu Al-Faqih, Tahdhib al-Khasa'il, Al-Istibsar*, etc. were compiled. These books now form the fundamentals of Shī'a learnings. In addition to these, you may read his biography and the *ahādīth* which he narrated in at-Tabari's *Tarikh*, in al-Balāthiri, as-Salami, al-Khattab, Abū Dāwūd's *Sunan*, al-Isfahani, az-Zamakhshari1, and in others.

---

1 He is "Abul-Qāsim" Mahmoud ibn (son of) Omer ibn Muhammed ibn Omer al-Zamakhshari, of Khawarizm (an area in Khurasan, Iran), a Mu'tazili Persian scholar, actually one of the imāms of the Mu'tazilis (Mu'tazilites). He was born in Rajab of 467 A.H./March 1075 A.D. and died in 538 A.H./1143 A.D. He is famous for two books which he wrote: "الكشاف" *Al-Kashāf* and "أساس البلاغة" *Asās al-Balāgha*. Although he mostly wrote in his mother tongue, Persian, he excelled in the writing of his Arabic works such as the ones referred to above. Al-Zamakhshari was born in Zamakhshar village, Khawarizm; he studied in Bukhara and Samarqand then moved to Baghdad seeking knowledge. From there, he moved to Mecca where he became famous as "Jar-Allah". After that he returned to Khawarizm where he died in its capital Jurjan (or Gorgan, a town in northern Iran). Jurjan is quite famous in Islamic history and

His moral excellences were admired even by his foes. A Syrian lived in Medīna and used to come to Imām al-Bāqir (ع) frequently declaring that he was opposed to the Household. Yet, despite his prejudice, he admitted that, "The high morality and eloquence of Imām al-Bāqir (ع) are too attractive to resist."

The author of *Tuhaf al-'Uqūl* quotes Imām as-Sādiq (ع) saying, "I entered the house of my father once and found him doling out eight thousand dinars as sadaqa to the poor, then he freed eleven slaves."

In a chapter on the merits of Imām Muhammed al-Bāqir (ع) in Vol. 3 of *Manaqib Ali Abi Talib*, and in Vol. 46 of al-Majlisi's *Bihār al-Anwār*, Sulayman ibn Qaram is quoted as saying, "Abū Ja'far Muhammed [ibn al-Hanafiyya], son of Imām Ali (ع), used to give us as much as five or six hundred or even a thousand *dirhams*, and he never felt tired of visiting his brethren."

Imām Ali ibn Abū Talib (ع) cooperated with his contemporary caliphs and offered sound counsel concerning the affairs of the Muslims. So did all the Imāms who succeeded him, each following his example. None of them hesitated to offer advice to their contemporary rulers, and Imām al-Bāqir (ع) was no exception. The Umayyad government had till then no currency of its own. The Byzantine currency of the eastern section of the then Roman Holy Empire was the valid tender in Damascus as well. But during the

---

literature, and it produced a good number of famous men such as: Abū Sa'īd al-Darīr al-Jurjānī, a 9th century A.D. astronomer and mathematician; Abū Sahl al-Masihi al-Jurjānī (al-Masihi, the Christian), a 10th century physician and teacher of Avicenna (Ibn Sina); Abd al-Qāhir al-Jurjānī, an 11th century grammarian and literary theorist; Zayn ad-Dīn al-Jurjānī, a 12th century royal physician; Fazlullāh Astar-Ābādī, a 14th century mystic and founder of Hurufism (a Sufi doctrine); Rustam Gorgani, a 16th century physician; Mir Damad, a 17th century Islamic scholar and Neoplatonic philosopher; Mirza Mehdi Khan Astar-Ābādī, an 18th century chief minister to King Nader (Nadir) Shah (founder of the Afsharid dynasty that ruled Iran from 1736 to 1796); Bibi Khatoon Astar-Ābādī, a notable writer and satirist and many others.

reign of al-Walid ibn Abdul-Malik, there rose a rift between him and the Byzantine ruler when the latter decided to stamp a new currency with a phrase which al-Walid considered as derogatory to the Holy Prophet (ص). This created suspense among the Muslims. Al-Walid convened a committee in which prominent Muslim scholars participated. Imām al-Bāqir (ع) expressed his opinion that the Muslim government ought to mint its own currency on one side of which it should stamp the statement "La Ilaha Illa Allāh" and on the other the statement "Muhammedun Rasul-Allāh," (There is no god but Allāh; Muhammed is the Messenger of Allāh). The opinion was unanimously approved and new Islamic coins were minted.

It was only during the caliphate of Omer ibn Abdul-Aziz, the only pious Umayyad caliph, that the Prophet's progeny enjoyed a brief period of peace which lasted for only two years and five months, the duration of Omer's government. He lifted from them a great deal of atrocities and prohibited the cursing of Imām Ali ibn Abū Talib (ع) on the pulpits on Friday, substituting it with this verse of the Holy Qur'ān: "Allāh commands justice, the doing of good, and liberality to kith and kin, and He forbids all shameful deeds, and injustice and rebellion: He instructs you, that ye may receive admonition" Qur'ān, 16:90 (Chapter an-Nahl, The Bees).

When the Imām met caliph Omer ibn Abdul-Aziz, he found him weeping for the injustice inflicted by his predecessors upon their subjects. The Imām admonished him with pieces of wisdom till the caliph sobbed, knelt down and begged the Imām for more. Then the Imām told Omer what wrongdoing he came to ask him to rectify, and it was none other than the estate of Fadak which the Messenger of Allāh (ص) had left as inheritance to his daughter Fatima (ع) and her descendants. According to Vol. 4 of *Bihār al-Anwār*, Omer wrote: "*In the Name of Allāh, the Most Gracious, the Most Merciful.* This is what Omer ibn Abdul-Aziz had given back to Muhammed ibn Ali to rectify the wrongdoing: Fadak."

Hisham ibn Abdul-Malik succeeded Omer ibn Abd ul-Aziz as the ruler, and he was a stone-hearted, immoral, miser and racist. His prejudice against non-Arab Muslims caused him to double the taxes non-Arabs had to pay, and his reign was a replay of the bloody days of Yazid ibn Mu'awiyah and those of the blood-thirsty al-Hajjaj ibn Yousuf at-Thaqafi[1]. It was then that the revolution of Zaid ibn Ali broke out as a continuation of the revolution of Imām Hussain ibn Ali ibn Abū Talib (ع), but Hisham was swift in crushing it. Dr. Hassan Ibrahim Hassan, in his book *Tarikh al-Islam* ("History of Islam"), quotes contemporary historians testifying that Hisham ordered to crucify Zaid ibn Ali and then burn his corpse and throw the ashes in the Euphrates.

Although Imām al-Bāqir (ع) never expressed any interest nor participated in political activities except when the rulers invited him to, since his peaceful way of living was devoted to people's spiritual guidance, he was not tolerated by the government. Hisham ibn Abdul-Malik wrote his governor over Medīna instructing him to send Imām al-Bāqir (ع) together with his son [later Imām] Ja'far as-Sādiq (ع) to Damascus, intending to insult them both. When they reached Damascus, he kept them waiting for three days. On the fourth day, he called them to his presence. He sat on a throne surrounded by his nobility, fully armed. In the center of the courtyard, a target was set on which the elite were shooting arrows on bet. Islam prohibits betting or gambling or any way of making money without working hard to earn it. As soon as the Imām entered, Hisham bluntly asked him to shoot arrows with others. Imām al-Bāqir (ع) asked to be excused, but Hisham insisted; he planned to ridicule the Imām. Since the Imām led a secluded life, Hisham thought that he might not have had anything to do with martial arts. Compelled by Hisham, Imām al-Bāqir (ع) took the bow. Handling it skillfully, he shot a few arrows continuously, all sitting straight in the very heart of the center. A shout of praise burst from

---

[1]The extent of al-Hajjaj's passion for shedding blood can be realized from this recorded and referenced incident: He entered once al-Heera's jail and commented about the prisoners saying, "I see heads the time for whose harvesting has come." They were all beheaded and their heads were brought to him at his government mansion. He ordered a carpet to be placed on the heads whereupon he sat and was served his lunch. Having finished eating, he said, "This has been the tastiest meal I have ever had." More about al-Hajjaj is stated in another footnote above. No wonder some Muslims do not teach Islamic history at all: It indicts them.

the throats of the astonished elites standing right and left. Hisham, thus outwitted, began to discuss the problems of Imāmate and the virtues of Ahl al-Bayt (ع). Now he clearly saw that the Imām's stay in Damascus might lead to popular respect for Ahl al-Bayt (ع), so he permitted the Imām to return home to Medīna. Inwardly, his enmity of the Prophet's family had increased.

Hisham harassed not only the Prophet's family but also their followers, dignitaries and scholars. He issued an order to execute Jābir ibn Yazid al-Ju'fi, the most distinguished among the Imām's scholars, but the Imām foiled his attempt by advising Jābir to feign madness as the only way to escape execution.

The more the Umayyads learned about the Imām's prestige and popularity, the more intolerable his existence became. At last they resorted to the same soundless weapon, poison, which used to be applied by those cunning monarchs quite often to eliminate their opponents or suspects. A saddle was presented to the Imām to which poison was skillfully applied. When he mounted on it, poison affected his whole body. After spending a few days suffering the pain of his ailment, he expired on the seventh of Thul-Hijja, 114 A.H./January 28, 733 A.D. He was laid to rest underneath the same dome in Jannat al-Baqi where Imām Hassan (ع) and Imām Zain al-Ābidīn (ع) already lay.

3) IMĀM JA'FAR AS-SĀDIQ (ع)
His name is Ja'far, and he is known as as-Sādiq and Abū Abdullāh, son of Imām Muhammed al-Bāqir (ع) son of Imām Zain al-Ābidīn (ع) son of Imām Hussain (ع). His mother was Umm Farwah daughter of Qasim son of Muhammed son of [first caliph] Abū Bakr who was one of the seven most prominent jurists of Medīna. Thus, the sixth Imām has an impressive lineage.

The Imām came to this world on Rabi' al-Awwal 17, 83 A.H./April 20, 702 A.D., the same lunar date when his great grandfather, the Holy Prophet (ص), was born. At his birth, his father, Imām al-Bāqir (ع), was 26, and his grandfather, Imām Zain al-Ābidīn (ع), was 44. The Prophet's family joyfully welcomed this auspicious addition.

220

Till the age of twelve, Ja'far was brought up under the guidance of his grandfather Imām Zain al-Ābidīn (ع) whose main concern was to worship his Maker and reflect on the tragic events of Kerbalā'. Twenty-two years had lapsed since then, yet the remembrance of that shocking tragedy was still quite fresh in his memory. So, as soon as Ja'far gained understanding, he was profoundly impressed by the continuous grief of his grandfather, so much so that he felt as if he himself was present during that tragedy. He also contemplated on the presence of his father, Imām Muhammed al-Bāqir (ع), although only three years old, at that gruesome scene. Ja'far as-Sādiq considered it as his duty to convene the recitation gatherings (majalis) about that sorrowful event.

He was twelve years old when his grandfather Imām Zain al-Ābidīn (ع) expired. From then on and till the age of 31, he spent his time under the supervision of his father Imām al-Bāqir (ع). It was the time when the Umayyad politics were tottering and Muslims who were approaching Imām Muhammed al-Bāqir (ع) by the thousands seeking his knowledge, wisdom and guidance. Whether at Medīna or in travels, Ja'far as-Sādiq was always with his father. When Hisham ibn Abdul-Malik summoned Imām Muhammed al-Bāqir (ع), Ja'far as-Sādiq accompanied him, as stated above.

In 114 A.H./732 A.D., Imām Muhammed al-Bāqir (ع) died, and the responsibilities of Imāmate devolved on the shoulders of now Imām Ja'far as-Sādiq. Hisham ibn Abdul-Malik was ruling in Damascus and political disturbances were rampant. The call for seeking revenge against Bani Umayyah was strong among the public, and several descendants of Imām Ali (ع) were preparing themselves in the hope of overthrowing their corrupt regime. Most prominent among them was Zaid bin Ali, the respected son of Imām Zain al-Ābidīn (ع). His religious zeal and piety were known throughout Arabia. He was a well versed *hafiz* of the Holy Qur'ān and had taken the field against the tyranny of the Umayyads.

This was a precarious juncture for Imām Ja'far as-Sādiq. As regarding hatred of the Umayyads, he agreed with his uncle Zaid for whom he had a great deal of respect. His far-sighted judgment could clearly see that his rising against the well-organized royal forces was of no avail; he, therefore, did not join him for all practical reasons. But he was compassionate towards him and sympathetic to his cause, and he asked him to be judicious. As a great host of Iraqis had sworn their allegiance to him, Zaid was now quite optimistic. He valiantly fought the royal forces but was in the end killed.

The vengeful enemies were not satisfied with Zaid's death. They exhumed his dead body from the grave, severed his head, sent it as a trophy to Hisham and hanged the body at the gate of Kūfa where it remained for several years. One year after Zaid's martyrdom, his son Yahya earned the same ancestral honor. Imām Ja'far was surely moved by these tragic events, but he was destined to carry out the duties of spreading the religious knowledge of Ahl al-Bayt (ع).

The last days of the Umayyads' reign of terror were ruffled by political disturbances. Imām Ja'far as-Sādiq witnessed the rise and fall of many of their kings. After Hisham, al-Walid ibn Yazid ibn Abdul-Malik, then Yazid ibn al-Walid, then Ibrahim ibn al-Walid, then Marwan al-Himar [the donkey] ascended the throne. The capture and death of the latter terminated the monarchy of tyrannical Umayyads.

During the last phase of tottering Umayyad rule, the Hashemites were actively engaged in their anti-Umayyad activities. The Abbāsides took advantage of their efforts and secretly formed an association whose members had sworn to transfer the government from the Umayyads to the Hashemites who really deserved it. It is clear that to rule the Islamic world was not the job of every Hashemite. It was the right of those divinely appointed descendants of the Holy Prophet and Imām Ali (ع) whom Allāh had chosen to lead humanity. But these high-thinking souls never wished to take undue advantage of the situation with the aid of cunning tactics.

In short, the Imāms who descended from the Commander of the Faithful, Imām Ali (ع), never tried to acquire power through political trickery and opportunism. But the Abbāsides, who also were Hashemites, no doubt took the opportunity by the forelock. Availing themselves of the silence shown by the Imāms, and of the compassion the people had for the Hashemites, the 'Abbāsides realized their chance to rise to power. But when they established themselves on the throne, they became enemies of Imām Ali's posterity in the same degree or more than that which had been adopted by the heartless Umayyads. Details of this will be narrated in the biographies of later Imāms.

The first to start the movement from among the Abbāsides was Muhammed ibn Ali ibn 'Abdullāh ibn al-Abbās who sent his agents throughout Persia to secretly obtain the oath of allegiance to the Hashemites' cause from the Persians. On Muhammed's death, his son Ibrahim succeeded him. Meanwhile, the martyrdom of Zaid and his son Yahya had fanned the flames of revolution against the Umayyads. The Abbāsides took advantage of it, increasing their influence in Iraq through Abū Salamah al-Khallal. Slowly but steadily, their power base increased. Through the sincere support of Abū Muslim al-Khurasani, all Western Persia and Khurasan came under their control and the Umayyad governor had to flee. The name of the Umayyad ruler was dropped from Friday sermons, having been replaced by that of Ibrahim ibn Muhammed.

The Umayyads till then were under the impression that the disturbances were merely local protests, but now the government spies reported that it was a full-fledged movement initiated by Ibrahim ibn Muhammed ibn Abbās who resided at Jabulqa. Soon Ibrahim was arrested, imprisoned and mercilessly killed. His family escaped the royal wrath with other Abbāsides and sought refuge with Abū Salamah in Iraq. When the news reached Abū Muslim al-Khurasani, he sent an army to Iraq which defeated the Umayyad forces and annexed Iraq.

Abū Salamah al-Khallal, dubbed "Minister of the Prophet's Progeny," was especially compassionate towards Imām Ali's offspring. He wrote letters to the prominent heads from among them inviting them to accept and share the royal power. One of such letters was addressed to Imām Ja'far as-Sādiq. In political struggles, such opportunities are considered golden, but the Imām declined the offer and remained devoted to his duty of disseminating knowledge.

Those who supported the Abbāsides' cause, in addition to the followers of Abū Muslim al-Khurasani, swore the oath of allegiance to Abul-Abbās as-Saffah. On Rabi' II 14, 132 A.H./November 30, 749 A.D., the latter was acknowledged as the ruler and caliph of the Muslim world. Establishing themselves in Iraq, the Abbāsides advanced towards Damascus. Marwan assembled his forces and confronted them, but his army was defeated. He had to flee for his life but was later captured in Egypt and killed.

Thereafter, a reign of terror followed: The Umayyads were massacred publicly; the dead bodies of the monarchs of their dynasty were exhumed and treated in a most shocking manner; thus, the revenge upon the oppressors, the law of nature, was implemented through the Abbāsides. In 136 A.H./753 A.D., as-Saffah, the first Abbāside caliph, died and was succeeded by his brother Abū Ja'far al-Mansūr, commonly known as al-Dawaniqi.

The Abbāsides raised the banner of standing and protecting the rights of Ahl al-Bayt (ع), thus succeeding to rally the public around them on this very pretext, and it was their war-cry as well. But when they came to power and destroyed the Umayyads, they naturally feared lest the world should be disappointed and disillusioned with them, or lest a movement should start demanding that the caliphate must be vested upon the descendants of Imām Ali (ع) and Fatima instead of the Abbāsides. Abū Salamah was inclined to the descendants, and he was a candidate to support such a movement; therefore, in spite of all the favours which he had done to the Abbāsides, he was the first to fall victim to their ingratitude. He was put to death during the reign of as-Saffah. Persia was under the control of Abū Muslim al-Khurasani. Al-Mansūr arranged to have him murdered most treacherously.

Al-Mansūr was no longer apprehensive of the interference of any influential person in his government. He, therefore, turned all his tyranny against the Sayyids, descendants of the Prophet (ص) themselves. On mere suspicion, al-Mansūr would begin to destroy the Sayyids. The prominent among them were subjected to atrocities. Muhammed son of Ibrahim, who was the most handsome among them and was, therefore, called the "silken", was walled alive[1].

Imām Ja'far as-Sādiq (ع) was sadly affected by those events. When the descendants of Imām al-Hassan ibn Ali (ع) were all fettered, shackled and banished from Medīna, he watched their plight with a saddened heart from the flat roof-top of his house. With flooded eyes he was heard saying, "Oh! Medīna is no longer a sanctuary or a haven of peace..." Then he expressed his sorrow for the descendants of the Ansār who stood idly by thus: "The early Medenites (Ansār) had invited the Holy Prophet to Medīna under the oath that they would protect him and his descendants just as they would protect their own kith and kin. But today the descendants of those very Ansār act as silent onlookers, and none stands up to protect the Prophet's offspring." Having said these words, he returned to his house and fell ill, unable to move from bed for twenty days.

Among the afore-mentioned prisoners was the aged Abdullāh Mahd son of Imām al-Hassan ibn Ali (ع) who had to suffer the hardships of a prolonged imprisonment. His son Muhammed (known as "Thul Nafs az-Zakiyya") rose against the oppressive government and fell fighting near Medīna in 145 A.H./762 A.D. The head of the young

---

[1]So that the reader may not misunderstand this statement, let him be informed that whenever the Abbāsides built a house or a mansion, they used to bring a number of descendants of the Prophet (ص) whom they would place inside the new structure's column. Then they would continue the construction, making these victims' bodies part of the building, thus slowly killing them by suffocation, keeping their corpses inside the structure... For numerous such incidents, the reader is referred to the book titled *Maqatil at-Talibiyyeen* by "Abul-Faraj" Ali ibn al-Hussain ibn Muhammed ibn Ahmed ibn Abdul-Rahman ibn Marwan ibn Abdullāh ibn Marwan ibn Muhammed ibn Marwan ibn al-Hakam ibn Abul-As ibn Umayyah ibn Abd Shams ibn Abd Munaf, of the Umayyads of Quraish, famous as "al-Isfahani." This great Sunni author was born in Isfahan, Iran, in 284 A.H./897 A.D. and died in 356 A.H./967 A.D. He wrote more than 31 books, the most famous of which are: *Al-Aghani, Jamharat Ansab al-Arab, Nasab Bani Taghlib*, and, of course, *Maqatil at-Talibiyyeen*. Mankind seldom produces writers as prolific and as fair as this Isfahani. May he be rewarded most generously by the Almighty, *Ameen*.

warrior was severed then sent to his aged father in prison, a shocking sight which the worn-out old man could not bear, falling dead shortly thereafter. Another son of Abdullāh Mahd, namely Ibrahim, also fought against al-Mansūr's army and fell fighting near Kūfa. In the same way, Abdullāh son of Thul Nafs az-Zakiyya, Mūsa and Yahya, brothers of Thul Nafs az-Zakiyya, were all killed mercilessly. Many Sayyids were used alive as part of the building materials of walls as explained in a footnote above.

In spite of all these atrocities which have been described very briefly here, Imām Ja'far as-Sādiq (ع) went on silently propagating the teachings of Ahl al-Bayt (ع). As a result, even those who did not acknowledge him as the Imām nor knew his prestige and lineage, bowed before his knowledge and prided in being counted among his students.

Al-Mansūr wanted to diminish the esteem in which Imām Ja'far as-Sādiq (ع) was held by the people. He tried to bring persons to compete with him who all proved incapable of arguing not with him but with his own students. These fellows admitted that their counterparts had acquired the religious learning from the Prophet's Progeny (ع). The haughty ruler, therefore, ignored them but continued to undermine the popularity of the Imām. Failing in all his efforts, he decided to harass, arrest or murder him. In every town and city, hired agents were posted to monitor the activities of the Shī'as so that anyone suspected of supporting the Imām would be arrested. Al-Mu'alla son of Khunais was one of the many Shī'as who were thus arrested and murdered in cold blood.

The Imām himself was summoned from Medīna to the royal palace five times, each time being in one way or another nothing but harassment. Al-Mansūr, however, could never find sufficient grounds to order his imprisonment or execution. On the other hand, the consequent stay of the Imām in Iraq only expanded the circle of those who wanted to learn the teachings of Ahl al-Bayt from him. Perceiving this, al-Mansūr ordered him to be sent back to Medīna. Even there, he was not spared persecution. Through saboteurs, his house was once set on fire but Providence put it out and nobody was harmed.

Imām Ja'far as-Sādiq (ع) was one of those Infallibles who were created by the Almighty to be role models of moral excellence. The particular virtues of Imām Ja'far as-Sādiq (ع), which were recorded by historians, included: hospitality, charity, the helping of the needy in secrecy, the fair treatment of the relatives, forgiveness, patience and fortitude.

Once a pilgrim visiting the Prophet's mosque in Medīna fell asleep there. On waking up, he hurriedly searched his belongings and found out that his purse containing one thousand dinars was missing. Looking around, he saw Imām Ja'far as-Sādiq (ع) performing his prayers in a corner of the mosque. Bewildered and ignorant of the greatness of the Imām, he accused him of having picked his purse. The Imām asked about its contents, and he was told that it contained one thousand dinars. The Imām asked the stranger to follow him to his house where he paid him the amount from his own money. When the stranger came back to the mosque satisfied, once more he checked his property and found his purse intact, wrapped in a bundle. Greatly ashamed of his conduct, he went back to the Imām's house, profusely apologized and asked him to take his money back. The Imām appeased him with these words: "We never take back what we once give away."

Another event of the Imām's trust in Allāh, the Sustainer, deserves mention here. During the days of scarcity and famine, one naturally tries to hoard up as much provisions as might suffice his needs for a long time. Once, the Imām asked his household's manager, Trenchab, "The price of corn is rising day by day. How much corn is there in our warehouses?" Trenchab said that the Imām should have no reason to worry since there was a large quantity of it to sustain them over a long period of time. The noble Imām then ordered him thus: "Sell out all the corn today and let us face the situation along with others." Then he directed him thus: "Pure wheat flour shall not be used in my kitchen. Let it be mixed with an equal quantity of oat flour. We must share the misfortune with the needy as long as it takes."

The Imām (ع) used to respect the poor more than the rich and value their hard work. Trade was his occupation, yet he liked to personally do manual work in his orchards. One day, while wielding the spade and sweating profusely from top to toe, someone offered to do the work for him, but the Imām (ع) said, "It is no insult to bear the heat of the summer's sun for the sake of my family."

To be kind to the slaves and bondmaids was the main characteristic of the Prophet's Progeny (ع). Sufyan at-Thawri has narrated a surprising event in this regard. He said, "Once I went to pay him a visit. I saw his complexion fading. On my asking him the reason, the Imām explained: I had forbidden my folk from ascending the stairs to the rooftop. Just now, as I entered the house, I saw a nursing maid with my babe in her arms ascending the stairs. She was so frightened that she became nervous, and the baby fell down and died. I do not grieve on the death of the baby as much as I grieve on her fright.'" Then he prepared to arrange for the shrouding and burial of his dead baby.

The Imām's profound knowledge of religious and other sciences was reputed throughout the entire Islamic world, and even Western scholars have paid him tribute, admiring his knowledge and character. One famous Western reference discussing the Imām is the renown *Encyclopedia Britannica* where he is discussed on p. 498, Vol. 5, of its *Micropedia*. People came to him from distant regions to quench their thirst for his ocean of knowledge. The number of his students reached once four thousand. Among them were scholars of jurisprudence, tafsir (exegesis), *hadīth*, etc. Theologies from other creeds also went there to debate with his students. When they went away vanquished and defeated, the Imām used to explain to his students their (the latter's) own weak points so that they might be more careful in the future.

Sometimes he himself debated with the opponents especially the atheists. Apart from religious sciences, he used to teach some students mathematics, chemistry, medicine, etc. Jābir ibn Hayyan[1]

---

[1]Jābir's name is immortalized in both the East and the West: it is from his first name that the science of Algebra is derived. He was its pioneer and founder.

of Tarsus, the famous pioneer of physics, chemistry and mathematics, was his disciple who wrote about four hundred treatises based on his mentor's instruction. The jurists who learned from him and authored several volumes of books on jurisprudence can be counted by the hundreds and their students by the thousands.

Such a great teacher and scholar can never be ambitious for power. But the government of his time regarded his popularity as a constant threat. It finally resorted to the use of their soundless weapon, poison, to put an end to this great man, just as other governments did to his ancestors and offspring. History always repeats itself; it is a wheel in an endless motion. The governor of Medīna was directed to offer him poisoned grapes the efficacy of which ended his life on Shawwal 15, 148 A.H./December 4, 765 A.D. when he was 65. His funeral was arranged by his son and successor, Imām Mūsa al-Kādhim (ع), who led the burial prayers. He was laid to rest in the same compound at Jannat al-Baqi where Imām al-Hassan (ع), Imām Zain al-Ābidīn (ع), and Imām al-Bāqir (ع) are buried...

4) IMĀM MŪSA AL-KĀDHIM (ع)
His name is Mūsa; "al-Kādhim" and "Abul-Hassan" are his titles.

He is usually called Mūsa al-Kādhim. Imām Ja'far as-Sādiq (ع) was his father whose lineage, by five generations, reaches the Holy Prophet (ص). His mother, Hamida Khatun, was a North African Berber. He was born on Safar 7, 128 A.H./November 8, 745 A.D. The knowledge of his father, Imām Ja'far as-Sādiq (ع), saturated the Islamic world. Although two elder sons, Isma'eel and Abdullāh, had already illuminated the house, the addition of the new-born brought unequalled happiness to the family, probably because Providence had decided to maintain the continuity of Imāmate through him. Photo (above) shows Imām al-Kādhim's shrine in al-Kādhimiyya, Baghdad, Iraq.

For twenty years, he remained under the care of his father Imām Ja'far as-Sādiq (ع). It was due to the virtues, teachings and the dissemination of the knowledge of the Prophet (ص) through Imām Ja'far as-Sādiq (ع) that Shī'a Muslims are called "Ja'faris," taught by

Imām Ja'far as-Sādiq (ع). The scholarly achievements of Imām Mūsa al-Kādhim (ع) were so conspicuous that the world acknowledged Imām Ja'far as-Sādiq (ع) had, indeed, appointed him as his successor as commanded by the Almighty. It is proven by this act that Imāmate does not, as a rule, go to the eldest son or be inherited. It is the blessing bestowed by the Almighty upon the Infallible ones who are gifted with divine knowledge. The principle is further established by the fact that such a great responsibility had once before passed from Imām Hassan (ع) to his brother Imām Hussain (ع) rather than to Hassan's descendants. The Imāmate of Mūsa al-Kādhim (ع), therefore, illustrates that Imāmate is based on personal perfection, not necessarily on descent.

In 148 A.H./765 A.D., upon the death of Imām Ja'far as-Sādiq (ع), the responsibilities of Imāmate devolved on Imam Mūsa al-Kādhim (ع). This was during the reign of al-Mansūr al-Dawaniqi, the tyrant who ordered the slaying of countless Sayyids, descendants of the Prophet of Islam (ع). The number of those imprisoned, oppressed, thrown into the dark cells of prisons or bricked up in the walls alive, was known only to Allāh. Imām Ja'far himself had been subjected to harassment, tyranny and intrigues, the last of which was poison which ended his life.

On his death-bed, Imām Ja'far as-Sādiq (ع) predicted that the life of his successor would also be ended in the same way. In order to avert this danger as much as he could, he nominated, in his will, five trustees to look after his family. Al-Mansūr, the Abbāside ruler, was one of them. The other four were: Muhammed ibn Sulayman, the then governor of Medīna, his son Abdullāh al-Aftah, (later Imām) Mūsa al-Kādhim (ع), and their respected mother Hamida Khatun.

Imām Ja'far's prediction was correct. When the news of his death reached al-Mansūr, the latter made a show of grief by thrice repeating these words: *Inna lillahi wa inn ilayhi rajioon*, "We are Allāh's and to Him is our return." He also said, "Who can be Ja'far's equal now...?" But secretly he wrote to the governor of Medīna saying, "If Ja'far, by way of a will, appointed any trustee, put him to death immediately." The governor replied: "He has appointed five trustees, the first of whom is your majesty." Having read this reply, al-Mansūr remained silent, since the sanctity of a will cannot be violated. Then, pondering over the situation, he said, "In this case, these persons cannot be slain."

Accordingly, for the next ten years, al-Mansūr did not try to harass Imām Mūsa al-Kādhim (ع) who carried out the duties of Imāmate peacefully. Al-Mansūr was, moreover, preoccupied with building the new capital, Baghdad, which he completed just one year before his death. He had, therefore, little time to think about harassing Imām Mūsa al-Kādhim (ع).

Al-Mansūr al-Dawaniqi died in 158 A.H./775 A.D. and was succeeded by his son al-Mahdi. In the beginning, al-Mahdi did nothing to humiliate or disrespect Imām Mūsa al-Kādhim (ع), but later he fostered the old enmity against Imām Ali's descendants. In 164 A.H./781 A.D., having performed the *hajj*, he took the Imām with him from Mecca to Baghdad where he imprisoned him. For one year, the Imām suffered the hardship of imprisonment. Then the ruler realized that he was mistreating a descendant of the Prophet (ص), so he released the pious Imām (ع). In 169 A.H./785 A.D., al-Mahdi died and was succeeded by his brother al-Hadi who ruled for only 13 months. On his death, Harūn ar-Rashīd ascended the throne. The latter's attitude towards Imām Mūsa al-Kādhim (ع) was very antagonistic, causing Imām al-Kādhim (ع) to die in prison.

Imām Mūsa al-Kādhim (ع) was one of the illustrious Imāms whom the Almighty Allāh had set as a paragon of moral excellence. Each member of this illustrious family personified the best of virtues and moral excellences. Each one of them was the embodiment of goodness. The Seventh Imām excelled in tolerance and forgiveness, so much so that he was titled al-Kādhim (ع), the suppressor of fury. Never was he heard speaking roughly or looking sternly. Even in the most unpleasant situations, he wore a smile. This was in accordance with the saying of his ancestor Imām Ali ibn Abū Talib (ع) that a believer keeps his grief confined in his chest while wearing a smile on his face.

One government official of Medīna was a persistent source of harassment to Imām Mūsa al-Kādhim (ع), even using abusive language regardig Imām Ali (ع). But the Imām always directed his followers not to abuse him in return. When his malicious conduct became too rude to be tolerated, they sought permission to retaliate against him. The Imām appeased them, promising to settle the matter himself.

Pacifying his followers thus, he went to the fellow's farm and treated him with such noble benevolence that the man felt ashamed of his conduct and subsequently changed his attitude and altered his conduct. Explaining this policy to his followers, the Imām asked them: "Was my behavior better than the methods you suggested?" They admitted that it was. He thus carried out the instruction of his great ancestor Imām Ali (ع) which is recorded in *Nahjul-Balāgha*: Subdue the enemy with kindness, since it is more effective than vanquishing him with force. Undoubtedly, this requires a correct judgment of the enemy's nature. With some enemies, one may say, good conduct does not bear any fruit; it is then that force must be met with equal or better force, rest assured. Imām Ali (ع) has, therefore, warned not to use this policy with the vile and the mean lest they should be encouraged to do more mischief. Consider this piece of advice when you deal with the enemies of Islam.

To vanquish the foe with goodness certainly requires the foresight the Imām possessed. Strictness is permissible only when the enemy's continuous vile conduct justifies retaliation or the use of force. If not, these dignified souls preferred to deal with him gently, so as to have a valid pretext against the opponent and leave no ground for him to justify his aggression.

Such was the noble method usually employed by the Fāmily of the Prophet (ص). Imām Ali (ع), even on his death-bed, behaved liberally with Ibn Muljim al-Muradi, his assassin who had dealt him a mortal blow only the day before. Imām Mūsa al-Kādhim (ع) showered his generosity on Muhammed ibn Isma'eel who carried out the orders of the Abbāside caliph to put an end to the Imām's life. It was Imām Mūsa al-Kādhim (ع) who aided him when he wanted to embark upon his journey with a grant of 400 dinars and 1,500 dirhams although he undertook this journey solely to poison the ears of the caliph against him.

Imām Mūsa al-Kādhim (ع) had to undergo a great deal of hardship. The academy of learning, which his father Imām Ja'far as-Sādiq (ع) had established, could no longer be maintained. Other means to disseminate knowledge were beyond his reach. It was only through his noble personal behavior that he was able to introduce the teachings of Prophet Muhammed (ص) and his Progeny (ع) to the public. This, indeed, is the best way to propagate Islam. You can talk about Islam as much as you want, but when one sees you doing something un-Islamic, your words will be forgotten, your reputation will be ruined, and your hypocrisy will be exposed. Talk is cheap; action is the true yardstick to measure one's piety; actions speak louder than words.

The Imām (ع) used to observe silence at gatherings or seminars, and he never spoke unless spoken to or someone asked him a question or requested him to solve a scientific problem. Nor did he ever initiate a conversation. In spite of this, he was held in very high esteem by friends and foes alike. All acknowledged his knowledge and noble personality. In view of his excessive worship at night, he was called "al-Abd as-Salih," i.e. the pious worshipper of Allāh. No less famed was his generosity. He used to secretly help the beggars and the destitute who never got to know who their benefactor was till he had died. After the *fajr* (pre-dawn) prayers, he used to lower his forehead in prostration and remain in that position till the sun rose high in the heart of the sky. His recitation of the Holy Qur'ān was attractive; he wept as he recited, and his audiences were deeply moved.

In 170 A.H./787 A.D., Harūn ar-Rashīd succeeded Abū Ja'far al-Mansūr as the caliph. His ancestors' traditional cruelty towards the descendants of Imām Ali (ع) and Fatima (ع) was well in his view. The revolt of Yahya ibn Abdullāh ibn al-Hassan broke out. Violating all agreements and covenants, as was always customary of the Umayyads and the Abbāsides, Harūn threw Yahya into the choking dark dungeons then had someone kill him. Imām Mūsa al-Kādhim (ع) was in no way connected with Yahya's uprising. Rather, he had actually advised him against opposing the tyrannical government. But Yahya's action served to intensify the enmity which Harūn harboured towards Imām Ali's descendants including, of course, Imām Mūsa al-Kādhim (ع). To make matters even worse, the Prime Minister, Yahya ibn Khalid al-Barmaki, poisoned Harūn's ears by pointing out that Ja'far ibn al-Ash'ath (tutor of Harūn's son, al-Amin, and a political rival of Yahya) was a follower of the Imām and that he planned to bring the Imām to power.

Although Yahya ibn Khalid intended just to entice Harūn against Ja'far ibn al-Ash'ath, his plan proved to be fatal to Imām Mūsa al-Kādhim (ع). In the same year, Harūn came to Mecca to perform the hajj, and so did Imām Mūsa al-Kādhim (ع). Here Harūn watched with jealous eyes the sublime popularity which the Muslim multitudes demonstrated towards that sage. It was sufficient to flare up his rage. Muhammed ibn Isma'eel's hostility worsened the situation.

To understand these complications, let us ponder on the following facts: Isma'eel, Muhammed's father, was the eldest son of Imām Ja'far as-Sādiq (ع), and he was expected to succeed his father as the Imām. But he died during the Imām's lefetime. The common notion was thus shattered. Yet some simpletons still held the view that Imām Ja'far's successor should be one of Isma'eel's offspring. Muhammed ibn Isma'eel and his followers, the Isma'eelis (or Isma'eelites, now a small off-shoot Shī'a sect), therefore, never acknowledged the Imāmate of Mūsa al-Kādhim (ع). Since his followers were a small minority, he outwardly expressed his loyalty to the fāmily.

To discuss all means to annihilate Imām Mūsa al-Kādhim (ع), Harūn consulted Yahya al-Barmaki whom he instructed to collect complete reports about the Imām through one of the descendants of Imām Ali (ع). Yahya, an avowed foe of the Prophet's Progeny, recommended Muhammed ibn Isma'eel as the person who would supply all the details correctly. Accordingly, he was summoned to Baghdad.

When Muhammed ibn Isma'eel received the caliph's letter, he considered it a passport to power, prestige, and prosperity. But he

234

was penniless and unable to prepare for the journey. He was, therefore, obliged to approach the same generous saint who demonstrated benevolence to friends and foes alike. The Imām knew fully well the motives behind the journey. He nevertheless inquired about its purpose. Muhammed explained that he was having hard times, being deeply in debt, and that he thought that the journey might bring him prosperity. The Imām said, "You need not go there; I promise to pay off all your debts and provide adequately for your sustenance." But Muhammed would not change his mind about going to Baghdad. Upon leaving, he paid the Imām a visit and requested a useful piece of advice. Imām Mūsa al-Kādhim (ع) remained silent. When he repeated his request, the Imām said, "Please see that you do not become a party in slaying me, and please do not be the cause of making my children orphans." Muhammed tried to turn from the point and asked for some appropriate advice. But the Imām refused to say anything more. When he got up to depart, the noble Imām gave him 450 gold dinars and 1,500 silver dirhams for the journey.

The result was exactly what the Imām had foreseen. Muhammed ibn Isma'eel reached Baghdad and stayed at the house of Prime Minister Yahya who introduced him to caliph Harūn. The latter surrounded him with honors and inquired about the pace of events in Medīna. Muhammed stated the circumstances most incorrectly, adding, "I never saw nor heard that a country is ruled by two kings." Asked to explain, he asserted: "As you are ruling here in Baghdad, Imām Mūsa al-Kādhim rules there in Medīna. From every town, revenues are delivered to him, and he claims to be your own equal in power."

These were the words Yahya al-Barmaki had instructed Muhammed to say to Harūn who felt provoked and challenged. He sent Muhammed back after granting him ten thousand dinars. But Allāh wished that Muhammed should not avail of this sizeable wealth. On that very night, he suffered from throat pain, and when the day dawned, the darkness of death closed on him. Harūn heard the news and ordered to retrieve the cash! Muhammed's statement was not erased from Harūn's memory and he was resolved to put an end to the Imām's life.

In 179 A.H./795 A.D., Harūn went to Mecca and Medīna. He stayed in the latter city for a day or two after which he sent his men to arrest Imām Mūsa al-Kādhim (ع). The Imām was not at home when the caliph's men came, so they went to the Prophet's tomb where he used to say his prayers. Having total disregard for the sanctity of the Prophet's grave, they arrested his descendant there and brought him before Harūn. It was on the 20th of Shawwal of 179 A.H./795 A.D. that the Prophet's pious son was being fettered and taken prisoner while not even one Medenite dared to raise a finger against the tyrant. This lethargy of the unfeeling Muslims had also been witnessed on several occasions before that incident. As a matter of fact, these Medenites have been politically lethargic ever since, especially after the Wahhabis took control, by force, of the politics of their country...

Being apprehensive of any attempt which might be made to rescue the Imām, Harūn ordered two camel-domes to be prepared in one of which he seated the Imām and sent him to Basra escorted by a sizeable military detachment. The other empty dome was sent to Baghdad with an equal number of soldiers in order to confuse any prospective rescuers and distract the attention of the people by keeping the place of imprisonment unknown. Was it not a shocking event that the Imām's family could not even see the Imām or bid him farewell? They only received the news that he had been imprisoned by the government. They were distressed to hear it and the Imām, too, was equally grieved for being separated from his loved ones without being able to bid them farewell.

Nobody knows what a zigzag route was followed; the journey to Basra took 47 days. There, the Imām remained in confinement for one year. The city's governor was ʿĪasa ibn Ja'far, a cousin of Harūn. In the beginning, he carried out Harūn's orders. But he often wondered about the reasons for the imprisonment of the pious descendant of Prophet Muhammed (ص). He, therefore, became curious about the Imām's life, character and personality. The more he studied them and noticed his forbearance, the more he was impressed by his noble conduct. He conveyed his views to Harūn in good faith, but the latter only became suspicious of the intentions of his own cousin. He, therefore, ordered the Imām to be transferred to

236

Baghdad where he put him under the custody of Fadl ibn ar-Rabi'. Having come to know that Fadl was sympathetic to the followers (Shī'a) of the Prophet's Progeny (ع), he put the Imām under the custody of Yahya al-Barmaki, the notorious enemy of Ahl al-Bayt (ع). It seems that the Imām's sacred personality impressed everybody, so the tyrant thought it necessary to change his jailers.

The Imām was finally imprisoned in a dungeon under the charge of as-Sindi ibn Shahik, the ruthless and stone-hearted Chief of Police of Harūn ar-Rashīd . The Imām died on the 25th of Rajab 183 A.H./September 2, 799 A.D. at the age of 55. No respect was awarded to him at the time of his burial either. Rather, the corpse was carried to the grave-yard by men who were announcing his death in degrading tones. By this time, the people felt depressed about the fate of the elevated Imām and sadly accompanied the coffin with a sincere display of grief and respect. They buried him in a northern suburb of Baghdad now bearing his name: al-Kādhimiyya, the city of Imām al-Kādhim (ع), where his magnificent mausoleum now houses a reputed school of theology coveted by scholars and seekers of knowledge.

5) IMĀM 'ALI AR-RIDHA (ع)
He is Imām Abul-Hassan II, Ali ibn Mūsa ar-Ridha, the eighth in the series of the Imāms from the Ahl al-Bayt (ع) of the Prophet. His birthplace is Medīna, and his resting place is Tus (Iran). He was born

in Medīna on Friday, or Thursday, Thul-Hijja 11, or Thul-Qi'da, or Rabaul-Awwal, of the Hijri year 148 or the year 153. He died on Friday, or Monday, near the end of the month of Safar, or the 17th of Safar, or Ramadan 21, or Jumada I 18, or Thul-Qi'da 23, or the end of Thul-Qi'da, of the year 202 or 203 or 206. In his *'Uyun Akhbar ar-Ridha*, as-Sadūq states: "What is accurate is that he died on the 13th of Ramadan, on a Friday, in the year 203." There is a great deal of dispute regarding the name of his mother. Some say she was called al-Khayzaran; others say she was Arwi and her nickname was "the blonde of

Nubia," while others say she was Najma and her nickname was "Ummul-Baneen." Others say she was called Sakan the Nubian; still others say she was called Takattum. Disputes exist also regarding the number of his offspring and their names. Some scholars say that they were five sons and one daughter, and that they were: Muhammed al-Qani', al-Hassan, Ja'far, Ibrahim, al-Hussain, and 'Aisha.

Sibt ibn al-Jawzi, in his book titled *Tathkiratul-Khawass*, says that the sons were only four, dropping the name of Hussain from the list. Al-Mufid inclines to believe that the Imām did not have any son other than Imām Muhammed al-Jawad (ع), and Ibn Shahr Ashub emphatically states so, and so does at-Tibrisi in his *A'lam al-Wara*. Author of *Al-'Udad al-Qawiyya* states that the Imām (ع) had two sons: Muhammed and Mūsa, and that he did not have other descendants. In his claim, he is supported by *Qurb al-Isnad* where the author says that al-Bazanti asked ar-Ridha, "For years I have been asking you who your successor is and you keep telling me that it is your son even when you had no son at all, but since Allāh has now blessed you with two sons, which one of them is he?" *'Uyun Akhbar ar-Ridha* indicates that he had a daughter named Fatima. His life was characterized by melancholy from its beginning till its painful end. At the onset of his life, he witnessed the trials and tribulations which filled the life of his father Imām Mūsa ibn Ja'far (ع).

The Abbāside caliph al-Mahdi III ordered the Imām (ع) to go to Baghdad so that the caliph would secure from him promises and pledges that he would not oppose his authority nor mobilize a revolution against him, and the Imām (ع) did not go back home till al-Mahdi went back to his Lord with his shoulders bent by the load of the regime's sins and immoral actions. He was succeeded by the Abbāside caliph al-Hadi who tried to put an end to the life of the Imām, but he did not live long enough, so ar-Rashīd acceded to the throne, thus the parching flames of the tragedy started incinerating the existence of the Alawis (Alawides) headed by Imām Mūsa ibn Ja'far (ع), and the dungeons of Baghdad, Basra, Wasit and other cities could not limit the regime's passion for seeking revenge against its opponents. Instructions issued by the government required the builders to fill the hollow building cylinders and columns with the still alive bodies of the elite from among Alawi youths as well as non-Alawi sympathizers. This ugly method of eliminating the government's opponents was not something invented by ar-Rashīd; it was a continuation of a custom started by al-Mansūr who sought revenge against some Alawi youths as history tells us.[1]

The Abbāside caliph al-Ma'mūn decided to use the Imām (ع) as a bargaining chip between him and the Abbāsides in Baghdad on one hand, and between him and the Alawis on the other, and also between him and the Shī'as of Khurasan as well. The ploy of relinquishing the throne was foiled when the Imām (ع) refused to accede to it.

It is worth mentioning here that when Imām ar-Ridha (ع) refused to accept the caliphate from the abdicating caliph, al-Ma'mūn, or to take charge of the post of heir apparent to the throne, he had no reason except his own awareness of the real depth of the goal al-Ma'mūn anticipated to achieve by his plan, and that the desire to abdicate was not to be taken seriously.

Imām ar-Ridha (ع) inherited the knowledge of his grandfather the Messenger of Allāh (ع). History narrates a great deal about his scholarly stances and intellectual discourses. Imām Mūsa a-Kādhim (ع) is reported to have often said to his sons, "Ali ibn Mūsa, your brother, is the learned scholar of the Descendants of Muhammed (ص); therefore, you may ask him about your religion, and memorize what he tells you for I have heard my father Ja'far ibn Muhammed more than once saying, The learned scholar of the family of

---

[1] Ibn al-Atheer, Vol. 4, p. 375. "Al-Mansūr," Muhammed ibn Ibrahim ibn al-Hassan, was brought in, and he was the most handsome man people ever saw. The Abbāside caliph asked him, "Are you the one nicknamed the yellow silk?" He answered, "Yes." He said, "I shall certainly kill you in a manner which I have not employed to anyone else," then he ordered him to be placed in a cylinder and it was built up on him while he was still alive; thus, he died inside it." al-Isfahani, *Maqātil at-Tālibiyyeen*, p. 136, indicates likewise.

Muhammed is in your loins. How I wish I had met him, for he is named after the Commander of the Faithful Ali (ع)." Ibrahim ibn al-Abbās as-Sali is reported as having said, "I never saw ar-Ridha (ع) unable to provide the answer to any question he received, nor have I ever seen any contemporary of his more learned than he was. Al-Ma'mūn used to put him to test by asking him about almost everything, and he always provided him with the answer, and his answer and parable was always derived from the Holy Qur'ān."

Raja' ibn Abul-Dhahhak, who was commissioned by al-Ma'mūn to escort ar-Ridha (ع) to his court, said once, "By Allāh! I never saw anyone more pious than him nor more often praising Allāh at all times, nor more fearful of Allāh, the Exalted. People approached him whenever they knew he was present in their area, asking him questions regarding their faith and its aspects, and he would answer them and narrate a great deal of hadīth from his father who quoted each of his forefathers till Ali (ع) who quoted the Messenger of Allāh (ع). When I arrived at al-Ma'mūn's court, the latter asked me about his behaviour during the trip and I told him what I observed about him during the night and the day, while riding or halting; so, he said, Yes, O son of al-Dahhak! This is the best man on the face of earth, the most learned, and the most pious.'"[1]

Al-Hakim is quoted in Tarikh Nishapur as saying that the Imām (ع) used to issue religious verdicts when he was a little more then twenty years old. In Ibn Majah's Sunan, in the chapter on "Summary of Cultivating Perfection," he is described as "the master of Banu Hashim, and al-Ma'mūn used to hold him in high esteem and surround him with utmost respect; he even made him his successor and secured the oath of allegiance for him."

Al-Ma'mūn said the following statement once in response to Banu Hashim: "As regarding your reaction to the selection by al-Ma'mūn of Abul-Hassan ar-Ridha (ع) as his successor, be reminded that al-Ma'mūn did not make such a selection except upon being fully aware of its implications, knowing that there is none on the face of

---

[1] *'Uyun Akhbār ar-Ridha*, Vol. 2, pp. 180-183.

earth more distinguished, more virtuous, more pious, more ascetic, more acceptable to the elite as well as to the commoners, or more God-fearing, than he (ar-Ridha) is."[1]

Abul-Salt al-Harawi is quoted as saying, "I never saw anyone more knowledgeable than Ali ibn Mūsa ar-Ridha (ع). Every scholar who met him admitted the same. Al-Ma'mūn gathered once a large number of theologians, jurists and orators and he (ar-Ridha [ع]) surpassed each and every one of them in his own respective branch of knowledge, so much so that the loser admitted his loss and the superiority of the winner over him."[2]

He is also quoted as saying, "I have heard Ali ibn Mūsa ar-Ridha (ع) saying, I used to take my place at the theological center and the number of the learned scholars in Medīna was quite large, yet when a question over-taxed the mind of one of those scholars, he and the rest would point at me, and they would send me their queries, and I would answer them all."[3]

After an intellectual discourse with al-Ma'mūn, 'Ali ibn al-Jahm said, "Al-Ma'mūn stood up to perform the prayers and took Muhammed ibn Ja'far, who was present there, by the hand, and I followed both of them. He asked him: What do you think of your nephew?' He answered, A learned scholar although we never saw him being tutored by any learned mentor.' Al-Ma'mūn said, This nephew of yours is a member of the family of the Prophet (ص) about whom the Prophet (ص) said, The virtuous among my descendants and the elite among my progeny are the most thoughtful when young, the most learned when adult; therefore, do not teach them for they are more learned than you are, nor will they ever take you out

---

[1]al-Majlisi, *Bihār al-Anwār*, Vol. 49, p. 211, as quoted by Ibn Maskawayhi's book *Nadam at-Taraf*.

[2]*Ibid.*, Vol. 49, p. 100. It is narrated from al-Hakim by Abū Abdullāh, the *hafiz* of Naishapur.

[3]*Ibid.*

of guidance, nor lead you into misguidance.'"[1]

Good manners constitute a significant part of one's personality. The Imām was characterized by a most noble personality which won him the love of the commoners as well as the elite. Ibrahim ibn al-Abbās as-Sali is quoted as saying, "I never saw Abul-Hassan ar-Ridha (ع) angering anyone by something he said, nor did I ever see him interrupting anyone, nor refusing to do someone a favour he was able to do, nor did he ever stretch his legs before an audience, nor leaned upon something while his companion did not, nor did he ever call any of his servants or attendants a bad name, nor did I ever see him spit or burst into laughter; rather, his laughter was just a smile. When he was ready to eat, he seated with him all his attendants, including the doorman and the groom." He added saying, "Do not, therefore, believe anyone who claims that he saw someone else enjoying such accomplishments."[2] A guest once kept entertaining him part of the night when the lamp started fading and the guest stretched his hand to fix it, but Abul-Hassan (ع) swiftly checked him and fixed it himself, saying, "We are folks who do not let their guests serve them."[3] The author of *Al-Manaqib* states that ar-Ridha (ع) once went to the public bath-house and someone asked him to give him a massage, so he kept giving the man a massage till someone recognized him and told that person who that dignitary was. The man felt extremely embarrassed; he apologized to the Imām (ع) and gave him a massage.[4] Muhammed ibn al-Fadl narrates the following anecdote regarding the Imām's simple personality. He says:

Ar-Ridha (ع), on the occasion of Eidul-Fitr, said to one of his attendants, "May Allāh accept your good deeds and ours," then he

---

[1]as-Sadūq, *'Uyun Akhbār ar-Ridha*, Vol. 1, p. 203.

[2]*Ibid*, Vol. 2, p. 184.

[3]Shaikh al-Mufid, *Al Kafi*, Vol. 6, p. 203.

[4]al-Maghazili, *Al-Manaqib*, Vol. 4, p. 362.

242

stood up and left. On the occasion of Eidul-Adha, he said to the same man, "May Allāh accept our good deeds and yours." I asked him, "O son of the Messenger of Allāh! You said something to this man on the occasion of Eidul-Fitr and something else on the occasion of Eidul-Adha; why?" He answered: "I pleaded to Allāh to accept his good deeds and ours because his action was similar to mine and I combined it with mine in my plea, whereas I pleaded to Allāh to accept our good deeds and his because we are capable of offering the ceremonial sacrifice while he is not; so, our action is different from his."[1]

Imām ar-Ridha (ع) defines for us the Islamic theory as the rules which govern the actual dealings of man with his brother man. From this can we be inspired that Islam abolishes the then class distinctions among individuals and groups in the areas of public rights and the safeguarding of man's dignity, and that the difference which we must recognize regarding these areas is the one between a person who obeys Allāh and another who does not. A man once said to the Imām: "By Allāh! There is nobody on the face of earth who is more honourable than your forefathers." The Imām responded by saying, "Their piety secured their honour, and their obedience of Allāh made them fortunate."[2] Another man said to him: "By Allāh! You are the best of all people!" He said to him: "Do not swear that like. Better than me is one who is more obedient to Allāh and more pious. By Allāh! The following verse was never abrogated: And We have made you nations and tribes so that you may know each other; verily the best of you in Allāh's sight is the most pious'" (Qur'ān, 49:13). Abul-Salt once asked him: "O son of the Messenger of Allāh! What do you say about something because of which people have been criticizing you?" He asked, "What is it?" He said, "They claim that you call people your slaves." He said, "Allāh! Creator of the heavens and the earth, You know what is hidden and what is manifest! I invoke Thee to testify that I have never said so, nor did I ever hear that any of my forefathers had said so! Allāh! You know

---

[1]Shaikh al-Mufid, *Al-Kafi*, Vol. 4, p. 81.

[2]as-Sadūq, *'Uyun Akhbār ar-Ridha*, Vol. 2, p. 226.

the many injustices this nation has committed against us, and this is just one of them..." Then he came to Abul-Salt and said, "O Abdul-Salam! If all people, as some claim, are our slaves, who did we buy them from?" Abul-Salt answered: "You are right, O son of the Messenger of Allāh..." Then the Imām said, "O Abdul-Salam! Do you deny the right which Allāh has allotted for us to be charged with the authority as others deny?" He said, "God forbid! I do acknowledge such right."[1] Abdullāh ibn as-Salt quotes a man from Balkh saying, "I accompanied ar-Ridha (ع) during his trip to Khurasan. One day he ordered preparations for his meal to which he invited all his attendants, blacks and non-blacks, so I said to him, May my life be sacrificed for yours! Maybe these should have a separate eating arrangement.' He said, Allāh Almighty is One; the father (Adam) and the mother (Eve) are the same, and people are rewarded according to their deeds.'"[2] Ibrahim ibn al-Abbās as-Sali is quoted as saying, "I heard 'Ali ibn Mūsa ar-Ridha saying, I swear by emancipation--and whenever I swore by it, I would emancipate one of my slaves till I emancipated each and every one of them--that I do not see myself as better than that (and he pointed to a black slave of his who remained in his service) on account of my kinship to the Messenger of Allāh (ع) except if I do a good deed which would render me better.'"[3] Yasir, one of his servants, said once, "Abul-Hassan said to us once: If I leave the table before you do, while you are still eating, do not leave on my account till you are through.' It may happen that he calls upon some of us to his service and he is told that they are eating, whereupon he says: Leave them to finish their meal first.'" Nadir, another servant, says, "Abul-Hassan did not require us to do anything for him except if we had finished eating our meal."[4]

---

[1]*Ibid.*, Vol. 2, p. 174.

[2]Shaikh al-Mufid, *Al-Kafi*, Vol. 4, p. 23.

[3]as-Sadūq, *'Uyun Akhbār ar-Ridha*, Vol. 2, p. 237.

[4]Shaikh al-Mufid *Al-Kafi*, Vol. 6, p. 298.

There is no doubt that, generally speaking, the Imāms (ع) were more distant than anyone else from the alluring wares of this vanishing world, and most distant from its ornamentations and allurements. But the concept of asceticism according to them was not limited to wearing modest coarse clothes or eating very simple food. Rather, its limits extended beyond that, for the ascetic person is the one who does not allow the pleasures of this world to take control over him without being able to take control of them, one who does not see this world as the ultimate goal he seeks; rather, when it comes towards him, the believer is entitled to enjoy its good things, and when it forsakes him, he contends himself that Allāh's rewards are more lasting.

Al-Ābi is quoted in *Nathr al-Durar* نثر الدرر as saying, "A group of Sufis visited ar-Ridha (ع) when he was in Khurasan, and they said to him, 'The commander of the faithful looked into the authority Allāh Almighty entrusted to him, and he found you, members of the Prophet's Ahl al-Bayt (ع), to be the most deserving of all people to be the leaders. Then he discerned you, members of the Prophet's Ahl al-Bayt (ع), and he found yourself the most worthy of leading the people, so he decided to entrust such leadership to you. The nation is in need of one who wears coarse clothes, eats the most simple food, rides the donkey and visits the sick.' Ar-Ridha (ع) was first leaning on his side, so he sat straight then said, 'Joseph (Yousuf) was a Prophet who used to wear silk mantles brocaded with gold. He sat on the thrones of the Pharaohs and ruled. An Imām is required to be just and fair; when he says something, he says the truth, and when he passes a judgement, he judges equitably, and when he promises something, he fulfills his promise. Allāh did not forbid (an Imām) from wearing a particular type of clothes or eating a particular type of food.' Then he recited the Qur'ānic verse: 'Say: Who has forbidden the beautiful (gifts) of Allāh which He has produced for His servants, and the good things, clean and pure (which He has provided) for sustenance?'"[1]

Imām al-Jawad (ع) was asked once about his view regarding musk.

---

[1] *Kashf al-Ghumma*, Vol. 3, p. 147; Sūrat Al A'raf:32.

He answered: "My father ordered musk to be made for him in a ben tree in the amount of seven hundred dirhams. Al-Fadl ibn Sahl wrote him saying that people criticized him for that. He worte back saying, "O Fadl! Have you not come to know that Joseph (Yousuf), who was a Prophet, used to wear silk clothes brocaded with gold, and that he used to sit on gilded thrones, and that all of that did not decrease any of his wisdom?" Then he ordered a galia moschata (perfume of musk and ambergris) to be made for him in the amount of four thousand dirhams.""[1]

Ibn Abbad tells us the following about Imām ar-Ridha's ascetic conduct: "Ar-Ridha used to sit on a leaf mat during the summer and on a straw sack during the winter; he used to put on coarse clothes, but when he went out to meet the public, he put on his very best."[2] So, when he is by himself, away from public life, his soul finds harmony with denying what is fake, that is, the decorations and allurements of this life. But when he goes out to meet people, he puts on his best for them following their own nature of holding the appearances of this world as significant, enjoying its good things. This realistically ascetic conduct of the Imām provides us with a glorious example of the truth regarding the Ahl al-Bayt (ع) and their pure view of life which is free from any disturbing fake or pretense.

The Imām (ع) tries to cause others to adorn themselves with the same trait of clemency and tolerance upon being wronged as an element of good relationship among them, justifying this by saying that it increases the dignity of man, for clemency and tolerance, when the ability to deal equal blows and effect equal retribution express the power of anger in man and his control over his rash temper upon being challenged, this causes others to respect and venerate such a person especially when that person shoulders the responsibilities of authority. Al-Ābi says:

A man sentenced to be beheaded was brought to al-Ma'mūn while ar-

---

[1]Shaikh al-Mufid, *Al Kafi*, Vol. 6, p. 516.

[2]as-Sadūq, *Uyun Akhbār ar-Ridha*, Vol. 2, p. 178.

Ridha (ﻉ) was among his train. Al-Ma'mūn asked him: Father of al-Hassan! What is your view?' He said, All I can say is that Allāh only increases the dignity of those whose good will causes them to forgive.' He, therefore, forgave the man.[1]

In a dialogue with al-Bazanti, the Imām said, "Anyone who receives a boon is in danger: He has to carry out Allāh's commandments in its regard. By Allāh! Whenever Allāh blesses me with something, I continue to be in extreme apprehension till (and here he made a motion with his hand) I take out some of it and spend it in the way Allāh has ordained in its regard." Al-Bazanti asked him: "May my life be sacrificed for yours! You, in your status of high esteem, fear that much?" He answered: "Yes, indeed! And I praise my Creator for the blessings He bestowed upon me."[2] When in Khurasan, he once distributed his entire wealth to the poor on the day of Arafat, so al-Fadl ibn Sahl said to him: "Now you are bankrupt!" he said, "On the contrary! I am now wealthier than ever. Do not consider trading my wealth for Allāh's rewards and pleasure as bankruptcy."[3] He did not give others in order to buy their affection or friendship; rather, he considered giving with generosity as a good trait whereby man gets nearer to his Maker by including His servants in the wealth with which He blessed him. This is the difference between his method of giving and that of others. Ya'qub ibn Ishāq an-Nawbakhti is quoted as saying,

A man passed by Abul-Hassan and begged him to give him according to the extent of his kindness. He said, "I cannot afford that." So he said, "Then give me according to mine,'" whereupon he ordered his servant to give the man two hundred dinars. [4]

The reason why the Imām abstained from giving the man according

[1] *Kashf al-Ghumma*, Vol. 3, p. 143.

[2] Shaikh al-Mufid, *Al Kafi*, Vol. 3, p. 502.

[3] Ibn al-Maghazili, *Al-Manaqib,* Vol. 4, p. 361.

[4] *Ibid.*, Vol. 2, p. 360.

to the extent of his own kindness, as the man asked him the first time, is probably due to the fact that he simply did not have as much money as he liked to give. As regarding his own affection towards the poor and the indigent, and his way of looking after them, Mu'ammar ibn Khallad narrates this anecdote:

Whenever Abul-Hassan ar-Ridha (ﻉ) was about to eat his meal, he would bring a large platter and select the choicest food on the table and put on it, then he would order it to be given away to the poor. After that he would recite the following verse: "But he hath made no haste on the path that is steep" (Qur'ān, 90:11). After that, he would say, "Allāh, the Exalted and the Sublime, knows that not everyone has the ability to free a slave; nevertheless, He found means for them to achieve Paradise (by feeding others)."[1]

Thus does the Imām sense the weight of deprivation under which the poor moan and groan; therefore, he shares his best food with them in response to the call of humanity and kindness and in harmony with the spirit of the message with which Allāh entrusted him. Al-Bazanti tells the story of a letter Imām ar-Ridha (ﻉ) once wrote to his son (later Imām) Abū Ja'far (ﻉ) which personifies the generosity and spirit of giving deeply rooted in the hearts of the Prophet's Ahl al-Bayt (ﻉ); he says: "I read the letter of Abul-Hassan Imām ar-Ridha (ﻉ) to Abū Ja'far which said, O Abū Ja'far! I have heard that when you ride, the servants take you out of the city through its small gate. This is due to their being miser so that nobody would ask you for something. I plead to you by the right I have upon you that every time you enter into or get out of the city, you should do so through its large gate, and when you ride, take gold and silver with you, and every time you are asked, you should give. If any of your uncles asks you for something, you should give him no less than fifty dinars, and you yourself may determine the maximum amount you would like to give; and if any of your aunts asks you for something, do not give her less than twenty-five dinars, and it is up to you to determine the maximum amount. I only desire that Allāh raises your status; therefore, keep giving away and do not fear that the Lord of

---

[1]as-Sadūq, *'Uyun Akhbār ar-Ridha*, Vol. 2, p. 264.

the Throne will ever throw you into poverty.'"[1] Yasir, one of the Imām's servants, narrates saying that the Imām's attendants were eating some fruit one day and they were throwing away a good portion of it uneaten. Abul-Hassan (ع) said to them: "Praise be to Allāh! If you have eaten to your fill, there are many who have not; so, you should feed them of it instead."[2] Sulaiman ibn Ja'far al-Jufi is quoted as saying, "I was in the company of ar-Ridha (ع) trying to take care of some personal business of my own when I wanted to go home. He said to me, Come with me and spend the night over my house.' So I went with him and he entered his house shortly before sunset. He noticed that his attendants were working with clay, probably mending stables, and there was a black man among them. He asked them, What is this man doing with you?' They said, He is helping us, and we will pay him something.' He asked, Did you come to an agreement with him regarding his wages?' They said, No. He will accept whatever we pay him.' He, thereupon, started whipping them and showing signs of extreme anger. I said to him, May my life be sacrificed for yours! Why are you so angry?' He said, I have forbidden them so many times from doing something like that and ordered them not to employ anyone before coming to an agreement with him regarding his wages. You know that nobody would work for you without an agreed upon wage. If you do not, and then you pay him three times as much as you first intended to pay him, he would still think that you underpaid him. But if you agree on the wage, he will praise you for fulfilling your promise and for paying him according to your agreement, and then if you give him a little bit more, he would recognize it and notice that you increased his pay."[3] Al-Bazanti is quoted as saying,

Ar-Ridha (ع) had one of his donkeys sent to convey me to his residence, so I came to the town and stayed with a dignitary for a part of the night, and we both had our supper together, then he ordered my bed to be prepared. A Tiberian pillow, a Caesarian sheet, and a Merv

[1] *Ibid.*, Vol. 2, p. 8.

[2] Shaikh al-Mufid, *Al-Kafi*, Vol. 6, p. 297.

[3] *Ibid.*, Vol. 5, p. 288.

blanket were brought to me. Having eaten my supper, he asked me, "Would you like to retire?"' I said, "Yes, may my life be sacrificed for yours." So he put the sheet and the blanket over me and said, "May Allāh make you sleep in good health," and we were on the rooftop. When he went down, I told myself that I had achieved a status with that man nobody else had attained before. It was then when I heard someone calling my name, but I did not recognize the voice till one of his (ar-Ridha's) servants came to me. He said, "Come meet my master;" so I went down and he came towards me, asked me for my hand to shake and he shook it with a squeeze, saying, "The Commander of the Faithful, Allāh's peace be with him, came once to visit Sa'sa'ah ibn Sawhan, and when it was time to leave, he advised Sa'sa'ah not to boast about his visit to him but to look after himself instead for he seemed to be about to depart from this world and that worldly hopes do not do a dying man any good, and he greeted him a great deal as he bid him good-bye."[1]

We can clearly be acquainted with the negative stance of Ahl al-Bayt (ع) towards their rulers by examining what al-Hassan ibn al-Hussain al-Anbari tells us about Imām Abul-Hassan ar-Ridha (ع). Says he, "I continued writing him for fourteen years asking his permission that I accept a job in the service of the sultan. At the conclusion of the last letter which I wrote him, I stated the fact that I was fearing for my life because the sultan was accusing me of being a *Rafidi* and that he did not doubt that the reason why I declined from working for him was due to my being a Rafidi. So Abul-Hassan wrote me saying, I have comprehended the contents of your letters and what you stated regarding your life being in jeopardy. If you know that should you accept the job, you would behave according to the commands of the Messenger of Allāh (ع) and your assistants and clerks would be followers of your faith, and if you use the gain you receive to help needy believers till you become their equal, then one deed will offset another; otherwise, do not.'"[2].

---

[1]*Qurb al-Isnad*, p. 222, and *Al-Kharaij wal Jaraih*, p. 237, with a slight textual variation.

[2]Shaikh al-Mufid, *Al-Kafi,* Vol. 5, p. 111.

The author of *Al-Ghaiba* الغيبة quotes al-Hassan ibn al-Hassan (al-Hassan II) saying, "I said to Abul-Hassan Mūsa (ع) once, Can I ask you a question?' He answered, You must rather ask your own Imām.' I inquired, What do you mean? I do not know of any Imām other than your own self.' He said, He is my son 'Ali to whom I gave my title (of Imām).' I said, Master! Please help me save myself from Hellfire! Abū Abdullāh (ع) had said that you yourself are the Qā'im, the caretaker of this issue.' He said, Was I not?' Then he added, O Hassan! No Imām preaches to a nation except when he is their Qā'im; so, when he leaves them (i.e. dies), his successor will be the Qā'im and the Hujja (Proof) till he too leaves. We (the Imāms) are all Qā'ims; therefore, from now on, redirect all your dealings to my son 'Ali, for by Allāh do I swear twice that I did not do that on my own accord but Allāh did out of His love for him.'"[1]

The Imām did his best to emphasize the error of that concept and how it collided with the reality by continuously stating that the Imāmate after his demise would be the responsibility of his son 'Ali, and he even made a number of his followers and family testify to it. For example, Haider ibn Ayyub says, "We were in Medīna at Quba, where we used to meet Muhammed ibn Zaid ibn Ali. He (the latter) came to us one day much later than anticipated, so we asked him what caused him to be so late. He said, Abū Ibrahim (Imām ar-Ridha [ع]) invited seventeen of our men, all descendants of Ali and Fatima, Allāh's blessings be upon both of them, and he required us to bear witness to his will and testimony that his son Ali would be his successor and representative during the remainder of his own life and after his demise.' Then Muhammed ibn Zaid said, By Allāh, O Haider! He has today tied the knot of Imāmate for him, and the Shī'as will accept him as the Imām after his father's demise.'"[2] Abdullāh ibn al-Harith said, "Abū Ibrahim called us to his presence and we responded. He said, Do you know why I have gathered you all here?' We answered in the negative. He said, Bear witness that this Ali, my son, is my regent, the executor of my will, and my

---

[1]Shaikh at-Tusi, *Al-Ghaiba*, p. 29.

[2]as-Sadūq, *Uyun Akhbār ar-Ridha*, Vol. 1, p. 28.

successor after me; whoever entrusted me with anything, let him take it back from him, and whoever insisted on seeking audience with me, let him obtain his written approval first.'"[1] Abdul-Rahman ibn al-Hajjaj is quoted as saying that Abul-Hassan Mūsa ibn Ja'far (ع) had nominated his son Ali for the Imāmate and wrote a statement to this effect in the presence of sixty witnesses from among the most distinguished dignitaries of Medīna.[2]

There are many narratives narrated by some advocates and inventors of Waqfism الوقفية أو الواقفة (*Waqfiyya* or *Waaqifa*) which clearly prove to us their false claims. For example, Ziyad ibn Marwan al-Qandi narrates the following:

Once I visited Abū Ibrahim, and his son Ali was with him. He said to me, "O Ziyad! His statements (referring to his son) are as good as mine, his speech is like my speech, and his instructions are as binding as mine."[3]

Ahmed ibn Muhammed al-Maithami, a Waqfi, says, "Muhammed ibn Isma'eel ibn al-Fadl al-Hashimi told me the following: I visited Abul-Hassan Mūsa ibn Ja'far (ع) when he was suffering from an acute illness. I asked him: If the matter regarding which I pray Allāh that it would not happen (Imām's death) comes to pass, who shall we follow?' He said, My son Ali; his writing is as though I wrote it, and he is my regent and successor after me.'"[4]

Ghannam ibn al-Qasim is quoted as saying, "Mansūr ibn Younus Barzaj told me that he had visited Abul-Hassan, that is, Mūsa ibn Ja'far (ع), and he said to him, Have you come to know what new undertaking I have undertaken today?' He answered in the negative,

---

[1]*Ibid.*, p. 27.

[2]*Ibid.*, p. 28.

[3]Shaikh al-Mufid, *Al-Kafi*, Vol. 1, p. 381; also al-Mufid's *Al-Irshad*, p. 286.

[4]Shaikh al-Mufid, *Uyun Akhbār ar-Ridha*, Vol. 1, p. 20.

so the Imām said, I have appointed my son Ali as my regent and successor after me; so, entered the room and congratulate him and tell him that I ordered you to do so.' He, therefore, entered Ali's room and congratulated him and informed him that his father had ordered him to do so, but al-Mansūr reneged after that, and he even confiscated the funds (of Muslims) entrusted to him."[1]

There is another stance for the Imām which is not without an exciting moment involving one of the main advocates of Waqfism. His stance was like a clear warning to those who created the controversy of this "sect" and promoted it; al-Bata'ini states the following:

I said to Abul-Hassan, "Your father had informed us of his successor, and we wish you could inform us of yours." So he took my hand and shook it, then he recited the verse: "Allāh will not mislead people after He had guided them, in order that He may make clear to them what to fear (and avoid)."[2]

The recitation of that verse came almost like a prophecy about the future of what that person and his friends would do and how they would fall into the slippery paths of misguidance; therefore, he shook his hand and recited a verse which predicted that those folks' deviation would take place after proof had been made manifest against them. The Imām, as a matter of fact, referred clearly to the Waqfi movement after him and even recited the epitaph of the faith of those who advocated Waqfism in a narrative transmitted by Muhammed ibn Sinan who says,

I visited Abul-Hassan one year before he was transported to Iraq, and his son was with him. He called upon me to be attentive, and I responded. Then he said, "There will be a movement this year..., but do not let it bother you." Then he lowered his head contemplating, picking the ground. Then he raised his head and recited this verse:

---

[1] al-Kashi's *Rijal*, p. 398.

[2] al-'Ayyashi, *Tafsir*, Vol. 2, p. 115 where verse 115 of Sūrat al Tawba is discussed.

"Allāh leads the oppressors astray and does whatever He pleases" (Qur'ān, 14:27). I said, "And what is that, may my life be sacrificed for yours?" He said, "Anyone who denies the right of this son of mine and refuses to recognize his Imāmate after me will be equal to one who denied the right of Ali ibn Abū Talib (ع) and did not recognize his Imāmate after Muhammed (ص)." So I understood that he was implying that his death was near, and that he was appointing his son as his successor.[1]

The Imām (ع) was briefly contemporary to ar-Rashīd 's regime during which he suffered the tragedy of the assassination of his father Imām Mūsa al-Kādhim (ع) and other Alawides. After the murder of his father, he was not safe from the schemes of some of those who flattered the rulers, followed their course, and pretended to show their loyalty by instigating enmity against the regime's opponents, encouraging their elimination, thinking that that would increase the rulers' liking for them and nearness to them, that it would strengthen their position, grant them unique distinctions, and raise them to the highest pinnacles.

Ja'far ibn Yahya says, "I heard asa ibn Ja'far say to Harūn (ar-Rashīd) upon leaving ar-Riqqa for Mecca, Remember your oath by the dignity of the descendants of Abū Talib that: should anyone after Mūsa (al-Kādhim [ع]) claim to be the Imām, you would strike his head with the sword. This Ali, his son, claims so, and people are addressing him in the same way they used to address his father.' He looked at him angrily and said, Why? Do you expect me to eliminate each and every one of them?'" Mūsa ibn Mahran says that when he heard Ja'far ibn Yahya say so, he went to him (i.e. to Imām ar-Ridha) and told him what he had heard. Ar-Ridha (ع) responded by saying, "What do I have to do with them? By Allāh, they cannot hurt me in the least."

Such instigation was not confined within a reasonable limit but went beyond it to where instigation might cause ar-Rashīd to pay serious attention, for the Barmakis were most antagonistic towards the

---

[1]as-Sadūq, 'Uyun Akhbār ar-Ridha, Vol. 1, p. 32.

Descendants of the Prophet (ص) and the most cruel among them in their grudge, so much so that it is reported that Yahya ibn Khalid al-Barmaki was the one who ordered Imām Mūsa ibn Ja'far (ع) to be murdered[1] when the Abbāside caliphate was under their mercy.[2] Imām ar-Ridha (ع) rendered Allāh's retribution against the Barmakis to their persecution and oppression the worst of which was suffered by Imām al-Kādhim (ع).[3] Suffices for proof is the fact that Yahya ibn Khalid was the one who plotted the ugly plot against Imām al-Kādhim (ع) after causing Harūn ar-Rashīd to be angry with him, instigating ar-Rashīd against the Imām (ع) and using some simpleton weaklings among the Alawides to achieve his goal.[4]

Finally, ar-Rashīd is surrounded by a large number of courtiers instigating him to kill Imām ar-Ridha (ع), and they succeeded in stirring his feelings against the Imām (ع). Abul-Salt al-Harawi narrates saying that one day he was sitting with the Imām (ع) at his house when a messenger from Harūn ar-Rashīd came in and ordered the Imām (ع) to present himself before the caliph. The Imām (ع) said, "O Abul-Salt! He does not call upon me at such time of the night except for trouble. By Allāh! He cannot do anything which I hate to me because of what I had come to know of certain statements said by my grandfather the Messenger of Allāh (ع)." Abul-Salt continues his narrative to say that he accompanied the Imām (ع) as he entered Harūn ar-Rashīd 's court. When the latter looked at him, ar-Ridha (ع) recited a certain supplication by the Prophet (ص). When the Imām (ع) stood before ar-Rashīd , the latter looked carefully at him and then said, "O Abul-Hassan! We have ordered a hundred thousand dirhams for you; write down of all your family's needs." When the Imām (ع) left the court, the caliph kept looking at him as he was leaving and said behind his back: "I wished

---

[1] as-Sadūq, 'Uyun Akhbār ar-Ridha, Vol. 2, p. 226.

[2] 'Umdat at-Talib, p. 185, 1st edition (Najaf, Iraq).

[3] al-Majlisi, Bihār al-Anwār, Vol. 48, p. 249.

[4] Shaikh at-Tusi, Al-Ghaiba, p. 22.

something, and Allāh wished otherwise, and what Allāh wished was good." Thus did Allāh save the life of the Imām (ع) who sought refuge with Him, seeking His assistance through the sincere words which he had come to know that his grandfather the Messenger of Allāh (ع) had articulated. Ar-Rashīd , on the other hand, went back to himself satisfied after destiny had opposed his vicious intention just to realize that what Allāh had done was, indeed, better than what he himself had intended to do.

Safwan ibn Yahya is quoted as saying, "When Abul-Hassan Mūsa (ع) passed away and ar-Ridha (ع) started preaching his mission, we were worried about his life (ar-Ridha's) and we said to him, You have declared something of great magnanimity, and we worry about your safety because of this tyrant.' He said, Let him try his best, for he shall not have the means to hurt me.'"[1] Muhammed ibn Sinan said, "During Harūn's reign, I said to Abul-Hassan ar-Ridha (ع), You have made yourself well-known because of this matter and followed in the footsteps of your father while Haroun's sword is dripping with blood.' He said, What made me bold in this regard is that the Messenger of Allāh (ع) had said, If Abū Jahl harms even one hair on my head, then bear witness that I am not a Prophet at all,' and I tell you that if Harūn took one hair away from my head, then bear witness that I am not an Imām at all.'"[2]

Some Waqfis tried to warn him against declaring himself as the Imām (ع) and openly acting as such, and he told them that such a matter did not require a warning, and that the fear that Harūn might hurt him was groundless. Those individuals had only one objective in mind: to discourage ar-Ridha (ع) from making his Imāmate public so that they might be able to promote their "sect" which claimed that the Qā'im was Imām Mūsa ibn Ja'far (ع) and that he was still alive as we mentioned above. Let us review the dialogue between the Imām (ع) and some of those Waqfis. Abū Masrooq has stated the

---

[1] Shaikh al-Mufid, *Al-Kafi*, Vol. 1, p. 487. It is also mentioned in as-Sadūq's book *'Uyun Akhbār ar-Ridha*, in *Al-Manaqib*, and in *Al-Irshad*.

[2] *Rawdat al-Kafi*, p. 257.

following:

"A group of Waqfis entered the house of the Imām (ع) once and among them were men like Abū Hamzah al-Bata'ini, Muhammed ibn Ishāq ibn Ammar, al-Hussain ibn Umran, and al-Hussain ibn Abū Sa'd al-Makari. Ali ibn Abū Hamzah said to him, "May my life be sacrificed for you! Tell us how your father is doing." He said, "He, peace be with him, passed away." He said, "Who did he recommend to succeed him?" He answered, "Myself." He said, "You are claiming something which none among your forefathers claimed, starting from Ali ibn Abū Talib downwards." He said, "It was said by the best of my forefathers and the most distinguished among them: the Messenger of Allāh (ع)." He asked, "Do not you fear for your safety?" He said, "Had I worried about my safety, I would have been in a position to do something to protect myself. The Messenger of Allāh (ع) was approached once by Abū Lahab who threatened him; the Messenger of Allāh (ع) said to him: If I am scratched by you even slightly, then I am, indeed, a liar.' That was the first time the Messenger of Allāh (ع) instigated someone, and this is the first time I do likewise and tell you that if I am scratched by Harūn even slightly, then I am, indeed, a liar." Hussain ibnMahran said to him, "If this comes to pass, then we will have achieved our objective." He said, "What do you exactly want? Should I go to Harūn and tell him that I am the Imām (ع) and that he is nobody? This is not how the Messenger of Allāh behaved at the onset of his mission; rather, he said so to his fāmily and followers and those whom he trusted from among the public. You believe that Imāmate belongs to my father, claiming that what stops me from admitting that my father is alive is my own fear. I do not fear you when I say to you that I am the Imām; so, how can I fear you if my father is, indeed, alive?"[1]

The Imām's expectation proved to be true; Ar-Rashīd breathed his last without hurting the Imām (ع) in the least.

---

[1]Sayyid Muhsin al-Amin, *A'yan ash-Shī'a* أعيان الشيعة, Vol. 4, Part I, p. 138.

As regarding the Imām's life during al-Amin's reign, we cannot recount any incident regarding the government's stance towards Imām ar-Ridha (ع), and this may be attributed to the confusing environment in which the Abbāside caliphate found itself due to internal dissents which led in the end to a serious split among the members of the ruling dynasty. Such split which was caused by al-Amin who deposed his brother al-Ma'mūn from the post of heir to the throne and the nomination of his son, Mūsa, in his place after listening to the advice of al-Fadl ibn ar-Rabi'' who had a personal vendetta against al-Ma'mūn and who feared him for his post should he become the caliph instead, since he had already opposed him openly.[1]

There is disagreement regarding caliph al-Amin's school of thought. Some think that he was Shī'a, while others think that he only pretended to be so out of his concern for Imām ar-Ridha's feelings and for those of other Alawides while in reality he was otherwise. But his discourses, debates, and his serious method whereby he challenged what was regarded as accepted facts by those who opposed his views dispel any doubts regarding his acceptance of Shī'aism. Moreover, there are certain noteworthy measures which he undertook supporting this view such as his belief that the Holy Qur'ān was the Word of Allāh created by Him, and his insistence that scholars and faqihs should indicate and promote this view, so much so that he stirred quite a reaction among contemporary Islamic circles to the extent that it was referred to as "the Holy Qur'ān's ordeal." His father, ar-Rashīd , differed from him in this regard. When he heard that Bishr al-Marisi endorsed the concept that the Holy Qur'ān was created by Allāh, he said, "If I ever lay my hand on him, I shall strike his neck with the sword."[2] Also, he believed in the temporary marriage of mut'a, and he refuted the views of the second caliph in this regard with arguments which have already been recorded by leading historians.

---

[1] Ibn al-Atheer, *At-Tarikh al-Kāmil* Vol. 5, p. 138.

[2] as-Sayyūti, *Tarikh al-Khulafa'*, p. 284.

Add to all this his preference of Ali ibn Abū Talib (ع) over all other companions of the Prophet (ص) and his view that Ali was more worthy of succeeding the Messenger of Allāh (ص) as the caliph. Yet another supporting argument is his serious attempt to make the cursing of Mu'awiyah a tradition and enforce it on his subjects; he announced to people once the following:

There shall be no pardon for anyone guilty of praising Mu'awiyah, and the best of creation after the Prophet (ص) is Ali ibn Abū Talib (ع).[1]

That was in response to Mu'awiyah who made the cursing of Ali a tradition which continued throughout the reign of all Umayyad rulers till the days of caliph Omer ibn Abdul-Aziz who put an end to it in order to safeguard the government of the Umayyads against the disgust people felt towards such an abominable tradition. He sympathized with the Alawides, and returned Fedak to them.

Al-Ma'mūn, in fact, sincerely felt guilty about the crimes committed by his predecessors against the Alawides as a letter he wrote to some Hashemites testified as stated above wherein he said, "The Umayyads killed anyone (among the Alawides) who unsheathed a sword, while we, the Abbāsides, have been killing them en masse; so, ask the great souls of the Hashemites what sin they committed, and ask those who were buried in Baghdad and Kūfa alive..."[2]

Al-Ma'mūn's inclination towards Shaism is the result of many factors of a permanent impact upon his way of thinking, starting with his childhood when a Shī'a educator planted deeply in his soul the allegiance to Ali and the family of Ali (ع), and ending with his residence in parts of Khurasan where mostly Shī'as lived. Al-Ma'mūn himself narrated an anecdote with a moral which taught him to sympathize with Shī'as. It involved an encounter with his

---

[1]*Ibid.*, p. 308.

[2]Al-Majlisi, *Bihār al-Anwār*, Vol. 49, p. 210 as quoted in Ibn Maskawayhi's book *Nadam al-Farid*.

father ar-Rashīd who was very well known for his cruelty, tyranny, arrogance and hatred of the Alawides, especially Imām Mūsa ibn Ja'far (ع) whom he poisoned. Al-Ma'mūn states that when Imām Mūsa ibn Ja'far (ع) met ar-Rashīd at Medīna, ar-Rashīd showed a great deal of humbleness before him and a great deal of respect to a degree which attracted his own attention; so, he continues to say, "When there was nobody else present, I said, O commander of the faithful! Who is this man whom you have held with such high esteem, respected a great deal, stood up to receive, and even seated in the most prominent place while seating yourself in front of him, and you even ordered us to hold the rein of his horse?!' He said, 'This is the Imām of the people, the Proof of Allāh's Mercy to His creation (Hujjatullah) and His caliph among His servants.' I asked, O commander of the faithful! Are not all these attributes yours and fulfilled in your person?' He replied, I am the Imām of the masses by force and through oppression, while Mūsa ibn Ja'far (ع) is the Imām in truth. By Allāh, son, he is more worthy of being the successor of the Messenger of Allāh (ع) as the caliph than I am and anyone else among the people! By Allāh! If you yourself attempt to take such caliphate from me, I shall take it away from you even if that means gouging your eyes, for power is blind!'"[1]

Harūn ar-Rashīd was still not satisfied till he divided the domains of the state into three sections, granting al-Amin authority over Iraq and Syria up to the end of his western possessions; to al-Ma'mūn he gave the territories from Hamadan up to the eastern borders of his domains; to al-Qasim he gave the peninsula, the sea ports, and the metropolises after having secured the oath of allegiance for him after his brother al-Ma'mūn and giving him the option to keep or depose al-Ma'mūn.[2] Thus, ar-Rashīd thought, the ghost of dissension would be averted, and the government after his death would be secured for all his sons since he gave each one of them a portion thereof whereby he would maintain a force strong enough to deter the aggression of the other.

---

[1]as-Sadūq, *'Uyun Akhbār ar-Ridha*, Vol. 1, p. 88.

[2]*Ibid.*, p. 112.

People predicted ominous consequences because of what ar-Rashīd had done. Some of them said that he sowed the seeds of evil and war among his sons.[1] Some wise men said that he caused them to fall into an inner conflict the perils of which victimized the subjects.[2] The conflict among the two brothers was worsened by the instigation of some top rank politicians in each party. On one hand, we find al-Fadl ibn ar-Rabi'', who caused the army to renege on its sworn promise of support for al-Ma'mūn in Khurasan as soon as ar-Rashīd died, marched to Baghdad in order to strengthen al-Amin's position, trying to aggravate the tension between al-Amin and his brother al-Ma'mūn, instigating the first to nullify the allegiance to al-Ma'mūn and change it to his son Mūsa, depending in so doing on various means of instigation which in the end pushed al-Amin to attack his brother. Al-Fadl, by doing so, was trying to get rid of al-Ma'mūn as the regent for fear that should he come to rule, he would certainly seek revenge against him due to his going back on his promise to support al-Ma'mūn whom he slighted and the oath of allegiance to whom he violated.[3]

Al-Irshād narrates that al-Ma'mūn discussed the subject of regency with ar-Ridha (ع), saying, "I have decided that you should be my successor." The Imām said, "Exempt me from that, O commander of the faithful, for I have neither the ability nor the strength for that." He said, "I have decided that you should be my successor." The Imām said, "Exempt me from that, O commander of the faithful." Al-Ma'mūn responded with a statement which was more of a threat than anything else; he said to him: "Omer ibn al-Khattab entrusted six persons to consult regarding the caliphate; one of them was your grandfather, Ali ibn Abū Talib (ع), and he preconditioned that anyone who went against their decision should be executed; therefore, you will have to accept what I have decreed for you, for I

---

[1]Ibn al-Atheer, *At-Tarikh al-Kāmil*, Vol. 5, p. 113.

[2]as-Sayyuti, *Tarikh al-Khulafa*, p. 290.

[3]Ibn al-Atheer, *At-Tarikh al-Kāmil*, Vol. 5, p. 138.

see no way that I can ever change my mind."[1]

The Imām (ع), therefore, had to agree.[2] It is also narrated that a lengthy discussion went on between both men in which al-Ma'mūn offered the Imām to be the caliph and the Imām refused to accept, then he offered him the regency and he again refused, so al-Ma'mūn said to him, "You always say what I hate to hear, and you think that you are safe from my might; therefore, I swear by Allāh that you should either accept the regency willingly or I shall force you to do so; therefore, accept out of your own will; otherwise, I shall certainly strike your neck with the sword."[3]

What proves the fact that al-Ma'mūn was not serious in his offer to the Imām to be the regent is a narration stating that al-Fadl an-Nawbakhti, who was an astronomer believed to be a Shī'a, wanted to test al-Ma'mūn's intentions, so he wrote him saying, "The order of the stars indicates that naming ar-Ridha (ع) as the regent at this time cannot be done; otherwise, the person named will suffer a catastrophe. Therefore, if al-Ma'mūn's intentions agree with what he proclaims in public, he ought to postpone this matter till a more opportune time." To this, al-Ma'mūn warned him against discouraging Thul-Riyasatayn from contracting that agreement at that time, and that if he did not, he would know that the postponement was instigated by an-Nawbakhti. He also ordered him to return his own letter back to him so that nobody else would come to find out about it. He then came to know that al-Fadl was aware of the fact that time was not ripe for contracting the regency because he himself had knowledge of the science of the stars; therefore, an-Nawbakhti feared that the change of mind of al-Fadl ibn Sahl was because of him personally, and he would thus be killed by al-Ma'mūn, so he rode to him and convinced him through his own

---

[1] al-Mufid, *Kitab al-Irshad*, p. 290. Abul-Faraj al-Isfahani, *Maqatil at-Talibiyyeen*, p. 375.

[2] al-Isfahani, *Maqatil at-Talibiyyeen*, p. 375.

[3] as-Sadūq, *Ilal ash-Shara'i* علل الشرائع, p. 266.

knowledge of astronomy that time was indeed ripe for it, contrary to the reality, because he was more knowledgeable than him in astrology, and he kept confusing him till he finally convinced him.[1]

Having failed to convince the Imām that he would abdicate the throne for him, al-Ma'mūn requested him to accept to be the regent and to name him the succeeding caliph after him, but the Imām again insisted on refusing, so much so that al-Ma'mūn had to seek the assistance of some of his best aides despite the fact that they themselves were not convinced that it was such a good idea, thinking that al-Ma'mūn was serious. In his book titled *Kitab Al-Irshād*, Shaikh al-Mufid states the following:

"A group of historians and court biographers who were contemporary to the [Abbāside] caliphs say that when al-Ma'mūn wanted to name Ali ibn Mūsa (ع) as his successor, and having thought seriously about the matter, he ordered al-Fadl ibn Sahl to come to him and he informed him of his intention, ordering him to seek the assistance of his brother al-Hassan ibn Sahl[2] in this regard, and he did just that. So they met with him, and al-Hassan kept pointing out the magnanimity of the consequences of his suggestion, acquainting him with the outcomes resulting from taking his family out of it and affecting his own life. Al-Ma'mūn, thereupon, said to him: "I pledged to Allāh that if I lay my hand on the person who deposed me, I would hand the caliphate over to the best person among the progeny of Abū Talib, and I do not know anyone better than this man on the face of earth." So, when both al-Fadl and al-

---

[1] as-Sadūq, `Uyun Akhbār ar-Ridha*, Vol. 2, P. 148.

[2] It appears that al-Hassan ibn Sahl was al-Ma'mun's ruler over Iraq at that time, and we cannot explain why the name of al-Hassan is mentioned in this story except in the case al-Ma'mun had called him to meet with him to consult regarding the issue of selecting Imām ar-Ridha (ع) as the regent as presumes Sayyid Muhsin al-Amin in his encyclopedic work titled *A'yan ash-Shī'a*. But al-Fadl's letter to his brother al-Hassan regarding regency, as Ibn al-Atheer and at-Tabari and other historians indicate, negates all that, and the addition may have been the action of the narrator who was ignorant of all of that, thus causing a major problem afflicting narratives.

Hassan saw his determination to carry out this matter, they stopped opposing him and he sent them to ar-Ridha (ع). They offered him the position, but he refused to accept it, and they continued pressing him till he finally agreed, so they went back to al-Ma'mūn and told him about his approval whereupon he was very pleased."[1]

Abul-Faraj al-Isfahani stated something similar to the above with this variation: "He dispatched them to Ali ibn Mūsa ar-Ridha (ع) and they offered it to him, and they continued pressing him while he was refusing till one of them said to him, If you agree, let it be so, but if you do not, we shall surely harm you,' and he threatened to kill him. Then one of them said, By Allāh he ordered me to strike your neck with my sword if you go against his wish.'"[2]

Imām ar-Ridha (ع) knew beforehand about al-Ma'mūn's intentions through his knowledgeable foresight of the circumstances which led al-Ma'mūn to vest the regency upon him, and he was contented that he would not actually accede to the throne in the future. Al-Madaini quotes one of his sources saying, "When ar-Ridha (ع) was seated during the regency celebration, with the orators and poets surrounding him and the flags fanning him, one individual who was present there and then said, I was close to him that day, and he looked at me and noticed my optimistic smile regarding the event, so he beckoned for me to come close. When I did, he said the following to me while nobody except me could hear him: Do not let this excite you, and do not be overly optimistic, for it will never materialize.'"[3]

Al-Ma'mūn was not satisfied with all of that; he went ahead and subjected the Imām (ع) to a strict surveillance whereby he was closely watching all his movements, and he indirectly restricted his contacts with others; ar-Rayyan ibn as-Salt narrates the following:

---

[1] al-Mufid, *Al-Irshad*, p. 291.

[2] al-Isfahani, *Maqatil at-Talibiyyeen*, p. 375.

[3] al-Mufid, *Kitab Al-Irshad*, p. 291.

"Hisham ibn Ibrahim ar-Rashīd i was the closest person to ar-Ridha (ع) before he was taken to the caliph's palace, and he was a courteous and brilliant scholar. Ar-Ridha's contacts used to be transacted through him and under his supervision, and he used to collect all monies on his behalf before he, Abul-Hassan, was taken away. When he was taken away to the palace, Hisham ibn Ibrahim contacted Thul-Riyasatayn and he tried his best to win his favour and started informing him and al-Ma'mūn about ar-Ridha's movements, thus he won their confidence and did not conceal anything regarding the Imām (ع) from them. Al-Ma'mūn, therefore, appointed him as the Imām's chamberlain, and nobody could have audience with the Imām (ع) except those whom he liked, and he enforced a tight surveillance on the Imām (ع), so much so that none of his supporters could reach him without Hisham's approval, and he used to inform al-Ma'mūn and Thul-Riyasatayn of anything and everything ar-Ridha (ع) said at home."[1]

What prompted al-Ma'mūn to take such a harsh measure was his great apprehension that the Alawides, who predominated Khurasan, encouraged and directed by the Imām (ع), might move topple his government.

Having evaluated the general status of the political policies of his government, which were surrounded by tumultuous events starting with Baghdad going back against its promise of support to him and passing by the Shī'a Alawide throngs surrounding his base of government in Khurasan and ending with the Alawide rebellions in Iraq, Hijaz and Yemen, al-Ma'mūn thought of curing this weak point by a brilliantly acceptable political move which would be something to divert the attention of the Alawides and the Shī'a residents of Khurasan and, at the same time, constituting a terrible threat to the Abbāside masses in Baghdad. All such measures, he hoped, would strengthen his influence and help him control all parties involved. This could not be accomplished without naming Imām Ali ibn Mūsa ar-Ridha (ع) as the successor to the throne. And so it happened; the caliph sent letters to the Imām (ع) ordering him to go to Merv. The

---

[1]as-Sadūq, *Uyun Akhbār ar-Ridha*, Vol. 2, p. 153.

Imām (ع) refused, and a great deal of correspondence ensured between both men till al-Ma'mūn finally convinced him to go there, sending a special force to escort him which included al-Dhahhak, or, according to al-Mufid and Abul Faraj al-Isfahani, al-Jalladi. History books do not say much about that trip except small bits and pieces which do not provide us with a clear vision of its nature and mission.

Al-Ma'mūn had already ordered his messenger to take a group of dignitaries who were descendants of Abū Talib to the Basra highway, then to al-Ahwaz and Persia, keeping in mind that the alternate route, which was Kūfa-al-Jabal-Kerman Shah-Qum, was mostly inhabited by Shī'as and it has their strongholds, and they might be carried away by their enthusiasm upon finding out that the Imām (ع) was among them and might decide to keep him there and thus involve the government in dangerous consequences which might cause its weakening and collapse.

When he entered Nishapur[1], he stayed at a neighbourhood called al-Qazwani where there were crowds of pigeons, the pigeons which they call today ar-Ridha (ع) pigeons, and there was a spring there the water of which had receded, so he hired workers who repaired it till its water became plentiful. He had a pool built on its outside where stairs were also built according to his instructions leading to the low level of the spring water, so the Imām (ع) went down, made his ablution, came out and said his prayers on the outside.

The Imām (ع) continued his trip till he finally reached Merv where al-Ma'mūn had prepared a comfortable place for him, surrounding him with respect and. It was then that al-Ma'mūn started to execute the plan which he had plotted for the regency.

Having been convinced to accept, the Imām (ع) said to al-Ma'mūn: "I also agree not to name anyone in a post nor remove anyone from a post, that I do not cancel any decree or custom, and to remain as an

---

[1]Founded in the third century A.D. by king Shapur I, Naishapur was a major cultural center under the Seljuks. It is the town where Omer al-Khayyam was born and buried.

266

advisor." The caliph agreed.[1]

In another encounter, al-Ma'mūn tried to press the Imām (ع) into participating in the state affairs. Mu'ammar ibn Khallad said that Abul-Hassan ar-Ridha (ع) had said to him, "Al-Ma'mūn said to me, O father of al-Hassan! You may suggest the names of some individuals whom you trust to be governors of the areas where corruption is manifest,' and I said to him, If you honour your part of the agreement, I shall certainly honour mine. I agreed to what I agreed on the condition that I do not issue orders nor overrule others, nor depose anyone nor appoint anyone, nor do I go anywhere except wherever Allāh sends me. By Allāh! Caliphate is something which I never desired, and I used to live in Medīna where I would go traverse its alleys on the back of my animal, and when its residents or others asked me to do them a favour, I would do them a favour, and thus they become like my own uncles. My letters still carry weight in various lands, and you have not increased me in the least in whatever blessing Allāh has bestowed upon me.' So he said, I shall honour it.'"[2]

One of the manifestations of the inaugural regency ceremony was the Eid prayers which al-Ma'mūn insisted that the Imām (ع) should conduct in person because he himself had caught a very bad cold, or he may have had another excuse. Al-Irshād quotes Ali ibn Ibrahim who, in turn, quotes Yasir the servant and ar-Rayyan ibn as-Salt saying that when the Eid approached, and ar-Ridha (ع) had already been named as the caliph's successor, al-Ma'mūn invited him to ride to the place where the occasion was to be celebrated and to lead the congregational prayers and deliver the sermon. Ar-Ridha (ع) sent him word saying, "You know what terms exist between both of us; so, please exempt me from conducting the prayers to people." Al-Ma'mūn answered saying, "My intention is that people's hearts must rest at peace regarding you and they should come to know your excellences." Messengers kept going between both men carrying

---

[1]as-Sadūq, *Ilal ash-Shara'i*, Vol. 1, p. 226.

[2]as-Sadūq, *Uyun Akhbār ar-Ridha*, Vol. 2, p. 167.

messages, and when al-Ma'mūn insisted on his suggestion, he sent him a message saying, "If you exempt me, I would appreciate it, and if you do not, I shall come out just as the Messenger of Allāh (ص) and the Commander of the Faithful Ali ibn Abū Talib (ع) did," whereupon al-Ma'mūn said, "Come out however you please." He ordered the commanders of the army and the chamberlains as well as the public at large to go early to ar-Ridha's house. People waited in the alleys and on rooftops to see Abul-Hassan ar-Ridha (ع), and women and children waited for him, too. The army commanders and their attending troops stood guard at his door mounted on their horses till the sun started rising. Abul-Hassan washed, put on his outdoor clothes. He wore a cotton turban, leaving a tassel of it drape down on his chest and between his shoulders. He rubbed his hands with some perfume, took a cane and told his servants to do likewise. So they all came out, and he was barefoot. He raised his trousers up to half the leg, and his clothes were hanging loosely on him. He walked for a short while, raised his head above and made the takbar and his servants did likewise. Then he walked till he reached his doorstep. When the leaders and their troops saw him looking like that, they all swiftly alighted, so much so that lucky was whoever happened to have a knife to cut the leather stirrups so that he could jump faster than the rest, take his sandals off and remain barefoot just as the Imām (ع) had done. Ar-Ridha (ع) made takbar again, and everyone else did likewise; it seemed as if the sky and the walls echoed with him, and Merv was shaken with the noise of weeping and hassle when its residents saw Abul-Hassan and heard him say *Allāhu Akbar! Allāhu Akbar!*...

Al-Ma'mūn came to know about all of that. Al-Fadl ibn Sahl Thul-Riyasatayn said to him, "O Commander of the faithful! If ar-Ridha (ع) reaches the mosque in such a condition, people will be fascinated by him and we all will have to fear for our lives; so, send him a messenger and tell him to return." Al-Ma'mūn sent him a message saying, "We have over-burdened you and wore you out, and we do not wish that you should suffer any hardship on our account; so, go back home, and let people say their prayers behind whoever they have been praying." Abul-Hassan, therefore, asked for his sandals back, put them on and went back. People on that day differed regarding their prayers, and he did not congregate with them.

Al-Ma'mūn's reign was plagued with dissensions and discords both at home and abroad, and part of the problem was the influence the caliph had awarded to his prime minister al-Fadl ibn Sahl. The latter did many things on his own, letting the caliph know what he wanted him to know. Many dignitaries, including top ranking government officials and commanders of the army, were not happy about such an influence. They were sincere in their intentions to save the deteriorating situation by requesting Imām ar-Ridha (ع) to disclose the reality of the status quo to al-Ma'mūn, since he was the only one who could not be harmed by al-Fadl nor could anyone instigate al-Ma'mūn against him. Ibn Khaldun writes the following:

"As discords took place in Iraq because of al-Hassan ibn Sahl (brother of al-Fadl), and due to people's resentment of his and his brother's excessive influence over al-Ma'mūn, then [their outrage at] the nomination of Ali ibn Mūsa ar-Ridha (ع) and the possibility of the caliphate slipping away from the Abbāsides' hands, al-Fadl ibn Sahl was meanwhile concealing all of that from al-Ma'mūn. He was going to extremes in such concealment for fear al-Ma'mūn might change his heart about him and about his brother. When Harthamah came, he knew that he was going to tell al-Ma'mūn about all of that, and that al-Ma'mūn trusted the advice of Harthamah; so, he perfected his instigation against him with al-Ma'mūn till he made him change his mind about the man and kill him, and he did not even listen to what he wanted to say; therefore, the displeasure of the Shī'as there, as well as that of the residents of Baghdad, intensified against him, and dissensions became widespread. The commanders of al-Ma'mūn's army started talking about it, but they could not inform him of it, so they approached Ali ar-Ridha (ع) and asked him to convey the matter to al-Ma'mūn. And so it was. He informed him of the rioting and killing in Iraq and that people criticized him for the favourite status which he had granted both al-Fadl and al-Hassan, and for his (ar-Ridha's) nomination. Al-Ma'mūn asked him, "Who else besides you knows all of that?" He said, "Yahya ibn Maad, Abdul-Aziz ibn Imran and other prominent army leaders." So he called them to him, and they did not reveal anything except after he had offered them sworn guarantees of their own security, so they told him exactly what ar-Ridha (ع) had already told him."[1]

At-Tabari provides us with a clear and more precise picture of Imām ar-Ridha's situation; he writes the following in his famous history book:

"It was rumoured that Ali ibn Mūsa ibn Ja'far ibn Muhammed [ar-Ridha], the Alawide, told al-Ma'mūn about the dissension and inter-killing among people, that since the assassination of his brother, al-Fadl was concealing the news from him, that his own fāmily and the public criticized him for certain reasons and said he was a bewildered madman, and that since they saw that he was doing all of that, they swore the oath of allegiance to his uncle Ibrahim ibn al-Mahdi as the caliph. Al-Ma'mūn said, "They did not swear the oath of allegiance to him; rather, they accepted him as a governor ruling them in the way al-Fadl had instructed him." He informed him that al-Fadl had indeed lied to him and that he cheated him as well, adding, "The war between Ibrahim and al-Hassan ibn Sahl is raging; people criticize him for the status which you gave him (al-Fadl) and his brother, and they criticize your nomination of myself as your successor." He asked him, "Who else in my army is aware of that?" He said, "Yahya ibn Mad, Abdul-Aziz ibn Imran, and a number of prominent military commanders." So he called them to his court, and they were Yahya ibn Mad, Abdul-Aziz ibn Imran and Mūsa and Ali ibn Abū Sa'd, who was son of al-Fadl's sister, and also Khalaf the Egyptian. He asked them about what he had heard, but they refused to tell him anything unless he guaranteed their safety against the threat of revenge by al-Fadl ibn Sahl. He guaranteed that for them, and he wrote each one of them a statement in his own handwriting to that effect. Then they told him about the discords among his subjects, about the deliberate misinformation he heard from al-Fadl regarding Harthamah, and that Tahir ibn al-Hussain had done an excellent job serving him and opened many lands to his government and strengthened his caliphate. When he accomplished all of that, he was "rewarded" by banishment to Riqqa where he was not permitted to receive funds from anyone, till his authority was undermined and

---

[1]Ibn Khaldūn, *Al-Muqaddima,* Vol. 3, p. 249.

his troops mutinied, that had his caliphate been in Baghdad, he would have had a better control and nobody would have dared to mislead him as al-Hassan ibn Sahl had. The land from one end to the other was shaking under his feet. Tahir ibn al-Hussain had been forgotten that year, since the murder of Muhammed in Riqqa, without being utilized in these wars while someone who was a lot less qualified was in charge...[1]

The picture now was turned upside down in the eyes of al-Ma'mūn, but he did not try to change the way how he was dealing with al-Fadl because the latter was in charge of the government base in both Khurasan and Baghdad. In Khurasan, the psychological war, which he waged by deposing Tahir ibn al-Hussain and by having Harthamah murdered, nurtured the desire among the commanders of the army for mutiny, pushing them to yield to his wishes and expectations after having felt that al-Ma'mūn represented no more than a magic wand in al-Fadl's hands. As regarding Baghdad, it was in the grip of his brother al-Hassan ibn Sahl who was considered as al-Fadl's right hand and the big stick whereby he threatened al-Ma'mūn.

As regarding those men who exposed to al-Ma'mūn the reality of al-Fadl's conduct and the dangers it implied, they were terrified when al-Fadl tore down the assurances which had been written by al-Ma'mūn guaranteeing their safety against his wrath and revenge upon coming to know about their instigation and their support of what Imām ar-Ridha (ع) had said about him. At-Tabari says,

"When that became certain to al-Ma'mūn, he ordered preparations to march to Baghdad, and when al-Fadl ibn Sahl came to know about those preparations, he came to know only about some of them, so he interrogated those men, whipping and jailing some of them and pulling the hair out of the beards of others. Ali ibn Mūsa [ar-Ridha] came to his court and told him what had happened to those men and reminded him of his assurances to them. He [al-Ma'mūn] answered

---

[1]at-Tabari, *Tarikh*, Vol. 8, p. 564.

him by saying that he was only tolerating."[1]

Al-Ma'mūn was now convinced that he had no choice except to get rid of al-Fadl ibn Sahl whose job in modern times is equivalent to prime minister. It is also interesting that chance should play a major role in the execution of al-Ma'mūn's plan to eliminate al-Fadl, and it may even have been arranged by al-Ma'mūn himself.

While on his way to Baghdad, al-Fadl, who was in the company of al-Ma'mūn, received a letter from his brother al-Hassan ibn Sahl in which he said, "I have looked in the changing of this year according to the calculations of the movements of the stars and I found out that you will in such and such month, on a Wednesday, taste the pain of red-hot iron and of the burning fire, and I am of the view that you should today go in the company of ar-Ridha (ع) and the commander of the faithful to the bath-house to take a bath and then pour blood over your body so that the ill luck of this omen may leave you." Al-Fadl, therefore, sent a letter to al-Ma'mūn asking him to go with him to the bath-house, and to request Abul-Hassan (ع) to join them too.

Al-Ma'mūn wrote a letter in that same meaning to ar-Ridha (ع) who wrote him back saying that he would not enter the bath-house the next day, nor would he recommend that the commander of the faithful should enter it either, nor even al-Fadl. But al-Ma'mūn repeated his request twice, and Abul-Hassan wrote him again saying, "I shall not enter the bath-house tomorrow for I saw in a vision the Messenger of Allāh (ع) last night telling me not to enter the bath-house tomorrow; therefore, I do not advise the commander of the faithful nor al-Fadl to enter the bath-house tomorrow," whereupon al-Ma'mūn wrote him saying, "You have, master, said the truth, and so has the Messenger of Allāh (ص); I shall not enter the bath-house tomorrow, and al-Fadl knows best what he should do..."[2] Al-Fadl entered the bath-house just to be received by the swords of the

---

[1]*Ibid.*, p. 565.

[2]Shaikh al-Mufid, *Al-Kafi*, Vol. 1, p. 491. Shaikh al-Mufid, *Al-Irshad*, p. 294.

assassins as the letter he had received from his brother al-Hassan ibn Sahl had "predicted," or was it really a prediction?!

We do not think it is unlikely that the letter prepared by al-Ma'mūn imitated the writing style of the al-Fadl's brother, al-Hassan, in order to avoid being accused of murdering his prime minister. It is also possible that al-Ma'mūn wished to get rid of both al-Fadl and Imām ar-Ridha (ع) by that method of assassination, but the Imām (ع) was alert in the face of al-Ma'mūn's cunning and scheming, so he resisted the insistence of al-Ma'mūn to enter the bath-house with him and with al-Fadl by tact and caution. The last paragraph of the anecdote tells us clearly that the letter was a plot by al-Ma'mūn to kill both al-Fadl and the Imām (ع); otherwise, why did al-Ma'mūn abstain from warning al-Fadl against entering the bath-house although the Imām (ع) had asked him to do just that? What provides evidence is the fact that those who killed al-Fadl were among the closest courtiers and train members of al-Ma'mūn and, according to one account, they later on faced al-Ma'mūn with their accusation that he was the one who asked them to do it. At-Tabari writes the following:

> When he [Ma'mūn] reached Sarkhas, some men assaulted al-Fadl ibn Sahl at the bath-house and struck him with their swords till he was dead, and that was on a Friday two nights before the end of Shaban in the year 202 A.H./817 A.D. They were arrested, and it became clear that those who assassinated al-Fadl were among al-Maman's closest courtiers. They were four in number: Ghalib al-Mas'udi, the black man, Qistantine (Constantine), Faraj al-Daylami, and Muwaffaq of Sicily; they killed him and he was sixty years old and they ran away. Al-Ma'mūn posted a reward of ten thousand dinars for anyone who would bring them to him, and they were brought to him by al-Abbās ibn Haitham ibn Bazar-Jamhar al-Daynari, and they said to al-Ma'mūn, "But you ordered us to kill him!" He ordered them to be killed. It is also said that when those who killed al-Fadl were arrested, al-Ma'mūn interrogated them, and some of them said that Ali ibn Abū Sa'd the son of al-Fadl's sister had dispatched them, while others among them denied that, and he ordered their execution. After that he ordered Abdul-Aiz ibn Imran, Ali, Mūsa, and Khalaf, to be brought to him, and he interrogated them. They denied having any knowledge of the matter, but he did not believe them and ordered their execution too,

sending their heads to al-Hassan ibn Sahl in Wasit as a trophy and informing him about his own pain because of the tragedy of the murder of al-Fadl and that he appointed him in his place.[1]

Thus did al-Ma'mūn get rid of the strongest power base within his government which threatened his authority and his fate, leaving only one obstacle in his way to guarantee to uproot the rebellion in Baghdad by dealing with its root causes which included the presence of Imām ar-Ridha (ع) who, according to the Abbāsides, was a difficult knot they could not be loyal to al-Ma'mūn except if he untied it, for its presence meant the end of the Abbāside rule and the beginning of the Alawide.

It was not politically feasible for al-Ma'mūn to reach Baghdad accompanied by Imām ar-Ridha (ع), for that would stir the winds of dissension against him which might not be strong enough to withstand. We are convinced that al-Ma'mūn was the one who plotted to end the life of the Imām (ع) by giving him poisoned grapes. Al-Ma'mūn's letter to the Abbāsides and the residents of Baghdad, which he wrote after the demise of Imām ar-Ridha (ع), lends credence to such a conviction. "He wrote the Abbāsides and their supporters as well as the people of Baghdad informing them of the death of Ali ibn Mūsa and that they had resented his nominating him as his successor, asking them now to go back to their loyalty to him."[2] This may be understood as a clear admission that the death of the Imām (ع) was not natural during those circumstances, and the text Ibn Khaldun provides in expressing the contents of this letter provides even clearer clues to accusing al-Ma'mūn of murdering him; he says the following in his Tarikh:

"... And al-Ma'mūn sent messages to al-Hassan ibn Sahl, to the people of Baghdad, and to his supporters apologizing for naming him his heir to the throne and inviting them to go back to his

---

[1]at-Tabari, Vol. 8, p. 565. Ibn Khaldūn mentions a similar story in Vol. 3, p. 250, of his work titled *Al-Muqaddima fil Tarikh*.

[2]at-Tabari, *Tarikh*, Vol. 8, p. 558, "Events of the Year 203 A.H.".

loyalty.[1]

As-Sadūq narrates saying, "While ar-Ridha (ع) was breathing his last, al-Ma'mūn said to him, "By Allāh! I do not know which of the two calamities is greater: losing you and parting from you, or people's accusation that I assassinated you...'"[2] In another narrative by Abul-Faraj al-Isfahani, al-Ma'mūn said to him, "It is very hard for me to live to see you die, and there was some hope hinging upon your stay, yet even harder for me is people saying that I have poisoned you, and Allāh knows that I am innocent of that."[3] This situation discloses the fact that the accusation of his own murder of the Imām (ع) was the subject of argument, maybe even of conviction, even then, for al-Ma'mūn asserts people's accusation of him and he tries to extract an admission from the Imām (ع) clearing him of it, as Abul-Faraj al-Isfahani mentions in his book *Maqatil at-Talibiyyin*.

Accounts regarding the method al-Ma'mūn employed to kill Imām ar-Ridha (ع) are abundant. Abul-Faraj al-Isfahani and Shaikh al-Mufid say that he killed him by poisoned pomegranate juice and poisoned grape juice. In his book *Al-Irshād*, al-Mufid quotes Abdullāh ibn Bashir saying, Al-Ma'mūn ordered me to let my nails grow as long as they could without letting anyone notice that; so I did, then he ordered to see me and he gave me something which looked like tamarind and said, Squeeze this with both your hands,' and I did. Then he stood up, left me and went to see ar-Ridha (ع) to whom he said, How are you?' He answered, I hope I am alright.' He said, I, too, by the Grace of Allāh, am alright; did any well-wisher visit you today?' He answered in the negative, so al-Ma'mūn became angry and called upon his servants to come, then he ordered one of them to immediately take the pomegranate juice to him, adding, ... for he cannot do without it.' Then he called me to him and

---

[1]Ibn Khaldūn, *Muqaddima*, Vol. 3, p. 250.

[2]as-Sadūq,*Uyun Akhbār ar-Ridha*, Vol. 2, p. 242.

[3]Abul-Faraj al-Isfahani, *Maqatil at-Talibiyyeen*, p. 380.

said, Squeeze it with your own hands,' and so I did. Then al-Ma'mūn handed the juice to ar-Ridha (ع) in person, and that was the reason for his death for he stayed only two days before he (ع) died.'"

Abul-Salt al-Harawi is quoted as saying, "I entered ar-Ridha's house after al-Ma'mūn had already left; he said to me, O Abul-Salt! They have done it...!' and he kept unifying and praising Allāh." Muhammed ibn al-Jahm is quoted as saying, "Ar-Ridha (ع) used to love grapes. Some grapes were said to be prepared for him; they were pierced with needles at their very tips and were kept like that for several days. Then the needles were taken out, and they were brought to him and he ate some of them and fell into the sickness to which we have referred. The grapes killed him, and it was said that that was one of the most effective methods of poisoning."[1] Al-Ma'mūn was, indeed, the one who killed Imām ar-Ridha (ع), there is no doubt about it.

His death occurred at Toos in a village called Sanabad, of the Nooqan area, and he was buried at the house of Hameed ibn Tahtaba under the dome where Harūn ar-Rashīd had been buried, and he was buried beside him facing the *qibla*.[2]

When ar-Ridha (ع) died, al-Ma'mūn did not disclose when it happened, leaving him dead for one day and one night, then he called for Muhammed ibn Ja'far ibn Muhammed and a group of descendants of Abū Talib. When they were present, he showed him [Imām] to them; his corpse looked alright; then he started weeping and addressed the corpse saying, "O Brother! It is indeed very hard for me to see you in such a condition, and I was hoping to go before you, but Allāh insisted on carrying out His decree," and he showed a great deal of agony and grief and went out carrying the coffin with others till he reached the place where it is now buried...[3]

---

[1]Shaikh al-Mufid, *Al-Irshad*, p. 297. A similar narrative is mentioned in al-Isfahani's book *Maqatil at-Talibiyyeen*, pp. 377-378.

[2]as-Sadūq, *Uyun Akhbār ar-Ridha*, Vol. 1, p. 18.

[3]al-Isfahani, *Maqatil at-Talibiyyeen*, p. 378.

... So al-Ma'mūn was present there before the grave was dug, and he ordered his [Imām's] grave to be dug beside that of his father, then he approached us and said, "he person inside this coffin told me that when his grave is dug, water and fish will appear underneath; so, dig..." They dug. When they finished digging, a spring of water appeared, and fish appeared in it, then the water dissipated, and ar-Ridha (ع) was then buried.[1]

In Yemen, in the aftermath of the Imām's assassination, Ibrahim ibn Mūsa ibn Ja'far rebelled and took control of the government after banishing al-Ma'mūn's governor. In Mecca, al-Hussain ibn al-Hassan al-Aftas revolted, and Muhammed ibn Ja'far was named caliph. In Basra, Zaid ibn Mūsa ibn Ja'far rebelled. He was nicknamed "Zaid of the fire" due to the number of the homes of the Abbāsides and of their followers which he had burnt. Whenever he came across a man draped in black, he would burn his home. Ali ibn Sa'd marched to him. Zaid requested him to guarantee his safety if he gave up, and Ali agreed. But he nevertheless arrested him[2] and sent him to al-Hassan ibn Sahl who ordered to have him executed while al-Hajjaj ibn Khaythamah was present, so he said, "Prince! Do not rush, for I have a piece of advice for you." He stopped the executioner and came close to him. He said, "Prince! Did you receive instructions from the commander of the faithful to do what you are about to?" He answered in the negative, so he asked again, "Then why are you executing the cousin of the commander of the faithful without his knowledge or consultation?" Then he narrated for him the story of Abū Abdullāh al-Aftas whom ar-Rashīd jailed under the watchful eyes of Ja'far ibn Yahya. Ja'far killed him without his knowledge and sent his head on a platter to him together with other Nawraz[3] presents. When ar-Rashīd ordered Masrar to kill

---

[1]*Ibid.*, p. 380.

[2]Ibn al-Atheer, *At-Tarikh al-Kāmil*, Vol. 5, pp. 175-177.

[3]Nawraz is the first day of Spring and, hence, the first day of the Persian (and Kurdish) new year. It is celebrated outdoors by enjoying the beauty of nature.

Ja'far, he said to him, "If Ja'far asked you about his crime for which you are killing him, tell him that you are killing him for his own killing of my cousin Ibn al-Aftas whom he killed without my knowledge." Then al-Hajjaj ibn Khaythamah said to al-Hassan ibn Sahl, "O Prince! Do you feel secure should anything happen between you and the commander of the faithful if you kill this man and use it as an excuse just as ar-Rashīd had done against Ja'far ibn Yahya?" Al-Hassan said to al-Hajjaj, "May Allāh reward you!" Then he ordered Zaid to be returned to his prison where he was kept till he was transported to al-Ma'mūn. Once he was there, al-Ma'mūn sent him to his brother ar-Ridha (ع) who set him free.[1] One of the interesting anecdotes narrated about him is the following:

"When he was brought to al-Ma'mūn, the latter said to him, "O Zaid! You led the uprising in Basra, and instead of starting with the homes of our common enemies: the Umayyads, Banu Thaqaf, Uday, Bahila and al Ziyad, you targeted the homes of your own cousins." Zaid, who had a humorous temper, said, "I, indeed, erred from each direction, O commander of the faithful! If I go back, I will start with our enemies!" Al-Ma'mūn laughed and sent him to his brother ar-Ridha (ع) saying, "I have pardoned him just to please you." When he was brought to the Imām (ع), he was reprimanded then released."[2]

What we try to get acquainted with by examining the Imām's stand towards his brother "Zaid of the fire" was the reality regarding the Imām's viewpoint of the revolutionary method employed by the Alawides in their revolutions against the Abbāsides. We find the Imām (ع) taking a strictly negative stand towards his brother Zaid. Yet he did not rebuke him and blame him simply because he had revolted against the government, but rather because he had committed several unlawful acts according to Islamic Shari'a such as looting, confiscating, burning, in which acts he did not distinguish between the innocent and the guilty. Other than that, the sincere Alawide revolutions which aimed at standing in the face of injustice

---

[1]as-Sadūq, *Uyun Akhbār ar-Ridha*, Vol. 2, p. 233.

[2]*Ibid.*

and oppression used to enjoy the support of the Imāms who considered them the only way to disclose to the nation how corrupt the government was, and to make them aware of its infringements and transgressions.

Al-Ma'mūn's tolerance towards those who rebelled against him was not in contradiction with his general conduct. On one hand, he wanted to compete with the Alawides in winning the public opinion to his side. On the other hand, he was trying to stay away from getting involved in shedding their blood and seeking revenge against them which did not agree with his inclination, though in theory, towards the Alawides.

The Imām (ع) had sided with the Alawide revolution of Ibn Tabataba under the command of Abul-Saraya; this is a fact. Muhammed ibn al-Athram, Medīna's chief of the police force of Muhammed ibn Sulayman al-Alawi during the days of Abul-Saraya, is quoted as saying, "His near in kin and some people from Quraish gathered around him and swore the oath of allegiance to him saying, If you send word to Abul-Hassan (ع), he will surely support us, and we will be thus united.' Sulayman said to me, Go to him and convey my greetings to him and tell him that his kinfolk have gathered and desired that he should join them; so, if you wish, please do so.' So I met him at al-Hamra and I conveyed the message to him. He said, "Convey my greeting to him and tell him that I will join him after twenty days." I conveyed to him the message with which I was sent. On the 18th day, Warqa, al-Jalladi's commander, marched towards us, whereupon I ran in the direction of the two Surs. When I heard someone calling me 'O Abū Athram!', I turned back, and it was Abul-Hassan (ع) asking me: 'Did the twenty days pass already?!'"[1]

Such cautious stand of the Imām (ع) was not due to evading his participation in the revolutionary movement but was the result of a realistic calculation of the development of events in the sphere of the movement of revolutions along the Abbāside rule and before them the Umayyad. For this reason, we cannot conclude that the Imām's

---

[1]as-Sadūq, *Uyun Akhbār ar-Ridha*, Vol. 2, p. 208.

lack of participation in a rebellion meant that he was not convinced of the principle of its necessity.

Now let us turn to the intellectual contributions of this great sage to Islam in particular and to humanity in general. Nobody can do justice to all the rich aspects of the intellectual life of Imām ar-Ridha (ع), but let us glance at his intellectual output in various fields of knowledge and scholarship.

Some historians doubted the scholarship of the Imāms, let alone their scholarly superiority, basing their doubts on the claim that had they been truly scholars, their books would have been made available to the public as is the case with all other scholars. Anyone who considers the revolution of Imām Hussain (ع) against Yazid as a mistake committed by the Imām (ع) and a gross miscalculation can be expected to make a statement like this which we cannot attribute to ignorance or to lack of the ability to know, but it is nothing other than the dark cloud of sectarian prejudice forming a curtain between a prejudiced person and his seeing events, issues, and reflections as they really are. This is true about Muslims and non-Muslims. A "fair-minded" historian is asked to tell us about the books authored by the *sahāba* and their works from whom he derived the principles and precepts of the creed of the Prophet (ص), or even the works of the tabieen whom he regards as the second class that is knowledgeable of the issues of the sharaa, custodians of its structure. What books did the "righteous caliphs" write?! Can you call the title of any of them besides *Nahjul-Balāgha* or Mushaf Fatima?! Let us stop here for a minute; surely many readers have heard and probably read *Nahjul-Balāgha*, but not many of them are familiar with Fatima's *mushaf*; so, let us shed some light on it here.

Linguistically, the word "mushaf" means: a collection of suhuf, plural of *sahifa*, a page or a tablet. The word "Qur'ān" means: a reading material, a written text. Both words are used at the present time to denote the Book of Allāh, the Holy Qur'ān, but that was not the case during the dawn of Islam. Mushaf Fatima, or Fatima's mushaf, is not a copy of the Holy Qur'ān as one may be tempted to believe. One of the scholars who sheds light on it is Thiqatul-Islam Muhammed ibn Ya'qub al-Kulayni. He does so on page 295 and following pages of Vol. 1 of his famous classic work titled *Usul al-Kāfi*. The edition consulted for this book was published by Dar at-Ta'aruf (Beirut, Lebanon) in 1411 A.H./1990 A.D. Al-Kulayni quotes a dialogue between Imām Ja'far as-Sādiq (ع) and his great companion, Abū Busayr, wherein the Imām (ع) details the most precious relics Ahl al-Bayt (ع) have, and the list includes, among others, Fatima's *mushaf*. The Imām (ع) described this *mushaf* as follows: "It is a *mushaf* three times the size of the Qur'ān, yet it does not contain even one Qur'ānic verse." The Imām (ع) continued to describe the extent of its contents to Abū Busayr. It contains, among others, a chronology of Islamic events, numerous traditions of the Prophet (ص), numerous *qudsi* traditions and many narratives related by arch-angel Gabriel to the Prophet (ص). Refer to this text for a description of "al-jami'a", a 70-yard long book written on ox skin by the Commander of the Faithful Imām Ali ibn Abū Talib (ع).

The legacy our Imāms, members of Ahl al-Bayt (ع) in various fields of knowledge is narrated about them by those with whom they associated, their admirers and sincere followers, and it is sufficient to acquaint us with the extent of their knowledge and superiority over all others barring none. Is it really possible that Ibn Khaldun did not review such legacy of *ahādīth* which reached us through them and recorded by scholars and thinkers and upon which the structure of their school of thought, in which a large section of the nation believes, stood? We doubt it; nay, we are sure about the unrealistic nature of such an odd question especially since Ibn Khaldun is one of the most knowledgeable, highly intellectual, and mature writers. A writer of such caliber is not expected to be so ignorant. Ignorant he was not, prejudiced he surely was, and so are millions others...

The Imāms were tested during various periods of their lives by pressing crises due to the trespassing of oppressive rulers on their civil liberties. They pursued their followers and sincere adherents, straitening on them in various aspects of their everyday life, so much so that the word "rafidi" or "rafidhi" came to represent in the eyes of the rulers the final indictment of anyone proven to be "guilty" of its context, a believer in its background. Because of that, the chance was lost for many of those who sought knowledge to derive from that leading fountainhead, and the chance to find the scholarly solutions for the intellectual problems because of which they were disturbing their minds. Despite all these pressures and violent trespassing, mankind is not intellectually deprived of a great deal of intellectual masterpieces which the Imāms (ع) dictated to their students and disciples in various aspects of scholarship.

Some of those students used to bribe the jailers so that they might agree to carry written questions to the jailed Imām (ع) and bring them back his answers. They only desired to benefit from the presence of the Imām (ع), and they aspired to be faithful to the trust of scholarship. They, moreover, wanted to protect the faith from the abyss of doubt and suspicion. The biography of the jailed Imām Mūsa ibn Ja'far (ع) bears witness to these facts according to the testimony of those who quoted him. Historians and biographers of Imām ar-Ridha (ع) do, in fact, mention some books authored by the Imām (ع) besides his narration of hadīth. They record what he dictated to those who asked him various questions and whatever he confided to his close companions who used to frequently question him about various types of knowledge which they could not fully comprehend and digest.

Among such books is *Al-Fiqh ar-Radawi* which الفقه الرضوي was for some time the object of debate among scholars. There are among the latter those who considered it to be authored by the Imām (ع), relied on it, and built their arguments on its premises. Among such scholars were: al-Majlisi (both al-Majlisi senior, the father, and his son, the renown author of *Bihār al-Anwār*, Sayyid Bahr al-Ulum, Shaikh an-Nawari, and others. The story of how this book surfaced is interesting. A a group of the residents of Qum brought a copy with them to Mecca where the ruler-judge (qadi-emir) Sayyid Hussain al-Isfahani saw it and testified to its being authored by ar-Ridha (ع) and made a copy of it for himself which he brought to Isfahan. There, he showed it to al-Majlisi (senior) who was, likewise, sure it was authored by the Imām (ع) and so was his son the second al-Majlisi (junior). The latter quoted the ahādīth it contained in his voluminous book Bihār al-Anwār, making the book one of his references, and this is how its fame spread.

In his Introduction to *Bihār al-Anwār*, al-Majlisi writes, "I was told about the book *Fiqh ar-Ridha* by the virtuous traditionist the ruler-judge Hussain, may Allāh be Gracious to his soul, after returning to Isfahan. He said to me, It happened that during the time when I was neighbouring the House of Allāh, a group of the residents of Qum visited me while performing their *hajj* and they had with them an old book the date of its writing agreed with the date during which ar-Ridha (ع) was alive.'" Al-Majlisi continues to say, "I heard my father saying that it was written in the handwriting of ar-Ridha (ع), and a large number of dignitaries testified to the same."

Among the Imām's scientific books is what is known as *Ar-Risala at-Thahabiyya fil Tibb* (the golden medical dissertation) for which sources are counted reaching sometimes to Muhammed ibn Jumhar, and sometimes to al-Hassan ibn Muhammed an-Nawfali who was accepted as trustworthy by an-Najjashi who described him as "highly esteemed and trustworthy; he narrated one text about ar-Ridha (ع)," which could be "the golden medical dissertation."

It is possible that the dissertation's fame among scholars, and their consensus in various centuries that the Imām (ع) was its author, and that nobody doubted such an authorship, are enough proofs leading the researcher to comfortably conclude that it was, indeed, from the intellectual output of Imām ar-Ridha (ع) himself. But what is this dissertation all about, anyway?

This dissertation is one of the most precious pieces of Islamic legacy dealing with the science of medicine. It is a summary of a number of medical sciences such as anatomy, biology, physiology, pathology and preventive medicine. Its contents are also relevant to the sciences of nutrition and chemistry, in addition to other medicine-related branches of science. The Imām (ع) sent this dissertation to the caliph al-Ma'mūn around the year 201 A.H./816 A.D., that is to say, when medicine was a primitive science and its research was not conducted scientifically but based on practice alone rather than on scientific discoveries. The science of bacteriology was not discovered yet, nor was there any significant knowledge of nutritional supplements such as vitamins, nor were there other significant medical discoveries for fighting microbes such as penicillin, streptomycin, oromycin, etc. On the surface, the dissertation seemed to be very simple in order to be in line with the mentality of that time, but it is quite deep and complicated in its implications and it is worthy of a serious scientific study and lengthy researches to unveil its secrets and uncover its treasures. It should be compared with modern scientific facts.[1] Al-Ma'mūn was very pleased to receive that dissertation and he expressed how much he cherished it by ordering to have it written down in gold and to be deposited at his "depository of wisdom," hence its name, "the golden dissertation." In praising it, al-Ma'mūn said, "I have reviewed the dissertation of my learned cousin, the loved and virtuous one, the logical physician, which deals with the betterment of the body, the conduct of bathing, the balance of nutrition, and I found it very well organized and one of the best blessings. I carefully studied it, reviewed and contemplated upon it, till its wisdom manifested itself to me, and its benefits became obvious, and it found its place to my heart, so I learned it by heart and I understood it by my mind, for I found it to be a most precious item to post, a great treasure, and a most useful thing, so I ordered it to be written in gold due to its being precious, and I deposited it at the depository of wisdom after I had it copied down by the descendants of Hashim, the youths of the nation. Bodies become healthy by balanced diets, and life becomes possible by overcoming disease, and through life wisdom is achieved, and through wisdom Paradise is won. It is worthy of being safeguarded and treasured... It is so because it came out of the house of those who derive their knowledge from the knowledge of the Chosen One (ﷺ), the missive of the prophets, the arguments of successors to the prophets, the manners of scholars, the cure to the hearts and the sick from among the people of ignorance and blindness..., may Allāh be pleased with them, bless and be merciful to them, the first of them and the last, the young and the old. I showed it to the elite from among my closest train who are known for their wisdom and knowledge of medicine, and who are authors of books, those who are counted among the people of knowledge and described with wisdom. Each one of them lauded it and thought highly of it, elevated it with esteem and evaluated it in order to be

---

[1]*Ibid.*, pp. 19-20.

284

fair to its author, submitting to him, believing in the wisdom he included therein."[1]

Al-Ma'mūn had a very inquisitive mind and a thirst for knowledge; he was always eager to obtain more and more knowledge. During one of his scientific debates, a group of physicians and philosophers in Nishapur, including Yuhanna (John) ibn Masawayh, the physician, Jibraeel (Gabriel) ibn Bakhtishoo[2], the physician, Salih ibn Salhamah, the Indian philosopher, in addition to others, had gathered. Discussion turned to medicine and how through it can the bodies be improved. Al-Ma'mūn and his attendants were involved in a very lengthy discussion of the subject. They were debating how Allāh created the human body and the contradictory things in it, the four elements, the harms and the benefits of various types of food. All this went on as the Imām (ع) kept silent and did not take part in any of it. Al-Ma'mūn, therefore, said to him, "What do you have to say, O father of al-Hassan, about today's subject of discussion?" Abul-Hassan (ع) said, "I have of it the knowledge of what I have personally tested and came to know about its accuracy by experience and by the passage of time in addition to what I was told by my ancestors of what nobody can afford to be ignorant of, nor excused for leaving out. I shall compile it with an equal portion of what everyone should know." Al-Ma'mūn, following that, had to go in a hurry to Balkh, now a province in northern Afghanistan the capital of which is Mazar Sharif[3], and Abul-Hassan (ع) did not accompany him; therefore, al-Ma'mūn sent him from there a letter asking him to

---

[1]Sayyid Muhsin al-Amin, *A'yan ash-Shī'a* أعيان الشيعة, Vol. 4, pp. 2, 143 and 144.

[2]The reader can correctly conclude that there were many Christian and Jewish scholars and scientists who received a great deal of respect and support from caliph al-Ma'mun who was a scholar in his own right. His time was, indeed, a golden period of learning and scholarship despite all contemporary political turmoils.

[3]"Mazar Sharif" means: a sacred mausoleum. It is named so because it houses the shrine of Khavajeh Abū Nasr Parsa, a pious man from the Persian region of Parsa who died and was buried there.

fulfill his promise and to make that compilation. Ar-Ridha (ع) wrote him saying,

In the Name of Allāh, Most Gracious, Most Merciful; My reliance is upon Allāh. I have received the letter of the commander of the faithful ordering me to acquaint him with what is needed of matters which I have tested and heard, about foods and drinks, medicines, venesection, blood letting, bathing, poisons, what should be avoided, and other things which manage the health of the body, and I explained what is needed to be done regarding one's own body, and Allāh is the One Who grants success.

After that he initiated his dissertation. A good number of scholars attempted to write commentaries on the dissertation; here is a partial listing of some of them so that the discreet reader may refer to them if he so wishes:

1. *Tarjamat al-Alawi lil Tibb ar-Radawi* ترجمة العلوي للطب الرضوي of Sayyid Diaud-Dan Abul-Ridha FadlAllāh ibn Ali ar-Rawandi (d. 548 A.H./1153 A.D.).

2. *Tarjamat at-Thahabiyya* ترجمة الذهبية by mawla FaydAllāh 'Usarah at-Tasatturi, an authority on medicine and astrology during the regime of Fath-Ali Khan. This book was written in secrecy in about 107 A.H./725 A.D. A handwritten copy of the manuscript dated 1133 A.H./1721 A.D. is available at the Mishkat Library of Tehran's University.

3. *Tarjamat at-Thahabiyya* ترجمة الذهبية by Muhammed Bāqir al-Majlisi. It is available at the private library of the late Sayyid Hassan as-Sadr in Kādhimiyya (north Baghdad, Iraq).

4. *'Afiyat al-Bariyya fi Sharh at-Thahabiyya* عافية البرية في شرح الذهبية by Mirza Muhammed Hadi son of Mirza Muhammed Salih ash-Sharazi. It was authored during the reign of Sultan Hussain as-Safawi (the Safavid). It is in handwritten manuscript form and is available at the Sayyid Hussain al-Hamadani Library, Najaf al-Ashraf (Iraq).

5. *Sharh Tibb ar-Ridha* شرح طب الرضا by mawla Muhammed Sharif al-Khatunabadi. He authored it around 1120 A.H./1709 A.D.

6. *Tarjamat at-Thahabiyya* ترجمة الذهبية by Sayyid Shamsud-Din Muhammed ibn Muhammed Bada ar-Radawi al-Mashhadi. Its writing was finished in 1155 A.H./1743 A.D. and is available at the Shaikh Muhammed Ali Akbar an-Nahawandi Library in Khurasan (Iran).

7. *Sharh Tibb ar-Ridha* شرح طب الرضا by Sayyid Abdulllah ash-Shubber who died in 1242 A.H./1827 A.D. Shaikh an-Nawari indicated in some of his writings that he had seen that copy himself.

8. *Sharh Tibb ar-Ridha* شرح طب الرضا by mawla Muhammed ibn al-Hajj Muhammed Hassan al-Mashhadi who taught at Mashhad and died in 1257 A.H./1842 A.D.

9. *Sharh Tibb ar-Ridha* شرح طب الرضا by mawla Nawraz Ali al-Bastami.

10. *Al-Mahmoodiyya* المحمودية by al-Hajj Kādhim al-Mūsawi az-Zanjani who died in 1292 A.H./1876 A.D. It is in manuscript form and is available with the author's grandsons.

There are others besides these scholars who explained and commented on it, revealing what is hidden of its secrets and obscure treasures. Probably the latest person to explain it and to conduct a comparative study between its theory and the latest modern scientific discoveries is Dr. Abdul-Sahib Zaini who did so in the "Multaqa al-Asrayn" periodical series.

Among other works, credit for which goes to this great Imām (ع), is Sahafat ar-Ridha which deals with fiqh. The author of *Mustadrak al-Wasa'il* described it as "among the well-known books which is relied upon and which no other book, before it or after it, is more esteemed or reliable."

Sayyid Muhsin al-Amin, in his encylopædic work titled A'yan ash-

Shī'a[1], mentions an isnad (ascription) related to it alone from Shaikh Abdul-Wasi' al-Yemani az-Zaydi for the copy brought by the said Shaikh from Yemen and published in Damascus, Syria. Also, some of its copies contain its ascription to Abū Ali at-Tibrisi.

Al-Mustadrak states the following: "The esteemed Mirza Abd-Allāh Afandi, in his *Riyad al-Ulema'*, has compiled all its sources and said, Among them is a copy of this *Saheefa* which I saw at the town of Ardabil (chief town of the Azerbaijan district, Iran), and its sanad was...,' then he goes on to indicate its *sanad*. Among other works attributed to the Imām (ع) is the book titled Mahd al-Islam wa Shara'i ad-Dan which is referred to by as-Sadūq in his Uyun Akhbar ar-Ridha through al-Fadl ibn Shathan, but he did not indicate that it was written in response to al-Ma'mūn's request.[2]

Ajwibat Mūsa'il Ibn Sinan ("Answers to ibn Sinan's Queries") can be described as one of the works of the Imām (ع). It contains his answers to questions put forth to him by Ibn Sinan. But this cannot be described as a book authored by the Imām (ع); otherwise, the collection of his answers to the questions of many others, which deal with various fields of knowledge and scholarship, must be also described as such. Ilal Ibn Shathan: This book contains the Imām's answers to questions relevant to ailments put forth to him by Ibn Shathan.

On various occasions, al-Ma'mūn tried to force Imām ar-Ridha (ع) into the arena of complex debates with various groups and creeds. He used to conduct scientific and intellectual sessions to which he

---

[1]This great encyclopedia falls in ten volumes, excluding its thorough and very well arranged Index which constitutes a volume by itself. The copy we have in our library is dated 1406 A.H./1986 A.D. and is published by Dar at-Ta'aruf lil Matbu'at (P.O. Box 8601, Beirut, Lebanon). It lists thousands of Shī'a men of letters, scholars, theologians, poets, authors, politicians, narrators of traditions, etc. It is edited by the author's son, the renown scholar Hassan al-Amin, author of many books probably the most famous of which is the 11-volume encyclopedia titled *Al-Ghadīr*..

[2]as-Sadūq, *Uyun Akhbār ar-Ridha*, Vol. 2, p. 121.

invited great thinkers, leading scientists, the atheists of the century, and debaters whose scientific caliber was feared, and before the stubbornness of whose complex arguments the evidence was muted, and due to the fierceness of whose doubt the proof was weakened. In all such debates, the Imām would come out victorious over his opponents due to the tremendous power of knowledge with which the Almighty endowed him, for such are the miracles of the Infallible Imāms. None of them ever had to force himself into the sophistry of arguments to which some might have resorted in order to smash his opponent's argument and weaken his ability to provide evidence. Rather, he depended in his debates on honest arguments in order to prove right to be right and on his miraculous ability of conviction and calm stylistic method.

An-Nawfali tried to warn the Imām against attempting to deal with the debates of such people when the Imām asked him why al-Ma'mūn had invited him to debate them, for al-Ma'mūn had asked the Catholic archbishop, the High Rabbi, the leading Sabians, the Hindu high priest, followers of Zoroaster, Nestus the Roman medical scientist, and a group of orators of his time, to engage in scientific debates with Imām ar-Ridha (ع).

He dispatched Yasir, the servant, to tell the Imām about the time when the debate would start, requesting him to attend. When Yasir went out and an-Nawfali was alone with the Imām, the Imām (ع) turned to him and asked him in the form of a dialogue, "O Nawfali! You are an Iraqi, and the heart of an Iraqi is not severe; so, what can you gain from causing your cousin to require us to meet with disbelievers and rhetoricians?" An-Nawfali answered, "May my life be sacrificed for yours! He wants to put you to test, and he loves to know how much knowledge you have. He has, indeed, built his assumption on a shaky foundation, and doomed, by Allāh, is what he has built." He asked him, "And what has he built?" He answered him saying, "Scholars of kalam and innovators are the antithesis of the scholars. A scholar does not deny the undeniable, whereas rhetoricians and polytheists are people who deny and try to prove what is not true. If you argue with them and tell them that Allāh is One, they would say, Prove His Oneness,' and if you say that Muhammed (ص) is the Messenger of Allāh, they would say,

Confirm his Message,' then they would press their lies on a person while he tries to disprove their lies, and they would continue to prove that he is mistaken till he abandons his argument; so, beware of them, may my life be sacrificed for you." The Imām (ع) smiled and asked him, "O Nawfali! Do you fear that they will disprove my argument?" He answered, "No, by Allāh! I have never worried about you, and I hope Allāh will enable you to have the upper hand over them." The Imām asked him again, "O Nawfali! Would you like to know when al-Ma'mūn will feel remorseful?" He answered, "Yes." He said, "When he hears me argue with the people of the Torah quoting their own Torah, with the people of the Gospel (Bible) quoting their own Gospel, with the people of the Psalms quoting their own Psalms, with Zoroastrians arguing in their Persian language, with the Romans in their own Latin, and with rhetoricians using their very rhetoric. So, if I closed all the avenues of argument in the face of each arguing party and disproved his claim, making him renounce his statement from its onset and referring to my own statement, then al-Ma'mūn will realize that he will not achieve what he aspires. It is then that he will feel regretful; We are Allāh's, and Unto Him is our return."

Thus does the Imām show that he was not concerned about such persons whom al-Ma'mūn wished to gather together against him trying to embarrass him with their falsification and arguments which he hoped might close for the Imām (ع) all the avenues of argument.

Cover of my book on Mary and Jesus

Whenever a session started and the Imām (ع) was invited to join it, discussion started and the Imām (ع) debated with the Catholics, making the Bible his reference to prove his own defense of the Unity of Allāh (versus their Trinity) and disprove the so-called godhead of Christ (ع). Then he would follow up with a magnificent discussion proving that the Bible in circulation today is not the same which Allāh had revealed to Christ (ع) and that it is authored by some of the disciples of Jesus (ع) who are the authors of the four gospels, not Jesus (ε), depending in his argument on the fact that the details presented by each one of them stand in flagrant contradiction with those of the other. To the right of this text is cover page of the author's book Mary and Jesus in Islam, a thorough research that proves, from "Christian" references, that Jesus (ε) was not the one who was crucified but that Judas Iscariot was, that he was not born on December 25, that the concept of Trinity crept into Christianity in the 3rd century..., in addition to evidences that Christianity has borrowed so much from ancient Babylonian, Greek, Roman Persian and Indian mythologies.

Let us digress here for a minute to tackle the issue of Christianity in brief, particularly that of Catholicism, then we will bring the reader a debate between Imām ar-Ridha (ε) and a Catholic archbishop.

The reader already knows that the only Bible accepted by Muslims is the one compiled by Saint Barnabas, a gospel which was not canonized at the famous Nicæa, N.W. Asia Minor, conference of 325 A.D. called for by Emperor Constantine who aspired to put an end to the sectarian differences among the Christians of his time. The next few paragraphs are excerpted from my book *Mary and Jesus in Islam*: According to the Gospel of Matthew, and to be exact Ch. 10, verse 4, the list of the twelve disciples of Jesus Christ is as follows:

Simon (or Peter), Andrew (Peter's brother), James (son of Zebedee), John (James' brother), Philip, Bartholomew, Thomas, Matthew (the tax collector), James (son of Alphaeus), Thaddaeus, another Simon who is said to be "a member of The Zealots,' a subversive political party," and Judas Iscariot. Why is the name of Saint Barnabas not among them, and how did he come to write his own Gospel, the only one accepted by Muslims as the true Bible? With all their prejudices, speculations, sectarian motivations, it is unwise to accept what today's or yesterday's Christians tell us about Saint Barnabas and his Bible, or about the other disciples. The Encyclopedia Britannica III, for example, describes those who believed that Christ was human and not divine as heretics, and so do many Christian writers and theologians. An independent research, therefore, will yield better results, that's for sure. One such research has been undertaken by

M.A. Yusseff who published his findings in a very interesting book titled The Dead Sea Scrolls, the Gospel of Barnabas, and the New Testament which was published in 1405 A.H./1985 A.D. by the American Trust Publications of Indianapolis, Indiana, U.S.A.[1] Saint Barnabas was originally called Joseph the Levite, or Joses the Levite, and is better known as Matthai, or Matthias. In the Christian document known as Recognitions, Matthias is identified as another name for Apostle Barnabas, which is correct. In another document known as Homilies, Barnabas is said to be a personal Apostle of Jesus, "a strict servant of the Law," and, hence, one of the original twelve Disciples (or Apostles) of Jesus Christ. The Jews, too, list his name among not twelve but five apostles, the remaining four being: Naki, Nester (perhaps Nestor after whom Nestorian Christians are named), Buni, and Todah. But we find the name "Lebbacus" among these disciples in Matthew 10:13, that of "Judas son of James" in Luke 6:16 and Acts 1:13, both contradicting other Biblical accounts; so, which one is correct and which one is not?!

Saint Barnabas was born in Cyprus in the first century A.D. Other references to him are recorded in the Bible in Acts 11:19 and 15:41. He is said as having joined the Jerusalem church "after the alleged crucifixion of Jesus[2]," which is not true, sold his property, and gave the proceeds as a donation to his community. He founded the church in Antioch (Turkish Antakya; see footnote above about the history of this city), where he preached. Inviting Paul of Tarsus (Turkey) to be his assistant, he undertook missionary activity and then went to Jerusalem. Shortly after 48 A.D., a conflict separated both men, and Barnabas sailed home to Cyprus. Where did he write his Gospel and when? Nobody seems to know. How did he die? Nobody seems to know, yet he is called a martyr... We are also told that he knew St.

---

[1] For the benefit of our reader, the full address of the said Publisher is: ATP, 10900 W. Washington Street, Indianapolis, IN 46231, U.S.A. This book should be in every personal and public library.

[2] This misleading statement exists in Vol. One of the world renown Encyclopedia Britannica III. How many other errors exist in this Encyclopedia?

Mark. In 488 A.D., his grave was discovered near the Monastery of St. Barnabas in the Cypriot city of Salamis. A copy of his Gospel was found buried with him[1]. The accurate list of the twelve disciples of Jesus exists in the Gospel of St. Barnabas himself who records the following:

Jesus, having returned to the region of Jerusalem, was found again of the people with exceedingly great joy, and they implored him to abide with them, for his words were not as those of the scribes, but were with power; for they touched the heart.

Jesus, seeing that great was the multitude of them that returned to their heart for to walk in the law of God, went up into the mountain, and abode all night in prayer. When the day came he descended from the mountain and chose twelve whom he called apostles, among whom is Judas, who was slain upon the cross[2]. Their names are: Andrew and Peter his brother, fishermen; Barnabas, who wrote this, with Matthew the publican, who sat at the receipt of custom; John and James, son of Zebedee; Thaddaeus and Judas[3]; Bartholomew and Philip; James, and Judas Iscariot the traitor. To these he always revealed the divine secrets. He made Judas Iscariot his dispenser of that which was given in alms, but he took the tenth part of everything. (The Gospel of Barnabas 14)

The Gospel of St. Barnabas is the one that contains the true teachings of Jesus Christ; it will be discussed later how it refers to

---

[1]That copy was later deposited at the Imperial Library at Vienna. It was at a much later date translated into English and edited by Lonsdale and Laura Ragg.

[2]This statement, among many others in the Gospel of St. Barnabas, agrees with what we, Muslims, have in the Holy Qur'an. Jesus Christ was not crucified.

[3]The reader can easily see that there were two men among the disciples of Jesus named Judas; one of them was crucified, so he was rewarded in heaven, and the other was not, so he was rewarded by the Romans for his treachery. The latter is Judas Iscariot.

Prophet Muhammed as the "Paraclete," a Greek word meaning "Messenger" and "Comforter," in Arabic al-Amin... Even if you set aside the Gospel of St. Barnabas, a good Greek translation of the original of John 14:16 will be: "And I will Pray the Patera, and he shall give you another Paraclete, that he may abide with you forever." The Greek word Patera is erroneously translated into "the Father," a reference to the Almighty, in a "modern" version of the Bible which gives the following text for John 14:16-17: "And I will ask the Father, and he will give you another Counselor to be with you forever—the Spirit of Truth."[1] No man of righteousness has earned the title of "the Spirit of Truth" (in Arabic al-Sadiq) more than Prophet Muhammed. A good scholar of Greek will do better than that; he will translate Patera into "Nourisher" or "Sustainer," and Paraclete into "Comforter," al-Amin in Arabic, a title given to Prophet Muhammed even before he had started his mission. The translation of what John has in 14:16-17 should instead run as follows:

"And I will request the Nourisher (God) to send you another Messenger, so that he may be (your) guide always, the inspired, the Truthful, whom the world at large will not welcome because it will not comprehend or appreciate him, but you (believers) will recognize him. He will dwell with you and (his message) will find a place in your hearts."

A testimony to the truth of the statement saying "... and (his message) will find a place in your hearts" is that most converts to Islam used to follow one sect of Christianity or another. Upon acceptance of Islam, such converts do not abandon Christ; they simply rediscover him and get to know the real Christ whose message has been and is still being distorted. The best Christians in the world are the Muslims. Muslims wholeheartedly honour Jesus Christ and his true and pristine message presented by Prophet Muhammed; read the following verses of the Holy Qur'ān and see for yourself how such message is described:

---

[1] *The Great News: The New Testament* (Colorado Springs, Colorado: International Bible Society, 1984).

Allāh said: O Jesus! I am going to terminate the period of your stay (on earth) and cause you to ascend unto Me and purify you of those who disbelieve and make those who follow you above those who disbelieve till the Day of Resurrection... (3:55)

Carefully examine the above verse especially this portion: "... and make those who follow you above those who disbelieve till the Day of Resurrection" and see how the Almighty raises the status of those who follow Jesus above those who disbelieve in him till the Day of Judgment. Those who believe in Jesus Christ and who follow his pristine message are none other than the Muslims, whereas the rest may be divided into two groups: 1) those who have distorted the message of Jesus Christ and lied about it one generation after another and are still doing so, and 2) the Jews who disbelieved in him and in his message and disbelieved in his virgin birth. Although the Jews now are the masters of the world, thanks to the West in general and to the U.S. in particular, but such power they will not keep forever. They will eventually weaken because the promise of the Almighty is true and irreversible; they will be exposed for what they really are: the anti-Christ, the Dajjal, the disseminator of falsehood through their absolute control over the news and information media.

The Imām (ﻉ) asked the Catholic, "O Christian! Are you familiar with a statement in the Bible wherein Jesus says: 'I am going to my Lord and your Lord, and the Paraclete is coming who shall testify to my truth just as I testified for him, and he shall explain everything to you, and he shall be the one to expose all the sins of nations, and he shall be the one to smash the pillar of apostasy'?[1] The Catholic said, 'We admit all what you have just quoted of the Bible." The Imām

---

[1]This is a rough translation of the original Arabic text. A thorough research of the Bible may yield better results and reveal the exact Biblical verse the Imām was referring to. Unfortunately, the Imām did not specify which of the four Gospels he was quoting. Consulting a Bible in Arabic may also produce the same anticipated result: the number of the exact verse and the name of the Gospel the Imām had in mind.

asked him, "Do you testify that such a statement is actually fixed in the Bible?" "Yes," said the Catholic. Imām ar-Ridha said, "O Catholic! Could you tell me about the first Bible, how you lost it then found it, and who put your existing Bible together?" The Catholic said, "We did not lose the Bible except for one single day then we found it fresh; John and Matthew brought it back to us." Imām ar-Ridha (ع) said, "How little your knowledge of the Bible and its scholars is! If such is your claim, then why do you dispute with one another about the Bible? Rather, controversy has always revolved around the Bible which is in your hands today. Had it been the same as the first one was, you would not have thus disputed (with one another) about it, but I shall inform you of such controversy myself."

The Imām went on to state the following:

"Be informed that when the first Bible was lost, the Christians gathered around their scholars and said to them: 'Jesus son of Mary has been killed, and we do not know where the Bible is. You are the scholars; so, what do you have with you?' Luke and Mark said to them, We have learned the Bible by heart; so, do not grieve in its regard, and do not forsake the churches, for we shall recite to you one Gospel after another on each Sunday till we put it all together.' Luke, Mark, John and Matthew sat together, and they put this Bible of yours for you after you had lost the first (original) one. These four men were students of the early disciples; are you aware of that?!" The Catholic answered, "This I did not know and now I do. It is also now clear to me how much you know about the Bible, and I have heard from you things with which I was familiar and to which my heart testifies to be the truth. I have, therefore, gained a better understanding." Imām ar-Ridha then said to him, "How do you, then, find the testimony of these men?" "Accurate," said the Catholic, "since they are the scholars of the Bible, and everything to which they testified is the truth." Imām ar-Rida then turned to al-Mamoon and his company and said, "Bear witness to what he has just said." They said, "We testify." Then the Imām turned to the Catholic and said, "I challenge you to swear by the son and his mother whether you know if Matthew had said, The Messiah is David son of Abraham son of Isaac son of Jacob son of Yehuda son of Khadrun', and that Mark said about the lineage of Jesus son of Mary that he was 'The word of God which He placed in the human body, so it became human', and that Luke said, 'Jesus son of Mary and his mother were humans of flesh and blood, so the Holy Spirit entered into them'. Then you testify that Jesus had himself said the following about his creation: 'I tell you the truth: Whoever ascends the heavens descends from it except the man who rides the camel, the seal of the prophets, for he shall ascend to the heavens then shall he descend;' so, what do you say about that?" The Catholic said, "This is the speech of Jesus, and we do not deny it." Imām ar-Ridha (ﻉ) said, "If so, what do you say about the testimony of Luke, Mark, and Matthew with regard to Jesus and what they had attributed to him?" The Catholic said, "They lied about Jesus..." Imām ar-Ridha (ﻉ) turned to the audience and said, "O people! Has he not (a moment ago) testified to their truthfulness, saying that they were the scholars of the Bible and what they said is the truth?!" The Catholic said to the Imām (ﻉ), "O scholar of the Muslims! I would like you to excuse me from discussing these men." After a while the Imām (ﻉ) turned to that Catholic, who was an arch-bishop, and said, "In the Bible, it is written: 'The son of the virtuous woman is departing, and the "Paraclete" is coming after him, and he shall lighten the burdens and explain everything to you, and he shall testify for me as I have testified to you. I have brought you the parables, and he shall bring you the interpretation.' Do you believe that such a text exists in the Bible?" The Catholic answered in the affirmative.[1]

The Holy Qur'ān, moreover, tells us in Sūrat as-Saff (Ch. 61) that "Jesus son of Mary said: 'O Children of Israel! I am the prophet of Allāh to you testifying to that which is before me of the Torah and giving the glad tidings of a Prophet who will come after me; his name is Ahmed; but when he came to them with clear arguments, they said: This is clear magic" (Qur'ān, 61:6). Compare this

---

[1]al-Majlisi, *Bihār al-Anwār*, Vol. 14, pp. 331-333. Again, since this text is my translation from the Arabic original, the Imām's quotations may not be exact. Consulting a Bible written in Arabic will be worthwhile and will provide the numbers of the chapters and verses to which the Imām here refers. Unfortunately, I do not have a copy of the Bible in Arabic.

Qur'ānic verse with the following text in the Gospel of St. Barnabas:

> Thereupon said the disciples, "O master, it is thus written in the book of Moses, that in Isaac was the promise made."

> Jesus answered with a groan, "It is so written, but Moses wrote it not, nor Joshua, but rather our rabbins (rabbis), who fear not God. Verily, I say to you that if you consider the words of the angel Gabriel, you shall discover the malice of our scribes and doctors. For the angel said: Abraham, all the world shall know how God loves you, but how shall the world know the love that you bear to God? Assuredly it is necessary that you do something for the love of God.' Abraham answered, 'Behold the servant of God ready to do all that which God shall will.'

> "Then spoke God, saying to Abraham, 'Take your son, your firstborn Ishmael, and come up the mountain to sacrifice him.' How is Isaac firstborn, if when Isaac was born Ishmael was seven years old?!"

> Then answered Jesus, "Verily I say to you that Satan ever seeks to annul the laws of God. Therefore he with his followers, hypocrites and evildoers, the former with false doctrine, the latter with lewd living, today have contaminated almost all things, so that scarcely is the truth found. Woe to the hypocrites, for the praises of this world shall turn for them into insults and torments in hell.

> "I, therefore, say to you that the messenger of God is a splendor that shall give gladness to nearly all that God has made, for he is adorned with the spirit of understanding and of counsel, the spirit of wisdom and might, the spirit of fear and love (of God), the spirit of prudence and temperance. He is adorned with the spirit of charity and mercy, the spirit of justice and piety, the spirit of gentleness and patience, which he has received from God three times more than He has given to all his creatures. O blessed time, when he shall come to the world. Believe me that I have seen him and have done him reverence, even as every prophet has seen him. Seeing that of his spirit God gives to them prophecy. And when I saw him my soul was filled with consolation, saying, O Muḥammed, God be with you, and may he make me worthy to untie your shoe latchet, for obtaining this I shall be a great prophet and holy one of God." (The Gospel of Barnabas 44)

"... unworthy to untie your latchet" above brings to memory what St. Mark said in 1:7: "And this was his message: After me will come one more powerful than I, the thongs of whose sandals I am not worthy to stoop down and untie." The speaker is undoubtedly Jesus and the one whose coming he is predicting is none other than Prophet Muhammed (ﷺ). But people look at things and make them appear as they would like them to. Such is the truth which all other disciples, with the exception of Barnabas, had deliberately hidden.

The reader is encouraged to obtain a copy of the Gospel of Saint Barnabas[1] and compare it with other existing Bibles, be they those accepted by the Catholics or those endorsed by the Protestants, and judge for himself as to how much distortion the message of Christ has suffered and is still suffering...

The Catholic archbishop slipped into an obvious self-contradiction; for he on one hand sanctified the authors of the four gospels and held them above lying while, on the other hand, he admitted to the Imām that they did tell lies about Christ (ﻉ).

Then the Imām (ﻉ) debated with the High Rabbi, the most distinguished scholar of the Jews, to prove the prophethood of Prophet Muhammed (ﷺ) from the previously revealed divine testaments, after which he follows with a very logical debate. Having argued with him that one of the requirements of a Prophet was to perform something all other creation are unable to perform, he asked him about the reason why they, the Jews, refrained from believing into the miracles of all prophets other than Moses (ﻉ) son of Imran (Amram), and the High Rabbi answered him by saying, "We cannot admit the prophethood of any who professes prophethood except after bringing us knowledge similar to that brought by Moses." Ar-Ridha (ﻉ) said to him, "Then how come you admitted the prophethood of other prophets who preceded Moses (ﻉ)

---

[1]Since there is no copyright on The Gospel of Barnabas, the copy of it consulted for this book does not contain the Publisher's name nor the place nor the date of publication.

who did not split the sea, nor did they cleave the stones so that twelve springs would gush forth from it, nor did they take their hands out shining white as Moses did, nor did they turn a cane into a snake?!" It was then that the High Rabbi overcame his stubbornness, submitted to the argument, and admitted that any supernatural act beyond human capacity was indeed a proof of prophethood.

The Imām (ع) then asked him about the reason why the Jews did not believe in the prophethood of Jesus (ع) despite the fact that he brought forth miracles beyond human capacity such as bringing the dead back to life, healing those who were born blind and the lepers, and about the reason why they did not believe in the prophethood of Muhammed (ص) despite his bringing an extra-ordinary miracle, the Holy Qur'ān, although he was neither a scholar nor a writer. The High Rabbi had no answer at all.

Then came the turn of the Zoroastrian high priest whom the Imām debated based on the priest's belief in the prophethood of Zoroaster. The Zoroastrian told the Imām (ع) that Zoroaster brought them what no other man had ever brought them before. "We did not see him," he continued, "but the tales of our ancestors informed us that he legalized for us what no other person before had made legal; so, we followed him." The Imām (ع) asked him, "You believed in the tales which came to you about him, so you followed him, didn't you?" "Yes," he answered. The Imām (ع) said, "This is the case with all other nations. Tales came to them about what the prophets had accomplished, what Moses (ع), Jesus (ع), and Muhammed (ص) had all brought them, so why did you not believe in any of these prophets, having believed in Zoroaster through the tales that came to you about him informing that he brought forth what others did not?" The Zoroastrian high priest had no more to say.

After that the Imām turned to the debate's witnesses, having finished debating with the chief representatives of those creeds, asking anyone else to go ahead and put forth any question to him. Everyone abstained from doing so. It was then that Imran the Sabian, who was one of the most distinguished scholars of the science of kalam of his time, approached the Imām (ع) and asked him how he could prove the existence of the Creator. The discussion between them delved into the deepest depths of this complex question, while the Imām answered the man's questions through clear scientific facts in a very simple way. Among the questions Imran asked the Imām (ﻉ) was: "Master! Was the Being known to Himself by His Own Self?" The Imām said, "Knowledge is acquired by something which would negate its antithesis (ignorance). So that the thing itself would be existing through what it is negated, without the existence of anything which contradicts its existence, a need arises to negate that thing about itself by defining what is known about it. Do you understand, O Imran?" He said, "Yes, by Allāh, master! Tell me, then, by what means did He come to know what He knew, by a pronoun or by something else?" The Imām (ﻉ) said, "If it had been by a pronoun, would He then find anyway not to establish for that pronoun a limit where knowledge ends?" Imran answered, "Yes, He will have to find such a way." The Imām asked him, "Then what is that pronoun?" Imran could not provide any answer. The Imām (ﻉ) said, "Is it alright if I ask you about the pronoun and you define it by another pronoun? If you answer in the affirmative, then you would make both your claim and statement void. O Imran! Ought you not come to know that the One cannot be described by a pronoun and would not be described except by a verb, a deed, an action, and He cannot be expected to be parts and kinds like human beings?" Imran asked him, "Master! The knowledge I have says that the being is changed in his essence by his action of creating..." The Imām (ﻉ) said, "Does your statement, O Imran, mean that the being does not in any way change its essence except when it affects its own essence in a way which changes it? O Imran! Can you say that the fire changes its own nature, or that the heat burns itself, or have you seen anyone seeing his own vision?" Imran said, "No, I have not seen that; could you please tell me, master, is it the creation, or is it the nature of creation?" The Imām (ﻉ) said, "Yes, O Imran, He is above all of that; He is not in the creation, nor is the creation in Him; He is elevated above that, and bad indeed is your knowledge about Him, and there is no might except in Allāh. Tell me about the mirror: are you in it or is it in you? If neither one of you is in the other, then how did you come to see your own reflection in it?" Imran said, "Through the light between myself and it." The Imām (ﻉ) said, "Can you see of that light more than what you can with your own eyes?" He answered, "Yes." The Imām (ﻉ) said to him, "Then show it to us..." It was then that the man was too baffled to say a word. The Imām (ع) said, "I do not see the light except leading you and the mirror to come to know each other without being in either one of you. There are many such examples which the ignorant simply cannot observe, and Allāh Has the greatest example."

Thus did the Imām face the challenge of Imran the Sabian's doubting method, smashing it and dispelling the ambiguity of the complex doubts which he could not understand till vision became clear to him. The Imām (ع) did not determine an evidence except after building it with simple, easy to understand, proofs derived from everyday life in order not to leave any room for the opponent to doubt after transforming a most complex theory into an easy and commonsense idea, all of that by employing a very beautiful and miraculously effective style.

In another session, al-Ma'mūn invited the Imām (ع) to debate Sulayman al-Marazi, Khurasan's scientist in kalam, and the debate between them dealt with some significant topics which were being debated then by scholars of the science of kalam. The starting-point of the discussion was the issue of *bada'*. The Imām (ع) explained its sound meaning, indicating that the Sublime and Dear God had innermost knowledge which nobody but He knew: that was the source of *bada'* and the knowledge whereby He taught His angels and Prophets.

To explain it in a way which would remove all confusion and ambiguity, we can say about *bada'* is that Allāh makes it clear that His Divine Will is always linked to an advantage, a benefit, that necessitates it, brings about such Will, carries it out..., whereas what is apparent is that His Will is hinging on what is opposite thereto. Then He, after that, makes manifest His actual Will when the advantage is satisfied from all aspects, and the reasons for which it was not previously manifested are removed, and it appears to the creation as if Allāh willed to abandon His first Will, hence it is in the view of creation, not in the reality of Will, *bada'*. This is the theory of *bada'* in its simple logical context which Imāmis (Shī'as) uphold and which some people misunderstood and misinterpreted, giving it a wrong meaning which necessitated attributing ignorance (!!!) to

302

the Almighty God, an excuse to wage an unfair campaign of defamation against Imāmi Shī'as by their opponents from among the followers of other sects.

First, the Imām (ﻉ) has proven the accuracy of *bada'* in which Ahl al-Bayt (ﻉ) believe by: First quoting the Holy Qur'ān where Allāh Almighty says, فَتَوَلَّ عَنْهُمْ فَمَا أَنتَ بِمَلُومٍ "So leave them alone, for you shall not be blamed for that" (Qur'ān, 51:54), meaning thereby that He intends to annihilate them. Then the Almighty, according to the *bada'* theory, says, وَذَكِّرْ فَإِنَّ الذِّكْرَى تَنفَعُ الْمُؤْمِنِينَ "So remind (them), for (such) reminding may avail the believers" (Qur'ān, 51:55), which indicates a shift from the first decision as observed from studying the context of both verses.

Second, he tries to prove it through traditions narrated from his forefathers citing the Messenger of Allāh (ﻉ) saying, "Allāh sent his wahi to one of His prophets to inform him that he would die on a particular day, and when that prophet was told of it, he plead toed Allāh, the King, while on his bed, and kept saying, Lord! Postpone my demise till I see my son growing up to carry out my will' till he fell from his bed, whereupon Allāh sent his wahi again to the same prophet to inform him that He decided to postpone it."

It is apparent that *bada'* in the meaning which we indicated requires no reason whatsoever to be alarmed, and it does not justify waging a campaign of defamation against those who believe in it by those who do not.

The same discussion led to discussing the will's eternity and transience, and the Imām (ﻉ) stood to disprove the theory which called for the eternity of the will, proving its being transient by revealing its self-contradiction, removing the confusion which may occupy anyone's mind in its regard.

Will, as the Imām (ﻉ) says, is one of the actions of the Almighty. It is not one of His attributes; therefore, it is transient, not perpetual, since an action is a form of event, and the deed cannot be identical to the doer, so the will cannot be identical to the willing person. Will is not like hearing, or seeing, or knowing as al-Marazi tried to prove; it does not make sense, the Imām says, to say that He "wanted" Himself. Does He want to be "something," or does He want to be alive, Seeing, Hearing, or Able?! If this is according to His Will, it would require the impossible which is the change occurring to the self, for the meaning then would be that He wanted Himself to be something which was not... Sublime is Allāh greatly above all of this sophistry.

Thus did the debates between the Imām and al-Marazi take place frequently about the eternity of the will versus its transience with regard to relevant matters.

In his debates with the Imām (ﻉ), al-Marazi kept arguing and coming back to the same point from which he had started his argument in an inflexible argumentative manner. While accepting that to desire something (to "will", to wish, to desire, to decide) is a verb, he goes back to deny that, claiming that it is an adjective, and he may admit something and say something else.

The Imām asked him, "O Abū Sulayman! Can you tell me if the will is a verb or not?" He said, "Yes, it is a verb." The Imām (ﻉ) asked him, "Is it causative, since verbs are?" "It is not a verb," came the answer. The Imām (ﻉ) asked him, "Is there anyone besides Him who, too, is eternal?" Sulayman answered, "Willing is doing." The Imām (ﻉ) said, "O Sulayman! This is the same (sophistry) because of which you criticized Dirar and his followers, saying that everything Allāh Almighty has created in His heavens and earth, ocean or land, dog or pig, monkey, human, or an animal, is Allāh's will, and that Allāh's will gives life and takes life away, and it goes here or drinks from there, marries, enjoys food, commits immoral acts, disbelieves and commits shirk..." Sulayman said, "It is like hearing, seeing, or knowing; that is, it is an adjective, an attribute." Having abstained from providing an answer to the Imām's question, Sulayman went back to the beginning of the argument regarding whether the will is an adjective, an attribute, or a verb, but the Imām nevertheless repeated his argument with him by following another route different from the one he took first. This indicates how commonsense the idea seems to him and demonstrates his ability to prove it however he willed.

304

The debate continued between them in the same calm manner in which the Imām (ʿ) coined his questions, which is the most magnificent method of debate. In his way of providing answers, the Imām never blocked the avenue before his opponent to continue the debate; rather, he left him completely free to debate in whatever manner he wished through his questions till he brought him to a dead-end where he could not proceed anymore just to go back to seek another route which the Imām himself wanted him to seek out of his own will, and after his own conviction.

But Sulayman kept fumbling about in his answers to the Imām's questions after the Imām had closed before him all avenues of argument, and al-Ma'mūn was quick to notice his fumbling about which indicated Sulayman's loss, so he rebuked the latter and criticized him. It is reported that during the debate, when ar-Ridha (ʿ) asked him to continue his questions, he said, "Will is one of His attributes." The Imām said, "How many times have you said that it is one of His attributes?! Is it a new attribute, or has it always been so?" Sulayman said, "New." The Imām (ʿ) said, "Allāhu Akbar! You are telling me that His attribute is new! Had it been one of His attributes, an eternal one, then He willed and He created as long as His will and His creation are eternal...! This means it is an attribute of someone who did not know what he did! Allāh is Elevated above this..." Sulayman said, "Things are not a will, and He did not will anything." Here the Imām said, "You have hissed, O Sulayman! He did and He created as long as His will and His creation are eternal...?! This is the attribute of someone who does not know what he is doing! Elevated is Allāh above all of that." Turning to al-Ma'mūn, Sulayman then said, "Master! I have already informed him that it is like hearing and seeing and knowing." Al-Ma'mūn said, "Woe unto you, Sulayman! How you have erred and how often you have repeated yourself! Stop it and take another route, for you seem to be unable to provide any answer better than that."

The debate continued after that till Sulayman's tongue was tied, whereupon al-Ma'mūn said, "O Sulayman! This is the most learned descendant of Hashim," and the session was terminated.

The Imām (ﻉ) also conducted a very magnificent debate with Ali ibn al-Jahm dealing with the infallibility of prophets in which he explained in a very beautiful way. He underscored the fact that the superficial meaning of some verses may give the impression of self-contradiction. The Imām (ﻉ) started his discussion with Ali ibn al-Jahm by criticizing him and those who interpreted the Book of Allāh according to their own viewpoints, stating that he and those folks have to refer to those whom Allāh endowed with the faculty of knowledge and understanding in order to learn the actual and accurate interpretation of such verses. This is according to the sacred verse which says, "And none knows its interpretation except Allāh and those deeply grounded in knowledge" (Qur'ān, Ali Imran:7). Then the Imām (ﻉ) started explaining the verses whose superficial meaning indicates the fallibility and possibility of sinning by prophets. He indicated that Adam's transgression took place while he was in Paradise, not on earth, and the infallibility in question is earthly, and that he did not commit any sinning act as long as he lived on earth which contradicted his infallibility as proven by the following sacred verse: "Allāh did indeed choose Adam and Noah, the family of Abraham, and the family of Imran above all people" (Qur'ān, Ali Imran:33). As regarding the verse which states the following: "And remember Thun-nan when he departed in wrath; he imagined that We had no power over him, but he cried through the depths of darkness, There is no God but You! Glory to You; I was indeed wrong"(Qur'ān, Al-Anbiya':87), what is meant by "he imagined that We had no power over him" is that he realized that Allāh was not going to sustain him." Had he thought that Allāh was unable to overpower him, he would have then committed kufr (apostasy) and he would have also committed 'isyan, transgression.

As regarding the verse "And (with passionate lust) did she desire him, and he would have desired her" (Qur'ān, Yousuf:24), the case regarding what the wife of al-'Aziz wanted, and what Yousuf (ﻉ) desired to do, are two different things, for she wanted to commit a sin while he desired to kill her if she forced him; therefore, Allāh saved him from the deed of killing her and its terrible consequences, and saved her from her own wishful desire to commit a sin.

As regarding prophet David (ﻉ), his statement that the defendant had committed injustice by asking for the ewe, it was an error only within the framework of the case, and it took place before he had asked the defendant about his defense against the plaintiff's claim, and it is not a transgression, for Allāh corrected his decision for him by bringing him the example of the two kings. As regarding his marriage with the widow of Uryah, which was regarded by people at that time as a sin and criticized him for it, it was done for the sake of effecting a legislative interest whereby David wanted to shatter the then prevalent custom of a widow not getting married after the death of her husband. It is similar to what happened to the Prophet with Zainab daughter of Jahsh, wife of Zaid ibn Harithah who had been adopted by the Prophet (ﷺ). By marrying Zainab after granting her divorce from Zaid, the Prophet (ﷺ) wanted to shatter the pre-Islamic custom whereby a man would not be permitted to marry the former wife of someone whom he had adopted, as is clear in the text of the Holy Qur'ān. The Prophet (ﷺ) was apprehensive of the criticism of the hypocrites of his action, so the Almighty addressed him by saying, "Do not fear people; it is more fitting that you should fear Allāh" (Qur'ān, Al Ahzab:37), since it was Allāh Who ordered him to marry her as we understand from the verse, "Then when Zaid had dissolved (his marriage) with her, with the necessary (formality), We joined her in marriage to you in order that (henceforth) there will be no difficulty to the believers in (the matter of) marrying the wives of their adopted sons, when the latter have dissolved with the necessary (formality, their marriage) with them, and Allāh's command must be fulfilled" (Qur'ān, Al Ahzab:37).

By providing such glorious knowledge of the exegesis of sacred Qur'ānic verses, and by giving such honest interpretations which safeguard the integrity of the context, the Imām (ع) used to dispel the confusion of those who did not have a deep actual understanding of the Glorious Book of Allāh.

In his book *Al-'Iqd al-Farid*, Ibn Abd Rabbih al-Andalusi recorded a debate on the subject of Imāmate between the Imām and caliph al-Ma'mūn which seems to be stamped with artificiality, and we think it is possible that some fanatics from among those who deviated from the line of the Ahl al-Bayt (ع) had fabricated it, for he stated the following in his book:

Al-Ma'mūn said to Ali ibn Mūsa (ع), "Why do you claim it (Imāmate) for your own selves?" The Imām (ع) answered, "Due to Ali and Fatima (ع) being near in kin to the Messenger of Allāh (ص)." Al-Ma'mūn said, "If it is only a matter of kinship, then the Messenger of Allāh (ص) had left behind him those who were closer in kinship to him than Ali or any of his relatives, and if you mean the kinship of Fatima (ع) to the Messenger of Allāh (ص), then the matter (Imāmate) after her should have belonged to al-Hassan and al-Hussain (ع) whose right was confiscated by Ali even while they were still alive, taking control of what was not his." Ali ibn Mūsa (ar-Ridha [ع]) could not provide an answer.

Let us record the following regarding this quotation:

The Imām did not claim his right to caliphate only on account of his kinship to the Prophet (ص), but rather on account of the clear statements made by the Prophet (ص) emphasizing that he was to be the caliph after him, in addition to the personal qualifications which adorned Imām Ali (ع) and which distinguished him above the rest of *sahāba*.

The concept of caliphate according to Ahl al-Bayt (ع) is that it is decreed according to a divine text, not dictated due to factors of kinship, politics, etc. Allāh is the One Who chooses, and His choice is conveyed by His Prophet (ص), whoever He sees to be most fit to safeguard the Message and the interest of the nation. The claim of those who said that they deserved caliphate due to their kinship to the Prophet (ص) is similar to the claim of those who said that the muhajiran (immigrants) were more qualified than the Ansār (supporters of Medīna) due to the nearness of the first party to the Messenger of Allāh (ص). The Imām, if this story is true at all, would not have been unable, as it suggests, to answer al-Ma'mūn's objection that there are among the Ahl al-Bayt (ع) those who had more priority than Ali (ع) or any of his relatives, an apparent reference to his grandfather al-Abbās ibn Abdul-Muttalib[1], to

---

[1]This is a direct reference to the Abbāsides who regarded themselves as more worthy of ruling the Muslims than all others although they proved to

caliphate. It was al-Abbās himself who approached the Imām requesting him to stretch his hand to him so that he would swear the oath of allegiance to him when he felt that the fate looked ominous and that the environment was threatening of a revolt. But the Imām refused to accept such an oath privately; rather, he preferred that such an oath be sworn to him in public and before eye witnesses after finishing the funeral rites for the Messenger of Allāh (ﷺ) whose corpse was still lying in state waiting to be bathed and buried[1]. If you suppose that al-Abbās had any right to the caliphate, he would then have relinquished it.

As regarding al-Hassan and al-Hussain, they were then very young; Hassan was 10 and Hussain was 9. Neither wilayat nor wisayat can be enforced on caliphate till they were old enough, for caliphate is a post which permits no wisayat at all; therefore, the issue of caliphate was confined to Ali (ﷺ) alone.

The fact that al-Ma'mūn's way of thinking regarding the issue of caliphate, and his views with which he confronted the faqihs in his debates, as the author of *Al-'Iqd al-Farid* العقد الفريد himself mentions, proving that caliphate was the legitimate right of only Ali rather than anyone else among the sahāba, this fact itself convinces us that this fabricated dialogue quoted above was written by some fanatic followers of other sects.

Imām ar-Ridha (ﷺ) did not write a book on exegesis, but he explained the meanings of the Qur'ānic verses about which he was asked, and we will indicate here some such explanations in order to acquaint you with the magnificent method and innovative style of

---

be among the very worst who ever ruled the Islamic nation. The title of the founder of their government, namely "as-Saffah," which means "the blood-shedder," says it all.

[1]The very fact that the so-called "election" of the first caliph, Abū Bakr, took place at Saqafat Bana Saida before the Prophet (ﷺ) had been buried opens the eyes even of the blind to the fact that those who were involved in such "election" masquerade were more concerned about power and politics than about burying the corpse of their Prophet (ﷺ).

the Imām (ع) in this regard.

Al-Ma'mūn asked him once to explain some Qur'ānic verses out of his curiosity about the knowledge which Allāh bestowed upon the Imām (ع). Among such verses was this one: "He it is Who created the heavens and the earth in six days, and His throne was over the water, so that He might try you which of you is best in conduct" (Qur'ān, Hud:7). He said, "The Praised and Exalted Allāh created the Throne, the water, and the angels before the creation of the heavens and the earth, and the angels used to know Allāh through their own creation, through the Throne and the water. Then He made His Throne over the water in order to manifest His might to the angels so that they might know that He is capable of doing whatever He pleased. Then He raised the Throne through His might, moved it and made it above the seven heavens. Then He created the heavens and the earth in six periods of time. He was capable of creating them in a twinkle of the eye, but the Exalted One created them in six periods in order to show the angels what He was creating, one creation after another, so that they would know time, and so that they would again know that Allāh was the absolute Originator of each and every thing. Allāh did not create the Throne because He was and is independent of it and of everything He created; He cannot be described by anything in the cosmos simply because He has no physical body; Exalted is He above the characteristics of what He created a great deal of Exaltation.

"As regarding His saying, ...so that He might try you which of you is best in conduct,' He has created them in order to test them through the responsibility of obeying and worshipping Him, not out of His desire to test or to try them, since He already knows all things."

Al-Ma'mūn also asked him about the meaning of this verse: "Had it been thy Lord's Will, they would all have believed, (so would have) all those on earth! Will you then compel mankind, against their will, to believe?! No soul can believe except by the Will of Allāh" (Qur'ān, Younus:99-100). Quoting his forefathers, ar-Ridha (ع) said, "Muslims said to the Messenger of Allāh (ص), We wish you forced those whom you have conquered, O Messenger of Allāh, to accept Islam, so that our number would increase, and we would become

310

stronger in the face of our enemies.' The Messenger of Allāh (ﷺ) said, I am not going to meet Allāh, the Almighty and the Exalted, having invented an innovation which He did not command me to do, nor am I the type of person who forces others to do anything at all.' It was then that this verse was revealed: Had it been thy Lord's Will, they would all have believed, (so would have) all those on earth,' by means of forcing them, or when they find no other choice while in this world, just as will those who will believe only after witnessing Allāh's might and retribution in the life after death. If I do such a thing to them, they would not deserve any reward, but I wish they accept it out of their own choice rather than being forced to do so in order that they may deserve to be close to me and blessed through me, and they will thus remain in Paradise forever.'

"As regarding the meaning of No soul can believe except by the Will of Allāh,' it does not mean that it is prohibited from believing (without a prior consent from Allāh); it simply means that Allāh invites it to believe without forcing it to do so."

The Imām (ع) said the following in his explanation of the verse which says, "[Allāh is He] Who has made the earth your couch, and the heavens your canopy" (Qur'ān, Al-Baqara:22): "He made the earth suitable to the creation of your nature, agreeable to your bodies; He did not make it too hot to burn you, nor too cold to freeze you, nor too windy to cause you dizziness, nor too stinky to damage your heads, nor as liquid as water to cause you to drown, nor too solid to enable you to build houses and graves for your dead; rather, the Exalted and the Sublime One made it strong enough to be useful for you, for your bodies, and for your buildings, making it usable in your homes and graves and a great deal of other advantages as well; thus, He made the earth a couch for you.

"As for the heavens, He made them like a protective ceiling above your heads in which He let the sun and its moon and the stars orbit for your own good. He ... 'sent down water from the heavens, and brought forth therewith fruits for your sustenance,' meaning thereby water which He caused to descend from a high altitude in order to reach the summits of your mountains and hills, valleys and plains. He caused it to descend as showers and as moisture which soil inhales, and He did not cause it to pour down at once to ruin your lands, trees and other vegetation and fruits. And brought forth therewith fruits for your sustenance' (Qur'ān, Al-Baqara:22) means whatever grows on earth for your sustenance, so Do not set up rivals unto Allāh while you know (the truth),' that is, rivals' such as similitudes and such things like idols which have no comprehension, hearing, sight, nor are they able to do anything at all, while you know that they cannot create any of these great blessings with which He, your Lord, the Exalted, the Most High, has blessed you."

About the subject of the infallibility of Prophets, the Imām (ع) was asked to explain the meanings of some verses whose superficial meanings suggest that Prophets were not infallible at all, that they were liable to commit sins. At one of the meetings arranged by al-Ma'mūn, the latter asked the Imām (ع): "O Son of the Messenger of Allāh (ص)! Don't you claim that Prophets are infallible?" The Imām (ع) answered in the affirmative. Al-Ma'mūn then asked him, "Then what is the meaning of this verse: Thus did Adam disobey his Lord and allow himself to be seduced'?" The Imām answered this question by explaining that Allāh had forbidden Adam and Eve from coming close to a particular tree without forbidding them from eating its fruit or the fruit of similar trees. They obeyed Allāh by not coming near that tree, but Iblis (Eblis) confused them in this regard and suggested that they should eat not from that tree but from other similar trees, swearing to them by Allāh that he was only providing them with advice. So they believed in his oath, and they ate the fruit of a similar tree, and that was before Adam was considered as a Prophet and before his descent to earth. What he did was not a sin for which the penalty is Hellfire, but it was a minor disobedience which could be forgiven and could be committed by Prophets before wahi (revelation) reaches them. When Allāh chose him and made him a Prophet, he became infallible and was not permitted to commit a sin, minor or major, telling him, "Thus did Adam disobey his Lord and allow himself to be seduced. But his Lord chose him (for His Grace); He turned to him, and gave him guidance.'"

Then he asked him about Ibrahim (Abraham) al-Khalil (ع), the Friend of Allāh, and about the stage of doubt through which he passed as appears on the surface in the Holy Qur'ān when he is mentioned, till truth became manifest to him and he believed therein. The Almighty says, "When the night covered him, he saw a star. He said, This is my Lord.' But when it set, he said, I do not love those that set.' When he saw the moon rising in splendour, he said, This is my Lord.' But the moon set, so he said, Unless my Lord guides me, I shall surely be among those who go astray.' When he saw the sun rising in splendour, he said, This is my Lord; this is the greatest (of all).' But when the sun set, he said, O my people! I am indeed free from your (guilt) of ascribing partners to Allāh. For me, I have set my face firmly and truly towards Him Who created the heavens and the earth, and never shall I attribue partners to Allāh'" (Qur'ān, Al An'am:76-79). About this issue, the Imām (ع) commented thus:

"Ibrahim (ع) never passed through a stage of doubt in Allāh; rather, his story may be summarized thus: He lived in a society where three types of worship dominated: the worship of Venus, the worship of the moon, and the worship of the sun. The outward pretense of Ibrahim (ع) to follow these religions before declaring his belief in Allāh was only to deny the validity of each one of them and to prove to others the fact that they were invalid, not due to his temporary belief in them. He simply wanted to prove to their fellows, through the method of argument which he employed in a spirit filled with belief in Him, that their type of creed and their norm of worship of Venus, the moon, and the sun, were not appropriate due to the variation which occurred to them and which is one of the attributes of the creatures, not of the Creator."

Then the Imām (ع) added saying, "What Ibrahim al-Khalil (ع) did was actually according to the inspiration which he had received from Allāh by the token of the verse that says, That was the reasoning about Us which We gave to Abraham (to employ) against his people' (Qur'ān, Al-An'am:83). What he did, therefore, was merely a method to win the argument against his people regarding the invalidity of their norms of worship and in their belief in gods other than Allāh, which is a unique method among Qur'ānic methods to invite others to believe."

Al-Ma'mūn then asked him about the meaning of the verse which says, "... till the apostles give up hope (of their people) and (their

313

people come to) think that they proved them to be liars, Our help will then come to them" (Qur'ān, Yousuf:110). The reason for questioning is attributing despair to Allāh's Messengers after being promised help from Allāh. Despair and despondency are forms of kufr (disbelief); the Almighty has said, "Never give up hope of Allāh's mercy; truly none despairs of Allāh's mercy except those who have no faith" (Qur'ān, Yousuf:87). So, how can despair find its way to the heart of a messenger of Allāh, or a prophet, knowing that, according to this verse, only kafirs can do so, and what is a greater sin than committing *kufr*?!

What is superficially obvious from the text of this verse is that the time when they despaired was after receiving the Message and inspiration. To this, the Imām (ع) answered by saying that the subject of despair in this verse is not Allāh's help promised to His messengers, but rather losing hope of their people ever believing in them and accepting their message; i.e. to believe in Him and renounce their previous disbelief and disobedience by their worship of gods other than Allāh. The meaning of this verse, then, will be something like this: When the messengers lost hope that their people would ever believe in them, and when those people thought that they succeeded in proving those messengers liars, it is then that Our help came to them.

Thus is the outward ambiguity of the verse removed, and thus does the Imām (ع), through providing such glorious explanations to the sacred verses of the Holy Qur'ān whose outward meaning is actually the opposite of that of the context, dispel the cloud of doubt which may come to one's mind regarding the infallibility of Prophets. They are not mere justifications or one's own personal opinions; rather, they are actual facts; to uphold to the contrary is not possible.

There are other verses the superficial meaning of which gives the impression that Allāh has limbs just as humans do which He uses to achieve His purpose. An example is His statement addressing Iblis when the latter refused to prostrate to Adam as commanded by Allāh: "What prohibited you from prostrating to what I have created with My own hands?" and also the verse saying, "When a leg will be uncovered and they are invited to prostrate..."

314

The Imām (ﻉ) explains the meaning of Allāh's hand to be His might. The meaning of the previous verse would be, "What prohibited you from prostrating to what I have created with My might and power?" Allāh does not have eyes, legs, hands, or any such things as we may imagine which would put limits to Allāh like those to man, and the revealed texts containing a reference to such things are given meanings which agree with conceiving Allāh to be Exalted above having physical dimensions a great deal of exaltation.

The "leg" is interpreted by the Imām as a barrier of light which, when removed, will cause the believers to fall prostrating, while the legs of the hypocrites become too stiffened to prostrate.

Thus does Imām ar-Ridha (ﻉ) portray for us an accurate picture which is honest in interpreting the meanings embedded in the Glorious Book if we wish to honestly and wisely interpret its verses.

One more thing remains. There are narratives which contain some interpretations of Qur'ānic verses attributed to Imām ar-Ridha (ﻉ) the authenticity of which is questioned simply because some of those who reported them are not free of the practice of distortion or fabrication. What we feel comfortable with is: if such narrations do not contain anything which disagrees with the beliefs of followers of the Ahl al-Bayt (ﻉ) regarding the interpretation of Qur'ānic verses, it will be a testimony to their authenticity. Add to this the fact that we think it is quite unlikely that some narrators would deliberately tell lies about the Imām (ﻉ) in cases where telling lies does not benefit the narrator a bit, particularly in the interpretations of the verses which we have quoted above. This is why we find scholars of exegesis rely on such narratives and their likes in explaining the Holy Qur'ān. If they contradict one another, they accept the one which seems to have the most sound meaning, or to the ones which agree with the basic principles of the School of Thought.

In the case where the interpretation of certain verses becomes the basis of a legislative rule, or in the process of deriving one, then the authenticity of narration or interpretation has to be verified first as one provided by the Prophet (ﺹ) or by members of his Ahl al-Bayt

(ε), and attempts should be made to make sure that the integrity of their narrators is not questioned.

Commander of the Faithful Imām Ali ibn Abū Talib (ε) justifies the existence of Qur'ānic verses which can be interpreted in more than one way by saying, "The Almighty has done so in order to foil the attempt of wrong-doers from among those who would take control over the legacy of the knowledge of the Book left by the Messenger of Allāh (ε), which he did not intend them to acquire, rendering them unable to explain the various possible meanings thereof." It is as if Allāh willed that the Prophet (ص) and those who would bear the Message after him would have a special distinction which is: the understanding of what others are not able to understand, so that people would resort to them when they are unable to understand certain verses of the Holy Qur'ān which they need to understand for the betterment of their life and the comprehension of their creed.

The Imām's answers to theological questions were all in harmony with the environment of the occasion surrounding their legislation. Causes may be to achieve a social benefit, when the social aspect of legislation is more apparent than any other, or for a health-related, spiritual or psychological benefit. For example, when he explains the causes for the prohibition of adultery, the Imām (ε) says, "Adultery is prohibited due to the corruption it causes such as murders, loss of lineage, child desertion, chaos regarding inheritance, and other such aspects of corruption." The Imām (ε) explains to us why usury (riba) is prohibited by saying, "The reason for prohibiting usury is because it eliminates favours, ruins funds, causes greed for profit, causes people to abandon their dealing with loans to each other or in paying with cash, or when they do each other favours, and due to all the bad consequences of corruption and oppression and the exhaustion of funds."

As regarding the prohibition of eating the meat of pigs, rabbits, dead animals, spleens, the Imām (ε) says, "As regarding pigs, their creation was distorted by Allāh in order to provide a moral lesson to man, and in order to remind man to fear Allāh, and as an evidence of Allāh's might to distort what He creates at will, and because the food they eat is the filthiest of filth, in addition to many other reasons. As regarding the rabbits, they are like cats: Their claws are like those of cats and like wild animals. Their behaviour, therefore, is equally wild, in addition to their own inner dirtiness and due to their bleeding which is similar to the bleeding of women during their menstrual period because they are miscreants. As regarding dead animals, the prohibition of eating their meat is due to the damage such meat will cause to the body, and due to the fact that Allāh has made lawful the meat of animals slaughtered in His name so that that would be a distinction between what is lawful and what is not. As regarding the spleen, it is prohibited because of the bad blood it contains, and the cause of its prohibition is similar to that of dead animals; it is equally bad in its consequences."

The Imām (ع) has said the following regarding the legislation of the pilgrimage (hajj): "The reason for the hajj is to seek to be the guest of Allāh, to request more blessings, to part with past sins, to feel repentant about the past, and to look forward to the future. It is due to spending on the trip seeking nearness to Allāh, tiring the body, abstaining from pleasures and desires, seeking nearness to Allāh by worshipping Him, yielding and submitting to Him, looking up towards Him in cases of hot weather and chilling cold, during security and fear, incessantly doing so, and due to all the benefits in it of desiring the rewards and fearing the wrath of Allāh, the Dear One, the Exalted."

As regarding marital relations between man and woman, the Imām (ع) justifies for us some legislative rules in this regard. For example, the reason why a man may marry up to four women, while a woman is prohibited from marrying more than one man, is that when a man marries four women, his children will all be related to him; had a woman married two husbands or more simultaneously, nobody would know for sure who fathered the sons she gave birth to, since they all were in cohabiting with her, and this causes a complete disorder for relating one to his father, and who should inherit who, and who is the kin of who.

The reason for repeating the divorce statement thrice is due to the time interval between each, and due to a possible desire for reconciliation or the calming of anger, if any, and to teach women to respect their husbands and deter them from disobeying them.

The reason why a husband can never remarry his wife whom he divorced thrice (articulating, in the process, the divorce statement nine times all in all), is that it is his right penalty so that men do not take divorce lightly or take advantage of women and think of them as weak, and so that the man would be considering his affairs, remaining awake and aware, so that he would lose all hope of a reunion after the ninth pronouncement of the divorce statement. The reason why a wife during her waiting period (iddat) cannot remarry her previous husband who had divorced her twice till she marries someone else, is due to the fact that Allāh had permitted divorce twice, saying, "A divorce is only permissible twice: after that, the parties should either hold together on equitable terms, or separate with kindness,"[1] that is, after he had already divorced her for the third time, due to his committing something which Allāh Almighty hates for him to do; therefore, He prohibited him from marrying her again except after she marries someone else in order to prohibit people from taking divorce lightly and in order to protect women's rights.

Regarding the monetary distribution of inheritance by allotting the male heir twice the share of that of the female, the Imām (ع) says the following: "The reason for giving women half what men get of inheritance is that when the woman marries, she receives, while the man gives; therefore, Allāh decided to assist the males to be able to give."

He provides another reason why the man is given twice as much as the woman: The woman is considered dependent on the man when she needs, and he has to take care of her living expenses and to spend on her, while the woman is not required to take care of the expenses of the man, nor can she be required to pay his expenses if he was in need; therefore, Allāh decreed to give the man more according to the Qur'ānic verse, "Men are the protectors and maintainers of women because Allāh has given the one more than

---

[1]Qur'an, Sūrat Al-Baqarah:229.

the other, and because they support them from their means."[1]

Regarding the common custom of defining the value of the dower to be equivalent to the value of five hundred dirhams, the Imām (ع) says in a narrative: "Allāh the Almighty and the Exalted has promised that if one believer pronounced *Allāhu Akbar!* one hundred times, and *Subhana-Allāh* one hundred times, and *Alhamdu-Lillah* one hundred times, and *La Ilaha Ila-Allāh* one hundred more times, and send blessings unto His Prophet (ص) yet a hundred more, then he pleads to Him to grant him in marriage the huris of Paradise with large lovely eyes, He would surely marry him to one, then He determined women's dowers to be five hundred dirhams. If any believer asks the hand of a woman from another Muslim brother, pays him the five hundred dirhams, and the brother does not marry him to that woman, he would have committed 'uqooq (disobedience of Allāh's commandments) towards him, and Allāh will not marry him to a huri."

The hadīth of Imām ar-Ridha (ع) contains precious jewels and invaluable treasures in which man senses the depth of the idea, the magnificence of tafsir, the beauty of performance, with neither the artificial manner of expression, nor the ambiguity of meaning, nor the stubbornness of instruction. When he is asked about the reasonable comprehension of some ahādīth of the Prophet (ص) in which a cloud of ambiguity hovers above their narration, he defines their actual objective with flexibility and ease, as if hadīth has no other connotation except the one he provides.

Some people asked him (ع) about the meaning of this tradition: "My companions are like the stars: If you follow any of them, you shall receive guidance," and another one saying, "Leave my companions to me." Both of these traditions are considered by Sunnis as the foundation of their generalization of judgement regarding all companions of the Prophet (ص) barring none, thus justifying even their acts which contradicted Islamic justice, calling what they could not justify as "an error in ijtihad." But the Imām (ع) provides us with

---

[1]Qur'an, Sūrat An-Nisa':34.

the actual explanation of these and other such ahādīth with honesty and integrity, outlining in an easy manner their exact meaning. In his answer regarding the first tradition, he said, "Yes; he did say this hadīth, meaning thereby the companions who did not make any alteration after him or any change (to the Islamic creed)." He was asked, "How can you tell that they altered and changed?" He said, "This is due to what is reported about him (ع) that he said, Certain individuals among my companions will be pushed away by force from my Pool (of Kawthar) on the Day of Judgement just as strange camels are pushed away from the watering place, and I shall cry, O Lord! My companions! My companions!' and it shall be said to me, You do not know what innovations they invented after you,' so they will be pushed away towards the left side (where Hell is), and I shall say, Away with them; ruined they shall be.'" The Imām continued to say, "Such will be the penalty of those who alter and change (the *hadīth* and the Sunnah)."

This *hadīth* is narrated, with a minor variation in its wording, by al-Bukhari who quotes Abdullāh ibn Mas'ud citing the Prophet (ص) saying, "I shall be the first to reach the Pool, then the souls of some men from among you will be resurrected and they shall be prohibited from coming near me, and I shall say, Lord! These are my companions!' And it shall be said to me, You do not know what they did after you...'"[1] A number of huffaz and narrators of hadīth reported this tradition in various wordings which maintained the same contextual meaning, proving thus that it is consecutively reported.

The Imām (ع), through his frank and proven answer, saved us the effort to look for lame excuses for the flagrant transgressions in which a number of the sahāba fell, and from far-fetched artificialities to justify the errors of conduct which they deliberately committed with determination and which the same *huffaz* could not justify except by saying that they were cases of "mistaken ijtihad" which, according to them, did not contradict the justice expected of them, having been pressed by their attempt to attribute absolute justice to

---

[1] *al-Bukhari, Sahīh, Vol. 8, p. 119, Amari edition.*

the sahabi no matter what he did...!

A companion (*sahabi*) of the Prophet (ﷺ) who was distinguished with the honour of being so close to the Prophet (ﷺ) is the custodian over the fruits of the Message and the protector of its structure through his faith and deeds. He is a man who ought to be taken as a role model of conduct. He is a man, as the Imām (ع) used to say, who does not alter or change any of the statements of the Prophet (ﷺ). As regarding those who altered and changed, these cannot be awarded a unique distinction, just because they were companions of the Prophet (ﷺ), which raised their status above that of other Muslims simply because they were not up to par with the level of responsibility of being honest, which is expected of them, to carry out after the demise of the Prophet (ﷺ) and the cessation of *wahi* (divine inspiration).

The *hadīth* which the Imām (ع) narrated about Ibn Mas'ud, and which is recorded by a number of those who learned the Holy Qur'ān and hadīth by heart in their books, is considered as an explanation of this hadīth and of its connotation. Moreover, it puts the sahāba on equal footing with the others in subjecting their behaviour to criticism and discussion, and it shatters the self-immunity which was granted to them in accordance with alleged Prophetic "statements" actually fabricated by a number of *huffaz* and traditionists without permitting themselves or others to discuss but take for granted.

In another *hadīth*, the Imām (ع) proves to us, through a clear tradition by the Prophet (ﷺ), that some individuals who were regarded as sahāba were not actually so, which shatters all the excuses used to justify the mistakes and the transgression committed by them. For example, Muhammed ibn Ishāq at-Taliqani reported that a man in Khurasan swore by divorce that Mu'awiyah was not among the true companions of the Messenger of Allāh (ﷺ), and this happened when Imām ar-Ridha (ع) was present there. The jurists there issued their verdict that the man had actually divorced his wife, and the Imām (ع) was asked to provide his own opinion in this regard. He decided that the man's wife was not divorced; therefore, those jurists wrote a statement and sent it to him. In it, they asked him, "How did you come to say, O son of the Messenger of Allāh (ﷺ), that the woman was not to be divorced?" He wrote down on the same sheet saying, "It is so because of what you yourselves narrate from Abū Sa'eed al-Khudri who quotes the Messenger of Allāh (ﷺ) saying about those who accepted Islam on the day of conquering Mecca, that is, Friday, the 20th of the month of Ramadan, 8 A.H., corresponding to January 14, 630 A.D., when he was surrounded by a large number of people, You are good; my companions are good; and there shall be no migration after this Fath (conquest),' without including these (meaning Mu'awiyah) among his companions." The jurists had to adopt the decision of the Imām (ﷺ).

Thus did the Imām (ﷺ) deny that Mu'awiyah was a companion of the Prophet (ﷺ). Such a claim used to surround this man with a halo of sanctity and was used to justify the very serious transgressions which he committed. Such transgressions left their terrible marks on the structure of the Islamic government since then. They justified such transgressions by saying that he was a sahabi, and that, as such, whatever he did or said could not possibly cast a doubt about his integrity, adding, "If we see the good aspect of his action missing, we may say that he attempted *ijtihad*, and he erred," even if such error was at the expense of the Prophet's Message itself...!

If we accept this argument, we would be justifying all the transgressions and erroneous behaviour of some companions of the Prophet (ﷺ) regardless of their motives or horrible consequences. The transgressions of Mu'awiyah and his norms of conduct, in which he departed from the line of the Islamic Message altogether, and which agreed with the attitude of animosity towards Islam, and whose motives and impulses were to cast doubts and suspicions, nobody is really obligated to defend and describe as within the Islamic Shari'a simply because they were the result of an erroneous ijtihad wherein the mujtahid is rewarded with one reward, due to his "immunity" which does not include Mu'awiyah simply because the latter was not a companion of the Prophet (ﷺ) but was just like any other Muslim whose conduct was subject to accountability and criticism, and the verdict in his regard is based on the anticipated results of his deeds.

322

The directive which the Imām (ﻉ) intended by denying that those who accepted Islam, including Mu'awiyah, were not all companions of the Prophet on the day when Mecca was conquered, is one of the strongest and deepest of his directives, for he drew a line between the Prophet (ﺹ) and his true companions on one hand, and those who accepted Islam after the conquest of Mecca and under the pressure of a superior power and authority on the other. Had it not been for their reaction to the precarious situation versus the might of their opponent, realizing that they had no choice except to make asylum and submit to the word of Islam, they would have otherwise dealt with Islam in a quite different manner...

Al-Ma'mūn once asked the Imām (ﻉ) why the Commander of the Faithful Imām Ali (ﻉ) is called the divider of Paradise and of Hell, and how that attribute came to be applied to him. The Imām (ﻉ) in turn asked him, "O commander of the faithful! Have you not narrated from your father from his forefathers quoting Abdullāh ibn Abbās saying that he had heard the Messenger of Allāh (ﻉ) saying, Loving Ali (ﻉ) is iman, and hating him is *kufr*?'" Al-Ma'mūn answered in the affirmative, so the Imām (ﻉ) said, "If the distribution of Paradise and of Hell is done according to loving or hating him, then he is the distributor of Paradise and of Hell." Al-Ma'mūn then said, "May Allāh never permit me to live after your demise, O father of al-Hassan! I testify that you are the heir of the knowledge of the Messenger of Allāh (ﺹ)."

Abul-Salt al-Harawi said, "After the Imām (ﻉ) had gone back home, I came to visit him, and I said to him, O son of the Messenger of Allāh! What an excellent answer you have given the commander of the faithful!' He said, O Abul-Salt! I spoke to him in the way he understood best, and I have heard my father telling hadīth from his forefathers about Ali (ﻉ) saying, The Messenger of Allāh (ﺹ) said, O Ali! You are the distributor of Paradise and of Hell on the Day of Judgement; you say to Hell: This is mine, and that is yours...'"

In another narrative, he asked the Imām (ﻉ) about the Commander of the Faithful Imām Ali (ﻉ) as to why he did not restore Fadak to its rightful owners after becoming the caliph. He answered him by saying, "We are members of a family who, upon becoming rulers, do not take their rights from those who confiscated them. Should we become in charge of the Muslims, we shall rule them and restore their confiscated rights to them, but we do not do so for our own selves."

Fadak remained the symbol of the lost justice according to the Ahl al-Bayt (ع); for az-Zamakhshari says the following in his great book titled *Rab'i' al-Abrar*: "Harūn ar-Rashīd kept pressing Mūsa ibn Ja'far (ع) to take Fadak back, and he kept refusing. When he insisted that he should, he said, "I shall not take it back except in its boundaries." He asked him, "And what are its boundaries?" He said, "The first is Aden;" ar-Rashīd 's face changed colour, yet he asked him, "And what is the second boundary?"" He said, "Samarkand;" now his face started shaking in anger. He asked him, "And what is the third boundary?" He said, "Africa;" and the caliph's face now turned black in outrage, yet he asked him, "And what is the fourth boundary?" He said, "The ocean, and whatever lies beyond the Caspian Sea and Armenia." Harūn ar-Rashīd then said, "There is nothing left for us; so, come and take my throne as well!" The Imām (ع) said, "I had told you before that if I defined its boundaries, you would refuse to give it back to me."

From this dialogue between Imām Mūsa ibn Ja'far (ع) and Harūn ar-Rashīd , we can comprehend the vast dimension of the significance of Fadak to Ahl al-Bayt (ع), and that it did not represent simply a piece of land and a few palm trees but a big missionary objective whose significance was linked to the significance of the Message itself in its connotation and depth.

Another person asked him about the Commander of the Faithful Imām Ali (ع) as to why people deserted him after knowing his distinction, his past feats, and the status he enjoyed in the eyes of the Messenger of Allāh (ص). He answered, "They deserted him and preferred others over him after having come to know his merits simply because he had killed a great number of their fathers, grandfathers, brothers, uncles, and other relatives who defied Allāh and His Messenger (ص); therefore, they kept their grudge against him inside their hearts and they did not like it when he became their

324

ruler. They did not have grudge against anyone else as much as they had against him, for nobody else was so forceful in making jihad in the defense of the Messenger of Allāh (ﷺ) as much as he was; so, they deserted him for someone else."

The Prophet (ﷺ) realized the seriousness of Ali's stand, the difficulty of the situation after his demise, and the dire consequences awaiting him due to his firm jihad in the Cause of Allāh. The statements he (ﷺ) made regarding Ali (ﻉ), therefore, were meant to deter those who were waiting for a chance to get even with him. Had they not been veiled by grudges, and by his own glorious past, they would have been described as the beginning of the tragedy of justice and righteousness.

We cannot find a better explanation for the change in public opinion regarding Ali's stand after the death of the Prophet (ﷺ) better than what Imām ar-Ridha (ﻉ) provided. If we set aside the clear ahādīth which named the Imām (ﻉ) as the caliph succeeding the Prophet (ﷺ) without any question and consulted the faculty of reason in all the criteria and logical orders to determine the person who should succeed the Prophet (ﷺ) as the caliph, the unavoidable outcome would certainly be none other than Ali (ﻉ). Besides, had the grudges and the past not been the cause of the removal of Ali from the post of ruler, the question would have remained unanswered by any honest and equitable person.

Another person asked the Imām (ﻉ), "Tell me, O son of the Messenger of Allāh! Why didn't Ali ibn Abū Talib (ﻉ) fight his enemies during the twenty-five years after the demise of the Messenger of Allāh (ﷺ) as he did during the days of his caliphate?" He answered, "It is due to his following the example of the Messenger of Allāh (ﷺ) who did not fight the polytheists of Mecca during the thirteen years after his Prophethood, or the ones in Medīna during the nineteen months period of his stay there; it is due to the number of his supporters being too small. Likewise, Ali (ﻉ) did not engage himself in fighting his enemies because his own supporters were too few. Since the Prophethood of the Messenger of Allāh (ﷺ) was not nullified by the fact that he did not make jihad during the period of thirteen years (in Mecca) and nineteen months (in Medīna), the Imāmate of Ali (ﻉ) was not nullified because he did not perform jihad for twenty-five years, for the deterring factor in both examples was one and the same."

Among the *ahādīth* of Imām ar-Ridha (ﻉ) is one narrated by Ibrahim ibn Muhammed al-Hamadani; he said, "I asked Abul-Hassan ar-Ridha (ﻉ), What is the reason for which the Almighty and Exalted Allāh drowned Pharaoh even after Pharaoh had believed in Him and admitted His unity?' He answered, Because he believed only when he saw Allāh's retribution, and belief to avoid danger is not accepted. This is Allāh's judgement regarding past and future generations. The Exalted and the Almighty has said, When they saw Our Punishment, they said, We believe in Allāh, the One God, and we reject the partners we used to associate with Him,' but their professing the faith when they (actually) saw Our Punishment was not going to benefit them' (Qur'ān, Al Mu'min [or Ghafir]:84-85). The Exalted and Almighty has also said, The day that certain Signs of thy Lord do come, no good will it do to a soul to believe in them then, if it did not believe before nor did it earn righteousness through its faith'" (Qur'ān, Al An'am:158). So when Pharaoh was about to be drowned, he said, "I believe that there is no God except the One in Whom the children of Israel believe, and I am of those who submit (to Allāh in Islam).' (It was then said to him), Ah now! But a little while before were you in rebellion! And you did mischief (and violence)! This day shall We save you in your body, so that you may be a Sign to those who come after thee!'" (Qur'ān, Younus:90-92).

This narrative has a moral for those who wish to learn, for iman is not that one believes and returns to his Lord only when he sees no avenue of salvation before him and despair overcomes him; rather, iman is belief in Allāh and going towards Him voluntarily in both cases of despair and of hope.

Another *hadīth* narrated by Imām ar-Ridha (ﻉ) stated the following: "Anyone who meets a poor Muslim and greets him in a greeting different from the one whereby he greets the rich, he would meet the Exalted and the Almighty on the Day of Judgement and He is angry with him." In this tradition, the Imām (ﻉ) provides us with a very beautiful example of humanity enjoined by genuine Islamic conduct governing the Muslim's conduct with his Muslim brother, for Islam united all members of the nation in its law of personal conduct; there is no distinction for the wealthy man over the deprived poor man, and all people are equal under the judgement of Islam.

Another *hadīth* of the Imām (ع) is one in which he was asked by Ibn as-Sikkit, "Why did the Almighty and Exalted God send Mūsa (Moses) ibn Imran (ع) with a miraculous cane and white hand and the tool of sorcery, asa (Jesus [ع]) with miraculous medicine, and Muhammed (ص) with miraculous speech and oratory?" The Imām (ع) said, "When the Almighty and the Exalted One sent Moses (ع), sorcery dominated the minds of people of his time. He, therefore, brought them from the Almighty and the Exalted One something which they never had, nor could they bring about anything like it, thus rendering their sorcery void and driving his argument against them home. When the Almighty and the Exalted God sent Jesus during a period of time when chronic diseases became widespread and people were in dire need of a cure, Jesus (ع) brought them from Allāh, the Almighty and the Exalted, something they never had, bringing the dead back to life, curing those born blind and the lepers by the Will of Allāh, proving his argument against them. And when the Almighty and the Exalted One sent Muhammed (ص) during the time when speeches and oratory (and I think he said with poetry, too), he brought them the Book of the Almighty and the Exalted God and with the wisdom and counsel, thereby voiding their arguments." Ibn as-Sikkit said, "By Allāh I have never seen anyone like you! What is the argument against people these days, then?" He answered, "Reason. Through it can you come to know who tells the truth about Allāh, so you believe in him, and who tells lies about Allāh, so you disbelieve in him." Ibn as-Sikkit said, "This, by Allāh, is the right answer..."

A miracle is a supernatural thing which the ordinary individual is unable to perform due to his limited energies and motivational powers. Miracles are different from sorcery. Sorcery is not an actual supernatural act but a swift movement which causes the viewer to see the realities turned upside down, or turns the visible picture into its contrary. This may take place by subjecting the viewer to obscure effects which veil from his sight a certain colour or a picture. What leads us to that conclusion is the statement of the Almighty in the context of narrating how Moses (ع) fared with the wizards from the descendants of Israel, saying, "So their ropes and canes seemed to him, because of their sorcery, as though they were crawling" (Qur'ān, Taha:66). Sorcery, then, is nothing more than stimulating the imagination, making things look different than they are, and causing one to fall under a magical spell. A miracle is an actual result of a super-natural deed intended to win the argument against people in the process of proving one's true prophethood and mission, and it is an act which Allāh causes to take place. It is different from sorcery because it is not subjected to psychological effects, or complications in the movement, but a broadening of the energy which affects matters viewed by man due to the effect of the Might of the Almighty. In narrating the story of Moses (ع), the Almighty states, "... and (appoint him) an apostle to the children of Israel, (with this message): I have come to you, with a Sign from your Lord, in that I make for you out of clay, as it were, the figure of a bird, and I breathe into it, and it becomes a bird by Allāh's leave; and I heal those born blind, and the lepers, and I bring the dead back to life by Allāh's leave'" (Qur'ān, Ali Imran:49). And the Almighty has also said, "And it was never the part of an apostle to bring a Sign except as Allāh permitted. For each period is a Book (revealed)" (Qur'ān, Al-Ra'd:38).

Every prophet had a miracle which distinguished him from other prophets and messengers and which was in harmony, in its own particular way, with the common phenomena prevailing upon the social condition of the time, so that the psychological effect caused by its miraculous effect would become a reality, as the Imām (ع) meant in the tradition stated above. The miracles of prophets, according to the contexts of the verses and narratives, were not the result of the effect of a natural human energy; rather, they were the results of a creative energy whereby Allāh distinguished His Prophets for the purpose of establishing the superiority of their argument when such a miracle was necessitated by their mission.

As regarding the miracles of the Imāms which are reported in order to testify to their Imāmate and to their being the most rightful for the post of caliphate, this is not something unusual about them since

328

they were selected by Allāh to be His vicegerents on earth. He entrusted them to carry out the responsibilities of the message after the demise of His Prophet (ﷺ), but what must be researched is that many such miracles were proven to have been performed by them and were attested to by an acceptable medium. But the Imāms never needed a miracle beyond the qualifications of knowledge and conduct which distinguished them in order to prove the authenticity of their Imāmate, for the qualifications which characterized them were by themselves the miracles proving their right.

Among the ahādīth of Imām ar-Ridha (ﷵ) which deal with the Islamic legislative system is one narrated by Abdullāh ibn Tawoos who said, "I told Abul-Hassan ar-Ridha (ﷵ) that I had a nephew whom I married off to my daughter and who used to frequently pronounce the divorce statement. He said, If he is a descendant of one of your (Shī'a) brethren, there is nothing to worry about, but if he is from these (Sunni) brothers, then recall your daughter, for they shall have to separate.' I said, But, may my life be sacrificed for yours, did not Abū Abdullāh (ﷵ) use to say, Beware of those divorced thrice at one time, for they shall marry more than once?' He said, Yes, this is the case if the man is one of your brethren, not one of these; whoever follows the creed of certain people is bound to follow their [juristic] rules.'"

As regarding the issue of divorce, which is the subject-matter of this hadīth, the school of thought of the Ahl al-Bayt (ﷵ) determines that if the divorce statement contains "thrice" in it, rather than being repeated twice again, is not considered binding but it would be if the statement were repeated twice provided it meets the other conditions such as the presence of two just witnesses, the absence of the use of force, and the woman being tahir (clean), that is, she has not cohabited with her husband prior to his pronouncement and has not taken her ghusul (ceremonial bath) yet, in addition to other conditions which validate divorce. This is what is commonly accepted, while others have decided that it will be void as the apparent understanding of this hadīth suggests. But if the husband repeats his statement, "She is divorced!" three times, it is, according to Imāmi (Shī'a) Muslims considered as one-time divorce with rendering the repetition null if such repetition is to be doubtful. The rest of Muslim sects regard divorce in both instands as binding and the husband cannot go back to her before she marries another husband.

Another *hadīth* narrated by the Imām (ﻉ) says, "The Almighty and Exalted One has decreed three rites each depends on yet another: He decreed the prayers and the payment of zakat; so, He does not accept the prayers of anyone who says his prayers but does not pay zakat; He decreed that one must thank Him and thank his parents, too; so, He does not accept the thanks of one who thanks Him but is not grateful to his parents; and He decreed that one should fear Him and remain in constant contact with his kin; so, anyone who does not remain in close touch with his relatives does not in turn fear Allāh, the Exalted, the Almighty." Still another says, "A believer (mu'min) cannot be truly so except after acquiring three attributes: from his Lord, from his Prophet (ﺹ), and from his fellow humans. From his Lord, he must learn how to keep a secret; the Almighty and the Exalted said, He (alone) knows the Unseen, nor does He make anyone acquainted with his Mysteries, except an apostle whom He has chosen' (Qur'ān, Al-Jinn:26-27). From his Prophet, he must learn patience while dealing with people; the Exalted and the Almighty ordered His Prophet to be patient with people saying, Uphold forgiveness; command what is right; but turn away from the ignorant (folks).' (Qur'ān, Al-Araf:199). From his fellows, he has to learn patience during periods of poverty and adversity, for the Dear and the Almighty One says, ... And to be firm and patient in pain and in adversity' (Qur'ān, Al- Baqara:177).

A man asked the Imām (ﻉ) once about the meaning of the verse saying, "Whoever relies on Allāh, He suffices him." He said, "Reliance on Allāh is in various degrees one of which is that you rely on Him in everything related to you, and when He does something to you which you know will not bring you anything good, you rely on His wisdom in doing it, so you nevertheless put your trust in Him willingly. Another is to believe in the Unseen regarding Allāh of which you have no knowledge, so you relied on Him and on His custodians, trusting in Him in their regard, and in others." He was also asked once about the extent of such reliance. He said, "It is that you fear none save Allāh." What the Imām here means is that

330

you submit to the Will of Allāh and accept His decree. Ahmed ibn Najm asked him about the pride which spoils one's deeds. He said, "Pride is degrees; among them is that one sees his bad deed as good, so he likes it and feels proud of it; another is that one believes in Allāh and feels he is doing Him a favour by believing in Him, whereas He is the One who enabled that person to believe in Him." He, peace be with him, said once, "If one lacks five attributes, do not expect to gain anything good out of him for your life in this world or for the life to come: if his lineage is known to be untrustworthy, if his nature lacks generosity, if his temper lacks balance, if he lacks a noble conduct, and if he lacks fear of his Lord."

He (ﷺ) was asked once who a lowly person is. He said, "Anyone who has something (a serious moral defect, habit, etc.) to distract him from Allāh."

Among the jewels of his wisdom are the following; read them, digest them, and share them with those whom you love:

"Allāh abhors hearsay, the loss of one's funds (through foolishness), and excessive questioning."

"To be courteous to people is to cross half the way to achieving wisdom."

"The discretion of a Muslim is not complete except after he acquires ten merits: Allāh accepts his good deeds, he is trustworthy, he sees as plentiful the little good that others do for him, while seeing his own abundant good as little; he does not fret from being asked for favours, nor does he feel tired of constantly seeking knowledge; poverty reached in order to please Allāh is better for him than wealth accumulated otherwise; to be subjected to power while trying to serve Allāh is better in his regard than achieving power over his foe, and obscurity he prefers over fame." Then he said, "And the third one..., do you know what the third one is?" It was said to him, "What is it?" He said, "Whenever he meets someone, he says to himself, He is better than me and more pious.' People are two types: a person better than him and more pious, and one who is more evil than him and more lowly. If he meets the one who is more evil than

331

him and more lowly, he says to himself, Maybe the goodness of this (statement) is implied, and it is better that he hears such a compliment, while my own goodness is apparent and it is detrimental to me.' And when he sees someone better than him and more pious, he would humble himself before him trying to raise himself to his level. So if he does that, his glory will be higher, his reputation will be better, and he will become distinguished above his contemporaries."

"Silence is one of the gates of wisdom. Silence wins the love of others. It is an indication of everything good."

"Everyone's friend is his reason; his enemy is his ignorance."

"Among the habits of Prophets is cleanliness."

"One who is blessed with plenty must spend generously on his family."

"If you mention someone who is present, use a kunya (surname) for him, and if he is absent, mention his full name."

"Time will come when one's safety lies in ten things nine of which are in staying aloof from people, and the tenth in staying silent."

"Whoever scrutinizes his behaviour wins; whoever does not do so loses. Whoever fears the consequences will live safely. Whoever learns a moral from others achieves insight, and whoever achieves insight achieves wisdom, and whoever achieves wisdom achieves knowledge. One who befriends the ignorant will be worn out. The best of wealth is that which safeguards one's honour. The best of reason is one's knowledge of his own self. If a true believer becomes angry, his anger does not cause him to abandon righteousness; when he is pleased, his pleasure will not tempt him into wrong-doing, and when he achieves power, he does not take more than what rightfully belongs to him."

"If one's attributes become plentiful, they will relieve him from having to win praise by mentioning them."

"Do not pay attention to the view of someone who does not follow your advice for his own good. Whoever seeks guidance from the appropriate source will never slip, and if he slips, he will find a way to correct himself."

"People's hearts are sometimes coming towards you, sometimes keeping away from you; sometimes they are active, sometimes they are relaxed. If they come along, they will achieve wisdom and understanding, and if they stay away, they will be exhausted and worn out; so, take them when they come to you and when they are active, and shun them when they stay away or are relaxed."

"Accompany with caution the person who has authority over you; be humble when in the company of a friend; stay alert when facing an enemy, and mingle with the public with a smile on your face."

"Postponement is detrimental to the fulfillment of desires. Fulfillment is the gain of the strict. Wastefulness is the calamity of one who can afford it. Miserliness tears up honour. Passion invites trouble. The best and most honourable of virtues is to do others favours, to aid the one who calls for help, to bring the hope of the hopeful to reality, not to disappoint the optimist, to have an ever increase of the number of friends when you are alive, and the number of those who will cry when you die."

"The miser one is never restful. The envious is never pleased. The grumbling is never loyal. The liar has no conscience."

"One who struggles to satisfy the needs of his family shall have more rewards than those who perform *jihad* in the Way of Allāh."

"Assisting the weak is better for you than your act of charity."

"No servant of Allāh achieves true belief except when he acquires three attributes: 1) He derives juristic deductions from the creed; 2) He is wise regarding his livelihood, and 3) He is patient while facing calamities."

333

"Beware of one who wants to offer you advice by speaking behind others' backs; he does not realize how bad his own end shall be."

He (ع) was asked once who the best of believers are; he said, "They are the ones who are excited with expectation when they do a good deed, who pray for Allāh's forgiveness when they commit a bad one, who show gratitude when they are granted something, who are patient when they are tried, who forgive those who anger them."

He (ع) was asked once, "How did you start your day?" He answered, "With a shorter life-span, with our deeds being recorded, with death round our necks, with Fire behind our backs, and we do not know what will be done to us."

He (ع) also said, "Wealth is not accumulated except by five means: extreme miserliness, a long-standing optimism, an overwhelming care, a boycott of the relatives, and a preference of this life over the life to come."

Ali ibn Shu'ayb said that he once visited Abul-Hassan Ali ar-Ridha (ع) who asked him, "O Ali! Do you know whose subsistence is the best?" He answered, "You, master, know better than me." He said, "It is that of the one through whom others' subsistence is improved. Do you know who has the worst subsistence?" Ali answered, "You know better than me!" The Imām (ع) answered saying, "It is that of the one who does not include others in it." Then he added, "O Ali! Be thoughtful to the boons for they are wild: if they leave people, they never come back to them. O Ali! The worst of people is someone who stops his contributions to charity, eats by himself, and whips his slave (or servant)."

When al-Hassan ibn Sahl died, He (ع) said, "To congratulate one for a reward in store for him is better than to console him on a swift calamity."

This is a truly magnificent bouquet of shining statements made by Imām a-Ridha (ع) which emanate with his wisdom, overflow with his iman, and over-brim with tasty intellectual fruits, but this book is too small to contain all of them. This book was originally meant to

334

be no more than a hundred pages, yet the Almighty has enabled it to grow, for He, and only He, helps promote and disseminate a good word and a good deed. In his statements, the Imām (ع) defines glorious ethical and educational manners and the upright conduct of a true belief, offering some glimpses of humanity for social cooperation and coexistence a Muslim is supposed to implement if he wants to be in harmony with the principles of Islam. They make up, if implemented, a milestone in the social change, turning an oppressive ignorant society into an advanced civilized one built upon virtue and love, justice and equity, respect and morality. But who is there to take upon himself such a task? Who has the power to implement the moral precepts provided by this great Imām (ع) and social reformer? The answer is too obvious to state...

We have to translate these statements into actions in our daily life and be in harmony with their ethical and humane practical implications if we wish to direct our individual and social conduct to the right direction which safeguards its principles and precepts in order to create a nation based on virtues and humanity, and build it from within in a firm spiritual structure. Such a structure is reflects its practical reality and affects its intellectual and social objectives so that it would be "the best nation that ever was" (Qur'ān, Sarat Aali 'Imran:110).

May the Almighty enable us and your own self to follow in the footsteps of Imām a-Ridha (ع), and may He strengthen our conviction, keep our feet firm on His Right Path, the Path of happiness in the life of this world and of salvation in the life to come, Allāhomma aammen.

6) IMĀM MUHAMMED AT-TAQI (ع)
His name is Muhammed; "Abū Ja'far," at-Taqi and al-Jawad are his titles. He is sometimes called Abū Ja'far II, the first being Imām Muhammed al-Bāqir (ع). His father's name is Imām Ali ar-Ridha (ع); his respected mother is known as Subaika or Sukayna. He was born in Medīna on the 10th of Rajab 195 A.H./April 8, 811 A.D. At that time, al-Amin son of Harūn ar-Rashīd was the monarch of Baghdad.

It is a sad story that Imām Muhammed at-Taqi (ع) had to face series of misfortunes since his early childhood. For only a very brief peaceful period, he enjoyed the love and availed himself of the teachings of his father. He was five years old when Imām Ali ar-Ridha (ع) was forced to leave Medīna for Khurasan. The sire never saw his son again since then, for Imām Ali ar-Ridha (ع) died in Merv three years after this separation. The astonishment of people knew no bounds when, a few years later, they saw the boy arguing and expostulating with the renowned scholars of fiqh, tafsir, hadīth and kalam, and subduing them in the presence of al-Ma'mūn. They had to admit that God-gifted knowledge never depends on material resources or on age.

Political exigencies had compelled al-Ma'mūn to cultivate relations with the descendants of Imām Ali and Fatima (ع) in order to win the support of the Shī'as. After all, being a Hashemite himself, he was related to them though remotely. He was aware of the political need to maintain close relations with them; therefore, at one of the gatherings relof heir-apparentship, he married his sister Umm Habiba to Imām Ali ar-Ridha (ع) and betrothed his daughter Umm al-Fadl to the son of Imām ar-Ridha (ع), this Muhammed at-Taqi (ع). He thought that those steps would enable him to win over Imām Ali ar-Ridha (ع) completely.

But al-Ma'mūn soon realized that Imām ar-Ridha (ع) continued to lead the same simple and saintly life which characterized the descendants of the Prophet (ص). The pattern of his true Islamic life, which was bound to disseminate the spirit of fraternity and equality, was obviously harmful to al-Ma'mūn's authority, especially when Imām Ali ar-Ridha (ع) was now a member of the royal family. It was at this point that he decided to put an end to the Imām's life. But as he thought it expedient that he should keep the Shī'as, particularly the Persians, on his side, he pretended to be very depressed at Imām Ali ar-Ridha's death, as the reader has already come to know. This was also necessary for him in trying his best to prove that he had no hand in killing him. In order to isolate himself from any suspicion, he summoned ar-Ridha's son, Muhammed at-Taqi, from Medīna to Baghdad to marry him off to his daughter Umm al-Fadl although she was already engaged.

The appointment of Imām Ali ar-Ridha (ع) as heir-apparent had been an intolerable dilemma for the Abbāsides; so, when ar-Ridha died, they sighed in relief. They also succeeded in causing al-Ma'mūn to appoint his son Trenchaman as his successor who later came to be known as caliph al-Muta'sim Billah. During the time when Imām ar-Ridha was the heir-apparent, the colour of the caliph's court and royal robes had been changed from black to green. After the Imām's death, they changed it again to black which signalled the restoration of Abbāside traditions. All these steps undertaken by al-Ma'mūn sufficiently satisfied the Abbāsides who thought that he was acting in accordance with their own desires. But when al-Ma'mūn procliam ed that he was going to marry his daughter off to the son of Imām Ali ar-Ridha (ع), their tribal attitude was stimulated. They could no longer hide their feelings, and their delegation approached al-Ma'mūn and complained in in the most unambiguous statements they could make, telling him that the honours which he had showered on Imām Ali ar-Ridha (ع) had grieved them, and that they tolerated it because the Imām could be respected in view of his age, learning and other virtues, and that he deserved those honours only to a certain extent. But elevating his son, who was quite young, so much as to prefer him over all other dignitaries and learned scholars did not befit the caliph. Furthermore, the marriage of al-Ma'mūn's sister to Imām Ali ar-Ridha (ع) did not prove prosperous. Why did the caliph, then, wish to offer the hand of the princess to ar-Ridha's son, anyway?

Al-Ma'mūn told them that ar-Ridha's son, Muhammed, was no doubt a boy of tender age, but he had inherited his father's virtues and qualities in full; the learned scholars of the Islamic world could not compete with him, and that if they doubted, they could put the boy to test. This reply, though totally said in jest, amounted to a challenge. Prompted by al-Ma'mūn's taunt, they consented to judge the boy's knowledge in a contest with the most learned authority of Baghdad then, namely Yahya ibn Aktham.

Al-Ma'mūn convened a pompous gathering for this open expostulation. There was anxiety to see this unequal match where a boy of eight was to contend with the seasoned and renowned Chief Justice

337

of the land. People crowded from every quarter. Historians have recorded that apart from dignitaries and the nobility, 900 seats were reserved only for scholars. Al-Ma'mūn's reign was described as the golden age of learning; experts from every trade and profession had assembled in that great capital from every corner of the world.

Al-Ma'mūn had a carpet laid by the side of his throne to seat Imām Muhammed at-Taqi. In front of him was accommodated the Chief Justice Yahya ibn Aktham. There was pindrop silence among the audience who waited to hear the arguments. Silence was broken by Yahya who said, "Will His Majesty allow me to put some questions to Muhammed at-Taqi?" Al-Ma'mūn answered: "You may seek that permission from Muhammed at-Taqi himself."

Yahya (to Muhammed at-Taqi): "Do you allow me to ask you a question?" Muhammed at-Taqi: "Yes, you may ask whatever you please." Yahya: "What is the atonement for a person who hunts a game while he is dressed in the pilgrimage garb?" The question itself indicated that Yahya underestimated the status of his opponent. Intoxicated with the pride of position and knowledge, he thought that the young boy might well be aware of simple daily routine problems of prayer or fasting, but the possibility that he might be totally ignorant of the statutes of pilgrimage or of the atonements of the sins or mistakes committed by a pilgrim never entertained his mind.

The sagacious, young Imām was clever enough to respond to the old seasoned inquirer. Instead of giving a general or a vague reply, he analyzed the different aspects of the question so aptly that the audience immediately had a true evaluation of the Imām's knowledge and of Yahya's shallow-mindedness. Yahya, too, was puzzled and felt humiliated when the Imām addressed him thus:

"Your question is utterly vague and lacks definition. You should first clarify whether the game killed was outside the sanctified area or inside it; whether the hunter was aware of his sin or did so in ignorance; did he kill the game purposely or by mistake? Was the hunter a slave or a free man? Was he an adult or a minor? Did he commit the sin for the first time or had he done so before? Was the

338

hunted game a bird or some thing else? Was it a small animal or a big one? Is the sinner sorry for his misdeed or does he insist on it? Did he kill it secretly at night or openly during daylight? Was he putting on the pilgrimage garb for hajj or for the umra?! Unless you clarify and define these aspects, how can you have a definite answer?"

Whatever Yahya's knowledge might have been, he was undoubtedly a well-read man specialized in jurisprudence. While the Imām was unfolding all such aspects of the problem, he had concluded that he was no match for his ingenious opponent. His face lost colour and the onlookers knew the situation as it was. His lips were sealed and he made no reply. Al-Ma'mūn fully assessed his condition and thought it useless to put any further pressure on him. He, rather, requested Imām Muhammed at-Taqi (ع) to solve all the aspects of the question one by one so that the listeners might gain knowledge. The Imām, in spite of his young age, explained the various aspects of the question. Yahya, silent and puzzled, gazed at him. But al-Ma'mūn was bent on carrying the matter to its very extreme. He, therefore, requested the Imām to put some questions to Yahya if he liked. The Imām accordingly said, "May I ask you a question?" Disillusioned, Yahya, who now had a correct idea about the Imām's ability and had now no misunderstanding about himself, said in a humble tone: "Your grace can ask; I shall reply if I can or I shall get it solved by your own self." Then the Imām put up a question in reply to which Yahya admitted his ignorance. The Imām explained it, too. Al-Ma'mūn's joy knew no bounds. Addressing the audience, he said, "Did I not tell you that this Progeny has been gifted by Allāh with unlimited knowledge? None can cope with even the children of this elevated House."

The excitement of the gathering was great: all unanimously exclaimed that al-Ma'mūn's assumption was correct and that Imām Muhammed at-Taqi (ع) was peerless. Al-Ma'mūn then thought it advisable to marry his daughter off to Imām Muhammed at-Taqi there and then. The Imām (ع) recited the marriage sermon in person. This sermon, as a remembrance, is being recited at weddings everywhere throughout the Muslim world ever since. Overjoyed at this auspicious occasion, al-Ma'mūn demonstrated his generosity by giving away millions in charity to the poor. Common people were given with regards to his grants.

One year after the marriage, Imām Muhammed at-Taqi (ع) lived in Baghdad. Then al-Ma'mūn allowed him to return to Medīna with his daughter Umm al-Fadl surrounded with great pomp.

Imām Muhammed at-Taqi (ع) occupied the highest position in human virtues and moral attainments, such is the Prophet's family. To meet everyone humbly, fulfill the needs of the poor, maintain Islamic equality and simplicity, help the destitute secretly, treat even the foes fairly, extend hospitality, impart knowledge to the scholars of religion and the like, all marked his saintly life.

Common people, who could not appreciate such heights of moral excellence, might have thought that the new relationship, i.e. to become son-in-law of the most influential monarch of his time, must influence the pattern of life of the Imām and change his manners altogether. Al-Ma'mūn, too, might have thought on the same lines because spiritualism, which was the chief characteristic of this Progeny, was against the practices of worldly rulers.

In order to uphold their imperialistic and luxurious norms of life, monarchs like al-Ma'mūn wanted to do away with these saints who personified righteousness, compassion, faith, piety, fraternity and justice as taught by Islam. Yazid's demanding obedience from Imām Hussain (ع) or al-Ma'mūn appointing Imām Ali ar-Ridha (ع) as his heir-appaent were two different aspects of one phenomenon. The procedures were different but the purpose was the same. Imām Hussain (ع) did not bow to pay homage, so he was slain on the battlefield. Imām Ali ar-Ridha (ع) did not serve the cause of Abbāside imperialism, so he was silenced with poison.

Undoubtedly, Imām ar-Ridha (ع) did not conform to al-Ma'mūn's designs, nor desires, but this did not disappoint him. Ar-Ridha's mature way of thinking and simple norm of life could not be changed. But there was the hope that in all probability a tender boy, who was brought up in the luxurious atmosphere of a royal palace, would grow up to be an ambitious, merry-making prince—altogether against his ancestral ways and views.

With the exception of a few enlightened persons, everybody would think on such lines. But the world stood aghast to see that the young son-in-law of the most distinguished monarch of his time refused to stay in the royal palace and lived instead in a rented house, thus maintaining his ancestral anti-monarchical conduct, leading a simple and modest life.

In the Middle East, it is usually seen that if the bride's people are fairly rich, they wish that the groom might live with them; if not in the same house, at least in the same town. The will-power of the Imām (ع) can be judged from the fact that he lived in a separate dwelling. After one year, when al-Ma'mūn realized that his son-in-law was not pleased with staying in Baghdad, he had to allow him to go to Medīna with Umm al-Fadl.

Having returned to Medīna, he maintained the same ancestral, unimposing behaviour: no body-guards, no pomp, no restrictions, no visiting times, no discrimination. He spent most of his time sitting at the Prophet's Mosque, where Muslims came to avail from his preaching. The narrators of hadīth and other students of theology came to inquire about religious sciences, and the Imām guided them by explaining every complicated issue. All the world saw that Imām Ja'far's successor, seated on the same mat, was guiding the people towards faith and piety.

Imām at-Taqi (ع) allowed the same amount of freedom to his wife Umm al-Fadl and imposed the same restrictions on her as his ancestors had done with their wives. He did not care much about the fact that Umm al-Fadl was a princess. Although she lived with him, he married another lady who was a descendant of Ammar ibn Yasir. Allāh had intended to continue the line of Imāmate through her, and she gave birth to (later) Imām Ali an-Naqi (ع), the tenth Imām. Umm al-Fadl complained about this to her father. Surely this would have passed heavily on al-Ma'mūn's heart but he could not interfere in the matter. He wrote his daughter saying, "Do not make such complaints to me in the future. I cannot stop Muhammed atTaqi from those things which Allāh has made lawful."

There are precedents, no doubt, that in view of the high personal virtues of a woman, her husband does not marry another lady. For example, while Khadija lived, the Holy Prophet did not marry any other wife. Similarly, Imām Ali (ع) married no other woman during the life-time of Fatima az-Zahra' (ع). But the same distinction could not be awarded to the daughter of a king because it was against the spirit of Islam which the Prophet's descendants were to safeguard, implement, and preserve.

Imām Muhammed at-Taqi's speech was very moving and effective. During the hajj season, he once addressed a gathering of Muslims, stating the commandments of the Divine Law of Sharaa. The audience included learned scholars who admitted that they had never heard such a comprehensive speech.

During the days of Imām ar-Ridha (ع), there was a group which believed that the Imāmate had come to an end with Imām Mūsa al-Kādhim (ع). They were called the Waqfiyya (Waqfism) الواقفة. Imām Muhammed at-Taqi (ع) admonished them so nicely, they abandoned their wrong beliefs for good. Nobody of that creed persisted in adhering to such beliefs.

Through Imām ar-Ridha (ع), scholars came to learn the teachings of Ahl al-Bayt (ع). A collection of brief and wise sayings is also among his legacy, resembling and ranking in wisdom next to the sayings of his ancestor Imām Ali ibn Abū Talib (ع). Some profound discourses on theology and monotheism are also to his credit.

Al-Ma'mūn died in 218 A.H./833 A.D. He was succeeded by his brother al-Mu'taman, the second heir apparent after Imām ar-Ridha (ع). He came to be known as al-Muta'sim Billah al-Abbāsi. His niece, Umm al-Fadl, now began to send him more complaining letters than she did during the days of her father. As al-Ma'mūn had given her in marriage to Imām at-Taqi (ع) in spite of the opposition of all the tribe, he paid no attention to her letters. Rather, he silenced her with disappointing replies. But al-Muta'sim was jealous of Imām ar-Ridha (ع). He had also led the opposition in the matter of Imām at-Taqi's marriage with his niece.

Al-Muta'sim now got a chance to settle his difference in this matter. Imām Muhammed at-Taqi's fame as a great scholar and people's gathering around him, as well as the fame of his world-renown noble character, annoyed him. The failure of the political tactics, too, intensified his resentment. All these factors intensified his enmity. In the second year of his reign, he summoned Imām Muhammed at-Taqi from Medīna to Baghdad, writing to the governor of Medīna expressly in this regard. Imām Muhammed at-Taqi had no choice except to set out for Baghdad leaving his son Imām Ali an-Naqi (ع) with his mother in Medīna.

Upon his arrival at Baghdad, Imām at-Taqi was not harmed by al-Muta'sim. But the Imām's stay in Baghdad was a forcible act which can be labelled as custody or house arrest. Imām Ali an-Naqi (ع), therefore, was killed with the very same soundless weapon which was quite frequently used against his ancestors. He was poison, so he died on the 29th of Thul-Qi'da, 220 A.H./November 24, 835 A.D. and was buried near his grandfather Imām Mūsa al-Kādhim (ع). It is due to these two saints' tombs that the place is called Kādhimain (the two Kādhims, the enduring ones). Inna Lillah wa Inna Ilayhi Rajian; surely we belong to Allāh, and to Him shall we return.

7) IMĀM 'ALI AN-NAQI (ع)
His name, Ali, is usually prefixed by his titles "Abul-Hassan" and "an-Naqi," the pure one.Since both Imāms Ali al-Murtada and Ali ar-Ridha (ع) were also called "Abul-Hassan" each, Imām Ali an-Naqi is known as "Abul-Hassan III." His mother's name is Sumana Khatun. He was born in Medīna on Rajab 5, 214 A.H./September 8, 829 A.D. He enjoyed the love of his father Imām at-Taqi (ع) for only six years because his father had to leave for Baghdad where he died on the 29th of Thu al-Qida 220 A.H./November 24, 835 A.D. and the responsibilities of Imāmate devolved on his young son's shoulders. Providence was the only tutor and instructor that reared and raised him to the extreme zenith of learning.

Imām Ali an-Naqi (ع) was still young when the Abbāside ruler al-Muta'sim Billah died and was succeeded by al-Wathiq Billah who died in 236 A.H./850 A.D. Al-Mutawakkil, the most cruel and deadly enemy of Ahl al-Bayt (ﻉ), ascended the throne in the same year then died in 250 A.H./864 A.D. and was succeeded by al-Muntasir Billah who ruled for only six months. On his death, al-Mustain was installed on the throne of the Abbāsides in Baghdad. The latter had to part with his crown, as well as with his head, in 253 A.H./867 A.D. and was succeeded by al-Mu'tazz Billah during whose regime Imām Ali an-Naqi (ﻉ) died.

Al-Muta'sim remained preoccupied with war against the Byzantines and had to deal with the troubles created by the Abbāside tribesmen in Baghdad. He did not harass the young Imām who carried out his responsibilities peacefully. After him, al-Wāthiq Billāh, too, treated Imām Ali an-Naqi (ﻉ) fairly. But when he was succeeded by his brother al-Mutawakkil son of al-Muta'sim, the period of persecution and misfortune began on a full scale. This ruler exceeded all his predecessors in bearing animosity towards Ahl al-Bayt (ﻉ).

During the 16 years of his Imāmate, Imām Ali an-Naqi (ﻉ) had become famous throughout the Islamic world. Those who loved to learn the teachings of Ahl al-Bayt (ﻉ) always flocked around him. In the 4th year of al-Mutawakkil's reign, the governor of Medīna, Abdullāh ibn Hakim, started harassing the Imām. After persecuting him personally, he sent hostile reports against him to Baghdad. He wrote the central government there saying that the Imām was assembling apparatuses of kingdom, and that his followers were in such numbers that he could rise against the government whenever he wished.

Imām Ali an-Naqi (ﻉ) became aware of such antagonism in sufficient time. In order to counteract, he, too, wrote a letter to al-Mutawakkil explaining the personal enmity the lying governor had borne against him. As a political step, al-Mutawakkil was quick to dismiss the governor. At the same time, he sent a regiment under the command of Yahya ibn Harthamah to explain to the Imām in a friendly way that the caliph wished him to stay in the capital for a few days before going back to Medīna.

The Imām knew very well the motives behind this request. He knew that the polite invitation actually meant his banishment from his

344

ancestral city. But to refuse was useless, as it would involve a forcible departure later. Leaving the sacred city was as painful to him as it had been for his respected forefathers, viz. Imām Hussain (ع), Imām Mūsa al-Kādhim (ع), Imām Ali ar-Ridha (ع) and Muhammed at-Taqi (ع). This type of harassment had almost become a legacy. Al-Mutawakkil's letter to the Imām was full of respect and terms of endearment. The military detachment sent to escort him as retinue or bodyguards was actually a deceitful ploy. So when the Imām reached Samarra' (Surra man Ra'a, "Pleased is one who sees it"), and al-Mutawakkil was informed, he neither arranged for his reception nor for his stay. He ordered to accommodate him in a wilderness where the city's beggars usually dwelt. Although the Prophet's descendants gladly associated with the poor and the destitute, and they did not covet luxurious living, al-Mutawakkil meant to thus insult the Imām who stayed there for three days; thereafter, al-Mutawakkil placed him under the custody of his secretary Razzaqi, banning his meetings with others.

It has been seen that during the imprisonment of Imām Mūsa al-Kādhim (ع), the Imām's moral charm had softened the guards' stone hearts. Likewise, Razzaqi was impressed by the greatness of Imām Ali an-Naqi (ع) and began to provide for his comfort. This leniency could not remain hidden from al-Mutawakkil who transferred the Imām (ع) to the custody of Sa'd, a cruel and ruthless man in whose jail Imām Ali an-Naqi (ع) spent twelve long years. In spite of all the hardships he had to suffer there, he spent his time worshipping his Maker, fasting during the day and praying during the night. Although confined within the four walls of a dark dungeon cell, his fame was on the wing. He was known in every house of Samarra', rather throughout all of Iraq. Millions hated the cruel ruler who had put such a man of noble character in prison.

Al-Fadl ibn Khaqan, who loved the Prophet's Progeny, had risen to the post of Minister in al-Mutawakkil's cabinet solely by virtue of his intellectual and administrative merits. On his recommendation, al-Mutawakkil ordered the Imām's imprisonment to be changed to house arrest, granting him a piece of land and allowing him to build his house on it to live therein. But Imām Ali an-Naqi (ع) was forbidden from leaving Samarra'. Sa'd was ordered to keep a tight

surveillance on the Imām's movements, contacts and correspondence.

During this period, too, Imām Ali an-Naqi (ع) set an admirable
example of trust in Allāh, ignoring all worldly gains. In spite of
permanent residence in the capital, he neither made a protest to the
caliph, nor did he ever ask him for a favour. He continued the same
worshipping and hermit-like life that he had led during his
imprisonment. The tyrant had changed his behaviour but the saint
had maintained his own. Even during such circumstances, Imām Ali
an-Naqi (ع) was not allowed to live peacefully. He was not harassed
physically but psychologically. His house was periodically searched
for arms or dissenting correspondence undermining the position of
the government. Such an act is certainly painful for a man of an
innocent and noble character. To top all this, the Imām was once
summoned to the royal palace where the cups of wine were in
rotation. Surrounded by his courtiers, al-Mutawakkil was very much
given to merry-making, so much so that in the excess of vanity and
lewdness, the arrogant and shameless ruler handed the cup of wine
to the Imām and asked him to drink. This order was surely more
painful than a thousand strokes of the sword, but the guardian of
faith said with unruffled dignity: "Spare me this order, for the flesh
and blood of my forefathers and my own have never mixed with
wine." Had there been a slight sense of faith in al-Mutawakkil, he
would have been impressed by the dignity of this saintly reply. But
he was dead to such a feeling; he, therefore, said, "Well, if you do
not like it, then sing a song for us." The Imām replied: "I do not
know that art, either." At last the haughty monarch said, "You shall
have to recite a few verses of poetry, then, in any tone you like."
This crude and ridiculous behaviour would have infuriated any
ordinary person, but the dignified Imām remained undisturbed and
sought to do what he was compelled to. He turned the ruler's order
for recitation of poetry into an opportunity for preaching, and he
recited the following poetic verses:

غلب الرجال، فلم تنفعهم القلل	باتوا على قلل الأجبال تحرسهم
و اسكنوا حفرا، يا بنسما نزلوا!	واستنزلوا بعد عز من معاقلهم
أين الأساور و التيجان و الحلل؟	ناداهم صارخ من بعد دفنهم:
من دونها تضرب الأستار و الكلل؟	أين الوجوه التي كانت منعمة

فافصح القبر عنهم حين ساءلهم: تلك الوجوه عليها الدود تقتتل

قد طال ما أكلوا دهرا وقد شربوا   واصبحوا اليوم بعد الأكل قد أكلوا

The glories of our blood and state
Are shadows, not substantial things.
There is no armour against the fate;
Death lays its icy hand on kings.
Sceptre and crown
Must tumble down.
And in the earth be equal made
To the labourer's scythe and spade.

No fortress on the mountain peak
Could save the kings from the jaws of death.
Their pomp and power proved too weak;
They lie in graves, deprived of breath.

The cold earth asks them in contempt:
"Whither is the robe, the crown, and the throne?!
"Did cruel Death thy beauty exempt?!
"Did it respect thy royal blood and bone?!"

The grave replies
With sorrowful sighs:

"Those beautiful forms
"Are now food for the worms!"

Having heard these lines recited by the Imām so profoundly, the gathering became spell-bound. The drunkards making merry just a moment ago now burst into tears. Even the proud king began to weep and wail. As soon as he recovered a bit, he allowed the Imām to go home.

Another incident that disturbed him a great deal was al-Mutawakkil's oppressive order forbidding the public from visiting Kerbalā' and Najaf. Throughout his territories ran the order that people should not go to visit the tombs of Imām Ali (ع) and Imām Hussain (ع). Anybody disobeying this order would do so under the

347

penalty of death. He further ordered that the buildings in Najaf and Kerbalā' be levelled to the ground, that all the mausoleums be razed and the land around Imām Hussain's tomb be ploughed. It was not, however, possible to stop those who loved Ahl al-Bayt (ع) from visiting those holy shrines. They disobeyed, and thousands of them were put to death indiscriminately. Undoubtedly, the Imām was as sorry for each one of them as he could have been on the death of a near relative of his. Due to this oppressive environment, he could not even preach or convey to the faithful the necessary instructions. This sorrowful situation lasted till al-Mutawakkil's death in 247 A.H./861 A.D.

At al-Mutawakkil's court, Imām Ali ibn Abū Talib (ع) was mimicked and mocked by the buffoons while al-Mutawakkil and his courtiers burst into laughter. It was such an insulting scene that once al-Mutawakkil's son could not help protesting thus: "It was somewhat tolerable if you spoke ill of Imām Ali (ع) yourself, but since you yourself say that he was related to you, how do you allow these wretched buffoons to mock him like that?" Instead of being sorry, al-Mutawakkil jested with his son and composed two couplets abusive of his mother which he instructed the singers to sing. They used to always sing those couplets as al-Mutawakkil laughed heartily.

Another event of those wretched times is equally painful. Ibn as-Sikkit of Baghdad, the acknowledged scholar of lexicography and syntax and the genius of his time, was the tutor of al-Mutawakkil's son. One day the cruel ruler asked this great scholar: "Are my two sons more respectable than Hassan and Hussain (ع)?" Ibn as-Sikkit loved Ahl al-Bayt. He could not control his feelings and flatly replied: "Not to speak of Imāms Hassan and Hussain (ع), Imām Ali's slave Qanbar is more respectable than both of your sons." Hearing these words, al-Mutawakkil flew into a passion and ordered that Ibn as-Sikkit's tongue be cut off. This barbaric order was carried out immediately, leading to the death of one of those who cherished the Prophet's Progeny (ع).

Imām Ali an-Naqi (ع) was not physically connected with these events. But each was like a blow of the sword, not striking his neck

348

but torturing his soul. Al-Mutawakkil's cruelties caused him to be the object of common hatred. Even his own children set their hearts against him. One of them, al-Muntasir, conspired with his chief slave Bāqir ar-Rumi to murder al-Mutawakkil while the latter was asleep, using his own sword, thus the world heard a sigh of relief and the population of hell increased by one; the death of the tyrant and the caliphate of al-Muntasir were proclaimed. After assuming the throne, al-Muntasir revoked the unjust orders of his father. Visiting the shrines of Najaf and Kerbalā' was permitted without any restriction. The tombs, moreover, received minor repairs. Al-Muntasir's conduct towards Imām Ali an-Naqi (ع) was fair. But the life of the new ruler proved to be mysteriously too short; he died in 248 A.H./862 A.D. after a brief rule of only six months. After him, caliph al-Mustaan Billah, too, did not mistreat the Imām (ع).

As stated above, Imām Ali an-Naqi (ع) had built a house in Samarra' and did not go back to Medīna either out of his own free will or under the orders of the rulers. Due to his continued stay there and the lack of interference by the regime, the students of the teachings of Ahl al-Bayt (ع) surrounded him. Al-Mustaan Billah died in 252 A.H./866 A.D. and was succeeded by al-Mu'tazz Billah who was alarmed by the Imām's popularity, so he put an end to his life.

Imām Ali an-Naqi's conduct and moral excellence were the same as those of each and every member of the sacred series of Infallibles. Imprisonment, confinement or freedom, in every case these sacred souls were engaged in worship, helping the poor, living a most ascetic and God-fearing life, disseminating knowledge and scholarship and promoting virtue. Totally refraining from succumbing to their own desires, greed or worldly ambitions, they lived dignified in misfortune. Dealing fairly even with the foes and helping the destitute were the qualities marking their conduct. The same virtues were reflected during the lifetime of Imām Ali an-Naqi (ع) as well.

During the period of his imprisonment, the Imām (ع) had a grave dug up for him and was ready by his prayer-mat. Some visitors expressed either apprehension or bewilderment thereat. The Imām explained thus: "In order to remember my end, I keep the grave

349

before my eyes." Be it so, but in reality, it was a silent, unspoken protest against those cruel rulers who wanted the Imām (ع) to give up his pure Islamic teachings. It was a negation of their demand of obeisance. It showed that the worldly rulers who can frighten common men with death can never bend a saint who is ready to embrace death at any moment. In spite of this fearlessness, he never took part in any secret or subversive activity against the government. Living permanently in a capital where daily conspiracies were sapping the roots of the Abbāsside regime, he could never be accused of treason by the strong secret intelligence of those kings.

Can you imagine the extent of the political turmoil of those unstable days? Al-Mutawakkil was opposed by his own son al-Muntasir and he ended in being slain by his own Turkish slave Bāqir ar-Rami. After al-Muntasir's death, the court nobility decided to take away the governemnt from the ruling dynasty. The regime of al-Mustaan was shaken by the uprising of Yahya ibn Omer ibn Yahya ibn Zaid al-Alawi in Kūfa, and by the occupation of Tabaristan by Hassan ibn Zaid (titled "Dai al-Haqq," the caller to justice) and his establishment of a permanent government there; the revolt of the Turkish slaves in Samarra' and al-Mustaan's flight to Baghdad to take refuge in its fort, and in the end his compulsory abdication and murder by al-Mu'tazz. Add to this list the Byzantine aggression during the reign of al-Mu'tazz who feared the danger of his own brother; Muayyad's demise; Muwaffaq's imprisonment in Basra—it was a continuous chain of chaos of which an opportunist could easily take advantage.

But Imām Ali an-Naqi (ع) could not be suspected even of taking part in any of these struggles for power. Any opportunist, excited by greed or revenge, will always take arms against a regime which not only harassed him but also exiled, insulted and imprisoned him. Yet, these sacred souls considered it below their spotless honour and dignity to partake in those vainglorious bids for power. They looked down upon all these struggles and always rose above the vile level of temporal temptations, declaring that all such acts were below them and their standard of virtue.

The Imām (ع) died during the reign of al-Mu'tazz Billah in Samarra'

350

on the 3rd of Rajab 254 A.H./June 28, 868 A.D. His death was attended only by his son Hassan al-'Askari who led the funeral prayers and arranged his burial, laying him to rest in his own residence. Now high stands his mausoleum which is being visited daily by tens of thousands of pilgrims from all over the world.

8) IMĀM HASSAN AL-'ASKARI (ع)

His name is al-Hassan, "Abū Muhammed." Being a resident of Askar, a suburb of Samarra', he is titled "al-'Askari." His father was Imām Ali an-Naqi (ع) and his mother was Salal Khatun, a role model of piety, adoration, chastity and generosity. He was born in Medīna on the tenth of Rabi' al-Akhir, 232 A.H./ December 4, 846 A.D. He lived under the care of his respected father upto the age of 11. Then his father had to leave for Samarra' and he was to accompany him and thus share the hardships of the journey with the fāmily. At Samarra', he spent his time with his father either in imprisonment or in partial freedom. He had, however, the opportunity to benefit from his father's teaching and instruction. His father died in 254 A.H./868 A.D. when he himself was twenty-two. Four months before his death, the father declared his son to be his successor and executor of his will, asking his followers to bear witness to the fact. Thus were the responsibilities of Imāmate vested upon him which he fulfilled even in the face of great difficulties and hostilities.

Imām Hassan al-'Askari partook in all misfortunes and hardships suffered by his father, whether imprisonment or confinement. In the early days of his Imāmate, al-Mu'tazz Billah, was the al-Abbāsi caliph who, when deposed in 255 A.H./869 A.D., was succeeded by al-Muhtadi. After The latter's brief reign of only eleven months and one week, al-Mu'tamid ascended to the throne. During these caliphs' regimes, Imām Hassan al-'Askari (ع) did not enjoy any peace of mind at all. Although the Abbāside dynasty was involved in constant complications and disorder, each and every king thought it necessary to keep the Imām imprisoned.

One of the Holy Prophet's traditions stated that the Prophet (ص) would be succeeded by twelve princes, the last of whom would be the Mahdi, Qā'im Ali Muhammed. The Abbāsides knew well that the true successors of the Prophet were these very Imāms (ع). With Imām Hassan al-'Askari (ع) being the eleventh of this series, his son would surely be the twelfth, the last. They, therefore, tried to put an end to the life of Imām Hassan al-'Askari (ع) so that nobody would succeed him. The house arrest once imposed on Imām Ali an-Naqi (ع) was considered inadequate for Imām Hassan al-'Askari (ع), so he was imprisoned, away from his family. Undoubtedly, the revolutionary intervals between two regimes gave him brief periods of freedom. Yet as soon as the new king came to the throne, he followed his predecessor's policy and imprisoned the Imām again. The Imām's brief life, therefore, was mostly spent inside dungeon cells.

The hardship of imprisonment reached its peak time during the reign of al-Mu'tamid Billah, although the latter knew the lineage, piety, knowledge and righteousness of the Imām as did all his predecessors.

Once, during a devastating drought, a Christian hermit was able to demonstrate that he could bring rain whenever he prayed to Allāh. This led many Muslims to convert to Christianity. In order to save Islam from this calamity, Imām Hassan al-'Askari (ع) was brought out of jail. He noticed how that Christian hermit raised his hands in prayers, and how as soon as he did so, rain started pouring down. He told the gathering that the piece of bone belonged to the corpse of one of the Prophets of Allāh, and he proved his point by raising it himself in his hand, and upon doing so, Lo, rain started pouring down again, as if the skies were weeping for the prophet! The Imām (ع) thus removed the common doubts from the minds of the people and kept them firmly on Islam. Al-Mu'tamid Billah was so impressed that he felt too ashamed to send the Imām back to prison; so, he put him under house arrest instead. Complete freedom, however, was not granted.

During all circumstances, the Imāms (ع) carried out their duties of guiding the people no matter what. Imām Hassan al-'Askari (ع) was subjected to numerous restrictions, so much so that those who sought to learn the teachings of Ahl al-Bayt (ع) and their Shī'a point of view could not reach him. In order to solve this problem, the Imām appointed certain confidants as his deputies in view of their knowledge of jurisprudence. These persons satisfied the curiosity of inquirers as much as they could. But if they could not solve certain theological problems, they would keep them pending the solutions provided by the Imām (ع) whenever they got the opportunity to see him. Of course, the visit to the Imām (ع) by a few individuals could be allowed by the government but certainly not by groups who wished to see the Imām on a regular basis.

The khums (1/5 of total savings), which was being paid to the Imāms by the believers who cherished them and regarded them as representatives of the Divine Law, was spent by these sacred saints on religious matters, and to sustain the Prophet's descendants. This khums was now secretly collected by these deputies who spent it according to the directives of the Imām (ع). They, accordingly, were in constant danger of being identified as such by the government's powerful secret intelligence service. In order to avert this danger, Othman ibn Sa'd and his son Abū Ja'far Muhammed, two prominent deputies of the Imām (ع) in the capital Baghdad, ran a large shop trading in oils. This provided them with free contact with the concerned people. It was thus that even under the very thumb of the tyrant regime, those devotees managed to run the system of the Divine law unsuspected.

Imām Hassan al-'Askari (ع) was one of the illustrious series of the immaculate Infallibles each member of whom displayed the moral excellence of human perfection. He was peerless in knowledge, forbearance, forgiveness, generosity, sacrifice, and piety. Whenever al-Mu'tamid Billah asked anybody about his captive Hassan al-'Askari, he was told that the Imām (ع) fasted during the day and adored his Lord during the night, and that his tongue uttered no word but remembrance of his Maker. During the brief periods of freedom and stay at home, people approached him hoping to avail from his benevolence, and they went back well rewarded. Once when the

Abbāside caliph asked Ahmed ibn Abdullāh ibn Khaqan, his Minister of Endowments (*awqaf*), about the descendants of Imām Ali (ع), he reported: "I do not know anybody among them who is more distinguished than Hassan al-'Askari. None can surpass him in dignity, knowledge, piety and abstinence, nor can anybody match him in nobleness, majestic grandeur, modesty and honesty."

When his father Imām Ali an-Naqi (ع) died and the family was busy arranging for his burial, some servants stole certain articles, thinking that none would notice it. When the burial was over, he called the servants and said to them, "I ask you about some missing items; if you tell me the truth, I will pardon you; but if you speak falsely, I shall get all those items from you then punish you." Then he asked each for the items which he had stolen. When they confessed their guilt, he got the articles back from them and spared them the penalty.

Imām Hassan al-'Askari (ع) had a brief span of life, only twenty-eight years, but even during this short period of time, which was ruffled by a chain of troubles and tribulations, several high ranking scholars benefitted from his ocean of knowledge. He also uprooted the atheism and disbelief which ensued from the philosophers of that age. One of those philosophers was the renown Ishāq al-Kindi who was then writing a book on what he called "self-contradictions" in the Holy Qur'ān. When the news reached the Imām, he waited for an opportunity to refute and rebut him. By chance, some of Ishāq's students came to visit him. The Imām (ع) asked them: "Is there anyone among you who can stop Ishāq from wasting his time in this useless effort fighting the Holy Qur'ān?" The students said, "Master! We are his students; how can we object to his teaching?" The Imām urged that they could at least convey to their teacher what he had to tell them. They replied that they would be ready to cooperate as much as they could.

The Imām (ع) then recited a few verses from the Holy Qur'ān which the philosopher considered as contradictory of one another. He then explained to them thus: "Your teacher thinks that some of the words in these verses have only one meaning. But according to the Arabic tongue, these words have other meanings too which, when taken into consideration, indicate no contradiction in the overall meaning. Thus, your teacher is not justified for basing his objections and allegations of contradictions on the premises of the 'wrong meaning' which he himself selects for such verses." He then put up some examples of such words before them so clearly that the students absorbed the point and comprehended the precedents of more than one meaning.

When these students visited Ishāq al-Kindi and, after routine discussions, reproduced the disputed points, he was surprised. He was a fair-minded scholar, and he attentively listened to his students' explanations. Then he said, "What you have argued is above your capacity; tell me truly who has taught you these points?" The students first said that it was their own reflection, but when he insisted that they could never have conceived those points, they admitted that they were explained to them by Abū Muhammed Imām Hassan al-'Askari (ﻉ). Al-Kindi said, "Yes; this level of knowledge is the heritage of that House, and only that House." Then he asked the students to set all such works of his to fire. This is a famous incident, and the reader is encouraged to research it on his own. This and so many other religious services were performed silently by the Prophet's descendants. The Abbāside dynasty, which unfairly claimed to be "the defender of the faith," was deeply drunk with lustful merriment. Had it ever recovered from its drunkenness and thus come to its senses, it would not have thought that those sincere and saintly souls were a "danger" to its power. It, therefore, issued orders to put some more restrictions on their movements. Imām Hassan al-'Askari (ﻉ), the lofty mountain of dignity and piety, put up with such unfair restrictions and unwarranted persecution with determined fortitude.

Imām Hassan al-'Askari (ﻉ) was a reliable authority on traditionists who have recorded several traditions in their collections on his own authority. One tradition about drinking runs thus: "The wine drinker is like an idolater." It has been recorded by Ibn al-Jawzi in his book Tahrim al-Khamr (prohibition of wine drinking) with continuous chain of references tracing its narrators. "Abū Na'im," namely Fadl ibn Waka, states that the tradition is true as it has been narrated by the Prophet's descendants and some of his companions such as Ibn

Abbās, Abū Hurayra, Anas, Abdullāh ibn 'Awf al-Aslami and others.

In his book titled *Kitab al-Ansab* (a geneaology book), as-Sam'ani indicates that "Abū Muhammed Ahmed ibn Ibrahim ibn Hashim al-Alawi al-Balāthiri heard many traditions in Mecca from the Imām of Ahl al-Bayt (ع), i.e. Imām Hassan al-'Askari (ع), which he recorded." The names of some of his prominent students who, availing of his discourses, speeches and addresses, became authors of some books, are given here:

1. "Abū Hashim," Dāwūd ibn Qasim al-Ja'fari, one of the deputies of the Imām, was a scholar of advanced age. He acquired knowledge from Imām ar-Ridha (ع), from his son Imām Muhammed at-Taqi (ع), from his son Imām Ali an-Naqi (ع), and from the latter's son Imām Hassan al-'Askari (ع).

2. Dāwūd ibn Abū Zaid an-Naishapuri[1]. He often visited Imām Ali an-Naqi (ع) and Imām Hassan (ع) al-'Askari (ع).

3. Abū Tāhir Muhammed ibn Ali ibn Bilāl.

4. Abul-Abbās Abdullāh ibn Ja'far al-Humairi al-Qummi. He was a scholar of a high caliber. He authored many books including *Qurb al-Isnad* which is a major source of *Al-Kāfi*, etc.

5. Muhammed ibn Ahmed ibn Ja'far al-Qummi was the Imām's chief deputy.

6. Ja'far ibn Suhail Saiqal was one of his most distinguished deputies.

7. Muhammed ibn Hassan as-Saffar al-Qummi was a high ranking scholar, author of several books including the famous classic work titled *Basā'ir al-Darajāt*. He sent written inquiries to the Imām (ع) and received their answers from him.

---

[1]A footnote above discusses the city of Naishapur for the curious reader.

8. Abū Ja'far Hamani al-Barmaki (Barmakid); he obtained written answers to his questions in jurisprudence from the Imām (ع) and compiled a book using their text.

9. Ibrahim ibn Abū Hafs, "Abū Ishāq," al-Katib is a companion of the Imām and author of a book.

10. Ibrahim ibn Mehr-Yar. He has a book to his credit.

11. Ahmed ibn Ibrahim ibn Isma'eel ibn Dāwūd ibn Hamdan al-Katib an-Nadīm. He was an authority on literature and lexicography, author of many books, and a confidant of the Imām (ع).

12. Ahmed ibn Ishāq al-Ash'ari, "Abū Ali," al-Qummi was an acknowledged scholar and author of several books including *Hilāl as-Sawm*.

These are only a few names; the details of all the students and companions would require a whole volume. The best reference the reader may consult is the encyclopedia titled *A'yān ash-Shī'ah* أعيان الشيعة, which is discussed above. "Abū Ali" Hassan ibn Khalid ibn Muhammed prepared a commentary of the Holy Qur'ān which should be considered the work of the Imām (ع) himself. The Imām (ع) used to dictate its contents and Abū Ali recorded them. Scholars indicate that the book consisted of 1,920 pages.

Unfortunately, these precious treasures of knowledge are not available now. Baghdad was repeatedly attacked by raiders from various nations that burnt or drowned thousands of precious books. A book recently published under the title *Tafsir Hassan al-'Askari* (exegesis of Hassan al-'Askari) is a separate work which was traced and rendered to the fourth century A.H. Shaikh as-Sadūq, namely Muhammed ibn Ali Babawayh al-Qummi, says that it was actually dictated by the Imām (ع). But the Shaikh's sources from which he copied are obscure. The biographers are not, however, sure about attributing it to the Imām (ع).

These are the details of the Imām's scholarly attainments, a wonderful performance when one reflects on the fact that he died at the young age of twenty-eight, having served as Imām for only six years, a period constantly disturbed by the troubles already stated above.

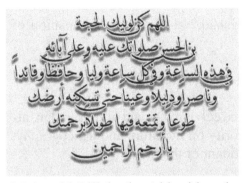

A busy man, who is engaged in the service of religion and scholarship, usually does not have time for politics or subversive activities. But the Imām's spiritual supremacy and his increasing popularity made him intolerable to his contemporary monarchs. Al-Mu'tamid Billah, the Abbāside ruler, administered his poisoning, so the Imām (ع) died on the 8th of Rabi' al-Awwal of 260 A.H./January 1, 874 A.D. and was buried in Samarra' by his father's side. His mausoleum, in spite of hostile circumstances, has been a sacred shrine for his admirers ever since and is visited daily by tens of thousands of pilgrims from all over the world.

9) THE AWAITED ONE, IMĀM AL-MAHDI (عج)

Muhammed son of Hassan al-'Askari (ع) is a facsimile of his name-sake and great ancestor, the Holy Prophet Muhammed (ص), in form and in manners. His mother was Nerjis Khatun, granddaughter of the contemporary Byzantine king who was a descendant of prophet Sham'un (Shemon, or Simon, trustee of Jesus Christ [ع]). He was born on the 15th of Sha'ban, 255 A.H./July 29, 869 A.D. His father, Imām Hassan al-'Askari (ع), gave away loaves of bread and meat as charity and sacrificed several goats for aqiqah, birth celebration. He also instructed his pious sister, Halīma Khatun, to tutor his child in the Divine Law.

Al-Mahdi (عج) is usually called by his titles rather than by his first name. These are numerous, second in number to those of Imām Ali ibn Abū Talib (ع). Famous among them are:

358

1. Al-Mahdi: المهدي This is the title which has acquired the status of a name to which reference is made in the prophecies of the Holy Prophet (ص). Hence, the concept of al-Mahdi, the Guided One, al-Muntazar, the Awaited One, is commonly acknowledge by Muslims. Undoubtedly, there are some differences of opinion among scholars

in his regard, but these deal with his life events or qualities. The belief in the reappearance of Imām al-Mahdi (عج) from his occultation is entertained by all except those who call themselves Muslims only for political or other necessities while not believing even in the unseen God. How can we expect such people to believe in the prophecies of the Holy Prophet (ص) regarding Imām al-Mahdi (عج)?

"Al-Mahdi" means: "the guided one." It indicates that Allāh is the real Guide; all creatures are guided by Him. In this sense, the Prophet and all Imāms are Mahdis, yet in reality, this title is exclusively used for the 12th Imām.

2. "Al-Qā'im." القائم This title is based on some traditions (ahādīth) where Prophet Muhammed (ص) asserts that, "This world will not come to its end unless there rises a Qā'im from my offspring who will fill it with equity and justice after its being filled with injustice and oppression."

3. "Sāhib az-Zamān" صاحب الزمان (master of the time). This is in view of the fact that he is the real guide of our time.

4. "Hujjatullāh." حجة الله Every Prophet or Imām is Hujjatullāh, the "proof" or "sign" of the Mercy Allāh, our Creator; he fulfills the responsibility of guiding humanity, thus leaving for people no excuse to commit wrongdoing. Since in our time the responsibility of guiding the world is fulfilled by the 12th Imām (ع), he will be called Hujjatullāh till Doomsday.

5. "Al-Muntazar" المنتظر (the expected or awaited one). All Muslim scholars have been repeating the prophecies regarding the

reappearance of Imām al-Mahdi (عج). Not only the Muslims but even people of other religions, too, believe in a "comer" to come in the last days. His name in various creeds may be different, but the coming of such a person is universally accepted. He was expected before his birth, and after birth and disappearance. Now his reappearance is awaited, hence his title.

Those who deny al-Mahdi (عج) base their denial on the incorrect claim that there is no reference to al-Mahdi (عج) in the Holy Qur'ān. There are two considerations to be borne in mind while studying the Holy Qur'ān:

First: Names of individuals are not always stated explicitly. For example, the holy Prophet of Islam (ص) is mentioned by name as: Muhammed, Ahmed, Taha and Yasin, whereas he is mentioned implicitly throughout the entire text of the Holy Qur'ān.

Second: Scholars of the Holy Qur'ān tell us that there are at least four meanings for each Qur'ānic verse: "ma'na zahir," an apparent or explicit meaning, "ma'na batin," a hidden or implicit meaning, "tanzeel," revelation (the circumstances under which that particular verse was revealed), and "ta'weel," interpretation. In order to fully comprehend a verse, we have to fathom all these four meanings; otherwise, our understanding of it will be extremely shallow, and "little knowledge is a dangerous thing."

The following references are all quoted from the most reliable Sunni sources:

On p. 443 of *Yanabi' al-Mawaddah* ينابيع المودة, the Hanafi *hafiz* Sulayman al-Qanduzi quotes Jābir ibn Abdullāh al-Ansāri narrating a lengthy hadīth in which a Jew named Jandal ibn Junadah ibn Jubair accepted Islam at the hands of the Prophet (ص) and the new convert asked the Prophet (ص) who his wasis were. The Prophet (ص) counted them for Jandal till he said, ".. and after him (i.e. Imām Hassan al-'Askari [ع]) his son Muhammed, who shall be called al-Mahdi and al-Qā'im and al-Hujjah. He shall occult, then shall he come back. When he comes back, he shall fill the world with justice and equity just as it was filled with injustice and iniquity; blessed are

360

those who persevere during his occultation (*ghayba*, or absence); blessed are those who persist in their love for them, for they are the ones whom Allāh described in His book saying, 'It is guidance sure, without doubt, to those who fear Allāh, who believe in the Unseen (*ghayb* الغيب)' (Qur'ān, 2:2-3)."

On p. 505 of the same work, the author, who belongs to the major Sunni sect the Hanafi, quotes Muhammed ibn Muslim who cites Imām Ja'far as-Sādiq (ع) explaining the meaning of verse 155 of the same Sura which states the following: "We shall test you with something of fear and hunger; some loss in goods or lives or the fruits (of your toil), but give glad tidings to those who patiently persevere (Qur'ān, 2:155)."

Imām Ja'far as-Sādiq (ع) indicated that there would be signs indicating the coming (reappearance) of al-Mahdi (عج) which are means whereby Allāh tests the faithful:

"Something of fear" is a reference to masses perishing by contagious diseases; "hunger" is a reference to high prices of foodstuffs; "some loss in goods" is reference to scarcity and famines; "lives" is reference to mass destruction (of human lives, probably due to global wars); "fruits" is reference to lengthy periods of droughts; so when all that happens, then "give glad tidings to those who patiently persevere".

"This is its interpretation," continued the Imām, quoting verse 7 of Ali 'Imran (Qur'ān, 3:7), which indicates that only those who are "firmly grounded in knowledge" are capable of interpreting the verses of the Holy Qur'ān, adding, "We (Ahl al-Bayt) are the ones firmly grounded in knowledge."

On p. 321 of the same work, the author quotes Imām Ja'far as-Sādiq (ع) interpreting verse 83 of Chapter 3 of the Holy Qur'ān then commenting thus: "When the Qā'im, al-Mahdi (عج), reappears, there will be no land on earth where the shahada (the testimony that *La ilaha illa-Allāh, Muhammedun rasulullāh*: There is no god but Allāh, Muhammed is the Messenger of Allāh) is not said." This could be a prediction that by the time al-Mahdi (عج) reappears, all continents of the world will have Muslim populations. They already do. At the end of Vol. 2 of *Fara'id as-Simtayn*, and on p. 269 of Ibn Khaldun's *Muqaddima* (Introduction), Ibn Abbās is quoted as saying that the Messenger of Allāh (ص) said, "Imām Ali ibn Abū Talib (ع) is the Imām of my nation and my successor therein after me; among his offspring is the awaited Qā'im who shall fill the world with justice and equity after it had been filled with injustice and iniquity. By the One Who sent me in truth a bearer of glad tidings, and a warner, I swear that those who persist adhering to his Imāmate even during his ghaybat (occultation) are more rare than red sulphur." Jābir ibn Abdullāh al-Ansāri stood up to ask the Messenger of Allāh (ص): "O Messenger of Allāh! Will there be a ghayba for that Qā'im from among your offspring?" He (ع) answered: "Ay by my Allāh! (then he quoted this verse:) 'Allāh desires to purify those that are true.' O Jābir! This is one of Allāh's orders and a secret of His which is obscure from His servants; therefore, beware of doubting, for to doubt the order of Allāh, the Mighty and the Sublime, is apostasy (*kufr*)."

On p. 507, the *hafiz* al-Qanduzi states in his book *Yanabi' al-Mawaddah* the explanation of verse 89 of Chapter 6 (al-An'am) quoting Muhammed ibn Ja'far as-Sādiq (ع) saying, "The person implied in this verse is the Qā'im, al-Mahdi (عج), who is safeguarded by Allāh; even if all people perish, Allāh will bring him and his companions out, for they are the ones entrusted by Allāh and who do not disbelieve."

Another author who follows the Shafi'i sect and who enjoys the title *'allama* is ash-Shiblinji, author of *Nur al-Absar*. He quotes Abū Ja'far (ع) explaining verse 86 of Chapter 11 (Hud) in a lengthy *hadīth* in which the Imām says, "When he (al-Mahdi (عج)) reappears, he shall lean on the Ka'ba, and three hundred and thirteen men of his companions shall join him there; the first statement he shall utter there will be: 'That which is left for you by Allāh is best for you (Qur'ān, 11:86).' Then he shall say: 'I am what is left you by Allāh, His vicegerent (a descendant of Adam), and His Proof (Hujjatullāh) over you;' so whenever someone greets him, he says, 'Peace be with you, O the one left for us by Allāh'."

The Shafi'i *faqih* Abd ar-Rahmān ibn Abū Bakr as-Sayyūti, quoting the *Sunan* of Abū Dāwūd, cites Abū Sa'īd al-Khudri on p. 50, Vol. 6, of his *Al-Durr al-Manthūr*, saying that the Messenger of Allāh (ﷺ) had said, "The Hour shall not come till al-Mahdi (ﷺ) takes charge on earth on my own behalf; he shall have a high forehead, a straight nose, and he shall fill the world with justice and equity after being filled with injustice and iniquity." He also indicates that Imām Ahmed ibn Hanbal (founder of one of the four Sunni sects, i.e. the Hanbali) quotes Abū Sa'īd al-Khudri quoting the Messenger of Allāh (ﷺ) saying, "I bring you the glad tidings of al-Mahdi (ﷺ); Allāh shall send him to my nation, in time quite different from your own, and after series of earthquakes, and he shall fill the world with justice and equity as it was filled before with injustice and iniquity, and all the residents of the world shall be pleased with him, and he shall distribute the wealth equitably." 'Allāma al-Bahrāni, quoting the Shāfi'i *faqīh* Ibrahim ibn Muhammed al-Hamawayni who in turn quotes Abdullāh ibn Abbās on p. 692 of *Ghayat al-Maram* saying that the Messenger of Allāh (ﷺ) had said, "My successors, wasis and hujaj are twelve: the first of them is my brother and the last is my son." He was asked: "O Messenger of Allāh! Who is your brother?!" He answered: "Ali ibn Abū Talib." "Then who is your son?" "Al-Mahdi (ﷺ) who shall fill the world with justice and equity after being filled with injustice and iniquity. By the One Who sent me in truth a bearer of glad tidings and a warner, I swear that if there is only one day left in this world, Allāh will prolong that day till my son (descendant) al-Mahdi (ﷺ) reappears, and the Spirit of Allāh, Jesus son of Mary, shall say his prayers behind him (then he quoted verse 69 of Chapter 39:) 'And the earth will shine with the glory of its Lord' and his domain shall encompass the East and the West."

Before the Imām's birth, predictions regarding him were put forth by the Holy Prophet and the Infallible Imāms. Several scholars of the Sunni School of Muslim Law have written volumes exclusively on this topic. For example, *hafiz* Muhammed ibn Yousuf al-Kanji ash-Shafi'i has compiled *Al-Bayan fi Akhbari Sahib az-Zaman* (the clear evidence regarding the tidings of the Master of Age). *Hafiz* Abū Na'im al-Isfahani has written *Na't al-Mahdi* (ﷺ) (title of al-Mahdi (ﷺ)). Abū Dāwūd as-Sijistani has devoted one complete chapter titled "Kitab al-Mahdi (ﷺ)" in his *Sunan* dedicated entirely to this subject. At-Tirmithi in his *Sahīh*, Ibn Majah in his *Sunan*, and al-Hakim in his *Mustadrak*, have all done likewise.

One tradition recorded by Muhammed ibn Ibrahim al-Hamawi (of Hama, Syria) which ash-Shafi'i cited in his work *Fara'id as-Simtayn* says, "Ibn Abbās heard the Prophet (ﷺ) saying, I am the chief of the Prophets, and Ali is the chief of the Trustees (*wasis*). My trustees (or successors) after me are twelve: the first of them is Ali and the last is al-Mahdi.'"

Jābir ibn Abdullāh al-Ansāri narrated saying that Fatima az-Zahra (ع) had a tablet (mushaf) on which the names of all the succeeding Imāms were written down; three of them were named "Muhammed" and four were named "Ali", all being her offspring, and the last was named al-Qā'im. Shaikh as-Sadūq, namely Muhammed ibn Ali ibn Babawayh al-Qummi, records in his book *Ikmāl ad-Dīn wa Itmām an-Ni'ma* a tradition on the authority of Imām ar-Ridha (ع) who narrated it from his ancestors. It states that Imām Ali (ع) addressed his son Imām Hussain (ع) once saying, "The ninth from your descendants shall rise defending the truth; he shall protect the faith and promote justice."

As-Sadūq, in his book *Ikmal al-Dīn*, also quotes the Prophet (ﷺ) as saying, "When the ninth among the descendants of my son Hussain is born, Allāh will extend his life-span during the period of absence (occultation) and will project him at the appointed time."

Imām Hussain (ع), the chief of martyrs, is quoted as saying, "The ninth of my descendants is the Imām who will rise with the truth. Allāh will grant life to earth through him after its death. The true faith will supersede all religions through him. His absence shall be lengthy during which multitudes would go astray. Only a few will be on the Right Path. They shall suffer painfully. People will oppress them, saying, Let us know when this promise is fulfilled!' Those who will bear the pain and deprivation patiently will get the same rewards as those who accompanied the Prophet during his expeditions for Jihad." Imām Zain al-'Ābidīn (ع) has said, "Of us one will be born whose birth will remain secret, so much so that people will say that he was not born at all." Imām Muhammed al-

Bāqir (ع) is quoted in *Al-Kāfi* by al-Kulayni as saying, "Nine Imāms after Hussain are destined; the last of them will be al-Qā'im."

Imām Ja'far as-Sādiq (ع) is quoted by Shaikh as-Sadūq in his book *'Ilal ash-Sharai'* as saying: "The fifth descendant of my son, Mūsa, will be the Qā'im, a descendant of the Prophet (ص)."

As recorded in *Ikmal ad-Din* of Shaikh as-Sadūq, Imām Mūsa al-Kādhim (ع) was asked once: "Are you the Qā'im with the truth?" The Imām replied: "I, too, rise truthfully, but the real Qā'im is he who will remove the enemies of Allāh from earth and will fill it with justice. He shall be my fifth descendant. His absence will be lengthy during which multitudes will turn away from the faith while only a few will uphold it."

When Du'bal al-Khuzā'i, the famous poet, recited his poem to Imām ar-Ridha (ع) which included these lines:

The Riser will appear, I do confess,
With grace he will rise, blessed and good:
And will deal with the faithful and the faithless
And will distinguish between truth and falsehood;

Imām ar-Ridha (ع) wept. Then, raising his head, he said, "O Du'bal, these lines have been inspired to you by Gabriel. Do you know who this Riser (Qā'im) is and when he shall rise?" Du'bal said that he did not know the details, but that he had been hearing that an Imām who would purge the world from evils and fill it with justice. The Imām explained: "O Du'bal, my son, Muhammed, will come when I am gone. After him, his descendant, al-Qā'im, will come. He will be awaited during his absence. When he appears, the world shall bow down before him."

Imām Muhammed at-Taqi (ع) has said, "The Qā'im will be from amongst us, the third of my descendants."

Imām Ali an-Naqi (ع) has said, "My successor is my son, Imām Hassan; but what will be your condition during the reign of Imām Hassan's successor?" Those who were present asked him: "Why, what do you mean by that?" Imām Ali an-Naqi (ع) said, "You will not have the opportunity to see him; later, you will not be allowed even to mention his name." Then he was asked as to how they should mention him. He said, "You may say that he is the last of Muhammed's (Infallible) descendants."

Some people asked Imām Hassan al-'Askari (ع): "Your revered forefathers have said that the earth would never be without a Sign of Allāh (Hujjat-Allāh) till Doomsday, and he who dies without knowing the Imām of his time dies the death of the days of ignorance." Imām Hassan al-'Askari (ع) said that that was as true as the shining day. They inquired as to who would be the Imām and who would be the Sign of the Mercy of Allāh after his death. Imām Hassan explained thus: "He will be my son, the namesake of the Holy Prophet. He who dies without knowing him will die the death of the days of ignorance. His absence will be so lengthy that the ignorant will wander puzzled and will surely stray; the false will fall into eternal destruction. Those who will foretell the exact date of his appearing will be wrong."

All these predictions were recorded since the time of the Holy Prophet who prophesied the advent of the Mahdi. The anecdote of Du'bal demonstrates that the concept was quite common. History tells us that friends and foes of Ahl al-Bayt (ع) knew the fact, and sometimes tried to take wrong advantage thereof. For example, one of the Abbāsides named Muhammed had assumed the title of al-Mahdi (ع). Muhammed son of Abdullāh Mahd, an offspring of Imām Hussain (ع), too, was considered by some people as the Mahdi. The Kaisanis had attributed the same to Muhammed ibn al-Hanafiyya. But these suppositions were refuted by the Imāms who condemned them and explained the qualities of the true Mahdi and asserted his absence. The aforementioned events clearly indicate that the idea about the advent of the Mahdi was unanimously acknowledged. Besides, the traditions of the Holy Prophet continuously affirmed that he would be succeeded by 12 persons. This number itself sufficed to refute the claims of the false pretenders. But when the eleventh Imām al-Hassan (ع) al-'Askari (ع) had come, people keenly awaited al-Mahdi (عج) who was sought even prior to his birth with the same eagerness as he is now awaited

366

since his absence.

Precedents existed that many Imāms did not have an opportunity for education; still, Providence Divine made arrangements to adorn them with learning and moral accomplishments which elevated them to Imāmate. For example, Imām Ali an-Naqi (ع) was six years old when his father Muhammed at-Taqi (ع) died. Imām at-Taqi (ع) was eight years old at the time of the death of his father Imām ar-Ridha (ع). Outwardly, a boy of this age cannot be proficient in learning. But once we acknowledge that Allāh had specially gifted the Prophet's Progeny, the question of age stands no more. If Jesus Christ could speak in his cradle and assert his prophethood (see the Holy Qur'ān, 19:24 and 19:30-33), a believer cannot think that the childhood of Imām al-Mahdi (عج) would negate or render his Imāmate faulty. Imām al-Mahdi (عج) could enjoy his father's love and instruction for a very short period of time because he was only five years old when his father died in 260 A.H./874 A.D. Even at that young age, Providence crowned him with Imāmate.

When the Pharaoh of Egypt heard the prophecy that a child would soon be born to destroy his kingdom, he tried his best to obstruct the child's birth or kill him after his birth. Likewise, the Abbāside ruler knew that a child would be born to Imām Hassan al-'Askari (ع) who would destroy his unjust kingdom. He, therefore, made every possible arrangement that the child would not be born, keeping Imām Hassan al-'Askari (ع) in continuous imprisonment away from his wife. But even the greatest worldly power cannot fight Providence. In spite of all the efforts of Pharaoh, Moses was born; similarly, in spite of the efforts of the Abbāside government, the awaited Imām came into the world.

His birth and upbringing were kept secret and, as Providence so wished, it remained so. Only a few moments did he appear in public. It was the time when his father's coffin was ready for the funeral prayers. All prominent Shī'ahs were present. The ranks had been formed. Imām Hassan al-'Askari's brother Ja'far stepped forward to lead the prayers and was at the point of reciting the Takbir when suddenly a boy came out from behind the curtains, passed the ranks quickly and took hold of Ja'far's robe and said, "Get back, Uncle; I am more than you worthy of leading the funeral prayers for my father." Ja'far at once withdrew and the boy led the prayers. Having performed this duty, the boy went back. It was not possible that the Abbāside ruler could remain ignorant of the fact. The search for him was carried out more seriously than ever before in order to arrest and slay the boy. Some may ask: "How can a boy lead the funeral prayers in the capacity of an Imām?" The question is provided by the Holy Qur'ān. Such skeptics should research the Holy Qur'ān to see how another boy, namely Yahya (John the Baptist), became a Prophet of Allāh even while being a young boy. See verse 12 of Chapter 19 (Sūrat Maryam).

The Prophet and the Imāms had predicted al-Mahdi's occultation (disappearance from public eyes, absence) as has already been narrated. His occultation is divided into two periods. The first period is known as the minor occultation. It extended from 260 A.H. to 329 A.H. (874-941 A.D.) when very pious persons nominated by the Imām himself acted as his deputies. Their duty was to convey to the Imām all problems of the Shī'as, get their solutions from the Imām or solve them themselves according to their own discretion, collect *zakat* and *khums* and spend them in the proper way, and convey the Imām's instructions to the trusted persons. Those deputies, four in number, were the most pious and learned, and they were the trusted confidants. Here are their names:

1. Abū Amr Othman ibn Sa'd ibn Amr al-Amri al-Assadi. He was a deputy of Imām Ali an-Naqi (ع), then of his son Imām Hassan al-'Askari (ع). Having performed the same duty for a few years for Imām al-Mahdi (عج), he died in Baghdad and was buried there.

2. Abū Ja'far Muhammed ibn Othman ibn Sa'd al-Amri (son of the above). Imām Hassan al-'Askari (ع) foretold his being deputized. Then his father, at the time of his death, proclaimed under the orders of the Imām his appointment as deputy. He died in Jumada I of 305 A.H./November 917 A.D.

3. Abul-Qasim Hussain ibn Ruh ibn Abū Bakr an-Nawbakhti. A member of the famous Nawbakhti family, he was distinguished for his knowledge, philosophy, astrology and kalam. He was a top

368

ranking scholar and a pious man. Under the directions of Imām al-Mahdi (عج), Abū Ja'far Muhammed ibn Othman appointed him as his successor. After having served for fifteen years in that capacity, he died in Shaban of 320 A.H./932 A.D.

4. "Abū Hassan," Ali ibn Muhammed as-Samari. He was the last deputy, succeeding Hussain ibn Rah as directed by the Imām. He performed this duty for nine years only and died on the 15th of Sha'ban of 329 A.H./May 15, 941 A.D. Having been asked on his deathbed as to who would succeed him, he replied: "Providence now wishes to give the matter another shape the duration of which is known by Allāh Alone."

After the demise of Abul-Hassan, there was no deputy. In this sorrowful year, i.e. 329 A.H./941 A.D., Imām Ali ibn Babawayh al-Qummi, the revered father of Shaikh as-Sadūq, and Muhammed ibn Ya'qub al-Kulayni, the learned compiler of Al-Kāfi, also expired. Besides these sad events, an extra-ordinary phenomenon was also witnessed. In the sky so many stars did shoot that it seemed as if Doomsday had come. That year was, therefore, named "the year of the dispersal of the stars." After this followed a dark period because none was left to approach Imām al-Mahdi (عج).

The period since 329 A.H./941 A.D. is called "the major occultation" because there is none deputized by the Imām. It was for this period that Imām al-Mahdi (عج) directed "to refer to those who know our traditions the lawful and the unlawful matters because they will guide you on our own behalf." It is in view of this advice that the scholars and mujtahids are called the Imām's successors. But this succession means general guidance of the people and is in no way by personal nomination. They are, therefore, quite different from the deputies who served as such during the minor occultation.

The predictions about these occultations had been made by the Infallible ones. The Holy Prophet affirmed: "He will have an occultation in which many groups will wander aimlessly; during this period, the number of those who believe in and follow him will be meager." Imām Ali ibn Abū Talib (ع) said, "The Qā'im will have a long period of absence (occultation). The scene is full in my view when the friends of Ahl al-Bayt (ع) will wander during his absence as animals wander in search of a meadow." Another tradition says that "He will reappear after such a long period of absence during which only true and sincere believers will uphold their religion."

Imām al-Hassan (ع) said, "Allāh will prolong his life-span during his absence." Imām al-Hussain (ع) said, "He will remain absent during which period so many parties will go astray." Imām Muhammed al-Bāqir (ع) said, "His absence will be so lengthy that many people will go astray."

Imām Ja'far as-Sādiq (ع) said, "Al-Mahdi (عج) will be the fifth descendant of the seventh Imām. He will remain unseen." On another occasion, he said that Sāhib al-Amr (the master of command) will have an occultation during which everybody must remember Allāh, do good deeds and uphold his religion.

Imām Mūsa al-Kādhim (ع) said, "His person will remain unseen to the eye but the believers will never forget him; he will be the Twelfth of our line."

Imām ar-Ridha (ع) predicted that he would be awaited during his absence. Imām Muhammed at-Taqi (ع) explained: "Al-Mahdi (عج) will be awaited during his absence and will be obeyed upon his reappearance."

Imām Ali an-Naqi (ع) clarified: "The Master of Command will be the one about whom people will say: He has not been born yet.'" Imām Hassan al-'Askari (ع) said, "My son's absence will cause doubts and disbeliefs in the minds of people except those whom Allāh guides."

Imām Muhammed al-Bāqir (ع) had also explained that the Qā'im of Ali Muhammed would have two periods of absence, a very lengthy one and a relatively short one. Imām Ja'far as-Sādiq (ع) had similarly predicted thus: "One of the two periods of absence will be quite lengthy."

It was due to these predictions that after the death of Imām Hassan al-'Askari (ع), his followers and sincere believers did not entertain any doubt about him. Instead of acknowledging the Imāmate of some present false claimant, they only believed in Imām al-Mahdi (عج), the Absent, the Occultant.

Although absent and unrepresented, Imām al-Mahdi (ع) still guides people and defends the faith. Even though unseen, he supervises the world's affairs and guides it. This curtain will exist as long as Providence deems it necessary; the time will come soon (though "soon" may occur to many too late) when the curtain of absence will be removed, Imām al-Mahdi (عج) will reappear and fill the world with justice and equity, discarding all the prevailing injustices and iniquities. May Allāh Almighty bring about his early reappearance and ease his coming, Allāhomma Aameen.

اللهم أرزقنا شفاعة الحسين
اللهم نتقرب اليك بالولاء لأهل بيت النبوة
و نتبرأ من أعدائهم الى يوم القيامة

CONCLUSION

Imām al-Hussain's revolution was not only for changing a government, as noble an objective as it was. Had it been so, it would have been wrong to call it a revolution. Imām al-Hussain (ع) advocated a drastic change in the social order, in the economic and political structure, and he enjoined the refining of the Islamic concepts from foreign ideas that had crept into them. In other words, Imām al-Hussain (ع) wanted to change the life of the Muslims for all time to come in conformity with the established Islamic laws and principles.

In our time and age, there are many Yazids ruling our Muslim world. This is why when the Muslim women were raped in Bosnia, massacred in Chechnya, Kashmir, Palestine, or southern Lebanon, very, very few Muslims stir to action while the rest remain in their slumber, preferring to close their eyes rather than see the horrors of what happens to their brethren. Yes, there are many Yazids

371

throughout our Islamic world, but there is no Hussain to lead the revolution against them; so, the oppression and the inequity shall continue unabated, and the Muslims shall remain the underdogs of the world till they take Islam more seriously and defend its pristine tenets with all their might and means. Meanwhile, the suffering continues.., *Inna Lillah wa Inna Ilayahi Raji'oon* (We belong to Allāh, and to Him shall we return).

It is sincerely hoped that the discreet reader has benefitted from this book, that it has brought him closer to His Maker, the One Who created him for one and only reason: to worship Him, and only Him. It is hoped that this book has brought him closer to Him, to His last Prophet (ص), and to the Prophet's Ahl al-Bayt (ع) and distanced himself from all those who do not denounce the murderers of Imām Hussain (ع), those who do not learn any lesson from his epic of heroism, who do not mourn his tragedy, who do not shed tears during the month of Muharram to commemorate this tragedy the like of which has never been recorded in history..., and unfortunately this description fits the majority of Muslims, for the majority is not always right. Seventy-two verses in the Holy Qur'ān condemn the majority. Let this be a lesson for all of us. Might and numerical superiority do not necessarily have to be right. In most instances, they are not.

For sure, whoever bases his belief in the Almighty on solid foundations will be the winner in this life and in the life to come, and the most solid of all foundations is one built on knowledge and conviction, not on ignorance, nor on taking things for granted, nor on hiding the truth or distorting it. This address is directed specifically to new Muslim converts in the West in general and in the U.S. in particular, those who have been taught to glorify certain sahāba and to forget about everyone else, to study the first few years of the dawn of Islam, and to forget about the rest. These converts should spare no time nor effort to study Islamic history and to find out who actually took Islam seriously and who did not, who shed the blood of innocent Muslims, including members of the Prophet's family, the very best of all families in the entire history of mankind, and altered the Sunnah to serve his own ambition.

372

One authentic *hadīth* says, "For everything there is a zakat, and the zakat of knowledge is its dissemination." The reader who reads this book ought not keep what he/she has learned to himself/herself but share it with others, believers or non-believers. It will then enhance the conviction of the believers and plant the seed of iman in the hearts of the unbelievers. Who knows? Maybe one day that seed will grow. It is the Almighty Who permits its growth, and He does so at the right time, the time which He chooses. Pass this book on to a relative or a friend. Translate it into another language. Let on-line computer services benefit from it. Make photocopies of some of its contents and distribute them to others. Write a dissertation or a thesis utilizing its text. Extract excerpts from it for inclusion in your newsletter or magazine, book or booklet. Or write one like it or better. All these options are yours; so, do not sit idle. Move to action, and let the Almighty use you as His tool for disseminating useful knowledge.

Do you, dear reader, think that you have a choice whether to disseminate the knowledge included in this book with others or not? If you think that you do, read the following statement of the great grandson of the Messenger of Allāh (ﷺ), namely Imām Mūsa ibn Ja'far (ﻉ), who quotes his forefathers citing the Messenger of Allāh (ﷺ) saying,

One who reneges from his oath of allegiance, or who promotes what misleads people, or who hides some knowledge with him, or who confines some wealth with him unjustly, or who knowingly aids an oppressor in committing oppression while being fully aware of his oppression, is outside the folds of Islam.

This tradition is recorded on p. 67, Vol. 2, of al-Majlisi's *Bihār al-Anwār*. It clearly demonstrates that one who hides knowledge is on the same level with that who deliberately assists oppressors and tyrants. We, therefore, should spare no means to share what we know with others, with those who listen and who follow the best of what they listen to. Earn rewards by bringing the servants of Allāh closer to their Creator Who made and sustained them, Who will try them and place them either in His Paradise or in His hell. If acts of worship are based on shallow conviction, they are as good as nothing. Strengthen your brethren's conviction through this book. They will surely appreciate it and, above all, Allāh, too, will.

If the reader appreciates the time and effort exerted in writing this book, I, the author, kindly request him/her to recite Sūrat al-Fātiha for the soul of my father, the late qari al-Hajj Tu'mah Abbās al-Jibouri who died in 1991 of diabetes, medicines for which were not available because of the "economic sanctions" imposed on the people of Iraq by the tyrants of the world, and for the souls of all believing men and women, the living and the dead. If you do so, rest assured that your rewards will be with the Most Generous of all those who reward, with Allāh Almighty Who appreciates even the smallest of good deeds. Why do I request the kind reader to recite Sūrat al-Fātiha for my parents? Well, this is the least a son can do for his deceased father who worked very hard to raise him as a Muslim. My father was a *qari* of the Holy Qur'ān who refused to read any other book besides the Qur'ān as long as he lived, a man who never intentionally hurt anyone all his life. Not only will my father receive blessings when you recite Sūrat al-Fātiha for his soul, but you, too, dear reader, will get your rewards as well. How will you be rewarded? Well, read on! Here is a glimpse of what you will Insha-Allāh receive:

On p. 88, Vol. 1, of *Mujma' al-Bayan fi Tafsir al-Qur'ān*, at-Tibrisi cites a tradition through a chain of narrator wherein the Prophet of Islam is quoted as saying, "Whoever recites Sūrat al-Fātiha will be rewarded as though he had read two thirds of the Holy Qur'ān and will be (in addition to that) given rewards as though he gave charity to each and every believing man and woman." Just imagine how generous the Almighty is! Ubayy ibn Ka'b is cited in the same reference saying, "I once recited Sūrat al-Fātiha in the presence of the Messenger of Allāh, peace and blessings of Allāh be upon him and his progeny, who said to me, I swear by the One Who controls my life, Allāh never revealed any chapter in the Torah, the Gospel, the Psalms, or (even) in the Qur'ān like it. It is the mother of the Book, and it is the seven oft-repeated verses. It is divided between Allāh and His servant, and His servant will get whatever he asks Him for.'" The Messenger of Allāh (ﻉ) said once to Jābir ibn Abdullāh al-Ansāri, one of his greatest sahāba, may Allāh be pleased with all his good *sahāba*, "O Jābir! Shall I teach you the merits of a Sura which Allāh revealed in His Book?" Jābir said, "Yes, O Messenger of Allāh! May both my parents be sacrificed for your sake! Please do!" The Messenger of Allāh (ﺹ) taught him Sūrat al-Hamd, the "Mother of the Book," then said to him, "Shall I tell you something about it?" "Yes, O Messenger of Allāh," Jābir responded, "May my father and mother be sacrificed for your sake!" The Messenger of Allāh (ﺹ) said, "It cures everything except death." Imām Ja'far as-Sādiq is quoted on the same page as saying, "Anyone who is not cured by the Book's Fātiha cannot be cured by anything else." Imām Ali ibn Abū Talib (ﻉ) has said,

The Messenger of Allāh (ﺹ) has said, "Allāh, the Exalted One, the Sublime, said to me: (O Muhammed!) We have bestowed upon you seven oft-repeated verses and the Great Qur'ān (verse 87 of Sūrat al-Hijr); so, express your appreciation for it by reciting the Book's Fatiha,' thus comparing it to the entire Qur'ān." Sūrat al-Fātiha is the most precious of the treasures of the Arsh. Allāh specifically chose Muhammed (ﺹ) to be honoured by it without having done so to any of His prophets with the exception of prophet Sulayman (Solomon) who was granted (only this verse) of it: Bismillahir-Rahmanir-Rahim (verse 30 of Chapter 27, Sūrat an-Naml); don't you see how He narrates about Balqees[1] saying, "O Chiefs (of

---

[1]Balqees Queen of Saba' (Sheba) belonged to the Arab tribe of Himyar which for centuries has been residing in Yemen. Her people used to worship the sun and the moon and other stars, and some of the ruins of the temples she had built for them can still be seen in Saba'. Solomon (Sulayman), on the other hand, was headquartered in Jerusalem (Ur-o-Shalom, the city of peace, as it is called in Hebrew; the Arabs used to refer to it as Eilya). The place where Balqees met Sulayman, that is to say, his palace, had been built in the 10th century B.C. Reference to the grandeur of this palace exists in 27:44: its glass-covered floor was so smooth, Balqees thought she was in front of a lake. Damascus, a very ancient city not far from Jerusalem, had by then established a reputation for its glass industry. Damascus, in 940 B.C. (around the same period of time when Sulayman was ruling in Jerusalem) was the city capital of the Aramaeans, the nations that spoke Aramaic, mother-tongue of prophet Jesus Christ (ﻉ). This is why Syria used to be called Aram, the land of the Aramaens. Aramaic is still spoken in some part of Syria even today.

Yemen's tribes)! Surely an honourable letter has been delivered to me; it is from Solomon, and it is: In the Name of Allāh, the Beneficent, the Merciful..." (27:29-30)? So whoever recites it sincerely believing that he/she is following in the footsteps of Muhammed and his progeny, ābidīng by its injunctions, believing in its apparent as well as hidden meanings, Allāh will give him for each of its letters a good deed better than all this world and everything in it of wealth and good things. And whoever listens to someone reciting it will receive a third of the rewards the reciter receives; so, let each one of you accumulate of such available goodness, for it surely is a great gain. Do not let it pass you by, for then you will have a great sigh in your heart about it."[1]

Rewards of reciting Sūrat al-Fātiha are also recorded on p. 132 of *Thawab al-A'mal wa Iqab al-A'mal* ثواب الأعمال و عقاب الأعمال cited above. Abū Abdullāh Imām Ja'far as-Sādiq has said, "Whoever recites Sūrat al-Baqara and Sūrat al-Fātiha, they will both shade him like two clouds on the Day of Judgment. And if the reader wishes to read more about the merits of the Basmala (Bismillahir-Rahmānir-Rahīm), he is referred to pp. 70-71 of my book *Fast of the Month of Ramadan: Philosophy and Ahkam* published by Ansāriyan (P.O. Box 37185/187, Qum, Islamic Republic of Iran). As for the merits of Sūrat al-Fātiha, I would like to quote for you here what is published on pp. 71-73 of the same book:

At-Tibrisi, in his exegesis *Mujma'ul-Bayan fī Tafsir al-Qur'ān*, provides nine names for the first chapter of the Holy Qur'ān, namely Sūrat al-Fātiha: 1) al-Fātiha الفاتحة, the one that opens, for it is like a gate: when opened, it leads one to the Book of Allāh; 2) al-Hamd الحمد, the praise, for its verses are clearly praising the Almighty; 3) Ummul-Kitāb أم الكتاب, the mother of the Book, for its status is superior to all other chapters of the Holy Qur'ān, or like the war standard: it is always in the forefront; 4) as-Sab' السبع, the seven verses, for it is comprised of seven verses and the only one whose verses are seven, and there is no room here to elaborate on the merits of the number 7 especially since most readers of this book are

_____

[2]at-Tabari, *Tarikh*, Vol. 1, p. 88.

already aware of such merits; 5) al-Mathāni المثاني, the oft-repeated Chapter, for no other Chapter of the Holy Qur'ān is repeated as often as this one; 6) al-Kāfiya الكافية, the chapter that suffices and that has no substitute; you simply cannot replace its recitation with that of any other chapter of the Holy Qur'ān in the first two rek'ats of the prayers, whereas it can substitute others; 7) al-Asās الأساس, the basis or foundation or bed-rock, a connotation of its being the foundation upon which the Holy Qur'ān stands just as the Basmala ("Bismillahir-Rahmānir-Rahīm") is the foundation of the Fātiha; 8) ash-Shifā' الشفاء, the healing, due to the fact that the Messenger of Allāh (ﷺ) has said that the Fātiha heals from all ailments except death, and 9) as-Salāt الصلاة, the prayers, or the basic requirement of the daily prayers, one without the recitation of which no prayer can be accepted. The Prophet has quoted the Almighty as saying, "The prayers have been divided between Me and My servant: one half for Me, and one for him;" so when one recites it and says, "Alhamdu lillahi Rabbil-Ālamīn," the Almighty says, "My servant has praised Me." And when he says, "Arrahmānir-Rahīm," the Almighty says, "My servant has lauded Me." And when he says, "Māliki Yawmid-Dīn," Allāh says, "My servant has exalted Me." And when he says, "Iyyaka Nabudu wa iyyaka nastaan," Allāh will say, "This is a covenant between Me and My servant, and My servant shall be granted the fulfillment of his pleas." Then if he finishes reciting the Fātiha to the end, Allāh will again confirm His promise by saying, "This is for [the benefit of] My servant, and My servant will be granted the answer to his wishes."

The Messenger of Allāh (ﷺ) is quoted by Abū Ali al-Fadl ibn al-Hassan ibn al-Fadl at-Tibrisi, may Allāh have mercy on his soul, saying that one who recites al-Fātiha will be regarded by the Almighty as though he recited two-thirds of the Holy Qur'ān and as though he gave by way of charity to each and every believing man and woman. "By the One in Whose hand my soul is," the Prophet continues, "Allāh Almighty did not reveal in the Torah, the Gospel, or the Psalms any chapter like it; it is the Mother of the Book and as-Sab' al-Mathāni السبع المثاني (the oft-repeated seven verses), and it is divided between Allāh and His servant, and His servant shall get whatever he asks; it is the best Sura in the Book of the most Exalted One, and it is a healing from every ailment except poison, which is death." He is also quoted by al-Kaf'ami as saying, "He (Allāh) bestowed it upon me as His blessing, making it equivalent to the Holy Qur'ān, saying, And We have granted you as-Sab' al-Mathāni السبع المثاني (the seven most often repeated verses) and the Great Qur'ān (Sūrat al-Hijr [Ch. 15], verse 87).' It is the most precious among the treasures of the Arsh." Indeed, Allāh, the most Sublime, has chosen Muhammed (ﷺ) alone to be honored by it without doing so to any other Prophet or Messenger of His with the exception of Solomon (Solomon) who was granted the Basmala. One who recites it, being fully convinced of his following in the footsteps of Muhammed (ﷺ) and his Progeny (ع), adhering to its injunctions, believing in its outward and inward meanings, will be granted by Allāh for each of its letters a blessing better than what all there is in the world of wealth and good things, and whoever listens to someone reciting it will receive one third of the reciter's rewards.

There is no doubt that you, dear reader, know that it is very costly to print books, and philanthropists in the Muslim world are rare and endangered species. Once you find one, you will find out that he is willing to spend money on anything except on a book! This is very sad, very tragic, very shameful. Islam spread through a Book: the Holy Qur'ān. That was all the early generations of Muslims needed besides the presence of the Messenger of Allāh. But times have changed; we do not have the presence of the Messenger of Allāh in our midst to ask him whenever we need to know, and his Sunnah has suffered acutely of alteration, addition, deletion, custom-designing and tailoring to fit the needs of the powerful politicians of the times, so much so that it is now very hard to find the pristine truth among all the numerous different views and interpretations. This is why the reader has to spend more effort to get to know the truth; nobody is going to hand it to you on a golden platter. You have to work hard to acquire it. "Easy come, easy go." Yet readers who would like to earn a place in Paradise through their dissemination of Islamic knowledge, such as the knowledge included in this book, are very much needed and are advised in earnest to send their contributions to the Publisher of this book in order to help him print more copies of it and make them available to those who cannot afford to purchase them. Some readers erroneously surmise that book publishers are wealthy people who make a lot of money selling books, but, alas, this applies ONLY to non-Muslim publishers. After all, Allāh will judge our actions according to our intentions, and if you help promote a book seeking the Pleasure of Allāh, rest assured that you will be richly rewarded. It remains to see how strong you are against the temptations of Satan who will try his best, and his worst, to dissuade you from doing so. He very well knows that nothing in the world stands between him and corrupting the minds of Muslims more than accurate knowledge about Allāh and the men of Allāh. May Allāh Taala include us among the latter, *Allāhomma Aameen.*

May Allāh Ta'āla accept our humble effort; may He forgive our sins and shortcomings; may He take our hands and guide us to what He loves and prefers, *Allāhomma Aameen, Wassalāmo Alaikom wa Rahmatullāhi wa Barakātuh.*

GLOSSARY OF ISLAMIC TERMS

A ا،أ، آ، ع

A'imma أئمة: Plural of امام imām, religious leader. There are many types of such leaders in Islam: The most common is the امام الجماعة *imām al-jama'a*, leader of congregational prayers. Imāmite Shī'ites follow 12 Imāms who start from Ali ibn Abū Tālib and end with the Awaited One, Imām al-Mahdi. The word امام imām is given a much broader meaning in verse 124 of Ch. 2, The Cow, of the Holy Qur'ān where it refers to an imām of an entire nation. Such imāms of entire nations, we are told in 17:71, will be gathered on the Judgment Day with their followers for questioning.

Abrashiyya أبرشية: parish, diocese

A.D.: stands for "Anno Domini" ("year of the Lord"). It is used to refer to pre-Hijra dates. Hijra is the migration of the Prophet from Mecca to Medīna. According to some reports, the Prophet entered Medīna on the 12th of Rabi` I which coincided with the 24th of September according to the Julian calendar or the 27th of September according to the Gregorian calendar of the year 622 A.D.

Adab or Aadaab آداب: ethics, rules of conduct, morals, arts

`Adil عادل: fair, just, equitable, impartial, unbiased

`Adl عدل: Usually, it refers to the concept of the justice of Allāh (God). This is one of the principles of the Islamic creed: The Almighty is fair and just to everyone and does not discriminate among His servants.

Ahadīth or Ahadeeth أحاديث: Pl.; singular: *hadīth*, a statement (usually stated/attributed either to the Prophet (ص) or to one of the members of his Progeny or companions); these are one of the two sources of the Sunna, the other being the Holy Qur'ān. But this Sunna has been distorted so much since the beginning of the Islamic history by politicians and interest seekers, so much so that it is very difficult now to sift through them and identify what is authentic, genuine, and what is fabricated. Umayyad rulers in general and Mu`awiyah in particular played a major role in distorting the Islamic creed by paying writers to tailor design "traditions" to serve their interests and legitimize their un-Islamic conduct.

Ahilla أهله: plural of *hilal*, crescent

Ahl ar-Ra'i أهل الرأي: people of opinion. It refers to qualified people who are consulted on Islamic matters.

Ahzab أحزاب: parties. "Ahzab" occurs in Ch. 33 of the Holy Qur'ān to describe the different tribes that fought the Muslims in the Battle of *Khandaq* (ditch, moat) which took place in 5 A.H./627 A.D. Refer to the meaning of *khandaq* below for full details.

Ala علا: rose, ascended; **علا على:** prevailed, overrode, predominated, triuphed over. It also means soared or indulged in pride, acted arrogantly, thought too much of himself. Other meanins: mounted, towered over.

`Ālim عالم: scholar, theologian, a highly knowledgeable person

Allāhu Akbar or Allāho Akbar, Allāhu Akber, Allāhoo Akber, Or Allāh Akbar الله أكبر: This statement is said by Muslims quite often and on various occasions. During the call for prayers, during prayers, when they are happy, when they wish to express their approval of what they hear, when they slaughter an animal, and when they want to praise a speaker…, Muslims utter this expression. Its means: "Allāh is the Greatest."

Almani or 'Ilmani علماني" secular, multi-confessional

A`mal أعمال: highly recommended acts of adoration

Amin or **Ameen** أمين: custodian or guardian, someone who is loyal, faithful, trustworthy, secretary

Amir or **Ameer** أمير: leader or commander, prince, one in charge

Amir al-Mumineen or **Ameerul-Mu'mineen** أمير المؤمنين: Commander of the Faithful: title of the caliphs, Islamic rulers. Followers of Ahl al-Bayt (ع), the Prophet's Progeny, apply it particularly to Imām Ali ibn Abū Tālib (ع) on account of the "Ghadīr Khumm Declaration". This Declaration took place on the 18ᵗʰ of Thul-Hijja of the year 11 A.H. which then coincided, according to the Gregorian Christian calendar, with the 9ᵗʰ of March (or the 6ᵗʰ of March according to the Julian Christian calendar) of the year 633 A.D. The Ghadīr, swamp or small lake of shallow water formed mostly by rainfall, is located in the Juhfa desert between Mecca and Medīna on the pilgrims' route to Mecca. It is there and then that the Prophet (ص) articulated his famous statement: "To whom I have been a *mawla*, master, this Ali is his master! Lord befriend whoever befriends him and be the enemy of whoever antagonizes him!" It is there and then that Ali was called "Amir al-Mu'mineen", commander of the faithful. Numerous classic books (mostly in Arabic) detail this incident. One of them is al-Bukhāri's book titled *At-Tarikh Al-Kabir* where the author details the incident in Vol. 1, Part 1, p. 375 (Hayderabad, India, edition). *Alhamdu-Lillah*, I have written an entire book about this incident which I titled *Ghadīr Khumm: Where Islam was Perfected*.

Ansār or **Ansar** أنصار: helpers, supporters. These were the people of Medīna who responded to the Prophet's call to Islam and helped establish Islam's first city-state power. One of the most famous of the Ansār is the great *sahabi* "Abū Ayyub" Khalid ibn Zaid (some say ibn Kulayb) al-Ansāri who hosted the Prophet (ص) upon his arrival at Medīna following his Hijra, migration, from Mecca.

Aqaba or **Aqabah** عقبه: Literally, this word means: obstacle, obstruction, stumbling block, hindrance. It also refers to a place in Mina just outside Mecca where the first Muslims of Yathrib (Medīna) pledged allegiance to the Prophet in the year 621 A.D. shortly before the migration (*hijra*). A similar meeting took place the next year when more Muslims from Yathrib pledged their allegiance to the Prophet (ص).

Aqiqa عقيقة: a dinner reception held after a child is born; relatives, friends, and neighbors are invited for such an occasion; sacrifice of a sheep or goat at the time of the ritual shaving of the baby's first grown hair

Arafat or Arafah or Arafa عرفه: a hill and plain north of Mecca. Muslims believe that it is on this hill and its surrounding plain that mankind will start their resurrection on the Judgment Day for questioning, judgment and settling accounts. During the *hajj* on the ninth day of the month of Thul-Hijja, Muslim pilgrims gather in this area for one day.

Arsh عرش: Literally, it means throne, symbol of the Almighty's Authority.

Asabiyya عصبيه: fanaticism, extremism, excessive tribal loyalty

Asāla or Asaalah أصالة: Purism, purity, genuineness, authenticity, excellence

Ashār أسحار: plural of *sahar*, the time immediately preceding daybreak

Assalāmu Alaikum or Assalāmo Alaikum, As-Salāmo Alaikom السلام عليكم" This is an expression which Muslims utter whenever they meet one another. It is a statement of greeting with peace. Its meaning is: "Peace be upon/with you" or "May the peace and the Mercy of Allāh be upon/with you," The complete statement is "Assalāmu Alalikum Wa Rahmatullāhi Wa Barakātuh," السلام عليكم و رحمة الله و بركاته which means: "May the peace, mercy, and blessings of Allāh be upon/with you."

Asr عصر" late afternoon, time for one of the five obligatory *salat*, prayer, rites

Astaghfirullāh or *Astaghfir-Allāh* أستغفرالله: This is an expression used by a Muslim when he pleads for Allāh's forgiveness. The meaning is: "I ask Allāh for His forgiveness." A Muslim utters this statement many times, even when he is talking to another person. When a Muslim abstains from doing wrong, or even when he wants to prove that he is innocent of an incident of which he is charged, he uses this expression, too. After every *salāt* (payer), a Muslim utters this statement at least three times. One *hadīth* (Prophet's tradition) says that *Istighfar*, the uttering of this statement, is the essence of adoration.

Ateeq عتيق: Literally, it means old, obsolete, antinquated, ancient. But the Venerable Ka'ba has always been referred to as البيت العتيق which has more than one meaning: the House which was spared the destruction of the flood of Prophet Noah (ع), that is, it was "freed" or spared the destruction caused by the flood. According to the famous lexicon *Lisan al-Arab*, what is عتيق is the best, the choicest, the most precious of everything. This fits the Ka'ba more than any other place or spot or monument on earth. *Lisan al-Arab* also says that the Ka'ba is described as البيت العتيق because the Almighty freed it from the hegemony of any tyrant in all human history: None could demolish it or obliterate its precincts or put an end to the pilgrimage to it which was first started by our father Adam, and it will continue till the Last Day. Adam was taught by arch-angel Gabriel how to perform the pilgrimage so he would be forgiven for having eaten of the forbidden fruit in Paradise. The time when Adam was kicked out of Paradise was in the late afternoon, so Gabriel taught him to pray 3 *rek'ats* (prostrations): one on behalf of himself, another on behalf of his wife, our mother Eve, and one on behalf of his offspring, our human species. This is why sunset prayers are performed in 3 rek'ats.

Athan or Adhan أذان: the call for prayers; *mu'aththin* is one who performs the *'athan*

Athbat أثبات: plural of *thabat* ثبت, one who is widely recognized as an authority in his field

Atiyya عطية: gift, present, grant, boon

A'uzu billahi minashaitanir-rajim or A'oodhu billahi minash-Shaitan ar-Rajeem أعوذ بالله من الشيطان الرجيم: This is a statement which Muslims have to recite before reciting the Holy Qur'ān, before speaking, before doing almost anything, even before making a supplication, performing the ablution or entering the wash room. Its meaning is: "I seek refuge with Allāh from the outcast Satan." "Allāh" is the Arabic name of God which the Muslims prefer over "God" simply because it is unique: You cannot derive a dual, plural, or feminine derivation from it. One of its meanings is: "The One about Whom the minds wonder" because nobody can grasp the essence or greatness of the Almighty. Satan is the source of evil and he always tries to misguide and mislead people, so one needs to seek refuge against the mischief of Satan with the omni-Potent and all-Powerful Lord of lords, Allāh.

Awl عول: one sought during the time of need, a reliable helper
Awqiyya أوقيه: weight, undefined measure for weighing items

Awra عورة: Private parts, body parts that are not supposed to be exposed to others, nudity, nakedness, intimate bodily parts, shame. For men, they are from the navel to the knee. For women, all the body except the hands, feet, and face.

Aya or Ayah or Ayat آيه: Verse (from a sacred scripture); plural: *ayat*. The literal meaning of "aya" is miracle or sign. The Qur'ān is considered to be a miracle by itself. Each verse is called an *ayat*, a miracle.

Azā' عزاء: consolation, comfort, solace, condolence; a ceremony held at one's death or martyrdom; عزاء الحسين (ع): Commemorations of the somber occasion of the martyrdom of Imām al-Hussain (ع) which include the recounting of the heroic epic of his martyrdom, lamentations, religious lectures, admonishments and other rites. They also include the distribution of traditional foods served on the occasion and other gifts to the attendants of the *majalis* where such commemorations are held.

B ب

Badā' بداء: starting point, the beginning/start of something, the onset

Bādiya باديه: desert or semi-arid environment

Badr بدر: Geographically, Badr is a highway station located 200 miles from Mecca and 80 miles from Medīna, and it is the site of the early Muslims' first battle in defense of the creed. The Muslims numbered only 313 men who had to fight mostly on foot because they had only 2 horses and 70 camels. Their enemies, the polytheists of Quraish, numbered between 900 and one thousand men. But the Muslims were fired with holy zeal and enthusiasm, so much so that they defeated their enemies, killing seventy of them and wounding many others. Their losses were: 14 from among the Muhajir fighters and 8 from the Ansār. The battle started on the 17th of the month of Ramadan in 2 A.H., which coincided with March 16, 624 A.D.

Bagha بغى: transgressed, behaved in an aggressive or unfairly hostile way, oppressed

Baghidh بغيض: hated, contemptible, abhorred

Ba'is بائس: destitute, needy, indigent, distressed, wretch, miserable

Bakka'in or Bakka'un or Bakka'oon بكائون: weepers. These were the people who could not accompany the Prophet on his TAbūk campaign because they lacked the resources. They started to weep when they realized that they could not go.

Balāgha or Balaaghah بلاغة: wise rhetoric, elocution, mastery of oratory and language

Baqi` or Baqee بقيع: the cemetery where some members of the Prophet's fāmily and many *sahāba* are buried. It is located in the south-east side of Medīna. The tomb of the Mother of the Faithful Khadija daughter of Khuwaylid, the Prophet's first wife and main supporter in spreading Islam, was also located there before it was demolished by Saudi authorities, and so was the grave of Hamzah, uncle and strong supporter of the Prophet. Only traces of both graves can now be seen at the Baqee'. A number of graves of other *sahāba* were gradually razed as well.

Bara'a or Baraa'ah براءة: dissociation, rejecting responsibility for; it also is one of the Chapters of the Holy Qur'ān and it has another name: Sūrat at-Tahreem, Chapter of Prohibition (Ch. 9). It was revealed to ban non-Muslims from entering the Haram of the Ka`ba in Mecca up to a certain perimeter. It is the only Qur'ānic chapter which does not start with the *basmala*.

Barak-Allāh or Barakalla, Barakalah بارك الله: This is an expression which means "May the blessings of Allāh (be upon/with you)." When a Muslim wants to thank another person, he uses different statements to express his thanks, appreciation and gratitude. One of them is to say "Bāraka Allāh."

Barakah or Baraka بركه: blessing, Divine Grace

Barzakh برزخ: barrier, separator, the place and time wherein the souls undergo a life of their own in the spiritual world till the Day of Judgment when each soul is re-outfitted with an eternal, indestructible, body, physical form or shape; see the Holy Qur'ān, 23:100, 55:20 and 25:53.

Basira or Baseerah بصيره: (intellectual) vision, insight, circumspection, discernment

Basmala بسمله: the uttering of *"Bismillahir-Rahmanir-Raham"* (In the Name of Allāh, the most Gracious, the most Merciful); see also ***Bismillah...*** below. **Basmala** (or Bismillah, Arabic بسملة) is an Arabic language noun which is used as the collective name of the whole of the recurring Islamic phrase *bismi-llahi ar-rahmani ar-rahim*. This phrase constitutes the first verse of every "sūra" (or chapter) of the Qur'ān (except for the ninth *sūra*, chapter), and is used in a number of contexts by Muslims. It is recited several times as part of Muslim daily prayers, and it is usually the first phrase in the preamble of the constitutions of Islamic countries.

بسم الله الرحمن الرحيم *bismi-llāhi ar-rahmāni ar-rahim*
"In the name of Allāh, the Most Gracious, the Most Merciful"
The word "basmala" itself was derived by a slightly unusual procedure in which the first four pronounced consonants of the phrase *bismi-llāhi...* were taken as a quadri-literal consonantal root b-s-m-l (ب س م ل). This abstract consonantal root was used to derive the noun *basmala*, as well as related verb forms which mean "to recite the *basmala*". The practice of giving often-repeated phrases special names is paralleled by the phrase Allāhu Akbar, which is referred to as the "Takbir تكبير" (also Ta'awwudh تعوذ etc.); and the method of coining a quadri-literal name from the consonants of such a phrase is paralleled by the name "Hamdala" for Alhamdulillāh.

In the Qur'ān, the phrase is usually numbered as the first verse of the first sūra, but according to the view adopted by at-Tabari, it precedes the first verse. It occurs at the beginning of each subsequent sūra of the Qur'ān, except for the ninth sūra (see, however, the discussion of the 8th and 9th chapters of the Qur'ān at eighth sūra), but is not numbered as a verse except, in the currently most common system, in the first sūra (chapter).

The *Basmala* occurs twice in the 27th sūra, at the beginning and in verse 30 (where it prefaces a letter from Sulayman (Prophet Solomon) to the Queen of Sheba, Balqees (or Balqis).

The *Basmala* has a special significance for Muslims, who are to begin each task after reciting the verse. It is often preceded by Ta'awwudh. In Arabic calligraphy, it is the most prevalent motif, more so even than the Shahada. The three definite nouns of the Basmala, Allāh, ar-Rahman and *ar-Rahim* correspond to the first three of the traditional 99 Names of Allāh in Islam. Both *ar-Rahmān* and *ar-Rahim* are from the same triliteral root, *rahm* "to feel sympathy or pity". According to Lane, *ar-rahmān* is more intensive, including in its objects the believer and the unbeliever, and may be

388

rendered as "The Compassionate", while *ar-rahim* has for its peculiar object the believer, considered as expressive of a constant attribute, and may be rendered as "The Merciful".

In a commentary on the Basmala in his *Tafsir*, at-Tabari writes: "The Messenger of Allāh (ﷺ) said that Jesus was handed by his mother Mary over to a school in order that he might be taught. [The teacher] said to him: 'Write "Bism (In the name of)".' And Jesus said to him: 'What is "Bism"?' The teacher said: 'I do not know.' Jesus said: 'The "Ba" is Baha'ullah (the glory of Allāh), the "Sin" is His Sana' (radiance), and the "Mim" is His Mamlakah (sovereignty)."

The total value of the letters of "Bismillāh ar-Rahmān ar-Rahim" according to one Arabic system of numerology is 786. There are two methods of arranging the letters of the Arabic alphabet. One method is the most common alphabetical order (used for most ordinary purposes), beginning with the letters Alif ١, ba ب, ta ت, tha ث etc. The other method is known as the "Abjad numerals' method" or ordinal method. In this method the letters are arranged in the following order:: Abjad, Hawwaz, Hutti, Kalaman, Sa'fas, Qarshat, Sakhaz, Zazagh; and each letter has an arithmetic value assigned to it from one to one thousand. (This arrangement was done, most probably in the 3rd century of Hijrah during the 'Abbāsid period, following the practices of speakers of other Semitic languages such as Aramaic, Hebrew, Syriac, Chaldean etc.)

Taking into account the numeric values of all the letters of the Basmala, according to the Abjad order, the total is 786. In the Indian subcontinent the Abjad numerals have become quite popular. Some people, mostly in India and Pakistan, use 786 as a substitute for *Bismillah* ("In the name of Allāh" or "In the name of God"). They write this number to avoid writing the name of God, or Qur'ānic verses on ordinary papers, which can be subject to dirt or come in contact with unclean materials. This practice does not date from the time of Muhammed and is not universally accepted by Muslims.

The *basmala*, or the phrase *bismillāh ar-Rahmān ar-Rahim*, is one of the most oft-recited phrases in the life of every single observant Muslim. It occupies a key place in the Qur'ān itself, for it is the only non-Qur'ānic phrase that all copies of the Qur'ān included, apparently as a 'marker' between the Sūras. Numerous works have been written specifically about the *basmala*. In this response, a brief linguistic and grammatical explanation will be offered, followed by a discussion of the name *ar-Rahmān*.

The Basmala as Portrayed in Early and Medieval Islamic Sources

The first verse of the Qur'ān has almost unanimously been portrayed as being Qur'ān, 96:1, 'Recite in the name of your Lord who created.' From this, some derived that the status of a rudimentary *basmala* was established, as the 'name of your Lord' is invoked. In another early Meccan Sūra, Noah is told to ride the Arc '...in the name of God' (Qur'ān, 11:41). In yet another Meccan Sūra, reputed to have been revealed after this one, Solomon writes a letter to the Queen of Sheba in which her advisors tell her, "This (letter) is from Solomon, and it (says): In the name of God, the *Rahman*, the *Rahim*" (Qur'ān, 27:30).

The fact that the *basmala* in its present form was introduced to the Meccan Arabs by the Prophet is quite explicitly mentioned in many sources. One incident, recorded in some canonical works of hadīth and the *Sirah* book of Ibn Ishāq (d. 150/767), mentions that during the writing of the Treaty of Hudaybiyyah in 6 A.H., one of the emissaries of Mecca, Suhayl ibn Amr, refused to allow the Prophet to begin the treaty with the *basmala*. His reputed reason was, "As for this '*ar-Rahman*', I do not know who He is, but rather, write as we are accustomed to write, 'In your name, O God! (*bismik Allāhumma*).'"

There are quite a few prophetic traditions that expound upon the blessings of this phrase and when it should be said. It might also have served a more mundane role: Ibn Abbās is alleged to have said that the Prophet was not able to recognize the end of one Sūra from the beginning of the next until the *basmala* was recited by Gabriel.

The *basmala* is the only phrase of the Qur'ān that Sunni scholars have disagreed about: is it a verse of the Qur'ān or not? There is agreement that it is a part of Qur'ān, 27:30, where it is mentioned in

390

Solomon's letter to Sheba, and there is also agreement that it does not form a part of Sūra 9. But there was a disagreement about its status at the beginning of all other Sūras, especially the first, *al-Fātiha*. This disagreement is found amongst the four canonical schools of law as well as the ten recitations (*qira'at*) of the Qur'ān. Some of them opined that the *basmala* was a separate verse at the beginning of every Sūra, others said it was part of the first verse. A third group claimed it was only a verse at the beginning of the *al-Fātiha*, while a fourth denied that it was a verse in any of these instances. And a fifth group posited that it was a verse by itself, not connected to any Sūra, which had been placed there as a 'divider' to separate two consecutive Sūras. This difference of opinion had a direct impact on certain rituals, such as whether one was obliged to recite the *basmala* out loud in every prayer or not.[6]

A Grammatical Breakdown and Exegetical Explanation of the *Basmala*

The *basmala* consists of four words, the first of which has a prepositional letter attached to it. All of these words are nouns; no verbs or verbal nouns are present. The first letter of the *basmala*, the '*b-*' is a prepositional letter (*harf jar*), thus causing the first word ('*bism*') to be in a genitive state The preposition *b-* has many uses, but over here appears to be for seeking help (*istianah*).[7] The word *ism* is the Arabic for 'noun'. Linguists differed whether it originated from *sumuw* (*s-m-w*), meaning 'to elevate', or from *wasam* (*w-s-m*), meaning 'to brandish'; the Basra school opted for the former, whilst the Kufa one preferred the latter.

Due to the fact that the phrase *bism* is in a genitive state, it needs some actor (*āmil*) to which it can be attached (*taalluq*). The Kufan school of grammar typically assumes that all missing actors must be verbs, as that is the basis of words for them. In contrast, the Basri school considers all missing actors to be nouns due to their position that nouns are the basis of words. The Kufans then split up amongst themselves in three specific issues regarding the *basmala*. Firstly: what was this missing verb? Was it, 'I recite,' or 'I begin,' or perhaps a verb that varied depending upon the action being done at that time? Secondly, what was the tense of the verb: was it a command or was it in present tense? In other words, is the one who

391

is reciting says, 'I recite with the name of God', or is God saying 'I command you to recite with the name of God?' Thirdly, what was the position of this missing verb: before the '*bism*' or after?

Most Kufans, as well as az-Zamakhshari in his *al-Kashshaf*, came to the conclusion that the verb is specific to the context of invoking the *basmala* (hence it can be used for any permissible act), that it was in the present tense (since the purpose of the *basmala* is to obtain God's blessings upon the recitor), and that the missing verb's place was after the '*bismi*' (since it is more blessed to begin with the name of God, and since it reminded one that the purpose of doing any act was for God, and because it is a clear refutation of the pagans who would begin by saying 'In the name of *al-Lat*').

The Basris, on the other hand, generally held that the missing noun was 'My recitation' (*qira'ati*), or 'My beginning' (*ibtida'i*), and that it was placed before the genitive. The question also arose: what does it mean seeking help from the 'name' (*ism*) of God? Specifically, the issue concerned the theological controversy over the implication of the Divine Names: are these Names God Himself, or do they belong to God, or originate from Him, or is the noun '*ism*' superfluous (*za'id*) and only needed for emphasis? The Ash'arites, Mu'tazilites and Ahl al-Hadīth (to name the more prominent groups) each had its own positions.

The next noun in the *basmala* is the divine name '*Allāh*'. This name raises a whole slew of questions, of which only a few will be dealt with here. There is no doubt that the name '*Allāh*' was the primary name of the Islamic divinity. The name appears more than 2,700 times in the Qur'ānic text, and there is an overwhelming amount of evidence to show that this name was used for many centuries by the pagan Arabs to refer to a Supreme God – a god that even they, with their permissive idolatry, refused to draw or carve images of.

The linguistic meaning and origin of this name has always been a topic of much discussed in Muslim scholarship. Although a minority of Sunni theologians and linguists considered this name to be a proper name, devoid of any meaning, the majority of them considered it to be derived from some three-letter root. Some suggested that it was a rare transmutation from *walaha*, which means 'to confound and confuse', as if the nature of God (*'Allāh'*) confuses and befuddles the minds of all those who try to grasp or understand Him. Others suggested that it is from *laha*, which means 'to conceal and cover', since the true nature of God is concealed from all. However, the most prevalent opinion, amongst linguistics, theologians, and exegetes, is that the name is derived from *alaha*, which means 'to show servitude and worship'; hence God (*"Allāh"*) is the only Being that is worthy of servitude and worship.

Some Western Islamists have posited Aramaic, Syriac or Hebrew origins for this name; strong evidence to substantiate this claim, however, remains lacking.

To summarize before moving on, the first two words of the *basmala* translate as, 'My recitation is with the name of *Allāh*' for the Basris, and as, 'With the name of *Allāh* I recite...' for the Kufans.

This name (viz., *'Allāh'*), is then followed by two other nouns, *ar-Rahman*, and *ar-Rahim*. Both can be derived from the root *r-h-m*, which means 'to have mercy, to be compassionate.' Both utilize known and common morphological forms: *falan* for the first and *fail* for the second. Before translating the *basmala*, it is crucial to understand the grammatical role of these two nouns, as that will decidedly determine the understanding of the *basmala*. We shall discuss the alleged origins of '*ar-Rahman*' in the next section.

Almost all classical works that I was able to reference (including works of theology, exegesis, and *shuruh al-hadīth*) appear to understand these two nouns as adjectives of the first noun, viz., '*Allāh*'. Many books of grammatical analysis do not even mention any other opinion. If these two nouns are understood as being adjectives (i.e., *nat*), it will imply that both *ar-Rahman* and *ar-Rahim* describe and characterize God (*'Allāh'*). So it is as if the *basmala* translates as (according to the Kufan understanding), "With the name of *Allāh*, who is ever Merciful (*ar-Rahman*) and extremely Compassionate (*ar-Rahim*), I begin this recitation."

Numerous opinions are found in classical sources regarding the difference between these two names. Most scholars (but not all) are in agreement that the two names are not synonymous or even as efficacious as each other, but rather that *ar-Rahman* is more indicative of God's mercy than *ar-Rahim*. Some opine that *ar-Rahman* is indicative of God's mercy to believers and unbelievers in this world, and *ar-Rahim* is indicative of His special mercy to believers in both worlds. Yet another opinion is that *ar-Rahman* indicates that God's Mercy is an essential part of His character, whereas *ar-Rahim* indicates that God's actions are always merciful.

Many scholars have sought to understand the wisdom of this particular order of names. At-Tabari posited that the reason these three names are in this order is that the Arabs typically start off with the primary name and then with its descriptions. God's primary name is '*Allāh*', hence it was used here. And since *ar-Rahman* was more specific to God than *ar-Rahim*, it was given precedence to it.

So far we have considered both nouns to be adjectives, and this is by far the 'standard' opinion. There seems to be another opinion, rarely expressed, that considers these two nouns to be substitutes (*badal*). As a substitute, the *basmala* would translate as (according to the Basri opinion this time, for ease of understanding), 'My recitation begins with the name of *Allāh*; my recitation begins with the name of *ar-Rahman*; my recitation begins with the name of *ar-Rahim*.' The purpose of these reiterations would obviously not be to express three distinct deities but rather to express three of God's 99 names. A modern theologian, Muhammed Abduh (or Abdoh), who appeared to lean towards such an explanation, claimed that this reiteration was meant as a refutation of the Trinity of the Christians, who began their rites with 'In the Name of the Father, the Son and the Holy Ghost.' By mentioning three of His Names, God intended to demonstrate to the Christians that even if He has many attributes, He is still One in His essence.

Some modern Islamists pose a third position, and that is that only the first of these two nouns is a substitute (*badal*), and the second is an adjective (*nat*) of it. If this understanding is taken, the *basmala* would translate as, 'My recitation begins with the name of *Allāh*, the merciful *ar-Rahman*.' I was not able to find any scholar within the Muslim tradition who understood it in this manner. Additionally, since both *ar-Rahman* and *ar-Rahim* are placed after the first noun, in the same grammatical context, one would have to show why one of these nouns should be given a different grammatical role than the other, as this would be an awkward rendering of the Arabic expression.

If this third position is taken, then obviously the question arises as to why two names are emphasized ('*Allāh*' and '*ar-Rahman*'), and what the relationship is between them. In order to do this, we need to first discuss the opinions regarding the origins of the name '*ar-Rahman*'.

Origin of the Attribute *ar-Rahman*
The discussion regarding the origins of the name *ar-Rahman* is an ancient one. The Qur'ān itself quite explicitly states that this name was unknown to the Quraish (as in Qur'ān, 25:60). Most scholars are of the opinion that *ar-Rahman* is a unique name of God, and so cannot be used to describe the creation, unlike most other Divine Names, including *ar-Rahim*. This is due to 17:110, where the two names '*Allāh*' and '*ar-Rahman*' appear to be equivalent in sanctity. There is also a tradition in the canonical works, a hadīth Qudsi, in which God is reported as saying 'I am *ar-Rahman*; I created the ties of kinship (*ar-Rahm*), and from it derived one of My Names.' This was one of the primary evidences used by those who claimed that this name is derived from *r-h-m*. On the other hand, a number of early Islamic authorities, such as al-Mubarrad, considered *ar-Rahman* to have a Jewish origin. Quite a few authorities are on record as stating that this name was a name given to 'ancients' as well.

It is clear that the Qur'ān itself considers the name *ar-Rahman* to be an ancient name. Apart from the reference in Solomon's letter (already given), this name is used as the God of all previous nations in Qur'ān, 43:45; Abraham beseeches God with it (Qur'ān, 19:44); Aaron uses it to remind the Israelites of their God (Qur'ān, 20:19); it appears on the tongue of an Israelite community (Qur'ān, 36:15);

and it appears on the tongue of Mary, mother of Jesus twice (in 19:18 and 19:26).

It is claimed by some that this name was a Meccan name that was later not emphasized as much, and perhaps even sidelined by later Muslims as a primary name of God. However, the name is mentioned in quite a few Medinan verses as well (for example, Qur'ān, 2:163, and 59:22). In addition, every single Sunni theologian who discussed the Divine Names considered the name 'ar-Rahman' as being one of those 99 names.

To conclude, as with many issues dealing with the academic study of religion, how one chooses to interpret the *basmala* has a lot to do with one's basic theological and historical premises. If one believes that Muhammed conjured up a new monotheistic system in order to unite the Arabs, then it is plausible to suggest that he might have wished to unite various factions of Arabia under the deities that they would be fāmiliar with, hence '*Allāh*' for the Arabs of Hijaz and '*ar-Rahman*' for the Arabs of Southern Arabia. And this is indeed the position of many modern Islamists. But such a position does lead to other questions, such as: why did he only choose the name of the god of one faction of Arabia (Southern Arabia), and not other areas and provinces? And why was he so stubbornly opposed to all the Meccan (and Hijazi) pagan deities, allowing no compromise with those deities whatsoever? Also the question arises as to how the name of this obscure divinity reached him. The claim that Muhammed was reaching out to convert Arabs in Southern Yemen while he was still in the early stages of his career at Mecca presupposes that he was envisioning this new religion to be a dominant force in the farthest corners of Arabia, even while being persecuted and rejected in his own city.

"That *ar-Rahman* should have been the name of a single God in central and southern Arabia is in no way incompatible with the fact that, when adopted by Islam, it assumes a grammatical form of a word derived from the root *rahm*."

Batil or Baatil باطل: false or falsehood, nullified, voided

Batsh بطش: Despotic behavior, tyranny

Batul or Batool بتول: ascetic. It is ascribed to Fātima (the Prophet's daughter) and Virgin Mary, mother of Christ.

Bawadi بوادي: plural of Badiya

Bay'a or Bay'ah بيعه: oath of allegiance, pledge to a man of authority or prominence

Bayan بيان: Statement, account, declaration, explanation, clarification, announcement

Bayt al-Mal بيت المال: State Treasury in the Islamic State

Beed بيض: plural of بيض/*abyad*, white

Bid`a or Bid`ah بدعه: innovation, novelty, (in religion) heresy

Bigha' بغاء: prostitution

Bismillahir-rahmanir-rahim بسم الله الرحمن الرحيم: This is a verse/statement from the Qur'ān which is articulated before the recitation of the Qur'ān. It is also recited before doing any daily activity, even when a husband starts making love to his wife, for love-making between legal spouses is as sacred as anything else can be, and it is rewardable by the Almighty, too, Who will surely punish those who permit themselves to have intercourse outside of the sacred limits of marriage unless they regret, repent and do good deeds to wipe out the bad ones. Islam is not just a religion, it is a way of life, the most clean and the most fulfilling, one which brings happiness in both this life and in the Hereafter. The Basmala means: "In the name of Allāh, the Most Beneficent, the Most Merciful." In the Fātiha, the first chapter of the Holy Qur'ān, the Basmala is a verse all by itself, whereas in all other chapters, with the exception of Bara'ah or Tawbah where it is not recited, it serves as an introduction to other verses. On pp. 39-40, Vol. 1, of his *Tafsir*, al-Qummi chronologically arranges the *isnad* of one particular statement made by Imām Ja'far as-Sādiq (ع) and recounts the longest list of narrators we have ever come across. The list of narrators ends with Abū Busayr, a well-known companion of this great Imām (ع), saying that he once asked Imām as-Sādiq (ع) about the exegesis of the Basmala. The Imām said the following: "The ب is derived from بهاء الله "baha-Allāh," the Splendor of Allāh; the س is derived from سناء الله "sanaa-Allāh," the Majesty of Allāh; the م is derived from ملك الله "mulk-Allāh," the Kingdom of Allāh; "Allāh" is the God of everything; الرحمان is the One Who is Merciful to all His creation; الرحيم is the One Who singles out those who believe in Him to receive the greatest share of His mercy." On p. 506 of *Misbah al-Kaf'ami* مصباح الكفعمي, the Messenger of Allāh (ص) is quoted as saying that when a teacher, who teaches a child to recite the Holy Qur'ān, tells the child to recite this Basmala, and when the child recites it, the Almighty will decree a clearance for the child, for his parents and for the teacher from hell, and that it is comprised of nineteen letters, the same number that corresponds to the number of the keepers of the gates of hell; therefore, whoever pronounces it, Allāh will permit these letters to close the gates of hell against him.

Bi'tha بعثه: the beginning of the Prophet's mission, his call to Prophethood, which started during the month of Ramadan, 13 years before the *hijra*, which coincided in the year 610 A.D.

Burda بردة: garment, gown

Busr بصر: partially ripe dates

Buhtan بهتان: falsehood, untruth

D د، ذ

Dafn دفن: burial. In Islam, there are numerous rules relevant to burying the dead. One is that their dead must not be buried together with followers of other creeds. Muslims have to have their own cemeteries when they live in non-Muslim countries. The corpses have to be given their burial bath then clothed in clean white cotton sheets, shrouds. It is highly recommended to write verses of the Holy Qur'ān on these shrouds. It is also recommended a small copy of the Holy Qur'ān be buried with the deceased person, and two will be even better, one on each of his/her sides. Visiting graves has always been an Islamic tradition especially on certain religious occasions when the Qur'ān is recited at the grave of a loved one whose soul, rest assured, will hear the recitation and appreciate it tremendously. The body dies, but the soul is immortal. Performing prayers on behalf of the dead, especially the parents, has numerous rewards of which only the Almighty is fāmiliar. Doing acts of charity on behalf of the dead has its rewards to both the doer and the person for whom they are done. Graveyards, cemeteries, burial grounds and the like have their own sanctity in Islam and must meet certain conditions to qualify to be called as such. There are also rules restricting the burying of Muslim dead to certain ways and certain places which must be distinguished from those of non-Muslims. A Muslim must not be buried at non-Muslims' cemetery. "Life" in the grave is a big topic in Islam and is worth researching. This text touches on it lightly due to space constrictions.

Dahr دهر: time, age, eternity, forever

Da'i داعي: Muslim missionary involved in *da'wa* دعوه, propagation of Islam. It can also have a general meaning referring to someone who calls others to a certain belief or ideology or to a gathering, meeting, banquet, wedding, etc.

Daim دائم: Permanent, continuous; if preceded by the definite article, i.e. الدائم, it will then refer to the Almighty Who is always there and neither time, nor place, nor anything material applies to Him, the One and only God of everyone and everything.

Da`iyy دعي: One whose father is unknown and someone joins him to his own lineage, a foundling, illegitimately born

Dajjal دجال: Impostor, charlatan, deceiver, pretender

Daleel دليل: evidence, proof, argument, indication, clue, guide, directory

Darij دارج: current, common, fāmiliar, parlance, colloquial, vernacular

Da'wa دعوه: inviting others to Islam, any missionary activity

Dayn دين: debt. It may be debt to other people or to the Almighty. Some people die leaving debts behind which they owe to others who had loaned them to the Almighty to Whom they owe everything and Who required them to do what is surely within their human ability. These debts, to people or to the Almighty, must be paid by the relatives of these unfortunate dead, and there is hardly one who leaves this temporary abode without leaving behind him/her many debts. This is why Islam emphasizes the need for writing wills. Remember that whatever you owe people, or you owe your Maker, in this life will be so hard for you to pay in the life to come.

Deen دين: religion, creed, faith. Islam is all of this and much more; it is a complete and perfect way of life. Islam is referred to as a "deen" while it is much, much more than that, it is a complete, perfect and flawless way of life which leads to one's happiness in the life of this world and in the Hereafter. It regulates one's relations with other people on one hand and with his/her Creator on the other. It is provides a complete social, political and economic system.

Deewan or Diwan Diwan ديوان: a collection of poem; also a place of meeting

Dhaleel ذليل: undignified, lowly, contemptible, one living in an undignified one

Dhamm ذم: slander, maligning, vilifying, speaking ill of someone. This is the habit of many people which will in the end lodge them in hell unless they regret, repent and amend. Beware of speaking ill of people unless they are publicly exposing their own sinning and perhaps even bragging about it. In such case, you should condemn them as should everyone else.

Dharee`ah ذريعه: pretext, excuse, ostensible motive, excuse

Dhikr or Thikr or Zikr ذكر: remembrance or the praising of Allāh.

Dhimmi or Thimmi or Zimmi ذمّي: a non-Muslim individual who lives under the protection of a Muslim state. He is exempt from Islamic duties and obligations, including military service, but he must pay a protection tax called *jizya*.

Dhurriyya ذريه: offspring, issue, progeny, descendants, children

Dinar or Deenar دينار: an Islamic (now Arab) gold currency varying in weight

Dirham درهم: (historically an) Islamic silver currency weighing approx. 3.12 grams

Diyya دية: blood money, monetary compensation for manslaughter or intentional murder

Du `a' دعاء: supplication, invocation, prayer

Du'at دعاة: plural of *da'iya* or *da`iyah*, a caller to Islam or any ideology

Dukhan دخان: smoke. Chapter 44 of the Holy Qur'ān is called "Al-Dukhan", the smoke. If you read the first 16 verses (out of a total of 59), you will notice how the Almighty warns those who disbelieve in the message brought from Him to Prophet Muhammed (ص): "Keep waiting, therefore, for the day when the sky brings an evident smoke that shall overtake men" (Qur'ān, 44:10-11). The Prophet, in a tradition dealing with the signs that denote the approach of the Day of Judgment, is quoted as having said, "The first of such signs is the smoke [to which reference is made in these verses]." He was asked what smoke it would be. He said, "It will cover the east of the earth and the west; it will remain for forty days and nights. It will affect the believer just like a cold [catarrh]. As to the unbeliever, he will feel as though he is intoxicated. It [smoke] will come out of his nostrils, ears and rear end." Imām Ja'far as-Sādiq (ع) is quoted as having said, "There will be a smoke that will overwhelm both ends of the earth (east and west or north and south), causing the death of two thirds of the world's population." This "smoke" can now be said as caused by the explosion of nuclear and hydrogen bombs and by the poison gases they release.

Dunya دنيا: this world or life as opposed to the Hereafter, mortality

ع E

Eid or Īd or `Eid or Eed عيد: an Islamic feast, a joyous celebration, a merry or festive occasion. The word 'Eid is an Arabic noun which means: a festivity, celebration, recurring happiness. In Islam, there are two major 'Eids: the feast marking the end of the fast of the month of Ramadan, which is called 'EId al-Fitr, and the Feast of Sacrifice, 'Eid al-Adhha. Friday is also regarded as the greatest of all feasts.

ف F

Fadak فدك : a garden oasis in Khaybar, a tract of land approximately thirty miles from Medīna, and it was known for its water-wells, dates, and handicrafts. When the Muslims defeated the people of Khaybar at the Battle of Khaybar, which took place in the year 628 A.D., the oasis of Fadak was part of the booty given to the Prophet Muhammed (ص). Upon his death, he bequeathed it to his daughter, Fātima. It became the object of dispute between Fātima and Abū Bakr (573 – 634 A.D.) after the latter had assumed power in the year 632 A.D. following the Prophet's death.

A brief history of Khaybar tells us that in the 7th century, this oasis was inhabited by Arab Jews who pioneered the cultivation of the oasis and made their living growing date trees as well as through commerce and craftsmanship, accumulating considerable wealth. The oasis was divided into three regions: an-Natat, ash-Shiqq الشّق, and al-Katiba الكتيبة, probably separated by natural diversions, such as the desert, lava drifts, and swamps. Each of these regions contained several fortresses or redoubts containing homes, storehouses and stables. Each fortress was occupied by a clan and surrounded by cultivated fields and palm-groves. In order to improve their defensive capabilities, the fortresses were raised up on hills or basalt rocks.

Prophet Muhammed (ﷺ) led the march on Khaybar oasis on Thul-Qa'da 6, 7 A.H., corresponding to May 7, 629 A.D., with approximately 1,500 men and one to two hundred horses. Primary sources, including the *Seerat Rasool Allāh* (Biography of the Prophet) of Ibn Ishāq, describe the conquest of Khaybar, detailing the agreement of Muhammed with the Jews to remain in Fadak and cultivate their land, retaining one-half of the produce of the oasis. This agreement was distinct from the agreement with the Jews of Khaybar, which essentially entailed the practice of share-cropping. It is not entirely clear how Muhammed managed his possession of Fadak. Some Muslim commentators agree that after the conquest of Fadak, the property belonged exclusively to the Prophet (ﷺ). Various primary sources describe the acquisition of Fadak in the following way:

An account indicates that eleven fruit trees in Fadak were planted by the Prophet (ﷺ) himself. Other scholars who accept the view of Fadak as belonging exclusively to the Prophet (ﷺ) after the conquest of Khaybar include Ali bn Ahmed as-Samhudi, Ibn Hisham and Abul-Fida.

Upon the death of the Prophet (ﷺ) on Rabi' I 2 or 12, 11 A.H./May 31st or June 12th, 632 A.D., his daughter Fātima declared her claim to inherit Fadak as the estate of her father. The claim was rejected by Abū Bakr on instigation from Omer ibn al-Khattab on the grounds that Fadak was public property and arguing that the Prophet had "no heirs". Sources report that Ali together with Umm Ayman testified to the fact that Muhammed granted it to Fātima when Abū Bakr required Fātima to summon witnesses for her claim. Various primary sources contend that Fadak was gifted by Muhammed to Fātima, drawing on the Qur'ān as evidence. These include narrations of Ibn 'Abbās who argued that when the Qur'ānic verse on giving rights to kindred was revealed, Muhammed called to his daughter and gifted the land of Fadak to her.

Various scholars commenting on the Qur'ān, Sūrat Al-Hashr (Chapter 59), verse 7, write that the Angel Gabriel came to the Prophet (ﷺ) and commanded him to give the appropriate rights to

"Thul Qurba" (near kin). The verse reads:

مَّا أَفَاء اللَّهُ عَلَى رَسُولِهِ مِنْ أَهْلِ الْقُرَى فَلِلَّهِ وَلِلرَّسُولِ وَلِذِي الْقُرْبَى وَالْيَتَامَى وَالْمَسَاكِينِ وَابْنِ السَّبِيلِ كَيْ لا يَكُونَ دُولَةً بَيْنَ الأَغْنِيَاء مِنكُمْ وَمَا آتَاكُمُ الرَّسُولُ فَخُذُوهُ وَمَا نَهَاكُمْ عَنْهُ فَانتَهُوا وَاتَّقُوا اللَّهَ إِنَّ اللَّهَ شَدِيدُ الْعِقَابِ

What Allāh has bestowed on His Messenger (and taken away) from the people of the towns, belongs to Allāh, to His Messenger, and to (the Prophet's) kindred and orphans, the needy and the wayfarers; so that it may not be taken in turn by the rich among you. So take what the Messenger assigns to you, and abstain from what he withholds from you. And fear Allāh, for Allāh is strict in punishment (59:7). When asked by the Prophet (ص) about who those "Thul Qurba" were referred to in that verse, Gabriel replied: "Fātima" and that by "rights" was meant "Fadak", upon which Muhammed called Fātima and presented Fadak to her.

When Omer became caliph, the value of the land of Fadak along with its dates was, according to some account, 50,000 dirhams. Ali again claimed Fātima's inheritance during Omer's era but was denied with the same argument as in the time of Abū Bakr. Omer, however, restored the estates in Medīna to `Abbās ibn `Abd al-Muttalib and Ali, as representatives of Muhammed's clan, the Banu Hashim. During Othman's caliphate, Marwan ibn al-Hakâm, his cousin, was made trustee of Fadak. After Othman, Ali became caliph but did not overturn the decision of his predecessor. He maintained Marwan's position as trustee of the Fadak. During Ali's caliphate, Fadak was regarded to be under the control of the Prophet's family, so the caliph did not make a formal declaration of personal possession in order to avoid resurrecting old feuds and jealousies and thus the causing of disunity regarding.

Under the Umayyads (661 – 750 A.D.), Mu'awiyah, their first self-impose ruler, the latter did not return Fadak to Fātima's descendants. This way was continued by later Umayyad Caliphs until the time of caliph Omer ibn Abd al-Aziz. When Omer ibn Abd al-Aziz, known as Omer II, became Caliph in 717 A.D., the income from the property of Fadak was 40,000 dinars. Fadak was returned to Fātima's descendants by an edict given by Omer II, but this decision was renounced by later caliphs and may have been the cause of Omer being killed as well. Omer II's successor, Yazid ibn Abd al-Malik (known as Yazid II) overturned his decision, and Fadak was again made public trust. Fadak was then managed this way until the Ummayad Caliphate expired.

Under the Abbāsids (750 – 1258 A.D.), in 747 A.D., a huge revolt against the Umayyad Caliphate took place. The Umayyad's were eventually defeated by the Abbāsid army under the rule of "Abū Abbās" Abdullāh as-Saffah (as-Saffah means in Arabic "blood-shedder" which perfectly describes him and his dynasty just as it describes the Umayyads as well. The last Umayyad ruler, Marwan II, was killed in a lesser battle a few months after the Battle of the Zab of 750 A.D., thus ending the Umayyad Caliphate. Historical accounts differ about what happened to Fadak under early Abbāsid rulers. Most likely they collected its revenues and spent it as they pleased. There is, however, consensus among Islamic scholars that Fadak was returned to the descendants of Fātima during Al-Ma'mun's reign (831-833 A.D.). Al-Ma'mun even decreed this to be recorded in his *diwāns*. Al-Ma'mun's successor, al-Mutawakkil (847-861 A.D.), repossessed Fadak, confiscating it from the descendants of Fātima. Al-Muntasir (861-862 A.D.), however, apparently maintained the decision of al-Ma'mun, thus allowing Fātima's offspring to manage Fadak. What happened thereafter is uncertain, but Fadak was probably seized by again and managed exclusively by the ruler of the time as his own personal property, and thus do some people behave.

In the 7th century, the Khaybar oasis was inhabited by Arab Jews who pioneered the cultivation of the oasis and made their living growing date palm trees as well as through commerce and craftsmanship, accumulating considerable wealth. Some objects found by the Muslims following their conquest of Khaybar and its fortresses included a siege-engine, 20 bales of Yemenite cloth, and 500 cloaks, an indication of an intense trade carried out by those Jews.

The oasis was divided into three regions: an-Natat, ash-Shiqq الشّق,

and al-Katiba الكتيبة, probably separated by natural diversions, such as the desert, lava drifts, and swamps. Each of these regions contained several fortresses or redoubts containing homes, storehouses and stables. Each fortress was occupied by a clan and surrounded by cultivated fields and palm-groves. In order to improve their defensive capabilities, the fortresses were raised up on hills or basalt rocks.

One may wonder what brought those Jews to Medīna. There are two theories. One says that those Jews were motivated by the desire to be the first to believe in the new Arabian Prophet whose name they have in their religious books and whose mission was about to start, so they made a mass immigration to Medīna. Their high rabbis told them that Medīna would be the place where the new Prophet, Muhammed (ص), would be preaching the divine message. This view is supported by verses 40 – 103 of Sūrat al-Baqara (Chapter of the Cow, i.e. Ch. 2) which repeatedly admonishes the Israelites and strongly rebukes them for seeing the truth but turning away from it. According to this theory, those Jews with religious fervor had come from Jerusalem in particular and Greater Syria (Sham) in particular.

The other theory seeks an explanation from the historic events that took place in southern Arabia, particularly Yemen, concluding that those Jews had migrated from there seeking religious freedom and better economic conditions. This is how advocates of this theory reason:

The immigration of the majority of Jews into Yemen from abroad appears to have taken place about the beginning of the 2nd century A.D., although the province is mentioned neither by Josephus, better known as Yoseph (Yousuf) ben (ibn, i.e. son of) Mattithyahu (37 – cir. 100 A.D.), a Romano-Jewish historian and hagiographer of priestly and royal ancestry, nor by the main books of the Jewish oral law, namely the Mishnah and Talmud. According to some sources, the Jews of Yemen enjoyed prosperity until the 6th century A.D. The Himyarite King, Abū-Karib Asad Toban, converted to Judaism at the end of the 5th century, while laying siege to Medīna. It is likely some of his soldiers preferred to stay there for economic and perhaps other reasons. His army had marched north to battle the

Aksumites who had been fighting for control of Yemen for a hundred years. The Aksumites were only expelled from the region when the newly Jewish king rallied the Jews together from all over Arabia, together with pagan allies. But this victory was short-lived.

In 518, the kingdom of Yemen was taken over by Zar'a Yousuf, who was of "royal descent" but was not the son of his predecessor, Ma'di Karib Ya'fur. Yousuf converted to Judaism and instigated wars to drive the Aksumite Ethiopians from Arabia. Zar'a Yusuf is chiefly known by his cognomen "Thu Nuwas", in reference to his "curly hair." The Jewish rule lasted till 525 A.D., only 85 years before the inception of the Islamic Prophetic mission. Some historians, however, date it later, to 530, when Christians from the Aksumites Kingdom of Ethiopia defeated and killed Thu Nuwas, taking power in Yemen. According to a number of medieval historians, Thu Nuwas announced that he would persecute the Christians living in his kingdom, mostly in Najran, because Christian states persecuted his fellow co-religionists (the Jews) in their realms. This persecution, which took place in the year 524 A.D., is blamed on one Dimnon in Najran, that is modern al-Ukhdud (or al-Okhdood) area of Saudi Arabia. Any reader of the Holy Qur'ān must have come across verse 4 of Sūrat al-Buruj (Chapter 85) of the Holy Qur'ān which refers to أَصْحَابُ الأُخْدُودِ, fellows of the Ukhdud, which is imprecisely translated as "the ditch self-destructed". To the author of this book, my dear reader, "the ditch self-destructed" does not make much sense at all. Actually, this "ukhdud" was a long ditch filled with firewood. It was lit and the believers were thrown into it if they refused to abandon their faith. Some ran away from this inferno, which may remind one of a similar situation which took place with Prophet Ibrahim (Abraham) at the hands of Nimrud of 13th Century B.C. Assyria. The survivors, most likely Christians and Jews, fled up north in the direction of Medīna which they made it home. The Almighty in 85:4 condemns this massacre in the strongest of terms.

According to some sources, after seizing the throne of the Himyarites, in 518 or 523 A.D., Thu Nuwas attacked the Aksumite (mainly Christian) garrison at Zafar, capturing them and burning their churches. He then moved against Najran, a Christian and Aksumite stronghold. After accepting the city's capitulation, he massacred those inhabitants who would not renounce Christianity in this *ukhdud* incident. Estimates of the death toll from this event range up to 20,000 in some sources. So, believers in God, Christians and Jews, had reasons to go somewhere else where they would practice their religion freely while enjoying better business opportunities among Arabs who, at the time, were mostly nomads.

Fa'izeen or Fa'izùn فائزين أو فائزون: winners, those who earn the Pleasure of the Almighty and His rewards

Fajir فاجر: unrepentant sinner, adulterer; according to p. 94, 94, Vol. 5 (Dar Sadir, Beirut, Lebanon, edition of 1997), of the famous lexicon *Lisan al-Arab* لسان العرب by Ibn Manzour, it also means one who commits too many sins while putting off repentance for them; another meaning is: wrongdoer

Fajr فجر: Daybreak, obligatory pre-sunrise *salat*, prayer rite; another meaning for it, according to p. 94, Vol. 5 (Dar Sadir, Beirut, Lebanon, edition of 1997), of *Lisan al-Arab* lexicon, is Abūndance of wealth.

Faqih فقيـه: jurist, one who is knowledgeable in Islamic jurisprudence (law), the *Shari`a*

Farasikh فراسخ: plural of *farsakh* فرسخ, parasang (a loan Persian word), a measure of distance. According to *Lisan al-`Arab* lexicon, it may be three to six miles. "It is called so," the author of the famous lexicon goes on, "because one who walks one *farsakh* will have to sit to rest," suggesting that the original meaning of the word is to halt, to come to a standstill, to rest.

Fard فرض: something which is obligatory on a Muslim. It is sometimes used in reference to the obligatory part of *salat*.

Fasiq فاسق: one of corrupt moral character who engages in various sins without feeling any sense of shame or regret

Fatawa فتاوى: plural of *fatwa*, a religious edict or decision

Fātiha, al- الفاتحه: The Prophet (ص) has quoted the Almighty as saying, "The prayers have been divided between Me and My servant: one half for Me, and one for him;" so when one recites it and says, "*Alhamdulillahi Rabbil-'Ālameen*," the Almighty says, "My servant has praised Me." And when he says, "*Arrahmānir Raheem*," the Almighty says, "My servant has praised Me." And when he says, "*Maaliki Yawmid-Deen*," Allāh says, "My servant has exalted Me." And when he says, "*Iyyāka Na'budu wa iyyāka nasta'een*," Allāh will say, 'This is a covenant between Me and My servant, and My servant shall be granted the fulfillment of his pleas." Then if he finishes reciting the Fātiha to the end, Allāh will again confirm His promise by saying, 'This is for [the benefit of] My servant, and My servant will be granted the answer to his wishes. The Messenger of Allāh (ص) is quoted by *Abū Ali al-Fadl ibn al-Hassan ibn al-Fadhl at-Tibrisi* الطبرسي, may Allāh have mercy on his soul, saying that one who recites al-Fātiha will be regarded by

the Almighty as though he recited two-thirds of the Holy Qur'ān and as though he gave by way of charity to each and every believing man and woman. "By the One in Whose hand my soul is," the Prophet (ص) continues, "Allāh Almighty did not reveal in the Torah, the Gospel, or the Psalms any chapter like it; it is the Mother of the Book and *al-Sab' al-Mathāni* (the oft-repeated seven verses), and it is divided between Allāh and His servant, and His servant shall get whatever he asks; it is the best Sūra in the Book of the most Exalted One, and it is a healing from every ailment except poison, which is death." He (ص) is also quoted by *al-Kaf'ami* الكفعمي as saying, "He (Allāh) bestowed it upon me as His blessing, making it equivalent to the Holy Qur'ān, saying, 'And We have granted you *as-Sab' al-Mathāni* and the Great Qur'ān (*Sūrat al-Hijr*, verse 87).' It is the most precious among the treasures of the '*Arsh*." Indeed, Allāh, the most Sublime, has chosen

Muhammed (ﷺ) alone to be honored by it without doing so to any other Prophet or Messenger of His with the exception of Sulayman (Solomon) نبي سليمان, peace be upon him, who was granted the Basmala البسمله (see Qur'ān, 27:30, i.e. verse 30 of Sūrat an-Naml, Chapter of the Ant). One who recites it, being fully convinced of his following in the footsteps of Muhammed (ﷺ) and his Progeny (ع), adhering to its injunctions, believing in its outward and inward meanings, will be granted by Allāh for each of its letters a blessing better than what all there is in the world of wealth and good things, and whoever listens to someone reciting it will receive one third of the rewards due to the one who recites it.

من بعض أسرار سورة الحمد (الفاتحة)

كتب قيصر الروم كتابا إلى خلفاء بني العباس وجاء فيه ((جاء في كتاب الإنجيل أنه من قرأ سورة خالية من سبعة أحرف ، حرم الله جسده من نار جهنم ، وهذه الأحرف عبارة عن :(ع) ث ، ج ، خ ، ز ، ش ، ظ ، ف (ع) . وفحصنا كثيرا فلم نعثر على هكذا سورة في كتب التوراة والزبور والإنجيل ، فهل يوجد في كتابكم السماوي تلك السورة؟

فجمع الخليفة العباسي جميع العلماء وعرض عليهم السؤال فعجزوا عن الجواب وأخيرا طرحوا هذا السؤال على الإمام علي الهادي (ع) فأجاب عليه السلام قائلا : هذه السورة هي سورة الحمد التي تكون خالية من الأحرف السبعة .

فسألوا الإمام ما فلسفة خلو هذه السورة من الأحرف السبعة ؟ فأجاب الإمام عليه السلام :

إن حرف (ث) إشارة إلى الثبور ، وحرف (ج) إشارة إلى الجحيم ، وحرف (خ) إشارة إلى الخبث ، وحرف (ز) إشارة إلى الزقوم ، وحرف (ش) إشارة إلى الشقاوة، وحرف (ظ) إشارة إلى الظلمة ، وحرف (ف) إشارة إلى الآفة .

فأرسل الخليفة هذا الجواب لقيصر الروم ، وشعر القيصر بالفرح بعد حصوله على الجواب واعتنق الإسلام وخرج من الدنيا مسلما. فأكثروا من قراءة سورة الحمد. لا تقرأ سورة الحمد (الفاتحة) بسرعة .... انظر لماذا؟

كثير من الناس يقرؤون سورة الفاتحة في الصلاة بسرعة وكأن الذئاب تلاحقهم ولا يعلمون ما فيها. روي عن رَسُولَ اللهِ صَلَّى اللهُ عَلَيْهِ وآله وَسَلَّمَ أنه قال: قَالَ اللهُ تَعَالَى: قَسَمْتُ الصَّلاةَ بَيْنِي وَبَيْنَ عَبْدِي نِصْفَيْنِ وَلِعَبْدِي مَا سَأَلَ فَإِذَا قَالَ الْعَبْدُ: {الْحَمْدُ للهِ رَبِّ الْعَالَمِينَ} قَالَ اللهُ تَعَالَى: حَمِدَنِي عَبْدِي وَإِذَا قَالَ: {الرَّحْمَنِ الرَّحِيمِ} قَالَ اللهُ تَعَالَى: أَثْنَى

410

عَلَيَّ عَبْدِي وَإِذَا قَالَ: ﴿مَالِكِ يَوْمِ الدِّينِ﴾ قَالَ: مَجَّدَنِي عَبْدِي وَقَالَ مَرَّةً: فَوَّضَ إِلَيَّ عَبْدِي فَإِذَا قَالَ: ﴿إِيَّاكَ نَعْبُدُ وَإِيَّاكَ نَسْتَعِينُ﴾ قَالَ: هَذَا بَيْنِي وَبَيْنَ عَبْدِي وَلِعَبْدِي مَا سَأَلَ فَإِذَا قَالَ: ﴿اهْدِنَا الصِّرَاطَ الْمُسْتَقِيمَ صِرَاطَ الَّذِينَ أَنْعَمْتَ عَلَيْهِمْ غَيْرِ الْمَغْضُوبِ عَلَيْهِمْ وَلَا الضَّالِّينَ﴾ قَالَ: هَذَا لِعَبْدِي وَلِعَبْدِي مَا سَأَلَ،،،،

Some mysteries about Sūrat al-Fātiha:

One of Rome's Caesars wrote a letter to an Abbāsid "caliph"—to use the word loosely since none of the Umayyads or Abbāsid rulers deserved to be called a caliph but a despotic ruler with the exception of only Caliph Omer ibn Abdul-Aziz, but we will use it here since it is quite commonly referred to those corrupt folks—saying, "It is written in the Bible that if anyone recites a chapter which does not contain seven letters, God will prohibit the Fire of Hell from consuming his body. These letters are: We have carefully examined in the Torah, Psalms and Bible but could not find such a chapter; so, is there in your divinely revealed Book such a Chapter?"

The Abbāsid caliph gathered all scholars and presented the question to them, but they could not provide an answer. Finally, they submitted this question to Imām Ali al-Hadi (ع) who answered saying that such a chapter is Sūrat al-Hamd, the Fātiha, which does not contain these alphabetical letters. The Imām (ع) explained the philosophy behind the exclusion of these alphabetical letters in the Fātiha Chapter as stated below, so the "caliph" sent this answer to Rome's Caesar who was very happy for having obtained it and immediately embraced Islam, departing from this world as a Muslim.

You, therefore, should recite Sūrat al-Hamd (Fātiha) quite often, but do not do so. Why? Many people recite the Fātiha in their prayers quickly as if the wolves are chasing them, not knowing what it really contains:

It has been narrated about the Messenger of Allāh, peace and blessings of Allāh be with him and his Progeny, has said, "Allāh Almighty has said: 'I have divided the prayer (supplication) between Myself and My servant into two halves: Whenever the servant says الْحَمْدُ لِلَّهِ رَبِّ الْعَالَمِينَ *Praise be to Allāh, the Cherisher and Sustainer of*

411

the worlds, I say that My servant has praised Me. When he says الرَّحْمَنِ الرَّحِيمِ *The Most Gracious, the Most Merciful*, I say that My servant has lauded me. When he says مَالِكِ يَوْمِ الدِّينِ *Master of the Day of Judgment*, I say that My servant has exulted me. In another narration of this tradition, the Almighty says, 'My servant has entrusted his (Hereafter) affairs to me'. When he says إِيَّاكَ نَعْبُدُ وَإِيَّاكَ نَسْتَعِينُ *You do we worship, and Your aid do we seek*, I say: 'This is between Myself and My servant, and My servant shall have what he pleads for'. And when he says اهدِنَا الصِّرَاطَ الْمُسْتَقِيمَ، صِرَاطَ الَّذِينَ أَنْعَمْتَ عَلَيْهِمْ غَيْرِ الْمَغْضُوبِ عَلَيْهِمْ وَلاَ الضَّالِّينَ *Guide us the Straight way, the way of those on whom You have bestowed Your Grace, those whose (portion) is not wrath, and who do not stray*, I say: 'This (too) is for My servant, and My servant shall be granted what he pleads for'."

Imām Ali al-Hadi (ع) was asked about the philosophy behind the Fātiha containing none of these seven alphabetical letters, so the Imām (ع) said: "The letter (ث) refers to ثبور destruction." The Almighty refers to it in the Holy Qur'ān in places such as these: 25:13 and 14, 84:11 and to one who is really ruined, Pharaoh, in 17:102. "The letter (ج)," the Imām (ع) went on, "refers to جحيم, hell." Numerous Qur'ānic verses refer to hell, warning those who heed the call about its torment. Some such verses are: 2:119, 5:10, 5:86, 9:113, 22:51, 26:91, 37:23, 37:55, 37:64, 37:68, 37:97, 37:163, 40:7, 44:47, 44:56, 52:18, 57:19, 69:31, 79:36, 81:12, 82:14, 83:16, 102:6, 73:12, to name few. The Imām (ع) added saying, "The letter (خ) refers to خبث" which is any bad thing, deed, person, thought, etc. to which references in the Holy Qur'ān exist in verses such as these: 7:58, 2:267, 3:179, 4:2, 5:100, 8:37, 24:26, 14:26, 7:157 and 21:74. The Imām (ع) went on to say, "The letter (ز) refers to زقوم Zaqqoom)" which is a tree in hell of which the sinners eat and to which references in the Holy Qur'ān exist in verses such as these: 37:62, 44:43 and 56:52. "The letter (ش)," went on the Imām (ع), "refers to شقاء", pain or suffering, a reference to the suffering of people, good or bad: The good people suffer in this life because of others unfairly and unjustifiably harming, hurting, oppressing belying them. They also suffer as they see things taking place and people behaving in an ungodly way and feel sorry for them. Some ordinary persons may suffer also during the period of the *barzakh* برزخ so the Almighty may punish them in the grave and forgive them later, while bad persons may suffer in this life and in the hereafter as well for their bad deeds. Its derivations exist in many verses such as these: 20:2, 20:117, 20:123, 11:105, 19:4, 19:32. 19:48, 87:11, 92:15, 91:12 and 23:106. The Imām (ع) went on in stating why these letters do not exist in the Fātiha and said, "The letter (ظ) refers to ظلمة", darkness, either physical, material, tangible, as is the darkness in the grave or in hell, or non-physical, immaterial, such as darkness of one's outlooks, attitudes, etc. Notice that the word ظلم which means oppression or injustice is associated with this same word ظلمة because people do not oppress others unless their mentality is dark. Hundreds of references in the Book of Islam, the Holy Qur'ān, refer to both types of such darkness and to people who oppress others or wrong them: These references are only few for you to check if you wish: 4:153, 13:6, 16:61, 4:75, 18:35, 25:27, 35:32, 37:113. This is just a drop in the bucket. Explaining the last letter, the Imām (ع) said, "The letter (ف) refers to آفة lesion, something which consumes, devours, spreads quickly like cancer cells, fire or a rash of bad deed in which many people are involved: This word fits many descriptions and applications, and it needs no further explanation.

The inquisitive reader may wonder who this Imām Ali al-Hadi (ع) is; after all, not many are familiar with the immediate family of the Prophet of Islam (ص); therefore, we have included his biography in this Glossary under "Hadi, al-" to which you may refer.

Fatwa فتوى: religious edict, which may be relevant to everyday matters or to the creed, issued by a *mujtahid* مجتهد

Fidya فدية: blood money, monetary compensation for either murder or a crime as serious as murder

Fiqh فقه: knowledge of the science of Islamic jurisprudence, the *Shari`a* شريعة. The literal meaning of the word *fiqh* is: understanding, comprehension, knowledge and familiarity with Islam's jurisprudence. A jurist is called *faqih*, one who is an expert in Islamic legal matters. A *faqih* فقيه issues verdicts within the rules of the Islamic Law, the *Shari`a* الشريعه. Any action or step in Islam falls within the following five categories of *fiqh*:

413

1. **Fardh فرض (must, obligatory, mandatory):** This category is a must for the Muslim to undertake such as the performance of the five daily prayers. Performing the *fardh* counts as a good deed, and not doing it is considered as a bad deed, a sin. It is also called *wajib*.

2. **Mandub مندوب (recommended, commendable):** This category is recommended for the Muslim to do such as additional prayers after the performance of the daily prayers. Doing what is *mandub* counts as a good deed, while not doing it does not count as a bad deed or a sin.

3. **Mubah مباح (allowed, permissible):** This category is optional and is left for the individual to decide such as partaking of food, etc. Doing or not doing the *mubah* does not count as a good or bad deed. One's intention can change *mubah* into a *fardh, mandub, makruh* or *haram*. Other things can also change the status of the *mubah*. For example, any *mubah* becomes *haram* if it is proven to be harmful, whether physically or spiritually, and any necessary thing to fulfill a *fardh* is a *fardh*, too.

4. **Makruh مكروه hated, not commendable:** This category includes acts that are detested, hated, things which one must stay away from such as letting his fingernails grow or sleeping on the stomach, etc. Not doing what is *makruh* counts as a good deed while doing it does not count as a bad deed.

5. **Haram حرام prohibited, banned:** This category includes things a Muslim is prohibited from doing such as stealing and lying. Doing what is *haram* counts as a sin, a bad deed, while not doing it counts as a good deed. Views of Islamic scholars about all the above vary.

Firdaws فردوس: Paradise, heaven, abode of the blessed, place of eternal peace and happiness, the garden of bliss. Some linguists think this word is Persian, whether others think it is Babylonian in origin, that is, a loan word.

Firqa فرقة: group, party, sect, division

Fitna or Fitnah فتنه: sedition, something which creates division, discord, disagreement, dispute, etc. among people. Numerous references exist in the Holy Qur'ān about *fitna*, warning the believers about falling into its traps. One such verse is this: الفتنة أشد من القتل *Sedition is harder than killing* (Qur'ān, 2:191), a warning which apparently was not heeded even when Islam was still in its infancy: Some "Muslims" went as far as plotting to assassinate the Prophet of Islam (ص) as he was returning from his last pilgrimage known as Hijjat al-Wadaa', Farewell Pilgrimage, as he himself points out in his Ghadīr sermon narrated for you in this Glossary. During the lifetime of the Prophet (ص), Muslims divided themselves into two communities: one following Ali (ع) whom they saw as the embodiment of everything Islam stands for, and one followed a handful of very affluent and influential companions of the Prophet (ص) in order to benefit from their money and prestige. As soon as the Prophet (ص) passed away, this division became much more evident: The first camp preferred to keep their pledge, which was made to the Prophet on Thul-Hijja 18, 10 A.H./March 19, 632 A.D., to obey Ali (ع) as the Commander of the Faithful أمير المؤمنين as granted this title by the Prophet of Islam (ص) who appointed him on that day at Ghadīr Khumm as his successor as ordered by the Almighty. Details of this subject are recorded in this Glossary under the "Ghadīr" item below. That was one of the earliest *fitnas* that divided the Muslims of the world and its effects can still be seen in our time and will continue to be so till the end of time.

The *fitna* of the succession to the Prophet (ص) almost led to Muslims killing each other, but Ali (ع) preferred to submit his will to the Almighty rather than go out to demand the implementation of the Ghadīr *wasiyya* (will) of the Prophet (ص). Abū Bakr, Omer ibn al-Khattab then Othman succeeded each other in ruling the Muslims, and during their governments many innovations found their way to Islam. The deliberate reluctance to follow the Prophet's will delivered in his Ghadīr sermon below, in which he appointed Imām Ali (ع) as his successor in response to a command which he had received from the Almighty, was later regretted as we know from the following text:

On pp. 428-9, Vol. 1/8 of the latest edition of *Bihār al-Anwār*, we read the following:

قال أبو الصلاح قدس الله روحه في تقريب المعارف: لما طعن عمر (بن الخطاب)، جمع بني عبد المطلب و قال: يا بني عبد المطلب، أراضون أنتم عني؟ فقال رجل من أصحابه: و من ذا الذي يسخط عليك؟ فأعاد اكلام ثلاث مرات، فأجابه رجل بمثل جوابه، فانتهره

عمر و قال: نحن أعلم بما أشعرنا قلوبنا، انا و الله أشعرنا قلوبنا ما ... نسأل الله أن يكفينا شره، و ان بيعة أبي بكر كانت فلتة نسأل الله أن يكفينا شرها.

و قال لابنه عبد الله و هو مسنده الى صدره: ويحك ضع رأسي بالأرض. فأخذته الغشية، قال: فوجدت من ذلك. فقال: ويحك ضع رأسي بالأرض. فأخذته الغشية، قال: فوجدت من ذلك. فقال: ويحك ضع رأسي بالأرض. فوضعت رأسه بالأرض فعفر التراب، ثم قال: ويل لعمر و ويل لأمه ان لم يغفر الله له.

و قال أيضا حين حضره الموت: أتوب الى الله من ثلاث: من اغتصابي هذا الأمر أنا و أبو بكر من دون الناس، و من استخلافي عليهم و من تفضيلي المسلمين بعضهم على بعض.

و قال أيضا: أتوب الى الله من ثلاث: من ردي رقيق اليمن، و من رجوعي عن جيش أسامة بعد أن أمره رسول الله (ص) علينا، و من تعاقدنا على أهل البيت ان قبض رسول الله أن لا نولي منهم أحدا.

Abul-Salah (man of righteousness), may Allāh sanctify his soul, has said in *Taqreeb al-Ma'arif* تقريب المعارف the following: "When Omer [ibn al-Khattab] was stabbed, he gathered the descendants of Abdul-Muttalib and said, 'O sons of Abdul-Muttalib! Are you pleased with me?' A man from among his fellows said, 'Who would be angry with you?' He (Omer) repeated his statement three times, getting the same response from the same man whom Omer rebuked and to whom he said, 'We know best how we made our hearts feel. We, by Allāh, made our hearts feel... what we plead to Allāh to spare us its evil. Allegiance to Abū Bakr was a slip [from the Right Path] the evil of which we plead to Allāh to spare us.'

"He (Omer) said to his son Abdullāh, who was helping his father recline on his chest, 'Woe on you! Put my head on the ground.' He was overtaken by a swoon. He (Abdullāh ibn Omer) said, 'I felt quite worried about it.' He (Omer) said, 'Woe on you! Put my head on the ground.' He was again overtaken by a swoon. He (Abdullāh ibn Omer) said, 'I felt quite worried about it.' He (Omer) said [for the third time], 'Woe on you! Put my head on the ground.' He (Abdullāh ibn Omer, a great reporter of *hadīth*) said, 'I put his head on the ground. Then he (Omer) said, 'Woe unto Omer, and woe unto his mother if Allāh does not forgive him.'

"He (Omer) also said at the time of his death: 'I repent to Allāh three

416

things: my sending the slaves of Yemen back, my abandonment of Usamah's army after the Messenger of Allāh (ص) had placed him in charge over us, and our agreement against Ahl al-Bayt (ع) that if the Messenger of Allāh died, we would not let any of them take charge.'"

Yet the most serious innovations, actually deviations from the right path of Islam, were practices by the government during Othman's time, so much so that Othman gradually lost all respect he had among the local Muslims and throughout the Islamic world. Among those who resented him was Mother of the Believers Āisha daughter of Abū Bakr and wife of the Prophet (ص).

On p. 794, Vol. 1/8 of the latest edition of *Bihār al-Anwār*, we read the following:

علي بن محمد الكاتب، عن الزعفراني، عن الثقفي، عن الحسن بن الحسين الأنصاري، عن سفيان، عن فضيل بن الزبير، عن فروة بن مجاشع، عن أبي جعفر (ع) قال: جاءت عائشة الى عثمان فقالت له: اعطني ما كان يعطيني أبي و عمر بن الخطاب. فقال: لم أجد لك موضعا في الكتاب و لا في السنة، و انما كان أبوك و عمر بن الخطاب يعطيانك بطيبة من أنفسهما، و أنا لا أفعل. قالت: فاعطني ميراثي من رسول الله (ص). فقال لها: أو لم تحسبي أنت و مالك بن أوس النضري فشهدتما أن رسول الله (ص) لا يورث حتى منعتما فاطمه (بنت النبي) ميراثها؟ أبطلتما حقها، فكيف تطلبين اليوم ميراثا من النبي (ص)؟ فتركته و انصرفت، و كان عثمان اذا خرج الى الصلاة أخذت قميص رسول الله (ص) على قصبة فرفعته عليها، ثم قالت ان عثمان قد خالف صاحب هذا القميص و ترك سنته.

Ali ibn Muhammed the scribe quotes az-Za'afarani quoting ath-Thaqafiquoting al-Hassan ibn al-Hussain al-Ansāri quoting Sufyan quoting Fudayl ibn az-Zubair quoting Farwah ibn Mujashi` from Imām [al-Bāqir] Abū Ja'far (ع) saying: "Āisha went to Othman and said to him: 'Give me what my father [Abū Bakr] and Omer ibn al-Khattab used to give me.' Othman said: 'I found no place for you in the Book of Allāh (Qur'ān) or in the Sunna [that you should get paid from *baytul-mal*]. Rather, your father and Omer ibn al-Khattab used to give you out of the goodness of their hearts, and I do not do that.' She said: 'Then give me my inheritance from the Messenger of Allāh (ص).' Othman said to her: 'Did you not think about it when you and Malik ibn Aws an-Nadari testified saying that the Messenger of

Allāh (ص) does not leave any inheritance, so much so that you prevented [through your testimony] Fātima (daughter of the Prophet (ص)) from getting her inheritance? You voided what was her legitimate right; so, how can you now demand any inheritance from the Prophet (ص)?' So she left him. Whenever Othman went out to pray, Āisha used to hand the shirt of the Messenger of Allāh (ص) on a reed and raise it high, then she would say: 'Othman has violated the owner of this shirt and has abandoned his Sunna'."

And on the same page we also read the following:

روى في كشف الغمة أن عائشة قالت لعثمان: يا نعثل يا عدو الله، انما سماك رسول الله (ص) باسم نعثل اليهودي الذي باليمن، فلاعنته و لاعنها، و حلفت أن لا تساكنه بمصر أبدا، خرجت الى مكة. ثم قال: قد نقل ابن أعثم صاحب الفتوح أنها (عائشة) قالت: اقتلوا نعثلا، قتل الله نعثلا، فلقد أبلى سنة رسول الله (ص): هذه ثيابه لم تبل، و خرجت الى مكة.

It has been narrated in *Kashf al-Ghumma* that Āisha said to Othman, "O Na'thal! O enemy of Allāh! The Messenger of Allāh called you 'Na'thal' after the Jew in Yemen.' She cursed him and he cursed her, and she swore never to stay in the same city where he was staying at all; she went out [of Medīna] to Mecca."

The narrator went on to say: "Ibn A'tham, author of *Al-Fitooh* [conquests], has transmitted saying that she (Āisha) said, 'Kill Na'thal, may Allāh kill Na'thal, for he has worn out the Sunna of the Messenger of Allāh (ص): Here are his clothes yet to wear out.' She went out for Mecca."

In the 1426 A.H./2005 A.D. Arabic edition of تأريخ الأمم و الملوك (History of nations and kings) (a fairly recent edition published by Al-Amira House for Printing, Publishing and Distribution, Beirut, Lebanon; this is the edition used for this book) by imām Abū Ja'far Muhammed ibn Jarir at-Tabari, which is more famous as Tabari's *Tarikh*, Vol. 3, p. 135:

قال محمد بن عمر: و حدثني محمد بن صالح، عن عبيد الله بن رافع بن نقاخة، عن عثمان بن الشريد، قال: مر عثمان على جبلة بن عمرو الساعدي و هو بفناء داره و معه جامعة فقال: يا نعثل، و الله لأقتلنك، و لأحملنك على قلوص جرباء، و لأخرجنك الى حرة

418

النار، ثم جاءه مرة أخرى و عثمان على المنبر فأنزله عنه.

حدثني محمد قال: حدثني أبو بكر بن اسماعيل عن أبيه عن عامر بن سعد قال: كان أول
من اجترأ على عثمان بالمنطق السيء جبلة بن عمرو الساعدي، مر به عثمان و هو
جالس في ندي قومه و في يد جبلة بن عمرو جامعة، فلما مر عثمان سلم، فرد القوم،
فقال جبلة: لم تردون على رجل فعل كذا و كذا؟! قال: ثم أقبل على عثمان فقال: و الله
لأطرحن هذه الجامعة في عنقك أو لتتركن بطانتك هذه. قال عثمان: أي بطانة؟! فو الله
اني لأتخير الناس. فقال جبلة: مروان تخيرته! و معاوية تخيرته! و عبد الله بن سعد
تخيرته! منهم من نزل القرآن بدمه، و أباح رسول الله دمه.

قال: فانصرف عثمان، فما زال الناس مجترئين عليه (يعني على عثمان) الى هذا اليوم.

Muhammed ibn Omer has said: "Muhammed ibn Salih has narrated
to me citing Ubaydullāh ibn Raafi` ibn Naqakhah from Othman ibn
ash-Sharid who said: "Othman passed by Jiblah ibn Amr as-Saa'idi
as he was in the courtyard of his home, and he had chains, so he
said, 'O Na'thal! By Allāh I shall kill you, and I shall carry you on a
scabby she-camel (not yet trained to carry anyone or anything), and I
shall get you out to the heat of the Fire.' Jiblah ibn Amr as-Saa'idi
also went once and saw Othman on the pulpit (preaching), so he
pulled him down it.

I [the author, at-Tabari, goes on to add] have been told by
Muhammed who said: I have been told by Abū Bakr ibn Isma'eel
who quotes his father citing Āmir ibn Sa'd saying: "The first person
to verbally Abūse Othman was Jiblah ibn Amr as-Saa'idi: Othman
passed by him once as he was sitting in his folk's meeting place.
Jiblah ibn Amr as-Saa'idi had a chain in his hand. When Othman
passed by, he greeted [those present at the meeting place]. The folks
responded [to the greeting], whereupon Jiblah said: 'Why do you
respond to a man who has done such and such?!' Then he went to
Othman and said: 'By Allāh, I shall place this chain round your neck
unless you abandon your train.' Othman said, 'What train?! By Allāh,
I choose from among people [for my close companions].' Jiblah said:
'You chose Marwan [ibn al-Hakam, Othman's young cousin and
bearer of his seal]! And you chose Mu'awiyah! And you chose
Abdullāh ibn Sa'd! Some of these have been condemned to death by
the Qur'ān, and some of them were condemned to die by the
Messenger of Allāh (ص)!' He went on to say: 'Othman left, and

people kept verbally Abūsing Othman till this day."

Why did the third caliph cause matters to deteriorate so badly? There is no room here to provide you with the detailed answer to this question, but we can refer you to a book written by one of Egypt's best intellectuals and scholars of the century, namely Dr. Taha Hussein, who worte الفتنة الكبرى *The Greater Sedition*. In it, you will find out that one of Othman's serious mistakes was giving his seal to his young and reckless cousin Marwan ibn al-Hakam, as you will read under the item "Hadi, al-" below, who greatly Abūsed the power that seal gave him. Taha Hussein details how the public funds deposited at the State Treasury known then as *baytul-mal* بيت المال were plundered and distributed among Othman's fāmily, relatives and supporters, so much so that Othman had three mansions built for him each of each cost more than three million dinars. Arabs do not have the word "million" in their language; instead, they use the term "a thousand thousands" to describe the gold dinars and the silver dirhams spent on building mansions for Othman and for his wife, Na'ila daughter of al-Qarafisa, who had so much jewelry, her jingle could be heard from a distance.

Another *fitna* was the falsification of *ahadīth* أحاديث, traditions, which make up one of the main sources of the Sunna which every Muslim must follow, the other being the Holy Qur'ān. Abū Bakr prohibited the writing of *hadīth* and most traditions were collected and burnt, so very few survived. Later, the Umayyad dynasty that ruled the Islamic world from 655 to 1031 A.D. was characterized by the flourishing of manufactures for making custom-designed traditions tailored to please various Umayyad rulers the first of whom was Mu'awiyah ibn Abū Sufyan ibn Harb. On pp. 332-3 of the 1426 A.H./2005 A.D. edition of تأريخ الأمم و الملوك (History of nations and kings) by imām Abū Ja'far Muhammed ibn Jarir at-Tabari, which is more famous as Tabari's *Tarikh*, we read the following:

و كانوا يعدون دهاة الناس حين ثارت الفتنة خمسة رهط، فقالوا: ذوو رأي العرب و مكيدتهم: معاوية بن أبي سفيان، و عمرو بن العاص، و المغيرة بن شعبة، و قيس بن سعد، و من المهاجرين عبد الله بن بديل الخزاعي.

Five men used to be regarded as the most cunning of all people when sedition erupted. People said that they were people of opinions and of scheming, and these are: Mu'awiyah ibn Abū Sufyan, Amr ibn al-Aas, al-Mughirah ibn Shu'bah and Qais ibn Sa'd, all from the Ansār, in addition to Abdullāh ibn Budayl al-Khuza'i from among the Muhajirun.

Who is this man, Mu'awiyah ibn Abū Sufyan ibn Harb?

On the 10th of Hijra/630 A.D., the date of the Conquest of Mecca, Abū Sufyan, father of this Mu'awiyah, had to choose either to accept Islam or be beheaded, so he pretended to accept Islam while all his actions and those of his family members proved that they never really did. Abū Sufyan was a wealthy and influential man who belonged to the Banu Umayyah clan of the once pagan tribe of Quraish of Mecca, Hijaz, that fought the spread of Islam relentlessly during the time of the Prophet of Islam (ص). He was contemporary to the Prophet of Islam (ص) whom he fought vigorously. His date of birth is unknown, but he died in 31 A.H./652 A.D. "Abū Sufyan" is his *kunya*, surname; his name is Sakhr ibn Harb ibn Umayyah. He is father of Mu`awiyah and grandfather of Yazid.

Abū Sufyan led pagan Quraish in its many wars against Prophet Muhammed (ص) and his small band of supporters, making alliances with other pagan tribes and with the Jews of Medīna against the new rising power of Islam. He kept leading one battle after another till the fall of Mecca to the Muslims in 630 A.D. It was then that he had to either accept the Islamic faith or face a sure death for all the mischief he had committed against the Muslims, so he preferred to live in hypocrisy as a "Muslim," though only in name, rather than accept death. He was the most cunning man in all of Arabia and one of its aristocrats and men of might and means. He saw Islam as the harbinger of the waning of his own personal power and prestige and those of his tribe, Quraish, not to mention the decline of his faith, paganism, and the pre-Islamic way of life to which he and his likes were very much accustomed, the life of promiscuity, lewdness and debauchery, with all the wine, women and wealth aristocrats like him very much enjoyed. His likes are present throughout the Islamic lands in our time and in every time and clime... This has always been so, and it shall unfortunately remain so...

Mu`awiyah son of Abū Sufyan was born out of wedlock in 602 A.D. during the *jahiliyya*, the time of ignorance, the period that preceded Islam. His mother, Maysun, was one of his father's slave-girls. Maysun had a sexual intercourse with one of Mu`awiyah's slaves and conceived Yazid by him. Mu`awiyah, in total disregard for Islamic or traditional Arab traditions, claimed Yazid as his son. A testimony to this fact is the well-documented tradition of the Prophet (ع) wherein he said, "The murderer of my [grand]son al-Hussain is a bastard." This tradition is quoted on p. 156, Vol. 1, of *Kanz al-`Ummal* of al-Muttaqi al-Hindi. The stigma of being a bastard applies actually not only to Yazid but also to both Shimr ibn Thul-Jawshan and `Ubaydullāh ibn Sa`d, the accomplices about whom the reader can read a great deal in my book titled *Kerbalā and Beyond*.

One glaring proof about the fact that Mu'awiyah never really accepted Islam is the following famous verse of poetry which Mu'awiyah composed:

جزع الخزرج من وقع الأسل	ليت أشياخي ببدر شهدوا
ثم قالوا يا يزيد لا تشل	لأهلوا و استهلوا فرحا
و عدلناه ببدر فاعتدل	قد قتلنا القرم من ساداتهم
خبر جاء و لا وحي نزل	لعبت هاشم بالملك فلا
من بني أحمد ما كان فعل	لست من خندف ان لم أنتقم

I wish my ancestors at Badr witnessed
Anxiety of the Khazraj as spears clamped
They would have made tahleel *in elation,*
Then they would have said:
May your hand, O Yazid, never be paralyzed!
We killed the mountain peaks of their masters,
Then we compared it with Badr,
And it surely was straight like Badr!
Hashim (clan) played with power:
Neither news came nor revelation descended.
I do not belong to Khandaf if I do not
Seek revenge on Ahmed's progeny
For what he had done to me.

Examine these verses of poetry and see how Yazid refers to the Battle of Badr when many of his apostate ancestors, for whom he still longs, were killed at the hands of "Ahmed's progeny," a reference to Imām Ali (ع), Hussain's father. Notice how he now feels that the record has been set straight by avenging the killing of those rotten ancestors of his, the *kafir* that they all were, with the killing of Hussain (ع) and his family members and supporters. Indeed, neither Yazid, nor his father Mu'awiyah nor his grandfather Sufyan ever accepted Islam truly. They only pretended to have done so in order to "go with the tide" and escape the penalty for apostasy. Their actions, all of them, testify to this fact. Yet you can find among the "Muslims" of our times and other times those who defend these Umayyads and justify the crimes which they had committed as well as the distortion of the true Sunna. May these defenders be lodged on the Day of Judgment in the company of Yazid and his ancestors and offspring, all of them, and may He lodge us, followers of Ahl al-Bayt (ع), in the company of the Prophet (ص) and his holy Ahl al-Bayt (ع), *Allāhomma Aameen* اللهم آمين. Those whose only weapon is to cast doubt about how un-Islamic and anti-Islamic the Umayyads were should read the verses cited above in their own original text as reported in the following list of references: *Al-Luhoof fi Qatla al-Tufoof*, p. 105; Ibn A'tham, *Al-Fitooh*, Vol. 5, pp. 150-51; al-Khawarizmi, *Maqtal al-Hussain*, Vol. 2, pp. 66-67; *Tathkirat al-Khawass*, p. 261; *Yanabi' al-Mawadda*, Vol. 3, p. 32; *Al-Nasaaih al-Kafiya*, p. 263; *Al-Bidaya wal Nihaya*, Vol. 8, p. 209 in the events of the year 61 A.H. as well as in other references which all are in Arabic.

Mu`awiyah played a major role in distorting the Islamic creed by paying writers to tailor design "traditions" to serve his interests and support his deviated views. He installed himself as ruler of Syria in 40 A.H./661 A.D. and ruled for twenty long years till his death at the age of seventy-eight. Shortly before his death, which took place in the month of Rajab of 60 A.H./May of 680 A.D., he managed to secure the oath of allegiance to his corrupt and immoral son Yazid as his successor. He did so by intimidation once and once by buying loyalty and favors, spending in the process huge sums of money that belonged to the Muslims. The weak-minded majority of the Muslims of his time swore allegiance to him. This proves that the majority does not necessarily have to be right. Imām al-Hussain (ع), together with a small band of devotees to the cause of truth, refused to bow their heads to the oppressive forces, hence this tale of heroism.

Mu`awiyah declared himself "caliph" in Syria when he was 59 years old and assumed authority by sheer force. He was not elected, nor was he requested to take charge. He did not hide this fact; rather, he bragged about it once when he addressed the Kufians saying, "O people of Kufa! Do you think that I fought you in order that you may establish prayers or give *zakāt* or perform the pilgrimage?! I know that you do pray, pay *zakāt* and perform the pilgrimage. Indeed, I fought you in order to take command over you with contempt, and Allāh has given me that against your wishes. Rest assured that whoever killed any of us will himself be killed. And the treaty between us of amnesty is under my feet."

Mu`awiyah's rule was terror in the whole Muslim land. Such terrorism was spread by many convoys sent to various regions. Historians have narrated that Mu`awiyh summoned Sufyan ibn Awf al-Ghamidi, one of the commanders of his army, and said to him, "This army is under your command. Proceed along the Euphrates River till you reach Heet. Any resistance you meet on your way should be crushed, and then you should proceed to invade Anbar. After that, penetrate deeply into Mada'in. O Sufyan! These invasions will frighten the Iraqis and please those who like us. Such campaigns will attract frightened people to our side. Kill whoever holds different views from ours; loot their villages and demolish their homes. Indeed, fighting them against their livelihood and taking their wealth away is similar to killing them but is more painful to their hearts."

Another of his commanders, namely Bishr ibn Arta'ah, was summoned and ordered to proceed to Hijaz and Yemen with these instructions issued by Mu`awiyah: "Proceed to Medīna and expel its people. Meanwhile, people in your way, who are not from our camp, should be terrorized. When you enter Medīna, let it appear as if you are going to kill them. Make it appear that your aim is to exterminate them. Then pardon them. Terrorize the people around Mecca and Medīna and scatter them around."

During Mu`awiyah's reign, basic human rights were denied, not simply violated. No one was free to express his views. Government spies were paid to terrorize the public, assisting the army and the police in sparing no opportunity to crush the people and to silence their dissent. There are some documents which reveal Mu`awiyah's instructions to his governors to do just that. For instance, the following letter was addressed to all judges: "Do not accept the testimony of Ali's followers (Shī'ites) or of his descendants in (your) courts." Another letter stated: "If you have evidence that someone likes `Ali and his fāmily, omit his name from the recipients of rations stipulated from the *zakāt* funds." Another letter said, "Punish whoever is suspected of following `Ali and demolish his house." Such was the situation during the government of Mu`awiyah, Yazid's infamous father. Historians who were recording these waves of terror described them as unprecedented in history. People were so frightened, they did not mind being called atheists, thieves, etc., but not followers of Imām `Ali ibn Abū Tālib (ع), the right hand of Prophet Muhammed (ص), confidant and son-in-law.

Another aspect of the government of Mu`awiyah was the racist discrimination between Arabs and non-Arabs. Although they were supposed to have embraced Islam which tolerates no racism in its teachings, non-Arabs were forced to pay *khiraj* and *jizya* taxes that are levied from non-Muslims living under the protection of Muslims and enjoying certain privileges, including the exemption from the military service. A non-Arab soldier fighting in the state's army used to receive bare subsistence from the rations. Once, a dispute flared up between an Arab and a non-Arab and both were brought to court. The judge, namely Abdullāh ibn `Āmir, heard the non-Arab saying to his Arab opponent, "May Allāh not permit people of your kind (i.e. Arabs) to multiply." The Arab answered him by saying, "O Allāh! I invoke You to multiply their (non-Arabs') population among us!" People present there and then were bewildered to hear such a plea, so they asked him, "How do you pray for this man's people to multiply while he prays for yours to be diminished?!" The Arab opponent said, "Yes, indeed, I do so! They clean our streets and make shoes for our animals, and they weave our clothes!"

Imām al-Hussain's older brother, Imām al-Hassan (ع), was elected in Medīna on the 21st of the month of Ramadan, 40 A.H./January 28, 661 A.D. as the caliph, but his caliphate did not last long due to the terrorism promoted by Mu`awiyah who either intimidated, killed, or bribed the most distinguished men upon whom Imām al-Hassan (ع) depended to run the affairs of the government. Finally, Mu`awiyah pushed Imām al-Hassan (ع) out of power after signing a treaty with him the terms of which were, indeed, honorable and fair, had they only been implemented. Finding his men too weak or too reluctant to fight Mu`awiyah, Imām al-Hassan (ع) had no alternative except to sign the said treaty with a man whom he knew very well to be the most hypocritical of all and the most untrustworthy.

This is the father. The mother is Maysun, Hind Having seen how his father, Abū Sufyan, became a "Muslim"—but never a Mu'min—, Mu'awiyah fled away to Bahrain where he sent his father a very nasty letter reprimanding him for accepting Islam...

Mu'awiyah son of Abū Sufyan was born out of wedlock in 602 A.D. during the *jahiliyya*, the time of ignorance, the period that preceded Islam. His mother, Maysun, was one of his father's slave-girls. Maysun had a sexual intercourse with one of Mu`awiyah's slaves and conceived Yazid by him. Mu`awiyah, in total disregard for Islamic or traditional Arab traditions, claimed Yazid as his son. A testimony to this fact is the well-documented tradition of the Prophet (a) wherein he said, "The murderer of my [grand]son al-Hussain is a bastard." This tradition is quoted on p. 156, Vol. 1, of *Kanz al-`Ummal* of al-Muttaqi al-Hindi. The stigma of being a bastard applies actually not only to Yazid but also to both Shimr ibn Thul-Jawshan and `Ubaydullāh ibn Sa`d, the accomplices about whom the reader will read later; all of these men were born out of wedlock.

Mu`awiyah played a major role in distorting the Islamic creed. He installed himself as ruler of Syria in 40 A.H./661 A.D. and ruled for twenty long years till his death at the age of seventy-eight. Shortly before his death, which took place in the month of Rajab of 60 A.H./May of 680 A.D., he managed to secure the oath of allegiance to his corrupt and immoral son Yazid as his successor. He did so by intimidation once and once by buying loyalty and favors, spending in the process huge sums of money that belonged to the Muslims. The weak-minded majority of the Muslims of his time swore allegiance to him. This proves that the majority does not necessarily have to be right. Imām al-Hussain (a), together with a small band of devotees to the cause of truth, refused to bow their heads to the oppressive forces, hence this tale of heroism.

The greatest damage Mu'awiyah caused to the Islamic creed is through falsification, fabrication and manufacturing of hadīth. He found in Abū Hurayra al-Dawsi his best tool to achieve this goal.

426

Who is this Abū Hurayra, and why did he manufacture as many as three thousand traditions during the three-year period when he was in the Suffa, a shelter for indigent Muslims, close to the Prophet's Mosque in Medīna?

In the year 7 A.H./629 A.D., a young and very poor man from the Daws tribe of southern Arabia (Yemen), met the Prophet immediately after the battle of Khaybar and embraced Islam. He is well known in history as "Abū Hurayra," the fellow of the kitten, after a kitten to which he was very much attached, reportedly carrying it wherever he went. His name shone neither during the lifetime of the Prophet nor of the four "righteous caliphs" but during the un-Islamic reign of terror of the Umayyads which lasted from 655, when Mu'awiyah seized power in Damascus, to 750 A.D., when Marwan II, the last Umayyad ruler in Damascus, died. It was during that period that the Islamic world witnessed an astronomical number of "traditions" which were attributed, through this same Abū Hurayra, to the Prophet of Islam (ﷺ). Since these traditions, known collectively as *hadīth*, constitute one of the two sources of the Islamic legislative system, the Shari`a, it is very important to shed a light on the life and character of this man even if some readers may consider this chapter as a digression from the main topic.

It is of utmost importance to expose the facts relevant to Abū Hurayra so that Muslims may be cautious whenever they come across a tradition narrated by him or attributed to him which, all in all, reached the astronomical figure of 5,374 "traditions," although he spent no more than three years in the company of the Prophet, a fact supported by the renown compiler al-Bukhāri, whenever such company did not involve any danger to his life, and despite the fact that Abū Hurayra did not know how to read and write... The reader can easily conclude that this figure is unrealistic when he comes to know that Abū Bakr, friend of the Prophet and one of the earliest converts to Islam, narrated no more than 142 traditions. Omer ibn al-Khattab, the story of whose conversion to Islam is narrated earlier in this book, narrated no more than 537 traditions. Othman ibn Affan narrated no more than 146 traditions. And Ali, the man who was raised by the Prophet and who was always with him, following him like his shadow, and whose memory and integrity nobody at all can question, narrated no more than 586 traditions. All these men, especially Ali and Abū Bakr, spent many years of their lives in the company of the Prophet and did not hide when their lives were in jeopardy, as is the case with Abū Hurayrah, yet they did not narrate except a tiny fraction of the number of "traditions," many of which cannot be accepted by logic and commonsense, narrated by or attributed to Abū Hurayra. This is why it is so important to discuss this man and expose the factories of falsification of *hadīth* established by his benefactors, the Umayyads, descendants and supporters of Abū Sufyan, then his son Mu`awiyah, then his son Yazid, all of whom were outright hypocrites and had absolutely nothing to do with Islam.

Abū Hurayra's name is said to be `Omayr ibn `Āmir ibn `Abd Thish-Shari ibn Tareef, of the Yemenite tribe of Daws ibn `Adnan1. His mother's name is Umaima daughter of Safeeh ibn al-Harith ibn Shabi ibn Abū Sa`b, also of the Daws tribe. His date of birth is unknown, but he is said to have died in 57, 58, or 59 A.H., and that he had lived to be 78. This would put the date of his birth at 677, 678 or 679 A.D.

When he came to the Prophet (ص), he was young and healthy and, hence, capable of enlisting in the Prophet's army. But he preferred to be lodged together with destitute Muslims at the Suffa referred to above. Most of the time which Abū Hurayra spent with the Prophet was during the lunches or dinners the Prophet hosted for those destitute. Abū Hurayra himself admitted more than once that he remained close to the Prophet so that he could get a meal to eat. Another person who used to shower the destitute of the Suffa with his generosity was Ja`fer ibn Abū Tālib (588 - 629 A.D.), the Prophet's cousin and a brother of Ali ibn Abū Tālib. He was, for this

---

[1]According to *Al-Munjid fil lugha wal a`lam* المنجد في اللغة و الأعلام, however, Abū Hurayra's name is recorded as `Abd ar-Rahman ibn Sakhr al-Azdi, and that he died in 59 A.H./678 A.D. The same reference indicates that this man spent "a long time in the company of the Prophet," which is not true at all; he accompanied the Prophet from time to time for only 3 years. The Publisher of this *Munjid*, namely Dar al-Mashriq of Beirut, Lebanon, is sponsored by the Catholic Press of Beirut. Undoubtedly, the information about Abū Hurayra in this Arabic-Arabic dictionary must have been furnished by Sunnis who try their best to elevate the status of Abū Hurayra even at the risk of sacrificing historical facts and data.

reason, called "Abul Masakeen," father of the destitute. This is why, Abū Hurayra used to regard Ja`fer as the most generous person next only to the Prophet. When the Prophet mandated military service for all able men in the Mu'ta expedition, Ja`fer ibn Abū Tālib did not hesitate from responding to the Prophet's call, but Abū Hurayra, who considered Ja`fer as his patron, preferred not to participate, thus violating the order of the Prophet. History records the names of those who did likewise.

In 21 A.H./642 A.D., during the caliphate of Omer ibn al-Khattab, Abū Hurayra was made governor of Bahrain. After two years, he was deposed because of a scandal. The details of that scandal are recorded in the books of Ibn `Abd Rabbih, the Mu`tazilite writer, and in Ibn al-Atheer's famous classic book *Al-Iqd al-Fareed*. A summary of that incident runs as follows:

When Abū Hurayra was brought to him, Omer said to him: "I have come to know that when I made you governor of Bahrain, you did not even have shoes to wear, but I am now told that you have purchased horses for one thousand and six hundred dinars." Abū Hurayra said, "I had horses which have multiplied, and I received some as gifts." Omer then said, "I would give you only your salary. This (amount) is a lot more than that (more than your salary for both years). Pay the balance back (to *baytul-mal*, the Muslim state treasury)!" Abū Hurayra said, "This money is not yours." Omer said, "By Allāh! I would bruise your back!" Saying this, Omer whipped Abū Hurayra till he bled. Then he thundered: "Now bring the money back!" Abū Hurayra replied: "I am to account for it before Allāh." Omer said, "This could be so only if you had taken it rightfully and had paid it back obediently. I shall throw you back to your mother as though you were dung so that she would use you to graze donkeys."

According to the sequence employed by Ibn Sa`d in his *Tabaqat*, Abū Hurayra ranks in the ninth or tenth class. He came to the Messenger of Allāh near the end of the seventh Hijri year. Hence, historians say that he accompanied the Prophet no more than three years[1] according to the best estimates, while other historians say it

---

[1] Al-Bukhari, *Sahīh*, Vol. 4, p. 175, where the author quotes Abū Hurayra talking about himself in a chapter dealing with the characteristics of Prophethood.

was no more than two years if we take into consideration the fact that the Prophet sent him to accompany Ibn al-Hadrami to Bahrain, then the Messenger of Allāh died while he was still in Bahrain.[2]

Abū Hurayra was not known for his *jihad* or valor, nor was he among those who were regarded as brilliant thinkers, nor among the jurists who knew the Qur'ān by heart, nor did he even know how to read and write... He came to the Messenger of Allāh in order to satisfy his hunger as he himself said, and as the Prophet came to understand from him, so he lodged him among the people of the Suffa to whom the Prophet used to send some food.

Yet he became famous for the Abūndance of *ahadīth* أحاديث which he used to narrate about the Messenger of Allāh. This fact attracted the attention of verifiers of *hadīth* especially since he had not remained in the company of the Prophet for any length of time and to the fact that he narrated traditions regarding battles which he had never attended.

Some critics and verifiers of *hadīth* gathered all what was narrated by the "righteous caliphs" as well as by the ten men given the glad tidings of going to Paradise in addition to what the mothers of the faithful and the purified Ahl al-Bayt, and they did not total one tenth of what Abū Hurayra had narrated all alone. This came despite the fact that among the latter was Ali ibn Abū Tālib who remained in the company of the Prophet for thirty years.

Then fingers were pointed to Abū Hurayra charging him with telling lies and with fabricating and forging *hadīth*. Some went as far as labeling him as the first narrator in the history of Islam thus charged. Yet some Muslims the extent of whose knowledge is apparently quite limited call him "Islam's narrator", so he is surrounded with a halo, a great deal of respect. They totally rely on him and even go as far as saying "Radiya Allhu `anhu," Allāh be pleased with him, whenever they mention his name. Some of them may even regard him as being more knowledgeable than Imām Ali ibn Abū Tālib (ع), who never parted with the Prophet (ص) and grew up in his lap, due

---

[2]This paragraph and the ones that follow are excerpted from my translation of Dr. Muhammed at-Tijani as-Samawi's book *Shi`as are the Ahl as-Sunnah* (New York: Vantage Press, 1996), pp. 207-215.

to one particular tradition which he narrates about himself and in which he says, "I said, `O Messenger of Allāh! I hear a great deal of your *hadīth* which I have been forgetting!' He said, `Stretch your mantle,' so I stretched it, whereupon he made a handful then said, 'Close upon it,' whereupon I closed upon it and never forgot of it a thing ever since," as we read on p. 38, Vol. 1, of al-Bukhāri's *Sahīh* where the author dedicates a chapter on acquiring knowledge.

Abū Hurayra kept narrating so many *ahadīth* that Omer ibn al-Khattab beat him with his cane and said to him, "You have quoted too many *ahadīth*, and it seems that you have been telling lies about the Messenger of Allāh." This was due to one particular narration which Abū Hurayra reported and in which he quoted the Prophet supposedly saying that Allāh had created the heavens, the earth and all creation in seven days. When Omer heard about it, he called him in and asked him to repeat that *hadīth*. Having heard him repeating it, Omer struck him and said to him, "How so when Allāh Himself says it was done in six days, while you yourself now say it was done in seven?!" Abū Hurayra said, "Maybe I heard it from Ka`b al-Ahbar..." Omer said, "Since you cannot distinguish between the Prophet's *ahadīth* and what Ka`b al-Ahbar says, you must not narrate anything at all."[1]

It is also narrated that Ali ibn Abū Tālib has said, "Among all the living, the person who has told the most lies about the Messenger of Allāh is Abū Hurayra al-Dawsi," as we read on p. 28, Vol. 4 of Ibn Abul-Hadeed's work *Sharh Nahjul-Balāgha*. Mother of the faithful Āisha, too, testified to his being a liar several times in reference to many *ahadīth* which he used to attribute to the Messenger of Allāh (ﷺ). For example, she resented something which he had once said so she asked him, "When did you hear the Messenger of Allāh say so?" He said to her, "The mirror, the kohl, and the dyestuff have all diverted you from the *hadīth* of the Messenger of Allāh," but when she insisted that he was lying and scandalized him, Marwan ibn al-Hakam interfered and took upon himself to verify the authenticity of the *hadīth* in question. It was then that Abū Hurayra admitted, "I did not hear it from the Messenger of Allāh; rather, I heard it from al-Fadl ibn al-`Abbās," according to al-Bukhāri, *Sahīh*, Vol. 2, p. 232, in a

---

[1]Refer to the book titled *Abū Hurayra* by the Egyptian author Mahmoud Abū Rayyah.

chapter dealing with a fasting person who wakes up finding himself in the state of *janaba*, and Malik, *Mawta'*, Vol. 1, p. 272. It is because of this particular narration that Ibn Qutaybah charged him with lying saying, "Abū Hurayra claimed that al-Fadl ibn al-'Abbās, who had by then died, testified to the authenticity of that tradition which he attributed to him in order to mislead people into thinking that he had heard it from him, according to at-Thahbi's book *Siyar A`lam an-Nubala*. In his book *Ta'weel al-Ahadīth* تأويل الأحاديث, Ibn Qutaybah says, "Abū Hurayra used to say: `The Messenger of Allāh said such-and-such, but I heard it from someone else." In his book A`lam an-Nubala, at-Thahbi says that Yazid ibn Ibrahim once cited Shu`bah ibn al-Hajjaj saying that Abū Hurayra used to commit forgery.

In his book *Al-Bidaya wal Nihaya* البداية و النهاية, Ibn Katheer states that Yazid ibn Haroun heard Shu`bah ibn al-Hajjaj accusing him of the same, that is, that he forges *hadīth*, and that he used to narrate what he used to hear from Ka`b al-Ahbar as well as from the Messenger of Allāh without distinguishing one from the other.

Ja`fer al-Iskafi has said, "Abū Hurayra is doubted by our mentors; his narrations are not acceptable," as we read on p. 68, Vol. 4, of Ibn Abul-Hadeed's book *Sharh Nahjul-Balāgha*.

During his lifetime, Abū Hurayra was famous among the *sahāba* of lying and forgery and of narrating too many fabricated ahadīth to the extent that some of the *sahāba* used to deride him and ask him to fabricate *ahadīth* agreeable with their own taste.

For example, a man belonging to Quraish put on once a new jubbah (a long outer garment) and started showing off. He passed by Abū Hurayra and [sarcastically] said to him, "O Abū Hurayra! You narrate quite a few traditions about the Messenger of Allāh; so, did you hear him say anything about my jubbah?!" Abū Hurayra said, "I have heard the father of al-Qasim saying, `A man before your time was showing off his outfit when Allāh caused the earth to cave in over him; so he has been rattling in it and will continue to do so till the Hour.' By Allāh! I do not know whether he was one of your people or not," as we read in Ibn Katheer's book *Al-Bidaya wal Nihaya*, Vol. 8, p. 108.

How can people help doubting Abū Hurayra's traditions since they are so self-contradictory? He narrates one "hadīth" then he narrates its antithesis, and if he is opposed or his previously narrated traditions are used against him, he becomes angry or starts babbling in the Ethiopian tongue.[1]

How could they help accusing him of telling lies and of forgery after he himself had admitted that he got traditions out of his own pouch then attributed them to the Prophet?

Al-Bukhāri, in his *Sahīh*, states the following:

"Abū Hurayra said once, 'The Prophet said, `The best charity is willingly given; the higher hand is better than the lower one, and start with your own dependents. A woman says: `Either feed me or divorce me.' A slave says, `Feed me and use me.' A son says, `Feed me for the woman who will forsake me.'" He was asked, "O Abū Hurayra! Did you really hear the Messenger of Allāh say so?" He said, "No, this one is from Abū Hurayra's pouch,'" as we read in Bukhāri, *Sahīh*, Vol. 6, p. 190, in a chapter dealing with spending on the wife and children.

Notice how he starts this "tradition" by saying, "The Prophet said," then when they refuse to believe what he tells them, he admits by saying, "... This one is from Abū Hurayra's pouch"! So congratulations to Abū Hurayra for possessing this pouch which is full of lies and myths, and for which Mu`awiyah and Banu Umayyah provided a great deal of publicity, and because of which he acquired position, authority, wealth, and mansions. Mu`awiyah made him the governor of Medīna and built him the Aqeeq mansion then married him off to a woman of honorable descent for whom he used to work as a servant...

Since Abū Hurayra was the close vizier of Mu`awiyah, it is not due to his own merits, honor, or knowledge; rather, it is because Abū Hurayra used to provide him with whatever traditions he needed to circulate. If some *sahāba* used to hesitate in cursing "Abū Turab," finding doing that embarrassing, Abū Hurayra cursed Ali in his own

---

[1]Al-Bukhari, *Sahīh*, Vol. 7, p. 31.

house and as his Shī'ites heard:

Ibn Abul-Hadeed says,

"When Abū Hurayra came to Iraq in the company of Mu`awiyah in the Year of the Jama`a, he came to Kufa's mosque. Having seen the huge number of those who welcomed him, he knelt down then beat his bald head and said, "O people of Iraq! Do you claim that I tell lies about the Messenger of Allāh and thus burn myself in the fire?! By Allāh! I heard the Messenger of Allāh saying, `Each prophet has a sanctuary, and my sanctuary is in Medīna from Eer [area] to [the mountain of] Thawr; so, anyone who makes it unclean will be cursed by Allāh, the angels, and all people, and I bear witness that Ali had done so." When Mu`awiyah came to hear this statement, he gave him a present, showered him with his generosity, and made him the governor of Medīna."[1]

Suffices us to point out to the fact that Abū Hurayra was made governor of Medīna by none other than Mu`awiyah. There is no doubt that verifiers and researchers, who are free of prejudice, will doubt anyone who befriended the enemy of Allāh and His Messenger and who was antagonistic towards the friends of Allāh and of His Messenger... would reward Abū Hurayra for nothing.

There is no doubt that Abū Hurayra did not reach that lofty position of authority, namely Governor of Medīna, then capital of the Islamic world, except by virtue of the services which he had rendered to Mu`awiyah and other authoritative Umayyads. Praise to the One Who changes the conditions! Abū Hurayra had come to Medīna with nothing to cover his private parts other than a tiny striped piece of cloth, begging passers-by to feed him. Then he suddenly became ruler of the sacred precincts of Medīna, residing in the Aqeeq Mansion, enjoying wealth, servants and slaves, and nobody could say a word without his permission. All of this was from the blessings of his "pouch"!

Do not forget, nor should you be amazed, dear reader, that nowadays we see the same stage plays being reenacted, and history certainly

---

[1]Ibn Abul-Hadeed, *Sharh Nahjul-Balagha*, Vol. 4, p. 67.

repeats itself. How many ignorant indigent persons sought nearness to a ruler and joined his party till they became feared masters who do and undo, issuing orders as they please, having a direct access to wealth without being accounted for it, riding in automobiles without being watched, eating foods not sold on the market...? One such person may not even know how to speak his own language, nor does he know a meaning for life except satisfying his stomach and sexual appetite. The whole matter is simply his having a "pouch" like the one Abū Hurayra used to have with some exception, of course, yet the aim is one and the same: pleasing the ruler and publicizing for him in order to strengthen his authority, firm his throne, and eliminate his critics.

Abū Hurayra loved the Umayyads and they loved him since the days of Othman ibn Affan, their leader. His view with regard to Othman was contrary to that of all *sahāba* who belonged to the Muhajirun and the Ansār; he regarded all the *sahāba* who participated in or encouraged the killing of Othman as being "apostates".

Undoubtedly, Abū Hurayra used to accuse Ali ibn Abū Tālib (ε) of killing Othman. We can derive this conclusion from the statement which he made at Kufa's Grand Mosque that Ali made Medīna unclean and that he, therefore, was cursed by the Prophet, the angels, and everyone else. For this reason, Ibn Sa`d indicates in his *Tabaqat* that when Abū Hurayra died in 59 A.H./679 A.D., Othman's descendants carried his coffin and brought it to the Baqee` to bury it as an expression of their appreciation of his having had high regards for Othman.[1]

Surely Allāh has his own wisdom in faring with His creation. Othman ibn Affan, the master of Quraish and their greatest, was killed although he was the Muslims' caliph bearing the title of "Thul-Noorayn", the man with two lights, and of whom, according to their claim, the angels feel shy. His corpse did not receive the ceremonial burial bath nor was it shrouded; moreover, it was not buried for full three days after which it was buried at Medīna's then Jewish cemetery.

---

[1] Ibn Sa`d, *Tabaqat*, Vol. 2, p. 63.

On p. 80, Vol. 3, of *Al-Isti'ab* by Ibn Abd al-Birr, we read the following: "When Othman was killed, his body was thrown on a pile of garbage for three days. When it was nighttime, twelve men went to his corpse. Among them were: Huwaitib ibn Abd al-Uzza, Hakeem ibn Hizam, Abdullāh ibn az-Zubair, Muhammed ibn Hatib and Marwan ibn al-Hakam. When they went to the cemetery to bury him, some people from Banu Mazin shouted at them saying, 'By Allāh! If you bury him here, we will tell people about it tomorrow [so they may dig the corpse up and remove it].' They had to carry his corpse till they reached Hash Kawkab, a wall in Medīna, where they dug up a grave for him. Āisha daughter of Othman [not to be confused with Āisha daughter of Abū Bakr] was carrying a lantern. When the men took him out to bury him, Āisha wailed, whereupon Abdullāh ibn az-Zubair said to her, 'By Allāh! If you do not remain silent, I will hit you on the head.' She stopped wailing, and he (Othman) was buried."

Ibn Abul-Hadeed quotes at-Tabari saying that Othman's corpse was kept for three days unburied. The author of this book has a copy of the 2005 A.H. edition of at-Tabari's voluminous Tarikh published by Al-Ameera house for publication and distribution of Beirut, Lebanon. He would like to quote *ver batim* what pp. 160-61 of Vol. 3 of this edition states with regard to Othman's burial:

نبذ عثمان ثلاثة أيام لا يدفن، ثم ان حكيم بن حزام القرشي ثم أحد بني أسد بن عبد العزى، و جبير بن مطعم بن عدي بن نوفل بن عبد مناف، كلما عليا في دفنه، و طلبا اليه أن يأذن لأهله في ذلك، ففعل، و أذن لهم علي، فلما سمع بذلك قعدوا له في الطريق بالحجارة، و خرج به ناس من أهله، و هم يريدون به حائطا بالمدينة، يقال له حش كوكب، كانت اليهود تدفن فيه موتاهم، فلما خرج به على الناس رجموا سريره، و هموا بطرحه، فبلغ ذلك عليا، فأرسل الى الناس يعزم عليه ليكفن عنه، ففعلوا، فانطلق حتى دفن في حش كوكب، فلما ظهر معاوية بن أبي سفيان على الناس أمر بهدم ذلك الحائط حتى أفضى به الى البقيع، و أمر الناس أن يدفنوا موتاهم حول قبره حتى اتصل ذلك بمقابر المسلمين.

The translation of this text is as follows:

"[The corpse of] Othman remained for three days without being buried. Then Hakeem ibn Hizam al-Qarashi (from the Quraish tribe)

436

and one of the offspring of Banu Asad ibn Abd al-Uzza, as well as Jubair ibn Mut'im ibn Adiyy ibn Nawfal ibn Abd Munaf, spoke with [then caliph] Ali (ع) about burying him, requesting him to permit his [Othman's] family to bury him, which he did. Ali (ع) permitted them. When people heard about it, they lurked in the streets with rocks in their hands. Some people from among Othman's family came out with his corpse and wanted to go to a wall in Medīna called Hash Kawkab where the Jews used to bury their dead. When people saw it [Othman's coffin], they pelted his coffin and were about to throw the body down. Ali (ع) came to know about it, so he sent a message to people to leave the corpse alone and not expose it to their harm, which they did. It was taken out till it was buried at Hash Kawkab. When Mu'awiya ascended to power, he ordered that wall to be demolished, joining its area with that of the Baqee`. He ordered people to bury their dead around his [Othman's] grave till the graves connected with the Muslims' graves."

These details and more are also narrated in Ibn al-Atheer's *Al-Kāmil* and in Ibn al-A'tham's *Tarikh*, in addition to the *Isti'ab* of Ibn Abd al-Birr. On the same page of the latter reference (p. 80, Vol. 3), the author indicates that Othman's body did not receive the ceremonial bathing and that he was shrouded in the same clothes which he was wearing when he was killed. Perhaps this much suffices to give the reader an idea about how angry people were with Othman and with the men whom he chose to run their affairs, plunder the state treasury and spread iniquity throughout the Muslim world.

Anyway, let us go back to Abū Hurayra who died after having enjoyed pomp and power. He was an indigent man whose lineage and tribal origins were not known to anybody. He had no kinship to Quraish. Despite all of this, the caliph's sons, who were in charge of running the affairs during Mu`awiyah's reign, took to bearing his corpse and to burying it at the Baqee`...! Let us now examine Abū Hurayra's attitude towards the Prophet's Sunna.

In his *Sahīh*, al-Bukhāri quotes Abū Hurayra saying, "I learned the fill of two receptacles [of *ahadīth*] from the Messenger of Allāh: I have disseminated only one of them; as for the other, if I disseminate it, this throat will be slit."[2]

---

[2]Al-Bukhari, *Sahīh*, Vol. 1, p. 38, in a chapter dealing with learning.

Here is Abū Hurayra revealing what erstwhile is hidden, admitting that the only traditions he quoted were the ones that pleased the ruling authorities. Building upon this premise, Abū Hurayra used to have two pouches, or two receptacles, as he called them. He used to disseminate the contents of one of them, the one which we have discussed here that contains whatever the rulers desired. As for the other, which Abū Hurayra kept to himself and whose *ahadīth* he did not narrate for fear his throat would be slit, it is the one containing the authentic traditions of the Prophet. Had Abū Hurayra been a reliable authority, he would have never hidden true *ahadīth* while disseminating illusions and lies only to support the oppressor, knowing that Allāh curses whoever hides the clear evidence.

Al-Bukhāri quotes him saying once, "People say that Abū Hurayra narrates too many *ahadīth*. Had it not been for two [particular] verses in the Book of Allāh, I would not have narrated a single hadīth: `Those who conceal what We have revealed of clear proofs and the guidance, after Our having clarified [everything] for people in the Book, these it is whom Allāh shall curse, and those who curse shall curse them, too' (Qur'ān, 2:159). Our brethren from the Muhajirun used to be busy consigning transactions at the market-place, while our brethren from the Ansār used to be busy doing business with their own money, while Abū Hurayra kept in the shadow of the Prophet in order to satisfy his hunger, attending what they did not attend, learning what they did not learn."[1]

How can Abū Hurayra say that had it not been for a couple of verses in the Book of Allāh, he would not have narrated a single *hadīth*, then he says, "I learned two receptacles [of *ahadīth*] from the Messenger of Allāh: I have disseminated one of them; as for the other, if I disseminate it, this throat will be slit"?! Is this not his admission of having concealed the truth despite both verses in the Book of Allāh?!

Had the Prophet not said to his companions, "Go back to your people and teach them"?[2] Had he not also said, "One who conveys is

---

[1]*Ibid.*, Vol. 1, p. 37.

[2]Al-Bukhari, *Sahīh*, Vol. 1, p. 30.

more aware than one who hears"? Al-Bukhāri states that the Prophet urged the deputation of `Abd Qays to learn belief and scholarship "... then convey what you learn to those whom you have left behind," as we read in the same reference. Can we help wondering: Why should the throat of a *sahabi* be slit if he quotes the Prophet (ﺹ)?! There must be a secret here which the caliphs do not wish others to know. Here, we would like to briefly say that "the people of the remembrance" was [a phrase in] a Qur'ānic verse revealed to refer to Ali's succession to the Prophet.

Abū Hurayra is not to blame; he knew his own worth and testified against his own soul that Allāh cursed him, and so did those who curse, for having hidden the Prophet's *hadīth*. But the blame is on those who call Abū Hurayra the narrator of the Sunnah while he himself testifies that he hid it then testifies that he fabricated it and told lies in its regard, then he further goes on to testify that it became confused for him, so he could not tell which one was the statement of the Prophet and which one was made by others. All of these *ahadīth* and correct admissions are recorded in al-Bukhāri's *Sahīh* and in other authentic books of *hadīth*.

How can anyone feel comfortable about a man whose justice was doubted by the Commander of the Faithful Ali ibn Abū Tālib who charged him with lying, saying that among the living, nobody told more lies about the Prophet than Abū Hurayra?! Omer ibn al-Khattab, too, charged him of the same; he beat him and threatened to expel him. Āisha doubted his integrity and many times called him a liar, and many other *sahāba* cast doubts about his accuracy and rejected his contradictory *ahadīth*, so he would once admit his error and would sometimes prattle in Ethiopian.[1] A large number of Muslim scholars refuted his traditions and charged him with lying, fabricating, and throwing himself at Mu`awiyah's dinner tables, at his coffers of gold and silver.

Is it right, then, for Abū Hurayra to become "Islam's narrator" from

---

[1]Abu Hurayra was bilingual. He spoke Arabic (his mother tongue) and Amharic. Historically speaking, during Abū Hurayra's time, Amheric was the language of "aristocrats" due to the fact that the Ethiopians had for many years colonized Yemen till they were kicked out of it at the hands of Sayf ibn Thi Yazun (or Yazin), Himyar's king who died in 574 A.D.

whom the religion's injunctions are learned?

Judaica and Jewish doctrines have filled the books of *hadīth*. Ka`b al-Ahbar, a Jew, may have succeeded in getting such doctrines and beliefs included into the books of *hadīth*, hence we find traditions likening or personifying Allāh, as well as the theory of incarnation, in addition to many abominable statements about the prophets and messengers of Allāh: all of these are cited through Abū Hurayra.

Mu'awiya was succeeded by his corrupt and equally sinner Yazid who is famous for staging the Kerbalā massacre of the immediate fāmily, relatives and some supporters of Imām Hussain son of Ali son of Abū Tālib, peace be with them all. The Imām felt obligated to rise against Yazid due to the depths to which the Islamic faith was driven at the hands of Yazid and his father Mu'awiyah, preferring to be martyred rather than endorse Yazid's illegitimate appointment as the "commander of the faithful" imposed on the Muslims. Full details can be found in my book titled *Kerbalā and Beyond* and in many other books written on the Kerbalā epic of heroism to which I would like to refer the seeker of the truth. In order to demonstrate to the reader how hostile Yazid was not only to Imām Hussain but also to his father and grandfather, the Prophet of Islam (ص), I would like to quote here verses of poetry which demonstrate this hostility:

كان يزيد جالسا في منظرة على "جيرون"، و لما رأى السبايا و الرؤوس على أطراف الرماح و قد أشرفوا على ثنية جيرون نعب غراب فأنشأ يزيد يقول:

تلك الرؤوس على شفا جيرون	لما بدت تلك الحمول و أشرقت
فقد اقتضيت من الرسول ديوني	نعب الغراب فقلت: قل أو لا تقل

Yazid was sitting at a surveillance outpost overlooking Jerun Mountain when he saw the captives with the severed heads planted atop spears as their throng came close and a crow croaked, so he composed these lines of poetry:

When those conveyances drew nigh
And the heads on the edge of Jerun,
The crow croaked, so said I:
"Say whatever you wish to say

440

"Or say nothing at all,
"From the Messenger have I today
"What he owed me he did repay."

Notice the last couple of verses and how Yazid considered the Prophet (ص) as owing him, and how what he did to Imām Hussain (ع) was the "repayment" of that debt! An in-depth study of what Yazid had in mind will take the reader back to the Battle of Badr in which many relatives of Mu'awiyah were killed, so the Umayyads were hostile to Islam and Muslims, including the Prophet (ص) himself, since then, and their actions prove that they really never accepted Islam wholeheartedly, and their offspring, who exist among us, in our time never will.

Fitra فطره: the amount (in cash or kind) paid to the needy at the end of the month of Ramadan; see text on this topic in my book titled *Fast of the Month of Ramadan: Philosophy and Ahkam* for more details. Another meaning for this word, فطرة, is: nature, the human nature, the way the Almighty created it

Fuqaha' فقهاء: plural of *faqih*, jurist

Furoo' or Furu' فروع: branches (of the faith, teaching, tree, company or anything else)

غ G, Gh

Ghadeer or Ghadīr غدير: pool, shallow water lake. The most famous shallow water lake in history is Gahdir Khumm, the place where the Prophet of Islam (ص) delivered a famous speech, nominating Ali ibn Abū Tālib (ع) as his successor.

Ghadīr Khumm غدير خم: Non-Muslims who like to attack Islam accuse the Prophet of Islam of having neglected to name his successor, not knowing that he actually did exactly so in accordance with the Divine order which he had received on Thul-Hijja 17, 10 A.H./March 18, 632 A.D., announcing the name of his successor the very next day, and here are the details:

441

In 10 A.H./632 A.D., immediately following *Hijjatul-Wada'* حجة الوداع (the Farewell Pilgrimage, the last pilgrimage performed by Prophet Mohammed), a divine order was revealed to the Prophet to convey the remaining Islamic tenets: the annual pilgrimage to Mecca and the Imāmate of the Twelve Infallible Imāms. The Prophet called upon the faithful to accompany him on his last pilgrimage; he knew that it would be his last and that he would soon have to leave this temporary abode for the eternal one. More than one hundred and twenty thousand Muslims responded to his call.

The Prophet and his company put on the ihram garbs at the appropriate time at Masjid ash-Shajara, a short distance from Mecca, his birthplace, which he entered on Thul-Hijja 5, 10 A.H./March 6, 632 A.D. The Prophet's call reached Yemen where Ali ibn Abū Tālib (ع) was acting as his representative. Twelve thousand Yemenite pilgrims came out headed by Ali in response to the Prophet's call to accompany him on his historic Pilgrimage, bringing the total number of those early pilgrims to more than one hundred and thirty-two thousand.

The Islamic pilgrimage starts in the month of Thul-Hijja (month of the pilgrimage), the last Islamic lunar calendar month, and continues for at least ten days. First, each pilgrim dons a special garb called ihram; males' *ihram* احرام consists of two white sheets or towels covering the upper and lower parts of the body, whereas females wear a full white cotton outfit, simple and modest. This ihram reminds the pilgrim of his/her death and of the equality of all before God. All pilgrims perform the same rituals; none receives any favorable treatment or distinction on account of his status, power, or wealth. The pilgrimage starts by the *tawaf*, the circling of the Ka'ba seven times. The Ka'ba is identified in Islamic literature as an earthly counterpart to the Almighty's Throne ('Arsh) in heaven where the angels circle it in adoration. Likewise, in imitation of those angels, Muslim pilgrims circle the Ka'ba in adoration of their Lord. The *tawaf* طواف is followed by the *Sa'i* سعي: the pilgrims run back and forth seven times between the -Safa and the Marwa in commemoration of Hagar (Hajar), mother of Ishmael, frantically searching for water for her newborn son Ishmael. After that, the pilgrims drink of the well of Zamzam which had appeared

442

miraculously for Hagar and Ishmael, wash with it or use it to make ablution for prayers at the Ka'ba but never to use it in the toilet; Zamzam is too sacred for such an application. Then the pilgrims leave Mecca for Muzdalifa, 'Arafa, and finally Mina to perform certain rites which fall outside the scope of this book which is intended to be a historical account of the Prophet of Islam, not one of *fiqh*. The author is a writer, a researcher, someone who, according to a friend of mine, "insists on finding out who the foundling's father is!" But he is not a faqih. Now let us go back to our original story after having cast a glimpse at the rite of the pilgrimage in Islam.

It was at Arafa that the divine command was received by Prophet Muhammed to appoint 'Ali as "Ameerul-Mo'mineen," أمـيـر المـؤمنيـن *the* Commander of the Faithful, title of the bearer of the highest temporal and religious powers in the Islamic State, one reserved solely for caliphs, those who are supposed to be the most knowledgeable of all people of secular and religious problems and of how to solve them. Muhammed was also ordered to convey to Ali the knowledge which the Almighty had bestowed upon him so that it would not be lost once he is dead. In Mina, the Prophet delivered two sermons in preparation for the great announcement to come. In the first, he referred to Ali's caliphate and reminded the audience of one particular *hadīth* which he had conveyed to them on various occasions and which is identified in books of *hadīth* as "*hadīth at-Thaqalain* حديث الثّقلين", tradition of the two weighty things (the first being the Holy Quran and the second being the Prophet's Progeny, the" Ahl al-Bayt" mentioned in verse 33 of Chapter 33 [al-Ahzab] of the Holy Qur'ān). He delivered his second sermon at Masjid al-Khaif, also located in Mina in the Meccan valley. In it, the Prophet reminded his audience of Ali's Imāmate, emphasizing the necessity of disseminating the contents of his sermon, announcing that those present were duty-bound to convey it to those who were absent. In both of these sermons, the Prophet publicly vested upon Ali both powers referred to above.

As soon as the rituals of the pilgrimage were completed, and to be exact on Thul-Hijja 17, 10 A.H./March 18, 632 A.D., the divine order came to the Prophet embedded in verse 67 of Chapter 5 (al-Ma'ida) quoted in the text of the Prophet's sermon to follow. The

Prophet immediately ordered Bilal ibn Rabah, his caller to prayers and one of his faithful *sahāba* صحابه, to convey the following order to the faithful: "Tomorrow, nobody should lag behind but should go to Ghadīr Khumm غدير خم."

The word "Ghadīr" means "swamp," an area where rain water gathers to form a shallow lake. Ghadīr Khumm is located near the crossroads of trade and pilgrimage caravans coming from Medīna, Egypt, Iraq, Syria, and Nejd on their way to Mecca. The presence of water and a few old trees there served as a resting place for trade caravans for centuries. A mosque, called Masjid al-Ghadīr, was later built on the same spot where the great gathering took place to commemorate that momentous event, an event which has unfortunately been forgotten by the vast majority of the Muslims who, by thus forgetting, forgot the most important part of their creed, one without which their faith is not complete at all according to the Prophet's sermon to follow and according to the text of the Holy Qur'ān...

The announcement conveyed by Bilal was transmitted by one person to another till it reached as far as Mecca proper, and people were wondering about what it could be. They had expected the Prophet to linger a little bit longer at Mecca where the pilgrims could meet him and ask him whatever questions they had about this new institution called "hajj" and about other religious matters.

In the morning of the next day, Thul-Hijja 18, 10 A.H./March 19, 632A.D., the Prophet and his 120,000 companions went to Ghadīr Khumm غدير خم, and so didAli with his 12,000 Yemenite pilgrims who had to change their route to the north instead of to the south where they would be home-bound. The Prophet also issued an order to four of his closest *sahāba*, namely Selman-al-Farisi, Abū Tharr al-Ghifāri, Miqdad ibn al-Aswad al-Kindi andAmmar ibn yasir, with whom the reader is already familiar, to clear the area where the old trees stood, to uproot the thorn bushes, collect the rocks and stones, and to clean the place and sprinkle it with water. Then these men took a piece of cloth which they tied between two of those trees, thus providing some shade. The Prophet told those *sahāba* that a ceremony that would last for three continuous days would be held in that area. Then the same men piled the rocks on top of each other and made a makeshift pulpit over them of camel litters as high as the Prophet's own length. They put another piece of cloth on the pulpit which was installed in the middle of the crowd, giving the Prophet an overview of the whole gathering. A man was selected to repeat loudly what the Prophet was saying so that those who stood the furthermost would not miss a word.

The *athan* أذان for the noon prayers was recited, and the congregational (*jama'a*) صلاة الجماعة prayers were led by the Prophet. After that, the Prophet ascended the pulpit and signaled to Ali ibn Abū Tālib (ع) to stand on his right. Ali did so, standing one pulpit step below the Prophet. Before saying anything, the Prophet looked right and left to make sure that people were prepared to listen to every word of his. The sun was so hot that people had to pull some of their outer mantles over their heads and under their feet in order to be able to somehow tolerate the heat. Finally the Prophet delivered his historic sermon which he intended, as the reader will see, to be not only for the assembled crowd but for all those who were not present at that gathering and for all their offspring, one generation after another, till the Day of Judgment.

Here is the text of the Prophet's sermon. We hope it will bring the reader guidance in the life of this world and happiness and success in the life to come through the intercession of Muhammed, the one loved most by Allāh, peace and blessings of the Almighty be upon him, his progeny, and true companions who obeyed him during his lifetime and after his demise and who did not forget or pretend to forget his following *khutba* (sermon):

PROPHET'S HISTORIC GHADĪR SERMON:
Below is the original Arabic text of this great sermon and below it you will find a humble translation by the author of this book. The text and translation were published through efforts of Darul-Salam Center in Annandale, Virginia, United States of America, in Thul-Hijja 1419/March 1999 when the author of this book was still living in the U.S. A copy of this translation is posted on the Internet, too. Here is the original Arabic text of this sermon:

نص خطبة الغدير المباركة

بِسْمِ اللهِ الرَّحْمَنِ الرَّحِيمِ

الحمد والثناء : الْحَمْدُ للهِ الَّذِي عَلاَ فِي تَوَحُّدِهِ وَدَنَا فِي تَفَرُّدِهِ وَجَلَّ فِي سُلْطانِهِ وَعَظُمَ فِي أَرْكانِهِ، وَأَحاطَ بِكُلِّ شَيْءٍ عِلْماً وَهُوَ فِي مَكانِهِ، وَقَهَرَ جَمِيعَ الْخَلْقِ بِقُدْرَتِهِ وَبُرْهانِهِ، مَجِيداً لَمْ يَزَلْ، مَحْمُوداً لاَ يَزَالُ. بارِئُ الْمَسْمُوكاتِ وَداحِي الْمَدْحُوّاتِ وَجَبّارُ الأرَضِينَ وَالسَّماواتِ، قُدُّوسٌ سُبُّوحٌ، رَبُّ الْمَلائِكَةِ وَالرُّوحِ، مُتَفَضِّلٌ عَلَى جَمِيعِ مَنْ بَرَأَهُ، مُتَطَوِّلٌ عَلَى جَمِيعِ مَنْ أَنْشَأَهُ. يَلْحَظُ كُلَّ عَيْنٍ وَالْعُيُونُ لاَ تَراهُ. كَرِيمٌ حَلِيمٌ ذُو أَناةٍ، قَدْ وَسِعَ كُلَّ شَيْءٍ رَحْمَتُهُ وَمَنَّ عَلَيْهِمْ بِنِعْمَتِهِ. لاَ يَعْجَلُ بِانْتِقامِهِ، وَلاَ يُبادِرُ إِلَيْهِمْ بِما اسْتَحَقُّوا مِنْ عَذابِهِ. قَدْ فَهِمَ السَّرائِرَ وَعَلِمَ الضَّمائِرَ، وَلَمْ تَخْفَ عَلَيْهِ الْمَكْنُوناتُ وَلاَ اشْتَبَهَتْ عَلَيْهِ الْخَفِيّاتُ. لَهُ الإِحاطَةُ بِكُلِّ شَيْءٍ، وَالْغَلَبَةُ عَلَى كُلِّ شَيْءٍ، وَالْقُوَّةُ فِي كُلِّ شَيْءٍ، وَالْقُدْرَةُ عَلَى كُلِّ شَيْءٍ، وَلَيْسَ مِثْلَهُ شَيْءٌ. وَهُوَ مُنْشِئُ الشَّيْءِ حِينَ لاَ شَيْءَ. دائِمٌ قائِمٌ بِالْقِسْطِ، لاَ إِلهَ إِلاَّ هُوَ الْعَزِيزُ الْحَكِيمُ. جَلَّ عَنْ أَنْ تُدْرِكَهُ الأبْصارُ وَهُوَ يُدْرِكُ الأبْصارَ وَهُوَ اللَّطِيفُ الْخَبِيرُ. لاَ يَلْحَقُ أَحَدٌ وَصْفَهُ مِنْ مُعايَنَةٍ، وَلاَ يَجِدُ أَحَدٌ كَيْفَ هُوَ مِنْ سِرٍّ وَعَلانِيَةٍ إِلاَّ بِما دَلَّ عَزَّ وَجَلَّ عَلَى نَفْسِهِ. وَأَشْهَدُ أَنَّهُ اللهُ الَّذِي مَلأ الدَّهْرَ قُدْسُهُ، وَالَّذِي يَغْشَى الأبَدَ نُورُهُ، وَالَّذِي يُنْفِذُ أَمْرَهُ بِلا مُشاوَرَةِ مُشِيرٍ، وَلاَ مَعَهُ شَرِيكٌ فِي تَقْدِيرٍ۞ وَلاَ يُعاوَنُ فِي تَدْبِيرٍ۞. صَوَّرَ ما ابْتَدَعَ عَلَى غَيْرِ مِثالٍ، وَخَلَقَ ما خَلَقَ بِلا مَعُونَةٍ مِنْ أَحَدٍ وَلاَ تَكَلُّفٍ وَلاَ احْتِيالٍ. أَنْشَأَها فَكانَتْ، وَبَرَأَها فَبانَتْ. فَهُوَ اللهُ الَّذِي لاَ إِلهَ إِلاَّ هُوَ الْمُتْقِنُ الصَّنْعَةِ، الْحَسَنُ الصَّنِيعَةُ، الْعَدْلُ الَّذِي لاَ يَجُورُ، وَالأكْرَمُ الَّذِي تَرْجِعُ إِلَيْهِ الأمُورُ. وَأَشْهَدُ أَنَّهُ الَّذِي تَواضَعَ كُلُّ شَيْءٍ لِقُدْرَتِهِ، وَخَضَعَ كُلُّ شَيْءٍ لِهَيْبَتِهِ. مَلِكُ الأمْلاكِ وَمُفَلِّكُ الأفْلاكِ وَمُسَخِّرُ الشَّمْسِ وَالْقَمَرِ، كُلٌّ يَجْرِي لأجَلٍ مُسَمّى. يُكَوِّرُ اللَّيْلَ عَلَى النَّهارِ وَيُكَوِّرُ النَّهارَ عَلَى اللَّيْلِ يَطْلُبُهُ حَثِيثاً. قاصِمُ كُلِّ جَبّارٍ عَنِيدٍ، وَمُهْلِكُ كُلِّ شَيْطانٍ مَرِيدٍ. لَمْ يَكُنْ مَعَهُ ضِدٌّ وَلاَ نِدٌّ، أَحَدٌ صَمَدٌ لَمْ يَلِدْ وَلَمْ يُولَدْ وَلَمْ يَكُنْ لَهُ كُفُواً أَحَدٌ. إِلهٌ واحِدٌ وَرَبٌّ ماجِدٌ، يَشاءُ فَيُمْضِي، وَيُرِيدُ فَيَقْضِي، وَيَعْلَمُ فَيُحْصِي، وَيُمِيتُ وَيُحْيِي، وَيُفْقِرُ وَيُغْنِي، وَيُضْحِكُ وَيُبْكِي، وَيَمْنَعُ وَيُعْطِي، لَهُ الْمُلْكُ وَلَهُ الْحَمْدُ، بِيَدِهِ الْخَيْرُ وَهُوَ عَلَى كُلِّ شَيْءٍ قَدِيرٌ. يُولِجُ اللَّيْلَ فِي النَّهارِ وَيُولِجُ النَّهارَ فِي اللَّيْلِ، لاَ إِلهَ إِلاَّ هُوَ الْعَزِيزُ الْغَفّارُ. مُجِيبُ الدُّعاءِ وَمُجْزِلُ الْعَطاءِ، مُحْصِي الأنْفاسِ وَرَبُّ الْجِنَّةِ وَالنّاسِ، لاَ يُشْكِلُ عَلَيْهِ شَيْءٌ، وَلاَ يُضْجِرُهُ صُراخُ الْمُسْتَصْرِخِينَ وَلاَ يُبْرِمُهُ إِلْحاحُ الْمُلِحِّينَ. الْعاصِمُ لِلصّالِحِينَ، وَالْمُوَفِّقُ لِلْمُفْلِحِينَ، وَمَوْلَى الْعالَمِينَ. الَّذِي اسْتَحَقَّ مِنْ كُلِّ مَنْ خَلَقَ أَنْ يَشْكُرَهُ وَيَحْمَدَهُ. أَحْمَدُهُ عَلَى السَّرّاءِ وَالضَّرّاءِ وَالشِّدَّةِ وَالرَّخاءِ وَأُومِنُ بِهِ وَبِمَلائِكَتِهِ وَكُتُبِهِ وَرُسُلِهِ. أَسْمَعُ لأمْرِهِ وَأُطِيعُ وَأُبادِرُ إِلَى كُلِّ ما يَرْضاهُ، وَأَسْتَسْلِمُ لِقَضائِهِ، رَغْبَةً فِي طاعَتِهِ وَخَوْفاً مِنْ عُقُوبَتِهِ، لأنَّهُ اللهُ الَّذِي لاَ يُؤْمَنُ مَكْرُهُ وَلاَ يُخافُ جَوْرُهُ.

أمر الهي في موضوع هام

وَأُقِرُّ لَهُ عَلَى نَفْسِي بِالْعُبُودِيَّةِ وَأَشْهَدُ لَهُ بِالرُّبُوبِيَّةِ، وَأُؤَدِّي ما أَوْحَى إِلَيَّ حَذَراً مِنْ أَنْ لاَ أَفْعَلَ فَتَحِلَّ بِي مِنْهُ قارِعَةٌ لاَ يَدْفَعُها عَنِّي أَحَدٌ وَإِنْ عَظُمَتْ حِيلَتُهُ؛ لاَ إِلهَ إِلاَّ هُوَ. لأنَّهُ قَدْ أَعْلَمَنِي أَنِّي إِنْ لَمْ أُبَلِّغْ ما أَنْزَلَ إِلَيَّ فَما بَلَّغْتُ رِسالَتَهُ، وَقَدْ ضَمِنَ لِي تَبارَكَ وَتَعالَى

446

العِصْمَةَ وَهُوَ اللهُ الكَافِي الكَرِيمَ. فَأَوْحَى إِلَيَّ: (بِسْمِ اللهِ الرَّحْمَنِ الرَّحِيمِ، يَا أَيُّهَا الرَّسُولُ بَلِّغْ مَا أُنْزِلَ إِلَيْكَ مِنْ رَبِّكَ ـ فِي عَلِيٍّ يَعْنِي فِي الخِلَافَةِ لِعَلِيِّ بْنِ أَبِي طَالِبٍ ـ وَإِنْ لَمْ تَفْعَلْ فَمَا بَلَّغْتَ رِسَالَتَهُ وَاللهُ يَعْصِمُكَ مِنَ النَّاسِ). مَعَاشِرَ النَّاسِ، مَا قَصَّرْتُ فِي تَبْلِيغِ مَا أَنْزَلَ اللهُ تَعَالَى إِلَيَّ وَأَنَا مُبَيِّنٌ لَكُمْ سَبَبَ نُزُولِ هَذِهِ الآيَةِ: إِنَّ جِبْرَئِيلَ عَلَيْهِ السَّلَامُ هَبَطَ إِلَيَّ مِرَاراً ثَلَاثاً يَأْمُرُنِي عَنِ السَّلَامِ رَبِّي ـ وَهُوَ السَّلَامُ ـ أَنْ أَقُومَ فِي هَذَا الْمَشْهَدِ فَأُعْلِمَ كُلَّ أَبْيَضَ وَأَسْوَدَ: أَنَّ عَلِيَّ بْنَ أَبِي طَالِبٍ أَخِي وَوَصِيِّي وَخَلِيفَتِي وَالإِمَامُ مِنْ بَعْدِي، الَّذِي مَحَلُّهُ مِنِّي مَحَلُّ هَارُونَ مِنْ مُوسَى إِلَّا أَنَّهُ لَا نَبِيَّ بَعْدِي وَهُوَ وَلِيُّكُمْ بَعْدَ اللهِ وَرَسُولِهِ. وَقَدْ أَنْزَلَ اللهُ تَبَارَكَ وَتَعَالَى عَلَيَّ بِذَلِكَ آيَةً مِنْ كِتَابِهِ: (إِنَّمَا وَلِيُّكُمُ اللهُ وَرَسُولُهُ وَالَّذِينَ آمَنُوا الَّذِينَ يُقِيمُونَ الصَّلَاةَ وَيُؤْتُونَ الزَّكَاةَ وَهُمْ رَاكِعُونَ)، وَعَلِيُّ بْنُ أَبِي طَالِبٍ أَقَامَ الصَّلَاةَ وَآتَى الزَّكَاةَ وَهُوَ رَاكِعٌ يُرِيدُ اللهَ عَزَّ وَجَلَّ فِي كُلِّ حَالٍ. وَسَأَلْتُ جِبْرَئِيلَ أَنْ يَسْتَعْفِيَ لِيَ عَنْ تَبْلِيغِ ذَلِكَ إِلَيْكُمْ ـ أَيُّهَا النَّاسُ ـ لِعِلْمِي بِقِلَّةِ الْمُتَّقِينَ وَكَثْرَةِ الْمُنَافِقِينَ وَإِدْغَالِ الآثِمِينَ وَحِيَلِ الْمُسْتَهْزِئِينَ بِالإِسْلَامِ، الَّذِينَ وَصَفَهُمُ اللهُ فِي كِتَابِهِ بِأَنَّهُمْ يَقُولُونَ بِأَلْسِنَتِهِمْ مَا لَيْسَ فِي قُلُوبِهِمْ، وَيَحْسَبُونَهُ هَيِّناً وَهُوَ عِنْدَ اللهِ عَظِيمٌ، وَكَثْرَةِ أَذَاهُمْ لِي غَيْرَ مَرَّةٍ، حَتَّى سَمُّونِي أُذُناً وَزَعَمُوا أَنِّي كَذَلِكَ لِكَثْرَةِ مُلَازَمَتِهِ إِيَّايَ وَإِقْبَالِي عَلَيْهِ، حَتَّى أَنْزَلَ اللهُ عَزَّ وَجَلَّ فِي ذَلِكَ قُرْآناً: (وَمِنْهُمُ الَّذِينَ يُؤْذُونَ النَّبِيَّ وَيَقُولُونَ هُوَ أُذُنٌ، قُلْ أُذُنٌ ـ عَلَى الَّذِينَ يَزْعُمُونَ أَنَّهُ أُذُنٌ ـ خَيْرٌ لَكُمْ، يُؤْمِنُ بِاللهِ وَيُؤْمِنُ لِلْمُؤْمِنِينَ). وَلَوْ شِئْتُ أَنْ أُسَمِّيَ بِأَسْمَائِهِمْ لَسَمَّيْتُ، وَأَنْ أُومِيَ إِلَيْهِمْ بِأَعْيَانِهِمْ لأَوْمَأْتُ، وَأَنْ أَدُلَّ عَلَيْهِمْ لَدَلَلْتُ، وَلَكِنِّي وَاللهِ فِي أُمُورِهِمْ قَدْ تَكَرَّمْتُ. وَكُلُّ ذَلِكَ لَا يَرْضَى اللهُ مِنِّي إِلَّا أَنْ أُبَلِّغَ مَا أُنْزِلَ إِلَيَّ. ثُمَّ تَلَا صَلَّى اللهُ عَلَيْهِ وَآلِهِ: (يَا أَيُّهَا الرَّسُولُ بَلِّغْ مَا أُنْزِلَ إِلَيْكَ مِنْ رَبِّكَ ـ فِي عَلِيٍّ ـ وَإِنْ لَمْ تَفْعَلْ فَمَا بَلَّغْتَ رِسَالَتَهُ وَاللهُ يَعْصِمُكَ مِنَ النَّاسِ).

الاعلان الرسمي بأمامة الأئمة الاثني عشر (عليهم السلام) وولايتهم

فَاعْلَمُوا مَعَاشِرَ النَّاسِ أَنَّ اللهَ قَدْ نَصَبَهُ لَكُمْ وَلِيّاً وَإِمَاماً مُفْتَرَضاً طَاعَتُهُ عَلَى الْمُهَاجِرِينَ وَالأَنْصَارِ وَعَلَى التَّابِعِينَ لَهُمْ بِإِحْسَانٍ، وَعَلَى الْبَادِي وَالْحَاضِرِ، وَعَلَى الأَعْجَمِيِّ وَالْعَرَبِيِّ، وَالْحُرِّ وَالْمَمْلُوكِ، وَالصَّغِيرِ وَالْكَبِيرِ، وَعَلَى الأَبْيَضِ وَالأَسْوَدِ، وَعَلَى كُلِّ مُوَحِّدٍ. مَاضٍ حُكْمُهُ، جَازٍ قَوْلُهُ، نَافِذٌ أَمْرُهُ، مَلْعُونٌ مَنْ خَالَفَهُ، مَرْحُومٌ مَنْ تَبِعَهُ، مُؤْمِنٌ مَنْ صَدَّقَهُ، فَقَدْ غَفَرَ اللهُ لَهُ وَلِمَنْ سَمِعَ مِنْهُ وَأَطَاعَ لَهُ. مَعَاشِرَ النَّاسِ، إِنَّهُ آخِرُ مَقَامٍ أَقُومُهُ فِي هَذَا الْمَشْهَدِ، فَاسْمَعُوا وَأَطِيعُوا وَانْقَادُوا لأَمْرِ رَبِّكُمْ، فَإِنَّ اللهَ عَزَّ وَجَلَّ هُوَ مَوْلَاكُمْ وَإِلَهُكُمْ، ثُمَّ مِنْ دُونِهِ مُحَمَّدٌ[1] وَلِيُّكُمُ الْقَائِمُ الْمُخَاطِبُ لَكُمْ، ثُمَّ مِنْ بَعْدِي عَلِيٌّ وَلِيُّكُمْ وَإِمَامُكُمْ بِأَمْرِ رَبِّكُمْ، ثُمَّ الإِمَامَةُ فِي ذُرِّيَّتِي مِنْ وُلْدِهِ إِلَى يَوْمِ تَلْقَوْنَ اللهَ وَرَسُولَهُ. لَا حَلَالَ إِلَّا مَا أَحَلَّهُ اللهُ، وَلَا حَرَامَ إِلَّا مَا حَرَّمَهُ اللهُ، عَرَّفَنِي الْحَلَالَ وَالْحَرَامَ وَأَنَا أَفْضَيْتُ بِمَا عَلَّمَنِي رَبِّي مِنْ كِتَابِهِ وَحَلَالِهِ وَحَرَامِهِ إِلَيْهِ. مَعَاشِرَ النَّاسِ، مَا مِنْ عِلْمٍ إِلَّا وَقَدْ أَحْصَاهُ اللهُ فِيَّ، وَكُلُّ عِلْمٍ عُلِمْتُ فَقَدْ أَحْصَيْتُهُ فِي إِمَامِ الْمُتَّقِينَ، وَمَا مِنْ عِلْمٍ إِلَّا عَلَّمْتُهُ عَلِيّاً، وَهُوَ الإِمَامُ الْمُبِينُ. مَعَاشِرَ النَّاسِ، لَا تَضِلُّوا عَنْهُ وَلَا تَنْفِرُوا مِنْهُ، وَلَا تَسْتَنْكِفُوا مِنْ وِلَايَتِهِ، فَهُوَ الَّذِي يَهْدِي إِلَى الْحَقِّ وَيَعْمَلُ بِهِ، وَيُزْهِقُ الْبَاطِلَ وَيَنْهَى عَنْهُ، وَلَا يَأْخُذُهُ فِي اللهِ لَوْمَةُ لَائِمٍ. ثُمَّ إِنَّهُ أَوَّلُ مَنْ آمَنَ بِاللهِ وَرَسُولِهِ، وَهُوَ الَّذِي فَدَى رَسُولَهُ بِنَفْسِهِ، وَهُوَ الَّذِي كَانَ مَعَ رَسُولِ اللهِ وَلَا أَحَدَ يَعْبُدُ اللهَ مَعَ رَسُولِهِ مِنَ الرِّجَالِ غَيْرُهُ. مَعَاشِرَ النَّاسِ، فَضِّلُوهُ فَقَدْ فَضَّلَهُ اللهُ، وَاقْبَلُوهُ فَقَدْ نَصَبَهُ اللهُ. مَعَاشِرَ النَّاسِ، إِنَّهُ إِمَامٌ مِنَ اللهِ، وَلَنْ يَتُوبَ اللهُ عَلَى أَحَدٍ أَنْكَرَ وِلَايَتَهُ وَلَنْ يَغْفِرَ

447

لَهُ، حَتْماً عَلَى اللهِ أَنْ يَفْعَلَ ذَلِكَ بِمَنْ خَالَفَ أَمْرَهُ فِيهِ وَأَنْ يُعَذِّبَهُ عَذَاباً شَدِيداً نُكْراً أَبَدَ الآبَادِ وَدَهْرَ الدُّهُورِ. فَاحْذَرُوا أَنْ تُخَالِفُوهُ، فَتَصْلُوا نَاراً وَقُودُهَا النَّاسُ وَالْحِجَارَةُ أُعِدَّتْ لِلْكَافِرِينَ. أَيُّهَا النَّاسُ، بِي وَاللهِ بَشَّرَ الأَوَّلُونَ مِنَ النَّبِيِّينَ وَالْمُرْسَلِينَ، وَأَنَا خَاتَمُ الأَنْبِيَاءِ وَالْمُرْسَلِينَ وَالْحُجَّةُ عَلَى جَمِيعِ الـ⃝مَخْلُوقِينَ مِنْ أَهْلِ السَّمَاوَاتِ وَالأَرَضِينَ. فَمَنْ شَكَّ فِي ذَلِكَ فَهُوَ كَافِرٌ كُفْرَ الْجَاهِلِيَّةِ الأُولَى، وَمَنْ شَكَّ فِي شَيْءٍ مِنْ قَوْلِي هَذَا فَقَدْ شَكَّ فِي الْكُلِّ مِنْهُ، وَالشَّاكُّ فِي ذَلِكَ فَلَهُ النَّارُ. مَعَاشِرَ النَّاسِ، حَبَانِيَ اللهُ بِهَذِهِ الْفَضِيلَةِ مَنَّاً مِنْهُ عَلَيَّ وَإِحْسَاناً مِنْهُ إِلَيَّ وَلا إِلَهَ إِلاَّ هُوَ، لَهُ الْحَمْدُ مِنِّي أَبَدَ الآبِدِينَ وَدَهْرَ الدَّاهِرِينَ وَعَلَى كُلِّ حَالٍ. مَعَاشِرَ النَّاسِ، فَضِّلُوا عَلِيَّاً فَإِنَّهُ أَفْضَلُ النَّاسِ بَعْدِي مِنْ ذَكَرٍ وَأُنْثَى. بِنَا أَنْزَلَ اللهُ الرِّزْقَ وَبَقِيَ الْخَلْقُ. مَلْعُونٌ مَلْعُونٌ، مَغْضُوبٌ مَغْضُوبٌ مَنْ رَدَّ عَلَيَّ قَوْلِي هَذَا وَلَمْ يُوَافِقْهُ. أَلا إِنَّ جَبْرَئِيلَ خَبَّرَنِي عَنِ اللهِ تَعَالَى بِذَلِكَ وَيَقُولُ: مَنْ عَادَى عَلِيَّاً وَلَمْ يَتَوَلَّهُ فَعَلَيْهِ لَعْنَتِي وَغَضَبِي، (وَلْتَنْظُرْ نَفْسٌ مَا قَدَّمَتْ لِغَدٍ وَاتَّقُوا اللهَ ـ أَنْ تُخَالِفُوهُ فَتَزِلَّ قَدَمٌ بَعْدَ ثُبُوتِهَا ـ إِنَّ اللهَ خَبِيرٌ بِمَا تَعْمَلُونَ). مَعَاشِرَ النَّاسِ، إِنَّهُ جَنْبُ اللهِ الَّذِي ذُكِرَ فِي كِتَابِهِ، فَقَالَ تَعَالَى مُخْبِراً: (أَنْ تَقُولَ نَفْسٌ يَا حَسْرَتَا عَلَى مَا فَرَّطْتُ فِي جَنْبِ اللهِ). مَعَاشِرَ النَّاسِ، تَدَبَّرُوا الْقُرْآنَ وَافْهَمُوا آيَاتِهِ وَانْظُرُوا إِلَى مُحْكَمَاتِهِ وَلا تَتَّبِعُوا مُتَشَابِهَهُ، فَوَ اللهِ لَنْ يُبَيِّنَ لَكُمْ زَوَاجِرَهُ وَلَنْ يُوضِحَ لَكُمْ تَفْسِيرَهُ إِلاَّ الَّذِي أَنَا آخِذٌ بِيَدِهِ وَمُصْعِدُهُ إِلَيَّ وَشَائِلٌ بِعَضُدِهِ وَمُعْلِمُكُمْ: أَنَّ مَنْ كُنْتُ مَوْلاهُ فَهَذَا عَلِيٌّ مَوْلاهُ، وَهُوَ عَلِيُّ بْنُ أَبِي طَالِبٍ أَخِي وَوَصِيِّي، وَمُوَالاتُهُ مِنَ اللهِ عَزَّ وَجَلَّ أَنْزَلَهَا عَلَيَّ. مَعَاشِرَ النَّاسِ، إِنَّ عَلِيَّاً وَالطَّيِّبِينَ مِنْ وُلْدِي هُمُ الثِّقْلُ الأَصْغَرُ، وَالْقُرْآنُ الثِّقْلُ الأَكْبَرُ، فَكُلُّ وَاحِدٍ مُنْبِئٌ عَنْ صَاحِبِهِ وَمُوَافِقٌ لَهُ، لَنْ يَفْتَرِقَا حَتَّى يَرِدَا عَلَيَّ الْحَوْضَ. هُمْ أُمَنَاءُ اللهِ فِي خَلْقِهِ وَحُكَّامُهُ فِي أَرْضِهِ. أَلا وَقَدْ أَدَّيْتُ، أَلا وَقَدْ بَلَّغْتُ، أَلا وَقَدْ أَسْمَعْتُ، أَلا وَقَدْ أَوْضَحْتُ. أَلا وَإِنَّ اللهَ عَزَّ وَجَلَّ قَالَ وَأَنَا قُلْتُ عَنِ اللهِ عَزَّ وَجَلَّ. أَلا إِنَّهُ لَيْسَ «أَمِيرُ الْمُؤْمِنِينَ» غَيْرُ أَخِي هَذَا. وَلا تَحِلُّ إِمْرَةُ الْمُؤْمِنِينَ بَعْدِي لأَحَدٍ غَيْرِهِ.

رفع علي (عليه السلام) بيدي رسول الله (صلى الله عليه وآله و سلم)

ثُمَّ ضَرَبَ بِيَ⃝⃝دِهِ إِلَى عَضُدِ عَلِيٍّ عَلَيْهِ السَّلامُ فَرَفَعَهُ، وَكَانَ أَمِيرُ الْمُؤْمِنِينَ عَلَيْهِ السَّلامُ مُنْذُ أَوَّلِ مَا صَعِدَ رَسُولُ اللهِ صَلَّى اللهُ عَلَيْهِ وَآلِهِ وَشَالَ عَلِيَّاً عَلَيْهِ السَّلامُ حَتَّى صَارَتْ رِجْلُهُ مَعَ رُكْبَةِ رَسُولِ اللهِ صَلَّى اللهُ عَلَيْهِ وَآلِهِ. ثُمَّ قَالَ: مَعَاشِرَ النَّاسِ، هَذَا عَلِيٌّ أَخِي وَوَصِيِّي وَوَاعِي عِلْمِي، وَخَلِيفَتِي فِي أُمَّتِي وَعَلَى تَفْسِيرِ كِتَابِ اللهِ عَزَّ وَجَلَّ، وَالدَّاعِي إِلَيْهِ وَالْعَامِلُ بِمَا يَرْضَاهُ وَالْمُحَارِبُ لأَعْدَائِهِ وَالْمُوَالِي عَلَى طَاعَتِهِ وَالنَّاهِي عَنْ مَعْصِيَتِهِ. خَلِيفَةُ رَسُولِ اللهِ وَأَمِيرُ الْمُؤْمِنِينَ وَالإِمَامُ⃝ الْهَادِي وَقَاتِلُ النَّاكِثِينَ وَالْقَاسِطِينَ وَالْمَارِقِينَ بِأَمْرِ اللهِ. أَقُولُ وَمَا يُبَدَّلُ الْقَوْلُ لَدَيَّ بِأَمْرِ رَبِّي، أَقُولُ: اللَّهُمَّ وَالِ مَنْ وَالاهُ وَعَادِ مَنْ عَادَاهُ وَالْعَنْ مَنْ أَنْكَرَهُ وَاغْضَبْ عَلَى مَنْ جَحَدَ حَقَّهُ. اللَّهُمَّ إِنَّكَ أَنْزَلْتَ عَلَيَّ أَنَّ الإِمَامَةَ بَعْدِي لِعَلِيٍّ وَلِيِّكَ عِنْدَ تِبْيَانِي ذَلِكَ وَنَصْبِي إِيَّاهُ بِمَا أَكْمَلْتَ لِعِبَادِكَ مِنْ دِينِهِمْ وَأَتْمَمْتَ عَلَيْهِمْ بِنِعْمَتِكَ وَرَضِيتَ لَهُمُ الإِسْلامَ دِيناً فَقُلْتَ: (وَمَنْ يَبْتَغِ غَيْرَ الإِسْلامِ دِيناً فَلَنْ يُقْبَلَ مِنْهُ وَهُوَ فِي الآخِرَةِ مِنَ الْخَاسِرِينَ). اللَّهُمَّ إِنِّي أُشْهِدُكَ وَكَفَى بِكَ شَهِيداً أَنِّي قَدْ بَلَّغْتُ. مَعَاشِرَ النَّاسِ، إِنَّمَا أَكْمَلَ اللهُ عَزَّ وَجَلَّ دِينَكُمْ بِإِمَامَتِهِ. فَمَنْ لَمْ يَأْتَمَّ بِهِ وَبِمَنْ يَقُومُ مَقَامَهُ مِنْ وُلْدِي مِنْ صُلْبِهِ إِلَى يَوْمِ الْقِيَامَةِ وَالْعَرْضِ عَلَى اللهِ عَزَّ وَجَلَّ فَأُولَئِكَ الَّذِينَ حَبِطَتْ أَعْمَالُهُمْ وَفِي النَّارِ هُمْ خَالِدُونَ، (لا يُخَفَّفُ عَنْهُمُ الْعَذَابُ وَلا هُمْ يُنْظَرُونَ). مَعَاشِرَ النَّاسِ، هَذَا عَلِيٌّ، أَنْصَرُكُمْ

لي وَأَحَقُّكُمْ بِي وَأَقْرَبُكُمْ إِلَيَّ وَأَعَزُّكُمْ عَلَيَّ، وَاللهُ عَزَّ وجلَّ وَأَنَا عَنْهُ رَاضِيَانِ. وَمَا نَزَلَتْ آيَةُ رِضاً إلاَّ فِيهِ، وَمَا خَاطَبَ اللهُ الَّذِينَ آمَنُوا إلاَّ بَدَأَ بِهِ، وَلاَ نَزَلَتْ آيَةُ مَدْحٍ فِي الْقُرآنِ إلاَّ فِيهِ، وَلاَ شَهِدَ اللهُ بِالْجَنَّةِ فِي (هَلْ أتى عَلَى الإنْسَانِ) إلاَّ لَهُ، وَلاَ أَنْزَلَهَا فِي سِوَاهُ وَلاَ مَدَحَ بِهَا غَيْرَهُ. مَعَاشِرَ النَّاسِ، هُوَ نَاصِرُ دِينِ اللهِ، وَالْمُجَادِلُ عَنْ رَسُولِ اللهِ، وَهُوَ التَّقِيُّ النَّقِيُّ الْهَادِي الْمَهْدِيُّ. نَبِيُّكُمْ خَيْرُ نَبِيٍّ وَوَصِيُّكُمْ خَيْرُ وَصِيٍّ وَبَنُوهُ خَيْرُ الأوْصِيَاءِ. مَعَاشِرَ النَّاسِ، ذُرِّيَّةُ كُلِّ نَبِيٍّ مِنْ صُلْبِهِ، وَذُرِّيَّتِي مِنْ صُلْبِ أمِيرِ الْمُؤْمِنِينَ عَلِيٍّ.

مَعَاشِرَ النَّاسِ، إنَّ إبْلِيسَ أَخْرَجَ آدَمَ مِنَ الْجَنَّةِ بِالْحَسَدِ، فَلاَ تَحْسُدُوهُ فَتَحْبَطَ أَعْمَالُكُمْ وَتَزِلَّ أَقْدَامُكُمْ، فَإنَّ آدَمَ أُهْبِطَ إلَى الأرْضِ لِخَطِيئَةٍ وَاحِدَةٍ، وَهُوَ صَفْوَةُ اللهِ عَزَّ وَجَلَّ، وَكَيْفَ بِكُمْ وَأَنْتُمْ أَنْتُمْ وَمِنْكُمْ أَعْدَاءُ اللهِ. ألاَ وَإنَّهُ لاَ يُبْغِضُ عَلِيّاً إلاَّ شَقِيٌّ، وَلاَ يُوَالِي عَلِيّاً إلاَّ تَقِيٌّ، وَلاَ يُؤْمِنُ بِهِ إلاَّ مُؤْمِنٌ مُخْلِصٌ. وَفِي عَلِيٍّ ـ وَاللهِ ـ نَزَلَتْ سُورَةُ الْعَصْرِ: (بِسْمِ اللهِ الرَّحْمنِ الرَّحِيمِ ● وَالْعَصْرِ ● إنَّ الإنْسَانَ لَفِي خُسْرٍ ● إلاَّ الَّذِينَ آمَنُوا وَعَمِلُوا الصَّالِحَاتِ وَتَوَاصَوْا بِالْحَقِّ وَتَوَاصَوْا بِالصَّبْرِ). مَعَاشِرَ النَّاسِ، قَدِ اسْتَشْهَدْتُ اللهَ وَبَلَّغْتُكُمْ رِسَالَتِي وَمَا عَلَى الرَّسُولِ إلاَّ الْبَلاغُ الْمُبِينُ. مَعَاشِرَ النَّاسِ، اتَّقُوا اللهَ حَقَّ تُقَاتِهِ وَلاَ تَمُوتُنَّ إلاَّ وَأَنْتُمْ مُسْلِمُونَ. مَعَاشِرَ النَّاسِ، (آمِنُوا بِاللهِ وَرَسُولِهِ وَالنُّورِ الَّذِي أُنْزِلَ مَعَهُ مِنْ قَبْلِ أنْ نَطْمِسَ وُجُوهاً فَنَرُدَّهَا عَلَى أَدْبَارِهَا أوْ نَلْعَنَهُمْ كَمَا لَعَنَّا أصْحَابَ السَّبْتِ). مَعَاشِرَ النَّاسِ، النُّورُ مِنَ اللهِ عَزَّ وَجَلَّ مَسْلُوكٌ فِيَّ ثُمَّ فِي عَلِيِّ بْنِ أبِي طَالِبٍ، ثُمَّ فِي النَّسْلِ مِنْهُ إلَى الْقَائِمِ الْمَهْدِيِّ الَّذِي يَأْخُذُ بِحَقِّ اللهِ وَبِكُلِّ حَقٍّ هُوَ لَنَا، لأنَّ اللهَ عَزَّ وَجَلَّ قَدْ جَعَلَنَا حُجَّةً عَلَى الْمُقَصِّرِينَ وَالْمُعَانِدِينَ وَالْمُخَالِفِينَ وَالْخَائِنِينَ وَالآثِمِينَ وَالظَّالِمِينَ مِنْ جَمِيعِ الْعَالَمِينَ. مَعَاشِرَ النَّاسِ، أُنْذِرُكُمْ أنِّي رَسُولُ اللهِ قَدْ خَلَتْ مِنْ قَبْلِيَ الرُّسُلُ، أَفَإنْ مِتُّ أوْ قُتِلْتُ انْقَلَبْتُمْ عَلَى أَعْقَابِكُمْ؟ وَمَنْ يَنْقَلِبْ عَلَى عَقِبَيْهِ فَلَنْ يَضُرَّ اللهَ شَيْئاً وَسَيَجْزِي اللهُ الشَّاكِرِينَ الصَّابِرِينَ. ألاَ وَإنَّ عَلِيّاً هُوَ الْمَوْصُوفُ بِالصَّبْرِ وَالشُّكْرِ، ثُمَّ مِنْ بَعْدِهِ وُلْدِي مِنْ صُلْبِهِ. مَعَاشِرَ النَّاسِ، لاَ تَمُنُّوا عَلَى اللهِ إسْلاَمَكُمْ فَيَسْخَطَ عَلَيْكُمْ وَيُصِيبَكُمْ بِعَذَابٍ مِنْ عِنْدِهِ، إنَّهُ لَبِالْمِرْصَادِ. مَعَاشِرَ النَّاسِ، إنَّهُ سَيَكُونُ مِنْ بَعْدِي أَئِمَّةٌ يَدْعُونَ إلَى النَّارِ وَيَوْمَ الْقِيَامَةِ لاَ يُنْصَرُونَ. مَعَاشِرَ النَّاسِ، إنَّ اللهَ وَأَنَا بَرِيئَانِ مِنْهُمْ.
مَعَاشِرَ النَّاسِ، إنَّهُمْ وَأنْصَارُهُمْ وَأَتْبَاعُهُمْ وَأَشْيَاعُهُمْ فِي الدَّرْكِ الأسْفَلِ مِنَ النَّارِ وَلَبِئْسَ مَثْوَى الْمُتَكَبِّرِينَ. ألاَ إنَّهُمْ أصْحَابُ الصَّحِيفَةِ، فَلْيَنْظُرْ أَحَدُكُمْ فِي صَحِيفَتِهِ!!

(قَالَ: فَذَهَبَ عَلَى النَّاسِ ـ إلاَّ شِرْذِمَةٌ مِنْهُمْ ـ أَمْرُ الصَّحِيفَةِ.)

مَعَاشِرَ النَّاسِ، إنِّي أَدَعُهَا إمَامَةً وَوِرَاثَةً فِي عَقِبِي إلَى يَوْمِ الْقِيَامَةِ، وَقَدْ بَلَّغْتُ مَا أُمِرْتُ بِتَبْلِيغِهِ حُجَّةً عَلَى كُلِّ حَاضِرٍ وَغَائِبٍ وَعَلَى كُلِّ أَحَدٍ مِمَّنْ شَهِدَ أوْ لَمْ يَشْهَدْ، وُلِدَ أوْ لَمْ يُولَدْ، فَلْيُبَلِّغِ الْحَاضِرُ الْغَائِبَ وَالْوَالِدُ الْوَلَدَ إلَى يَوْمِ الْقِيَامَةِ. وَسَيَجْعَلُونَ الإمَامَةَ بَعْدِي مُلْكاً وَاغْتِصَاباً، ألاَ لَعَنَ اللهُ الْغَاصِبِينَ الْمُغْتَصِبِينَ، وَعِنْدَهَا (سَنَفْرُغُ لَكُمْ أَيُّهَا الثَّقَلاَنِ)، وَ(يُرْسَلُ عَلَيْكُمَا شُوَاظٌ مِنْ نَارٍ وَنُحَاسٌ فَلاَ تَنْتَصِرَانِ). مَعَاشِرَ النَّاسِ، إنَّ اللهَ عَزَّ وَجَلَّ لَمْ يَكُنْ لِيَذَرَكُمْ عَلَى مَا أَنْتُمْ عَلَيْهِ حَتَّى يَمِيزَ الْخَبِيثَ مِنَ الطَّيِّبِ، وَمَا كَانَ اللهُ لِيُطْلِعَكُمْ عَلَى الْغَيْبِ. مَعَاشِرَ النَّاسِ، إنَّهُ مَا مِنْ قَرْيَةٍ إلاَّ وَاللهُ مُهْلِكُهَا بِتَكْذِيبِهَا وَكَذَلِكَ يُهْلِكُ الْقُرَى وَهِيَ ظَالِمَةٌ، وَهَذَا عَلِيٌّ إمَامُكُمْ وَوَلِيُّكُمْ وَهُوَ مَوَاعِيدُ اللهِ، وَاللهُ مُصَدِّقٌ وَعْدَهُ. مَعَاشِرَ النَّاسِ، قَدْ ظَلَّ قَبْلَكُمْ أَكْثَرُ الأوَّلِينَ، وَاللهُ لَقَدْ أَهْلَكَ الأوَّلِينَ، وَهُوَ مُهْلِكُ الآخِرِينَ. قَالَ اللهُ تَعَالَى: (أَلَمْ

449

نُهْلِكُ الأَوَّلِينَ • ثُمَّ نُتْبِعُهُمُ الآخِرِينَ • كَذلِكَ نَفْعَلُ بِالْمُجْرِمِينَ • وَيْلٌ يَوْمَئِذٍ لِلْمُكَذِّبِينَ). مَعَاشِرَ النَّاسِ، إِنَّ اللّهَ قَدْ أَمَرَنِي وَنَهَانِي، وَقَدْ أَمَرْتُ عَلِيّاً وَنَهَيْتُهُ. فَعِلْمُ الأَمْرِ وَالنَّهْيِ مِنْ رَبِّهِ عَزَّ وَجَلَّ، فَاسْمَعُوا لأَمْرِهِ تَسْلَمُوا، وَأَطِيعُوهُ تَهْتَدُوا، وَانْتَهُوا لِنَهْيِهِ تَرْشُدُوا، وَصِيرُوا إِلَى مُرَادِهِ وَلاَ تَتَفَرَّقْ بِكُمُ السُّبُلُ عَنْ سَبِيلِهِ. مَعَاشِرَ النَّاسِ، أَنَا صِرَاطُ اللّهِ الْمُسْتَقِيمُ الَّذِي أَمَرَكُمْ بِاتِّبَاعِهِ، ثُمَّ عَلِيٌّ مِنْ بَعْدِي، ثُمَّ وُلْدِي مِنْ صُلْبِهِ أَئِمَّةٌ يَهْدُونَ إِلَى الْحَقِّ وَبِهِ يَعْدِلُونَ. ثُمَّ قَرَأَ: (بِسْمِ اللّهِ الرَّحْمنِ الرَّحِيمِ • الْحَمْدُ للّهِ رَبِّ الْعَالَمِينَ...) إِلَى آخِرِهَا، وَقَالَ: فِيَّ نَزَلَتْ وَفِيهِمْ نَزَلَتْ، وَلَهُمْ عَمَّتْ وَإِيَّاهُمْ خَصَّتْ، أُولئِكَ أَوْلِيَاءُ اللّهِ لاَ خَوْفٌ عَلَيْهِمْ وَلاَ هُمْ يَحْزَنُونَ، أَلاَ إِنَّ حِزْبَ اللّهِ هُمُ الْغَالِبُونَ. أَلاَ إِنَّ أَعْدَاءَ عَلِيٍّ هُمْ أَهْلُ الشِّقَاقِ وَالنِّفَاقِ وَالْحَادُّونَ وَهُمُ الْعَادُونَ وَإِخْوَانُ الشَّيَاطِينِ الَّذِينَ يُوحِي بَعْضُهُمْ إِلَى بَعْضٍ زُخْرُفَ الْقَوْلِ غُرُوراً. أَلاَ إِنَّ أَوْلِيَاءَهُمُ الَّذِينَ ذَكَرَهُمُ اللّهُ فِي كِتَابِهِ، فَقَالَ عَزَّ وَجَلَّ: (لاَ تَجِدُ قَوْماً يُؤْمِنُونَ بِاللّهِ وَالْيَوْمِ الآخِرِ يُوَادُّونَ مَنْ حَادَّ اللّهَ وَرَسُولَهُ وَلَوْ كَانُوا آبَاءَهُمْ أَوْ أَبْنَاءَهُمْ أَوْ إِخْوَانَهُمْ أَوْ عَشِيرَتَهُمْ، أُولئِكَ كَتَبَ فِي قُلُوبِهِمُ الإِيمَانَ...). أَلاَ إِنَّ أَوْلِيَاءَهُمُ الَّذِينَ وَصَفَهُمُ اللّهُ عَزَّ وَجَلَّ فَقَالَ: (الَّذِينَ آمَنُوا وَلَمْ يَلْبِسُوا ايمَانَهُمْ بِظُلْمٍ أُولئِكَ لَهُمُ الأَمْنُ وَهُمْ مُهْتَدُونَ). أَلاَ إِنَّ أَوْلِيَاءَهُمُ الَّذِينَ يَدْخُلُونَ الْجَنَّةَ بِسَلاَمٍ آمِنِينَ، تَتَلَقَّاهُمُ الْمَلاَئِكَةُ بِالتَّسْلِيمِ يَقُولُونَ: سَلاَمٌ عَلَيْكُمْ طِبْتُمْ فَادْخُلُوهَا خَالِدِينَ. أَلاَ إِنَّ أَوْلِيَاءَهُمُ الَّذِينَ قَالَ لَهُمُ اللّهُ عَزَّ وَجَلَّ (يَدْخُلُونَ الْجَنَّةَ يُرْزَقُونَ فِيهَا بِغَيْرِ حِسَابٍ). أَلاَ إِنَّ أَعْدَاءَهُمُ الَّذِينَ يَصْلَوْنَ سَعِيراً. أَلاَ إِنَّ أَعْدَاءَهُمُ الَّذِينَ يَسْمَعُونَ لِجَهَنَّمَ شَهِيقاً وَهِيَ تَفُورُ وَلَهَا زَفِيرٌ. أَلاَ إِنَّ أَعْدَاءَهُمُ الَّذِينَ قَالَ اللّهُ فِيهِمْ: (كُلَّمَا دَخَلَتْ أُمَّةٌ لَعَنَتْ أُخْتَهَا). أَلاَ إِنَّ أَعْدَاءَهُمُ الَّذِينَ قَالَ اللّهُ عَزَّوَجَلَّ: (كُلَّمَا أُلْقِيَ فِيهَا فَوْجٌ سَأَلَهُمْ خَزَنَتُهَا أَلَمْ يَأْتِكُمْ نَذِيرٌ قَالوا بَلَى قَدْ جَاءَنَا نَذِيرٌ فَكَذَّبْنَا وَقُلْنَا مَا نَزَّلَ اللّهُ مِنْ شَيْءٍ، إِنْ أَنْتُمْ إِلاَّ فِي ضَلاَلٍ كَبِيرٍ). أَلاَ إِنَّ أَوْلِيَاءَهُمُ الَّذِينَ يَخْشَوْنَ رَبَّهُمْ بِالْغَيْبِ، لَهُمْ مَغْفِرَةٌ وَأَجْرٌ كَبِيرٌ. مَعَاشِرَ النَّاسِ، شَتَّانَ مَا بَيْنَ السَّعِيرِ وَالْجَنَّةِ. عَدُوُّنَا مَنْ ذَمَّهُ اللّهُ وَلَعَنَهُ، وَوَلِيُّنَا مَنْ مَدَحَهُ اللّهُ وَأَحَبَّهُ. مَعَاشِرَ النَّاسِ، أَلاَ وَإِنِّي مُنْذِرٌ وَعَلِيٌّ هَادٍ.

مَعَاشِرَ النَّاسِ، إِنِّي نَبِيٌّ وَعَلِيٌّ وَصِيِّي. أَلاَ إِنَّ خَاتَمَ الأَئِمَّةِ مِنَّا الْقَائِمُ الْمَهْدِيُّ. أَلاَ إِنَّهُ الظَّاهِرُ عَلَى الدِّينِ. أَلاَ إِنَّهُ الْمُنْتَقِمُ مِنَ الظَّالِمِينَ. أَلاَ إِنَّهُ فَاتِحُ الْحُصُونِ وَهَادِمُهَا. أَلاَ إِنَّهُ قَاتِلُ كُلِّ قَبِيلَةٍ مِنْ أَهْلِ الشِّرْكِ. أَلاَ إِنَّهُ الْمُدْرِكُ بِكُلِّ ثَارٍ لأَوْلِيَاءِ اللّهِ. أَلاَ إِنَّهُ النَّاصِرُ لِدِينِ اللّهِ. أَلاَ إِنَّهُ الْغَرَّافُ فِي بَحْرٍ عَمِيقٍ. أَلاَ إِنَّهُ يَسِمُ كُلَّ ذِي فَضْلٍ بِفَضْلِهِ وَكُلَّ ذِي جَهْلٍ بِجَهْلِهِ. أَلاَ إِنَّهُ خِيَرَةُ اللّهِ وَمُخْتَارُهُ. أَلاَ إِنَّهُ وَارِثُ كُلِّ عِلْمٍ وَالْمُحِيطُ بِكُلِّ فَهْمٍ. أَلاَ إِنَّهُ الْمُخْبِرُ عَنْ رَبِّهِ عَزَّ وَجَلَّ وَالْمُنَبِّهُ بِأَمْرِ إِيمَانِهِ، أَلاَ إِنَّهُ الرَّشِيدُ السَّدِيدُ. أَلاَ إِنَّهُ الْمُفَوَّضُ إِلَيْهِ. أَلاَ إِنَّهُ قَدْ بَشَّرَ بِهِ مَنْ سَلَفَ بَيْنَ يَدَيْهِ. أَلاَ إِنَّهُ الْبَاقِي حُجَّةً وَلاَ حُجَّةَ بَعْدَهُ، وَلاَ حَقَّ إِلاَّ مَعَهُ، وَلاَ نُورَ إِلاَّ عِنْدَهُ. أَلاَ إِنَّهُ لاَ غَالِبَ لَهُ وَلاَ مَنْصُورَ عَلَيْهِ. أَلاَ وَإِنَّهُ وَلِيُّ اللّهِ فِي أَرْضِهِ، وَحَكَمُهُ فِي خَلْقِهِ، وَأَمِينُهُ فِي سِرِّهِ وَعَلاَنِيَتِهِ.

مَعَاشِرَ النَّاسِ، قَدْ بَيَّنْتُ لَكُمْ وَأَفْهَمْتُكُمْ، وَهذَا عَلِيٌّ يُفْهِمُكُمْ بَعْدِي. أَلاَ وَإِنِّي عِنْدَ انْقِضَاءِ خُطْبَتِي أَدْعُوكُمْ إِلَى مُصَافَقَتِي عَلَى بَيْعَتِهِ وَالإِقْرَارِ بِهِ، ثُمَّ مُصَافَقَتِهِ بَعْدِي. أَلاَ وَإِنِّي قَدْ بَايَعْتُ اللّهَ وَعَلِيٌّ قَدْ بَايَعَنِي، وَأَنَا آخُذُكُمْ بِالْبَيْعَةِ لَهُ عَنِ اللّهِ عَزَّ وَجَلَّ. (إِنَّ الَّذِينَ يُبَايِعُونَكَ إِنَّمَا يُبَايِعُونَ اللّهَ، يَدُ اللّهِ فَوْقَ أَيْدِيهِمْ. فَمَنْ نَكَثَ فَإِنَّمَا يَنْكُثُ عَلَى نَفْسِهِ، وَمَنْ أَوْفَى بِمَا عَاهَدَ عَلَيْهِ اللّهَ فَسَيُؤْتِيهِ أَجْراً عَظِيماً). مَعَاشِرَ النَّاسِ، إِنَّ الصَّفَا وَالمَرْوَةَ مِنْ شَعَائِرِ اللّهِ، (فَمَنْ حَجَّ الْبَيْتَ أَوِ اعْتَمَرَ فَلاَجُنَاحَ عَلَيْهِ أَنْ يَطَّوَّفَ بِهِمَا). مَعَاشِرَ النَّاسِ، حُجُّوا الْبَيْتَ،

فَمَا وَرَدَهُ أَهْلُ بَيْتٍ إِلاَّ اسْتَغْنَوْا، وَلاَ تَخَلَّفُوا عَنْهُ إِلاَّ افْتَقَرُوا. مَعَاشِرَ النَّاسِ، مَا وَقَفَ بِالْمَوْقِفِ مُؤْمِنٌ إِلاَّ غَفَرَ اللهُ لَهُ مَا سَلَفَ مِنْ ذَنْبِهِ إِلَى وَقْتِهِ ذَلِكَ، فَإِذَا انْقَضَتْ حَجَّتُهُ اسْتَأْنَفَ عَمَلَهُ. مَعَاشِرَ النَّاسِ، الْحُجَّاجُ مُعَانُونَ وَنَفَقَاتُهُمْ مُخْلَفَةٌ عَلَيْهِمْ، وَاللهُ لاَ يُضِيعُ أَجْرَ الْمُحْسِنِينَ.

مَعَاشِرَ النَّاسِ، حُجُّوا الْبَيْتَ بِكَمَالِ الدِّينِ وَالتَّفَقُّهِ، وَلاَ تَنْصَرِفُوا عَنِ الْمَشَاهِدِ إِلاَّ بِتَوْبَةٍ وَإِقْلاَعٍ. مَعَاشِرَ النَّاسِ، أَقِيمُوا الصَّلاَةَ وَآتُوا الزَّكَاةَ كَمَا أَمَرَكُمُ اللهُ عَزَّ وَجَلَّ فَإِنْ طَالَ عَلَيْكُمُ الْأَمَدُ فَقَصَّرْتُمْ أَوْ نَسِيتُمْ فَعَلِيٌّ وَلِيُّكُمْ وَمُبَيِّنٌ لَكُمْ، الَّذِي نَصَبَهُ اللهُ عَزَّ وَجَلَّ لَكُمْ بَعْدِي وَمَنْ خَلَّفَهُ اللهُ مِنِّي وَمِنْهُ يُخْبِرُونَكُمْ بِمَا تَسْأَلُونَ عَنْهُ وَيُبَيِّنُونَ لَكُمْ مَا لاَ تَعْلَمُونَ. أَلاَ إِنَّ الْحَلاَلَ وَالْحَرَامَ أَكْثَرُ مِنْ أَنْ أُحْصِيَهُمَا وَأُعَرِّفَهُمَا فَآمَرَ بِالْحَلاَلِ وَأَنْهَى عَنِ الْحَرَامِ فِي مَقَامٍ وَاحِدٍ، فَأُمِرْتُ أَنْ آخُذَ الْبَيْعَةَ مِنْكُمْ وَالصَّفْقَةَ لَكُمْ بِقَبُولِ مَا جِئْتُ بِهِ عَنِ اللهِ عَزَّ وَجَلَّ فِي عَلِيٍّ أَمِيرِ الْمُؤْمِنِينَ وَالأَئِمَّةِ مِنْ بَعْدِهِ الَّذِينَ هُمْ مِنِّي وَمِنْهُ إِمَامَةً فِيهِمْ قَائِمَةً، خَاتِمُهَا الْمَهْدِيُّ إِلَى يَوْمٍ يَلْقَى اللهَ الَّذِي يَقْضِي بِالْحَقِّ.

مَعَاشِرَ النَّاسِ، وَكُلُّ حَلاَلٍ دَلَلْتُكُمْ عَلَيْهِ، وَكُلُّ حَرَامٍ نَهَيْتُكُمْ عَنْهُ؛ فَإِنِّي لَمْ أَرْجِعْ عَنْ ذَلِكَ وَلَمْ أُبَدِّلْ. أَلاَ فَاذْكُرُوا ذَلِكَ وَاحْفَظُوهُ وَتَوَاصَوْا بِهِ، وَلاَ تُبَدِّلُوهُ وَلاَ تُغَيِّرُوهُ. أَلاَ وَإِنِّي أُجَدِّدُ الْقَوْلَ: أَلاَ فَأَقِيمُوا الصَّلاَةَ وَآتُوا الزَّكَاةَ وَأْمُرُوا بِالْمَعْرُوفِ وَانْهَوْا عَنِ الْمُنْكَرِ. أَلاَ وَإِنَّ رَأْسَ الْأَمْرِ بِالْمَعْرُوفِ وَالنَّهْيِ عَنِ الْمُنْكَرِ أَنْ تَنْتَهُوا إِلَى قَوْلِي وَتُبَلِّغُوهُ مَنْ لَمْ يَحْضُرْ، وَتَأْمُرُوهُ بِقَبُولِهِ عَنِّي، وَتَنْهَوْهُ عَنْ مُخَالَفَتِهِ فَإِنَّهُ أَمْرٌ مِنَ اللهِ عَزَّ وَجَلَّ وَمِنِّي. وَلاَ أَمْرَ بِمَعْرُوفٍ وَلاَ نَهْيَ عَنْ مُنْكَرٍ إِلاَّ مَعَ إِمَامٍ مَعْصُومٍ.

مَعَاشِرَ النَّاسِ، الْقُرْآنُ يُعَرِّفُكُمْ أَنَّ الأَئِمَّةَ مِنْ بَعْدِهِ وُلْدُهُ، وَعَرَّفْتُكُمْ أَنَّهُمْ مِنِّي وَأَنَا مِنْهُ، حَيْثُ يَقُولُ اللهُ فِي كِتَابِهِ: (وَجَعَلَهَا كَلِمَةً بَاقِيَةً فِي عَقِبِهِ)، وَقُلْتُ: (لَنْ تَضِلُّوا مَا إِنْ تَمَسَّكْتُمْ بِهِمَا). مَعَاشِرَ النَّاسِ، التَّقْوَى، التَّقْوَى، وَاحْذَرُوا السَّاعَةَ كَمَا قَالَ اللهُ عَزَّ وَجَلَّ: (إِنَّ زَلْزَلَةَ السَّاعَةِ شَيْءٌ عَظِيمٌ). اُذْكُرُوا الْمَمَاتَ وَالْمَعَادَ وَالْحِسَابَ وَالْمَوَازِينَ وَالْمُحَاسَبَةَ بَيْنَ يَدَيْ رَبِّ الْعَالَمِينَ وَالثَّوَابَ وَالْعِقَابَ. فَمَنْ جَاءَ بِالْحَسَنَةِ أُثِيبَ عَلَيْهَا وَمَنْ جَاءَ بِالسَّيِّئَةِ فَلَيْسَ لَهُ فِي الْجِنَانِ نَصِيبٌ.

مَعَاشِرَ النَّاسِ، إِنَّكُمْ أَكْثَرُ مِنْ أَنْ تُصَافِقُونِي بِكَفٍّ وَاحِدٍ، وَقَدْ أَمَرَنِيَ اللهُ عَزَّ وَجَلَّ أَنْ آخُذَ مِنْ أَلْسِنَتِكُمُ الْإِقْرَارَ بِمَا عَقَدْتُ لِعَلِيٍّ أَمِيرِ الْمُؤْمِنِينَ، وَلِمَنْ جَاءَ بَعْدَهُ مِنَ الْأَئِمَّةِ مِنِّي وَمِنْهُ، عَلَى مَا أَعْلَمْتُكُمْ أَنَّ ذُرِّيَّتِي مِنْ صُلْبِهِ. فَقُولُوا بِأَجْمَعِكُمْ: «إِنَّا سَامِعُونَ مُطِيعُونَ رَاضُونَ مُنْقَادُونَ لِمَا بَلَّغْتَ عَنْ رَبِّنَا وَرَبِّكَ فِي أَمْرِ إِمَامِنَا عَلِيٍّ أَمِيرِ الْمُؤْمِنِينَ وَأَمْرِ وُلْدِهِ مِنْ صُلْبِهِ مِنَ الْأَئِمَّةِ. نُبَايِعُكَ عَلَى ذَلِكَ بِقُلُوبِنَا وَأَنْفُسِنَا وَأَلْسِنَتِنَا وَأَيْدِينَا. عَلَى ذَلِكَ نَحْيَى وَعَلَيْهِ نَمُوتُ وَعَلَيْهِ نُبْعَثُ. وَلاَ نُغَيِّرُ وَلاَ نُبَدِّلُ، وَلاَ نَشُكُّ وَلاَ نَجْحَدُ وَلاَ نَرْتَابُ، وَلاَ نَرْجِعُ عَنِ الْعَهْدِ وَلاَ نَنْقُضُ الْمِيثَاقَ. نُطِيعُ اللهَ وَنُطِيعُكَ وَعَلِيّاً أَمِيرَ الْمُؤْمِنِينَ وَالْأَئِمَّةَ الَّذِينَ ذَكَرْتَهُمْ مِنْ ذُرِّيَّتِكَ مِنْ وُلْدِهِ بَعْدَهُ، الْحَسَنَ وَالْحُسَيْنَ. ... فَالْعَهْدُ وَالْمِيثَاقُ لَهُمْ مَأْخُوذٌ مِنَّا، مِنْ قُلُوبِنَا وَأَنْفُسِنَا وَأَلْسِنَتِنَا وَضَمَائِرِنَا وَمُصَافَقَةِ أَيْدِينَا. مَنْ أَدْرَكَهَا بِيَدِهِ وَإِلاَّ فَقَدْ أَقَرَّ بِلِسَانِهِ وَلاَ يَبْغِي بِذَلِكَ بَدَلاً وَلاَ يَرَى اللهُ مِنْ أَنْفُسِنَا عَنْهُ حِوَلاً أَبَداً. نَحْنُ نُؤَدِّي ذَلِكَ عَنْكَ، الدَّانِيَ وَالْقَاصِيَ مِنْ أَوْلاَدِنَا وَأَهَالِينَا، وَنُشْهِدُ اللهَ بِذَلِكَ وَكَفَى بِاللهِ شَهِيداً وَأَنْتَ عَلَيْنَا بِهِ شَهِيدٌ».

451

مَعَاشِرَ النَّاسِ، مَا تَقُولُونَ؟ فَإِنَّ اللّهَ يَعْلَمُ كُلَّ صَوْتٍ وَخَافِيَةٍ كُلِّ نَفْسٍ، (فَمَنِ اهْتَدى فَلِنَفْسِهِ وَمَنْ ضَلَّ فَإِنَّمَا يَضِلُّ عَلَيْها)، وَمَنْ بَايَعَ فَإِنَّمَا يُبَايِعُ اللّهَ، (يَدُ اللّهِ فَوْقَ أَيْدِيهِمْ). مَعَاشِرَ النَّاسِ، فَاتَّقُوا اللّهَ وَبَايِعُوا عَلِيًّا أَمِيرَ الْمُؤْمِنِينَ وَالْحَسَنَ وَالْحُسَيْنَ وَالْأَئِمَّةَ كَلِمَةً طَيِّبَةً بَاقِيَةً؛ يُهْلِكُ اللّهُ مَنْ غَدَرَ وَيَرْحَمُ مَنْ وَفى. (فَمَنْ نَكَثَ فَإِنَّمَا يَنْكُثُ عَلَى نَفْسِهِ وَمَنْ أَوْفى بِمَا عَاهَدَ عَلَيْهِ اللّهُ فَسَيُؤْتِيهِ أَجْراً عَظِيماً). مَعَاشِرَ النَّاسِ، قُولُوا الَّذِي قُلْتُ لَكُمْ وَسَلِّمُوا عَلَى عَلِيٍّ بِإِمْرَةِ الْمُؤْمِنِينَ، وَقُولُوا: سَمِعْنَا وَأَطَعْنَا غُفْرَانَكَ رَبَّنَا وَإِلَيْكَ الْمَصِيرُ، وَقُولُوا: الْحَمْدُ لِلّهِ الَّذِي هَدَانَا لِهذَا وَمَا كُنَّا لِنَهْتَدِيَ لَوْلاَ أَنْ هَدانَا اللّهُ. مَعَاشِرَ النَّاسِ، إِنَّ فَضَائِلَ عَلِيِّ بْنَ أَبِي طَالِبٍ عِنْدَ اللّهِ عَزَّ وَجَلَّ ـ وَقَدْ أَنْزَلَهَا فِي الْقُرْآنِ ـ أَكْثَرُ مِنْ أَنْ أُحْصِيَهَا فِي مَقَامٍ وَاحِدٍ، فَمَنْ أَنْبَأَكُمْ بِهَا وَعَرَّفَهَا فَصَدِّقُوهُ. مَعَاشِرَ النَّاسِ، مَنْ يُطِعِ اللّهَ وَرَسُولَهُ وَعَلِيّاً وَالْأَئِمَّةَ الَّذِينَ ذَكَرْتُهُمْ فَقَدْ فَازَ فَوْزاً عَظِيماً.

مَعَاشِرَ النَّاسِ، السَّابِقُونَ إِلى مُبَايَعَتِهِ وَمُوَالاَتِهِ وَالتَّسْلِيمِ عَلَيْهِ بِإِمْرَةِ الْمُؤْمِنِينَ أُولئِكَ هُمُ الْفَائِزُونَ فِي جَنَّاتِ النَّعِيمِ. مَعَاشِرَ النَّاسِ، قُولُوا مَا يَرْضَى اللّهُ بِهِ عَنْكُمْ مِنَ الْقَوْلِ، فَإِنْ تَكْفُرُوا أَنْتُمْ وَمَنْ فِي الْأَرْضِ جَمِيعاً فَلَنْ يَضُرَّ اللّهَ شَيْئاً. اَللّهُمَّ اغْفِرْ لِلْمُؤْمِنِينَ وَاغْضَبْ عَلَى الْكَافِرِينَ، وَالْحَمْدُ لِلّهِ رَبِّ الْعَالَمِينَ.

Here is my humble translation of this most important text:

"All Praise is due to Allāh Who is Exalted in His Unity, Near in His Uniqueness, Sublime in His Authority, Magnanimous in His Dominance. He knows everything; He subdues all creation through His might and evidence. He is Praised always and forever, Glorified and has no end. He begins and He repeats, and to Him every matter is referred. Allāh is the Creator of everything; He dominates with His power the earth and the heavens. Holy, He is, and Praised, the Lord of the angels and of the spirits. His favors overwhelm whatever He creates, and He is the Mighty over whatever He initiates. He observes all eyes while no eye can observe Him. He is Generous, Clement, Patient. His mercy encompasses everything, and so is His giving. He never rushes His revenge, nor does He hasten the retribution they deserve. He comprehends what the breast conceals and what the conscience hides. No inner I thought can be concealed from Him, nor does He confuse one with another. He encompasses everything, dominates everything, and subdues everything. Nothing is like Him. He initiates the creation from nothing; He is everlasting, living, sustaining in the truth; He is greater than can be conceived by visions, while He conceives all visions, the Eternal, the Knowing.

None can describe Him by seeing Him, nor can anyone find out how He is, be it by his intellect or by a spoken word except through what leads to Him, the Sublime, the Mighty that He is.

"I testify that He is Allāh, the One Who has filled time with His Holiness, the One Whose Light overwhelms eternity, Who effects His will without consulting anyone; there is no partner with Him in His decisions, nor is He assisted in running His affairs. He shaped what He made without following a preexisting model, and He created whatever He created without receiving help from anyone, nor did doing so exhaust Him nor frustrated His designs. He created, and so it was, and He initiated, and it became visible. So He is Allāh, the One and Only God, the One Who does whatever He does extremely well. He is the Just One Who never oppresses, the most Holy to Whom all affairs are referred.

"I further testify that He is Allāh before Whom everything is humbled, to Whose Greatness everything is humiliated, and to Whose Dignity everything submits. He is the King of every domain and the One Who places planets in their orbits. He controls the movements of the sun and of the moon, each circles till a certain time. He makes the night follow the day and the day follow the night, seeking it incessantly. He splits the spine of every stubborn tyrant and annihilates every mighty devil.

"Never has there been any opponent opposing Him nor a peer assisting Him. He is Independent; He never begets nor is He begotten, and none can ever be His equal. He is One God, the Glorified Lord. His will is done; His word is the law. He knows, so He takes account. He causes death and gives life. He makes some poor and others rich. He causes some to smile and others to cry .He brings some nearer to Him while distancing others from Him. He withholds and He gives. The domain belongs to Him and so is all the Praise. In His hand is all goodness, and He can do anything at all. He lets the night cover the day and the day cover the night; there is no god but He, the Sublime, the oft-Forgiving One. He responds to the supplication; He gives generously; He computes the breath; He is the Lord of the jinns and of mankind, the One Whom nothing confuses, nor is He annoyed by those who cry for His help, nor is He fed-up by those who persist. He safeguards the righteous against sinning, and He enables the winners to win. He is the Master of the faithful, the Lord of the Worlds Who deserves the appreciation of all those whom He created and is praised no matter what. I praise Him and always thank Him for the ease He brings me and for the constriction, in hardship and in prosperity, and I believe in Him, in His angels, in His Books and messengers. I listen to His Command and I obey, and I initiate the doing of whatever pleases Him, and I submit to His decree hoping to acquire obedience to Him and fear of His penalty, for He is Allāh against Whose designs nobody should feel secure, nor should anyone ever fear His "oppression."

"I testify, even against my own soul, that I am His servant, and I bear witness that he is my Lord. I convey what He reveals to me, being cautious lest I should not do it, so a catastrophe from Him would befall upon me, one which none can keep away, no matter how great his design may be and how sincere his friendship. There is no god but He, for He has informed me that if I do not convey what He has just revealed to me in honor of Ali in truth, I will not have conveyed His Message at all, and He, the Praised and the Exalted One, has guaranteed for me to protect me from the (evil) people, and He is Allāh, the One Who suffices, the Sublime. He has just revealed to me the following (verse): *In The Name of Allāh, the Most Gracious, the Most Merciful. O Messenger! Convey what has (just) been revealed to you (with regard to 'Ali), and if you do not do so, you will not have conveyed His Message at all, and Allāh shall protect you from (evil) people; surely Allāh will not guide the unbelieving people* (Qur'ān, 5:67).

"O people! I have not committed any shortcoming in conveying what Allāh Almighty revealed to me, and I am now going to explain to you the reason behind the revelation of this verse: Three times did Gabriel command me on behalf of the Peace, my Lord, Who is the source of all peace, to thus make a stand in order to inform everyone, black and white, that: Ali ibn Abū Tālib is my Brother, *Wasi*, and successor over my nation and the Imām after me, the one whose status to me is like that of Aaron to Moses except there will be no prophet after me, and he is your master next only to Allāh and to His Messenger, and Allāh has already revealed to me the same in one of the fixed of His Book saying,ₗverses "Your Master is Allāh and His Messenger and those who believe, those who keep up prayers and pay *zakāt* even as they bow down" (Qur'ān, 5:55), and, Ali ibn Abū Tālib the one who keeps up prayers, who pays *zakāt* even as he bows down, seeking to please Allāh, the Sublime, the Almighty, on each and every occasion.

"I asked Gabriel to plead to the Peace to excuse me from having to convey such a message to you, O people! Due to my knowledge that the pious are few while the hypocrites are many, and due to those who will blame me, and due to the trickery of those who ridicule Islam and whom Allāh described in His Book as saying with their tongues contrarily to what their hearts conceal, thinking lightly of it, while it is with Allāh magnanimous, and due to the Abūndance of their harm to me, so much so that they called me "ears" and claimed that I am so because of being so much in his (Ali's) company, always welcoming him, loving him and being so much pleased with him till Allāh, the Exalted and the Sublime One, revealed in this regard the verse saying: " And there are some of them who harm the (feelings of the) Prophet and say: He is an ear (*uthun* أُذُن; i.e. he always listens to Ali). *Say: One who listens (to Ali) is good for you; He believes in Allāh and testifies to the conviction of the believers and a mercy for those of you who believe; and those who (thus) harm the Messenger of Allāh shall have a painful punishment"* (Qur'ān, 9:61). Had I wished to name those who have called me so, I would have called them by their names, and I would have pointed them out. I would have singled them out and called them by what they really are, but I, by Allāh, am fully aware of their affairs. Yet despite all of that, Allāh insisted that I should convey what He has just revealed to me in honor of Ali. Then the Prophet recited the following verse:) *O Messenger! Convey what has (just) been revealed to you (with regard to 'Ali), and if you do not do so, you will not have conveyed His Message at all, and Allāh shall protect you from (evil) people* (Qur'ān, 5:67).

"O people! Comprehend (the implications of) what I have just said, and again do comprehend it, and be (further) informed that Allāh has installed him (Ali) as your Master and Imām, obligating the Muhajirun and the Ansār and those who follow them in goodness to

455

obey him, and so must everyone who lives in the desert or in the city, who is a non-Arab or an Arab, who is a free man or a slave, who is young or old, white or black, and so should everyone who believes in His Unity. His decree shall be carried out. His (Ali's) word is binding; his command is obligating; cursed is whoever opposes him, blessed with mercy is whoever follows him and believes in him, for Allāh has already forgiven him and forgiven whoever listens to him and obeys him.

"O people! This is the last stand I make in such a situation; so, listen and obey, and submit to the Command of Allāh, your Lord, for Allāh, the Exalted and the Sublime One, is your Master and Lord, then next to Him is His Messenger and Prophet who is now addressing you, then after me 'Ali is your Master and Imām according to the Command of Allāh, your Lord, then the lmams from among my progeny, his offspring, till the Day you meet Allāh and His Messenger. Nothing is permissible except what is deemed so by Allāh, His Messenger, and they (the Imāms), and nothing is prohibitive except what is deemed so by Allāh and His Messenger and they (the Imāms). Allāh, the Exalted and the Sublime One, has made me acquainted with what is permissible and what is prohibitive, and I have conveyed to you what my Lord has taught me of His Book, of what it decrees as permissible or as prohibitive.

"O people! Prefer him (Ali) over all others! There is no knowledge except that Allāh has divulged it to me, and all the knowledge I have learned I have divulged to Imām al-Muttaqin امام المتقين (leader of the righteous), and there is no knowledge (that I know) except that I divulged it to Ali, and he is *al-Imām al-Mubin* امام مبين (the evident Imām) whom Allāh mentions in Sūrat Ya-Sin: "*... and everything We have computed is in (the knowledge of) an evident Imām*" (Qur'ān, 36:12).

"O people! Do not abandon him, nor should you flee away from him, nor should you be too arrogant to accept his authority, for he is the one who guides to righteousness and who acts according to it. He defeats falsehood and prohibits others from acting according to it, accepting no blame from anyone while seeking to please Allāh. He is the first to believe in Allāh and in His Messenger; none preceded him as such. And he is the one who offered his life as a sacrifice for the Messenger of Allāh and who was in the company of the Messenger of Allāh while no other man was. He is the first of all people to offer prayers and the first to worship Allāh with me. I ordered him, on behalf of Allāh, to sleep in my bed, and he did, offering his life as a sacrifice for my sake.

"O people! Prefer him (over all others), for Allāh has preferred him, and accept him, for Allāh has appointed him (as your leader). O people! He is an Imām appointed by Allāh, and Allāh shall never accept the repentance of anyone who denies his authority, nor shall He forgive him; this is a must decree from Allāh never to do so to anyone who opposes him, and that He shall torment him with a most painful torment for all time to come, for eternity; so, beware lest you should oppose him and thus enter the fire the fuel of which is the people and the stones prepared for the unbelievers.

"O people! By Allāh! All past prophets and messengers conveyed the glad tiding of my advent, and I, by Allāh, am the seal of the prophets and of the messengers and the argument against all beings in the heavens and on earth. Anyone who doubts this commits apostasy similar to that of the early *jahiliyya*, and anyone who doubts anything of what I have just said doubts everything which has been revealed to me, and anyone who doubts any of the Imāms doubts all of them, and anyone who doubts us shall be lodged in the fire.

"O people! Allāh, the most Exalted and the Almighty, has bestowed this virtue upon me out of His kindness towards Ali and as a boon to Ali and there is no god but He; to Him all praise belongs in all times, for eternity, and in all circumstances. O people! Prefer Ali (over all others), for he is the very best of all people after me, be they males or females, so long as Allāh sends down His sustenance, so long as there are beings. Cursed and again cursed, condemned and again condemned, is anyone who does not accept this statement of mine and who does not agree to it. Gabriel himself has informed me of the same on behalf of Allāh Almighty Who he said (in Gabriel's words): "Anyone who antagonizes Ali and refuses to accept his *wilayat* shall incur My curse upon him and My wrath." "... *and let every soul consider what it has sent forth for the morrow, and be careful of (your duty to) Allāh"* (Qur'ān, 59:18), *"And do not make your oaths a means of deceit between you lest a foot should slip after its stability" (Qur'ān, 16:94), " Allāh is fully aware of all what you do"* (Qur'ān, 58: 13).

"O people! He (Ali) is *janb-Allāh* mentioned in the Book of Allāh, the Sublime One: The Almighty, forewarning his (Ali's) adversaries, says, *"Lest a soul should say: O woe unto me for what I fell short of my duty to Allāh, and most surely I was of those who laughed to scorn"* (Qur'ān, 39:56).

"O people! Study the Qur'ān and comprehend its verses, look into its fixed verses and do not follow what is similar thereof, for by Allāh, none shall explain to you what it forbids you from doing, nor clarify its exegesis, other than the one whose hand I am taking and whom I am lifting to me, the one whose arm I am taking and whom I am lifting, so that I may enable you to understand that: Whoever among you takes me as his master, this, Ali is his master, and he is Ali ibn Abū Tālib, my Brother and *wasi*, and his appointment as your *wali* is from Allāh, the Sublime, the Exalted One, a commandment which He revealed to me.

"O people! Ali and the good ones from among my offspring from his loins are the Lesser Weight, while the Qur'ān is the Greater One: each one of them informs you of and agrees with the other. They shall never part till they meet me at the Pool (of Kawthar). They are the Trustees of Allāh over His creation, the rulers on His earth. Indeed now I have performed my duty and conveyed the Message. Indeed you have heard what I have said and explained. Indeed Allāh, the Exalted One and the Sublime, has said, and so have Ion behalf of Allāh, the Exalted One and the Sublime, that there is no *Ameerul-Mo'mineen* أمير المـؤمنين (Commander of the Faithful) *save this Brother of mine*; no authority over a believer is permissible after me except to him."

Then the Prophet patted Ali's arm, lifting him up. Since the time when the Messenger of Allāh ascended the pulpit, *Ameerul-Mo'mineen* was one pulpit step below where the Messenger of Allāh had seated himself on his pulpit. As Ali was on his (Prophet's) right side, one pulpit step lower, now they both appeared to the gathering to be on the same level; the Prophet lifted him up. The Prophet then raised his hands to the heavens in supplication while Ali's leg was touching the knee of the Messenger of Allāh. The Prophet continued his sermon thus:

"O people! This is Ali, my Brother, *Wasi*, the one who comprehends my knowledge, and my successor over my nation, over everyone who believes in me. He is the one entrusted with explaining the Book of Allāh, the most Exalted One, the Sublime, and the one who invites people to His path. He is the one who does whatever pleases Him, fighting His enemies, befriending His friends who obey Him, prohibiting disobedience to Him. He is the successor of the Messenger of Allāh and *Ameerul- Mo'mineen*, the man assigned by Allāh to guide others, killer of the renegades and of those who believe in equals to Allāh, those who violate the Commandments of Allāh. Allāh says, *"My Word shall not be changed, nor am I in the least unjust to the servants"* (Qur'ān, 50.29), and by Your Command, O Lord, do I (submit and) say, O Allāh! Befriend whoever befriends him (Ali) and be the enemy of whoever antagonizes him; support whoever supports him and abandon whoever abandons him; curse whoever disavows him, and let Your Wrath descend on whoever usurps his right.

"O Lord! You revealed a verse in honor of Ali, Your *wali*, in its explanation and to effect Your own appointment of him this very day did You say, *"This day have I perfected your religion for you, completed My favor on you, and chosen for you Islam as a religion"* (Qur'ān, 5.3); "And whoever desires a religion other than Islam, it shall not be accepted from him, and in the hereafter he shall be one of the losers" (Qur'ān, 3:85). Lord! I implore You to testify that I have conveyed (Your Message).

"O people! Allāh, the Exalted and the Sublime, has perfected your religion through his (Ali's) Imāmate; so, whoever rejects him as his Imām or rejects those of my offspring from his loins who assume the same status (as lmams) till the Day of Judgment when they shall all be displayed before Allāh, the Exalted and the Sublime, these are the ones whose (good) deeds shall be nil and void in the life of this world and in the hereafter, and in the fire shall they be lodged forever, " ...*their torture shall not be decreased, nor shall they be given a respite"* (Qur'ān,2:162).

"O people! Here is Ali, the one who has supported me more than anyone else among you, the one who most deserves my gratitude, the one who is closest of all of you to me and the one who is the very dearest to me. Both Allāh, the Exalted and the Sublime, and I are pleased with him, and no verse of the Holy Qur'ān expressing Allāh's Pleasure except that he is implied therein, nor has any verse of praise been revealed in the Qur'ān except that he is implied therein, nor has the Lord testified to Paradise in the (Qur'ānic) Chapter starting with *"Has there not come over man a long period of time when he was nothing (not even) mentioned?"* (Qur'ān, 76:1) nor was this Chapter revealed except in his praise.

"O people! He is the one who supports the religion of Allāh, who argues on behalf of the Messenger of Allāh. He is the pious, the pure, the guide, the one rightly guided. Your Prophet is the best of all prophets, and your *wasi* is the best of all *wasis*, and his offspring are the best of *wasis*. O people! Each prophet's progeny is from his own loins whereas mine is from the loins of Arneerul-Mo'mineen Ali.

"O people! Iblis caused Adam to be dismissed from the garden through envy; so, do not envy him lest your deeds should be voided and lest your feet should slip away, for Adam was sent down to earth after having committed only one sin, and he was among the elite of Allāh's creation. How, then, will be your case, and you being who you are, and among you are enemies of Allāh? Indeed, none hates Ali except a wretch, and none accepts Ali's wilayat except a pious person. None believes in him except a sincere *mu'min*, and in honor of, Ali was the Chapter of Asr (Ch. 103) revealed, I swear to it by Allāh: "In the Name of Allāh, the Beneficent, the Merciful. I swear by time that most surely man is in loss" (Qur'ān, 103:1-2) except Ali who believed and was pleased with the truth and with perseverance.

"O people! I have sought Allāh to be my Witness and have conveyed

460

my Message to you, and the Messenger is obligated only to clearly convey (his Message). O people! *"Fear Allāh as Re ought to be feared, and do not die except as Muslims"* (Qur'ān, 3:102). O people! *" ...Believe in what We have revealed, verifying what you have, before We alter faces then turn them on their backs or curse them as We cursed the violators of the Sabbath"* (Qur'ān, 4:47). By Allāh! Redid not imply anyone in this verse except a certain band of my *sahāba* whom I know by name and by lineage, and I have been ordered (by my Lord) to pardon them; so, let each person deal with Ali according to what he finds in his heart of love or of hatred.

"O people! The *noor* from Allāh, the Exalted One and the Sublime, flows through me then through 'Ali ibn Abū Tālib then in the progeny that descends from him till al-Qā'im al-Mahdi القائم المهدي (عج), who shall effect the justice of Allāh, and who will take back any right belonging to us because Allāh, the Exalted and the Sublime, made us Hujjat over those who take us lightly, the stubborn ones, those who act contrarily to our word, who are treacherous, who are sinners, who are oppressors, who are usurpers, from the entire world.

"O people! I warn you that I am the Messenger of Allāh; messengers before me have already passed away; so, should I die or should I be killed, are you going to turn upon your heels? And whoever turns upon his heels shall not harm Allāh in the least, and Allāh shall reward those who are grateful, those who persevere. 'Ali is surely the one described with perseverance and gratitude, then after him are my offspring from his loins.

"O people! Do not think that you are doing me a favor by your accepting Islam. Nay! Do not think that you are doing Allāh such a favor lest He should void your deeds, lest His wrath should descend upon you, lest He should try you with a flame of fire and brass; surely your Lord is ever-watchful.

"O people! There shall be Imāms after me who shall invite people to the fire, and they shall not be helped on the Day of Judgment. O people! Allāh and I are both clear of them. O people! They and their supporters and followers shall be in the lowest rung of the fire;

miserable, indeed, is the resort of the arrogant ones. Indeed, these are the folks of the *sahifa* [a covenant written by a number of very prominent Muslims, some of whom are sanctified by some Muslims, pledging to assassinate the Prophet; it was written and signed then buried at one of the walls of the Ka'ba]; so, let each one of you look into his *sahifa*! [This reference to the *sahifa* has been overlooked by most people with the exception of a small band, and I, author of this book, will *Insha-Allāh* shed light on this *sahifa* in my later writings. The Prophet continued his historic sermon thus:]

"O people! I am calling for it to be an Imāmate and a succession confined to my offspring till the Day of Judgment, and I have conveyed only what I have been commanded (by my Lord) to convey to drive the argument home against everyone present or absent and on everyone who has witnessed or who has not, who is already born or he is yet to be born; therefore, let those present here convey it to those who are absent, and let the father convey it to his son, and so on till the Day of Judgment. And they shall make the Imāmate after me a property, *a usurpation*; may Allāh curse the usurpers who usurp, and it is then that you, O jinns and mankind, will get the full attention of the One Who shall cause a flame of fire and brass to be hurled upon you, and you shall not achieve any victory!

"O people! Allāh, the Exalted and the Sublime, is not to let you be whatever you want to be except so that He may distinguish the bad ones from among you from the good, and Allāh is not to make you acquainted with the unknown. O people! There shall be no town that falsifies except that Allāh shall annihilate it on account of its falsehood before the Day of Judgment, and He shall give al-lmam al-Mahdi (ﷺ) authority over it, and surely Allāh's promise is true.

"O people! Most of the early generations before you have strayed, and by Allāh, He surely annihilated the early generations, and He shall annihilate the later ones. Allāh Almighty has said, *"Did We not destroy the former generations? Then did We follow them up with later ones. Even thus shall We deal with the guilty. Woe on that Day to the rejecters!"* (Qur'ān, 77: 16-19).

462

"O people! Allāh has ordered me to do and not to do, and I have ordered 'Ali to do and not to do, so he learned what should be done and what should not; therefore. you should listen to his orders so that you may be safe, and you should obey him so that you may be rightly guided. Do not do what he forbids you from doing so that you may acquire wisdom. Agree with him, and do not let your paths be different from his. O people! I am as-Sirat al-Mustaqeem (the Straight Path) of Allāh whom He commanded you to follow, and it is after me Ali then my offspring from his loins, the Imāms of Guidance: They guide to the truth and act accordingly."

Then the Prophet recited the entire text of Sūrat al-Fātiha and commented by saying: "It is in my honor that this (Sūra) was revealed, including them (the Imāms) specifically; they are the friends of Allāh for whom there shall be no fear, nor shall they grieve; truly the Party of Allāh are the winners. Indeed, it is their enemies who are the impudent ones, the deviators, the brethren of Satan; they inspire each other with embellished speech out of their haughtiness. Indeed, their (Imāms') friends are the ones whom Allāh, the Exalted One, the Great, mentions in His Book saying, *"You shall not find a people who believe in Allāh and in the latter Day befriending those who act in opposition to Allāh and to His Prophet, even though they may be their own fathers or sons or brothers or kinsfolk; these are they into whose hearts He has impressed conviction"* (Qur'ān, 58:22). Indeed, their (Imāms') friends are the *mu'mins* (believers) whom Allāh, the Exalted One, the Sublime, describes as: *"Those who believe and do not mix up their faith with iniquity, those are the ones who shall have the security, and they are the rightly guided"* (Qur'ān, 6:82).

"Indeed, their friends are those who believed and never doubted. Indeed, their friends are the ones who shall enter Paradise in peace and security; the angels shall receive them with welcome saying, "Peace be upon you! Enter it and reside in it forever!" Indeed, their friends shall be rewarded with Paradise where they shall be sustained without having to account for anything. Indeed, their enemies are the ones who shall be hurled into the fire. Indeed, their enemies are the ones who shall hear the exhalation of hell as it increases in intensity, and they shall see it sigh. Indeed, their enemies are the ones thus described by Allāh: *"Whenever a nation enters, it shall curse its sister..."* (Qur'ān, 7:38). Indeed, their enemies are the ones whom Allāh, the Exalted One and the Sublime, describes thus: *"Whenever a group is cast into it, its keepers shall ask them: Did any warner not come to you? They shall say: Yea! Indeed, there came to us a warner but we rejected (him) and said: Allāh has not revealed anything; you are only in a great error. And they shall say: Had we but listened or pondered, we would not have been among the inmates of the burning fire. So they shall acknowledge their sins, but far will be forgiveness) from the inmates of the burning fire"* (Qur'ān, 67:8-11). Indeed, their friends are the ones who fear their Lord in the unseen; forgiveness shall be theirs and a great reward.

"O people! What a difference it is between the fire and the great reward! O people! Our enemy is the one whom Allāh censures and curses, whereas our friend is everyone praised and loved by Allāh. O people! I am the Warner (*nathir* نـذير) and Ali is the one who brings glad tidings (*basheer* بشير). O people! I am the one who warns (*munthir*) while 'Ali is the guide (*hadi* هادي). O people! I am a Prophet (*nabi* نبي) and Ali is the successor (*wasi* وصي). O people! I am a Messenger (*rasool* رسول) and Ali is the Imām and the *wasi* after me, and so are the Imāms after him from among his offspring. Indeed, I am their father, and they shall descend from his loins. Indeed, the seal of the lmams from among us is al-Qā'im al-Mahdi. He, indeed, is the one who shall come out so that the creed may prevail. He, indeed, is the one who shall seek revenge against the oppressor. He, indeed, is the one who conquers the forts and demolishes them. He, indeed, is the one who subdues every tribe from among the people of polytheism and the one to guide it. He is the one who shall seek redress for all friends of Allāh. He is the one who supports the religion of Allāh. He ever derives (his knowledge) from a very deep ocean. He shall identify each man of distinction by his distinction and every man of ignorance by his ignorance. He shall be the choicest of Allāh's beings and the chosen one. He is the heir of all (branches of) knowledge, the one who encompasses every perception. He conveys on behalf of his Lord, the Exalted and the Sublime, who points out His miracles. He is the wise, the one endowed with wisdom, the one upon whom (Divine) authority is

464

vested. Glad tidings of him have been conveyed by past generations, yet he is the one who shall remain as a Hujja, and there shall be no Hujja after him nor any right except with him, nor any *noor* except with him. None, indeed, shall subdue him, nor shall he ever be vanquished. He is the friend of Allāh on His earth, the judge over His creatures, the custodian of what is evident and what is hidden of His.

"O people! I have explained (everything) for you and enabled you to comprehend it, and this Ali shall after me explain everything to you. At the conclusion of my *khutba*, I shall call upon you to shake hands with me to swear your allegiance to him and to recognize his authority, then to shake hands with him after you have shaken hands with me. I had, indeed, sworn allegiance to Allāh, and Ali had sworn allegiance to me, and I on behalf of Allāh, the Exalted One and the Sublime, I require you to swear the oath of allegiance to him: *"Surely those who swear (the oath of) allegiance to you do but swear allegiance to Allāh; the hand of Allāh is above their hands; therefore, whoever reneges (from his oath), he reneges only to the injury of his own soul, and whoever fulfills what he has covenanted with Allāh, He will grant him a mighty reward"* (Qur'ān,48:10).

"O people! The pilgrimage (*hajj*) and the 'umra are among Allāh's rituals; *"So whoever makes a pilgrimage to the House or pays a visit (to it), there is no blame on him if he goes round them [Safa and Marwa] both"* (Qur'ān, 2:158). O people! Perform your pilgrimage to the House, for no members of a family went there except that they became wealthy, and receive glad tidings! None failed to do so except that their lineage was cut-off and were impoverished. O people! No believer stands at the standing place [at 'Arafa] except that Allāh forgives his past sins till then; so, once his pilgrimage is over, he resumes his deeds. O people! Pilgrims are assisted, and their expenses shall be replenished, and Allāh never suffers the rewards of the doers of good to be lost.

"O people! Perform your pilgrimage to the House by perfecting your religion and by delving into *fiqh*, and do not leave the sacred places except after having repented and abandoned (the doing of anything prohibited). O people! Uphold prayers and pay the *zakāt* as Allāh, the Exalted One and the Sublime, commanded you; so, if time lapses and you were short of doing so or you forgot, Ali is your *wali* and he will explain for you. He is the one whom Allāh, the Exalted and the Sublime, appointed for you after me as the custodian of His creation. He is from me and I am from him, and he and those who will succeed him from my progeny shall inform you of anything you ask them about, and they shall clarify whatever you do not know. *Halāl* and *harām* things are more than I can count for you now or explain, for a commandment to enjoin what is permissible and a prohibition from what is not permissible are both on the same level, so I was ordered (by my Lord) to take your oath of allegiance and to make a covenant with you to accept what I brought you from Allāh, the Exalted One and the Sublime, with regards to Ali *Ameerul-Mo'mineen* and to the *wasis* after him who are from me and from him, a standing Imāmate whose seal is al-Mahdi till the Day he meets Allāh Who decrees and Who judges.

"O people! I never refrained from informing you of everything permissible or prohibitive; so, do remember this and safeguard it and advise each other to do likewise; do not alter it; do not substitute it with something else. I am now repeating what I have already said: Uphold the prayers and pay the *zakāt* and enjoin righteousness and forbid abomination. The peak of enjoining righteousness is to resort to my speech and to convey it to whoever did not attend it and to order him on my behalf to accept it and to (likewise) order him not to violate it, for it is an order from Allāh, the Exalted and the Sublime, and there is no knowledge of enjoining righteousness nor prohibiting abomination except that it is with a *ma'soom* (infallible) Imām امام معصوم.

"O people! The Qur'ān informs you that the Imāms after him are his (Ali's) descendants, and I have already informed you that they are from me and from him, for Allāh says in His Book, *"And he made it a word to continue in his posterity so that they may return "* (Qur'ān, 43:28) while I have said: "You shall not stray as long as you uphold both of them (simultaneously)." O people! (Uphold) piety, (uphold) piety, and be forewarned of the Hour as Allāh, the Exalted and the Sublime, has said, *"O people! Guard (yourselves) against (punishment from) your Lord; surely the violence of the Hour is a grievous thing"* (Qur'ān, 22:1).

"Remember death, resurrection, the judgment, the scales, and the account before the Lord of the Worlds, and (remember) the rewards and the penalty. So whoever does a good deed shall be rewarded for it, and whoever commits a sin shall have no place in the Gardens. O people! You are more numerous than (it is practical) to shake hands with me all at the same time, and Allāh, the Exalted and the Sublime, commanded me to require you to confirm what authority I have vested upon Ali *Ameerul-Mo'mineen* and to whoever succeeds him of the Imāms from me and from him, since I have just informed you that my offspring are from his loins. You, therefore, should say in one voice: 'We hear, and we obey; we accept and we are bound by what you have conveyed to us from our Lord and yours with regard to our Imām Ali *Ameerul-Mo'mineen*, and to the Imāms, your sons from his loins. We swear the oath of allegiance to you in this regard with our hearts, with our souls, with our tongues, with our hands. According to it shall we live, and according to it shall we die, and according to it shall we be resurrected. We shall not alter anything or substitute anything with another, nor shall we doubt nor deny nor suspect, nor shall we violate our covenant nor abrogate the pledge. You admonished us on behalf of Allāh with regard to Ali *Ameerul-Mo'mineen*, and to the Imāms whom you mentioned to be from your offspring from among his descendants after him: al-Hassan and al-Hussain and to whoever is appointed (as such) by Allāh after them. The covenant and the pledge are taken from us, from our hearts, from our souls, from our tongues, from our conscience, from our hands. Whoever does so by his handshake, it shall be so, or otherwise testified to it by his tongue, and we do not seek any substitute for it, nor shall Allāh see our souls deviating there from. We shall convey the same on your behalf to anyone near and far of our offspring and families, and we implore Allāh to testify to it, and surely Allāh suffices as the Witness and you, too, shall testify for us.'

"O people! What are you going to say?! Allāh knows every sound and the innermost of every soul; *"Whoever chooses the right guidance, it is for his own soul that he is rightly guided, and whoever strays, it is only to its detriment that he goes astray"*

(Qur'ān, 17:15). O people! Swear the oath of allegiance to Allāh, and swear it to me, and swear it to Ali *Ameerul-Mo'mineen*, and to al-Hassan and al-Hussain and to the Imāms from their offspring in the life of this world and in the hereafter, a word that shall always remain so. Allāh shall annihilate anyone guilty of treachery and be merciful upon everyone who remains true to his word*: "Whoever reneges (from his oath), he reneges only to the harm of his own soul, and whoever fulfills what he has covenanted with Allāh, He will grant him a mighty reward"* (Qur'ān, 48:10).

"O people! Repeat what I have just told you to, and greet Ali with the title of authority of "*Ameerul-Mo'mineen*" and say: *"We hear, and we obey, O Lord! Your forgiveness (do we seek), and to You is the eventual course"* (Qur'ān, 2:285), and you should say: *"All praise is due to Allāh Who guided us to this, and we would not have found the way had it not been for Allāh Who guided us"* (Qur'ān, 7:43).

"O people! The merits of Ali ibn Abū Tālib with Allāh, the Exalted and the Sublime, the merits which are revealed in the Qur'ān, are more numerous than I can recount in one speech; so, whoever informs you of them and defines them for you, you should believe him. O people! Whoever obeys Allāh and His Messenger and Ali and the Imāms to whom I have already referred shall attain a great victory. O people! Those foremost from among you who swear allegiance to him and who pledge to obey him and who greet him with the greeting of being the Commander of the Faithful are the ones who shall win the Gardens of Felicity. O people! Say what brings you the Pleasure of Allāh, for if you and all the people of the earth disbelieve, it will not harm Allāh in the least. O Lord! Forgive the believers through what I have conveyed, and let Your Wrath descend upon those who renege, the apostates, and all Praise is due to Allāh, the Lord of the Worlds."

Thus did the Prophet of Allāh (ﺹ) speak on behalf of the Almighty Who sent him as the beacon of guidance not only for the Muslims but for all mankind. But the question that forces itself here is: "What happened after that historic event? Why did the Muslims forget, or pretend to have forgotten, their Prophet's instructions with regards to

468

Ali and supposedly "elected" someone else in his stead?" To answer this question requires the writing of another book and, indeed many such books have been written. May the Almighty grant all of us guidance, and may He count us among His true servants who recognize the truth when they see it, who abide by His tenets, Who revere His Prophet and follow his instructions in all times, in all climes, *Allāhomma Ameen* اللهم آمين.

The reader may wonder what happened following this Ghadīr incident. The answer is very simple: The most prominent Muslims of the time prtended to have forgotten it, so they met at سقيفة بني ساعدة the shed of Bani Sā'ida, few meters from the Prophet's Mosque, where they kept for days fussing with each other about who would succeed the Prophet (ص) as the caliph while the corpse of the Prophet (ص) was lying in state waiting to be buried... And the rest is history.

The Ghadīr incident is immortalized in Arabic poetry. Hassan ibn Thabit, the Prophet's poet, was there and then witnessing the appointment of Ali as أمير المؤمنين Commander of the Faithful, so he composed the following lines of poetry on the occasion which I roughly translated below:

بخم، و أكرم بالنبي مناديا	يناديهم يوم الغدير نبيهم
فقالوا و لم يبدوا هناك التعاديا:	يقول: فمن مولاكم و وليكم
و لن تجدن منا لك اليوم عاصيا	الهك مولانا و أنت ولينا
رضيتك من بعدي اماما و هاديا	فقال له: قم يا علي فانني
لعينيه مما يشتكيه مداويا	و كان علي أرمد العين يبتغي
فبورك مرقيا و بورك راقيا	فداواه خير الناس منه بريقه

Their Prophet on the Ghadīr Day calls upon them all
At Khumm, how great the Prophet is when he does call!
He said, "Who is your Master and Wali?"
They said, showing on that day no hostility,
"Our Master is our God while our Wali is you,
You shall find today none to disobey you."
He said to him, "Stand up, O Ali, for I did find
"You to be and Imām after me and a guide."
Ali was sore in the eyes and did seek a remedy

For that from which was complaining Ali,
So he was doctored with the saliva of the best of all,
So the one who received it and who gave it are blessed by all.
(Reference: al-Qanduzi, *Yanabi al-Mawadda* ينابيع المودة, p. 120)

For those who have the habit of casting doubt about anything in which they do not wish to believe, we would like to state below some mostly classic references where this *Khutba of the Ghadīr* is quoted. In these references the reader can deliberate on the various portions of this historic sermon as quoted in bits and pieces in these references. Most of these references are considered reliable by the majority of Muslims, Sunnis and Shī'ites:

1. Jalal ad-Deen as-Sayyuti, *Kitab Al-Itqan*, Vol. 1, p. 31.
2. al-Majlisi, *Bihar.al-Anwar*, Vol. 21, pp. 360-90, Vol. 37, pp. 111-235, and Vol. 41, p. 228.He Quotes book *Al-Ih'tijaj* by at-Tibrisi (vol.2)
3. *Al-Bidaya wal Nihaya*, Vol. 5, p. 208.
4. *Badeeal-Ma'ani*, p. 75
5. *Tareekh Baghdad*, V01. 1, p. 411 and V01. 8, p. 290.
6. *Tareekh Dimashq*, Vol. 5, p. 210.
7. Ibn al-Jawziyya, *Tadh'kirat al-Khawas*, pp. 18-20.
8. Ibn as-Sa'ud's *Tafseer*, Vol. 8, p. 292.
9. At-Tibari, *Tafseer al-Qur'ān*, Vol. 3, p. 428 and Vol. 6, p. 46.
10. al-Fakhr ar-Razi, *At-Tafseer al-Kabeer*, Vol. 3, p. 636.
11. *At-Tamhid fi USool al-Deen*, p. 171.
12. *Tayseer al-Wusul*, Vol. 1, p. 122.
13. Ghiyath ad-Din ibn Hammam, *Tareekh Habib as-Siyar*, V01. 1, p. 144.
14. al-Maqrizi, *Khutat*, p. 223.
15. as-Sayyuti, *Al-Durr al-Manthur*, Vol. 2, pp. 259, 298.
16. *Thakha'ir al-'Uqba*, p. 68.
17. *Ruh al-Ma'ani*, Vol. 2, p. 348.
18. Mohibb at-Tabari, *Al-Riyadh an-Nadhirah*, Vol. 2, p.169. Look it up also in his *Tarikh*.
19. *As-Siraj al-Munir*, Vol. 4, p. 364.
20. al-Hakim, *As-Seera al-Halabiyya*, Vol. 3, p. 302.
21. *Shar'h al-Mawahib*, V01. 7, p. 13.

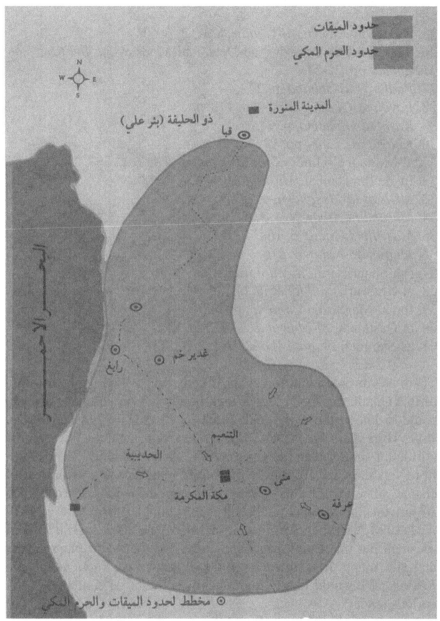

حدود الميقات
حدود الحرم المكي

المدينة المنورة ◼

ذو الحليفة (بئر علي)   قبا ◉

البحر الأحمر

رابغ ◉   ◉ غدير خم

التنعيم

الحديبية

منى ◉

مكة المكرمة ◼   عرفة ◉

◎ مخطط لحدود الميقات والحرم المكي

A road map showing location of Ghadīr Khumm almost in the center

22. Ibn Hajar al-Asqalani, *As-Sawa'iq al-Muhriqa*, p. 26.
23. Ibn al-Badriq, *Al-'Umda*, p. 52.

24. Badr ad-Deen, *'Umdat al-Qari fi Shar'h al-Bukhāri*, V01. 8, p. 584.

25. Hassan al-Ameen, *Al-Ghadīr*, V01. 2, p. 57.

26. Sharafud-Deen Sadr ad-Deen al-Mousawi, *Al-Fusul al-Muhimma*, pp. 25-27.

27. *Fadha 'il as-Sahāba*, p. 272.

28. *Faydh al-Ghadīr*, V01. 6, p. 218.

29. *Kashf al-Ghumma*, p. 94.

30. *Kifayat al- Tālib*, pp. 17, 28.

31. al-Muttaqi al-Hindi, *Kanz al-'Ummal*, Vol. 6, p. 397.

32. Imām Ibn Hanbal, *Musnad*, V01. 4, p. 281.

33. *Mishkat al-Masabeeh*, p. 272.

34. *Mushkil al-Athar*, Vol. 3, p. 196.

35. *MaTālib as-Su'ul*, p. 16.

36. *Muftah an-Najat*, p. 216.

37. ash-Shahristani, *Al-Milal wal Nihal*, V 01. 1, p. 220.

38. al-Khawarizmi, *Manaqib*, pp. 80, 94.

39. Ibn al-Maghazli, *Manaqib*, p. 232.

40. al-Qastalani, *Al-Mawahib*, Vol. 2, p. 13.

41. as-Samhudi, *Wafaal-Wafa'*, Vol. 2, p. 173.

There is a question that forces itself here, folks: What is the location of this Ghadīr and how does it look like now? As you have already come to know, the event took place in 10 A.H./632 A.D., that is, 1,422 Hijri years ago, 1,379 Christian Era years ago; the Hijri year is a little bit shorter than the CE (or A.D., Anno Domini, "Year of our Lord", as they call it). Surely the site has undergone a great deal of change since then. Kamal al-Sayyid has conducted a research which Ansāriyan Publications published it in a booklet form first in 1419 A.H./1998 A.D. then reprinted it in 1424 A.H./2003 A.D. It falls in 45 small but interesting pages plus nine pages of color photographs and site maps. It is titled الطريق الى غدير خم *The Road to Ghadīr Khumm*. We would like to quote below some of its contents for the curious reader:

The "Ghadīr Khumm" area is located midway on the route between Mecca and Medīna near the Juhfa. Our Prophet (ص) passed through it during his historic *hijra*, or Hegira, migration, in September of 622 A.D. then on the 18th of Thul-Hijja of the 10th Hijri year (March 16,

472

632 A.D. according to the Julian calendar or the 19th of March of the same year according to the Gregorian calendar) during his return from the Farewell Pilgrimage حجة الوداع. Sands have covered the ancient caravan routes in this area which is now called the Ghurba غربة, but a water spring still gushes out of the core of stones in a spacious valley bordered by two mountain series from the north and the south. One who leaves the port city of Jidda on the Red Sea will arrive at the Juhfa junction near Rabigh city مدينة رابغ where there is a local air port on the route's right side. The distance between the said junction and the Miqat Mosque مسجد الميقات, which was built on the ruins of an ancient mosque, extends to 10 kilo meters. From this Miqat Mosque, one can head in the direction of the Alyaa Mansion قصر علياء across a route full of sand dunes where the blessed migration route can still be seen. This Mansion is located on the borders of the Juhfa village in the direction that leads to Medīna and to Rabigh city, whereas the Miqat Mosque is located, in the direction that leads to Mecca. The distance between the Miqat Mosque and the Alyaa Mansion is about five kilo meters. Sand dunes and torrential rains have created sand dams between both areas where there are mountain heights that form the path leading to an open valley where routes diverge. From there, one can go in the direction of the Ghurba, which is not easy to get to because of the sand dunes. As for the Ghadīr area itself, it falls at the borders of the Harra, an area filled with black stones where it is impossible for anything to grow, at the end of which the broad valley opens and leads to the Ghadīr water spring. It is in this very spot that the Prophet (ص) stopped to convey the caravans of pilgrims and the entire Islamic nation, then, now and till the Judgment Day, the last of the Almighty's directives to the faithful.

Because of violent torrential floods during rainy seasons, the area's features keep changing. One who seeks the blessing of this spot, where the very last of the Almighty's prophets and their very best, Muhammed (ص), stopped to make history, can go via one of two routes: either the Juhfa or the Rabigh: The first route starts from the Juhfa junction at the Rabigh Airport where there is a paved road extending up to nine kilo meters to the Juhfa village, where there is a large mosque, and from there he takes a route to the right to a distance of two kilo meters of sand dunes and dark rocks, as dark as the hearts of all those Muslims who forgot, or pretended to have forgotten, the Ghadīr Declaration and left it behind their backs and will continue to do so for all time to come. At the end of that route, the Ghadīr valley starts.

The second route starts from the Mecca-Medīna junction in the direction of Rabigh. After a distance of ten kilo meters, the road leading to the Ghadīr diverges; the distance from Rabigh to the Ghadīr is about 26 kilo meters. The Ghadīr valley is located, generally speaking, to the east of the Miqat Mosque in the Juhfa at the distance of eight kilo meters, or to the south from Rabigh city at the distance of 26 kilo meters. In this sacred spot, a mosque was built. Its structure has for long been covered by sands and torrential waters. Winds and other soil erosion factors have all taken their toll on it. This mosque may have remained up to the beginning of the 8th century; only its walls remain as indicted in books of *fiqh* and history as well as texts of *ziyara* of those who seek Allāh's blessings at it, supplicating to the Almighty and pleading to Him to keep their firm on the footsteps of the Prophet of Islam (ص) and to count them among those who act upon the last will of His beloved Prophet and Messenger (ص) who never spoke a word of his own but only conveyed the Divine Message which he received from his Lord and Maker.

It is a shame that only Shī'ite Muslims now joyously celebrate the Eid al-Ghadīr feast, as if the Prophet (ص) singled them out to do so rather than generalizing the message to all those who testify that لا اله الا الله، محمد رسول الله *There is no god save Allāh, Muhammed (ص) is the Messenger of Allāh.* And do not be surprised, dear reader, if someone, a Muslim, of course, tells you that all what is said about Ghadīr Khumm is simply "old hags' tales", for there are such people in all times and climes. May the Almighty keep us away from such folks. May He forgive them and lead them to His Path, *Allāhomma Aameen* اللّهم آمين.

Ghara غاره: raid, incursion, sudden descent (upon something), (predatory) invasion

Ghawi غـاوي: aberrant (individual or group), deviate, stray,

474

misguided

Ghazi غازي: Muslim soldier, warrior

Ghazwa غزوة: military expedition, campaign, invasion

Ghulat غلاة: plural of *ghali*, an extremist, one whose views and/or actions are excessive, the name of a renegade sect; noun: غلو ghulu; the best (worst) example of extremists these days are the Takfiris who follow to the letter the philosophy of Ibn Taymiyyah.

Ghusul غسل: ceremonial bath conducted in certain ways, physical purification, for occasions such as Friday ghusul, *Janaba* ghusul, Burial ghusul, etc.

ح،ه H

Habs حبس: confinement, imprisonment, detention, jail

Hadas حدس: conjucture, presumption, a sense of something

Hadd حد: penalty imposed by the Shari`a, border, adjoin, margin, frontier, barrier, ceiling, limit

Hadi هادي: guide, one who shows the right path to others: It may be any ordinary person who guides others towards what is good for them, something which is righteous, useful and beneficial. If the definite article "the " is added to it, it will have a special meaning, a much broader one: It will then refer to the Almighty Who guides His servants to His Right Path, or it may be one of the Infallible Imāms who, in turn, are guided by the Almighty and instructed to show the right way to people. Here are two examples for you:

One is **"Al-Hadi الهادي"**, the Almighty God, Allāh, سبحانه و تعالى Praise and Exaltation belong to Him and only Him. The Most Glorified and Exalted One has said, ... *and sufficient is your Lord as a Guide and a Helper* (Qur'ān, 25:31). "Al-Hadi" is an Attribute derived, linguistically, from hidaya, guidance, which means: to attract someone to something, such as attracting the heart of a believer to al-Hadi, to the One Who provides such guidance. Guidance means bringing the hearts closer to the Almighty. Guidance is the following of one's sound reason and common sense and the graceful way of bringing someone to the anticipated goal. He guides the elite from among His servants whom He has chosen to know His Essence, so much so that they see things through Him, and He guides the commoners among them to witness His creatures, so much so that they have seen them as signs of His being their Creator and Sustainer. He has guided everything He created to whatever means whereby it can satisfy its needs. He has guided the baby to suck the breast of its mother, the young birds to pick the seeds, and the bees to build their honey-combs in hexagonal shapes which are the best to suit the forms of their bodies, and such examples are quite lengthy indeed. Al-Hadi guides the guilty to repentance, and those blessed with knowledge to the facts regarding nearness to Him.

Al-Hadi occupies the hearts by truthfulness and equity, the bodies by life and death. Al-Hadi has given everything He has created its shape and characteristics, and He guides whom He creates to the goals behind His creating them, to issues related to their life in this world and to those related to their creed, in addition to everything else related to them. He guides the hearts to know Him and the souls to obey Him; He guides the guilty to the path of repentance, the sincere ones to nearness to Him after being far from it. He keeps the hearts filled with love for equity and truth; He enables them to treat people justly. Al-Hadi is in all reality Allāh. Al-Hadi has guided the elite from among His servants to wisdom and knowledge. Whenever the Messenger of Allāh woke up during the night for prayers, he would supplicate to his Lord saying, "Lord! God of Gabriel, Michael and Israfil, Originator of the heavens and the earth, Knower of the unknown and the Witness! You judge between Your servants regarding that wherein they dispute! I plead to You to guide me to that wherein they have differed, by Your will, for You guide whomsoever You please to a straight path." We know that the Almighty is the source of all guidance, but we also know that He works through mediums, agents, servants of His who obey His commandments and guide others to His Path, the Path of happiness in this life and in the life to come. These guides can be ordinary men and they can be scholars of theology who dedicate years of their life to studying His Holy Book, the Qur'ān, and His Prophet's Sunna.

Below is information about one of His servants who dedicated his life to serving his Creator and the servants of this Creator; he is Infallible Imām Ali al-Hadi, peace be with him and with all Imāms from among the Prophet's Progeny:

The other is **Imām al-Hadi (ع):** His first name is Ali which is usually prefixed by one of his many titles the most famous of which are: an-Nasih, al-Muftah, an-Najib, al-Murtada, al-Hadi, an-Naqi, al-Alim, al-Faqih, al-Amin, al-Mu'taman, at-Tayyib, al-Mutawakkil, a title which he avoided very much during the Abbāsid ruler who also was called "al-Mutawakkil", and the "Askari *Faqih*". Because both Imāms Ali ibn Abū Tālib, al-Murtada, and Ali ar-Ridha, peace be with both of them, were called "Abul-Hassan" each, Imām Ali al-Hadi (ع) is referred to as "Abul-Hassan III". His mother's name is Sumana Khatun. He was born in Saria, a suburb of Medīna, now "Saudi Arabia", on Rajab 5, 214 A.H./September 8, 829 A.D. He enjoyed the love of his father, Imām at-Taqi and also al-Jawad (ع), for only six years because his father had to leave for Baghdad where he was martyred on the 29th of Thu al-Qi`da 220 A.H./November 24, 835 A.D. and the responsibilities of Imāmate devolved on his young son's shoulders. Providence was the only tutor and instructor that reared and raised him to the extreme zenith of learning. For more information about Imām al-Hadi (ع), refer to our discussion above of the nine Imāms who descended from the hero of this book (ع).

Hadīth or Hadeeth حديث: A report on a statement or tradition (action) of Prophet Muhammed (ص) or what he witnessed and approved of is called *hadīth* (sing.; plural: *ahadīth*). These are the explanations, interpretations and living examples of the Prophet (ص) as he taught the nation and/or explained the teachings of the Qur'ān. Other meanings of this word include: modern, new, talk, speech, conversation, fresh, novel

Hadīth Qudsi حديث قدسي: one of *ahadīth* in which the Prophet cites the Almighty; i.e. the speech of the Almighty as worded by His Prophet Muhammed. The meaning of these *ahadīth* indicates revelations to the Prophet which the Prophet (ص) put in his own words, unlike the Qur'ān which is the word of Allāh Almighty as conveyed to the Prophet (ص) exactly, *verbatim*.

Hafiz حافض: one who has learned the entire text of the Holy Qur'ān by heart; plural *huffaz*; another meaning refers to an angel in charge of protecting a human's life till it is time for his/her demise

Hajib حاجب: doorkeeper, usher

Hajiz حاجز: barrier, curtain, separator, obstruction, check or control post

Hajj or Haj or Hijj حج: Hajj is an Arabic word which means: the performance of the Islamic pilgrimage to Mecca in Hijaz, northern Saudi Arabia. It is one of the five pillars of Islam. A Muslim is to perform *hajj* at least once in his/her life, if he has the means (of health and financial ability) to do so. There are rules and regulations as well as specific outfits related to the performance of this rite. The Islamic pilgrimage takes place during the last month of the Islamic lunar calendar, namely the month of Thul-Hijja.

Hajz حجز: seizure, sequestration, garnishment, confinement, impounding

Halal حلال: something which is lawful, permissible, in Islam, the opposite of *haram*

Halif or Haleef حليف: ally, one who enjoys the protection of a tribe but does not belong to it

Hakim حاكم: ruler, governor, judge, magistrate

Halaqa حلقة: ring, circle, cycle, a group of students involved in the study of Islam

Hamid or Hameed حميد : praiseworthy, commendable, laudable

Hamim or Hameem حميم: intimate, very close (friend); another meaning refers to the boiling water or pus given to the residents of hell whenever they ask for water

478

Hamiya حاميه: garrison, protection force

Hāmil حامل: bearer, carrier, conveyor, , holder, expectant, pregnant

Hanan حنان: affection, tenderness, sympathy, compassion

Hanif or Haneef حنيف: *Haneefs* are people who, during the pre-Islamic period of *jahiliyya*, rejected the worship of idols. These people were in search for the true religion of Prophet Abraham.

Hanith حانث: perjurer, guilty of perjury

Hannata (v.) حنط: embalmed, (n.) embalming حنوط. A word of caution here: Do not confuse what the Muslims do to corpses of their dead with that of non-Muslims, mostly the Christians who embalm their dead by draining them of blood then injecting a liquid in them. This is not permissible in Islam. Instead, Muslims anoint/oil the corpse with a special mixture of herbs which preserve the freshness of the corpse for some time. The best who excelled in this art are the Pharaohs of ancient Egypt. The hardest period that follows death (which, in Islam, means: the separation of the eternal and indestructible soul from the temporal and decaying body) is the first three days of our own counting. Researching true life, eternal life, that is, life after death, is from my viewpoint a most fascinating research. For those who wish to research this subject, the best reference I have come across is Sheikh (mentor) Abbās al-Qummi's *Manazil al-Akhira* which was originally written in Farsi then translated into Arabic by Dr. Abdul-Mahdi Yargari who, by the way, did an outstanding job. The edition I read was published in 1990 by the Balagh Foundation of Beirut, Lebanon. It falls only in 124 pages, yet it draws a road map for you and explains what you should expect, and how to be prepared for, as the stages on the very long and rough road to eternity succeed each other. To my deep dismay, not a single Publisher has till now asked me to translate this precious book, and I do not know if I will live long enough to see this great book translated into English...

Haqq حق: the truth, what is right, an obligation, a responsibility, what belongs to someone

Harām or Haraam حرام: a thing or action which is forbidden, prohibited, made unlawful by Islam

Haram حرم: sanctuary, a sacred territory. Mecca has been a *haram* since time immemorial. All things within the limits/boundaries of the *haram* are protected and considered inviolable; non-Muslims are not supposed to enter them. Medīna was also declared a *haram* by the Prophet (ص). The term "Haramain" refers to both sanctuaries of Mecca and Medīna.

Hassana or Hasaanah حصانه: immunity, privilege, exemption, liberty

Hashd حشد: crowd (of people, etc.), throng, multitude (of persons, etc.), riotous assembly

Hashr حشر: crowding, grouping, gathering together, assembling يوم الحشر (such as for the Day of Judgment). Speaking of the Day of Judgment, here is the picture I have drawn in my imagination for the Gathering on that Day: First of all, the place where I believe the Judgment will take place will be on our Planet Earth since we all are earthlings. The globe will change its form considerably: The mountains will be crushed and made to look like cotton being worked by a cotton carder (نداف) as we are told in 101:5 (Chapter 101, Verse 5) of the Holy Qur'ān and the oxygen will be separated from the hydrogen in water and the oxygen is set ablaze, so much so that you will see oceans set on fire as we are told in verses such as 81:6 and 52:6, till the entire earth is flattened like a computer's storage CD. This completely circular disk will be split into at least 128,000 triangles, this number corresponding to the number of prophets whom the Almighty sent to various nations of the human species. If you place many triangles side by side, you will come up with a circle. On tip of each pyramid will be the prophet who will face the nation to whom he was sent as those closest to him will be the nearest followed those who emulated them, and so on and so forth. For example, immediately facing the prophet will be his *wasis* الأوصياء (successors to prophets), then the *walis* الأولياء, then the martyrs الشهداء, then the scholars العلماء, that is, the people of

480

knowledge who did not profit by their knowledge, who did not sell their religion, who did not become wealthy or politically powerful (or who gained both wealth and power while losing all their balance with God), those who did not write for fame or reputation but to benefit the public and hopefully earn the Almighty's Pleasure and rewards. Another tough condition for these scholars is that they should have acted upon what they had taught the people, a condition which not many of them can meet, and this includes the writer of this book who, therefore, needs your prayers and supplications, perhaps these prayers and supplications will benefit him on the Day of Gathering يوم الحشر. These will be followed by others and others who disseminated knowledge or who in some way benefited the people especially in assisting them in getting closer to know and to worship their Maker rather than worship their ego, whims and desires. Within each triangle, there will be numerous groups. Each group will share one or more characteristic. People, we are told by a number of *ahadīth* (traditions), will be gathered in the company of those whom they love the most, and "love" here does not mean only emotional but in actuality, in practicality, in reality, in degree of emulation and following. So, it is now up to you to give your heart to whomsoever you please: the movie stars, the singers, the dancers and their likes, or those who sacrificed their lives for the sake of humanity, setting immortal models for self-denial and self-sacrifice, rather than self-worship, such as the prophets and messengers of God who we, Muslims, respect and revere without making distinctions, as we are instructed to do in the Holy Qur'ān. Now, and only now, you have an option. When the Day of Gathering comes, there will be no options left. The angels will know exactly where to place you for judgment; they are the judgment angels, for each angel has a function for which the Almighty creates him, and "him" here is used loosely since angels in Islam have no gender nor will have the souls. After the judgment is done and the accounts are settled (make sure you do not die while owing people some money or a past due apology!), the fortunate ones will be transported, in groups or individually, to the gardens of bliss جنات النعيم, which I think will occupy the vast cosmos at that time—and only God knows if that cosmos will be similar to this cosmos, and most likely it will not— whereas those doomed will remain on earth. At that time, the earth will take another shape, becoming an inferno with numerous methods and chambers of torture described vividly in the Holy Qur'ān for our admonishment. This is just an imagined picture, that is all, and you can say that I have a "wild imagination"! If you have a better idea, let us hear it! Surely Allāh knows best.

Hasra or Hasrah حسره: regret, sorrow, remorse

Hawza حوزه: place of acquisition (of higher learning), religious seminary; among the world's most famous *hawzas* are located in Najaf, Iraq, and Qum, Iran.

Haya' حياء: timidity, shyness, feeling of decorum or propriety, modesty

Hayawan حيوان: animal. It also means "eternal life", everlasting life, eternity, as we read in Ch. 29 (Al-AnkAbūt, Spider), Verse 64. Most Arabic words have more than one meaning.

Hayawi حيوي: vital, full if vitality and energy, of utmost importance, essential

Hayawiyya حيويه: vitality, energy

Hayd or Haydh or Hayz حيض: menstruation period

Hayta or Heeta حيطه" precaution, safeguard; *al-ahwat* الأحوط refers to what is regarded by the creed as the most precautionary measure

Hazan (or Huzn) حزن: grief, agony, sorrow

Hazim حازم: strict, stringent, stern

Hifz حفظ: preservation, protection from loss, memorization (usually of the Holy Qur'ān). Anyone who memorizes the entire text of the Holy Qur'ān is called *hafiz*.

Hila or Heelah حيله: trick, cunning, ruse, artifice, stratagem, ingenuity, contrivance

Hijab حجاب: veil, curtain, barrier

Hijama or Hijaamah حجامه: cupping

Hikma حكمه: wisdom, sagacity, prudence

Hilal هلال: crescent, singular of *ahilla*

Hilf حلف: alliance, confederation, an oath

Hijra هجره: migration. The *hijra* or hegira refers to the Prophet's migration from Mecca to Madinah. This journey took place in the 13th year of his mission (which coincided at the time with the month of September of 622 A.D.). This is the beginning of the Muslim calendar. The word *"hijra"* means: leaving a place in order to seek sanctuary or freedom from persecution or to go where there is freedom of religion, or for any other purpose. *Hijra* can also mean to leave a bad way of life for a good or more righteous way, or to leave the company of bad folks and choose that of good folks.

Hiqd حقد: grudge, animosity, intense hatred, hostility, malice. (Do not let any of these diseases eat your heart up. Instead, pray for the wrongdoers to see the light of the Right Path so they may return to their senses, amend their ways and spare people their mischief. Do not harbor such negative feelings towards any human being, animal, plant or even stone, for all these are servants of the Almighty. Direct such sentiments towards bad actions caused through the insinuations of the Devil, arch-enemy Satan, Lucifer, and those of his tribe. Direct your contempt towards the deed rather than the doer for the doer may not be aware of what he does or why he does it. Empty your heart of hatred and fill it with love for everyone and everything, and this love will return back to you multiplied many times. Those who sow good seeds will reap a good harvest. Try it! It comes with a guarantee!)

Hisab حساب: accounting, accounting (or right and wrong, etc.), arithmetic, computation

Hisar حصار: siege, boycott, blockade, embargo

Hiwar حوار: dialogue, conversation (usually between two persons or groups)

Hizb حزب: literally, it means party (plural *ahzab*); another meaning is each 60th portion of the text of the Holy Qur'ān

Hisn حصن: fortress, fortified place, chateau, citadel, protection against or a protective place or measure, security against, immunity

Hudud or Hudood حدود: limits ordained by Allāh. This includes the punishment for crimes; it also refers to the plural of *hadd* حد, specific penalty

Hujja حجة: proof, argument, evidence, authority

Huri حوري: heavenly wives known for their extreme whiteness and large lovely eyes married to the male residents of Paradise

Hurr حر: free, liberal, open-minded

I ع،إ

I`ara or I`aarah إعاره: lending, loaning

Ibada عباده: worship, adoration, religious service, rite, cult; Muslims feel honored when described as "obedient servants of Allāh". They testify that Prophet Muhammed (ص), the very best not only of mankind but of all creation, is the servant and Messenger of Allāh. Anyone who serves anyone else other than Allāh is a mean, humiliated and miserable loser in both this life and the life to come, whereas a sincere servant of the Almighty is a winner of both.

Ibaha or Ibaahah إباحة: Sufferance, tolerance or toleration, passive consent, disclosure, divulgence and sometimes it means: promiscuity, pornography إباحية

Ibham or Ibhaam إبهام: ambiguity, obscurity; it also means thumb

484

Ibtal or Ibtaal إبطال: nullification, annulment, voiding

Ibtihal ابتهال: supplication, invocation

Ida or Idha or Iza عظه: admonition, lesson, warning sermon

Iddi`a' إدعاء: allegation, claim, contention, assertion, declaration

Idman إدمان: addiction

Iffa عفه: uprightness, probity, modesty, honesty, incorruptibility, continence

Iftar إفطار: time or meal for breaking the fast; breakfast

Ifti`al إفتعال: contriving, designing, scheming

Iftirad إفتراض: supposition, hypothesis, assumption

Ihram إحرام: pilgrimage garb, white unwoven cotton shroud worn by pilgrims

Ihsan or Ihsaan إحسان: benevolence, charity, beneficence, kindness

Ihtifal احتفال: festivity, celebration, a merry occasion; plural: احتفالات *ihtifalat* Islamic Festivities: Other than the two major Islamic feasts or `Ids, there are few festivities which Muslims enjoy. These are related to different activities or special occasions. Some of these special occasions are:

1)   عقيقة **Aqiqa**: It is a dinner reception held after a child is born. Relatives, friends, and neighbors are invited for such an occasion.
2)   وليمة **Walima**: It is a dinner reception during or after marriage is consummated. It is offered by the parents and/or the married couple. Friends, relatives, and neighbors are also invited.

Ihtijaj or Ihtijaaj إحتجاج: protesting, remonstrance, under protest, the producing of evidence, proof, rebuttal

485

Ihtikar or Ihtikaar إحتكار: monopoly, monopolization

Ihtiraz or Ihtiraaz إحتراز: taking precaution, precautionary measure

Ihtiyat or Ihtiyaat إحتياط: precaution, taking precautionary measures, advance care/measure

Ijhaf or Ijhaaf إجحاف: injustice, inequity

Ijma` or Ijmaa` إجماع: **unanimity, consensus**

Ijtihad or Ijtehad, Ijtihad, Ijtehad إجتهاد: the degree one reaches in order to be qualified as a *mujtahid*, one who is capable of deriving religious decisions on his own. It is exerting one's total ability to uncover Allāh's rulings on issues from their sources (Qur'ān, Sunnah, consensus, etc.).

Ikhtilaq or Ikhtilaaq إختلاق: fabrication, invention, innovation

Ikrah or Ikraah إكراه: coercion, imposition, forcing

Ikram or Ikraam إكرام: honoring, being generous to, revering, respecting, esteeming, recognizing, venerating

Ilhaf or Ilhaaf الحاف: insistence, importunity, soliciting or requesting while being too pushy

`Illiyeen or `Illiyoon عليون: the highest pinnacle of Paradise; see Holy Qur'ān, 83:18.

`Ilm علم: knowledge, learning, knowing, science; علم الأجواء : aerology; علم أمراض الجلد: dermatology; علم الأمراض : pathology; علم; علم الأمراض النفسيه: psychiatrics; أمراض النساء : gynaecology; علم الأنساب : genealogy; علم الأنسان : anthropology; علم البيئه : ecology; علم التربيه : agrology; علم التشريح : anatomy; علم الجرائم : criminology; علم الزراعيه : entomology; علم الحشرات: agrostology; الحشائش; hygiene; علم الصحه : geology; علم طبقات الأرض : petrology; علم الطبيعيـات الأرضيه : geophysics; علم الفلك : astronomy; علم الفنـون الصناعيه : technology; علم; علم الصخور

486

الكونيـات : cosmology; علم النفس : psychology; علم النوويات: nucleonics; علم الوراثه : genetics.

Iltibas or Iltibaas إلتباس: confusion, complication, predicament

Imām or Imām, Emam, Emaam إمام: leader of an *ummah*, a group of people (small or big); he may be the one who leads others in congregational prayers, or a supreme religious or political authority or both, or one of the Twelve Infallible Imāms (ع). An *imām* is a religious community leader. Any person who leads a congregational prayer is called an *imām*. A religious leader who also leads his community in the political affairs may be called an *imām*, an *amir* (or *emir*) or caliph.

Iman or Iman, Eman إيمان: faith and trust in Allāh, conviction

Imtiyaz or Emtiyaaz إمتيـاز: distinction, excellence, eminence, privilege, concession, franchise

Infilaq or Infilaaq إنفلاق: cleaving, fission (of nucleus, molecules, etc.)

Infirat or Infiraat إنفراط: dispersal, breaking down (of group, coalition, etc.), disruption, separation, falling apart

Injil إنجيل: the revelations that were sent down during the time of Prophet Isa (Jesus). It is referred to as the New Testament.

Inna lillahi wa inna ilahi raji'un or Inna Lillahi Wa Inna Ilahi Rajioon إنـا لله و إنـا إليـه راجعون: When a Muslim is struck with a calamity, such as when he loses one of his loved ones, or when he becomes bankrupt, he should be patient and utter this statement with full conviction. It means: "We are from Allāh and to Him do we return." Muslims believe that Allāh is the One who gives and who takes away. He tests us. A true Muslim submits himself to Allāh wholeheartedly, during good times and bad times. He is grateful and thankful to Allāh for whatever He decrees for him. He is patient and says this expression during times of turmoil and calamity.

487

Insha-Allāh or **Insha** *Allāh, In Sha' Allāh* بِإِنْشَاء الله: When a person wishes to plan to do something in the future, when he promises someone to do something for him or to give him something, when he makes resolutions, and when he makes a pledge..., he does so only with permission of the Almighty Who enables him to do so, Who provides him with the means, tools, resources, etc., to achieve this end. For this reason, a Muslim uses the Qur'ānic instructions by saying "In-Sha' Allāh", which means: "If Allāh so wills." Muslims are supposed to strive hard and to trust in Allāh, not in themselves, not in anyone else. They leave the results in the hands of Allāh.

Inshiqaq or Inshiqaaq إِنْشِقَاق: separating from, breaking open, cleaving, breaking apart; title of Ch. 84 of the Holy Qur'ān

Inshitar or Inshitaar إِنْشِطَار: fission, cleaving, splitting, dividing, tearing apart

Intihal or Intihaal إِنْتِحَال: impersonation, simulation

Intikas or Intikaas إِنْتِكَاص: recanting, repudiation, renunciation (of a previous assertion or conviction)

Iq'ad إِقْعَاد: paralysis in the lower half of the body

Iqama or Iqamah إِقَامه: the pronouncement of certain statements in preparation for the performing of the prayers. It usually follows the *athan*. *Iqama* means that the prayer ritual is ready to start, to be performed, whether individually or collectively (in a congregation). It is to be recited in Arabic before every obligatory prayer.

Iqna` إِقْنَاع: convincing, persuading, inducing

Irhab إِرهاب: terrorism, terrorizing, intimidation

Irtidad إِرْتِداد: reneging, defection, apostasy, reversion

Irtiyab إِرْتِياب: suspicion, doubt, apprehension

Isha or Isha' عشاء: nighttime, evening, time for obligatory evening

488

salat, prayer, after sunset, later in the evening. It also means supper.

Ishtiqaq إشتقاق: derivation, deduction

Islam إسلام: Islam is an Arabic word the root of which is "silm", peace, and "salam", which also means peace. Among its other meanings are these: greeting, salutation, obedience to the Almighty, loyalty, allegiance, and submission to the will of the Creator of the Universe. Islam is the last and final religion to all mankind and to all generations irrespective of color, race, nationality, ethnicity, language or one's social, political or any other position. The religion of Islam is not to be confused with so-called "Mohammedanism", a misnomer created by some ignorant folks in order to tarnish the image of this pristine faith. Muslims do not accept this name as it gives wrong information about Islam and Muslims. If you really wish to know what Islam is all about, ask Muslims, not those who are hostile to the adherents to this religion of peace, and unfortunately there are many such folks.

Isnad إسناد: the method whereby one *hadath* is traced and in the end attributed to a *muhaddith*, traditionist, one who first transmitted it

Isra' إسراء: night journey; usually a reference to the Prophet's night journey from Mecca to Jerusalem, an incident which took place in the year 622 A.D.

Israf إسراف: extravagance, eccessiveness, going to extremes

Ithbat or Ithbaat إثبات: proof or proving, evidence (or presenting an evidence)

Ith`an إذعان: surrender, submission, obedience, resignation, succumb-ing, acceding

Ithna-Asheris or Ithna-Ashariyya الاثنا عشرية: Shī'ite (or Shī'a or Shī'i) Muslims who follow the path of the 14 Infallibles, namely the Prophet of Islam (ص), Fātima (ع) daughter of the Prophet (ص) and the Infallible Imāms who descended from Ali (ع). Ithna-Asheris are also called Ja'faris, after Imām Ja'far as-Sādiq (ع) whose biography is detailed in this book. Here is a brief narrative of their biographies for you:

THE 14 INFALLIBLES
1. **Prophet Muhammed:** He is Muhammed ibn (son of) Abdullāh ibn Abdul-Muttalib ibn Hashim ibn Abd Munaf ibn Qusayy ibn Kilab ibn Murrah ibn Ka`b ibn ibn Ghalib ibn Fahr ibn Malik ibn Nadar ibn Kinanah ibn Khuzaymah ibn Mudrikah ibn Ilyas ibn Mazar ibn Nazar ibn Ma`ad ibn Adnan ibn Isma`eel (Ishmael) ibn Ibrāhim (Abraham), peace and blessings of Allāh be upon him, his progeny, and righteous ancestors, especially his great grandfathers Isma`eel and Ibrāhim. **PROPHET'S FATHER:** Abdullāh ibn Abdul-Muttalib (545 - 570 A.D.). The Blessed Prophet's father, Abdullāh ibn Abdul-Muttalib, was born in 545 A.D., 25 years before the Year of the Elephant. Abū Tālib and az-Zubair were his brothers by the same father and mother. So were the girls, except Safiyya. When his father died, the Prophet of Allāh (ص) was two months old, though reports about this differ. Abdul-Muttalib loved `Abdullāh immensely because he was the best of his children, the most chaste and the most noble among them. Once Abdul-Muttalib sent his son on business, and when the caravan passed by Yathrib (Medīna), Abdullāh died there. He was buried in the house of Arqam ibn Ibrāhim ibn Surāqah al-Adawi. **PROPHET'S FOSTER FATHER:** Al-Hārith son of Abd al-Uzza ibn Rifā`ah ibn Millān ibn Nāsirah ibn Fusayya ibn Nasr ibn Sa`d ibn Bakr ibn Hawāzin. **PROPHET'S FOSTER MOTHERS:** Thawbiyya; she was a bondmaid of Abū Lahab, the paternal uncle of the Messenger of Allāh (ص). She breast-fed him with the milk of her son Masruh. **Halima**, the Prophet's foster mother. She was the daughter of "Abū Thu'aib" Abdullāh ibn Shajnah ibn Jābir ibn Rizām ibn Nāsirah ibn Sa`d ibn Bakr ibn Hawāzin al-Qaisi. She breast-fed the Messenger of Allāh (ص) with the milk of her son Abdullāh and reared him (ص) for four years (till the year 574 A.D.). **PROPHET'S CHILDREN:** 1) Ibrāhim, 2) Abdullāh; 3) al-Qāsim; 4) stepdaughter (some say daughter) Zainab (d. 629 A.D.); 5) stepdaughter (some say daughter) Ruqayya (d. 624 A.D.), 6) stepdaughter (some say daughter) Umm Kulthum (d. 630 A.D.); 7) the Prophet's daughter Fātima, peace be upon her

and her progeny. For more details, refer to my book titled *Muhammed: Prophet and Messenger of Allāh.*

2. Fātima (ع) Daughter of Muhammed (ص): Fātima (615 – 632 A.D.), mother of the Imāms (ع), is the daughter of the Messenger of Allāh (ص) by his first wife, Khadija daughter of Khuwaylid, may the Almighty be pleased with her. Fātima was
born in Mecca on a Friday, the 20th of Jumada II in the fifth year after the declaration of the Prophetic message which corresponds, according to the Christian calendar, to the year 615. She was only 18 and 75 days when she died in Medīna few days only (some say 75) after the death of her revered father (ص): The Prophet (ص) passed away on Safar 28/May 28 according to the Christian Gregorian calendar, or the 25th according to the Julian calendar, of the same year. Fātima passed away on the 14th of Jumada I of 11 A.H. which corresponded to August 7, 632 A.D. She was buried somewhere in the graveyard of Jannatul-Baqi' in Medīna in an unmarked grave. According to her will, her husband, Imām Ali (ع), did not leave any marks identifying her grave, and nobody knows where it is. According to Shī'ite Muslims, she was the only daughter of the Holy Prophet (ص).

Fātima has nine names/titles: Fātima فاطمة, al-Siddiqa الصديقة (the truthful one), al-Mubaraka المباركة (the blessed one), al-Tahira الطاهرة (the pure one), al-Zakiyya الزكية (the chaste one), al-Radhiayya الرضية (the grateful one), al-Mardhiyya المرضية (the one who shall be pleased [on Judgment Day]), al-Muhaddatha المحدثة (the one, other than the Prophet, to whom an angel speaks) and al-Zahra الزهراء (the splendid one).

The Prophet (ص) taught Fātima (ع) divine knowledge and endowed her with special intellectual brilliance, so much so that she realized the true meaning of faith, piety, and the reality of Islam. But Fātima (ع) also was a witness to sorrow and a life of anguish from the very beginning of her life. She constantly saw how her revered father was mistreated by the unbelievers and later how she herself fell a victim to the same abuse, only this time by some "Muslims".

A number of chronicles quote her mother, Khadija, narrating the following about the birth of her revered daughter: "At the time of Fātima's birth, I sent for my neighboring Quraishite women to assist me. They flatly refused, saying that I had betrayed them by marrying and supporting Muhammed. I was perturbed for a while when, to my great surprise, I saw four strange tall women with halos around their faces approaching me. Finding me dismayed, one of them addressed me thus, 'O Khadija! I am Sarah, mother of Ishāq (Isaac). The other three are: Mary mother of Christ, Asiya daughter of Muzahim and Umm Kulthum sister of Moses. We have all been commanded by God to put our nursing knowledge at your disposal.' Saying this, all of them sat around me and rendered the services of midwifery till my daughter Fātima was born."

The motherly blessings and affection received by Fātima (ع) were only for five years after which Khadija left for her heavenly home. The Holy Prophet brought her up thereafter.

The Holy Prophet said: "Whoever injures (bodily or otherwise) Fātima, he injures me; and whoever injures me injures Allāh; and whoever injures Allāh practices unbelief. O Fātima! If your wrath is incurred, it incurs the wrath of Allāh; and if you are pleased, it makes Allāh pleased, too."

M.H. Shakir writes the following: "Fātima, the only daughter of the Holy Prophet of Islam, was born in Mecca on 20th of Jumada al-Thaniya 18 B.H. (Before Hijra). The good and noble lady Khadija and the Apostle of Allāh bestowed all their natural love, care and devotion on their lovable and only child, Fātima, who in her turn was extremely fond of her parents. The Princess of the House of the Prophet was very intelligent, accomplished and cheerful. Her speeches, poems and sayings serve as an index to her strength of character and nobility of mind. Her virtues gained her the title 'Our Lady of Light'. She was moderately tall, slender and endowed with great beauty which caused her to be called 'az-Zahra' (the Lady of Light)".

Fātima (ع) was called az-Zahra' because her light used to shine among those in the heavens. After arriving in Medīna, she was

492

married to Ali in the first year of Hijra, and she gave birth to three sons. Her sons were: Hassan, Hussain, Masters of the youths of Paradise, and Muhsin. Muhsin never saw the light because he was aborted as his mother was behind her house door fending for herself while rogues were trying to break into it and force her husband to swear the oath of allegiance to Abū Bakr. She had two daughters, Zainab, the heroine of Kerbalā, and Umm Kulthum. Her children are well-known for their piety, righteousness and generosity. Their strength of character and actions changed the course of history.

The Holy Prophet said فاطمة بضعة مني, "Fātima is part of me". He would go out to receive his daughter whenever she came from her husband's house. Every morning on his way to the Mosque, he would pass by Fātima's house and say, *"as-Salamu `alaykum ya Ahla Bay annnubuwwah wa ma`din arr-risala "* (Peace be with you, O Ahl al-Bayt (Household of the Prophet) and the Substance of the Message).

Fātima (ع) is famous and acknowledged as the "Sayyidatu nisa '1-`alamin" (Leader of all the women of the world for all times) because the Prophethood of Muhammad would not have been everlasting without her. The Prophet is the perfect example for men, but could not be so for women. For all the verses revealed in the Holy Qur'ān for women, Fātima is the perfect model, who translated every verse into action. In her lifetime, she was a complete woman, being Daughter, Wife and Mother at the same time.

Fātima inherited the genius and wisdom, the determination and will power, piety and sanctity, generosity and benevolence, devotion and worship of Allāh, self-sacrifice and hospitality, forbearance and patience, knowledge and nobility of disposition of her illustrious father, both in words and in actions. "I often witnessed my mother," says Imām Husain, "absorbed in prayer from dusk to dawn." Her generosity and compassion for the poor was such that no destitute or beggar ever returned from her door empty-handed. She (ع) worked, dressed, ate and lived very simply. She was very generous; and none who came to her door ever went away empty handed. Many times she gave away all the food she had had, staying without any food at all. As a daughter, she loved her parents so much that she won their

493

love and regard to such an extent that the Holy Prophet (ص) used to stand up whenever she came to him.

Marriage: When Fātima came of age, a number of hopefuls sought her hand in marriage. The Holy Prophet was awaiting the Divine order in this respect until Imām `Ali approached him and asked for her hand in marriage. The Holy Prophet came to Fātima (ع) and asked, "My daughter! Do you consent to be wedded to `Ali, as I am so commanded by Allāh?" Fātima (ع) thereupon bowed her head in modesty. Umm Salamah narrates the following: "Fātima's face Fātima bloomed with joy and her silence was so suggestive and conspicuous that the Holy Prophet stood up to shout: *Allāhu Akbar'* (Allāh is great)! Fātima's silence is her acceptance." On Friday, Thul Hijja 1, 2 A.H., which corresponded to May 25, 624 A.D. according to the Julian Christian calendar or to the 28th of May of the same year according to the Gregorian Christian calendar which is widely used in the text of this book, the marriage ceremony took place. All the Muhajirun (emigrants) and Ansār (supporters) of Medīna assembled in the mosque while Imām `Ali was seated before the Holy Prophet with all the ceremonious modesty of a bridegroom. The Holy Prophet first recited an eloquent sermon then declared: "I have been commanded by Allāh to get Fātima wedded to `Ali, and so I do hereby solemnize the matrimony between `Ali and Fātima on a dower of four hundred *mithqal* of silver." Then he asked Imām Ali, "Do you consent to it, O Ali? " "Yes, I do, O Holy Prophet of Allāh!" replied Imām Ali (ع). Then the Holy Prophet raised his hands and supplicated thus: "O Lord! Bless both of them, sanctify their progeny and grant them the keys of Your beneficence, Your treasures of wisdom and genius; and let them be a source of blessing and peace to my *umma*." Her children; Imām Hassan, Imām Hussain, Zainab and Umm Kulthum, are well-known for their piety, righteousness and generosity. Their strength of character and actions changed the course of history and fortified Islam which otherwise would have been lost to mankind.

As a wife, she was very devoted. She never asked Ali for anything in her entire life. As a mother, she cared for and brought up wonderful children; they have left their marks on the pages of world history which time and the plots of enemies of Ahl al-Bayt (ع) will never be able to erase.

AFTER THE PROPHET'S DEMISE

قال ابن الجوزي (أبو الفرج عبد الرحمن بن أبي الحسن علي بن محمد القرشي التيمي البكري، الفقيه الحنبلي الحافظ المفسر الواعظ المؤرخ الأديب المعروف بابن الجوزي، رحمه الله رحمة واسعة، وأدخله فسيح جناته، فقيه حنبلي محدث ومؤرخ ومتكلم [510هـ/1116م - 12رمضان 592هـ] ولد وتوفي في بغداد) : روي عن علي (عليه السلام) قال: لما مات رسول الله (صلى الله عليه وآله وسلم) جاءت فاطمة (عليها السلام) فأخذت قبضة من تراب القبر فوضعته على عينيها، فبكت وأنشأت تقول:

يا ليتها خرجت مع الزفرات   نفسي على زفراتها محبوسة

أبكي مخافة أن تطول حياتي   لا خير بعدك في الحياة وإنما

Ibn al-Jawzi, namely Abul-Faraj Abdul-Rahman ibn Abul-Hassan Ali ibn Muhammed al-Qarashi (or Quraishi, of Quraish tribe) al-Taymi al-Bakri, was a Hanbali *faqih* who knew the Holy Qur'ān by heart, an orator, historian and a man of letters. He was born in Baghdad in 510 A.H./1117 A.D. and died there on the 12th of the month of Ramadan of 592 A.H. which coincided with August 16, 1196 A.D. according to the Gregorian Christian calendar or the 9th of the same month and year according to the Julian calendar. May the Almighty shower him with His broad mercy and admit him into His spacious Paradise. He quotes Imām Ali (ع) saying that when the Messenger of Allāh (ص) died, Fātima (ع) went to his gravesite, took a handful of its dust, put it on her eyes, wept and composed these verses of poetry:

My soul is confined with every sigh,
How I wish it departed as sighs depart.
No good is there in life after you so I
For fear my life will prolong do I cry.

PROPERTY OF FADAK:

The Prophet (ص) taught Fātima (ع) divine knowledge and endowed her with special intellectual brilliance, so much so that she realized the true meaning of faith, piety, and the reality of Islam. But Fātima (ع) also was a witness to sorrow and a life of anguish from the very beginning of her life. She constantly saw how her revered father was mistreated by the unbelievers and later how she herself fell a victim to the same Abūse, only this time by some "Muslims". For more details about Fadak, refer to its proper place in this Glossary.

KHUTBA OF FĀTIMA ZAHRA (A.S.) DEMANDING FADAK

خطبـة فاطمـة الزهـراء بنـت النبي محمـد (ص) عند مطالبتها بفدك و ميراثها من أبيها:

روى عبد الله بن الحسن باسناده عن آبائه ، أنه لما أجمع أبوبكر وعمر على منع فاطمـة عليها السلام فدكا و بلغها ذلك لاثت خمارها على رأسها و اشتملت بجلبابها وأقبلت في لمةٍ من حفدتها ونساء قومها تطأ ذيولها، مـا تخرم مشيتها مشية رسول الله (ص)، حتى دخلت على أبي بكر وهو في حشد من المهاجرين والأنصار وغيرهم فنيطت دونها ملاءة فجلست ثم أنَت أنَةً أجهش القوم لها بالبكاء فأرتج المجلس ثم أمهلت هنيئـة حتى إذا سكن نشيج القوم وهدأت فورتهم افتتحت الكلام بحمد الله و الثناء عليه والصلاة على رسوله فعاد القوم في بكائهم فلما أمسكوا عادت في كلامها فقالت عليها السلام:

الحمد لله على مـا أنعم ولـه الشكر على مـا ألهم والثنـاء بمـا قدم من عمـوم نعم ابتداها وسبوغ آلاء أسداها وتمام منن أولاها جم عن الإحصاء عددها ونأى عن الجزاء أمدها وتفاوت عن الإدراك أبدها وندبهم لاستزادتها بالشكر لاتصالها واستحمد إلى الخلائـق بإجزالها وثنى بالندب إلى أمثالها وأشـهد أن لا إلـه إلا الله وحده لا شريك لـه كلمـة جعل الإخلاص تأويلها وضمن القلوب موصولها وأنار في التفكر معقولها الممتنع من الأبصار رؤيته ومن الألسن صفته ومن الأوهام كيفيته ابتدع الأشياء لا من شـيء كان قبلها وأنشأها بلا احتذاء أمثلة امتثلها كونها بقدرته وذرأها بمشيته من غير حاجة منه إلى تكوينها ولا فائدة له في تصويرها إلا تثبيتا لحكمته وتنبيها على طاعتـه وإظهارا لقدرتـه تعبدا لبريته وإعزازا لدعوته ثم جعل الثواب على طاعته ووضع العقاب على معصيته ذيادة لعباده من نقمته وحياشة لهم إلى جنته وأشهد أن أبي محمدا عبده ورسوله اختاره قبل أن أرسله وسماه قبل أن اجتباه واصطفاه قبل أن ابتعثه إذ الخلائـق بالغيب مكنونـة وبستر الأهاويل مصونة وبنهاية العدم مقرونة علما من الله تعالى بمآيل الأمور وإحاطـة بحوادث الدهور ومعرفة بمواقع الأمور ابتعثه الله إتمامـا لأمره وعزيمـة على إمضاء حكمـه وإنفـاذا لمقادير رحمتـه فـرأى الأمم فرقـا في أديانها عكفا على نيرانها عابـدة لأوثانها منكرة لله مع عرفانها فأنار الله بأبي محمد ص ظلمها وكشف عن القلوب بهمها وجلى عن الأبصار غممها وقام في النـاس بالهدايـة فأنقذهم من الغوايـة وبصرهم من العمايـة وهداهم إلى الدين القويم ودعاهم إلى الطريق المستقيم ثم قبضه الله إليه قبض رأفة واختيار ورغبة وإيثار فمحمد (ص) من تعب هذه الدار في راحة قد حف بالملائكة الأبرار ورضوان الرب الغفار ومجاورة الملك الجبار صلى الله على أبي نبيه وأمينه وخيرته من الخلق وصفيه والسلام عليه ورحمة الله وبركاته.

ثم التفتت إلى أهل المجلس وقالت : أنتم عباد الله نصب أمره ونهيه وحملة دينه ووحيه

وأمناء الله على أنفسكم وبلغاءه إلى الأمم زعيم حق له فيكم وعهد قدمه إليكم وبقية استخلفها عليكم كتاب الله الناطق والقرآن الصادق والنور الساطع والضياء اللامع بينة بصائره منكشفة سرائره منجلية ظواهره مغتبطة به أشياعه قائدا إلى الرضوان اتباعه مؤد إلى النجاة استماعه به تنال حجج الله المنورة وعزائمه المفسرة ومحارمه المحذرة وبيناته الجالية وبراهينه الكافية وفضائله المندوبة ورخصه الموهوبة وشرائعه المكتوبة فجعل الله الإيمان تطهيرا لكم من الشرك والصلاة تنزيها لكم عن الكبر والزكاة تزكية للنفس ونماء في الرزق والصيام تثبيتا للإخلاص والحج تشييدا للدين والعدل تنسيقا للقلوب وطاعتنا نظاما للملة وإمامتنا أمانا للفرقة والجهاد عزا للإسلام والصبر معونة على استيجاب الأجر والأمر بالمعروف مصلحة للعامة وبر الوالدين وقاية من السخط وصلة الأرحام منساة في العمر ومنماة للعدد والقصاص حقنا للدماء والوفاء بالنذر تعريضا للمغفرة وتوفية المكاييل والموازين تغييرا للبخس والنهي عن شرب الخمر تنزيها عن الرجس واجتناب القذف حجابا عن اللعنة وترك السرقة إيجابا للعفة وحرم الله الشرك إخلاصا له بالربوبية فاتقوا الله حق تقاته ولا تموتن إلا وأنتم مسلمون وأطيعوا الله فيما أمركم به ونهاكم عنه فإنه إنما يخشى الله من عباده العلماء.

ثم قالت: أيها الناس اعلموا أني فاطمة و أبي محمد ص أقول عودا وبدوا ولا أقول ما أقول غلطا ولا أفعل ما أفعل شططا ، لَقَدْ جَاءَكُمْ رَسُولٌ مِنْ أَنْفُسِكُمْ عَزِيزٌ عَلَيْهِ ما عَنِتُّمْ حَرِيصٌ عَلَيْكُمْ بِالْمُؤْمِنِينَ رَؤُفٌ رَحِيمٌ ، فإن تعزوه وتعرفوه تجدوه أبي دون نسائكم وأخا ابن عمي دون رجالكم ، ولنعم المعزى إليه دون فبلغ الرسالة صادعا بالنذارة مائلا عن مدرجة المشركين ضاربا ثبجهم آخذا بأكظامهم داعيا إلى سبيل ربه بالحكمة والموعظة الحسنة يجف الأصنام وينكث الهام حتى انهزم الجمع وولوا الدبر حتى تفرى الليل عن صبحه وأسفر الحق عن محضه ونطق زعيم الدين وخرست شقاشق الشياطين وطاح وشيظ النفاق وانحلت عقد الكفر والشقاق وفهتم بكلمة الإخلاص في نفر من البيض الخماص وكنتم على شفا حفرة من النار مذقة الشارب ونهزة الطامع وقبسة العجلان وموطئ الأقدام تشربون الطرق وتقتاتون القد و الورق أذلة خاسئين تخافون أن يتخطفكم الناس من حولكم فأنقذكم الله تبارك وتعالى بمحمد ص بعد اللتيا واللتي وبعد أن مني ببهم الرجال وذؤبان العرب ومردة أهل الكتاب كلما أوقدوانارا للحرب أطفأها الله أو نجم قرن الشيطان أو فغرت فاغرة من المشركين قذف أخاه في لهواتها فلا ينكفئ حتى يطأ جناحها بأخمصه ويخمد لهبها بسيفه مكدودا في ذات الله مجتهدا في أمر الله قريبا من رسول الله سيدا في أولياء الله مشمرا ناصحا مجدا كادحا لا تأخذه في الله لومة لائم وأنتم في رفاهية من العيش وادعون فاكهون آمنون تتربصون بنا الدوائر وتتوكفون الأخبار وتنكصون عند النزال وتفرون من القتال. فلما اختار الله لنبيه دار أنبيائه ومأوى أصفيائه ظهر فيكم حسكة النفاق وسمل جلباب الدين ونطق كاظم الغاوين ونبغ خامل الأقلين وهدر فنيق المبطلين فخطر في عرصاتكم وأطلع الشيطان رأسه من مغرزه هاتفا بكم فألفاكم لدعوته مستجيبين وللعزة فيه ملاحظين ثم استنهضكم فوجدكم خفافا وأحمشكم فألفاكم غضابا فوسمتم غير إبلكم ووردتم غير مشربكم هذا والعهد قريب والكلم رحيب والجرح لما يندمل والرسول لما يقبر ابتدارا زعمتم خوف الفتنة ألا في الفتنة سقطوا وإن جهنم لمحيطة بالكافرين فهيهات فهيهات منكم وكيف بكم وأنى تؤفكون وكتاب الله بين أظهركم أموره ظاهرة وأحكامه زاهرة وأعلامه باهرة وزواجره لائحة وأوامره واضحة وقد خلفتموه

497

وراء ظهوركم أرغبة عنه تريدون أم بغيره تحكمون بئس للظالمين بدلا ومن يتبع غير الإسلام دينا فلن يقبل منه وهو في الآخرة من الخاسرين ثم لم تلبثوا إلا ريث أن تسكن نفرتها ويسلس قيادها ثم أخذتم تورون وقدتها وتهيجون جمرتها وتستجيبون لهتاف الشيطان الغوي وإطفاء أنوار الدين الجلي وإهمال سنن النبي الصفي تشربون حسوا في ارتغاء وتمشون لأهله وولده في الخمرة والضراء ويصير منكم على مثل حز المدى ووخز السنان في الحشا وأنتم الآن تزعمون أن لا إرث لنا ، أ فحكم الجاهلية تبغون ومن أحسن من الله حكما لقوم يوقنون أفلا تعلمون ، بلى قد تجلى لكم كالشمس الضاحية أني ابنته أيها المسلمون أأغلب على إرثي يا ابن أبي قحافة أفي كتاب الله ترث أباك ولا أرث أبي لقد جئت شيئا فريا أفعلى عمد تركتم كتاب الله ونبذتموه وراء ظهوركم إذ يقول " :وَوَرِثَ سُلَيْمَانُ دَاوُدَ" وقال فيما اقتص من خبر يحيى بن زكريا إذ قال : "فَهَبْ لِي مِنْ لَدُنْكَ وَلِيًّا يَرِثُنِي وَ يَرِثُ مِنْ آلِ يَعْقُوبَ" وقالِ : "وَ أُولُوا الْأَرْحَامِ بَعْضُهُمْ أَوْلَى بِبَعْضٍ فِي كِتَابِ اللَّهِ" وقال:"يُوصِيكُمُ اللَّهُ فِي أَوْلَادِكُمْ لِلذَّكَرِ مِثْلُ حَظِّ الْأُنْثَيَيْنِ" وقال : "إِنْ تَرَكَ خَيْرًا الْوَصِيَّةُ لِلْوالِدَيْنِ وَ الْأَقْرَبِينَ بِالْمَعْرُوفِ حَقًّا عَلَى الْمُتَّقِينَ"، وزعمتم أن لا حظوة لي ولا إرث من أبي ولا رحم بيننا أفخصكم الله بآية أخرج أبي منها أم هل تقولون إن أهل ملتين لا يتوارثان أو لست أنا وأبي من أهل ملة واحدة أم أنتم أعلم بخصوص القرآن وعمومه من أبي وابن عمي فدونكها مخطومة مرحولة تلقاك يوم حشرك فنعم الحكم الله والزعيم محمد والموعد القيامة وعند الساعة يخسر المبطلون ولا ينفعكم إذ تندمون ولكل نبأ مستقر وسوف تعلمون من يأتيه عذاب يخزيه ويحل عليه عذاب مقيم.

ثم رمت بطرفها نحو الأنصار فقالت:
يا معشر النقيبة وأعضاد الملة وحضنة الإسلام، ما هذه الغميزة في حقي والسنة عن ظلامتي أما كان رسول الله أبي يقول المرء يحفظ في ولده سرعان ما أحدثتم وعجلان ذا إهالة ولكم طاقة بما أحاول وقوة على ما أطلب و أزاول أتقولون مات محمد (ص) فخطب جليل استوسع وهنه واستنهر فتقه وانفتق رتقه وأظلمت الأرض لغيبته وكسفت الشمس والقمر وانتثرت النجوم لمصيبته وأكدت الآمال وخشعت الجبال وأضيع الحريم وأزيلت الحرمة عند مماته، فتلك والله النازلة الكبرى والمصيبة العظمى لا مثلها نازلة ولا بائقة عاجلة أعلن بها كتاب الله جل ثناؤه في أفنيتكم وفي ممساكم ومصبحكم يهتف في أفنيتكم هتافا وصراخا وتلاوة وألحانا ولقبله ما حل بأنبياء الله ورسله حكم فصل وقضاء حتم "وَ ما مُحَمَّدٌ إِلَّا رَسُولٌ قَدْ خَلَتْ مِنْ قَبْلِهِ الرُّسُلُ أَ فَإِنْ ماتَ أَوْ قُتِلَ انْقَلَبْتُمْ عَلى أَعْقابِكُمْ وَ مَنْ يَنْقَلِبْ عَلى عَقِبَيْهِ فَلَنْ يَضُرَّ اللَّهَ شَيْئاً وَ سَيَجْزِي اللَّهُ الشَّاكِرِينَ ." إيها بني قيله أأهضم تراث أبي وأنتم بمرأى مني ومسمع ومنتدى ومجمع تلبسكم الدعوة وتشملكم الخبرة وأنتم ذوو العدد والعدة والأداة والقوة وعندكم السلاح والجنة توافيكم الدعوة فلا تجيبون وتأتيكم الصرخة فلا تغيثون؟ أنتم موصوفون بالكفاح معروفون بالخير والصلاح والنخبة التي انتخبت والخيرة التي اختيرت لنا أهل البيت قاتلتم العرب وتحملتم الكد والتعب وناطحتم الأمم كافحتم البهم لا نبرح أو تبرحون نأمركم فتأتمرون حتى إذا دارت بنا رحى الإسلام ودر حلب الأيام وخضعت ثغرة الشرك وسكنت فورة الإفك وخمدت نيران الكفر وهدأت دعوة الهرج واستوسق نظام الدين فأنى حزتم بعد البيان وأسررتم بعد الإعلان ونكصتم بعد الإقدام وأشركتم بعد الإيمان؛بؤسا لقوم نكثوا أيمانهم من بعد عهدهم وهموا بإخراج الرسول وهم بدءوكم أول مرة أ تخشونهم فالله أحق أن

498

تخشوه إن كنتم مؤمنين ألا وقد أرى أن قد أخلدتم إلى الخفض وأبعدتم من هو أحق
بالبسط والقبض وخلوتم بالدعة ونجوتم بالضيق من السعة فمججتم ما وعيتم ودسعتم
الذي تسوغتم فإن تكفروا أنتم ومن في الأرض جميعا فإن الله لغني حميد ألا وقد قلت ما
قلت هذا على معرفة مني بالجذلة التي خامرتكم والغدرة التي استشعرتها قلوبكم ولكنها
فيضة النفس ونفثة الغيظ وخور القناة وبثة الصدر وتقدمة الحجة فدونكموها فاحتقبوها
دبرة الظهر نقبة الخف باقية العار موسومة بغضب الجبار وشنار الأبد موصولة بنار الله
الموقدة التي تطلع على الأفئدة ، فبعين الله ما تفعلون وسيعلم الذين ظلموا أي منقلب
ينقلبون وأنا ابنة نذير لكم بين يدي عذاب شديد فاعملوا إنا عاملون و انتظروا إنا
منتظرون.

Abullah son of Imām al-Hassan (ع) quotes his forefathers saying that
Abū Bakr and Omer decided to prevent Fātima (ع) from her Fadak
property. When she came to know about it, she put her veil on her
head, wrapped herself with her outer cloak and, accompanied by
some of her relatives and men of her folks, stepping on her gown,
her gait not differing from that of the Messenger of Allāh (ص), went
till she entered [the Mosque of the Prophet] where Abū Bakr was.

Abū Bakr was in the company of a crowd of the Muhajirun and
Ansār and others. A curtain was placed behind which she sat and
moaned. Hearing her thus moaning, everyone present burst in tears,
so much so that the meeting place shook. She waited for a moment
till the sobbing stopped and the fervor abated. She started her speech
by praising Allāh and lauding Him, sending blessings to His
Messenger, whereupon people resumed their cries. When they
stopped, she resumed her speech saying,

"Praise to Allāh for that which He bestowed (us). We thank and laud
Him for all that which He inspired and offered, for the Abūndant
boons which He initiated, the perfect grants which He presented.
Such boons are too many to compute, too vast to measure. Their
limit is too distant to grasp. He commended them (to His beings) so
they would gain more by being grateful for their continuity. He
ordained Himself praiseworthy by giving generously to His
creatures. I testify that there is no God but Allāh, the One without a
partner, a statement which sincere devotion is its interpretation, the
hearts guarantee its continuation, and in the minds and hearts is its
perpetuation. He is the One Who cannot be perceived with vision,
nor can He be described by tongues, nor can imagination

comprehend how He is. He originated things but not from anything that existed before them, created them without pre-existing examples. Rather, He created them with His might and spread them according to His will. He did so not for a need for which He created them, nor for a benefit (for Him) did He shape them, but to establish His wisdom, bring attention to His obedience, manifest His might, lead His creatures to humbly venerate Him and exalt His decrees. He then made the reward for obedience to Him and punishment for disobedience so as to protect His creatures from His Wrath and amass them into His Paradise.

"I also testify that my Father, Muhammed, is His servant and messenger whom He chose and prior to sending him when the [souls of all] beings were still concealed in that which was transcendental, protected from anything appalling, associated with termination and nonexistence. Allāh the Exalted One knew that which was to follow, comprehended that which would come to pass and realized the place of every event. Allāh sent him (Muhammed) to perfect His commands, a resolution to accomplish His decree, and an implementation of the dictates of His Mercy. So he (Muhammed) found nations differing in their creeds, obsessed by their fires [Zoroastrians], worshipping their idols [Pagans], and denying Allāh [atheists] despite their knowledge of Him. Therefore, Allāh illuminated their darkness with my Father, Muhammed, uncovered obscurity from their hearts, and cleared the clouds from their insights. He revealed guidance to the people. He delivered them from being led astray, taking them away from misguidance, showing them the right religion and inviting them to the Straight Path (*as-Sirat al-Mustaqeem*).

"Allāh then chose to recall him mercifully, with love and preference. So, Muhammed is now in comfort, released from the burden of this world, surrounded angels of devotion, satisfied with the Merciful Lord and with being near the powerful King. So, peace of Allāh with my Father, His Prophet, the trusted one, the one whom He chose from among His servants, His sincere friend, and peace and blessings of Allāh with him."

Fātima (ع) then turned to the crowd and said:

500

"Surely you (people) are Allāh's servants at His command and prohibition, bearers of His creed and revelation. You are the ones whom Allāh entrusted to fare with your own selves, His messengers to the nations. Amongst you does He have the right authority, a covenant which He brought forth to you and an legacy which He left to guard you: The eloquent Book of Allāh, the Qur'ān of the truth, the brilliant light, the shining beam. Its insights are indisputable, its secrets are revealed, its indications are manifest and those who follow it are surely blessed. (The Qur'ān) leads its adherents to righteousness. Listening (and acting upon) it leads to salvation. Through it are the enlightening divine arguments achieved, His manifest determination acquired, His prohibited decrees avoided, His manifest evidence recognized, His convincing proofs made apparent, His permissions granted and His laws written. So Allāh made belief (in Islam) a purification for you from polytheism. He made prayers an exaltation for you from conceit, Zakāt purification for the soul and a (cause of) growth in subsistence, fasting an implantation of devotion, pilgrimage a construction of the creed and justice (Adl) the harmony of the hearts. And He made obedience to us (Ahl al-Bayt) the management of the affairs of the nation and our leadership (Ahl al-Bayt) a safeguard from disunity. He made *jihad* (struggle) a way for strengthening Islam and patience a helping course for deserving (divine) rewards. He made commending what is right (Amr Bil Ma'ruf) a cause for public welfare, kindness to parents a safeguard from (His) wrath, the maintaining of close ties with one's kin a cause for a longer life and for multiplying the number of offspring, in-kind reprisal (*qisas* قصاص) to save lives, fulfillment of vows the earning of mercy, the completion of weights and measures a cause for avoiding neglecting the rights of others, forbidding drinking wines an exaltation from atrocity, avoiding slander a veil from curse, abandoning theft a reason for deserving chastity. Allāh has also prohibited polytheism so that one can devote himself to His Mastership. Therefore; Fear Allāh as He should be feared, and die not except in a state of Islam; Obey Allāh in that which He has commanded you to do and that which He has forbidden, for surely those truly fear among His servants, who have knowledge.'

"O People! Be informed that I am Fāṭima, and my father is Muhammad I say that repeatedly and initiate it continually; I say not what I say mistakenly, nor do I do what I do aimlessly. Now has come unto you an Apostle from amongst yourselves; It grieves him that you should perish; ardently anxious is he over you; To the believers he is most kind and merciful. Thus, if you identify and recognize him, you shall realize that he is my father and not the father of any of your women; the brother of my cousin (Ali (ﻉ)) rather than any of your men. What an excellent identity he was, may the peace and blessings of Allāh be upon him and his descendants Thus, he propagated the Message, by coming out openly with the warning, and while inclined away from the path of the polytheists, (whom he) struck their strength and seized their throats, while he invited (all) to the way of his Lord with wisdom and beautiful preaching He destroyed idols, and defeated heroes, until their group fled and turned their backs. So night revealed its dawn; righteousness uncovered its genuineness; the voice of the religious authority spoke out loud; the evil discords were silenced; The crown of hypocrisy was diminished; the tightening of infidelity and desertion were untied, So you spoke the statement of devotion amongst a band of starved ones; and you were on the edge of a hole of fire;(you were) the drink of the thirsty one; the opportunity of the desiring one; the fire brand of him who passes in haste; the step for feet; you used to drink from the water gathered on roads; eat jerked meat. (Lady Fāṭima (ﻉ) was stating their lowly situation before Islam) You were despised outcasts always in fear of abduction from those around you. Yet, Allāh rescued you through my father, Muhammad after much ado, and after he was confronted by mighty men, the Arab beasts, and the demons of the people of the Book Who, whenever they ignited the fire of war, Allāh extinguished it; and whenever the thorn of the devil appeared, or a mouth of the polytheists opened wide in defiance, he would strike its discords with his brother (Ali, (ﻉ)), who comes not back until he treads its wing with the sole of his feet, and extinguishes its flames with his sword. (Ali is) diligent in Allāh's affair, near to the Messenger of Allāh, A master among Allāh's worshippers, setting to work briskly, sincere in his advice, earnest and exerting himself (in service to Islam); While you were calm, gay, and feeling safe in your comfortable lives, waiting for us to meet disasters, awaiting the

502

spread of news, you fell back during every battle, and took to your heels at times of fighting. Yet, When Allāh chose His Prophet from the dwell of His prophets, and the abode of His sincere (servants); The thorns of hypocrisy appeared on you, the garment of faith became worn out, The misguided ignorant(s) spoke out, the sluggish ignorant came to the front and brayed. The he camel of the vain wiggled his tail in your courtyards and the your courtyards and the Devil stuck his head from its place of hiding and called upon you, he found you responsive to his invitation, and observing his deceits. He then aroused you and found you quick (to answer him), and invited you to wrath, therefore; you branded other than your camels and proceeded to other than your drinking places. Then while the era of the Prophet was still near, the gash was still wide, the scar had not yet healed, and the Messenger was not yet buried. A (quick) undertaking as you claimed, aimed at preventing discord (trial), Surely, they have fallen into trial already! And indeed Hell surrounds the unbelievers. How preposterous! What an idea! What a falsehood! For Allāh's Book is still amongst you, its affairs are apparent; its rules are manifest; its signs are dazzling; its restrictions are visible, and its commands are evident. Yet, indeed you have cast it behind your backs! What! Do you detest it? Or according to something else you wish to rule? Evil would be the exchange for the wrongdoers! And if anyone desires a religion other than Islam (submission to Allāh), it never will it be accepted from him; And in the hereafter, he will be in the ranks of those who have lost. Surely you have not waited until its stampede seized, and it became obedient. You then started arousing its flames, instigating its coal, complying with the call of the misled devil, quenching the light of the manifest religion, and extinguished the light of the sincere Prophet. You concealed sips on froth and proceeded towards his (the Prophet) kin and children in swamps and forests (meaning you plot against them in deceitful ways), but we are patient with you as if we are being notched with knives and stung by spearheads in our abdomens, Yet-now you claim that there is not inheritance for us! What! "Do they then seek after a judgment of (the Days of) ignorance? But How, for a people whose faith is assured, can give better judgment than Allāh? Don't you know? Yes, indeed it is obvious to you that I am his daughter. O Muslims! Will my inheritance be usurped? O son of Abū Quhafa! Where is it in the

Book of Allāh that you inherit your father and I do not inherit mine? Surely you have come up with an unprecedented thing. Do you intentionally abandon the Book of Allāh and cast it behind your back? Do you not read where it says: And Solomon (Sulayman) inherited David (Dawood)'? And when it narrates the story of Zacharias and says: `So give me an heir as from thyself (One that) will inherit me, and inherit the posterity of Jacob (Yaqoob)' And: `But kindred by hood have prior rights against each other in the Book of Allāh' And: Allāh (thus) directs you as regards your children's (inheritance) to the male, a portion equal to that of two females' And, If he leaves any goods, that he make a bequest to parents and next of kin, according to reasonable usage; this is due from the pious ones.' You claim that I have no share! And that I do not inherit my father! What! Did Allāh reveal a (Qur'ānic) verse regarding you, from which He excluded my father? Or do you say: `These (Fātima and her father) are the people of two faiths, they do not inherit each other?!' Are we not, me and my father, a people adhering to one faith? Or is it that you have more knowledge about the specifications and generalizations of the Qur'ān than my father and my cousin (Imām Ali)? So, here you are! Take it! (Ready with) its nose rope and saddled! But if shall encounter you on the Day of Gathering; (thus) what a wonderful judge is Allāh, a claimant is Muhammad, and a day is the Day of Rising. At the time of the Hour shall the wrongdoers lose; and it shall not benefit you to regret (your actions) then! For every Message, there is a time limit; and soon shall ye know who will be inflicted with torture that will humiliate him, and who will be confronted by an everlasting punishment. (Fātima then turned towards the Ansār and said:) O you people of intellect! The strong supporters of the nation! And those who embraced Islam; What is this shortcoming in defending my right? And what is this slumber (while you see) injustice (being done toward me)? Did not the Messenger of Allāh, my father, used to say: A man is upheld (remembered) by his children'? O how quick have you violated (his orders)?! How soon have you plotted against us? But you still are capable (of helping me in) my attempt, and powerful (to help me) in that which I request and (in) my pursuit (of it). Or do you say: "Muhammad has perished;" Surely this is a great calamity; Its damage is excessive its injury is great, Its wound (is much too deep) to heal. The Earth became darkened with his departure; the stars eclipsed for his calamity; hopes were seized; mountains submitted; sanctity was violated, and holiness was encroached upon after his death. Therefore, this, by Allāh, is the great affliction, and the grand calamity; there is not an affliction-which is the like of it; nor will there be a sudden misfortune (as surprising as this). The Book of Allāh-excellent in praising him-announced in the courtyards (of your houses) in the place where you spend your evenings and mornings; A call, A cry, A recitation, and (verses) in order. It had previously came upon His (Allāh's) Prophets and Messengers; (for it is) A decree final, and a predestination fulfilled: "Muhammad is not but an Apostle: Many were the apostles that passed away before him. If he died or was slain, will ye then turn back on your heels? If any did turn back on his heels, not the least harm will he do to Allāh; but Allāh (on the other hand) will swiftly reward those who (serve Him) with gratitude." O you people of reflection; will I be usurped the inheritance of my father while you hear and see me?! (And while) You are sitting and gathered around me? You hear my call, and are included in the (news of the) affair? (But) You are numerous and well equipped! (You have) the means and the power, and the weapons and the shields. Yet, the call reaches you but you do not answer; the cry comes to you but you do not come to help? (This) While you are characterized by struggle, known for goodness and welfare, the selected group (which was chosen), and the best ones chosen by the Messenger for us, Ahlul-Bayt. You fought the Arabs, bore with pain and exhaustion, struggled against the nations, and resisted their heroes. We were still, so were you in ordering you, and you in obeying us. So that Islam became triumphant, the accomplishment of the days came near, the fort of polytheism was subjected, the outburst of was subjected, the outburst of infidelity calmed down, and the system of religion was well-ordered. Thus, (why have you) become confused after clearness? Conceal matters after announcing them? Do you thus turn on your heels after daring, associating (others with Allāh) after believing? Will you not fight people who violated their oaths? Plotted to expel the Apostle and became aggressive by being the first (to assault) you? Do ye fear them? Nay, it is Allāh Whom you should more justly fear, if you believe! Now I see that you are inclined to easy living; having dismissed one who is more worthy of guardianship [referring to Ali (ع)]. You secluded yourselves with

505

meekness and dismissed that which you accepted. Yet, if you show ingratitude, ye and all on earth together, yet, Allāh free of all wants, worthy of all praise. Surely I have said all that I have said with full knowledge that you intent to forsake me, and knowing the betrayal that your hearts sensed. But it is the state of soul, the effusion of fury, the dissemination of (what is) the chest and the presentation of the proof. Hence, Here it is! Bag it (leadership and) put it on the back of an ill she camel, which has a thin hump with everlasting grace, marked with the wrath of Allāh, and the blame of ever (which leads to) the Fire of (the wrath of Allāh kindled (to a blaze), that which doth mount (right) to the hearts; For, Allāh witnesses what you do, and soon will the unjust assailants know what vicissitudes their affairs will take! And I am the daughter of a warner (the Prophet) to you against a severe punishment. So, act and so will we, and wait, and we shall wait.'"

فأجابها أبو بكر وقال : يا بنت رسول الله لقد كان أبوك بالمؤمنين عطوفا كريما رءوفا رحيما وعلى الكافرين عذابا أليما وعقابا عظيما إن عزوناه وجدناه أباك دون النساء وأخا إلفك دون الأخلاء آثره على كل حميم وساعده في كل أمر جسيم لا يحبكم إلا سعيد ولا يبغضكم إلا شقي بعيد فأنتم عترة رسول الله الطيبون الخيرة المنتجبون على الخير أدلتنا وإلى الجنة مسالكنا. وأنت يا خيرة النساء وابنة خير الأنبياء صادقة في قولك سابقة في وفور عقلك غير مردودة عن حقك ولا مصدودة عن صدقك والله ما عدوت رأي رسول الله ولا عملت إلا بإذنه والرائد لا يكذب أهله وإني أشهد الله وكفى به شهيدا أني سمعت رسول الله (ص) يقول نحن معاشر الأنبياء لا نورث ذهبا و لا فضة و لا دارا و لا عقارا و إنما نورث الكتاب والحكمة والعلم والنبوة. وما كان لنا من طعمة فلولي الأمر بعدنا أن يحكم فيه بحكمه وقد جعلنا ما حاولته في الكراع والسلاح يقاتل بها المسلمون ويجاهدون.

فقالت عليها السلام ، سبحان الله ما كان أبي رسول الله (ص) عن كتاب الله صادفا ولا لأحكامه مخالفا بل كان يتبع أثره ويقفو سوره؛ أفتجمعون إلى الغدر اعتلالا عليه بالزور وهذا بعد وفاته شبيه بما بغي له من الغوائل في حياته هذا كتاب الله حكما عدلا وناطقا فصلا يقول يَرِثُنِي وَ يَرِثُ مِنْ آلِ يَعْقُوبَ و يقول وَ وَرِثَ سُلَيْمانُ داوُدَ وبين عز وجل فيما وزع من الأقساط وشرع من الفرائض والميراث وأباح من حظ الذكران والإناث ما أزاح به علة المبطلين وأزال التظني والشبهات في الغابرين كلا بل سولت لكم أنفسكم أمرا فصبر جميل والله المستعان على ما تصفون . فقال أبو بكر: صدق الله ورسوله وصدقت ابنته معدن الحكمة وموطن الهدى والرحمة وركن الدين وعين الحجة لا أبعد صوابك ولا أنكر خطابك هؤلاء المسلمون بيني وبينك قلدوني ما تقلدت وباتفاق منهم أخذت ما أخذت غير مكابر ولا مستبد ولا مستأثر وهم بذلك شهود.

فالتفتت فاطمة عليها السلام إلى الناس و قالت:

معاشر المسلمين المسرعة إلى قيل الباطل المغضية على الفعل القبيح الخاسر أفلا تتدبرون القرآن أم على قلوب أقفالها كلا بل ران على قلوبكم ما أسأتم من أعمالكم فأخذ بسمعكم وأبصاركم ولبئس ما تأولتم وساء ما به أشرتم وشر ما منه اغتصبتم لتجدن والله محمله ثقيلا وغبه وبيلا إذا كشف لكم الغطاء وبان بإورائه الضراء وبدا لكم من ربكم ما لم تكونوا تحتسبون و خسر هنا لك المبطلون.

Abū Bakr responded to her by saying, "O daughter of the Messenger of Allāh! Your father was always affectionate with the believers, generous, kind and merciful, and towards the unbelievers was a painful torment and a great punishment. Surely the Prophet is your father, not anyone else's, the brother of your husband, not any other man's; he surely preferred him over all his friends and (Ali) supported him in every important matter, no one loves you save the lucky and no one hates you save the wretched. You are the blessed progeny of Allāh's Messenger, the chosen ones, our guides to goodness our path to Paradise, and you-the best of women-and the daughter of the best of prophets, truthful is your sayings, excelling in reason. You shall not be driven back from your right... But I surely heard your father saying: `We the, group of prophets do not inherit, nor are we inherited Yet, this is my situation and property, it is yours (if you wish); it shall not be concealed from you, nor will it be stored away from you. You are the Mistress of your father's nation, and the blessed tree of your descendants. Your property shall not be usurped against your will nor can your name be defamed. Your judgment shall be executed in all that which I possess. This, do you think that I violate your father's (will)?"

Fātima then refuted Abū Bakr's claim that the Prophet had stated that prophets cannot be inherited, and said: "Glory be to Allāh!! Surely Allāh's Messenger did not abandon Allāh's Book nor did he violate His commands. Rather, he followed its decrees and adhered to its chapters. So do you unite with treachery justifying your acts with fabrications? Indeed this—after his departure—is similar to the disasters which were plotted against him during his lifetime. But behold! This is Allāh's Book, a just judge and a decisive speaker, saying: `One that will (truly) inherit Me, and inherit the posterity of Yaqub,' (19:6) and 'And Sulaiman (Solomon) inherited Dawood

507

(David).' (27: 16) Thus, He (Glory be to Him) made clear that which He made share of all heirs, decreed from the amounts of inheritance, allowed for males and females, and eradicated all doubts and ambiguities (pertaining to this issue which existed with the) bygones. Nay! But your minds have made up a tale (that may pass) with you, but (for me) patience is most fitting against that which ye assert; it is Allāh (alone) whose help can be sought." It is apparent that Abū Bakr chanced the mode with which he addressed Lady Fātima (ع) after delivering her speech. Listen to his following speech; which is his reply to Fātima's just reported speech.

Abū Bakr said: "Surely Allāh and His Apostle are truthful, and so has his (the Prophet's) daughter told the truth. Surely you are the source of wisdom, the element of faith, and the sole authority. May Allāh not refute your righteous argument, nor invalidate your decisive speech. But these are the Muslims between us-who have entrusted me with leadership, and it was according to their satisfaction that 1 received what 1 have. I am not being arrogant, autocratic, or selfish, and they are my witnesses." Upon hearing Abū Bakr speak of the people's support for him, Lady Fātima Zahra (ع) turned towards them and said:

"O people, who rush towards uttering falsehood and are indifferent to disgraceful and losing actions! Do you not earnestly seek to reflect upon the Qur'ān, or are your hearts isolated with locks? But on your hearts is the stain of the evil, which you committed; it has seized your hearing and your sight, evil is that which you justified cursed is that which you reckoned, and wicked is what you have taken for an exchange! You shall, by Allāh, find bearing it (to be a great) burden, and its consequence disastrous. (That is) on the day when the cover is removed and appears to you what is behind it of wrath. When you will be confronted by Allāh with that which you could never have expected, there will perish, there and then, those who stood on falsehoods." Although parts of Abū Bakr's speeches cannot be verified with authentic evidence, and despite the fact that we have already mentioned part of the actual speech, which Abū Bakr delivered after Lady Fātima's arguments, it appears certain that Abū Bakr was finally persuaded to submit Fadak to her. Nevertheless, when Fātima was leaving Abū Bakr's house, Omer suddenly appeared and exclaimed: "What is it that you hold in your hand?"

Abū Bakr replied: 'A decree I have written for Fātima in which I assigned Fadak and her father's inheritance to her." Omer then said: "With what will you spend on the Muslims if the Arabs decide to fight you?!"

وفي سيرة الحلبي ج 3 ص 391 -: أن عمر أخذ الكتاب فشقه.

According to p. 391, Vol. 3, of al-Halabi's *Seera* book, Omer [ibn al-Khattab] seized the decree and tore it to pieces…

ثم عطفت على قبر النبي (ص) و قالت:

لو كنت شاهدها لم تكثر الخطب	قد كان بعدك انباء و هنبثة
واختل قومك فاشهدهم فقد نكبوا	انا فقدناك فقد الارض وابلها
من البرية لا عجم و لا عرب	و قد رُزينا بما لم يرزه أحد
يوم القيامة أنى سوف ينقلب	سيعلم المتولي ظلم حامتنا
وسيم سبطاك خسفاً فيه لي نصب	ضاقت عليَّ بلادي بعدما رحبت
عند الاله على الأدنين مقترب	و كل أهل له قربى و منزلة
لما مضيت و حالت دونك الترب	أبدت رجال لنا نجوى صدورهم
اذ غبت عنا فنحن اليوم نغتصب	تجهمتنا رجال و آستخف بنا
عليك ينزل من ذي العزة الكتب	وكنت بدرا و نورا يستضاء به
فقد فقدت و كل الخير محتجب	قد كان جبريل بالآيات يؤنسنا
لما مضيت و حالت دونك الكثب	فليت قبلك كان الموت صادفنا
بقيت من العيون بتهمال لها سكب	فسوف نبكيك ما عشنا وما
صافي الضرائب و الأعراق و النسب	و قد رزينا به محضا خليقته
و أصدق الناسحين الصدق و الكذب	فأنت خير عباد الله كلهم

After you, reports and momentous chaotic events we found,
Had you witnessed them, calamities would not abound.
We missed you as sorely as earth would miss its rain,
Your folks lost balance, see how from the creed they did refrain,
We, like no others, have suffered affliction,
Unlike all Arabs, or others from among Allāh's creation.
One who has oppressed us will come on Judgment Day
To know what fate will be awaiting him.
My homeland is now narrow after its great expanse indeed,

Both your grandsons have been wronged, so my heart is grieved,
Every family has relatives and a place
With the Almighty Who is close to those of grace,
Certain men what their chests hid did they to us reveal,
When you went, and now you from our sights did a grave conceal,
Men assaulted and slighted us, when you became far away
So, now what rightfully belongs to us is being taken away.
You were the moon, your light showed us what we should heed,
Messages from the Exalted One were to you revealed.
With the Verses did Gabriel make our day,
Now you are gone, every good thing is kept away.
How we wish in our direction death did the Almighty guide
Before you left us, and you did the dunes from us hide.
We shall cry over you so long as our tears can pour,
So long as floods of tears can withstand and endure.
We have been afflicted with tragedy on his account
One who is pure in peers, folks and lineage,
For you are the best of Allāh's creation and
Most truthful of those who only the truth defend.

ـ من أشار إلى خطبة الصدّيقة فاطمة (عليها السلام) أو روى شيئاً منها نذكر بعضاً منهم على سبيل المثال لا حصر، وهم كالتالي:

1ـ الخليل بن أحمد الفراهيدي (ت 175 هـ) في كتاب العين: 8 / 323 في كلمة اللمّة، وقال: وفي الحديث جاءت فاطمة (عليها السلام) إلى أبي بكر في لُميمة من حفدتها ونساء قومها.
2ـ جار الله محمد بن عمر الزمخشري (ت 538 هـ).
في الفائق: 3 / 331 في مادة اللمة أيضاً قال: وفي حديث فاطمة (عليها السلام): إنّها خرجت في لمة من نسائها تتوطأ ذيلها، حتى دخلت على أبي بكر.
3ـ أبو الفرج عبد الرحمن بن علي بن الجوزي، (ت 597 هـ.)
في غريب الحديث: 2 / 333 وقال: وفي الحديث: أنّ فاطمة (عليها السلام) خرجت في لمّة من نسائها إلى أبي بكر فعاتبته. أي في جماعة ؛ وقيل: من الثلاث إلى العشر.
4ـ مجد الدين أبو السعادات ابن الأثير (ت 606 هـ.)
في النهاية في غريب الحديث والأثر: 4 / 273 وقال: في حديث فاطمة (عليها السلام): إنّها خرجت في لمة من نسائها تتوطأ ذيلها، إلى أبي بكر فعاتبته.
5ـ أبو الفضل جمال الدين بن منظور (ت 711 هـ).
في لسان العرب: 12 / 548 وقال: وفي حديث فاطمة (عليها السلام): إنّها خرجت في لمة من نسائها تتوطأ ذيلها إلى أبي بكر فعاتبته. ذكرها في مادة لمم.

References to this speech by the Truthful One, Fātima, peace with her, including some who cited excerpts of it, include the following:

1. Al-Khalil ibn Ahmed al-Farahidi الخليل بن أحمد الفراهيدي (d. 175 A.H./792 A.D.) on p. 323, Vol. 8, of *Kitab al-Ayn*,
2. Jarallāh Muhammed ibn Omer al-Zamakhshari[1] الزمخشري (d. 538 A.H./1144 A.D.) on p. 331, Vol. 3, of Al-Faiq;
3. Abul-Faraj Abdul-Rahman ibn Ali ibn al-Jawzi ابن الجوزي (d. 597 A.H./1201 A.D.),
4. Majd ad-Deen Abū al-Sa'adat Ibn al-Atheer ابن الأثير (d. 606 A.H./1210 A.D.) on p. 273, Vol. 4 of his book titled *Al-Nihaya*,
5. Abul-Fadl Jamal ad-Deen ibn Manzour ابن منظور (d. 711 A.H./1312 A.D.) on p. 548, Vol. 12 (old edition) of his lexicon titled *Lisan al-Arab*.

FĀTIMA FURTHER OPPRESSED

Throughout her life, Fātima (ع) never spoke to those who had oppressed her and deprived her of her rightful claims. She kept her grief to herself. During her sickness which preceded her death, she requested that her oppressors should be kept away even from attending her funeral. Her ill-wishers even resorted to physical violence. Once the door of her house was pushed on her, and the child she was carrying was hurt and the baby-boy was stillborn. This incident took place, and it is very well documented by Shī'ite and Sunni historians and chroniclers, when Omer ibn al-Khattab was urging, sometimes even beating, people to go to the Prophet's Mosque to swear allegiance to his friend, Abū Bark. Omer promoted Abū Bakr to the seat of "caliph", being the very first person to swear allegiance to him after being convinced that it would not be long before he, too, would occupy the same seat. Fātima's house was set on fire. Having been mistreated and stricken with grief, which crossed all limits of forbearance and endurance, she expressed her sorrows in an elegy which she composed to mourn her father the Holy Prophet (ص). In that elegy, she makes a particular reference to her woeful plight saying, after having taken a handful of earth from her father's grave, putting it on her eyes, crying and saying,

---

[1] Refer to a footnote about al-Zamakhshari above.

ماذا على من شمَّ تربةً أحمد أن لا يشمَّ مدى الزمان غواليا؟
صُبّت عليَّ مصائبٌ لو أنّها صُبّت على الأيَّام صرْنَ ليَاليا
قد كنت ذات حمى بظل محمد لا أختشي ضيماً و كان جماليا
فاليوم أخشع للذليل وأتقي ضيمي، و أدفع ظالمي بردائيا
فإذا بكت قمرية في ليلها شجناً على غصن بكيت صباحيا
فلأجعلن الحزن بعدك مؤنسي و لأجعلن الدمع فيك وشاحيا

What blame should be on one who smells Ahmed's soil
That he shall never smell any precious person at all?
Calamities have been poured on me (like waters boil)
Were they poured on days, they would become nights.
In the shade of Muhammed, I enjoyed all protection
And he was my beauty, and I feared no oppression,
But now I surrender to the lowly and fear I am done
Injustice, pushing my oppressor with only my gown.
So, if a dove cries during its night, forlorn,
Out of grief on its twig, I cry in my morn.
So, I shall after you let grief be a companion for me,
And my tears that mourn you my cover they shall be.

On p. 218, Vol. 2, of al-Tabari's *Tarikh* (Dar al-Amira for Printing, Publishing and Distribution, Beirut, Lebanon, 2005), it is stated that when Fātima could not get her inheritance, Fadak, from Abū Bakr, she boycotted him and never spoke to him till her death.

The death of the Apostle, affected her very much and she was very sad and grief-stricken and wept her heart out crying all the time. Unfortunately, after the death of the Prophet, the Government confiscated her famous land of Fadak. Fātima (ع) was pushed behind her home door (when they

512

attacked Ali's house and took him away in order to force him to accept the caliphate of Abū Bakr), so the fetus she was carrying, namely Muhsin, was subsequently aborted. Omer ibn al-Khattab ordered his servant, Qunfath, to set her house on fire, an incident which is immortalized by verses of poetry composed by the famous Egyptian poet Hafiz Ibrahim which is reproduced here but without English translation. The author has preferred not to translate it in order not to hurt the feelings of his Sunni brethren, especially non-Arabs:

اللهم
كما سترت ذنوبنا وعيوبنا
فى الدنيا
فاسترها يوم القيامة
يوم الحسرة والندامة
يوم يرى كل إنسان منا
عمله أمامه

وقـولـــة لـ (علـى) قـالـها (عـمـر)   مـا نَحـنُ فيـهِ بقـايـا مـن مآسـيهـا
حَرَقْـتُ دارَكَ لا أُبـقـى عَلَيـــكَ بهـا   إِن لَـم تُبـايـعْ وبنـتُ المُصطَفى فيهـا
ومـا أَتى دارَ وَحى اللّــه مُنـتَـفِـضـا   بـالنّـار بـوعـدُها خـرقـاً يُعَنّفـهـا
قالـوا لَـه:(فاطِـمٌ) فى الدّار قـال:(وإن)   بِغَظـة أَعجَـزت حَتّى مُداريهـا
فقـولـة أَفصَحَتْ عن دين صاحِبها   هَـل كـانَ بـالحَـقِّ أَم بـالظُّـلم مُلقِيها؟
وقـل لِمـن عَـدَّ هـذا القـولَ مَكرُمَـة   للمَكـرُمـات بِسَـهم الإفك تَرمِيهـا
سائـل (أَبا حفصٍ) هَـل كـانَتْ مَقولَتُـه   وفـى الشُّـريفَـة؟ أَم حُكمـاً تُنافِيهـا؟
أَفى الكِتـاب؟ وذا القـرآن مُشـاهـدة   آبـائَـه أَنّهـا للكُـفـر تَنمِيهـا
أَم سُنّةُ المَصطَفى جـاءتْ بهـا وَلَـه   عِلـمٌ بِمـا دَرارِها فَتُضـاعَ يُخزِيهـا
إنّ الـذى يَهتَـكُ (الـزّهـراء) حُرمَتَهـا   مـا كـانَ يَومـاً لآي الـذّكـر تالِيهـا
أَنَسى قـولُ رسـول اللّـه: فاطِمَـةٌ   بَقِيتى فيكـم بـالفَضـل يُصَفيهـا
و(فاطِـمٌ) بِضـعَـة مِنّى فيَـؤلِمُـنى   مـا كـان يؤلِمُها يا بِئسَ مؤذيهـا
يا لَهـفَ (فاطِـم) خَلـفَ البـاب إِذ وَقَفتْ   تَـدعـو أَبـاهـا عسى يأتى فَيَحمِيهـا
لَـم يَبـلُ جِسمُكِ والأَحكـامُ قَـد بُلِيَـتْ   و(السّـامِرى) بِحُكم الجَـوز ماحِيهـا
قَـد كـان بعدَكَ أَنبـــاءٌ وهَنبَثَـــة   لَـو كُنتَ شـاهـدَها هـاقتْ دواهِيهـا
قَتـلُ الجَنِيــن وكَسـرُ الضّلـع أَعظَمُهـا   أَم غَضبٌ حقّى وأَمسـولٌ أُلاقِيهـا؟
يا بـابَ (فاطِـم) ما لاقَيتَ مِن مِحَـن   نُشـجى الكِـرامَ ومـا زالَـتْ تُقـاسِيهـا

513

On p. 220, Vol. 2, of al-Tabari's *Tarikh* (Arabic text), it is stated that the Holy Prophet (ص) remained unburied for three days. His sacred body finally received the burial bath by his cousin and son-in-law, Fātima's husband Ali (ع). Besides Ali (ع), those who attended the burial of the Prophet (ص) were: al-Abbās ibn Abdul-Muttalib, his son al-Fadhl, Qutham ibn al-Abbās, Usamah ibn Zaid, and Shuqran, a freed slave of the Prophet (ص), according to the same page. According to Ibn Ishāq, Aws ibn Khawli, who had taken part in the Battle of Badr, earnestly requested Ali (ع) to let him assist in burying the Messenger of Allāh (ص) which the Commander of the Faithful accepted (ع).

The tragedy of her father's death and the unkindness of her father's followers, were too much for the good, gentle and sensitive lady and she breathed her last on Jumda I 14, 11 A.H., exactly seventy-five days after the death of her revered father, the Holy Prophet of Islam. Grieved about the way she was treated by certain "sahāba" of the Prophet (ص), the confiscation of her property, Fadak, the aborting of her son, Musin, and the confiscation of the right to caliphate from her husband, Ali, were all too much for her, so much so that they eventually put an end to her life when she was in the prime of her life at the age of eighteen, although historians provide different dates, and was buried in Jannatul-Baqi', Medīna.

FĀTIMA'S DEATH
On p. 218, Vol. 2, of al-Tabari's *Tarikh*, al-Tabari says,

فدفنها علي ليلا، و لم يؤذن بها أبا بكر

"Ali buried her at night, and Abū Bakr did not call the *athan* (to announce her death)."

Fātima (ع) did not survive more than seventy-five days after the demise of her father. She breathed her last on the 14th Jumdi I, 11 A.H. Before her demise, she told her will to her husband, Imām Ali (ع), thus:

1. O Ali, you will personally perform my funeral rites.

514

2. Those who have displeased me should not be allowed to attend my funeral.
3. My corpse should be carried to the graveyard at night.

Thus, Imām Ali (ع), in compliance with her will, performed all the funeral rites and accompanied exclusively by her relatives and sons carried her at night to Jannatu'l-Baqi ', where she was laid to rest and her wishes fulfilled.

Having buried her, in the darkness of the night, her husband, the Commander of the Faithful Ali (ع) composed these verses of poetry:

هذي قصيدة الامام علي بن ابي طالب عندما كان عند قبر فاطمة الزهراء (ع):

قبر الحبيب فلم يرد جوابي؟	ما لي وقفت على القبور مُسلما
أنسيت بعدي خلّة الأحباب؟	أحبيب، ما لك لا ترد جوابنا
و أنا رهين جنادل و تراب؟	قال الحبيب: وكيف لي بجوابكم
وحجبت عن أهلي وعن أترابي	أكل الترابُ محاسني فنسيتكُم
مني و منكم خلّة الأحباب	فعليكم مني السلام تقطعت

Why did I stand at the graves to greet,
The tomb of the loved one, but it did not respond?
O loved one! Why do you not answer us?
Have you forgotten the friendship among loved ones?
The loved one said: How can I answer you
While I am held hostage by soil and stones?
Earth has eaten my beauties, so I forgot about you,
And I now am kept away from family and peers;
So, peace from me to you, the ties are now cut off
And so are the ties with loved ones.

On p. 136 of Dalaa'il al-Imāma دلائل الامامة, we are told that those who attended Fātima's burial in the darkness of the night were, besides her husband Ali (ع), none other than both her sons al-Hassan and al-Hussain (ع), her daughters Zainab and Umm Kulthum, her maid Fidda and Asmaa daughter of Umays. The author, as quoted on p. 92, Vol. 10 of the newly published edition of *Bihār al-Anwār*, adds the following:

و أصبح البقيع ليلة دفنت و فيه أربعون قبرا جددا، و ان المسلمين لما علموا وفاتها جاءوا الى البقيع فوجدوا فيه أربعين قبرا، فأشكل عليهم قبرها من سائر القبور، فضج الناس و لام بعضهم بعضا و قالوا: لم يخلف نبيكم فيكم الا بنتا واحدة تموت و تدفن و لم تحضروا وفاتها و الصلاة عليها و لا حتى تعرفوا قبرها.

ثم قال ولاة الأمر منهم: هاتم من نساء المسلمين من ينبش هذه القبور حتى نجدها فنصلي عليها و نزور قبرها. فبلغ ذلك أمير المؤمنين صلوات الله عليه، فخرج مغضبا قد احمرت عيناه و درت أوداجه و عليه قباه الأصفر الذي كان يلبسه في كل كريهة و هو متوكيء على سيفه ذي الفقار حتى ورد البقيع، فسار الى الناس النذير و قال: هذا علي بن أبي طالب قد أقبل كما ترونه يقسم بالله لئن حول من هذه القبور حجر ليضعن السيف على غابر الآخر.

فتلقاه عمر (بن الخطاب) و من معه من أصحابه و قال له: ما لك يا أبا الحسن؟ و الله لننبشن قبرها و لنصلين عليها. فضرب علي (ع) بيده الى جوامع ثوبه (يعني ثوب عمر) فهزه، ثم ضرب به الأرض و قال: يا ابن السوداء! أما حقي (في الخلافة) فقد تركته مخافة أن يرتد الناس عن دينهم، و أما قبر فاطمة، فو الذي نفس علي بيده، لئن رمت و أصحابك شيئا من ذلك، لأسقين الأرض من دمائكم. فان شئت، فأعرض يا عمر.

فتلقاه أبو بكر فقال: يا أبا الحسن بحق رسول الله و بحق من (هو) فوق العرش الا خليت عنه، فانا غير فاعلين شيئا تكرهه. فتخلى عنه و تفرق الناس و لم يعودوا الى ذلك.

In the morning of the eve in which she (Fātima) was buried, al-Baqi' was found to have forty new graves. When the Muslims came to know about her death, they went to al-Baqi' where they found forty freshly built graves, so they were confused and could not identify her grave from among all of them. People fussed and blamed each other. They said, "Your Prophet left only one daughter among you. She dies and is buried while you do not attend her demise or perform the prayers for her or even know where her grave is."

Those in authority among them said, "Bring from among the Muslims' women those who would inter these graves till we find her, perform the prayers for her and visit her grave." The report reached the Commander of the Faithful, Allāh's blessings with him, so he came out furious, his eyes reddened, his veins swollen and wearing his yellow outer garment which he always put on whenever there was trouble, leaning on his sword, Thul-Fiqar, till he reached al-Baqi'. A warner rushed to people to warn them saying, "Here is Ali ibn Abū Tālib has come as you can see, swearing by Allāh that if

516

anyone moves a brick of these graves, he will kill each and every one of them."

He was met by Omer [ibn al-Khattab] and some of his companions and said, "What is wrong with you, O father of al-Hassan?! By Allāh, we shall inter her grave, and we shall perform the [funeral] prayers for her." Ali (ع) took hold of Omer's garment, shook him and threw him on the ground and said, "O son of the black woman! As regarding my right [to succeed the Prophet as the caliph], I have abandoned it for fear people might revert from their religion. As for Fātima's grave, I swear by the One Who holds Ali's soul in His hands that if you and your fellows want to do any such thing, I shall let the earth drink of your blood, all of you; so, if you want, stay away from it, O Omer."

Abū Bakr met him and said, "O father of al-Hassan! By the right of the Messenger of Allāh (ص) and by the right of the One on the Arsh, leave him, for we shall not do anything which you dislike." Ali (ع) left Omer alone. People dispersed and did not make any further attempt. This incident shows the reader how Abū Bakr was blessed with a higher degree of wisdom than Omer.

هذه الابيـات مـن قصيدة فاطمـة سيدة نساء العالمين للمرحوم الشيخ محسن أبو الحب الكبير أهديها الى كل الفاطميات:

أو قـيل مـريم قلت فـاطم أفضل	فإن قـيل حـوّا قلت فاطم فخرها
أم هـل لمـريم مـثل فاطم أشبل؟	أفـهل لحـوّا والـد كـمحمّد
مـنها عـقول ذوي البـصائر تـذهل	كـلّ لهـا عـند الولادة حـالةً
رطـبا جنيّاً فـهي مـنه تأكـل	هـذي لنـخلتها التجت فتسـاقطت
أنّـي وحـارسها السّـرىّ الأبسل؟	وضعت بـعيسى وهي غـير مـروعةٍ
بنـت النّـبيّ فأسـقطت مـا تـحمل	وإلى الجدار وصفحةُ البـاب التجت
مـن كـلّ ذي حسب لئيم جـحفل	سـقطت وأسـقطت الجنـين وحـولها
و يـردها هـذا و هـذا يـركل	هـذا يـعنّفها وذاك يـدعّها
بـالحبل قـنفذ، هـل كـهذا معضل؟	و أمـامها أسـد الأسـود يـقوده
تشكـو الى رب السـماء و تـعول	و لسـوف تأتـي في القيامة فاطم
بشكـايةٍ مـنها السّـما تـتزلزل:	ولتـعرفنّ جنـينها و حـنينها
غـصبوا، و أبـنائي جـميعاً قتّلوا	ربّـاه مـيراثي و بـعلي حقّه

517

Following are verses of poetry in honor of Fātima, Head of the Women of Mankind, composed by the late Shaikh Muhsin Abū al-Hubb Senior presented to all ladies who descended from Fātima:

When they mention Eve, I say that Fātima is her pride,
Or if Mary is mentioned, I say that Fātima is superior.
Can anyone underestimate a father such as Muhammed?
Or does Mary have a lion cub more brave than Fātima's?
Each had a status at her birth that puzzles sages' minds:
This to her date tree resorted, so of fresh ripe dates she ate,
Giving birth to Jesus without fright, how so when the guard
Is the most brave night sojourner?
And to the wall and the door's slab did this resort,
Prophet's daughter, so she aborted what she was bearing.
She fell, and her fetus [Muhsin] fell with her, surrounded by
Every one of a mean descent and lowly birth:
This rogue rebukes her, that one reprimands her,
This one dismisses her, that one even kicks her...
Though before her was the lion of lions being led
By the rope..., so, is there a greater calamity?
Fātima will come on the Judgment Day to complain
To the Lord of the Heavens, and she will wail,
And you will know who her fetus was, why she wails
Why she presents a complaint from which the heavens shake:
"Lord! My inheritance and my husband's right did they confiscate
"And, moreover, all my sons did they kill, O Lord!"

قصيدة للشاعر المسيحي عبد المسيح الأنطاكي يمدح فيها فاطمة الزهراء (ع) فالسيدة الزهراء (ع) قد شهد بفضلها المخالف والمؤالف لأنها سيدة نساء العالمين من الأولين والأخرين:

بنتُ لحواءَ تدنو من معاليها	و إنها فزَّةٌ بين النساء فلا
و لا ثُلالي إذا لاحت كلاليها	ومن يُشعُ شَعاعَ الشمس جبهتُها
مَن بالمفاخرِ و العُليا يُحاكيها	هي الجديرةُ بالكُفءِ الكريم لها
بناتها، سَنيةً تأبى تعذَيْها	والغَرْبُ تطلبُ أكفاءً تَزَوجُهُمْ
عاراً عليها لدى الأقرانِ يُخزيها	وكُلُّ عقدٍ بغير الكُفءِ تحسَبُهُ
ومَن من العَرَب العَرباءَ كافيها؟	فمن يليقُ ببنتِ المُصطفى حسباً
وهي المصاهرةُ المسعودُ مُلقيَها؟	و مَن يناسَب طه كي يُصاهرَه
سَبَقُ الهدايةِ مُذ نادى مناديها	غيُر العليّ حبيب المصُطفى و له

518

فانه بعدَ طه خيرُ من ولَدَتْ   قُريشَ مُنذ برا الباري ذراريها

و أنه بطلُ الإسلامِ تعرفُهُ تلك   الحروب التي أمسى مُجليّها

Here is a poem composed by the Christian poet Abdul-Maseeh al-Antaki (of Antioch city) in praise of Fātima al-Zahra (ع), for those who agree with our [religious] views and those who do not have all testified to Fātima's distinction: She is the Mistress of all Women of Mankind from the early generations to the very last:

Among women, hers is a unique birth:
No other daughter of Eve comes to her distinctions close.
One from whose forehead the sun's rays shine,
From her standing places glitter glows.
She is the peer of the honored one and only who
In his feats and supreme honors is her only match.
Arabs seek competent peers for daughters to marry
A tradition which they refuse to forgo.
Any marriage without a competent peer they regard
As a shame on them that debases them among peers.
Who can match in lineage the daughter of the Chosen one?
Who among the Arabs in honors matches her?
Who suits Taha (ص) to be his son-in-law,
A marriage tie that brings happiness to one who wins it
Other than Ali, the one loved by the Chosen One?
He accepted Guidance since the Messenger called for it.
Next to the Chosen One, he is the best of Quraish
Since the Almighty created its souls.
And he is the hero of Islam well known
By those wars that raised his status.

ما هو ''مصحف فاطمة''؟

((وخلفت فاطمة عليها السلام مصحفاً، ما هو قرآن، ولكنه كلام من كلام الله، أنزله عليها، إملاء رسول الله، وخط على عليه السلام))(بحار الأنوار ج26 ص41 رواية73 باب1) ولذا سمّيت فاطمة، فهي مظهر فاطر السموات والأرض. وحيث أن الملك المرسل من قِبَله تعالى يحدّثها، سمّيت المحدّثة، كما مرّ أنه كان يخبرها عمّا سيحدث بعدها في ذريّتها من المصائب والبلايا، والأهم من ذلك ما ستكتسبها الذرية، من انتصارات عظيمة، ونجاح كبير في عصر الغيبة، ومن ثَم ظهور ابنها المهدي المنتظر، عجّلّ الله تعالى فرجه الشريف.

عليٌ عليه السلام كاتبُ المصحف

519

أنَّ الزهراء، سلام الله عليها، كانت تحسُّ بالملك، وتسمع صوته، ولم تكن تشاهده، فبمجرَّد أن حصل ذلك، شكت إلى أمير المؤمنين علي، عليه السلام، حيث لم تكن تتوقَّع هذا الأمر بهذه الصورة المستمرَّة. اذن كان أمير المؤمنين علي، عليه السلام صاحب فكرة كتابة المصحف، حيث يسمع صوت روح الأمين، فيكتب كلما يسمعه، إلى أن اجتمع في مصحف متكامل، وهو مصحف الزهراء عليها السلام. ولا يخفى عليك ، أنَّه ليس من السهل كتابة ما يلقيه جبرئيل، بل كان ذلك ضمن العلوم الخاصَّة الإلهيَّة التي امتاز بها أمير المؤمنين، عليه السلام، فهو الذي كتب من قبل ما أملاه رسول الله عليه، وهو الذي مع القرآن الكريم في المصحف الشريف كما هو ثابت في محلِّه.

محتوى المصحف

إنَّ المصحف يشتمل على أمورٍ كثيرةٍ تتلخص في كلمة واحدة وهي: استيعابه لجميع الحوادث الخطيرة الآتية، خصوصاً ما سيواجه ذريتُها، من المصائب والبلايا، وأيضاً الانتصارات، ويشتمل على أسماء جميع الملوك والحكَّام إلى يوم القيامة، كما ورد في الحديث: ((ما من نبي و لا وصي ولا ملك إلا وفي مصحف فاطمة)) (بحار الأنوار ج47 ص32 رواية29 باب4). ويحتوى على أمور ترجع إلى شخص رسول الله، صلى الله عليه وآله وسلم، وأيضاً يشتمل على وصيتها سلام الله عليها.

((ابن هاشم عن يحيى بن أبي عمران عن يونس عن رجل عن سليمان بن خالد قال : قال أبو عبد الله عليه السلام.. فإن فيه وصية فاطمة عليها السلام..))(بحار الأنوار ج26 ص43 رواية76 باب1). ومن الطبيعي أنَّ الوصيَّة تشتمل على أمورٍ خاصَّة، تتعلَّق بحزنها عليها السلام، وبالمصائب الواردة عليها، من أعدائها، لتُنفذها ابنها الإمام الثاني عشر المهدي المنتظر، عجَّل الله تعالى فرجه الشريف، لأنَّه هو الإمام مبسوط اليد، الذي به يملأ الله الأرض قسطاً وعدلاً، كما مُلئت ظلماً وجوراً.

الأئمَّة عليهم السلام ومصحف فاطمة

كان الإمام الصادق عليه السلام، يؤكِّد دائماً على علوم أهل البيت عليهم السلام، ففي الحديث أنَّه كان يقول "أنَّ علمهم عليهم السلام غابر ومزبور ونكتٌ في القلوب ونقر في الأسماع" وأنَّهم يمتلكون "الجفر الأحمر، والجفر الأبيض، ومصحف فاطمة، والجامعة" فهم عليهم السلام رغم ارتباطهم وسماعهم صوت الملائكة ورغم تبعيّتهم لمصحف الإمام عليّ الذي هو الجامعة المشتملة على جميع الأحكام حتى أرش الخدش، ورغم معرفتهم بعلم الجفر الذي يشتمل على "علم ما يحتاج إليها الناس إلى يوم القيامة من حلال و حرام" إلّا أنَّهم كانوا يعتمدون في فهم الحوادث الخطيرة على مصحف فاطمة عليها السلام كما ورد في الحديث "فنحن نتبع ما فيها فلا نعدوها" حيث يشتمل على الحوادث الخارجية جميعاً. وأيضاً أسماء الملوك إلى يوم القيامة، ففي الحديث: ((سئل عن محمد بن عبد الله بن الحسن فقال عليه السلام: ما من نبي ولا وصى ولا ملك إلّا وهو في كتاب عندي. يعنى مصحف فاطمة، والله ما لمحمد بن عبدالله فيه اسم)) (بحار الأنوار ج47 ص32 رواية29 باب4).

لقد وصل المصحف إلى مستوى من الرفعة والسموّ بحيث صار مصدر سرورهم

واستبشارهم، كما يستفاد من جملة قرت عينه في الحديث التالي: ((عن فضيل بن عثمان عن الحذاء قال: قال لي أبو جعفر عليه السلام يا أبا عبيدة كان عنده سيف رسول الله صلى الله عليه وآله وسلم ودرعه ورايته المغلبة ومصحف فاطمة عليها السلام قرَّتْ عينُه)) (بحار الأنوار ج26 ص211 رواية22 باب16).

هل مصحف فاطمة هو القرآن؟

إنَّ الكثير من الناس كانوا ولا زالوا يتصوَّرون أنَّ المصحف يشتمل على الآيات القرآنية الشريفة، أو أنَّ هناك قرآناً آخر عند الشيعة، كما يزعم بعضُ الجُهال من العامَّة. ولكنَّ الواقع هو خلاف ذلك، فإنَّ المصحف لا يشتمل حتى على آية واحدة من آيات القرآن الكريم، كما هو المستفاد من الأحاديث الكثيرة ،كما أنَّه ليس من قبيل القرآن ولا يشبهه من ناحية المحتوى أصلاً، فهو من مقولة أخرى، فأحاديثنا صريحةٌ في ذلك فقد ورد في حديث: ((...عن على بن سعيد عن أبي عبد الله عليه السلام... ما فيه آيةٌ من القرآن)) (بحار الأنوار ج26 ص42 رواية74 باب1).

وفي أحاديث أخر: ((...عن على بن الحسين عن أبى عبد الله عليه السلام .. عندنا مصحف فاطمة، أما والله ما فيه حرفٌ من القرآن))(بحار الأنوار ج26 ص46 رواية84 باب1).

- ((عبد الله بن جعفر عن موسى بن جعفر عن الوشاء عن أبي حمزة عن أبي عبد الله عليه السلام قال: مصحف فاطمة عليها السلام ما فيه شيء من كتاب الله..))(بحار الأنوار ج26 ص48 رواية89 باب1).

- ((عن عنبسة بن مصعب قال: كنا عند أبي عبد الله عليه السلام.. ومصحف فاطمة أما والله ما أزعم أنه قرآن))(بحار الأنوار ج26 ص33 رواية50 باب1).

عند ملاحظة الأحاديث تعرف أنَّ الشبهة كانت منتشرة في عصر الأئمة عليهم السلام، ولهذا نراهم يستنكرون بكلّ حزم وجدّ، ويتوسَّلون بالقسم لنفي ذلك، غير أنَّ هناك حديثا يدلّ على أنَّ المصحف:

((فيه مثل قرآنكم هذا ثلاث مرات))(بحار الأنوار ج26 ص38 رواية70 باب).

والظاهر أنَّ المقصود هو من ناحية الكميّة وحجم المعلومات، لا من حيث المحتوى. ثُمَّ لا يخفى عليك ما في كلمة قرآنكم من معانٍ فتأمَّل جيِّداً.

وأيضاً:

المستفاد من أحاديث كثيرة أنَّ مصحف الزهراء عليها السلام ليس فيه شيء من الحلال والحرام أصلاً، ومن تلك الأحاديث قوله عليه السلام: ((أما إنَّه ليس من الحلال والحرام))(بحار الأنوار ج26 ص44 رواية77 باب1).

WHAT IS FĀTIMA'S *MUSHAF*?

Fātima (ع) has left us a book behind her which is not a Qur'ān but speech of the Almighty revealed to her, dictated by the Messenger of Allāh (ص) and written down by Ali (ع), according to p. 41, Vol. 26 of *Bihār al-Anwār*. This is why she is named "Fātima": the one who manifests the speech of the Fatir (Creator) of the heavens and earth.

Since the angel sent by Him speaks to her on behalf of the Almighty, she is called "muhaddatha المحدّثة", one spoken to. Also, the angel used to tell her the calamities and afflictions that will happen after her death to her progeny and, more importantly, the gains such progeny will achieve, the great victories and success during the Time of Occultation then during the time when her descendant, al-Mahdi, the Awaited One, may the Almighty speed up his holy ease, reappears.

Ali (ع) was the scribe of this *mushaf*. Al-Zahra used to sense the presence of the angel and hear his voice, but she did not see him. When this took place, she complained about it to the Commander of the Faithful Ali (ع) because she did not expect the matter would thus continue taking place.

Ali (ع), then, was the one who thought about writing the *mushaf* down since he heard the voice of the trusted angels, so he would write down what he heard till a complete *mushaf* was gathered which is al-Zahra's *mushaf*, peace with her. You realize that it is not easy to write down what Gabriel was dictating; rather, this was among the special divine sciences which characterized the Commander of the Faithful (ع). He was the one who used to write down what the Messenger of Allāh (ص) used to dictate to him, and he was the one who compiled together the Holy Qur'ān as is confirmed.

MUSHAF'S CONTENTS

Fātima's *mushaf* (book) contains many matters which can be summarized thus: It absorbs all upcoming serious events, especially the calamities and afflictions her progeny would face as well as the victories. It contains names of all kings and rulers till Judgment Day, according to this tradition which is recorded on p. 32, Vol. 47, of *Bihār al-Anwār*: "There is no prophet or *wasi* or king except that he is mentioned in Fātima's *mushaf*." It also contains matters relevant to the person of the Messenger of Allāh (ص) as well as her own will (ع).

Ibn Hisham quotes Yahya ibn Abū Omran quoting other sources

citing Abū Abdullāh (Imām Ja'far al-Sādiq [ع]) saying that it contains the will of Fātima (ع) as stated on p. 43, Vol. 26, of *Bihār al-Anwār*. Naturally, the said will contains personal matters relevant to her grief and the predicaments she had to go through which her enemies caused so her descendant, the 12th Imām, the Awaited Mahdi, may Allāh Almighty hasten his sacred ease, would carry it. This is so because the Mahdi is the one who will have the power to do so, who will be empowered by Allāh to fill the earth with justice and equity after having been filled with injustice and iniquity.

THE IMĀMS (ع) AND FĀTIMA'S *MUSHAF*

Imām Ja'far al-Sādiq (ع) used to always emphasize the significance of the sciences of Ahl al-Bayt (ع). In one tradition, he used to say, "Their knowledge, peace with them, transcends time, comprehended and recorded, effective in the hearts, having an impact on those who hear it," that they have الجفر الأحمر و الجفر الأبيض, the Red Wide Well (or pool) and the White one, Fātima's *mushaf* and al-Jami'a." The red and white wells or pools referred to above are connotations of what is prohibitive and permissible in Islam. As for al-Jami'a , it is a collection of writings by the Commander of the Faithful Ali (ع) who held them so precious, he attached them to his sword, Thul-Fiqar. The contents of this Jami'a were recorded on animal's skin and used to be inherited, as is the case with Fātima's book, by the immediate family of the Prophet (ص), the Ahl al-Bayt (ع), who were subjected to untold trials and tribulations, persecution, imprisonment, poisoning, beheading and a host of injustices because of which these precious writings are now lost. Ahl al-Bayt (ع) used to maintain connection with the angels and adhere to the contents of Imām Ali's book, the Jami'a which contained all judicial rulings, including the penalty for one slightly scratching someone else's cheek. Their knowledge included the "science of Jafr" which contains branches of knowledge relevant to what is permissible in Islam and what is not needed by people of all times till the Judgment Day. But they used to depend in understanding serious events on Fātima's book according to a tradition that says, "We follow its contents and do not go beyond them." Such contents include all external [beyond the Household of the Prophet {ص}] incidents as well as the names of kings till the Day of Judgment. One tradition states that Muhammed son of Abdullāh son of Imām al-Hassan (ع) was once asked and he said this in his answer: "The names of every prophet, *wasi*, king... is with me in a book," meaning Fātima's book, adding, "By Allāh! It does not contain any mention of [Prophet] Muhammed ibn Abdullāh," according to p. 32, Vol. 47, of *Bihār al-Anwār*.

This *mushaf* reached a high level of loftiness, so much so that it became a source of happiness and optimism as is concluded from the phrase "apple of his eyes" in the following tradition: "Fudhail ibn Othman quotes al-Haththa saying that Imām Abū Ja'far [al-Bāqir] (ع) said to him, 'O Abū Ubaidah! He used to have the sword of the Messenger of Allāh (ص), his shield, winning banner and Fātima's *mushaf*, the apple of his eyes," as indicated on p. 211, Vol. 26, of *Bihār al-Anwār*.

IS FĀTIMA'S MUSHAF THE HOLY QUR'ĀN?

Most people used to, and still do, imagine that this *mushaf* contains the sacred Qur'ānic verses, or that there is another Qur'ān the Shī'as have, as ignorant commoners claim. But the reality is contrary to this: This *mushaf* does not contain a single verse of the verses of the Holy Qur'ān, as is understood from many traditions. Also, it is not similar to the Qur'ān, nor is it like it from the standpoint of context at all. It tells quite a different tale. Traditions are clear in this regard: One tradition says, "... quoting Ali ibn Sa'eed citing Abū Abdullāh (ع), 'It does not contain any verse of the Qur'ān,'" according to p. 42, Vol. 26, of *Bihār al-Anwār*.

In another tradition, it is indicated that "... from Ali son of al-Hussain who quotes Abū Abdullāh (ع), 'We have Fātima's *mushaf*. By Allāh! It does not contain a single syllable of the Qur'ān," as stated on p. 46, Vol. 26, of *Bihār al-Anwār*.

❖ Abdullāh ibn Ja'far quotes Mousa ibn Ja'far quoting al-Washa citing Abū Hamzah citing Abū Abdullāh (ع) saying, 'The *mushaf* of Fātima, peace with her, does not contain anything of the Book of Allāh,'" according to p. 48, Vol. 26, of *Bihār al-Anwār*.

❖ Anbasah ibn Mus'ab has said, "We were in the company of Abū Abdullāh (ع)... and Fātima's *mushaf*; by Allāh, he did not claim at all that it is a Qur'ān," as we read on p. 33, Vol. 26, of *Bihār al-Anwār*.

When examining these traditions, you will come to know that this confusion spread even during the time of the Imāms (ع); therefore, we find them strictly and seriously denouncing it, swearing about denying it. There is one tradition which indicates that this *mushaf* "contains three times the like of your Qur'ān," according to p. 38, Vol. 26, of *Bihār al-Anwār*. It is quite obvious the comparison is with regard to the quantity and size of information, not from that of context. You can conclude that from the phrase "your Qur'ān"; so, carefully ponder.

Many traditions conclude that the *mushaf* of al-Zahra (ع) does not contain anything about what is permissible and what is not; among such traditions is this statement (by Imām al-Sādiq, peace with him): "It is not about what is permissible and what is not," as stated on p. 44, Vol. 26, of *Bihār al-Anwār*.

The list of the other Infallible Fourteen (ع) is as follows:

3. Ali ibn Abū Tālib (ع)
4. Al-Hassan ibn Ali (ع)
5. Al-Hussain ibn Ali (ع)
6. Ali ibn al-Hussain (ع)
7. Muhammed ibn Ali al-Bāqir (ع)
8. Ja'far ibn Muhammed al-Sādiq (ع)
9. Mousa ibn Ja'far al-Kādhim (ع)
10. Ali ibn Mousa al-Ridha (ع)
11. Muhammed ibn Ali al-Taqi (ع)
12. Ali ibn Muhammed al-Naqi (ع)
13. al-Hassan ibn Ali al-Askari (ع)
14. Muhammed ibn al-Hassan al-Mahdi (ع).

The author of this book, his family and ancestors up to about 150 years back are followers of the Shī'a Ithna-Asheri faith. Earlier than that, his ancestors were Sunnis, and the conversion of his first ancestor took place in al-Kādhimiyya city following a bloody incident which shook him. Details of this incident and the persecution to which early Jibouri (author's tribesmen) Shī'as were exposed, as well as the prejudice the author received from Sunnis in Atlanta, Georgia, where he was studying for his higher degree, are all recorded in his Memoirs. These Memoirs are available for all to read on an Internet web page by clicking on this link: http://www.scribd.com/yasinaljibouri/.

Istidrak إستدراك: retraction, catching up (with), overtaking (somebody ahead)

Istighfar إستغفار: seeking Allāh's forgiveness

Istihqaq إستحقاق: entitlement, worth, value, merit, maturity (of debt, etc.)

Istihsan إستحسان: preference, finding something to be valuable, worthwhile, commending, advising

Istihtar إستهتار: rash behavior, disregard (for laws, customs, traditions, ethics, etc.), wantonness, recklessness, disregard for others' feelings, sentiments, interests, etc.

Istimnaa or Istimnaa' or Istimnā' استمناء: masturbation. What does Islam say about it? Following is quoted from p. 106, Vol. 1, of *Al-Khisal* (tradition 68):

(الخصال) عن أبيه عن سعد عن الطيالسي عن عبد الرحمن بن عوف عن ابن أبي نجران التميمي عن ابن حميد عن أبي بصير قال: سمعت أبا عبد الله (ع) يقول: ثلاثة لا يكلمهم الله يوم القيامة و لا ينظر اليهم و لا يزكيهم و لهم عذاب أليم: الناتف شيبه و الناكح نفسه و المنكوح في دبره.

(*Al-Khisāl*) from his father from Sa'd from al-Tayālisi from Abdul-Rahmān ibn Awf from Ibn Abu Najrān al-Tamimi from Ibn Hameed from Abu Busayr said: "I heard Abu Abdullāh (ع) [Imām Ja'far as-Sādiq] saying: 'Three [types of men] to whom Allāh shall not speak on the Judgment Day, nor will He look at them nor purify them [of their sins], and they shall have a painful torment: one who removes his gray hair, one who masturbates and one who lets another man penetrate his anus."

Istinsakh إستنساخ: copying, duplicating, cloning

Istintaj إستنتاج: reaching conclusion, deduction (from certain events or facts) by inference

Istitan إستيطان: settling (usually on someone else's land)

Istithna' إستثناء: exception, exclusion

I'tikaf إعتكاف: the act of remaining most of the time at a mosque for prayers and supplications

Itrat عترة: progeny (usually) of Prophet Muhammed

Itmam or Itmam إتمام: Completion, conclusion, consummation

Ittikal or Ittikaal إتكال: reliance (on), dependence on, dependency

Ittizan or Ittizan إتـزان: rationality, sobriety, the keeping of sedateness (of conduct), balance, poise

Izdiwajiyya إزدواجيـة: duplicity, duality (of control, allegiance, jurisdiction, etc.), measuring by two scales, judging by double standards

ج J

Jadaf جدف: (v. or n.) to blaspheme (the name of God) or blashempy, to revile or reviling, to swear to a lie

Jahannam جهنم: Hell; reference to and description of it has already been made in my book titled Mary and Jesus in Islam. However, if you do not have a copy of it, here is what I wrote in explaining the Hebrew origin of this word: "Ge hen Hinnom," Hebrew for "the valley of the son of Hinnom." Jews believe that this valley is a place near Jerusalem where, according to Jeremiah 19:5, [Gentile] children were burnt in sacrifice to Baal. The latter was the fertility god of then polytheist Canaanites (Arabs, descendants of Ken`an, who inhabited Greater Syria. According to Vol. 1, p. 24 of *Civilization: Past and Present*, "'Phoenician' is the name which the Greeks gave to those Canaanites who dwelt along the Mediterranean coast of Syria, an area that is today Lebanon."). The Greeks, then, were the ones who called those Arabs "Phoenicians". *Ge hen Hinnom* is Arabized as "Jahannam." Before the advent of Islam, Arabs believed neither in heaven nor in hell; they had no clear concept of the afterlife. They, therefore, had no words for Paradise or hell in their very rich and extensive vocAbulary. "Janna جنة," by the way, means: a garden, an orchard, but it really does not describe Paradise fully. Paradise is a lot more than an orchard or a garden. It is a whole world by itself. Incidentally, the word "Paradise" (*firdaws*) is also a loan word, some say from Persian, others from Babylonian.

Jahid جاحد: ingrate, unappreciative, denies favors, denies the existence of the Creator (apostate), atheist

Jahil جاهل: ignorant, illiterate, unlettered

Jahiliyya جاهليه: period of overwhelming ignorance, a reference to the conditions of the Arabs before the advent of Islam. It implies is a combination of views, ideas, and practices that totally defy and reject commonsense and the guidance sent down by God through His Prophets.

Ja'ir جائر: oppressive, unfair, unjust, inequitable, transgressing, encroaching, transgressing

Ja'iz جائز: permissible, allowable, admissible, possible, probable

Jalbab جلباب: long loose fitting garment worn by the Arabs

Jalda or Jaldah جلده: lash, whip

Jallad جلاد: executioner, headsman, hangman

528

Jami `a جامعه: inclusive, universal, university; it also means handcuffs

Janaba جنابه: uncleanness caused by seminal discharge

Jannat or Jannah جنه: heaven, Paradise, garden, the eternal abode of those with whom the Almighty is pleased; plural: *jannaat*

Janih جانح: devious, errant, delinquent, misdemeanant

Jami` جامع: mosque, house of congregational worship, same as *masjid مسجد*; literally, it means "place where people *gather for* يتجمع prayers"

Janin جنين: fetus

Jard جرد: stock-taking, inventory

Jarrada جرد: stripped one (of property, clothes, etc.), deprived of, despoiled, denuded

Jariya جاريه: bondmaid, slave girl, servant

Jasha` جشع:** greed, avarice, avidity; one who is greedy is called **jashi` جشع

Jaza'i جزائي: punitive, penal, vindicatory

Jazak Allāhu khayran or Jazak Allāhu Khairan, Jazak Allāh Khair, Jazak Allāhu Khair جزاك الله خيراً: This is a statement of thanks and appreciation said to the person who does a favor. Instead of saying "thanks" (Shukran), the Islamic statement of thanks is to say this phrase. Its meaning is: " May Allāh reward you for the good deed which you have done." It is understood that human beings can't repay one another enough, especially and particularly his parents and educators. Hence, it is better to plead to the Almighty, Allāh, to reward the person who did you a favor to grant him what is best for him.

Jawhara جوهره: jewel, precious (stone, etc.)

Jazim جازم: positive, sure, categorical

Jidal جدال: arguing, argument, debate, discussion

Jihad or Jihaad جهاد: It is an Arabic word the root of which is "jaahada" which implies one who has strived for a worthy cause, a better way of life, etc. The nouns from which the word is derived are: *juhd* (effort, endeavor, exertion, exhaustion), mujahid (one who exerts himself or defends the creed, provided such defense is not done through aggression or through any means not allowed by Islam), jihad (struggle, defense of the Islamic creed) and ijtihad (ultimate effort in order to derive a solution for a problem related to jurisprudence; one who does so is called *mujtahid*, a highly learned jurist capable of deriving Islamic rulings). The other meanings are: strain, exertion, effort, diligence, fighting to defend one's life, land and religion. Jihad has commonly been mistranslated or misrepresented to the world to mean "holy war". In the absence of the Prophet, such a war does not exist in Islam, nor will Islam allow its followers to be involved in this so-called "holy war". Unfortunately, the past few years have witnessed the rising of a number of extremist movements that justify the shedding of the blood not only of non-Muslims but even of Muslims who do not agree with their ideologies. Those who are hostile to Islam have utilized the acts of terrorism committed by these groups, mostly identified as Takfiri groups, groups that label all others as "kafirs", apostates, to tarnish Islam's image. They use Islam as a pretext for their criminal acts just as the crusaders had done during the Middle Ages when even some crusaders shed the blood of their own Christian brethren. Jihad is not a war to force the Islamic faith on others, as many ignorant people think or portray. Contrariwise, there is an explicit verse in the Qur'ān that says the following: "There is no compulsion in religion" (Chapter Al-Baqarah, verse 2256). Jihad is not only a defensive war but a struggle, through peaceful means, against any unjust regime or any injustice, period. If such a regime exists—and there are many which do exist—such an effort has to be exerted against the leaders, the decision-makers, not against the people. Islam strongly prohibits terrorism, kidnapping, hijacking and depriving one of his freedom, even if this "one" is an animal or a bird. One statement made by the Prophet of Islam (ص) says, "A woman entered hell because of a cat which she confined, neither feeding it nor letting it eat of what is available on the ground." As for some "Muslim" political figures, leaders and rulers who waged wars against non-Muslims in the pretext of "spreading Islam", they were further from Islam than the earth is from the sun and did what they did for political, economic or selfish reasons. They were ignorant of the true message of Islam. Unfortunately, there are many such "Muslims" in our time and in all times and climes.

Jinaya or Jinayah جنايه: serious crime, felony

Jinn or Jin, Ginn جن: These are spiritual beings, "genies", that inhabit the world and, like humans, are required to follow the commandments of their Creator. They are held accountable for their deeds. Some of them are good while most of them are not, as is the case with humans. The meaning of the word "jinn" in Arabic is "hidden", invisible, because they cannot be seen by most humans. They were created by the Almighty from smokeless fire. I discussed the jinns in more detail in my book titled *Allāh: The Concept of God in Islam*.

Jirab جراب: pouch, bag, sack

Jizya or Jizyah جزيه: tribute, protection tax paid to Muslims by non-Muslims residing in areas under Islamic control. The Muslims collect this tax in exchange for protecting the lives and possessions of these non-Muslims, exempting them from the military service and awarding them full freedom to practice their religion, whatever it may be. If the Islamic State cannot protect those who have paid the *jizya*, they are entitled to get it back. In all reality, such tax is hardly collected because even in Pakistan, where the majority are Muslims living with mostly Hindu and Buddhist minorities, the latter do not pay any *jizya*.

Jumood جمود: stagnation, freezing, inaction, inactivity, passiveness (to influence, change, etc.)

Junha or Junhah جنحه: misdemeanor

Junoon or Jinoon جنون: madness, insanity

Jutham جذام: leprosy

Juzaf جزاف: at random, haphazard, casual

خ،ك K, Kh

Ka'bah or Kaaba كعبه: the first house of worship built for mankind, the cubic-shaped structure which is the most sacred to the Muslims of the world. It was originally built by Adam and was rebuilt by Abraham and his son Ishmael because it was damaged by torrential rain. It has the Black Stone which is believed as having been brought by an angel for Adam from another planet. The stone has been subjected to tests and analyses which all proved that it was unlike any other on our planet, thus proving the Muslims' claim that it is not earthly but cosmic. It is located in Mecca, the city located in Hijaz to which all Muslims of the world turn as they perform their five daily prayers and all other prayers, obligatory or optional. Mecca now is a very modern city with luxury hotels, malls, commercial centers and all modern facilities, and its people are most courteous, kind, generous and hospitable. Many pilgrims did not like to leave it once they had completed their pilgrimage rituals, so they married there and lived happily ever after.

Kaffara كفاره: atonement from sin, a penalty for wrongdoing. It is great if sinners pay for their sins in this short life for the price they will have to pay in the Hereafter will be quite dear. Kaffara sometimes is done by paying a certain amount of money determined by a jurist which will be distributed to the poor and needy. Other ways of paying it may be with performance of rituals such as prayers, fast, pilgrimage, etc.; so, dear reader, if you have committed a sin—who has not?! —, try to atone for it before it is too late.

Kafir كافر: infidel, apostate, atheist, one who does not believe in the existence of the Creator. The noun *kufr* denotes a person who refuses to submit to the will of Allāh (God), who disbelieves in God. It also means one who deliberately covers up the truth while fully knowing it.

Kalam or Kalaam كلام: Talk or speech as in "kalamu-Allāh". It also means logic or philosophy.

Kalima or Kalimah كلمـه: Synonymous to "*shahada*," it is a Muslim's declaration of faith (that is, to testify that there is no god except Allāh, and that Muhammed is the Messenger of Allāh), and it is always pronounced in Arabic.

Kantar قنطار: in Arabic, it is *qintar*, a varying weight of 100 *ratls* (rotls); a *ratl* in Syria is roughly 3.202 kg., whereas in England it is 449.28 grams, and in Lebanon it is 2.566 kg.

Khabir or Khabeer خبير: expert, learned, informed, connoisseur (of), specialist

Khafaqan خفقان: palpitation (of heart, etc.)

Khala`a or Khalaa`ah خلاعه: indecency, immorality, debauchery

Khaleefa or Khalifah خليفه: caliph; the word "khalifah" refers to the successor of Prophet Muhammed (ص) or simply to any ruler who claims that he rules the Muslims according to the will of the Almighty, whether he is justified in his claim or not. History has proven that most of these claims are false! This person sees himself as the head not only of his country but of the entire Muslim nation, so let us leave him enjoying this thought! Another title for the khalifah is "Amir Al-Mu'mineen", Commander of the Faithful, which is explained above.

Khalis خالص: whole, clear, pure, candid, genuine, exclusive

Khandaq خندق: ditch, moat. This word reminds the Muslims of the "Battle of the Khandaq" which took place during Islam's early years, that is, in 627 A.D. First of all, there are two theories about how contemporary Jews went to and settled in Mecca and Medīna. One theory says that they fled the persecution of the Romans who had by then subjected Jerusalem, which Jews call Ur-shalom, the city of peace, and went to Arabia where they felt confident that the Romans would not chase them there. Arabia at that time did not have much to attract foreign invaders. Another theory says that these Jews, who spoke Arabic besides Hebrew and Yiddish, had actually fled away from the persecution of cruel and fanatical Christian rulers of Nejran, southern Yemen, who were at the time appointed by the emperors of Abyssinia (Ethiopia). In Medīna, most Jews settled within small fortified towns. Upon settling down at Khaibar, one of their tribes, Banu Nadir, decided to seek revenge against the Muslims because of an incident which had taken place at Medīna's main bazaar: A Jewish shop owner went from behind a Muslim woman and pulled her gown up, exposing her private parts. A Muslim man noticed the incident, attacked the Jew and killed him. The Jews went into a riot and contacted the Meccans. Twenty Jewish leaders and 50 others from pagan Quraish made a covenant in the Ka`ba that as long as they lived, they would fight Muhammed and the Muslims. Then the Jews and Quraish contacted their allies and sent emissaries to a number of tribes. Banu Ghatfan, Banu Asad, Banu Aslam, Banu Ashja`, Banu Kinanah and Banu Fizarah readily responded. The Meccans, four thousand strong, including three hundred cavaliers and fifteen hundred camels, were joined by six thousand allies from among the Jews and the bedouin tribes. The three armies set out, ten thousand strong, under the command of Abū Sufyan in the beginning of the month of Shawwal, 5 A.H. (the end of February 627 A.D.) to attack Medīna.

When news of these preparations reached Medīna, the Prophet consulted his companions, as he always did during such situations. There was hardly sufficient time to make preparations for the war. He decided this time to remain within the city and fight back. The stone houses of the city were built adjacent to one another so as to make a high and continuous strong wall for a long distance except in the north-west where a wide open space could afford the enemy an easy entry. At this place, with the suggestion of Salman al-Farisi, who was familiar with the mode of defending cities in other countries such as his home country (Persia), a trench, fifteen feet in width and fifteen feet in depth, was dug up. Muslims were divided into parties of 10 each, and each party was allotted 10 yards to dig. The Prophet himself participated in this task, carrying the excavated earth away. The *khandaq* (moat) was completed in the nick of time: just 3 days before the host of the enemies reached Medīna. The houses outside the city were evacuated, and the women and children were accommodated for safety on the tops of the double-storied houses at the entrenchment. Muslims could muster only three thousand men to face this huge army, and they immediately took cover behind the ditch. The Propeht camped in the center of the entrenchment in a tent of red leather on a space shaped like a crescent. The camp had the rising ground of Sila` on its rear and the trench in the front.

Huyaiy ibn Akhtab, head of Banu Nadir Jews of Medīna, met secretly with Ka`b ibn Asad, head of Banu Quraizah, another Jewish tribe which was still in Medīna. Huyaiy was the most antagonistic Jew towards the Prophet (ص). Banu Quraizah, on his instigation, tore down the treaty which they had concluded with the Muslims. The Jews decided that they would assist the pagan Quraishites after ten days' preparations and would attack the rear of Muhammed's army from the north-western side of the city which was located on the south-east side of their fortress and which was easily accessible to them.

Rumours reached the Prophet about the Jews' schemes, so he sent two chiefs, one from the Aws and one from the Khazraj, namely Sa`d ibn Mu`ath and Sa`d ibn `Abadah (by the way, the reader may remember this same Sa`d ibn `Abadah whom I mentioned in my book titled *Allāh: The Concept of God in Islam* while discussing the jinns) respectively, to ascertain the truth. Both men proceeded to meet the Jews. Having made searching inquiries and some scouting of their own, they returned to report to the Prophet that the temper of the Jews was even worse than it had been feared. This news alarmed the Prophet. It was then necessary to take precautions against any surprise attack or treachery from the side of those Jews. The north-western part of the city, which was located on the side of the Jewish stronghold, was the weakest of all defenses. In order to protect the families of his followers throughout the city, the Prophet, as a meager measure of precaution, had no choice except to send a considerable number of his men from his already small army of three thousand to afford them such protection. His men's supplies were hardly adequate due to the length of the siege of the entrenchment which formed his defense line. Still, he had no choice except to detach two parties, one of three hundred men under the command of Zayd ibn Harithah, his freed slave whom he raised since childhood, and another of two hundred men under the command of a chieftain from Medīna. Their job was to patrol the streets and the alleys of the city night and day.

This treachery and danger from inside Medīna, when Muslims were surrounded by the combined armies of pagans and Jews of all of Arabia on the outside, had a telling effect on the Muslims. The enemy was astonished to see the moat because it was a novel military tactic for the Arabs. They camped on the outside for 27 (or 24) days. Their number increased day by day, and many Muslims were extremely terrified, as the Qur'ān portrays for us. Sūrat al-Ahzab (Chapter 33 of the Holy Qur'ān) describes various aspects of this siege. For example, read the following verses:

When they came upon you from above you and from below, and when the eyes turned dull, and the hearts rose up to the throats, you began to think diverse thoughts about Allāh. There, the believers were tried, and they wee shaken a tremendous shaking. (Qur'ān, 33:10-11)

At that time, many hypocrites, and even some Muslims whose faith was weak and who are unfortunately described by some scholars as being *sahāba*, companions of the Prophet, asked permission to leave the ranks of the Muslims and to go home:

A party of them said: O people of Yathrib! There is no place for you to stand. And a party of them asked permission of the Prophet saying: Verily our houses are exposed, and they were not exposed; they only (thus) described (them in order) to flee away. (Qur'ān, 33:13)

The bulk of the army, however, steadfastly withstood the hardship of inclement weather and rapidly depleting provisions. The coalition's

536

army hurled arrows and stones at the Muslims.

Finally, a few of Quraish's more valiant warriors, `Amr ibn Abdwadd, Nawfal ibn Abdullāh ibn Mughirah, Dhirar ibn Khattab, Hubairah ibn Abū Wahab, `Ikrimah ibn Abū Jahl (an unbelieving cousin of the Prophet) and Mirdas al-Fahri, succeeded in crossing the moat.

`Amr called for battle; nobody responded; he was considered equal to one thousand warriors. History accounts state that all the Muslims were as though birds were sitting on their heads: they were too afraid to raise their heads.

Three times did the Prophet exhort the Muslims to battle `Amr. Three times it was only Ali who stood up. In the third time, the Prophet allowed Ali to go. When Ali was going to the battlefield, the Prophet said: "The whole faith is going to fight the whole infidelity; the embodiment of the former bounds is to crush the entirety of the latter." The Prophet put his own turban on Ali's head, his own coat of mail over Ali's body, and he armed Ali with his own sword, Thul-Fiqar, then he sent him to meet his opponent. Then the Prophet raised his hands to supplicate thus: "O Allāh! `Obaydah, my cousin, was taken away from me in the Battle of Badr, Hamzah, my uncle, in Uhud. Be Merciful, O Lord, not to leave me alone and undefended. Spare Ali to defend me. You are the best of defenders."

Ali invited `Amr to accept Islam or to return to Mecca, or to come down from his horse since Ali had no horse and was on foot.

"Nephew," said `Amr to Ali, being a friend of Ali's father Abū Tālib, "By God I do not like to kill you." Ali replied, "By God, I am here to kill you!" `Amr, now enraged at this reply, alighted from his horse. Having hamstrung his horse, a token of his resolve never to run away from the battlefield but either to conquer or to perish, he advanced towards Ali. They were immediately engaged in a duel, turning the ground underneath them into a cloud of dust, so much so that for a good while, only the strokes of their swords could be heard while they themselves could not be seen. `Amr succeeded once in inflicting a serious cut on Ali's head. At last, Ali's voice was heard

537

shouting, "*Allāhu Akbar! Allāhu Akbar!*" That was his cry of victory. It always is Muslims' cry of victory. Seeing how the most brave among them has been killed by Ali, the other pagans who crossed the moat now took to their heels with the exception of Nawfal whose horse failed to leap; it fell into the moat. As the Muslims showered him with a hail of stones, he cried out thus: "I rather die by the sword than by the stones!" Hearing this, Ali leaped into the moat and fulfilled his last wish, dispatching him to hell!

Ali, contrary to the Arab custom then, did not, however, strip either men from their armor or clothes. When `Amr's sister came to her brother's corpse, she was struck with admiration at the noble behavior of her slain brother's adversary and, finding out who he was, she felt proud of her brother having met his fate at the hands of the person who was known as the unique champion of spotless character. She said, as recorded in *Tarikh al-Khamis*, "Had his conqueror been someone else other than the one who killed him, I would have mourned `Amr for the rest of my life. But his opponent was the unique spotless champion." Ali, the "Lion of God," thus distinguished himself as on previous occasions: in the battles of Badr and of Uhud. About this battle, the Prophet said: "Verily, one attack of Ali in the Battle of Khandaq is better than the worship of all human beings and jinns up to the Day of Resurrection."

No further activity was attempted by the enemy that day, but great preparations were undertaken during the night. Khalid ibn al-Walid, with a party of cavaliers, attempted during the night to clear the ditch for crossing the next day. The next morning, the Muslims found the entire enemy force arrayed in fighting formations along their line of entrenchment. The enemies tried to overrun the Muslim side of the trench but were repelled at every point. The ditch served its purpose; it could not be crossed. During the entire military campaign, by the way, only five Muslims were martyred. The Muslims' vigilance paralyzed the enemies despite their numeric superiority. Numeric superiority is not always a prerequisite for victory. The Almighty grants victory to whosoever He pleases.

But the Muslims were running out of provisions. The Prophet had to tie a stone on his stomach in order to minimize the pangs of hunger.

Abū Sa`eed al-Khudri said: "Our hearts had reached our throats in fear and in desperation." On the other hand, the besieging army was getting restive, too; it could not put up any further with the rain and cold; its horses were perishing daily and provisions nearing depletion. The Prophet went to the place where the Mosque of Victory (Masjidul-Fath) now stands and prayed to Allāh. The Prophet said, "O Lord! Revealer of the Sacred Book, the One Who is swift in taking account, turn the confederate host away! Turn them to flight, O Lord, and make the earth underneath them quake!"

A fierce storm raged, uprooting the tents of the enemies; their pots and belongings went flying in all directions; it blew dust in their faces, extinguished their fires, and their horses were running around as though they were possessed. An unbearable terror was cast in their hearts. In the fourth night, after having finished his prayers, Muhammed asked Abū Bakr if he would go to the enemy's camp to discern and report their activities. He replied saying, "I ask pardon of Allāh and of His Messenger." The Prophet promised Paradise to be the reward of anyone who would venture out for that purpose, then asked `Omer ibn al-Khattab if he would do it. `Omer's answer was similar to that of Abū Bakr. The Prophet's request is actually an order, a divine one, since it is coming from one who does not say anything or do anything without the Will of the Almighty. These facts are recorded in *Tafsir al-Durr al-Manthur, As-Sira al-Muhammediyya, As-Sira al-Halabiyya, Tarikh al-Khamis,* and *Rawdat al-Ahbab* for all to review. The third person the Prophet asked was Huthayfah al-Yemani who readily responded to the request and proceeded to the enemy camp in the darkness of the night where he saw the devastation wrought by the storm. He saw Abū Sufyan looking very depressed. When he came back to his camp and reported in detail to the Prophet what he had seen, the Prophet was delighted to find out that his plea to Allāh was answered.

Either feeling the pain of the severity of the weather or struck with terror at that storm which was interpreted as a manifestation of the Divine Wrath, Abū Sufyan decided to lift the siege and to march back at once. Summoning the chiefs of his allies, he announced his decision to them, issuing orders to dismantle the camp. He and all the Meccans with him, as well as the pagan tribes that allied themselves under his command, fled away. The first to flee was Abū Sufyan himself who was so upset that he tried to ride his camel without first untying its rope. Khalid ibn al-Walid guarded the rear of the armies with two hundred cavaliers against a pursuit. The Ghatfan tribesmen and the bedouin allies returned to their deserts; not a single person remained on the battlefield in the morning. It was with great joy that in the morning the Muslims discovered the sudden disappearance of the enemy, finding themselves unexpectedly relieved. The siege lasted for twenty-four long days and ended in March of 627 A.D.

This episode is referred to in the Qur'ān in this *ayat*:

O ye who believe! Remember the bounty of Allāh unto you when came upon you the hosts, so We sent against them a strong wind and hosts that ye saw not, and Allāh sees all what you do. (Qur'ān, 33:9)

And also in *ayat* 25 which says:

And God turned back the unbelievers in their rage; they did not achieve any advantage, and Allāh sufficed for the believers in fighting, and Allāh is Strong, Mighty (Qur'ān, 33:25).

Abdullāh ibn Mas`ud was interpreting this thus: "And God sufficed the believers (through Ali ibn Abū Tālib) in their fight," as we read in *Tafsir al-Durr al-Manthur*.

As a direct result of this defeat of the infidels' combined forces in the Battle of Khandaq (moat, or the Battle of Ahzab, coalitions), Quraish's influence waned, and those tribes who were till then hesitating to accept Islam out of fear of Quraish began to send deputations to the Prophet. The first deputation came from the tribe of Mazinah, and it consisted of four hundred persons. They not only accepted Islam but were ready to settle down in Medīna. The Prophet, however, advised them to return to their homes.

Likewise, a deputation of a hundred persons came from the Ashja` and embraced Islam. The tribe of Juhainah lived near them, so they were influenced by their conversion. One thousand of the latter's men came to Medīna to join the fraternity.

Kharab خراب: destruction, ruin, desolation, doom, waste

Khardal خردل: mustard

Khariq خارق: extraordinary, exceptional, remarkable, piercing, penetrating

Khasir خاسر: loser, loss-making, unprofitable

Khaskhasa خصخصه: privatization

Khasm خصم: opponent, disputant, foe

Khat خط: line, path, method, style, writing, route

Khatib or Khateeb خطيب : orator, speaker, one who delivers the "khutba", sermon, whether during the Friday prayer service or any other service

Khawarij خوارج: defectors, apostates, renegades, an extinct group of individuals who split from the Islamic nation and declared a rebellion on elected Caliph Ali ibn Abū Tālib (ع). Literally, the word means "Those who Went Out"): a controversial term which is described by some Muslim scholars differently, each according to his level of education and extent of bias and prejudice. If you are sincere about researching who these rogues were, you can start with p. 278, Vol. 3, of Tabari's famous book *Tarikh al-Umam wal Mulook* (famous as simply *Tarikh*). There are many editions of this book available for reviewers, but the one I have is the newest; it is published by the Dar Al-Amira for Publication and Distribution, Beirut, Lebanon, and is dated 1426 A.H./2005 A.D. Their history started in the year 37 A.H. (which then corresponded to the year 658 A.D.) when they first reverted against the then elected caliph, Ali, but returned to obedience after he had reasoned with them just to revolt against him again and one of them, namely Ibn Muljim, killed caliph Ali on a Friday, 11th, 13th or 17th of the month of Ramadan of

40 A.H., according to various narratives. Their ideology could not withstand the intellectual challenges of the time, so it gradually weakened and died away. I think they do not deserve more space than this much here! To hell with them and with all those who apply this term to any Muslims, whoever they may be and from any sect at all, presently or in the future. The خوارج Khawarij and their ideology are both dead and decayed; so, there is no need to beat on a dead horse.

Khayr خير: good, goodness, well-being, welfare, prosperity, benefit; in some verses of the Holy Qur'ān, it means "money" which, of course, can be a good tool for the doing of righteousness and for helping people.

Khazaf خزف: ceramic

Khida` خداع: deceit, deception, trickery, cheating, fooling, double-dealing

Khilaf خلاف: dispute, disagreement, feud, variance (of opinion, etc.), discrepancy

Khilafa or Khilaafah خلافه: succession, [Islamic] caliphate

Khiraj خراج: religious tax collected at the end of the Islamic lunar year for *baytul-mal*

Khitam ختام: conclusion, end, termination

Khitan ختان: circumcision

Khiyara خيره: choice, option, prime, best

Khulud or Kholood خلود: immortality, eternity, forever

Khums خمس: one-fifth of one's savings and is now paid only by Shi`a Muslims; see Chapter 8, verse 41 of the Holy Qur'ān. It is set aside from one's annual income or increase in wealth. It is divided into 2 equal parts: One, called "sahm as-Sadat", is payable to needy

Sadat (or Sayyids), descendants of the Prophet who are not allowed to receive charity (*sadaqa*) and are too dignified to ask for it. The other half, called "sahm al-Imām (ع)", is to be spent on promoting the Islamic creed, such as paying expenses for writing, translating, editing, publishing and printing of books or the building of schools, religious seminaries, libraries, etc. *Khums*, moreover, is collected from one's profits or gains which he earn, as well as from the following: minerals, treasure troves, amalgamation of *halal* (permissible) wealth with what is *haram* (prohibitive), gems obtained from sea diving, spoils of war, land which a *thimmi* (a non-Muslim living under the protection of Islamic Government) purchases from a Muslim. There are many rules and regulations about the collection of, exemption from and distribution of this *khums* which, according to 8:41 of the Holy Qur'ān is not optional, as some ill-informed individuals claim, but compulsory. Here is this verse for you: وَاعْلَمُواْ أَنَّمَا غَنِمْتُم مِّن شَيْءٍ فَأَنَّ لِلّهِ خُمُسَهُ وَلِلرَّسُولِ وَلِذِي الْقُرْبَى وَالْيَتَامَى وَالْمَسَاكِينِ وَابْنِ السَّبِيلِ إِن كُنتُمْ آمَنتُمْ بِاللّهِ وَمَا أَنزَلْنَا عَلَى عَبْدِنَا يَوْمَ الْفُرْقَانِ يَوْمَ الْتَقَى الْجَمْعَانِ وَاللّهُ عَلَى كُلِّ شَيْءٍ قَدِيرٌ And know that out of all the booty that you may acquire (in war), a fifth share is assigned to God! and to the Messenger, and to near relatives, to the orphans, the needy, and the wayfarer! if you believe in Allāh and in the Revelation We sent down to Our servant on the day of testing! the day of the meeting of the two forces, for Allāh has power over all things. (Qur'ān, 8:41). What is stated in the Holy Qur'ān as permissible or not permissible remains so till the Day of Judgment, and if you disagree, it is your own burden which you will carry and not mine. If you have the *risala* (compilation of edicts) of Grand Ayatollah Sayyid Ali al-Hussaini as-Sistani, refer to his "Kitab al-Khums" (Chapter on the *khums*) which starts on p. 387, Vol. 1, of the Arabic text of his 4-volume *Minhaj as-Saliheen* (published in the Hijri year 1427 which coincides with the year 2006 A.D. by the Grand Ayatollah's office in Holy Mashhad, Iran). If you do not have a copy of the said *risala*, the Internet can provide you with a wealth of information on this subject.

Khushu` خشوع: state of submission and full attention, humility, of being in reverence

Khusuf or Khosoof (القمر) خسوف: eclipse of the moon

Khutba خطبه: a speech or sermon. It is sometimes used to refer to the sermon given during the Friday congregational prayer.

Kuffar كفار: plural form of *kafir*, apostate

Kufr كفر: showing ungratefulness to Allāh and not to believe in Him and in His religion, to deliberately hide the truth while fully knowing it with the ability to show the truth

Kunya كنيه: the use of "Abū " (father of) or "Umm " (mother of) someone, often used as a prefix for one's name

Kursi كرسي: Literally, it means "chair", theologically, however, it refers to the symbol of the Almighty's Seat of Judgment and Authority; see Holy Qur'ān, 2:255 (*ayat al-Kursi*, verse of the Throne).

Kusuf (الشمس) كسوف: eclipse of the sun

Khutba خطبه: lecture, sermon; a speech delivered on a specific occasion

Kufr كفــر: apostasy, infidelity, disbelief, the deliberate covering/hiding of the truth

ل L

Lat لات: a chief deity in the religion of pre-Islamic Arabs during the days of *jahiliyya*

La hawla wa la quwwata illa billah لا حول و لا قوة إلا بالله: The meaning of this expression is: "There is neither power nor strength save in Allāh." This expression is articulated by a Muslim when he is struck by a calamity or is taken over by a situation beyond his control. A Muslim puts his trust in the hands of Allāh, and submits himself willingly to Allāh.

La ilaha ilal-Allāh or *La Ilaha Ill-Allāh* لا إلـه إلا الله: This expression

544

is very important in Islam. It is part of the first pillar of Islam which is called *tawhid*, the belief in the unity of God. It means: "There is no god worthy of worship except Allāh." The second part of this first pillar is to say "Muhammedun Rasul-Allāh" which means: "Muhammed (ص) is the messenger of Allāh." This statement is called the "key to Paradise". Before you close your eyes and slepp, pronounce it three times because you do not know for sure whether you will wake up at all.

Labbayk !لبيك: an exclamation conveying the meaning of "At your service!" or "Here I am!"

M م

Ma`ad معاد: the return: a reference to the returning of the souls to new bodies/forms after the period of *barzakh* برزخ (see above), their ultimate return to their Maker for judgment; generally, it is used to refer to death and the life hereafter.

Mahlaj محلج: cotton gin, gin

Maqam مقام: standing or staying place, a place where one usually stands to preach or address the public; "Maqam Ibrahim" is a small area in the precincts of the Ka'ba Mosque which shows footprints of Abraham (prophet Ibrahim [ع] where he used to stand to rebuild the Ka'ba.

Medīna or Madeenah مدينه: city, the first city-state that came under the banner of Islam. It is a city in Hijaz, northern part of presently Saudi Arabia, where the Prophet's *masjid* and grave are located.

Maghazi مغازي: Prophet's military campaigns

Maghrib مغرب: sunset, time for the obligatory sunset prayer ritual, *salat*

Mahdi مهدي: Rightly guided in order to guide others; preceded by the definite article "ال", it means المهدي (عج) the Awaited Imām, al-Qā'im, al-Hujja, Savior of Mankind, the 12th in the series of the Infallible Imāms followed by Twelver Shī'ites, may the Almighty hasten his re-appearance. We owe it to the reader to introduce him to this great personality, perhaps he will wake up from his slumber and realize that he has a lot of work to do in preparation for the re-appearance of the Savior of Mankind. Needless to say, Sunni and Shī'ite sects believe in al-Mahdi but differ among themselves about his family lineage, birth and other issues which are not regarded as being major.

More details about Imām al-Mahdi (ﻉ) are already stated above.

Mahr ﻣﻬﺮ: dowry paid by the groom to the bride (or *vice versa* in some cultures). It is part of the Muslim marriage contract. It can never be demanded back except when the bride refuses to cohabit with her groom in the absence of any legitimate excuse. In this case, she may be entitled to receive half the dower or none of it once the divorce takes place. By the way, do you know what dowry our father Adam paid our mother, Eve?! Did he pay it in cash, check or credit card?! If you do not, read my book titled *Allāh: The Concept of God in Islam.*

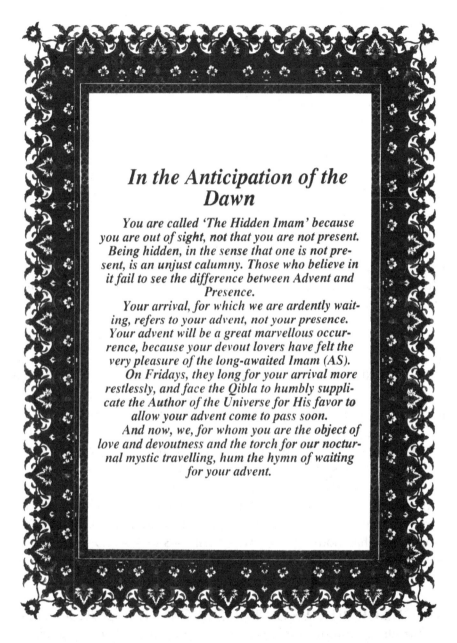

In the Anticipation of the Dawn

You are called 'The Hidden Imam' because you are out of sight, not that you are not present. Being hidden, in the sense that one is not present, is an unjust calumny. Those who believe in it fail to see the difference between Advent and Presence.

Your arrival, for which we are ardently waiting, refers to your advent, not your presence. Your advent will be a great marvellous occurrence, because your devout lovers have felt the very pleasure of the long-awaited Imam (AS).

On Fridays, they long for your arrival more restlessly, and face the Qibla to humbly supplicate the Author of the Universe for His favor to allow your advent come to pass soon.

And now, we, for whom you are the object of love and devoutness and the torch for our nocturnal mystic travelling, hum the hymn of waiting for your advent.

Mahram or *Mahrim* محرم: "mahram" refers to people who are unlawful for a woman to marry due to blood relationships. These people include:

1.   Her **permanant** *mahrams* on account of blood relationship: her father, son, brother, paternal uncle, maternal uncle, step-son and nephew.

2.   Her *radha' رضاع mahrams* on account of sharing the nursing milk when she was an infant; their status is similar to the permanent *mahrams* referred to above.

3.   Her (in law) *mahrams* because of marriage; these are: her husband's father (father in law), husband's son (step-son), her mother's husband (step-father) and her daughter's husband. These categories of people, along with the woman's husband, are permitted to escorts Muslim women when they travel as required by some countries such as Saudi Arabia.

Majalis مجالس: meetings or gatherings held to commemorate certain religious occasions, mostly applied to those held during the month of Muḥarram or to recite the *Fatiha* for a deceased person; singular: *majlis*, a place where people sit

Manzil منزل: (sing.) home, residence, abode; منزلة *manzila*: status, position, esteem; (pl.) منازل *manazil*: homes, positions, stages, phases. منازل الآخرة Stages or phases of the life in the hereafter: Brace yourself, Dear Reader, for the following text may not make you happy; shed a tear now before your tears later on will not avail you a bit. You will notice that there are so many supplications in the following text. This is due to the significance Islam, or any other religion, awards supplication. One authentic *hadīth* حديث (tradition) says: الدعاء مخ العبادة Supplication is the pith (or essence) of adoration." As for the Holy Qur'ān, it tells you in the following verse that had it not been for people supplicating to their Creator, He would have had nothing to do with them: " قُلْ مَا يَعْبَأُ بِكُمْ رَبِّي لَوْلَا دُعَاؤُكُمْ Say: 'Had it not been for your prayers (supplications), my Lord would not have cared about you'" (Qur'ān, 25:77):

STAGES OR PHASES OF THE HEREAFTER: منازل الآخرة These are the phases through which one has to pass on his/her way to either eternal happiness in Paradise or endless doom in Hell, may the Almighty keep it away from us and from your own self اللهم آمين *Allāhumma Ameen*. Following is a list of these stages or phases from some of which very few are exempted such as those who are very close to the Almighty on account of their being very deeply knowledgeable and ascetic such as the *anbiya,'* prophets الأنبياء, *awliya',* walis الأولياء, `*ulema',* scholars العلماء, *salihun,* righteous الصالحون and the *shuhada',* martyrs الشهداء. If you are none of these, and most of us are not, brace yourself for the following phases. Of course, due to self-deception, every Muslim who performs his daily prayers thinks that he is included among the righteous, not knowing whether his/her prayers are accepted or not, forgetting that performing the daily prayers is only the very first step along a very lengthy and thorny path to salvation. Those included in the categories listed above will not taste any painful death, nor will they have to go anywhere in the company of hordes of angels except to Paradise and to nearness to the Almighty. Others have to go through the following:

An-Naza` al-Akheer النزع الأخير Drawing the Last Breath: Another name is سكرات الموت, Stupors of Death. Reference to these stupors of death exists in this Qur'ānic verse: وَجَاءَتْ سَكْرَةُ الْمَوْتِ بِالْحَقِّ ذَلِكَ مَا كُنتَ مِنْهُ تَحِيدُ *"And the stupor of death will bring truth (before his eyes): "This was the thing which you were trying to escape!"* (Qur'ān, 50:19). These are the moments when the dying person bids this vanishing world goodbye, casts a last look at it, mostly at his own self: Life will pass before his eyes like a flash, and he will realize how short it really was, how he wasted it, how he did not perform the purpose behind his very creation: to worship the Almighty his Lord and the Lord of all creation. How will one naturally die? The answer is in verses 88-96 of Sūrat al-Waqi`a (Chapter 56): فَأَمَّا إِن كَانَ مِنَ الْمُقَرَّبِينَ، فَرَوْحٌ وَرَيْحَانٌ وَجَنَّةُ نَعِيمٍ: وَأَمَّا إِن كَانَ مِنَ أَصْحَابِ الْيَمِينِ فَسَلَامٌ لَّكَ مِنْ أَصْحَابِ الْيَمِينِ، وَأَمَّا إِن كَانَ مِنَ الْمُكَذِّبِينَ الضَّالِّينَ فَنُزُلٌ مِّنْ حَمِيمٍ وَتَصْلِيَةُ جَحِيمٍ: إِنَّ هَذَا لَهُوَ حَقُّ الْيَقِينِ، فَسَبِّحْ بِاسْمِ رَبِّكَ الْعَظِيمِ: *Thus, then, if he is of those nearest to Allāh, (there is) rest and satisfaction (for him) and a Garden of delights. And if he is of the companions of the right Hand, (for him there is salutation:) "Peace be unto you!" from the companions of the right Hand. And if he is one of those who treat (truth) as falsehood, who commit wrong, for him there is* **entertainment** *of boiling water and burning in Hell-Fire. Truly this is the very truth, so celebrate with praise the Name of your Lord, the Supreme* (Qur'ān, 56:88-96). See how the Almighty in these verses classifies three methods of death perhaps the first of which is particularly interesting: One who is near to his Maker will smell fragrance which will turn death into a very pleasant and pleasūrable experience. Of course an opposite type of death awaits those who are not close to Him and who apparently will experience death by way of suffocation. According to some traditions, two angels pull life out of each and every cell of the dying person's body, and it will not be fun at all. During these moments, the dying person will have a moment of contemplation on what he has just left behind: worries about the little ones, separation from wealth, estates, precious items, homes on which he spent fortunes, wealth which he amassed without making sure where it exactly came from, etc. And there will be worries about how much he fell short of carrying out with regard to his duties to others and to his Maker. In *Nahjul-Balāgha*, the Commander of the Faithful Imām Ali (ع) has summarized it thus:

«يتذكر أموالاً جمعها أغمض في مطالبها وأخذها من مُصرّحاتها ، ومشتبهاتها قد لزمته تبعات جمعها وأشرف على فراقها، تبقى لمن وراءه ينعمون بها فيكون المهنأ لغيره والعبءُ على ظهره».

"He shall remember wealth which he had overlooked where it had come from, accepting its sources as they were claimed to be, or as they were thought to be, the consequences of having collected it now are round his neck, haunting him, as he is about to leave it behind him for those who will now enjoy it, thus the pleasure will be for others while he bears the burden." Verse 22 of Sūrat Qaf states the following:

لَقَدْ كُنتَ فِي غَفْلَةٍ مِّنْ هَذَا فَكَشَفْنَا عَنكَ غِطَاءَكَ فَبَصَرُكَ الْيَوْمَ حَدِيدٌ

"You were heedless of this, so We have removed your veil, and your sight is sharp (on) this Day!" (Qur'an, 50:22). Indeed, the sight of the dying person during the stupors of death will be quite sharp: He will for the first time be able to see angels, who are created of light that can easily blind any human eye, and the *jinns* who are created of smokeless fire. He will be able to see and hear his fāmily, relatives, friends and strangers who are around him at the time of death and who will soon bear his casket to the cemetery. But he will not be able to show any reaction because he has lost control over his temporal body and his soul روح now takes over. On the other hand,

there will be a tremendous transformation in the process of changing from one form into quite another which now enables him to see what he could never see before: According to p. 170, Vol. 6 of *Bihār al-Anwār*,

فيرى رسول الله وأهل بيته الأطهار صلوات الله عليهم وملائكة الرحمة وملائكة العذاب حاضرين عنده ليحكموا فيه وأنّه يترقب ايّ حكم يحكمون به ، وأي شيء سوف يوصون به ؟ ومن جهة أخرى قد اجتمع ابليس واعوانه ليوقعوه في الشك ، وهم يحاولون جاهدين أن يسلبوا إيمانه ليخرج من الدنيا بلا إيمان. ومن جهة أخرى يعاني من هول حضور ملك الموت ، وبأي صورة وهيئة سوف يجيئه به ، وبأي نحو سوف يقبض روحه . الى غير ذلك.. قال أمير المؤمنين عليه السلام: "فاجتمعت عليه سكرات الموت ، فغير موصوف ما نزل به".

"He will see the Messenger of Allāh and his Pure Fāmily, peace and blessings of Allāh be with them all, the angels of mercy and those of torment, all present near him as he awaits their verdict and what they will decide. On the other hand, the army of Satan and his helpers (will also be present in order to prevent him by all means from saying *La ilaha illa-Allāh* لا إله إلا الله, There is no god save Allāh, which is the key to salvation), to cast doubt in his heart and try hard to rob him of his belief (*iman*ايمان) so he will come out of this life without *iman*. At the same time, he is overwhelmed by expecting the presence of the angel of death: In what form it will approach him and how he will take his life away, etc. The Commander of the Faithful (ع) has said: 'The stupors of death surround him, so no description can be made for what has afflicted him.'" What about the *munjiyat* المنجيات during this very critical and dangerous phase, the acts of adoration which one can form during his lifetime so they may help ease or even cancel his pain of death? We are told on p. 9 of Abbas al-Qummi's precious work منازل الآخرة *Manazil al-Akhira*, which is the main source for this text material, that it is reported that the Messenger of Allāh (ص) was present during the death of a young man. The Prophet (ص) told the dying youth to testify that لا إله إلا الله *La ilaha illa-Allāh* (There is no god save Allāh), but his tongue was tied and he could not. Whenever the Prophet (ص) repeated his تلقين *talqeen* (instruction to the dying person to make a pronouncement), the dying young man could not respond. The Prophet (ص) asked a woman who was sitting at the head of the dying young man if she was his mother, and she answered in the affirmative. He again asked her if she was angry with her young son, and she again answered in the affirmative, adding that she had not spoken to him for the past six years. The Prophet (ص) asked her to be pleased with her son now, so she said, "May Allāh be pleased with him on account of you being pleased with him, O Messenger of Allāh." When the mother thus expressed her pleasure with her dying son, the latter was able to pronounce *La ilaha illa-Allāh* لا إله إلا الله. The Prophet (ص) then asked the youth to tell him about what he saw. The youth said, "I see a very dark man, very ugly, extremely smelly, wearing very filthy outfits, emitting a stench, coming in my direction, pressing on my mouth and respiratory passages." The Prophet (ص) ordered him to say:

يا من يقبل اليسير ويعفو عن الكثير، إقبل مِنّي اليسير وآعف عنّي الكثير، إنَّك أنت الغفور الرحيم.

"O One Who accepts little (of good deeds) while forgiving a lot (of sinning), do accept what is little [of the good deeds which I have done] and forgive a lot (of my sins); surely You are the Forgiving, the most Merciful." The young man did as instructed by the Prophet (ص), so the Prophet (ص) asked him again about what he now saw. The dying young man said, "I now see a man with a glowing face, pleasant, smelling very nicely and wearing clean outfits coming in my direction, whereupon the dark one is going away and getting ready to depart." The Prophet (ص) ordered the young man to repeat the statement which he had taught him then asked him once more about what he then saw. "The dark one has already gone, leaving no traces," the young man said, adding, "while the one having a glowing face remains beside me." It was at that moment that the young man passed away. This is recorded on p. 92, Vol. 1 of *Mustadrak Wasa'il ash-Shi`ah*. We also read on p. 380, Vol. 74 of *Bihār al-Anwār* that Imām Ja`far as-Sādiq (ع) has said, "One who gives an outfit to his [believing] brother, whether for the summer or for the winter, it will be incumbent upon the Almighty to outfit the first with one of the outfits of Paradise, ease the stupors of death for him and expand his resting place." The greatest Prophet (ص) has said:

من أطعم أخاه حلاوه، أزال الله عنه مرارة الموت

"One who feeds his Muslim brother something sweet, Allāh will remove from him the bitterness of death." What also helps the dying person and eases his pain is hearing the recitation of Sūrat Ya-Sin (Chapter 36 of the Holy Qur'an) and Sūrat as-Saffat (Chapter 37) as well as "du'a al-faraj" which is:

لا إله إلا الله الحليم الكريم، لا إله إلا الله العليم العظيم، سبحان الله رب السماوات السبع و رب الأرضين السبع و ما فيهن و ما بينهن و رب العرش العظيم و سلام على المرسلين، و الحمد لله رب العالمين:

"There is no god save Allāh, the Clement, the Great; there is no god save Allāh, the all-Knowing, the Great; praise to Allāh, Lord of the seven heavens, Lord of the seven earths and everything in them and everything between them, and the Lord of the Great `Arsh; peace be with the Messengers, and praise be to Allāh, Lord of the worlds." We read on p. 33, Vol. 97, of *Bihār al-Anwār* that according to Imām as-Sādiq (ع), as we are told by the mentor as-Saduq, "One who fasts the last day of the month of Rajab will be placed by Allāh in security against the intense pain of the stupors of death and the horror after death as well as the torment in the grave." As quoted by al-Kafami on p. 397, Vol. 2, p. 397 of his *Musbah*, the Prophet (ص) is quoted as having said that if one recites the following supplication ten times every day, ten thousand of his major transgressions will be forgiven by Allāh Who will also save him from the stupors of death and from the constriction of the grave as well as grant him security from one hundred thousands of the horrors of the Judgment Day; He will also protect him from the evil of Satan and his hosts, will pay his debts on his behalf and remove his worries and concerns; this very precious supplication, which you should share with all the ones you love, is as follows:

«أعددتُ لكُلّ هولٍ لا إله إلاّ الله ، ولِكُلّ هَمٍّ وَغَمٍّ ما شاء الله ، ولِكُلّ نعمَةٍ الحَمدُ لله ، ولِكُلّ رخاءٍ الشُّكرُ لله ، ولِكُلّ أعجوبَةٍ سُبحان اللهِ ، ولِكُلّ ذَنبٍ أستَغفِرُ الله ، ولِكُلّ مُصيبَةٍ إنا لله وإنا اليه راجعون ، ولِكُلّ ضيقٍ حَسبِيَ اللهُ و نعم الوكيلُ ، ولِكُلّ قَضاءٍ وقَدَرٍ تَوَكَّلتُ على اللهِ ولِكُلّ عَدُوٍّ اعتَصَمتُ باللهِ ، ولِكُلّ طاعَةٍ وَمَعصِيَةٍ لا حَولَ ولا قوةَ إلاّ باللهِ العَلِيّ العظيم.

"I have prepared for every horrific thing "There is no god save

Allāh", for every worry and distress "The will of Allāh be done", for every blessing "Praise to Allāh", for every prosperity "Thanks to Allāh", for every amazing thing "Blessed be Allāh", for every sin "I seek forgiveness of Allāh", for every transgression "We belong to Allāh, and to Him shall we return", for every hardship "Allāh suffices me, and how good a Helper He is!", for every decree and destiny "I have relied on Allāh", for

every enemy "I have sought refuge with Allāh" and for every obedience and disobedience "There is neither power nor might save in Allāh, the most Sublime, the most Great". Another supplication has as many as seventy merits one of which is that one who recites it will be given glad tidings at the time of his/her death; it is this:

«يا أسمع السامعين ويا أبصر الناظرين ويا أسرع الحاسبين ويا أحكم الحاكمين»

"O You, the most Hearing of those who hear, the most Seeing of those who see, the most Wise of those who decree!" Al-Kulayni has quoted Imām as-Sādiq (ع) as saying, "Do not ever be bored with reciting Sūrat az-Zalzala (Chapter 99 of the Holy Qur'an), for if one recites it in the voluntary prayers, Allāh will keep earthquakes away from him; he will not die because of an earthquake or be struck by lightning or any of this life's catastrophes; a glorious angel will descend upon him, sit at his head and address the angel of death thus: 'Be kind to him, for he is a servant of Allāh who used to recite me quite often,'" as we read on p. 331, Vol. 92, of *Bihār al-Anwār*. Remember that in the life hereafter, there will be personification of everything: Each and every action or intention, good or bad deed, will have a form, a shape, an entity. Every verse of the Holy Qur'an, every chapter and the Qur'an as a whole will also have forms. So will desires, wishes, hopes, aspirations, remorse, regret, prayer, fast and all other norms of adoration: All will have forms. How one will distinguish one from the other is a faculty which will be created with him as he is re-created, re-formulated, re-born in a new form, for the hereafter is the true life awaiting all of us, so get ready for it; there is no escape from it. But if you do not believe in the Hereafter, this book is not written for you, and it is a pity it fell in your hands; someone else can make better use of it. Also, some non-Muslims may feel "sorry" for what the Muslims will have to go through in the

554

Afterlife, feeling happy with the thought placed in their heads by their clergymen that they had nothing to worry about, that nothing but many good things await them after they die. Muslims, however, think that all followers of religions, or those who do not follow any religion at all, are entitled to their own wishful thinking.

2)   **The *Adeela* at the Time of Death العديله عند الموت** It means one turning from right to wrong as he dies due to the presence of Satan at the time of his death who will cast doubts in his heart through his evil insinuations in order to get him out of the right creed. There are many supplications to seek protection for such عديله: For example, the pride of all critics, may Allāh have mercy on his soul, has said that if one seeks security against Satan, he must bring into his presence the proofs of conviction and the five basic principles of Islam through irrevocable evidences, with ease of conscience, then he hands them all over to Allāh Almighty so He may return them to him at the time of his death. Having stated all the right doctrines, he should say the following:

»اللّهمَّ يا أرحم الراحمين انّي قد اودعتك يقيني هذا وثبات ديني وأنت خير مستودع قد أمرتنا بحفظ الودائع فردّه عليّ وقت حضور موتي«.

"O Lord, the most Merciful of those who show mercy: I have entrusted You with this conviction of mine, with the firmness of my creed. Since You are the best of trusted ones, and You commanded us to safe keep the trusts, do return it to me at the time when I am to die." What also helps is performing the prayer rites on time; doing so helps during such a critical stage. According to one tradition, the angel of death looks at all people five times a day, that is, during the five daily prayers, so he may teach those who perform them on time the *shahada* and spare him the evil of the cursed Satan. It is also highly recommended to recite the following supplication/ Qur'anic verse on every Sunday during the month of Thil-Qi'da:

رَبَّنَا لاَ تُزِغْ قُلُوبَنَا بَعْدَ إِذْ هَدَيْتَنَا وَهَبْ لَنَا مِن لَّدُنكَ رَحْمَةً إِنَّكَ أَنتَ الْوَهَّابُ

"Our Lord!" (they say,) "do not let our hearts deviate now that You have guided us, but grant us mercy from Your Own

Presence, for You are the Giver of unlimited bounties" (Qur'an, 3:8). Other Qur'anic Chapters that have the same effect include Suras 23 and 109.

3) *Wahshat al-Qabr* وحـشة القبـر **Grave's Loneliness:** According to the book titled من لا يحضره الفقيه *Man la Yahdhuruhu al-Faqih*, there are tremendous horrors in the grave; therefore, when the deceased person is taken to his burial spot, he must not be entered into it suddenly. He must be placed near the pit for a while so the dead person may get ready to enter it. Then one must bring him closer to it and wait a short while again after which the deceased person is to be placed in the grave. Al-Majlisi, the father, has explained the wisdom in these steps. He says that, true, the soul has already left the body, the الروح الحيوانية "animal spirit" (*spiritus animalis* in Latin) or the moving soul; as for the الروح الناطقة "articulate soul", it is yet to sever its ties with the body: There is fear about the grave's constriction, the questioning by Munkir and Nakeer, Ruman who tries to cause the dead to slip away into the torment, and the البرزخ *barzakh*; so, the deceased person has a lot to worry about. Ar-Rawandi has narrated saying that Jesus Christ (ع) once addressed his mother, Maryam (Mary) (ع), after her death saying, "Speak to me, Mother! Do you wish to return to the abode of the living?" She said, "Yes, so I may perform the prayers during an extremely cold night, and so I may fast during a very hot day. O Son! This path [of the dead] is frightful, horrific." It has also been narrated that Fatima az-Zahra (peace be with her) said once to her revered husband, Commander of the Faithful Ali (ع), by way of her will:

وروي : انَّ فاطمة عليها السلام لمّا احتضرت أوصت عليًا عليه السلام فقالت : «اذا أنـا مت، فتقول أنت غسلي وجهّزني ، وصلّ عليَّ وانزلني قبري وألحدني ، وسوّ التراب عليَّ، واجلـس عنـد رأسي قُبالـة وجهـي ، فـأكثر مـن تـلاوة القرآن والدعاء فانّها ساعة يحتاج الميت فيها الى أُنس الأحياء»

"When I die, wash my body and outfit me [with the shrouds], perform prayers for me, get me inside the grave, place the grave stone, bury me in the earth, sit at my head facing me, recite the Book of Allāh and recite many supplications, for it is time when the deceased person needs the company of those alive." We are told on p. 148, Vol. 1, of *Mustadrak al-Wasa'il* مستدرك الوسائل that Ibn Tawoos, may Allāh have mercy on his soul, has quoted the Prophet (ص) as saying:

«لا يأتي على الميت ساعة أشدّ من أول ليلة فارحموا موتاكم بالصدقة ، فان لم تجدوا فليصل أحدكم ركعتين يقرا فيهما فاتحة الكتاب مرّة وآية الكرسي مرّة ، وقل هو الله احد مرّتين ، وفي الثانية فاتحة الكتاب مرّة والهاكم التكاثر عشر مرّات ويسلم ويقول : اللّهمّ صلّ على محمّد وآل محمّد وابعث ثوابها الى قبر ذلك الميت فلان بن فلان ، فيبعث الله من ساعته الف ملك الى قبره مع كل ملك ثوب وحلة ويوسع في قبره من الضيق الى يوم ينفخ في الصور ويعطى المصلي بعدد ما طلعت عليه الشمس حسنات ويرفع له أربعون درجة»

"There is nothing harder for the deceased person than the first night in the grave; so, send mercy to your dead by offering charity on his behalf, and if one does not have charity to offer, let him perform two *rek'ats* (prostrations) in the first of which he should recite Sūrat al-Fātiha, the Verse of the Throne and twice Sūrat at-Tawhid (al-Ikhlas). In the second, he should recite Sūrat al-Fātiha followed by reciting ten times Sūrat at-Takathur (Chapter 102 of the Holy Qur'an). Then he should offer the *tasleem* [greeting the Prophet of Allāh (ص)] and say, "Lord! Bless Muhammed and the Progeny of Muhammed, and send the rewards [of this prayer] to the grave of the deceased person so-and-so." Allāh Almighty will then instantly send a thousand angels to the grave of that dead person. Each angel will be carrying an outfit. His grave will be widened till the trumpet is blown. The person who performs this prayer will be granted good deeds as many as the expanse of what is under the sun, and he will be raised forty stations." What also helps lessen the pain of loneliness in the grave is one during his lifelong perfecting *rukoo'* ركوع (bowing down) very well during the prayers. Imām al-Bāqir (ع) is quoted as having said: من أكمل الركوع لا يدخل الى قبره وحشة "One who perfects his bowing down [during the performance of the daily prayers] will not feel lonely in his grave," according to p. 244, Vol. 6 of *Bihār al-Anwār*. Actually, the doers of good do not have to worry about such loneliness, for angels will keep them company and they will be permitted to visit their relatives, the living or the dead, escorted by these angels, and this will be a diversion for them. Another act of *munjiyat* منجيات is repeating a hundred times this beautiful statement: لا الـه الا الله الملك الحق المبين There is no god save Allāh, the true and obvious King. Such act will save one from poverty in his lifetime and from loneliness in the grave in the Hereafter. He will be wealthy in this life and the gates of Paradise will be opened for him in the next. According to p. 217, Vol. 8 of *Bihār al-Anwār*, one who fasts 12 days during the month of Sha`ban will be visited in his grave every day by seventy thousand angels till the trumpet is blown. Here we must point out that "every day" means days of our own counting, days of this short life, for the *barzakh* period precedes the Judgment Day. Starting with that Day, time will bear a different dimension. And one who goes to visit a sick person will be rewarded by Allāh Who will assign an angel to visit him in his grave till the Day of Gathering, the Assembling Day. Also, it is recorded in Rawandi's *Da`awat* دعوات that the Prophet (ص) has said that if one recites the following supplication three times when a deceased person is buried, the torment from the latter will be lifted till the Trumpet is blown:

(اللّهمَّ إنِّي أسألكَ بحق محمدٍ وآل محمدٍ أن لا تُعَذِبَ هذا المَيِتَ)

Lord! I plead to You through the status reserved with you for Muhammed (ص) and the Progeny of Muhammed (ص) not to torment this deceased person till the Day when the trumpet is blown."

4)   Grave's Constriction (pressure) ضـغطة القبر: This is a very terrifying phase to the extent that it is difficult for the living to imagine. Commander of the Faithful Imām Ali ibn Abū Talib (ع) has said the following about it:

»يا عِباد الله ما بَعدَ المَوتِ لمَن لا يُغفَر له أشدُّ منَ المَوت: القبر، فاحذروا ضِيقَةُ وضَنكَهُ وظُلمَتَهُ وغُربتَهُ ، إنَّ القَبرَ يقولُ كُلَّ يَوم: أنـا بَيتُ الغربـة! انـا بيتُ الوَحشَة! أنا بَيتُ الدّودِ! ، والقَبرُ روضَةٌ من رياض الجنّـةِ أو حُفرةٌ من حُفر النّار... الى أن قالَ : وإنَّ مَعيشَةَ الضّنكَ الّتي حَذَّرَ اللهُ منها عَدُوَّهُ (هي) عذابُ القبر ، إنـّهُ يُسلّطُ على الكـافِر فـي قَبره تِسعةً وتِسعين تنيناً فَينهشنَ لَحمـهُ ويكسِرنَ عِظمـهُ، يَتردَّدنَ عليه كذلك الى يوم

558

يبعث ؛ لَو اَنَّ تِنيناً مِنها نَفَخَ في الأرض لَم تُنبِت زَرعاً. يا عِبـاد الله: إنَّ انفسَكُم الضّعيفة وأجسادكُم النّاعمة الرّقيقة التي يكفيها اليسيرُ تَضعُفُ عن هذا».

"O servants of Allāh! There is nothing harder, on those who are not forgiven, than death save the grave: So, beware of its constriction, darkness and loneliness. Each day, the grave says: 'I am the abode of loneliness! I am the abode of worms!' And the grave is either like one of the gardens of Paradise or one of the pits of Hell... Indeed, the "life of hardship" about which Allāh has warned those who are hostile to Him is the torment in the grave: The unbeliever is assaulted as he is in his grave by ninety-nine dragons that tear up his flesh, crush his bones and keep visiting him thus till the Day of Resurrection. Had one of these dragons blown on earth, no vegetation would have ever grown in it. O servants of Allāh! Your weak selves, tender and soft bodies which are satisfied with little, are too weak to withstand all of this." As indicated above, the sins, transgressions and wrongdoings will each take a form in the hereafter, and the worse one is the worse its form will be. What will help during this difficult situation? Page 327, Vol. 4 of *Usul al-Kafi* أصول الكـافي, tradition No. 13, says that whenever Imām as-Sādiq (ع) woke up at the end of the night, he would raise his voice so his family members could hear him saying the following:

«اللّهمّ أعنِّي على هول المطلع ، و وسع علي ضيق المضجع، اللّهُمَّ بارك لي في الموتِ ، و ارزقني خير مـا قبل الموتِ، و ارزقني خير مـا بعد الموتِ؛ اللّهُمَّ أعنِّي علـى سَكرات المَوتِ، اللّهُمَّ أعنِّي على غمّ القَبرِ ، اللّهُمَّ أعنِّي على ضيقِ القَبرِ، اللّهُمَّ أعنِّي علـى وَحشَةِ القَبرِ، اللّهُمَّ زوّجني مِن الحور العين»

"Lord! Help me with regard to the horror of what is awaiting me [after death] and expand for me the narrowness of the grave. Lord! Grant me a blessing at the time of death, and grant me goodness before death, and grant me goodness after death. Lord! Help me during the time of the stupors of death. Lord! Help me against the agonies of the grave. Lord! Help me against the constriction of the grave. Lord! Help me against the loneliness of the grave. And Lord! Do marry me to the *huris* with large, lovely eyes." Be informed, dear reader, that most torment in the grave is due to one not paying enough attention and care while using the toilet, taking lightly the sources of نجاسة uncleanness, and also due to committing calumny and backbiting as well keeping a distance from his family, according to p. 222, Vol. 6 of *Bihār al-Anwār*. From a narration by Sa'eed ibn Jubair, another cause is one having bad manners with his wife, speaking to her roughly rather than with kindness and consideration. Whatever the reason may be, we are assured by Imām Ja`far as-Sādiq (ع) that لا ينجو أحد من المؤمنين من ضغطة القبر "No believer is spared the grave's constriction," according to p. 221, Vol. 6 of the same reference. On p. 221, Vol. 6 of *Bihār al-Anwār* and on p. 74, Vol. 2 of *Safeenat al-Bihar*, Imām as-Sādiq (ع) is quoted as having said: "ان ضغطة القبر كفارة عن نعمه ضيعها المؤمن" The grave's constriction is atonement for a bliss wasted by a believer." Now let us review what helps in this terrible phase of the afterlife: Luckily, there are many acts of adoration which one can perform during his lifetime which will help him in the life to come, and the book titled منازل الآخرة *Manazil al-Akhira* by Abbas al-Qummi counts 15 of them. But we, in order to be brief, would like to cite the following for you: 1) Commander of the Faithful Imām Ali (ع) has said

من قرأ سورة النساء من القرآن في كل يوم جمعة أمن من ضغطة القبر

"One who recites Sūrat an-Nisaa (Chapter 4 of the Holy Qur'an) every Friday will have security against the grave's constriction," according to p. 330, Vol. 74 of the same reference. 2) It is recorded on p. 397, Vol. 2 of *Safeenat al-Bihar* that

من داوم على قراءة سورة الزخرف، آمنه الله تعالى في قبره من حشرات الأرض و الحيوانات و ضغطة القبر

"One who recites Sūrat an-Nisaa (Chapter of the Women [Chapter 4] of the Holy Qur'an) every Friday will be granted security in his grave from the earth's insects, animals and the grave's constriction." 3) According to the same reference and page, some traditions of the Prophet (ص) indicate that

من قرأ سورة "ن و القلم" في فريضة الصلاة أو النافلة، آمنه الله من ضغطة القبر

"If one recites Sūrat Noon (Chapter 68 of the Holy Qur'an which is also called Sūrat al-Qalam), during obligatory or optional prayers, Allāh will grant him security from the grave's constriction." 4) On pp. 221 and 243, Vol. 6 of *Bihār al-Anwār*, we are told that Imām ar-Ridha (ع) has said:

من مات بين زوالي الخميس و الجمعه، آمنه الله من ضغطة القبر

"One who dies between the periods of *zawal* زوال (midday) of Thursday and Friday, he will be secured by Allāh from the grave's constriction." 5) Imām ar-Ridha (ع) is also quoted as having said:

عليكم بصلاة الليل، فما من عبد مؤمن قام آخر الليل فصلى ثماني ركعات صلاة الليل، و ركعتين صلاة الشفع، و ركعة صلاة الوتر، و استغفر في قنوت الوتر سبعين مرة، الا و آمنه الله من عذاب القبر، و من عذاب النار، و طال عمره، و توسعت معيشته

"Uphold the Night Prayer; no believing servant of Allāh stands at the end of the night to offer 8 *rek'ats* (prostrations), two *Shaf` rek'ats* ركعتا الشفع, one *Witr Rek`a* ركعة الوتر, then he seeks forgiveness of Allāh in the *Qunoot* (invocation) of the Witr seventy times except that Allāh will grant him security against the torment of the grave and against the torture of the Fire, grants him a longer lifespan and expands his means of livelihood for him", as we are told on p. 397, Vol. 2 of *Safeenat al-Bihar* where the subject of the grave is discussed.

5) Questioning by Munkir and Nakeer سؤال منكر و نكير: On p. 223, Vol. 6 of *Bihār al-Anwār*, Imām Ja`far as-Sādiq (ع) is quoted as having said:

«ليس من شيعتنا مَن أنكر ثلاثة أشياء: المعراج، المساءَلة في القبر، والشفاعة»

"Not among our followers (Shī'as) is one who denies three things: the ascension [to heavens], the questioning in the grave (by Munkir and Nakeer) and the intercession." In the same reference on p. 261, we are told the following:

روي أن الملكين (منكر و نكير) يأتيان في هيئة هائلة، لهما صوت كالرعد و أعين كالبرق، يسألان: من ربك؟ و من نبيك؟ و ما دينك؟ و يسألان عن وليه و امامه، و بما أن الاجابة، في تلك الحال، صعبة على الميت، و أنه لا جرم يحتاج الى مساعدة، تعين التلقين في موضعين: أحدهما حين وضعه في القبر، و يستحسن أن يؤخذ كتفه الأيمن باليد اليمنى، و كتفه الأيسر باليد اليسرى، و يحرك و يلقن في حالة الاهتزاز و الادخال

في القبر، و الثاني بعد وضعه في القبر و دفنه، يستحب أن يجلس أقرب أنسبائه، و هو ولي الميت، على رأس الميت، بعد أن تركه الباقون و غادروا المكان، و يلقن الميت بصوت مرتفع، و يستحسن به أن يضع (الملقن) كفيه على القبر، و يقرب فاه من القبر، أو يفعل ذلك من ينوب عنه، فلقد ورد أن الملكين حينما يسمعان هذا التلقين، يقول منكر لنكير: دعنا نعود، فلقد لقنوه تلقين الحجة، و لا يحتاج الى سؤال، فيتركان السؤال و يعودان.

It has been reported that the two angels (Munkir and Nakeer) come in a terrifying form: Their voice is like thunder and their eyes like lightening. They will ask the dead person: "Who is your God? Who is your Prophet? What is your religion?" And they will ask him about his *wali* and Imām. Since the answers under such conditions will be very difficult for the dead person, and he undoubtedly needs help, the *talqeen* becomes a must in two places: One of them when he is placed inside the grave, and it is recommended that his right shoulder be held by the *mulaqqin* and his left shoulder by the left hand and moved then instructed with *talqeen* when his body is being shaken and entered into the grave. The other place is after the deceased person is put in the grave and buried: It is recommended that the *mulaqqin*, who is a close relative and a *wali* of the deceased person, sits at the area of the head after everyone else had left. He should raise his voice as he conducts the *talqeen*, and it is recommended that the *mulaqqin* places both his hands on the grave and brings his mouth close to the grave. Someone else who acts on behalf of the *mulaqqin* may do so. It is reported that when both angels hear the *talqeen*, Munkir will say to Nakeer: "Let us go back, for they have taught him the *talqeen* of evidence, and he needs no question," whereupon they both leave. On p. 183, Vol. 1 of *Mustadrak al-Wasa'il* مستدرك وسائل الشيعة, we are told that Imām as-Sādiq (ع) has said the following:

"اذا دخل المؤمن القبر، حضرت الصلاة الى يمينه، و الزكاة الى شماله و أشرف عليه البر و الاحسان: أما الصبر فيستقر في جانب، فاذا حضر الملكان ليسألاه، يخاطب الصبر الصلاة و الزكاة و البر (قائلا): أعينوا صاحبكم، يعني الميت، فان عجزتم عن ذلك، فأنا مستعد لذلك"

If the believer enters the grave, prayer come at his right and *zakat* at his left as kindness and benevolence look on. As for perseverance, it will stand aside. When both angels (Munkir and Nakeer) come to question him, perseverance will address prayer, *zakat* and kindness saying, 'Help your fellow,' meaning the deceased person, 'and if you cannot, I am ready.'" Also,

في بصائر الدرجات للصفار : ص 145 ـ 146 الطبعة الحجرية بالإسناد عن زر بن جبيش قال : روي في المحاسن بسند صحيح عن احدهما عليهما السلام ـ يعني الامام الصادق أو الامام الباقر ـ قال: «اذا مات العبد المؤمن دخل معه في قبره ستة صور ، فيهنّ صورة أحسنهنّ وجهاً ، وأبهاهنّ هيئة ، وأطيبهنّ ريحاً ، وأنظفهنّ صورة . قال : فتقف صورة عن يمينه وأخرى عن يساره وأخرى بين يديه ، وأخرى خلفه ، وأخرى عند رجله . وتقف التي هي أحسنهنّ فوق رأسه . فإن أوتي عن يمينه منعته التي عن يمينه، ثم كذلك الى أن يؤتى من الجهات الست. قال : فتقول أحسنهنّ صورة : ومن أنتم جزاكم الله عنّي خيراً؟ فتقول التي عن يمين العبد : أنا الصلاة. وتقول التي عن يساره : أنا الزكاة. وتقول التي بين يديه : أنا الصيام. وتقول التي خلفه : أنا الحجّ والعمرة . وتقول التي عند رجليه : أنا برّ مَن وصلت من اخوانك. ثم يقلن : مَن أنت ؟ فأنت أحسننا وجهاً وأطيبنا ريحاً ، وأبهانا هيئة . فتقول : أنا الولاية لآل محمّد صلوات الله عليهم أجمعين».

On pp. 145-146 of the old edition of as-Saffar's *Basa'ir al-Darajat*, through isnad which goes back to Zurr ibn Jubaish narrating an authentic tradition in the *Mahasin* book from one of them, peace be with them, namely Imāms as-Sādiq and al-Bāqir, saying, "When a believer dies, six faces (forms or shapes, i.e. personifications) enter the grave with him, each is more beautiful, more fragrant and more clean than the rest. These faces settle in six positions: on his right side, on his left, behind him, in front of him and at his feet. The most beautiful and the most fragrant one rests at his head. If questioning or torture approaches him from all sides, it will be prevented by one of the six faces. The most beautiful face will ask the other faces saying: 'Who are you, may Allāh reward you well on my behalf?!' The face settling at the believer's right side will say, 'I am the prayers.' The face settling on the believer's left side will say, 'I am the *zakat*.' The face settling opposite to the believer's face will say, 'I am the fast.' The one settling behind the believer will say, 'I am the pilgrimage', while the one settling at his feet will say, 'I am kindness and benevolence towards the believing brothers.' Everyone will then ask him about himself thus: 'And who are you with your dazzling beauty and extra-ordinary fragrance?' He will say, 'I am the *wilaya* (mastership) of the Progeny of Muhammed (peace and blessings of Allāh be with them all).'"

563

The *Barzakh* البرزخ (Purgatory?) It is one of the terrifying phases or stages through which the vast majority of people will pass. Exceptions are two kinds: People with whom the Almighty is very pleased, and these go straight to Paradise, and people with whom He is very displeased, and these go straight to hell. Neither group will go through whatever goes on in the grave as indicated above. The *barzakh* is mentioned in the Holy Qur'an in places such as this: وَمِن وَرَائِهم بَرْزَخٌ إِلَى يَوْم يُبْعَثُونَ "(There) is a barrier before them till the Day they are raised up (from their graves for judgment)" (Qur'an, 23:100). This barrier separates this short temporal life as we know it from the other everlasting one awaiting us, but it is also one of its phases or stages, a station, if you will. On p. 71, Vol. 1 of *Safeenat al-Bihar* سفينة البحار we are told that Imām as-Sādiq (ع) pointed out to the *barzakh* once saying, "By Allāh, I fear for you the *barzakh*." He was asked, "What is the *barzakh*?" He said, "It is the grave from the moment of death till the Day of Judgment."

قال الامام الصادق عليه السلام في حديث: «ولكني والله اتخوف عليكم من البرزخ. قيل له: وما البرزخ ؟ قال: القبر منذ حين موته الى يوم القيامة.

It has been cited from ar-Rawandi's book *Lubb al-Lubab* لب اللباب that those in the graves go to call upon their fāmilies, offspring and relatives and tearfully plead to them saying: "O our children!! O our fāmilies! O our relatives! Have mercy on us and bestow upon us of the good things with you and the good deeds, and do remember us, may Allāh have mercy on you. We have sat in narrow prisons, bearing many worries and concerns; so, do not be too miser to pray for us and to pay alms on our behalf before your fate becomes similar to ours, perhaps Allāh will have mercy on us all. Alas! We used to be like you, enjoying blessings, but we did not spend in the way of Allāh, so our wealth turned into a calamity on our heads while others benefited from it; so, listen to us and do not forget to do us a favor with a dirham or a loaf of bread or whatever you wish, for you shall join us; you shall weep and your tears will not do you any good, just as we do although we find doing so to be futile. Work hard and seize the opportunity before it is gone and before your condition will be similar to ours."

ونقل عن لبّ اللباب للقطب الراوندي قـال: وفي الخبر كـان المـوتى يـأتون فيقفون ، وينادي كلّ واحد منهم بصوت حزين باكياً : يـا أهلاه ! يـا ولداه ! ويـاقرابتـاه ! اعطفوا علينا بشيء يرحمكم الله ، واذكرونـا ولا تنسونـا بالـدعاء وارحمـوا علينا وعلى غربتنـا ، فاننـا قد بقينا فـي سـجن ضـيق ، وغمّ طويـل وشـدّة ، فـارحمونـا ، ولا تبخلـوا بالـدعاء والصدقة لنا لعل الله يرحمنا قبل أن تكونوا مثلنا. فواحسرتاه قد كنّـا قادرين مثل مـا أنتم قادرون فيا عباد الله : اسمعوا كلامنا ولا تنسونا فـانّكم ستعلمون غداً فانّ الفضول التـي في ايديكم كانت في أيدينا فكنّا لاننفق في طاعة الله ، ومنعنـا عن الحقّ ، فصار وبالاً علينـا ومنفعةً لغيرنا . اعطفوا علينا بدرهم أو رغيف أو بكسرة. ثم ينادون مـا أسرع مـا تبكون على انفسكم ولا ينفعكم كما نحن نبكي ولا ينفعنا فاجتهدوا قبل أن تكونوا مثلنا.

Is the *barzakh* similar to the purgatory? Catholics believe that the purgatory is a place where the souls of the dead are cleansed before receiving God's grace, and such cleansing includes atonement through pain. This seems to be close to the Islamic concept because the Almighty punishes many of His servants in the grave in order to affect justice so He may not punish them again in hell. This does not apply to everyone, however, because some sinners are punished in this life, in the grave and in hell as well. This "purging" in which the Catholics believe may be close to the "grave's constriction" detailed above. It is also stated in some traditions that this constriction, or the torment in the grave, is one of the manifestations of the Almighty Who does not wish to torment His servants twice; so, the grave is the last phase where they have to "pay" for some of their sins. But it is better, of course, to avoid such torment by doing simple things in this life that will spare you having to go through it, in other words, the *munjiyat* المنجيات, acts bringing salvation, the easiest of which is recitation of supplications on a regular basis and helping others morally and financially, that is, those who deserve to be helped as explained in the Qur'an and Sunna. The best way to offer charity, of course, is to give with the right hand what the left does not know, that is, let it be a secret you keep to yourself; do not make a show of it and thus lose its rewards. In the reference *Jami` al-Akhbar* جامع الأخبار, we read the following on p. 197:

ذكر صحابي عن الرسول الأعظم (ص) أنه قال: "إبعثوا بهداياكم إلى موتاكم" فسئل عن هدايا الموتى، فقال: "الصدقه و الدعاء".

A companion of the Greatest Prophet (ص) cited the Prophet (ص) as saying, "Send your gifts to your dead." He was asked about what gifts could be sent to the dead, so he said, "Charity and supplication." If you read the classic reference written by al-Harrani titled *Thawab al-A`mal* ثواب الأعمـال, you will see how rewards for good deeds multiply by many times, starting from the tenfold promised in the Almighty for a good deed and go up the ladder till they reach an astronomical figure of one hundred thousand times. Who will be rewarded so many times and for what? One who offers charity on behalf of both his deceased parents will receive them. If his parents still living, he will receive in the hereafter ten thousand times as much as he gives away as charity in the life of this world on their behalf. But if you have no money to pay charity, supplications will do. A combination of both is the best, though, if you really want to shun many horrors awaiting us in the hereafter and to live a very happy and blissful life here and hereafter.

و فيه أيضا عن النبي الكريم (ص) أنه قال: إذا تصدق أحدكم لميت، فإن ملكا يحملها في طبق من نور، تمتد إشعته حتى تبلغ السماوات، فيقف على حافة القبر، و ينـادي بـأعلى صوته: السلام عليكم يا أهل القبور، هذه هديـة أهلكم إليكم! فيتسلمها الميت، و يدخلها قبره، و يتسع بها مضجعه. .... ثم قال رسول الله (ص): إعلموا أنه من ترحم على ميت بصدقه، فله أجر عند الله مثل جبل أحد، و هو يوم القيامـه تحت ظل عرش الله، إذ لا ظل سواه يومذاك و ينجو بالصدقه الأموات و الأحياء.

In the same reference, that is, *Jami` al-Akhbar* جامع الأخبار, we read the following on the same page: "The Revered Prophet (ص) has been quoted as saying, 'If one of you offers charity on behalf of a deceased person, an angel carries it on a platter of *noor* (celestial light) the rays of which extend and reach the heavens. He stands at the edge of the grave and calls out as loudly as he can, saying: Peace be with you, O people of the graves! This is a gift sent to you by your fāmily! The deceased person receives it and takes it with him inside his grave: It expands his resting place..." Then the Messenger of Allāh (ص) added saying, "Be informed that when someone seeks mercy for a deceased person through offering charity on his behalf, he will get rewards as large as the Uhud Mountain, and he will be on the Judgment Day under the shade of Allāh's `Arsh when, on that Day, there will be no shade other than it, and charity will be the salvation of the dead and of the living." Here we must point out that many writers write about the thirst and hunger of the Judgment Day but do not say much about the darkness which will engulf the bad ones. There are many references to the *noor* نور, celestial light, that will shine through and for the good ones on that Day, whereas the bad ones will be terrified because they will have no *noor* that will enable them to see what is around them, and they will most likely suffer from the stench of the pus coming out of the bodies of many in their company whose bodies will be smitten by the angels of torture. Contrary to their condition is enjoyed by those whom the Almighty will bless on that Day: These will have *noor*, shade on their heads rather than heat and be brought drinks and fruits from Paradise as they watch others being tried, that is, court marshaled! On p. 59, Vol. 74 and on pp. 573-4 of *Zad al-Ma`ad* زاد المعاد, we read the following statement by Imām as-Sādiq (ع):

قـال الامـام الـصادق (ع) يرد الـصوم و الـصلاة و الـصدقة و الـحـج و الأدعيـة و الـخيرات
على الميت في قبره، و يكتب ثواب جميع الأعمال للميت و لفاعل الخير معا

"Fast, prayers, charity, pilgrimage, supplications and good deeds reach the deceased person inside his grave, and the rewards of all deeds done on behalf of the deceased person will be recorded as they are for the doer of these deeds."

6) *Qiyama*: **Judgment Day** القيامـه Belief in the Day of Judgment is one of the basic principles of the Islamic creed and of almost all other creeds, including primitive non-divine ones. For example, if you ask an Eskimo in the North Pole what will happen when one of his folks dies, he will tell you that he will be placed in his husky dog-pulled chariot with plenty of food and clothes. The dogs will be told to pull it wherever they want, and he will be taken to a place reserved for the dead with which the huskies are familiar. There, he will return to life and, if he is good, the Eskimo will go on, the place to which the dogs will take him will be very nice and warm: The food and clothes will keep recreating themselves indefinitely. And we know how the ancient Egyptians used to bury their dead with food, clothes and jewelry due to their belief in the hereafter. Such belief is innate, natural, instinctive, deeply ingrained in the human nature. Islam portrays the Judgment Day as follows:

القيامة من منازل الآخره المهوله، بل هولها أشد الأهوال و أعظمها، و فزعها أكبر فزع،
و قد وصفها الله (تبارك و تعالى) في القرآن: "يَسْأَلُونَكَ عَنِ السَّاعَةِ أَيَّانَ مُرْسَاهَا قُلْ

567

إِنَّمَا عِلْمُهَا عِندَ رَبِّي لاَ يُجَلِّيهَا لِوَقْتِهَا إِلاَّ هُوَ ثَقُلَتْ فِي السَّمَاوَات وَالأَرْض لاَ تَأْتِيكُمْ إِلاَّ بَغْتَةً يَسْأَلُونَكَ كَأَنَّكَ حَفِيٌّ عَنْهَا قُلْ إِنَّمَا عِلْمُهَا عِندَ اللَّهِ وَلَكِنَّ أَكْثَرَ النَّاسِ لاَ يَعْلَمُونَ

They ask you about the Hour (of Resurrection) when its appointed time will be. Say: 'The knowledge of this is with my Lord (alone): None but He can reveal when it will occur; its burden will be weighty throughout the heavens and the earth. It will come but suddenly to you'. They ask you as if you were solicitous of it; say: 'The knowledge of it is with Allāh (alone), but most men do not know'" (Qur'an, 7:187). On p. 312, Vol. 6 of *Bihār al-Anwār*, we read the following:

روى الراوندي عن الصادق من آل محمد (عليهم السلام) إن عيسى بن مريم (عليه السلام) سأل جبرائيل: متى تقوم القيامة؟ فارتعش جبرائيل حتى سقط على الأرض مغشيا عليه و أغمي عليه، و لما صحا، قال: يا روح الله، ليس المسؤول بأعلم من السائل عن أمر القيامة، ثم تلى الآيه التي مر ذكرها

"Ar-Rawandi has quoted Imām as-Sādiq (ع) saying that Jesus son of Mary (peace be with him) asked Gabriel once: "When shall the Judgment Day be?" Gabriel shook till he fell on the ground conscious, and he lost his consciousness. When he woke up from it, he said, "O Ruhullah (Spirit of Allāh)! The asked person does not know about it more than the questioner." Then he recited the above verse.

روي أنه لما كان النبي (ص) يذكر القيامة، يتغير صوته و يشتد، و يحمر وجهه الشريف

It has been narrated that whenever the Prophet (ص) mentioned the Judgment Day, his voice would change and intensifies, and his holy face would change color. There are many *munjiyat* المنجيات, acts of salvation, that can help during this terrifying Day about which so many Chapters and verses of the Holy Qur'an warn. Here are some of them: 1) On p. 293, Vol. 7 of *Bihār al-Anwār*, we read the following:

روي أنه من قرأ سورة يوسف (ع) كل يوم أو كل ليلة، يبعث يوم القيامة جميلا كجمال يوسف (ع)، و لا يستولي عليه فزع يوم القيامة الأكبر

"One who recites Sūrat Yousuf (Chapter 12 of the Holy Qur'an) every day or every night will be resurrected on the Judgment Day as beautiful as Yousuf (Joseph) (peace be with him) used to be, and he will not be overtaken by the greatest fright of the Judgment Day." On p. 295 of the same reference, Imām al-Bāqir (ع) is quoted as having said:

من قرأ سورة الدخان في فرائضه و نوافله، فإن الله تعالى يبعثه مع الآمنين المطمئنين

One who recites Sūrat al-Dukhan (Smoke, i.e. Chapter 44 of the Holy Qur'an) in his obligatory as well as voluntary prayers will be resurrected by Allāh in the company of those who will be secure and contented." And the Imām (ع) has also said the following as we read on p. 298 of the same reference:

من قرأ سورة الأحقاف كل ليلة أو كل جمعة، لا يستولي عليه الخوف في الدنيا، و يجعله الله تعالى في أمان يوم القيامة

"Whoever recites Sūrat al-Ahqaf (Chapter 46 of the Holy Qur'an) every night or every Friday will not be overtaken by fear in the temporary life, and Allāh Almighty will grant him security on the Judgment Day." On p. 298, Vol. 7 of the same reference, the Imām (ع) is quoted as having said:

من قرأ سورة "و العصر" في نوافله، يبعث يوم القيامة ناصع الوجه، مشرق المحيا، قرير العين، تبدو على شفتيه البسمة الى أن يدخل الجنة

One who recites Sūrat al-Asr (Chapter 103 of the Holy Qur'an) in his voluntary prayers will be resurrected on the Judgment Day with a bright face, shiny forehead, cooled eyes and a smile painted on his lips till he enters Paradise." 2) On p. 302, Vol. 7 of the same source, al-Kulayni cites Imām as-Sādiq (ع) as having said that the Messenger of Allāh (ص) has said:

من إحترم الذي بيض شعره في الإسلام، جعله الله في أمان من فزع القيامة الأكبر، و لا يخاف منه

"One who shows respect to a person who grows grey hair while being Muslim will be granted by Allāh security against the greatest fright of the Judgment Day and he will not fear that Day." 3) He is also quoted, as stated in the same reference and on the same page, as having said:

من مات في طريق مكه في ذهابه إليها أو إيابه عنها، كان آمنا من فزع القيامة الأكبر، و لا يخاف منه "

One who dies on his way going to Mecca or returning from it will be secure against the greatest fright of the Judgment Day, and he will not fear that Day." And on p. 57 of the same source, as-Sadūq quotes him as having said:

من مات في أحد الحرمين، أي حرم مكة و حرم المدينة، زادهما الله شرفا و تعظيما، بعثه الله مع الذين لا يخافون، و هم في أمان يوم القيامه

"One who is buried in the holy precincts of Mecca the Venerable or in Medīna, may the Almighty increase their honor and glory, will be secure and resurrected by Allāh in the company of those who do not fear and will enjoy security on the Judgment Day." 4) On p. 303, Vol. 7 of *Bihār al-Anwār*, it is indicated that as-Sadūq has narrated saying that the Messenger of Allāh (ص) said:

من تهيأت له فاحشه أو شهوه، فتخلى عنها و تجنب التورط فيها خوفا من الله تعالى جل و علا، حرم الله عليه نار جهنم، و جعله في أمان من هول القيامة و خوفها

"If one had the opportunity to commit a sin or satisfy a lustful desire but he let it pass by and avoided being involved in it out of his fear of Allāh, the most Sublime, the most Great, Allāh will prevent the fire of Hell from coming near him and will grant him security against the horror of the Judgment Day and of its fright." 5) The same source cites the Prophet (ص) as having said:

من عادى نفسه و لم يعاد الناس، جعله الله في أمان من فزع يوم القيامه

"If one opposes his desires while not being hostile to people, Allāh will grant him security against the greatest fear of the Judgment Day." 6) The great mentor, Sheikh Ali ibn Ibrahim al-Qummi, as we read in Vol. 62 of the same reference, has quoted Imām Muhammed al-Bāqir (ع) as having said:

من كظم غيظه و هو قادر على تنفيذه و تطبيقه، ملأ الله تعالى قلبه بالإيمان و الأمان

"If one suppresses his anger while being able to carry its dictates out and implement them, Allāh will fill his heart with conviction and security." 7) Allāh Almighty has said the following in the Holy Qur'an: "مَن جَاءَ بِالْحَسَنَةِ فَلَهُ خَيْرٌ مِّنْهَا وَهُم مِّن فَزَعٍ يَوْمَئِذٍ آمِنُونَ" Whoever does a good deed will be rewarded with better than it, and these will be secure against the fright of that Day" (Qur'an, 27:89). A footnote on p. 117, Vol. 7 of *Bihār al-Anwār* cites the Commander of the Faithful Ali ibn Abū Talib (ع) commenting about the word الحسنة in this verse by saying: الحسنه في هذه الإيه المعرفة و الولاية و محبتنا نحن أهل البيت "The doing of good in this verse is knowing about, accepting the mastership of and loving us, we Ahl al-Bayt (ع) (immediate family of the Prophet (ص))." 8) In the same reference, we are told that as-Sadūq has quoted Imām as-Sādiq (ع) as saying:

من أعان أخاه المغموم الظمآن بما في وسعه، و أراحه من همه و غمه، أو أعانه في قضاء حاجته، فله من الله تعالى إثنتان و سبعون رحمة، يعطيه الله في الدنيا رحمة واحدة، و بها يصلح الله أمر معاشه، و يدخر له إحدى و سبعين رحمة الباقيه لأهواله و فزعه يوم القيامة

"One who helps his distressed and thirsty brother as much as he can, or if he relieves him of his worry and concern, or if he helps him take care of something, he will receive from Allāh Almighty seventy-two blessings: Allāh will grant him in the life of this world one blessing whereby He repairs his livelihood while saving his remaining seventy-one blessings for the horrors and fright of the Judgment Day." More *munjiyat* منجيات, acts of adoration that result in one's salvation, are stated on the pages of al-Qummi's *Manazil al-Akhria* منازل الآخرة to which we refer the reader.

7)   *Al-Hashr* الحشر The Gathering: It is a terrifying phase which starts when one comes out of his grave, having a new form with which he is not familiar, and it is one of the three most critical times through which a human being has to go. Prophet Isa (Jesus Christ), peace be with him, refers to these three phases during which he will see nothing but peace as we read in verse 33 of Sūrat Maryam, a chapter in the Holy Qur'an named after his saintly

mother, Maryam (Mary), where Jesus is quoted by the Almighty as saying on the very first day when he was born, a miracle which testified to his extra-ordinary birth to an extra-ordinary Lady, the Mistress of the world of her time, the following: وَالسَّلاَمُ عَلَيَّ يَوْمَ وُلِدتُّ وَيَوْمَ أَمُوتُ وَيَوْمَ أُبْعَثُ حَيًّا "So peace is upon me the day I was born, the day I die, and the day I shall be raised up to life (again)!" (Qur'an, 19:33). In Sūrat al-Ma`arij (Chapter 70 of the Holy Qur'an), the Almighty says the following:

فَذَرْهُمْ يَخُوضُوا وَيَلْعَبُوا حَتَّى يُلاَقُوا يَوْمَهُمُ الَّذِي يُوعَدُونَ، يَوْمَ يَخْرُجُونَ مِنَ الأَجْدَاثِ سِرَاعًا كَأَنَّهُمْ إِلَى نُصُبٍ يُوفِضُونَ ، خَاشِعَةً أَبْصَارُهُمْ تَرْهَقُهُمْ ذِلَّةٌ ذَلِكَ الْيَوْمُ الَّذِي كَانُوا يُوعَدُونَ

"So leave them to plunge into vain talk and play until they encounter the Day they have been promised. (It is) the Day on which they will come out of their sepulchers in sudden haste as if they were rushing to a goal-post (fixed for them), their eyes lowered in dejection, ignominy covering them (all over). Such is the Day they are promised" (Qur'an, 70:42-4). On p. 111, Vol. 7, of *Bihār al-Anwār*, we read the following text:

روي عن ابن مسعود أنـه قـال: كنت جالسا فـي محضر أمير المؤمنين (عليه السلام)، فقال: في القيامة خمسون موقفا، و كل موقف ألف سنة. الموقف الأول هو الخروج من القبر، يحبس الناس فيه ألف سنة حفاة عراة جياعا عطاشى، فمن خرج من جدثه مؤمنـا بـالله و الجنـة و النـار و البعث و القيامـة، و مقرا بـالله، و مصدقا لنبيه و مـا أنزل من الله تعالى، نجا من الجوع و العطش.

"In the Hereafter, there will be fifty stations: Each station lasts a thousand years. The first station is getting out of the grave. People will be confined in it for a thousand years barefoot, hungry and thirsty. Whoever comes out of his grave believing in Allāh, in Paradise and Hell, in the Accounting and the Judgment, admitting Allāh as the Lord, believing in His Prophet and in what Allāh Almighty had revealed to him, will be saved from hunger and thirst." The Holy Qur'an refers to these fifty thousand years in the following verse:

تَعْرُجُ الْمَلائِكَةُ وَالرُّوحُ إِلَيْهِ فِي يَوْمٍ كَانَ مِقْدَارُهُ خَمْسِينَ أَلْفَ سَنَةٍ

572

"It is the Day on which Allāh gathers the early generations and the last to discuss settling accounts and to reward good deeds. People will be submissive as they stand stifled by sweat, the earth having shaken underneath their feet. The best condition among them all is one who can find a foothold and a space." Obviously, the reckoning will take place on the same earth on which humans have been living for many years, but the earth will not be the same: All mountains will be then be flattened, all water in the seas and the oceans would have been turned into fire: The oxygen will be separated from the hydrogen and set ablaze:

وَإِذَا الْجِبَالُ سُيِّرَتْ وَإِذَا الْعِشَارُ عُطِّلَتْ وَإِذَا الْوُحُوشُ حُشِرَتْ وَإِذَا الْبِحَارُ سُجِّرَتْ

"When the mountains vanish (like a mirage); when the she-camels, ten months with young, are left untended; when the wild beasts are gathered together, and when the oceans boil over with a swell" (Qur'an, 81:3-6). Notice the verse saying: "And when the wild beasts are gathered together" which indicates that the Day of Gathering will not be confined to humans but also to animals as well: All those who, without a justifiable cause, harmed these animals will have to account for their sins on that horrific Day, and this proves to you how Islam cares so much not only about humans but also about animals. One can write a book about "animal rights in Islam" and compare these rights with the abuse these servants of the Almighty receive at the hands of either ignorant or selfish humans, but let us not get into that now. As for the last verse, No. 6, the one referring to the oceans "boiling over with a swell", I think it is a weak translation of what should be something like this: "And when the oceans are set ablaze." The earth will be flattened in order to make room for all billions of humans and animals and perhaps birds as

573

well; it will be like a thin disk. Mentor al-Kulayni, as cited on p. 197, Vol. 7 of *Bihār al-Anwār*, quotes Imām al-Bāqir (ع) as saying:

ان الله تبارك و تعالى يبعث يوم القيامة أناسا من قبورهم، غلت أيديهم و ربطت إلى أعناقهم لدرجة أنهم لا يستطيعون أن يأخذوا بأيديهم قدر أنمله، و معهم ملائكة يلومونهم بشدة و يقولون: هؤلاء منعوا الخير القليل عن الخير الكثير، و هؤلاء هم الذين منحهم الله من عطاياه، فامتنعوا عن أداء حقوق الله من أموالهم

"Allāh, the most Blessed and the most Exalted One, will send on the Judgment Day people out of their graves: Their hands are tied to their necks to the extent they cannot take an iota of anything in their hands. The angels will be with them chastising them harshly and saying: "These (folks) prevented the doing of small acts of goodness while plenty was at their disposal. These are the ones whom Allāh granted out of His boons, yet they did not pay what belonged to Allāh from their wealth." In the same reference and on the same page, mentor as-Sadūq quotes the Messenger of Allāh (ص) as saying the following in a lengthy tradition:

من وشى بين شخصين، سلط الله عليه في قبره نارا تحرقه إلى يوم القيامه، و إذا ما خرج من قبره و حفرته، سلط الله عليه حيه سوداء تقطع لحمه إلى أن يدخل النار

"If one drives a wedge between two persons, Allāh sends a fire in his grave that burns him till the Judgment Day. Once he gets out of his grave, Allāh will send on him a black snake that will tear his flesh apart till he enters hell." The Prophet (ص) is also quoted in the same reference as having said:

من ملأ عينه من النظر إلى المرأة الغريبه، حشره الله يوم القيامه مسمرا بمسامير ناريه حتى يحكم الله بين الناس، فيحكم عليه أن يؤخذ الى النار

"If one fills his eyes with looking at a stranger woman, Allāh will gather him on the Judgment Day nailed with nails of fire till Allāh judges among the people. He will then rule to throw that man into the fire of hell." He (ص) is also quoted on the next page of the same reference as having said the following:

شارب الخمر يحشر يوم القيامة مسود الوجه، مائل العينين معتمة، معوج الفم، يسيل اللعاب منه، و قد أخرج لسانه من قفاه

"One who drinks wine will be gathered on the Judgment Day with a black face, his eyes are dark and slanted, his mouth twisted, saliva pouring down his mouth and his tongue sticking out of his back." Sheikh as-Sadūq, as stated on p. 198 of the same reference cited above, has quoted Imām as-Sādiq (ع) as saying:

أنه من أزال عن مؤمن همه و غمه، أزال الله عنه هموم الآخرة و غمومها، و يخرج من قبره مفرح القلب مثلجه

"If one removes the worry and the agony of another believer, Allāh will remove from him the worries and the agonies of the Hereafter, and he shall come out of his grave with a happy and cooled heart." Both al-Kulayni and as-Sadūq, as stated in the same reference, narrate a lengthy tradition from Sadeer, the money exchanger, citing Imām as-Sādiq (ع) saying:

يحشر الله المؤمن من قبره و معه تمثال و نظير، و كلما رأى المؤمن من أهوال القيامة، قال له التمثال: لا تخف و لا تحزن فإن لك البشرى من الرحمن. و يديم على بشارته حتى يبلغ موقف الحساب، فيحاسبه الله حسابا يسيرا و يأمر له بالجنة و التمثال أمامه. فيقول المؤمن للتمثال: رحمك الله، فقد كنت لي خلا حسنا، خرجت معي من القبر، و داومت على بشارتي بالسرور و كرامة الله تعالى إلى أن تحققت لي، فمن أنت؟ فيجيبه التمثال: أنا السرور الذي أدخلته في قلب أخيك المؤمن في الدنيا، و قد خلقني الله لأبشرك بالسرور الدائم و الفرح المداوم .

"Allāh gathers a believer, once he is out of his grave, in the company of an image and a like form. Whenever the believer sees horror in the Hereafter, the image says to him, "Do not worry and do not grieve, for you have the glad tidings from the most Merciful One." He keeps telling him such glad tidings till he takes his place for the judgment. Allāh will then be easy on him as He judges him. He will order him to be lodged in Paradise. The image will still be standing in front of him, so the believer will ask it, "May Allāh have mercy on you! You have been a good companion to me: You came out with me from the grave and continued to give me glad tidings of happiness and honor from Allāh Almighty till this became a reality for me; so, who are you?!" The image will answer him saying, "I am the pleasure which you entered into the heart of your believing brother in the temporary life, and Allāh created me so I may inform you of the continuous happiness and incessant pleasure." On p. 168, Vol. 7 and p. 380, Vol. 74 of the same reference, mentor al-Kulayni narrates saying that Imām as-Sādiq (ع) has also said:

مـن كـسـا أخـاه الـمـؤمـن كسـوة الشتاء أو الـصيف، فقد أوجب الله عـلى نفسـه أن يكسـوه ملابـس الجنـة و يـسهل علـيـه مـشاق الـمـوت، و يوسـع عـلـيـه قبـره، و تبـشره الملائكـة بالبشـرى حين خروجـه مـن قبـره إشـارة إلى هذه الآيـة الكريمـه: "لا يَحْزُنُهُمُ الْفَزَعُ الأَكْبَرُ وَتَتَلَقَّاهُمُ الْمَلائِكَةُ: هَذَا يَوْمُكُمُ الَّذِي كُنتُمْ تُوعَدُونَ .

"One who gives his believing brother an outfit for the winter or for the summer obligates Allāh to clothe him from the outfits of Paradise, removes the hardships of death from him, expands his grave for him and the angels convey the glad tiding to him when he comes out of his grave as referred to in this sacred verse: 'The angels welcome them saying: This is your Day which Allāh promised you!' (Qur'an, 21:103)."

8) الميزان **Al-Mizan: The Scales of Deeds** It is one of the terrifying phases/stages of the hereafter; the Almighty says the following in Sūrat al-A`raf:

وَالْوَزْنُ يَوْمَئِذٍ الْحَقُّ، فَمَن ثَقُلَتْ مَوَازِينُهُ فَأُولَئِكَ هُمُ الْمُفْلِحُونَ، وَمَنْ خَفَّتْ مَوَازِينُهُ فَأُولَئِكَ الَّذِينَ خَسِرُواْ أَنفُسَهُم بِمَا كَانُواْ بِآيَاتِنَا يَظْلِمُونَ .

"And truly We shall recount their whole story with knowledge, for We were never absent (at any time or place). The balance that Day will be (absolutely) true: Those whose scales (of good deeds) will be heavy will prosper" (Qur'an, 7:8-9). Following is Sūrat al-Qari`a, Chapter of the noise and clamor that announce the reckoning:

بسم الله الرحمن الرحيم: الْقَارِعَة: مَا الْقَارِعَةُ؟ وَمَا أَدْرَاكَ مَا الْقَارِعَةُ؟ يَوْمَ يَكُونُ النَّاسُ كَالْفَرَاشِ الْمَبْثُوثِ وَتَكُونُ الْجِبَالُ كَالْعِهْنِ الْمَنفُوشِ فَأَمَّا مَن ثَقُلَتْ مَوَازِينُهُ فَهُوَ فِي عِيشَةٍ رَّاضِيَةٍ، وَأَمَّا مَنْ خَفَّتْ مَوَازِينُهُ فَأُمُّهُ هَاوِيَةٌ، وَمَا أَدْرَاكَ مَا هِيَ؟ نَارٌ حَامِيَةٌ.

In the name of Allāh, Most Gracious, Most Merciful. The (Day) of noise and clamor: What is the (Day) of noise and clamor? And what will explain to you what the (Day) of noise and clamor is? (It is) a Day on which men will be scattered about like moths, and the mountains will be like carded wool. It is then that one whose balance (of good deeds) will be (found) heavy, he will be in a life of good pleasure and satisfaction. But if one's balance (of good deeds) will be (found) light, he will have his home in a (bottomless) pit (of hell). And what will explain to you what this (pit) is? (It is) a fiercely blazing Fire" (Qur'an, 101:1-11). It is called so because it hammers on the hearts with fear and terror. We read the following on p. 64 of al-Qummi's book منازل الآخرة *Manazil al-Akhira*:

إعلم أنه ربما لا يساوي عمل لترجيح كفة الميزان في ثقله مثل الصلاة على النبي الكريم و آله البررة (صلوات الله عليهم أجمعين) و مثل الخلق الحسن

Be informed that perhaps there is nothing that tilts the scales of good deeds due to its weight like blessing the Venerable Prophet and his righteous progeny, peace and blessings of Allāh be with them all, and like good manners. On p. 49, Vol. 2 of *Safeenat al-Bihar*, we read the following:

سأل من روى الحديث : كيف نصلي على محمد وآله؟ فقال الصادق (عليه السلام): تقول: صلوات الله وصلوات ملائكته وانبيائه ورسله وجميع خلقه على محمد وآل محمد والسلام عليه وعليهم ورحمة الله وبركاته . قال الراوي : فسألت الامام: ما ثواب من صلى على النبي هكذا؟ فقال الصادق (عليه السلام): ثوابه الخروج من معاصيه وسيناته، اي انه يتطهر منها كمن ولد من أمه.

"The person who narrated this tradition asked Imām as-Sādiq (ع): 'How should we bless Muhammed and his progeny?' The Imām (ع) said, 'You should say: Blessings of Allāh, of His angels, prophets and messengers and all creation be with Muhammed and the progeny of Muhammed; greeting upon him and upon them, the mercy of Allāh and His blessing.' The narrator said, 'I asked the Imām (ع): What is the reward of one who thus blesses the Prophet (ص)? The Imām (ع) said: Its reward is one coming out of his transgressions and sins, that is, he will be purged of them as though he has just been born." On p. 443, Vol. 4 of the *Tafsir* book by Sheikh Abū al-Fitooh ar-Razi, we read the following text:

روى الشيخ أبو الفتوح الرازي عن رسول الله (صلى الله عليه و آله و سلم) أنه قال: في ليلة المعراج، عندما وصلت الى السماء، رأيت ملكا له ألف يد، وفي كل يد ألف إصبع، كان يعد بأصابعه. فسألت جبرائيل عن إسمه و وظيفته وعمله، فقال: إنه ملك موكل على عد قطرات المطر النازلة الى الأرض. فسألت الملك: هل تعلم عدد قطرات المطر الساقطة

على الأرض منذ أن خلق الله تعالى الأرض؟ فاجاب الملك قائلا: يا رسول الله (صلى الله عليه و آله و سلم)، و الذي بعثك بالحق نبيا الى الخلائق، إني لأعلم عدد قطرات المطر النازلة من السماء الى الأرض عامة، كما أعلم الساقطة في البحار والقفار والمعمورة والمزروعة و الأرض السبخة والمقابر. قال النبي (صلى الله عليه و آله و سلم): فتعجبت من ذكائه وذاكرته في الحساب. فقال الملك: يا رسول الله (صلى الله عليه و آله و سلم)، ولكني بما لدي من الأيدي والأصابع وما عندي من الذاكرة والذكاء، فاني أعجز من عد أمر واحد. فقلت له: وما ذاك الامر؟ قال: اذا اجتمع عدد من أفراد أمتك في محفل وذكروا اسمك فصلوا عليك، فحينذاك أعجز عن حفظ ما لهؤلاء من الأجر والثواب إزاء صلواتهم عليك.

Sheikh Abū al-Fitooh ar-Razi has quoted the Messenger of Allāh, peace and salutation of Allāh be with him and his progeny, saying, "In the Ascension Night, when I reached the heavens, I saw an angel having a thousand hands. In each hand he had a thousand fingers. He was counting with his fingers. I asked Gabriel about his name, function and job. Gabriel said, 'He is an angel in charge of counting the drops of water that fall to the ground.' I asked the angel, 'Do you [really] know the number of rain drops that fall on the earth since Allāh Almighty created the earth?' The angel answered saying, 'O Messenger of Allāh (peace and salutation of Allāh be with him and his progeny), by the One Who sent you in truth as a Prophet to the creation, I know the number of the rain drops that fall from the sky to the earth, all of it. I also know those that fall in the seas, on the deserts, on inhabited areas, on farms, on salty land and on the grave sites.' The Prophet (peace and salutation of Allāh be with him and his progeny) said, 'I was amazed at his intelligence and memory in calculation.' The angel, therefore, said, 'O Messenger of Allāh (peace and salutation of Allāh be with him and his progeny), but despite all the hands, fingers, memory and intelligence, I am unable to count one thing.' I said to him, 'What is it?' He said, 'If some members of your nation gather together, mention your name and bless you, it is then that I am unable to calculate how many rewards they will receive for having blessed you.'" Also, al-Kulayni, the mentor, articulated the following after having performed the prayers ritual in the afternoon of a Friday:

روى الشيخ الكليني ذيل صلوات عصر الجمعة: اللهم صلي على محمد وآل محمد الأوصياء المرضيين بأفضل صلواتك وبارك عليهم بأفضل بركاتك، والسلام عليه وعليهم

و رحمة الله وبركاته. إنه من قرأ هذه الصلوات سبع مرات، فإن الله يرد عليه بعدد كل عبد حسنة، وعمله مقبول يوم القيامة، ويأتي يوم القيامة و بين عينيه نور.

Lord! Send Your peace upon Muhammed and the progeny of Muhammed, the *wasis*, the pleased ones, bless them with the best of Your blessings, peace be with him and with them, the mercy of Allāh and His blessings. Anyone who recites this supplication seven times will be rewarded by Allāh with rewards the number of which equals that of all of His servants; his good deeds will be accepted on the Judgment Day, and he will come out on the Judgment Day with *noor* (celestial light) shining between his eyes." On p. 49, Vol. 2 of *Safeenat al-Bihar*, we read the following text:

روي أنه من قال بعد صلاة الصبح والظهر: اللهم صلي على محمد وآله وعجل فرجهم واحشرنا معهم وارزقنا شفاعتهم، فانه لا يموت الا و مدرك القائم من آل محمد (عليهم السلام)

"One who recites the following after the morning and afternoon prayers will not die before seeing al-Qā'im [al-Mahdi عج] from among the progeny of Muhammed, peace be with them: 'Lord! Bless Muhammed and his progeny, speed up their ease, gather us in their company and grant us their intercession.'"

9)   *Al-Hisab* الحساب **The Reckoning**: It is one of the most terrifying of all phases/stages of the hereafter, so much so that the hereafter is often referred to, as a whole, as "the Day of Reckoning". Numerous verses in the Holy Qur'an refer to it, emphasizing its significance and urging the faithful to prepare themselves for it with good deeds and acts of adoration, the latter cannot be accepted if the former are not. Some of the verses which refer to reckoning and to the fact that people take it lightly are these:

بسم الله الرحمن الرحيم. اقْتَرَبَ لِلنَّاسِ حِسَابُهُمْ وَهُمْ فِي غَفْلَةٍ مُّعْرِضُونَ، مَا يَأْتِيهِم مِّن ذِكْرٍ مِّن رَّبِّهِم مُّحْدَثٍ إِلاَّ اسْتَمَعُوهُ وَهُمْ يَلْعَبُونَ، لاهِيَةً قُلُوبُهُمْ وَأَسَرُّواْ النَّجْوَى الَّذِينَ ظَلَمُواْ: هَلْ هَذَا إِلاَّ بَشَرٌ مَّثْلُكُمْ؟ أَفَتَأْتُونَ السِّحْرَ وَأَنتُمْ تُبْصِرُونَ؟ قَالَ رَبِّي يَعْلَمُ الْقَوْلَ فِي السَّمَاء وَالأَرْضِ وَهُوَ السَّمِيعُ الْعَلِيمُ، بَلْ قَالُواْ أَضْغَاثُ أَحْلامٍ، بَلِ افْتَرَاهُ، بَلْ هُوَ شَاعِرٌ، فَلْيَأْتِنَا بِآيَةٍ كَمَا أُرْسِلَ الأَوَّلُونَ: مَا آمَنَتْ قَبْلَهُم مِّن قَرْيَةٍ أَهْلَكْنَاهَا، أَفَهُمْ يُؤْمِنُونَ؟

"In the name of Allāh, the Most Gracious, the Most Merciful. Mankind's reckoning comes closer and closer: Yet they do not heed, and they turn away. (Nothing) ever comes to them of a renewed message from their Lord except that they listen to it as in jest, their hearts toying with trifles. The wrongdoers conceal their private counsels (saying), 'Is this more than a man like your own selves? Will you yield to witchcraft with your eyes open?' Say: 'My Lord knows (every) word (spoken) in the heavens and the earth: He is the One Who hears and knows (all things).' 'No,' they say, '(these are) medleys of dreams! No, he forged it! No, he is (but) a poet! Then let him bring us a Sign like the ones that were sent to (Prophets) of old!' (As for those) before them, not one of the populations which We destroyed believed: Will these believe?" (Qur'an, 21:1-6). Another reference is this:

وَكَأَيِّن مِّن قَرْيَةٍ عَتَتْ عَنْ أَمْرِ رَبِّهَا وَرُسُلِهِ فَحَاسَبْنَاهَا حِسَابًا شَدِيدًا وَعَذَّبْنَاهَا عَذَابًا نُّكْرًا، فَذَاقَتْ وَبَالَ أَمْرِهَا وَكَانَ عَاقِبَةُ أَمْرِهَا خُسْرًا: أَعَدَّ اللَّهُ لَهُمْ عَذَابًا شَدِيدًا فَاتَّقُوا اللَّهَ يَا أُولِي الأَلْبَابِ الَّذِينَ آمَنُوا قَدْ أَنزَلَ اللَّهُ إِلَيْكُمْ ذِكْرًا: رَّسُولا يَتْلُو عَلَيْكُمْ آيَاتِ اللَّهِ مُبَيِّنَاتٍ لِّيُخْرِجَ الَّذِينَ آمَنُوا وَعَمِلُوا الصَّالِحَاتِ مِنَ الظُّلُمَاتِ إِلَى النُّورِ، وَمَن يُؤْمِن بِاللَّهِ وَيَعْمَلْ صَالِحًا يُدْخِلْهُ جَنَّاتٍ تَجْرِي مِن تَحْتِهَا الأَنْهَارُ خَالِدِينَ فِيهَا أَبَدًا، قَدْ أَحْسَنَ اللَّهُ لَهُ رِزْقًا

How many generations that insolently opposed their Lord's command and (that) of His Prophets did We call to account, to a severe account? And We imposed on them an exemplary punishment. Then they tasted the evil result of their conduct, and the end of their conduct was perdition. Allāh has prepared a severe punishment for them (in the hereafter). So fear Allāh, O you men of understanding who have believed, for Allāh has indeed sent down a message for you, a Prophet who rehearses God's Signs to you, containing clear explanations, so that he may lead forth those who believe and do righteous deeds from the depths of darkness into the light. And those who believe in Allāh and do righteous deeds He will admit into gardens beneath which rivers flow to dwell therein forever: Allāh has indeed granted a most excellent provision for them" (Qur'an, 65:8-11). Just as there are numerous references to reckoning in the Holy Qur'an, there are also numerous references to it in the Sunna of the Prophet (ص): Many traditions warn the believers about its woes and perils. On p. 258, Vol. 7 of Bihār al-Anwār, we read the following:

روى الشيخ الصدوق (رحمة الله عليه) عن طريق أهل البيت (عليهم السلام) أنه قال رسول الله (صلى الله عليه و آله و سلم): لا تتحرك قدما عبد من عباد الله، إلا و أن يسأل عن أربعه: عن عمره فيم أفناه، و عن شبابه فيم قضاه، و عن ماله من أين وجده، و فيم صرفه، و عن محبتنا نحن أهل البيت

Sheikh as-Sadūq (may Allāh have mercy on him) has narrated through the path of Ahl al-Bayt (peace be with them) saying that the Messenger of Allāh (peace and salutation of Allāh be with him and his progeny) said: "The feet of a servant of Allāh do not move before he is asked about four things: his lifespan and how he spent it, his youth and what he did during it, his wealth and where he found it and how he spent it and about love for us, we Ahl al-Bayt (ع)." On p. 267 of the same reference, we read the following:

روى الشيخ الطوسي (رحمة الله عليه) عن الامام الباقر (عليه السلام أنه قال: أول ما يحاسب عنه العبد الصلاة، إن قبلت قبل ما سواها

Sheikh at-Tusi (may Allāh have mercy on him) has narrated from Imām al-Bāqir (peace be with him) saying: "The first thing about which a servant of Allāh is questioned is prayer. If it is accepted, everything else is accepted." On p. 274 of the same reference, we read the following:

روى الشيخ الصدوق أن الدائن يأتي يوم القيامة و يشتكي، فاذا كان للمدين حسنات، تؤخذ منه للدائن، و ان لم تكن له حسنات، فتؤخذ من معاصي الدائن و تضاف الى معاصي المدين.

"Sheikh as-Sadūq has narrated saying that the creditor comes on the Judgment Day and complains. If the borrower has good deeds, they (some of them if not all) will be taken away and given to the creditor. But if he has no good deeds, some of the sins of the creditor will be taken and added to those of the borrower." On p. 82 of *Manazil al-Akhira*, we read the following:

إعلم أن بعض المحققين قد قال: لا ينجو من مخاطر الحساب و دقائق الميزان إلا من حاسب نفسه في الدنيا و آختبر شخصه بميزان الشرع الاسلامي و كذلك أعماله و أقواله و أفعاله و سيئاته و لحظاته و حركاته و سكناته، فقد قالوا: حاسبوا أنفسكم قبل أن تحاسبوا

"Be informed that some critics have said: Nobody is spared the perils of reckoning and the precisions of the scales except one who holds himself to account in the short life and tests his person according to the scales of the Islamic *Shari`a*, applying the same to his actions, statements, deeds, sins, looks, motion and stillness, for they have said: Hold yourselves to account before you yourselves are held to account."

10) تسليم صحيفة الأعمال *Tasleem Safeet al-A`mal*: **Delivering the Book of Deeds:** It is one of the terrifying phases of the Judgment Day when the list of deeds is delivered to the one it belongs to. The Almighty has made a number of references to this book of deeds; here are some of them: وَإِذَا الصُّحُفُ نُشِرَتْ، "When the scrolls are laid open" (Qur'an, 81:10); and also these verses:

فَأَمَّا مَنْ أُوتِيَ كِتَابَهُ بِيَمِينِهِ فَسَوْفَ يُحَاسَبُ حِسَابًا يَسِيرًا وَيَنْقَلِبُ إِلَى أَهْلِهِ مَسْرُورًا، وَأَمَّا مَنْ أُوتِيَ كِتَابَهُ وَرَاءَ ظَهْرِهِ فَسَوْفَ يَدْعُو ثُبُورًا وَيَصْلَى سَعِيرًا

"He who is given his book in his right hand, soon his account will be taken by an easy reckoning, and he will turn to his people, rejoicing! But whoever is given His record behind his back, He will soon cry for perdition, and he will enter a blazing Fire" (Qur'an, 84:7-12). On p. 314, Vol. 7 of *Bihār al-Anwār*, al-Ayyashi quotes Imām as-Sādiq (ع) saying:

إذا قامت القيامة، تعطى لكل واحد قائمة أعماله و يقال له: إقرأ، و يذكره الله جميع أعماله بالنظر إلى تلك الصحيفة، و كذلك جميع أقواله، و خطواته و غيرها و كأنه قالها و فعلها و خطاها في الحال، فيقولون: "يا ويلتنا، ما لهذا الكتاب لا يغادر صغيرة و لا كبيرة إلا أحصاها"؟"

When it is Judgment Day, everyone will be handed over his list of deeds, and it will be said to him, 'Read!' Allāh will remind him of all his deeds through looking at this tablet, and the same applies to his statements, steps and everything else, as if he said, did or treaded them instantly. People will say, 'Woe unto us! Why does this book not leave out the recording of anything, be it small or big?!'" (Qur'an, 18:49). Ibn Qawlawayh has quoted Imām as-Sādiq (ع) as saying:

من زار قبر الحسين (عليه السلام) في شهر رمضان و مات في سفر زيارته للحسين (عليه السلام)، فلا يتعرض لأمر أو حساب و يقال له: أدخل الجنة لا خوف عليك

"If one visits the gravesite of Imām al-Hussain (ع) during the month of Ramadan and dies during his trip to visit al-Hussain (ع), he will not be exposed to anything, nor will he be held to account, and it will be said to him, "Enter Paradise, you shall not fear." `Allama al-Majlisi, may Allāh have mercy on him, has quoted Imām ar-Ridha (ع) through two reliable *isnads* as saying:

من زارني على بعد قبري، أتيته في مواطن ثلاثة: يوم القيامة لأنقذه من أهوالها، و عند تطاير كتب المحسنين إلى يمينهم، و صحائف المجرمين إلى شمائلهم، و على الصراط، و على الميزان

"If one comes from a distance to visit my gravesite, I shall go to him on three occasions: on the Judgment Day to save him from its woes, when the books of the doers of good are flown to their right hands, when the tablets of the criminals are flown to their left, on the Sirat [path between Paradise and Hell] and at the Mizan (scales of deeds)." In the book titled *Al-Haqq al-Yaqeen* الحق اليقين, it is indicated that al-Hussain ibn Sa'eed has quoted Imām as-Sādiq (ع) as having said:

إذا أراد الله أن يحاسب مؤمنا، أعطاه كتابه بيمينه، و يحاسبه فيما بينه و بينه دون أن يطلع على حسابه أحد، و يقول له: عبدي، لقد فعلت كذا و كذا، فيجيب العبد: إلهي، لقد فعلته. و يقول الله تعالى: غفرت لك و بدلته إلى حسنات. فيقول الناس: سبحان الله! إن هذا العبد لم يقترف ذنبا، و لم يرتكب قبيحا، و هذا معنى قوله تعالى: " فَأَمَّا مَنْ أُوتِيَ كِتَابَهُ بِيَمِينِهِ فَسَوْفَ يُحَاسَبُ حِسَابًا يَسِيرًا وَيَنقَلِبُ إِلَى أَهْلِهِ مَسْرُورًا" (الإنشقاق، 7-9) . فسأل الراوي: أي أهل يقصد بهذا الأهل؟ هل يصحب المؤمن من أهله الذين كانوا معه في الدنيا؟ قال الصادق (ع): إذا أراد الله بعبد سوءا حاسبه جهرا أمام الخلائق و أتم عليه حجته و أعطاه كتابه إلى شماله، كما قال الله تعالى: " وَأَمَّا مَنْ أُوتِيَ كِتَابَهُ وَرَاء ظَهْرِهِ فَسَوْفَ يَدْعُو ثُبُورًا وَيَصْلَى سَعِيرًا، إِنَّهُ كَانَ فِي أَهْلِهِ مَسْرُورًا " – يعني في الدنيا—، " إِنَّهُ ظَنَّ أَن لَّن يَحُورَ" يعني أنه لن يعود — و هذا يشير إلى أن أيدي الكفار و المنافقين تغل و تقيد و تسلم صحائفهم إلى شمالهم، و إلى هاتين الحالتين أشير في أدعية الوضوء عند غسل اليدين: "اللهم أعطني كتابي بيميني و خلودي في الجنه بشمالي، و حاسبني حسابا يسيرا، و لا تعطني كتابي عن شمالي و لا وراء ظهري، و لا تغل يدي إلى عنقي".

"If Allāh wants to hold a believer to account, he gives him his book [of deeds] in his right hand and judges him between Himself and the believer without anyone seeing it. He will then say to him, 'My servant! You have done this and that.' The servant will say, 'Lord, I have done it.' Allāh Almighty will say, 'I have forgiven you and change it into good deeds.' People will say, 'Blessed be Allāh! This servant of Allāh did not commit a sin, nor did he do anything contemptible!' This is the meaning of the verse of the Almighty: Then whoever is given his record in his right hand, soon his account will be taken by an easy reckoning, and he will turn to his people, rejoicing!' (Qur'an, 84:7-9). The narrator asked, 'What is meant by *his people* (his family)? Does the believer accompany his folks who used to be with him in this life?' Imām as-Sādiq (ع) said, 'If Allāh wants something bad to afflict His servant [on account of the latter's deeds], He will try him before all creations, complete His argument against him then gives him his book in his left hand as Allāh Almighty has said: Truly he thought that he would not have to return (to Us)!' (Qur'an, 84:14). This points towards the hands of the unbelievers and hypocrites being tied and chained and their tablets delivered on their left side. It is to both these conditions that the supplications related to ablution refer: 'Lord! Give me my book in my right hand and my eternity in Paradise on my left; do judge me easily and do not give me my book on my left or behind my back, and do not tie my hands to my neck."

11) *As-Sirat al-Mustaqeem* الصراط المستقيم **The Straight Path** is also one of the most terrifying phases/stages of the Hereafter if not the very most. It is described in both Holy Qur'an and authentic Sunna in numerous verses and traditions (أحاديث) due to its significance, so much so that the faithful are reminded of it ten times a day in their obligatory daily prayers and in all optional ones (نوافل) when they recite Sūrat al-Fātiha, the Opening Chapter to the Book of Allāh, the Qur'an. Following is a good deal of more information about this Sirat; so, keep reading.

On pp. 103-105, Vol. 46 of *Bihār al-Anwār*, we read detailed descriptions of this Sirat, and additional text is indicated on pp. 69-71 of the same reference. Here is some of the text on the latter pages:

584

هو جسر ممدود على جهنم، لا يدخل الجنـة إلا مـن اجتـازه. و جـاء فـي الروايـات أنـه أدق
من الشعرة و أحد من السيف و أصلى من النار. يعبره خـالص المؤمنين كالبرق الخـاطف،
و بعضهم يعبره بصعوبة لكنه يجتازه و ينجو بنفسه. و بعض المـارة يسقطون فـي جهنم
من بعض عقبات الصراط. و هو نموذج من صراط الدنيا المستقبـل حيث الدين الحق و
طـريق الولايـة، و متابعـة أميـر المـؤمنين و ذريتـه الأئمـة الطـاهرين (صلوات الله عليهم
أجمعين)، فمن مال عن هذا الصراط الدنيوي و عدل عنـه إلى الباطل قـولا أو عمـلا، فقد
ارتجف من عقبة صراط الآخرة و سقط الى الجحيم، و الصراط المستقيم الـذي تجده فـي
سورة الحمد في القرآن الكريم يشير إلى صراط الدنيا و صراط الآخرة كليهما.

"It is a bridge extended over Hell: Nobody enters Paradise without
successfully passing over it. Traditions indicate that it is thinner than
hair, sharper than the sword and hotter than fire. Sincere believers
cross over it like lightning that snatches the eyes. Some of them pass
over it with difficulty but they pass it and are thus saved, whereas
others fall into Hell from one of the obstacles on this Sirat. It is a
sort of this life's *As-Sirat al-Mustaqeem* where true faith, the path of
the *wilaya* ولاية, is to follow in the footsteps of the Commander of
the Faithful and the Purified Imāms (peace of Allāh be with all of
them): Anyone who swerves from this worldly path and leans
towards falsehood by speech or by action, the obstacle of the
Hereafter's Sirat will shake under his feet, causing him to fall into
hell. *As-Sirat Al-Mustaqeem* which you find in Sūrat al-Hamd in the
Holy Qur'an points out to both Sirats: the one in this life and the one
in the hereafter."

In his book titled *Al-Haqq Al-Yaqeen* الحق اليقين , where he quotes *Al-
`Aqa'id* العقائد by Sheikh as-Sadūq, may Allāh have mercy on his
soul, al-Majlisi states the following:

إننا نعتقد أن كل عقبـة مـن العقبـات التـي تعترض سبيل المحشر هو إسم لفريضة مـن
الفرائض—الأوامر و النـواهي—فـإذا وصل الإنسان الى عقبة مسماة بإسم فريضة، و
كـان مقصرا فـي ذلك الواجب، اوقف فـي تلك العقبـة و طلب منـه تأديـة حق الله تعـالى
بالنسبة لذلك الواجب. فإن إستطاع الخروج من تلك العقبة بالأعمال الصالحة التي قدمها،
أو برحمة من الله تشمله، فقد خرج و اجتاز تلك العقبـة بالـذات، و مدة التوقيف فـي كل
عقبة ألف سنة، و تتوالى العقبات، و تتواصل التوقيفات و تنهال الأسئلة و الإستنطاق
عما يعود إلى مسمى إسم تلك العقبة من الواجب و الفريضة، حتى إذا أجاب عن جميع مـا
عليه بما يجب من حسن الإجابة، إنتهى من العقبـة الأخيرة إلى دار البقاء و سرح سـراحا
جميلا، و يحيى حياة خالـدة لا موت فيها و لا بـوار، و يسعد سعادة لا شقاء فيها و لا

دمـار، و يسكن إلـى جـوار رحمـة ربـه مـع النبيـين و الحجـج و الـصديقين و الـشفعاء و
الصالحين و حسن أولئك رفيقا. أما إذا استجوب في عقبـة مـن العقبـات، و طلب منـه حق
قصر فـي تأديتـه فـي الدنيا، و لم يقدم عملا صالحا يكافىء ذلك التقصير، و لا تدركه رحمـة
من الله تعالى لينجو من تلك العقبة، فتزل قدمه في تلك العقبة و يسقط منهـا إلى الهاويـة و
الجحيم، و نعوذ بالله من ذلك الأمر. و جميع هذه العقبـات علـى الـصراط،، تسمى واحده
منها الولاية، يتوقف فيهـا جميع الخلائق، فيـسأل عـن ولايـة أميـر المـؤمنين علـي بـن أبـي
طالب و الأئمة الطاهرين من بعده، فإذا كان قـد أتاهـا و إتبعهـا فقـد نجـا و اجتـاز هـذه العقبـة،
و إلا فقد هوى إلى الجحيم. قال تعالى: "وَقِفُوهُمْ إِنَّهُم مَّسْئُولُونَ" (الصافات: آيه 24)، و
أهم العقبـات هـي المرصـاد: "إِنَّ رَبَّكَ لَبِالْمِرْصَادِ" (الفجـر: آيـة 14). يقول الله تعـالى:
بعزتـي و جلالـي لا يفـوتني ظلـم ظـالم. و تـسمى عقبـة أخـرى بعقبـة الـرحم، و أخـرى
بالأمانة، و أخرى بالصلاة، و هكذا فـ‍إن لكل فريضة أو أمر من أوامر الله، أو نهـي مـن
نواهيه، يقف المرء ليجيب عما هو مسؤول عنه.

"We believe that each of the obstacles along the path to the
Gathering represents the name of one of the obligations, i.e. what the
Almighty has commanded or prohibited. If someone reaches an
obstacle bearing the name of an obligation, and if he had fallen short
of performing that obligation, he will be stopped at it and will be
required to pay what he owes Allāh Almighty. If he can get out of
that obstacle through the good deeds which he had done, or there
may be mercy from Allāh which will include him, he will get out
and pass that particular obstacle. The time period of keeping anyone
at each of these obstacles is a thousand years. The obstacles
continue, following each other; questions go on and arguments are
pursued about what each station represents: the obligations and the
commandments. If one answers duly, he will pass by the last station
to the abode of eternity and will be released most beautifully: He
will live a perpetual life where there is neither death nor loss, and he
will taste happiness where there is neither misery nor destruction. He
will live beside the mercy of his Lord with the prophets, the Signs of
Allāh, the Truthful Ones, the ones who can intercede on behalf of
others, the righteous ones whose company is truly the very best. But
if he is asked at one of the obstacles and required to make up for
falling short of performing it during his lifetime, if he did not offer
an act of righteousness to make up for that shortcoming, and if he is
not saved through mercy from Allāh Almighty that rescues him from
that obstacle, his feet will slip in that area and he will fall from it
into the abyss and into Hell, we seek refuge with Allāh against this.
All these obstacles are on the Sirat. One of them is called the *wilayat*

(mastership of or loyalty to the Imāms from among the Ahl al-Bayt (ع)): All people will be stopped at it and asked about the *wilayat* of the Commander of the Faithful Ali ibn Abū Talib and the Pure Imāms after him (ع). If one was observing this *wilayat*, adhering to it, he will pass this obstacle; otherwise, he will fall into Hell. Allāh Almighty has said وَقِفُوهُمْ إِنَّهُم مَّسْئُولُونَ "But stop them, for they must be asked" (Qur'an, 37:24). And the most important of these obstacles is the Mirsad: إِنَّ رَبَّكَ لَبِالْمِرْصَادِ "For your Lord is (as a Guardian) on a watch-tower" (Qur'an, 89:14). Allāh Almighty says: بعزتي و جلالي لا يفوتني ظلم ظالم "By My Honor and Greatness (do I swear) that no oppression committed by an oppressor escapes My knowledge." Another obstacle is called the kinship obstacle. Another is called *amana* أمانة, trust (something entrusted for safe keep to someone), another is called *salat* صلاة, prayer, and so on:

لكل فريضه من الفرائض—الأوامر و النواهي—يوقف العبد عندها ليجيب عما هو مسؤول عنه

Each obligation—what is commanded and what is prohibitive—has an obstacle at which the servant of Allāh is stopped to answer about his responsibility towards it."

On p. 65, Vol. 8 of *Bihār al-Anwār*, we read the following:

فترى الناس على الصراط يسقطون كالفراش المبثوث، و ترى آخرين قد تعلقوا بأيديهم أو بيد واحده أو بأرجلهم و هم يمسكون خوفا من الهبوط و الملائكة حولهم واقفون يدعون و ينادون: أيها الرب الحليم، اغفر لهؤلاء و اعف عن هؤلاء بفضلك و جودك، و سلمهم ليجاوزوا الصراط و يقطعوا الصراط. فمن اجتاز الصراط برحمة الله الواسعة، قال: الحمد لله، و بنعمة الله تتم صالحات الأعمال، و تنمو الحسنات، و أحمد الله الذي نجاني منك بفضله و منه، بعد أن كنت قد يئست، ان ربنا لأعمال العباد لغفور شكور

"So you would see people on the Sirat falling like scattered butterflies while others are holding to it with their hands or feet or even with one foot fearing they would fall down as the angels around them stand, call upon the Almighty and plead to Him saying: 'O Clement Lord! Forgive these people, overlook them through Your favor and generosity, let them safely pass on the Path and cross it.' Whoever passes the Path does so through wide mercy from Allāh and says, 'Praise to Allāh and through a blessing from Allāh that good deeds are sealed and blessed actions grow, and I praise Allāh Who saved me from you through His favor and boon after I had lost all hope; surely our Lord forgives the servants' [sinful] deeds, appreciative [of good deeds]'." On p. 410, Vol. 22 of the same reference, we are also told that the great *sahabi* Abū Tharr al-Ghifāri (رض) has cited the Messenger of Allāh (ص) saying:

الـرحم و الأمانـه عـلى طرفـي الـصراط، فمـن وصـل الـرحم و أدى الأمانـة، سـار عـلى الصراط، فإن طرفي الصراط يحفظانه من السقوط و الهبوط في النار

"Kinship and trust are at both ends of the Path: Whoever maintains good relations with his kinsfolk and returns the trust safely will pass over the Path, for both ends of the Path shall protect him against falling into the Fire." In another narrative, Imām al-Bāqir (ع) said:

إذا ورد قاطع الرحم و خـائن الأمانـة الصراط، فإن أعمالـه الحسنة لا تنفعه مـا دامت لـه هاتان الخصلتان و تسقطانه في النار

"If one who severed his ties and betrayed the trust reaches the Path, his good deeds will not avail him so long as both these characteristics were in him, and they will cause him to fall into the Fire (of hell)."

May the Almighty have mercy on us in this life and the life to come and enable us to keep our feet firm on His الصراط المستقيم Straight Path and admit us into His Paradise, *Allāhomma Āmeen* اللهم آمين.

أعمـال لتسهيل المـرور على الصراط: Good deeds that make the passage on the Sirāt easy:

According to p. 639 of the book إقبال الأعمال *Iqbāl al-A'mā* by Ibn Tawoos, one who offers 21 *rek'as* after the sunset prayers in the eve of the first of the month of Rajab in each *rek'a* of which he recites both Sūrat al-Hamd (Chapter 1) and Sūrat at-Tawhīd (Chapter 112), then he recites the *tasleem* after each couple of prostrations will be protected by the Almighty, and his family, wealth and children will be protected, too, and he will be granted security from the torment in the grave. Moreover, he will pass over the Sirat without any questioning like lightning.

من صلَّى أول ليلة من شـهر رجب بعد صلاة المغرب عشرين ركعة بالحمد والتوحيد ، ويسلم بين كل ركعتين ليحفظ في نفسه وأهله وماله وولده، وأجير من عذاب القبر، وجاز على الصراط كالبرق الخاطف.

2. On p. 136 of *Thawab al-A`mal*, we are told that one who fasts six days during the month of Rajab will be secure on the Day of Reckoning and will pass over the Sirat without being asked any questions.

من صام من رجب ستة أيّام ... بعث من الآمنين يوم القيامة حتّى يمرّ على الصراط بغير حساب.

3. Ibn Tawoos also narrates that one who performs ten *rek'as* during the 29th eve of the month of Sha'ban, reciting in each rek'a Sūrat al-Hamd once and at-Takathur (Chapter 102) ten times, in addition to both Chapter 113 and Chapter 114 ten times each and Sūrat at-Tawhid (Chapter 112), he will be granted by the Almighty rewards of those who exert their utmost in learning the creed and in teaching it, making his scale of good deeds heavier and easing for him to pass over the Sirat like lightning.

مَن صلَّى في الليلة التاسعة والعشرين من شعبان عشر ركعات يقرأ في كل ركعة فاتحة الكتاب مرّة وألهاكم التكاثر عشر مرّات ، والمعوذتين عشر مرّات، وقل هو الله أحد عشر مرّات، أعطاه الله تعالى ثواب المجتهدين، وثقل ميزانه، ويخفف عنه الحساب، ويمرّ على الصراط كالبرق الخاطف.

4.   On p. 102, Vol. 34 of *Bihār al-Anwār*, we are told that one who performs the *ziyara* of Imām ar-Ridha (ع) despite his grave being so far, the Imām will visit him at three places on the Judgment Day in order to save him from their horrors, and one of these horrors is the Sirat.

من زار الامام الرضا عليه السَّلام على بعد قبره الشريف، فانّه يأتي عنده يوم القيامة في ثلاثة مواطن ليخلصه من أهوالها ، وانّ أحدها عند الصراط .

What will happen after all of these phases/stages? The answer is very simple: One will be led either to eternal happiness in Paradise or to damnation in hell. And surely Allāh knows best.

Marji` taqlid مرجع تقليد: the highest theological authority-referee followed

Marwa or Marwah مروه: a mound near the Ka'ba referred to in the Qur'an as a place one of Islam's rites, the *sa`i* between the Safa and the Marwa, is performed 7 times during the pilgrimage or the `umra

Masjid مسجد: a place of worship, a mosque, where people can perform the *salat* rite. The life of the early Muslims used to revolve around the *masjid*. Meetings were held there and discussions took place.

Mash `ar مشعر: a place where certain rites are conducted, a sacred area or place or precinct

Ma`soom معصوم: infallible, divinely protected against sinning

Mawla مولى: It is a word with dual meaning: Depending on its usage, it may mean either "master" or "slave," or it may mean one who is most fit for a specific position of honor and prestige. Derived from the adjective *awla* (one who is best qualified), it denotes the person who is best suited to be the religious and/or temporal leader of the Muslims. It also means a person/slave who does not have tribal protection.

Mawlaya مولاي!: a form of address to a ruler who is referred to as the protector

Mihrab محراب: a recess/area in the *masjid*, mosque that indicates the direction of the Qibla

Mina or Minaa منى: a plain within the limits of the *haram*, precincts, of Mecca, about five kilometers outside the city limits. During the *hajj*, the pilgrims pass the night between the eighth and ninth day before proceeding to Arafat on the ninth day.

Minbar منبر: pulpit, podium

Mi`raj معراج: Prophet's ascension from Jerusalem to the heavens

Mithqal مثقال: a weight equivalent to 24 karats or 4.68 grams

Mu'adh-dhin or Muaththin مؤذن: the person who calls the *athan*, the call for prayers

Mufassir مفسر: theologian who is well-versed in the exegesis of the Holy Qur'an and is capable of interpreting its verses

Mufti مفتي: a judge who enjoys the power to issue binding legal opinions relevant to the Islamic faith

Muhaddith محدث: traditionist, one who tracks and quotes statements of Prophet Muhammed (ص)

Muhajir مهاجر: person who undergoes *hijra*, migration

Mujahid مجاهد : one who practices *jihad* (se *jihad* above), someone who is active and who struggles for the dignity and honor of Islam, a Muslim struggler

Mujtahid مجتهد: one who acquires the degree of *ijtihad* and thus becomes capable of deriving religious decisions/verdicts on his own

Mu'min مؤمن: believer, one who has *iman*, conviction, true belief, a person who has deep faith in Allāh and is a righteous and obedient servant of His

Munafiq منافق: hypocrite, one whose external appearance is Islamic (with regard to performing the rituals or to promoting the creed) but whose inner reality conceals *kufr*—often unknown to the persons themselves. (See Al-Baqarah, verses 8-23). A *munafiq* is more dangerous to the society and the religion and worse than a *kafir*: plural: *munafiqun*, hypocrites; refer to Ch. 63 of the Holy Qur'an titled al-Munafiqoon المنافقون, the hypocrites, which refers to interest-seekers and loafers from among the *sahāba*, companions,

591

who used to hang around the Prophet not out of their love for Islam (ص) but for other un-Islamic reasons of their own.

Murabit مرابط: a person who disseminates and propagates for the Islamic creed

Mustad'afin or Mustad`afun or Mustad`afoon: مـستظعفين أو مستظعفون a downtrodden, weak and oppressed person

Mushaf مصحف: a book, a sacred book, usually refers to a copy of the Qur'an but linguistically it refers to any book; a book manuscript (*Mushaf Fatima*, the very first book written in Islam; it contained some traditions of the Prophet (ص), narratives about some important contemporary incidents, explanations of some verses of the Holy Qur'an and other very interesting and valuable information; it seems that this great book was lost; it must not be confused with the Holy Qur'an simply because it is not) on which the names of all the succeeding Imāms were written down; three of them were named Muhammed and four were named Ali, all being her offspring, and the last was named al-Qā'im (عج) القائم. Fatima's Mushaf مصحف فاطمـة must not be confused with the Holy Qur'an. It is not a Qur'an; refer to what is stated about Fatima (ع) daughter of the Prophet (ص) above for details.

Mushawarah مشاوره: consultation, consulting

Mushrik مـشرك: polytheist, a person who ascribes partners to Allāh or believes in the existence of many gods

Musnad مـسند: compilation of traditions (*ahadīth*) which are consecutively and chronologically traced back to their transmitters

Mutawatir متـواتر: consecutively reported, traced by a perfect chronological chain of ascertained narrators of *hadīth*

Mu'aththin مؤذن: caller to prayers (usually at a mosque)

Mut`a متعة: literally it means: enjoyment; temporary marriage; refer to verse 24 of Chapter 4 (an-Nisaa) of the Holy Qur'an:

$$\text{فَمَا اسْتَمْتَعْتُمْ بِهِ مِنْهُنَّ فَآتُوهُنَّ أُجُورَهُنَّ فَرِيضَةً}$$

where the root word for it is: اسْتَمْتَعْتُمْ, that is, "you enjoyed". Temporary marriage existed during the time of the Prophet (ص), of first caliph Abū Bakr and part of second caliph, Omer ibn al-Khattab who, because of a certain incident, banned it although his son, the famous and highly respected narrator of *hadīth*, namely Abdullāh ibn Omer, kept practicing despite his father's prohibition. He is reported as having regarded *mut'a* as being Islamically permissible. Ahmed, *Musnad*, No. 2, p. 95; Ali ibn Abū Bakr al-Haithami, *Mujma' Az-Zawaaid*, Vol. 7, pp. 332-33; Sa'eed ibn Mansour, *Sunan*, Vol. 1, p. 252 and Abū Ya'li, *Musnad*, Vol. 10, p. 68 quote Abdullāh ibn Omer (son of caliph Omer ibn al-Khattab) saying, " (ص) و الله ما كنا على عهد رسول الله زانين و لا مسافحين By Allāh! During the time of the Messenger of Allāh (ص), we were neither adulterers nor fornicators." In two places of his Sahīh, al-Tirmithi indicates on p. 143, Vol. 3 and p. 175, Vol. 1, that a man from Syria asked Abdullāh ibn Omer about the *mut'a*. Ibn Omer said, "It is *halal* (lawful, permissible)." The man said, "But your father banned it." Ibn Omer said, أرأيت ان كان أبي "نهى عنها، و وضعها رسول الله، أنترك السنة و نتبع قول أبي؟! Do you see that if my father bans something which the Messenger of Allāh (ص) permitted, should we abandon the Sunna and follow what my father says?!" This statement is also quoted by imām Ahmed ibn Hanbal in his *Musnad* in three places: on p. 95 and 104 of Vol. 2 and p. 436, Vol. 4. Likewise, it is cited on p. 365, Vol. 2 of al-Qurtubi's *Tafsir* and on p. 21, Vol. 5 of al-Bayhaqi's *Sunan*. Also, refer to p. 185, Vol. 1 of *Mujma' al-Zawad* where it is quoted. Although all these references are reliable classic Sunni references, only Shī'ites now perform this marriage

The reader may think that only the renown renown of hadīth, Abdullāh son of second caliph Omer ibn al-Khattab, insisted on practicing the mut'a marriage, but a review of other classic Arabic books reveals contrariwise. Read the following as an example:

روى مسلم عن قتادة عن أبي نضرة قال: كان (عبد الله) ابن عباس يأمر بالمتعة و كان (عبد الله) ابن الزبير ينهى عنها، قال: فذكرت ذلك لجابر بن عبد الله (الأنصاري)، فقال: على يدي دار الحديث، تمتعنا مع رسول الله (ص) فلما قام عمر قال: ان الله كان يحل لرسوله ما شاء بما شاء، و ان القرآن قد نزل منازله فأتموا الحج و العمرة كما أمركم

الله عز و جل و اثبوا نكاح هذه النساء فلن أوتى برجل نكح امرأة الى أجل الا رجمته بالحجارة.

Muslim has narrated from Qatadah from Abū Nadhra saying that [Abdullāh] ibn Abbās enjoined the practice of *mut'a*, whereas [Abdullāh] ibn az-Zubair used to prohibit it. He said: I mentioned this to Jābir ibn Abdullāh [al-Ansāri]. He [Jābir] said, "I witnessed the talk. We practiced *mut'a* during the time of the Messenger of Allāh (ص). When Omer came to power, he said, "Allāh used to permit His Messenger whatever He willed however He willed. The Qur'an has reached its full stages, so you should complete the pilgrimage and the *umra* as Allāh, the most Exalted, the most Great, commanded you and keep away from cohabiting with these women, for I shall never be brought a man who cohabited with a woman for a set period of time without stoning him."

Refer to p. 206, Vol. 7 of al-Bayhaqi's *Sunan* where the author says that Muslim has quoted it in his *Sahīh* through other sources from Humam.

Mut'a marriage is never a substitute for the blessed institution of permanent marriage. As a matter of fact, top Shī'a *faqihs* and scholars caution the faithful about abusing this institute which provides a bitter pill for a much, much more bitter ailment. On p. 720, Vol. 2 of *Man la Yahdhuru al-Faqih* من لا يحضره الفقيه by *'allama* Shaikh al-Sadūq, the following is stated:

روى الحسن بن محبوب عن أبان عن أبي مريم عن أبي جعفر (ع) قال: انه سئل عن المتعة، فقال: ان المتعة اليوم ليست كما كانت قبل اليوم، انهن كن يؤمن يومئذ، فاليوم لا يؤمن فاسألوا عنهن.

"Al-Hassan ibn Mahbūb narrated from Aban from Abu Maryam who quotes (Imām) Abu (father of) Ja'far (al-Bāqir) (ع). He said that al-Bāqir was asked about the mut'a. He (Imām al-Bāqir) said, "Mut'a now is not what used to be. They (women) used to believe then; nowadays, they do not believe; so, ask about them.""

What the Imām (ع) means is that women used to be closer to the fountains of true Islamic knowledge, but nowadays they are not;

they are quite distant from them. This is why he recommended that one should inquire about a woman's Islamic conduct which reflects the depth of her *imān*, conviction, before considering marrying her for a pre-determined period of time. Imagine how the status of women has suffered, deteriorated, from the time of Imām al-Bāqir (ع) and till now!

On the same page of the reference cited above, we read the following about the founder of the Shī'a Ja'fari *fiqh*, namely Abu Abdullāh Imām Ja'far al-Sādiq (ع) also cautioning about getting involved in this type of marriage with women who are not famiłiar with its *ahkam*, rules and regulations:

روى داود بن اسحاق عن محمد بن الفيض قال: سألت أبا عبد الله(ع) عن المتعة فقال: نعم اذا كانت عارفة، قلت: جعلت فداك، فان لم تكن عارفة؟ قال: فاعرض عنها، و قل لها، فان قبلت فتزوجها، و ان أبت و لم ترض بقولك فدعها، و اياكم و الكواشف و الدواعي و البغايا و ذوات الأزواج، فقلت: ما الكواشف؟ فقال: اللواتي يكاشفن و بيوتهن معلومة و يؤتين، فقلت: فالدواعي؟ قال: اللواتي يدعون الى أنفسهن و قد عرفن بالفساد، قلت: فالبغايا؟ قال: المعروفات بالزنا، قلت: فذوات الأزواج؟ قال: المطلقات على غير السنة.

Dawūd ibn Ishāq narrated from Muhammed al-Faydh saying, "I asked (Imām) Abu Abdullāh (al-Sādiq) (ع) about the *mut'a*. He said, 'Yes, if she knows it.' I said, 'May I be sacrificed for your sake, what if she does not?' He said, "Then turn away from her and speak to her; if she accepts, marry her, but if she refuses and does not accept your statement, leave her alone. Beware of women who reveal themselves, who solicit, who are prostitutes and who practice polyandry.' I said, 'Who are those who reveal themselves?' He said, "They are those who reveal their ornaments and whose houses are well known (to the public), and they are visited (by stranger men).' I said, 'Who are the solicitors?' He said, 'They are the ones who try to attract others to themselves, and they are known to be corrupt.' I said, 'Who are the prostitutes?' He said, 'They are the ones known to be committing adultery.' I asked, 'Who are those who take many husbands?' He said, 'They are the ones whose divorces are not conducted according to the Sunna.'"

As you can see from this quotation, many categories of women must be excluded when one contemplates on getting married for an agreed about term. Nowadays, we see many married and single "solicitors" walking down streets with make-up, tight clothes and making suggestive gestures. It is one of the signs of the time, folks, the last period of time before the end of time, so beware.

Some Shī'a Muslims still practice *mut'a* marriage the rules, regulations, permissions and prohibitions, rights and obligations, etc. for which are available in *fiqh* books. They do so on a very limited basis, i.e. in rare situations. They do not encourage it except when there are legitimate reasons for it. For example, adult students who study in non-Muslim countries are prone to surrender to temptation, and many of them fall victims to temptation. Some businessmen stay abroad for extended periods of time. The sexual urge of both of these categories of strangers in foreign lands has to be met legitimately in both of these situations; it is not healthy to suppress this perfectly natural urge. Another situation is one who has no financial ability to bear the expenses of a permanent marriage. Temporary marriage must be dealt with as a bitter medicine for a much, much more bitter situation. On the other hand, some Sunnis, notably Shafi'is, seem to have found a number of almost similar types of marriage the most famous of which is زواج المسيار *misyar* (or *misyaar*) marriage, as well as marriage with the intention to divorce, coworker's marriage, etc. Have they found a verse in the Holy Qur'an similar to 4:24 or a tradition of the Prophet (ص) referring to *misyar* or other types of newly invented temporary marriages?

ن N

Nabi or Nebi, Nabee نبي: The meaning of the word Nabi is a prophet. To be a prophet he should receive a revelation from Allāh that does not necessarily mean a revealed book. When a prophet is instructed to deliver his message to a certain group of people, he is a messenger. It is stated in the Qur'an that there are no more prophets and messengers after Muhammed (ص).

Naddaf نداف: cotton carder, cotton teaser, one who works cotton into some usable form

Nafaqa نفقـة: maintainence expenses; *nafaqa* applies to the obligation of the husband towards the wife while they are married. *Alimony,* on the other hand, applies in the West to the "spousal support" which the ex-husband has to pay his divorced wife.

Nafl نفل: (also **Nafila نافلة)** optional, non-compulsory, supererog-atory, highly recommended act of worship; plural *nawafil*

Najasa نجاسه: uncleanness, impurity; adjective *najis*

Najwa نجوى: silent supplication, invocation, the time when one pleads silently to his Maker; recommended periods for such supplications are: evenings, before dawn, during times of trials and tribulations or when one is sick

Nasab نسب: lineage or genealogy

Nasiha or Naseehah نصيحه: sincere good advice

Nathr نذر: one's pledge to do something to show appreciation for the Almighty's favorable response to his supplication and the attainment of his worldly wish; plural: *nuthur*

Nikah نكاح: Islamic marriage

Nisab نصاب: amount of savings or capital or product a Muslim has so the payment of zakat becomes obligatory on him; it is also applied in courts where it means "legal quorum"

Nifas نفاس: period of a woman's pre-natal bleeding

Noor نور: divine or celestial light; Muslims believe that the angels are created of such *noor*. Human eyes cannot withstand the intensity of their light, so they are veiled by their Maker from being seen by humans. Humans will see the angels starting from the moment when the soul starts its journey out of the body and into the afterlife.

Nubuwwah نبوه: prophethood, the belief in prophets and their messages

P

P.B.U.H.
These acronyms refer to the phrase "Peace Be Upon/with Him" which mean in Arabic: "'*Alaihis Salam*" عليه السلام, an expression articulated when the name of a prophet is mentioned. This expression does not convey the meaning of "*Salla Allāhu 'Alaihi Wa Alihi wa Sallam*" صلى الله عليه وعلى الـه و سلم which means: Allāh blesses him and his family and sends them His greetings."

Q ق

Qadi or Qadhi قاضي: judge.

Qa`ideen or Qa`idoon قاعدين أو قاعدون: people who remain inactive and do not actively fight; the opposite of *mujahid*

Qaniteen or Qanitoon قانتون: those who constantly supplicate

Qanitun or Qanitoon قانطون: those who lose hope of the mercy of Allāh

Qard قرض: a loan given for a good cause in the name of Allāh, in hopes of repayment or reward in the Hereafter

Qari قاريء: someone who recites the Qur'an being knowledgeable of the rules of such recitation

Qayyim قيم: person in charge of something, one charged with authority or responsibility

Qaza قضاء: compensatory, making up for a missed rite

Qibla قبلة: the direction that Muslims face when they perform their *salat*. It is in the direction of the Ka'bah in Mecca

Qisas قصاص: retaliation/reprisal in kind (an eye for an eye). In Islam, though, retaliation should be forgone as an act of charity; see

Sura 5, Aya 48 (5:48). According to some Muslim jurists, *qiyas* is a method, a yardstick, for measuring or reaching a legal decision on the basis of evidence (precedent) in which a common reason, or an effective cause, is applicable.

Qiyam قيام: standing (usually, but not necessarily, during the performance of the prayers)

Qiyama or Qiyaamah قيامة: Day of Judgment, resurrection, the dead rising from their graves and are herded for their Judgment

Qudat قضاة: plural form of *qadi*, judge

Qudsi قدسي: divine, related to the Almighty

Qunoot قنوت: optional but very highly recommended supplication

Quraysh or Quraish قريش: the Arabian tribe of the Prophet of Islam; for the meaning of "quraish", refer to my book titled *Muhammed: Prophet and Messenger of Allāh.*

Qur'an or Koran or Kuran قرآن: The holy book of Islam is called the Qur'an. It was revealed to Prophet Muhammed (ص) through arch-angel Gabriel (Jibril) during a period of 23 years. There is only one Qur'an in the whole world and it is in Arabic. The Qur'an has one text, one language, and one dialect. It has been memorized by millions of Muslims in different parts of the world. The Qur'an is composed of 114 *suras* (chapters). Rules and regulations apply to its methods of recitation and chanting. The authenticity and pristine originality of the Qur'an have been documented and recognized. It is the ultimate source of guidance for people in all aspects of their spiritual and material lives. It also is described as being bounteous, glorious, mighty, honored, exalted, purified, wonderful, blessed, and confirming the truth of previous revelations to prophets who preceded Muhammed (ص).

ر R

Rabb رب: Owner, master, head, owner; *ar-Rabb* الرب refers to the

Almighty, Lord, Creator, Master of all, the Adored One. In Arabic, He is referred to as "Allāh" which literally means "the One and Only God": It has no gender, and you cannot derive from it a plural form. As for *rabb*, one can be the *rabb*, head, of his family, or owner of home, business, etc.

Rabeeb ربيب: foster-child, step-child, someone brought up by another parent or parents. Islam does not permit adoption but strongly encourages custody, and the guardian is not supposed to give his last name to anyone other than children of his own loins.

Radhi Allāhu 'Anhu or Razhi Allāhu 'Anhu رضي الله عنه: This is an expression used by Muslims whenever a name of a good and respectful companion of the Prophet Muhammed (ص) is mentioned. Not all the companions of the Prophet are worthy of praise and veneration; contrarily, some of them are condemned by the Almighty in Chapter 63 of the Qur'an titled "Al-Munafiqoon المنافقون", the hypocrites. These hypocrites were some companions of the Prophet (ص). The Messenger of Allāh (ص) was too nice and too polite to tell some leeches, loafers and seekers of interests to get off his back, go somewhere else and get lost. Believe it or not, some "companions" went as far as plotting to kill the Prophet by throwing rocks at him from mountains. They even signed a pledge, covenant, to commit their conspiracy and buried their covenant at one of the walls of the Ka`ba in order to swear to it solemnly. Keeping these hypocrites aside, not all believers will escape the fire of hell: Read verses in which the Almighty addresses the believers, those who believe, المؤمنون, or الذين آمنوا where there are stern warnings of the Almighty's wrath on them or where they are warned not to take their conviction إيمان for granted. One such verse is this: "O you **who believe** [يا ايها الذين آمنوا]! Save yourselves and your fāmilies from a fire whose fuel is men and stones, over which stern (and) strong angels are appointed, (angels) who do not flinch (from executing) the commands they receive from Allāh but do (precisely) what they are commanded" (Qur'an, 66:6). So, let the believers watch their conduct, fear their Lord and not look down at others as being inferior to them or harm them or others (unbelievers) in any way at all. The road to Paradise is not strewn with rose petals but with thorns.

Rafida or Rafidha or Rafidhis رافضة أو رافضي: Literally, it means "rejecters" or "rejectionists"; a misnomer used to insult Shī'ites by reminding them (as if they forgot!) that they rejected the governments established by the first three "righteous caliphs". These days, Saudi Arabia's Wahhabis in general and Takfiri extremists in particular, are circulating this misnomer in order to stir hostility against Shī'ite Muslims and thus justify beheading them, raping their women, killing their children, destroying their mosques…, etc. The best answer we provide for these ignorant Wahhabis and Takfiris are these poetic verse by none other than one of the four main imāms of the Sunnis, namely Imām ash-Shafi'i (150 – 206 A.H./767 – 206 A.D.; notice how he founded this sect one century and a half after the *hijra*, migration, whereas Ali (ع), cousin and son-in-law of the Prophet (ص), was there a long time before then):

واهتف بقاعد خيفها والناهض	يا راكبا قف بالمحصب من منى
فيضا كملتطم الفرات الفائض	سحرا إذا فاض الحجيج إلى منى
فليشهد الثقـــلان أني رافضي	إن كان رفضا حب آل محمــد

O rider! Stop at the Muhassab in Mina and shout
At one who sits at its Kheef (Mosque) and who stands
At the time of sahar, when pilgrims flood Mina
A flood like the Euphrates when it floods
That if loving Muhammed's Progeny is Rafdh,
Let both humans and jinns testify that I am Rafidhi.

The "Muhassab" is an area in Mina, one of the stations where pilgrims perform the rituals of the pilgrimage. The "Thaqalan" is a collective word that refers to jinns and mankind. Imām ash-Shafi'i, may Allāh be pleased with him, used to recite these verses with tears in his eyes whenever he was on top of any hill or mountain while performing the pilgrimage.

Rak`at or Rakat or Rek`a ركعة: an individual unit of *salat*

Ramadan or Ramadhan or Ramazan رمضان: the holy month of prescribed fasting for the Muslims. It was during this month that the Qur'anic revelations began. For details about this month, refer to my book titled *Fast of the Month of Ramadan: Philosophy and Ahkam*.

Rashid راشد: adult, adolescent, the age of distinguishing between right and wrong through commonsense and instinct, the age of responsibility, of accountability, of questioning on the Day of Questioning; it also means wise, sage.

Rasul or Rasool رسول: The meaning of the word Rasul is: a messenger. Allāh sent many prophets and messengers to mankind. Amongst them, the names of twenty-five are mentioned in the Qur'an. From within the list, the Qur'an states the names of five *rasuls*, messengers, who are the mighty ones and who are known as "*ulul-azm*", prophets of determination and resolution: Nuh (Noah), Ibrahim (Abraham), Musa (Moses), Isa (Jesus), and Muhammed (ص). What is the difference between a Rasool and a *Nabi*, prophet? A messenger carries a message for people, some people or all people, while the prophet does so and more: He foretells them of things to happen to them or to others, i.e. he makes a prediction according to divine inspiration which he receives from the Almighty. The word "prophet" in Islam carries much more weight than it does in other religions.

Riba ربا: usury, lending for an exorbitant interest, which is prohibited in Islam for both giver and taker

Rijs رجس: defilement, uncleanness, evil or Islamically prohibitive thought or act; Satan is believed to be the source of inspiring such thoughts to people; so, beware of his insinuations!

Risala رسالة: Literally, it means an oral "message" or a written letter; also: published collection of religious rulings by a *marji`*; dissertation containing what is permissible or prohibitive in Islam

Rooh or Ruh روح: spirit, soul, essence, an animating or life-giving principle or material. Some say that the origin of this word is ريح which means "wind" or "air": It cannot be seen but felt through motion. A human body is created of two main ingredients: the body and the soul. Most people look after their bodies while ignoring their souls, their need for spiritual nourishment, thus creating an imbalance between these two components which will eventually cause them either serious psychological or physical problems or both. In Islam, the soul never dies; only the material body does. Scientists tell us that bodily cells are constantly born and die. Death is the separation of the soul from the body. The soul has much more faculties than the body: Souls of the dead can see, hear, feel and react to causes and causations, but it they have no means to show all these faculties to us since the means, the body, has expired. What will happen to all the dead when the time comes for them to stand on the Day of Judgment to answer to what they had done in this life? Another question: How will life return to the dead when the resurrection process starts? Scientists tell us that the DNA (DeoxyriboNucleic Acid) never dies, is never extinct, indestructible. There are numerous verses in the Holy Qur'an which paint a picture of how all the dead buried in our planet will be brought back to life as the resurrection process starts in preparation for the big Day, the Judgment Day. On that Day, all outstanding accounts are settled and those who call others bad names or harm them in any way get what they deserve. One of these verses is 35:9 which reads: "It is Allāh Who sends forth the winds so that they raise up the clouds, and We drive them [clouds] to a land that is dead, and revive the earth with them after its death: *Even so (will be) the Resurrection!*" Do you get the picture?! It seems that when that time comes, the Almighty will send a cloud the "rain water" of which will fall on the earth and will rearrange the DNA of each and every human being, and perhaps non-human beings, too, such as those of animals as we are told in 81:5 which reads: "And when the beasts (animals) are herded together (for Judgment)", in preparation for an eternal life either in bliss or in damnation. Just as a seed receives rain and it sprouts and brings about a new life, the dead will receive this "rain water", which most likely be different than water as we know it in this life, and life will start sprouting in them again. This water will infuse a new life in each DNA. At that time, the souls will be clothed with new bodies, forms, shapes, of some sort. How will these forms or shapes or bodies be, only the Creator knows. Will they be similar to ours? We do not know for sure, but we know that just as the soul during the *barzakh* برزخ period needs spiritual nourishment, these bodies will need food, fuel, something to keep them going. And we know that there will be eating and drinking in both Paradise and hell;

so, will our stomachs be similar to the way they are now, we simply do not know; most likely they will not.

Ruku' or Ruku or Rukoo` ركوع: The root of this word is *raka'a* ركع which means: to bow down. During prayers (*salat*), a Muslim make *ruku'* before Allāh to express veneration to him, he bows forward at the waist, stands with the hands on knees and the back parallel to the ground. While in the position of *ruku'*, a Muslim glorifies Allāh three times.

Rushd رشد: adolescence, mental maturity, the ability to distinguish right from wrong

Rutab رطب: ripe dates, opposite: *busr*

S س،ص

Sabeel سبيل: path, way, avenue, same as Sirat

Sabirin or Sabiroon صابرين أو صابرون: people who are patient and steadfast, who persevere

Sabr صبر: patience, steadfastness, perseverance

Sadaq or Sedaq صداق: same meaning as *mahr*, dower

Sadaqa صدقة: (singular) charity offered voluntarily; plural: *sadaqat*

Sadeed صديد: pus collected from bleeding wounds and served to the sinners in hell to drink when they ask for water to quench their thirst

Safa صفا: a mound near the Ka'bah referred to in the Qur'an as one of the spots held sacred by Allāh. It is in conjunction with Marwah.

Safawis or Safavids or as-Safawiyyoon الصفويون: Some ignorant fanatics apply the misnomer "Safawis" to taunt Shī'ite Muslims, not even knowing exactly what the word means. For this reason, we decided to go into details to narrate to you the history of these Safawis, perhaps one of these fanatics will wake up. The Internet's

Wikipedia tells us that the Safavids (Persian: صفویان; Azerbaijani: Səfəvilər) formed one of the most significant ruling dynasties in Iran's history. They ruled one of the greatest Persian empires since the Muslim conquest of Persia and established the Twelver school of Shī'a Islam as the official religion of their empire, marking one of the most important turning points in Muslim history. This Shī'i dynasty was of mixed ancestry (Kurdish and Azerbaijani, with intermarriages with Georgian and Pontic Greek dignitaries), ruling Iran from 1501 to 1722 A.D.

The Safavid dynasty had its origin in the Safaviyya Sufi order which was established in the city of Ardabil in the Azerbaijan region. From their base in Ardabil, the Safavids established control over all of Greater Iran and reasserted the Iranian identity of the region, thus becoming the first native dynasty since the Sassanid Empire to establish a unified Iranian state.

Despite their demise in 1736 A.D., the legacy that they left behind was the revival of Persia as an economic stronghold between East and West, the establishment of an efficient state and bureaucracy based on "checks and balances", their architectural innovations and patronage of fine arts. The Safavids have also left their mark down to the present era by spreading Shī'a Islam in major parts of the Caucasus and West Asia. Perhaps this is why the Wahhabis of Saudi Arabia are so hostile to the Shī'ites in general and to Iranians in particular.

Even though the Safavids were not the first Shī'a rulers in Iran, they played a crucial role in making Shī'a Islam the official religion in all of Iran. There were large Shī'a communities in some cities like Qum and Sabzevar as early as the 8th century. In the 10th and 11th centuries, the Buwayhids, who were of the Zaidiyya branch of Shī'a Islam, ruled in Fars, Isfahan and Baghdad. As a result of the Mongol conquest and the relative religious tolerance of the Ilkhanids, Shī'a dynasties were re-established in Iran, Sarbedaran in Khorasan being the most important. The Ilkhanid ruler Öljaitü and converted to Twelver Shī'ism in the 13th century.

Following his conquest of Iran, Isma'il I made conversion mandatory for the largely Sunni population. The Sunni ulema, clergy, were reportedly either killed or exiled. Isma'il I, despite his heterodox Shī'a beliefs, brought in Shī'a religious leaders and granted them land and money in return for loyalty. Later, during the Safavid, especially the Qajar period, the Shī'a ulema's power increased, and they were able to exercise a role, independent of or compatible with the government. Despite the Safavid's Sufi origins, most Sufi groups were prohibited, except the Ni'matullahi order.

Iran became a feudal theocracy: The Shah was held to be the divinely ordained head of state and religion. In the following centuries, this religious stance cemented both Iran's internal cohesion and national feelings, provoking attacks by its Sunni neighbors. After the disastrous invasion of the Mongols, in the 1200s, migrated Turks and Mongolian tribes adopted the Persian customs and even language. In the 1300s, the Ilkhanids, a dynasty founded by "Genghis Khan's" grandson, Holagu Khan, had been an influential factor in Persia. During these turbulent years of 13th century, the Persians had submerged themselves deeper in Islamic devotion and Sufism.

Towards the end of the 14th century, Timur (Tamberlane) claimed to be a descent from Genghis Khan's fāmily. The disturbed conditions in Mongol Transoxania gave him in the town of Kish the chance to build up a kingdom in Central Asia. He entered Iran in 1380, and in 1393 he reduced the Jalayirids' power and domination after taking their capital, Baghdad. In 1402 A.D., he captured the Ottoman Sultan Bayezid at Ankara and conquered Syria then turned his attention to campaigns to the east of his quickly acquired and ill-cemented empire. He died in 1405 on an expedition to China. He showed interest in Sufism, a form of mysticism. Timur may have hoped to find popular leaders whom he could use for his own purposes. But he encountered ill-treated Iranians who proved that they knew him perhaps better than he knew himself. His legacy was the reverse of stability to Iran; and division of his ill-assimilated conquests among his sons ensured that an integrated Timurid Empire would never be achieved.

Shah Esma'il killing Uzbek leader Mohammed Sheybani in a battle near Merv, 1510 A.D.

The Timurid state came to being an integrated Iranian empire under Timur's son, Shahrokh Shah (1405-47), who endeavored to weld Azerbaijan, which demanded three military expeditions, as well as western Persia to Khurasan (which means in Persian "land of sunshine") and eastern Persia in order to form a united Timurid state for a short and troubled period of time. He only succeeded in loosely controlling western and southern Iran from his beautiful capital at Herat. He made Herat the seat of a splendid culture, the atelier of great miniature painters of Herat school, Behzad notable among them, and the home of a revival of Persian poetry and philosophy. This revival was not unconnected with an effort to claim for an Iranian center once more the leadership in the propagation of Sunni ideology; Herat used to send copies of Sunni canonical works on request to Egypt. The reaction in Shī'ism's ultimate victory under the Safavid shahs of Persia was, however, already in preparation.

In the mean time, the *"Qara Qoyunlu"* (Black Sheep) Turkman, used to dominate Western Iran. In Azerbaijan they had replaced their former masters, the Jalayirids. Timur had put these Qara Qoyunlu to run away, but in 1406, they regained their capital, Tabriz. On Shahrokh's death, Jahan Shah (reigned c. 1438-67) extended Qara Qoyunlu rule out of the northwest deeper into Iran. The Timurids relied on their old allies, the Qara Qoyunlus' rival Turkman of the *"Aq Qoyunlu"* (White Sheep) clans, whose Jahan Shah was

607

destroyed by the Uzun Hassan of Aq Qoyunlu by the end of 1467.

Uzun Hassan (1453-78) achieved a short-lived Iranian empire, but under his son Yaqub (1478-90), the state was subjected to fiscal reforms associated with a government-sponsored effort to reapply hard purist principles of orthodox Islamic rules for revenue collection. Yaqub attempted to purge the state of taxes introduced under the Mongols and not sanctioned by the Muslim canon. His Sunni fanaticism was discredited when the inquiries made into his activities by the orthodox religious authorities.

The attempts to revive religious orthodoxy through revenue reform gave momentum to the spread of Safavid Shī'a faith. Economic decline, which had resulted from fiscal reforms introduced by Yaqub, must have been another factor as well.

Shaikh Jonayd's son, Shaikh Heydar (or Haider), led a movement that had begun as a Sufi order under his ancestor, Shaikh Safi ud-Din Ardabili (of Ardabil 1252-1334). This order may be considered to have originally represented a puritanical, but not legalistically so, reaction against the corruption of Islam, the staining of Muslim lands, by the Mongol infidels. What began as a spiritual, unearthly reaction against irreligion and the betrayal of spiritual aspirations developed into a manifestation of the Shī'a quest for dominion over Islamic authority. By the 15th century, the Safavid movement could draw on both the mystical emotional force and the Shī'a appeal to the oppressed masses to gain a large number of dedicated adherents. Shaikh Heydar toke his numerous followers to warfare by leading them on expeditions from Ardabil into the nearby Caucasus. He was killed on one of these campaigns in 1488. His son Esma'il, then was one year old, was to avenge his death and lead his devoted army to a conquest of Iran whereby Iran gained a great dynasty, a Shī'a regime, and in most essentials its shape as a modern nation state. Yaqub did not kill Shaikh Heydar's sons, whose mother was Yaqub's sister, but instead sent them to exile in Fars province. Death of Yaqub in 1490 caused turmoil and paved the path for Esmail and his brothers to leave their exile and secretly taking refuge in Lahijan, Gilan province, as its governor had sympathy toward Shī'a.

A militant Islamic Sufi order, the Safavids, appeared among Turkish speaking people of west of the Caspian Sea, at Ardabil. The Safavid order survived the invasion of Timur to that part of the Iran in the late 13th century. By 1500 the Safavids had adopted the Shī'a branch of Islam and were eager to advance Shī'ism by military means. Safavid males used to wear red headgear. They had great devotion for their leader as a religious leader and perfect guide as well as a military chieftain, and they viewed their leaders position as rightly passed from father to son according to the Shī'a tradition. In the year 1500, Esma'il the thirteen-year-old son of a killed Safavid leader, Shaikh Heydar, set out to conquer territories and avenge death of his father. In January 1502, Esma'il defeated the army of Alvand Beig of Aq Qoyunlu, ruler of Azerbaijan, and seized Tabriz and made this city his capital. Safavids went on and conquered rest of Azerbaijan, Armenia and Khorasan; They became the strongest force in Iran, and their leader, Esma'il, now fifteen, was declared Shah (King) on 11 March 1502.

In that era Iran had a variety of settled peoples; in addition to Persians it had Kurds, Arabs, Turkmans and Baluchis to name a few. Safavid's power over various tribes was not strong enough to consolidate an absolute supremacy; tribal leaders remained those who had been tribal chieftains and consider their tribes to be independent. However, the Safavids laid claim to authority over all that had been Persia.

Turkish language was spoken at Shah Esma'il's court, but having adopted Persian as official language and much of Persian culture the Safavids were mistakenly thought by outsiders to be Persian, but they were truly Iranian with a unifying spirit. To help organize the state the Safavids used Persian bureaucrats with a tradition in administration and tax collecting, and they tried to create a religious unity. Shah Esma'il described himself as a descendant, on their father's side, of the Prophet Mohammad and claimed to have royal Sassanian blood as well. Shī'ism became the state religion, Esma'il ignored the Sunni branch of Islam and tried to force people to become Shī'a, which was a difficult task with a variety of tribes and less than complete authority.

The newly established Iranian Empire lacked the resources that had been available to the Islamic Caliphs of Baghdad in former times through their dominion over Central Asia and the West in order to consolidate their power over the Islamic authority. Asia Minor and Transoxania were gone, and the rise of maritime trade in the West was unfavorable to a country whose wealth had depended greatly on its position on important east-west overland trade routes like the famous Silk Road. The rise of the Ottomans held back Iranian westward advances and contested with the Safavids' control over both the Caucasus and Mesopotamia. By 1506, Shah Esma'il had conquered Arak, Esfahan, Fars, Kerman, Yazd, Kashan, Semnan, Astarabad (Gorgan or Jurjan) and, in 1507, he added Shī'a holy cities of Najaf and Kerbalā to Iran.

In 1507, the Portuguese invaded what is called the "Persian Gulf" and captured Hormuz Island. It became a naval base and a trade outpost which lasted for more than a hundred years. Shah Esma'il, having no navy, reluctantly accepted this European presence. In the mean time, the Safavids extended their rule by capturing Baghdad and Iraq in 1508. Later on, after defeating the Uzbeks and killing their leader, Mohammad Sheybani (Shaibani), nicknamed Sheibak Khan, in a battle near Merv on December 1510, Shah Esma'il absorbed the large province of Khorasan into his state as well as Merv, Herat and Qandahar. But Uzbeks remained a formidable rival to the Safavids' domination of Northern Khorasan throughout the 16th century.

In his message, the Ottoman sultan Bayezid II congratulated Shah Esma'il on his victories and advised him to stop destroying the graves and mosques of Sunni Muslims. Shah Esma'il was convinced of the righteousness of his cause, ignoring the request. With many Shī'a Muslims in Asia Minor under the authority of the Ottoman sultan, Bayezid II was concerned about the power of the Safavids. The new sultan in Constantinople after 1512, Sultan Selim (Salim), fought against Shī'a Muslims under his rule, killing thousands and displacing others. Sultan Selim waged war also against the Safavids. On August 23, 1514, just west of Tabriz in the Chalderan plain, the army of Shah Esma'il suffered a crushing defeat. His cavalry and infantry were armed with spears, bows and swords and were fighting against Ottoman's superior numbers as well as field artillery and musketeers. Shah Esma'il and his followers firmly believed that Allāh was on their side, but they were confused by their military setback. Tabriz, their capital, was briefly occupied. This battle and defeat of Safavid Shah paved the path for the Ottoman conquest of Diyarbakr, Erzinjan and other parts of eastern Anatolia as well as northern Iraq. Shah Esma'il himself found relief from psychological depression in wine and died ten years later at the age of only thirty-seven.

Shah Esma'il's descendants, namely Shah Tahmasp I (1524-1576), Shah Esma'il II (1576-1577) and Shah Muhammed (1577-1587), ruling in succession, recovered some of the original Safavid confidence and expanded in the opposite direction of the Ottomans, as far as Transoxania. Safavid shahs tightened their controls over Iran; each district had its own Safavid leader, a "Qezelbash" chief who answered to the shah. In time of war, the Qezelbash chiefs were responsible for providing soldiers for the shah's army and to collect revenues to pay for war. The local Qezelbash chiefs grew wealthy in land and in collecting taxes. Shah Tahmasp I the eldest son of Shah Esma'il ascended the throne at the age of ten, and for the first ten years of his reign, real power was held by a number of leaders of competing Qezelbash factions, which caused much political instability. In 1533, Shah Tahmasp I asserted his authority. One of his legacies was the introduction of converted slaves into court and the military. They were drawn from thousands of Georgian, Circassian and Armenian prisoners captured in campaigns fought in the Caucasus in the 1540s and 1550s. Female slaves entered the royal harem, becoming mothers of princes and a force in court politics and dynastic quarrels. Some of the male slaves began to acquire positions of influence, under Shah Abbas I, reaching high offices that challenged the supremacy of the Qezelbash.

During the reign of Shah Tahmasp I, Uzbeks launched as many as five major invasions of Khorasan with the intent of retaking the area. Safavids were successful in driving back the Uzbeks threat; and in 1545 they captured of Qandahar from the Mughal Empire. The Safavid capital was moved to Qazvin in 1548, following the temporary capture of Tabriz by the Ottomans. Despite periodic wars between Iran and the Ottoman Empire, they maintained an extensive trade, especially in the highly prized Iranian silk, which large quantities of silk were shipped from Iran to commercial centers such as Aleppo and Bursa and from there re-exported to Marseilles, London, and Venice.

Shah Tahmasp I, encouraged carpet weaving on the scale of a state industry. The exquisite miniatures illustrating the Iranian national epic known as the "Shahnama" (Epic of Kings) were painted at the request of Shah Tahmasp. This masterpiece is known as "Shahnameh of Tahmaspi" and was presented by the Safavid ruler to the Ottoman sultan Selim II in 1568.

In 1576 Qezelbash faction interested in a prince whose mother was Turkman rather than Circassian or Georgian, brought Shah Esma'il II son of Shah Tahmasp I to power. Shah Esma'il II reign was marked by brutality and a pro-Sunni policy. Consequently in November 1577, he was poisoned with the participation of his sister Pari Khan Khanom.

Mohammad Shah was the only surviving brother of Shah Esma'il II, proved to be a weak leader. His wife Mahd-e Olya initially dominated him; but after her assassination in 1579 the Qezelbash took control. Meanwhile Ottomans took advantage of Iran's political turmoil to launch a major invasion of the country. Consequently extensive territories were lost to Ottomans, including most of Azerbaijan, with Tabriz, and Georgia.

With their self-esteem and power derived from their increased wealth, some local Qezelbash chiefs wished to have more freedom from the shah's authority. They tried to convince Mohammad Shah that he should select a successor agreeable to them. Some of these chiefs tried to reduce the chances of another choice by executing the heir apparent, his mother and some other possible heirs within the royal family. As often happens, politics by murder was less than efficient. The younger brother of the murdered heir apparent was secretly send away to Khorasan, and Qezelbash chiefs loyal to the royal family fought and defeated Qezelbash chiefs who were not, and full power was returned to the old dynasty of shahs.

Abbas I (1587-1629), who succeeded Mohammad Shah, learnt from his family's experience with the local Qezelbash chiefs, and he broke their power and confiscated their wealth. He extended state-owned lands and lands owned by the shah. Provinces were now to be administered by the state replacing the Qezelbash chiefs. He strengthened his government's bureaucracy and managed to relocate tribes in order to weaken their power. The Sufi bands, Qezelbash, which had been formed into artificial tribal units mainly for military purposes during the dynasty's formative period, as a source of recruitment, were replaced by a standing strong army of his own. He recruited soldiers from Persian villages and from among Christians, Georgians, Circassian, Armenians and others, equipped them with artillery and muskets. The Christians were proud to serve the shah and to call themselves "*Ghulams*" (slaves) of the shah although slaves they were not. To finance the new army, Shah Abbas converted large pieces of land traditionally granted to tribal chiefs as assignments into crown lands that he taxed directly. This new military force was trained on European lines with the advice of Robert Sherley. Sherley was an English adventurer expert in artillery tactics who, accompanied by a party of cannon founders, reached Qazvin (the Caspian Sea) with his brother Anthony Sherley in1598. In a short time Shah Abbas created a formidable army, consisting of cavalry, infantry and artillery.

Shah Abbas was open to the ideas and was mentally active as well. He was curious and in ways more tolerant than his predecessors. Previously, "infidels" (foreigners and non-Muslim subjects) had been denied entry to the shah's court. He welcomed foreigners and his non-Muslims subjects to his court, and enjoyed discussing with foreigners the complexities of religious ideology. He took an unusual step among Islamic rulers by allowing Christians to wear what they wanted and allowing them to own their own home and land.

Shah Abbas defeated the Uzbeks in April 1598 and recovered Herat and territories in Khorasan, including Mashhad, lost several years earlier. He consolidated the Safavid power strongly in Khorasan. He rebuilt and developed the shrine of Ali ar-Reza (Imām Reza or

Ridha) at Mashhad, the eighth Shī'a Imām, as a pilgrim, which was damaged by the Uzbeks. The shrine became a major center for Shī'a pilgrimage, and a rival to Shī'a holy places in Mesopotamia like Najaf and Kerbalā where visiting pilgrims took currency and attention out of Safavid into Ottoman territory.

The Safavids had earlier moved their capital from the vulnerable Tabriz to Qazvin. Since the Uzbek threat from east of the Caspian had been overcome, Shah Abbas could move to his newly built capital at Esfahan (or Isfahan) in 1598, more centrally placed than Qazvin for control over the whole country and for communication with the trade outlets of the Persian Gulf.

Under Shah Abbas I, Iran prospered; he also transplanted a colony of industrious and commercially astute Armenians from Jolfa in Azerbaijan to a new Jolfa next to Esfahan. He patronized the arts, and he built palaces, mosques and schools, Esfahan becoming the cultural and intellectual capital of Iran. Shah Abbas encouraged international trade and the production of silks, carpets, ceramics and metal ware for sale to Europeans. Shah Abbas also founded a carpet factory in Esfahan. Royal patronage and the influence of court designers assured that Persian carpets reached their zenith in elegance during the Safavid period. He advanced trade by building and safeguarding roads. He welcomed tradesmen from

Ali Qapou Palace in Shah Square, Esfahan (or Isfahan)

Britain, the Netherlands and elsewhere to Iran. His governmental monopoly over the silk trade enhanced state revenues. Merchants of the English East India Company established trading houses in Shiraz and Esfahan. After Shah Abbas ousted the Portuguese from the island of Hormuz at the entrance to the Persian Gulf in 1622, Bandar Abbas (Port of Abbas) became the center of the East India Company's trade. But Later the Dutch East India Company received trade capitulations from Shah Abbas. The Dutch soon gained supremacy in the European trade with Iran, outdistancing British competitors. They established a spice-trading center at Bandar Abbas. In 1623-24 Shah Abbas I launched an offensive against Ottomans and established control over Kurdish territories, Baghdad and the Shī'a Holy Cities of Najaf and Kerbalā.

During his reign, Shah Abbas I paid considerable attention to the welfare institutions in Esfahan and other cities like establishing hospitals. Medical practice was still depended on medieval guides for the treatment of most illnesses. The standard reference work remained the Canon of Ibn Sina (Avicenna) (d. 1037), but new clinical works were written during the Safavid period as well. In the 17th century, a unique work, The Treasury of Surgery, was written by an army surgeon known as Hakim Mohammad and was dedicated to Shah Safi I. It included a detailed list of the instruments available to surgeons, including a special device for the removal of bullets; outlined various forms of anesthesia; and advocated surgery for cancerous tumors.

The bureaucracy, too, was carefully reorganized, bold reforms in the military, administrative, and fiscal structures helped to centralize state authority to a degree not achieved by Shah Abbas I predecessors. But the seeds of the sovereignty's weakness lay in the royal house itself, which lacked an established system of inheritance by primogeniture. One of Shah Abbas I innovations, however, weakened the Safavid state in the long run; fear of revolts by his sons led him to abandon the traditional practice of employing the princes to govern provinces. Instead, he instituted the practice of confinement of infant princes in the palace gardens away from the direct reach of conspiracies and the world at large. A reigning shah's nearest and most acute objects of suspicion were his own sons. Among them, brother plotted against brother over who should succeed on their father's death; and conspirator, ambitious for influence in a subsequent reign, supported one prince against another. The new practice, followed also by his successors, resulted in ill-educated, indecisive shahs of lower competence, easily dominated by powerful religious dignitaries to whom the Safavids had accorded considerable influence in an attempt to make Shī'ism the state religion

After the death of Shah Abbas I in 1629, his son, Shah Safi I, who ruled from 1629 to 1642, known for his cruelty, sat on the throne. He was the first of the Safavid shahs to be raised in the palace gardens. Shah Safi I put to death potential rivals to the throne as well as some of his male and female relatives on his accession. He executed most of the generals, officers and councilors he had inherited from his father's reign. The dominant influence of Mirza Taqi, known as Saru Taqi, the Grand Vezir (chancellor, prime minister) at the Safavid court allowed the government to be run smoothly despite the shah's lack of interest in affairs of state.

On May 17, 1639, a peace treaty with the Ottomans was signed which established the Ottoman-Safavid frontier and put an end to more than a hundred years of sporadic conflict. The treaty forced Shah Safi I to accept the final loss of Baghdad in Mesopotamia, recaptured by the Ottomans in 1638, and instead gave Yerevan in the southern Caucasus to Iran.

The era of Shah Abbas II, who ruled from 1642 to 1667, was the last fully competent period of rule by a Safavid shah. Shah Abbas II took an active role in government matters. Under his rule Iran revived, and some of Persia's glory in the eyes of the outside world returned. He increased the central authority of the state by increasing crown lands and often intervened in provincial affairs on the side of the peasants, but with peace on the frontiers the army declined in size and quality. He stuck to the notion that the Safavid ruler was sacred and perfect and openly disputed with members of the Shī'a religious establishment who had begun to articulate the idea that in the absence of the occult Imām Zaman (twelfth Shī'a Imām, al-Mahdi), true temporal authority rightly belonged to the mujtahid who merited emulation by the faithful. Safavid Shī'ism had not improved monarchy as an institution, but instead recognized the state as a theocracy. The *'ulema*, religious leaders, rebuked the shahs, questioned the religious legitimacy of their power and claimed that the mujtahids had a superior claim to rule.

After Abbas II died in 1667, decline set in again when Shah Soleyman (Sulayman, Solomon) (Safi II), who ruled from 1667 to 1694, took power. He was renamed, superstitiously, to Soleyman because the first year and half of his reign was so disastrous. Shah Soleyman was not a competent ruler, and shortly after his accession food prices soared and famine and disease spread throughout the country. Although pressing problems faced him, he increasingly retreated into the harem and left his grand vezir to cope with affairs of state.

Shah Sultan Hossein (Hussain or Hussein), who ruled from 1694 to 1722, have been described as the most incompetent shah of Safavids. He was similar to some others who had inherited power by accident of birth. Indifferent to affairs of state, Shah Sultan Hossein effectively brought Safavid Empire to its sudden and unexpected end. He was of a religious temperament and especially influenced by the Shī'a religious establishment. At their insistence, he issued decrees forbidding the consumption of alcohol and banning Sufism in Esfahan. In 1694 Shah Sultan Hossein appointed Mohammad Bāqir Majlesi, the most influential member of Shī'a religious establishment, to the new office of "*Mulla Bashi*" (Head Mulla). Majlesi wrote "Bihār al-Anwār" (The Seas of Light), an encyclopedic work dedicated to the preservation of the prophet Mohammad's words and deeds. He devoted himself to the propagation of a legalistic form of Shī'ism and to the eradication of Sufism and Sunni Islam in Iran. Under his guidance specifically Shī'a popular rituals, such as mourning for the martyred third Shī'a Imām Hossein (d. 680), Ashora, were encouraged, as were pilgrimages to the tombs of holy Shī'a personages. Majlesi's policies also included the persecution of non-Muslims in Iran, including Zoroastrians, Jews, and Christians. Unchecked by the Safavid regime, Majlesi and the Shī'a clergy emerged with increased strength and independence from the ruling government in the 17th and 18th centuries.

The Safavid Empire had also declined militarily, leaving it more vulnerable to invasion, which came out of the east. In 1722 Afghan invaders under Mahmoud, a former Safavid vassal in Afghanistan, captured Esfahan and murdered Shah Sultan Hossein. The Afghan invasion was disastrous for Iran, which consequently in 1723 the Ottomans took advantage of the disintegration of the Safavid realm and invaded from the west, ravaging western Persia as far as Hamadan, while the Russians seized territories around the Caspian Sea. In June 1724 the two powers agreed on a peaceful partitioning of Iran's northwestern provinces.

From this extensive research in the Safavid empire, one can conclude that those who taunt Shī'ite Muslims and call them "Safavids" prove, by so doing, that their brains are not bigger than those of birds, yet they are a lot more harmful. Birds are useful servants of Allāh, whereas some "Muslims", certainly not "mu'mins", have throughout history harmed Islam's reputation while thinking that they, and only they, are the true Muslims...!

Safh صفح: pardon, forgiveness, excuse

Sahāba صحابة: companions of the Holy Prophet Muhammed (ص); singular *sahabi*

Saheefa or Sahīfa صحيفة: page, tablet, scroll, parchment, manuscript, written document

Sahīh صحيح: literally: authentic, correct, accurate; it is generally used to refer to the collection, group of collections, or book, of verified and authenticated *ahādīth* of Holy Prophet (ص)

Sajda سجدة: prostration; it is also the title of Chapter 32 of the Holy Qur'an

Salat or Salah صلاة: *Salāt* is an Arabic word which mean: a spiritual relationship and communication between the servant/being and his

Creator. *Salat* is one of the five pillars of Islam. It is performed five times a day at these times: *fajr* (pre-dawn or pre-daybreak), *dhuhr* noon, *'asr* (afternoon), maghrib (sunset) and *'isha'* (late night). *Salat* is to be performed with mental concentration, verbal communication, vocal recitation, and physical movement to attain spiritual upliftment, peace of mind, harmony with the soul and with the Creator and concord. Congregational prayer services are held on Fridays at noon which they include a sermon (*khutba*) delivered by a religious leader (Imām) called *khatib*. To perform the *salat* ritual, a Muslim has to first perform the ablution (*wudhu'*). He/she should make sure about that cleanliness of the body, clothing, and place before performing the *salat*. How many types of prayers are there in Islam? There are many besides the daily prayers: The Ghufaila Prayers, the Sahu (forgetfulness or miscalculation while performing obligatory prayers), the Janaza Prayers for a deceased person whose coffin is being witnessed, the Ghaayib Prayers for the deceased person whose coffin is not present, Salat al-Wahsha which is performed for a deceased person in the same night of his death, Salat al-Layl which is performed from the time after midnight and before Fajr, Salat al-Aayaat which is performed at the time of eclipse of the sun or the moon, Salat al-Shukr, a form of thanks giving prayer, Salat al-Haja, a prayer performed when one wants to plea to his Maker so he may attain a certain objective, Salat al-Istikhara when one needs guidance from his Maker regarding a particular complex issue, a prayer to remove one's worries and concerns, Salat al-Tasabeeh in which one praises the Almighty a great deal, Eid prayers, prayers on certain other occasions such as Laylatul-Qadr, etc..., to name only a few. Each of these prayers has its own rules and regulations. Refer to your *mujtahid* for details. But if you have no *mujtahid* to guide you, for sure you are lost...!

**Salatul-`Id صلاة العيد**: late morning prayers comprised of two *rek`at* (prostrations) performed on the first day of `Id al-Fitr (the feast of fast-breaking) which signals the end of the fast of the month of Ramadan

Sall Allāhu 'alaihi wa Aalihi wa sallam صلى الله عليه وعلى اله و سلم: This is an expression which Muslims articulate whenever the name of Prophet Muhammed (ص) is mentioned or written. The meaning is: "May the blessings and the peace of Allāh be with him (Muhammed (ص)".

Saqifah or Saqifa or Saqeefa سقيفه: a shelter from the sun, a shed with a roof. The companions of the Prophet (ص) met in such a place in Medīna known as "Saqifat Bani Sa`idah سقيفة بني ساعد ه" to "elect" the first successor to the Prophet (ص). The attendants actually represented a fraction of the Muslim community of the time and many dignitaries boycotted that "elections" and later cast doubts about its legitimacy, igniting a division among the Muslim the effects of which can still be felt even in our times and in all times to come. Many books have been written about this "saqifa" incident, and the controversy will most likely never dissipate. On p. 215, Vol. 2 of Tabari's *Tarikh* (Dar al-Amira for Publication and Distribution, Beirut, Lebanon, 1426 A.H./2005 A.D.), we are told that the sacred body of the Prophet (ص) remained without being buried for three full days because some people were arguing with each other at the *saqifa* of Bani Sa'idah about who should be the successor to the Prophet (ص). How many Muslims were there when the Prophet (ص) was buried? On p. 408, Vol. 6/2 (combined edition published in 1427 A.H./2006 A.D. by the Ihyaa al-Kutub al-Islamiyya, Qum, Iran) of al-Majlisi's *Bihār al-Anwār* بحـار الأنـوار, we read precise details about who gave the Prophet (ص) his burial bath and buried him. The sacred body of the Prophet (ص) was given the burial bath by none other than his son-in-law, cousin and the man whom he raised in his lap: Ali ibn Abū Talib (ع). A handful of the Prophet's closest relatives and true companions buried him, and these included, in addition to Ali, Aws ibn Khawli, "Abū Talhah" Zaid ibn Sahl, al-Abbas ibn Abdul-Muttalib and his son al-Fadl ibn al-Abbas, Abū Ubaidah ibn al-Jarrah and Usamah ibn Zaid ibn Harithah. As for the rest, they were too busy fussing and arguing, almost fighting, with each other about who would be the next caliph to be concerned about burying the Prophet of Allāh (ص)…

Saraya سرايا: (plural) military campaigns personally ordered by Prophet Muhammed (ص); singular: *sariya*

Sarmadi سرمدي: eternal, everlasting, perpetual

620

Sawm صوم: Sawm or Siyam implies a total abstinence from partaking of food, water or any liquid, smoking, intercourse, etc. from dawn till sunset for one whole lunar month. Sawm (fasting) takes place during the ninth month of the lunar calendar called Ramadan. It is one of the five pillars of Islam. How many types of fast are there in Islam? If you really want to know the answer, read my book Fast of the Month of Ramadan: Philosophy and Ahkam where you will find out that there are as many as forty types of fast in Islam. Muslims take their religion very seriously.

Sa'yee or Sa'ee or Sa'i سعي: the going back and forth seven times between the Safa and the Marwa during the *hajj* or *umra*. It symbolizes Hajar's search for water for her son Ishmael.

Sayyid سيد: leader, head or chief; also: a descendant of the Prophet (ص)

Shafeer شفير: brink, verge, brim, edge

**Shafee` شفيع:** intercessor, preemptioner, one who intercedes on behalf of another. May the Almighty accept the Prophet of Islam (ص) as our Shafee` and yours, *Allāhomma Ameen*.

Shahada شهادة: martyrdom; it also means testimony, declaration of faith. A person must recite the *shahada* in Arabic to convert to Islam. The *shahada* in Islam is: *Ashhadu an La Ilaha illa-Allāh wa anna Muhammedan Rasul Allāh*, that is, "I testify that there is no god except Allāh and that Muhammed (ص) is the Messenger of Allāh." Other meanings for this word: certificate, testimonial; **Shahadat Ashum شهادة أسهم أو حصص:** share certificate or scrip; شهادة أسهم الحامل: share-warrant to bearer; شهادة أسهم امتياز: certificate of preferred stock; شهادة اكتتاب (بأسهم): stock certificate; أمان (سفينه): شهادة: certificate of safety (of a ship/vessel); شهادة ايداع : certificate of deposit; شهادة تأسيس : certificate of incorporation; شهادة تسجيل سفينه : certificate of registry; شهادة تفريغ: unloading certificate; شهادة سوابق : certificate of police record (criminal record)

Shaheed or Shahid شهيد: a martyr, someone who dies in the way of Allāh

621

Shahr شهر: month

Shī'a or Shī'i or Shī'ite شيعي: a follower of the Islamic faith according to the teachings of the Prophet's immediate family, the Ahl al-Bayt (ع). The largest Shī'ite sect is the Ithna-Asheri one which is detailed for you above.

Shaikh or Sheikh شيخ: The word "shaikh" is a title of an elderly person or a religious leader. This title is also given to a wise person, and it means, in this case, a mentor.

Shaitan or Shaitan شيطان: Shaitan (Satan) is the source of evil in the world. The plural name is Shayatin, devils or demons. His other name is Iblis or Eblis which means "one who has lost everything". The origin of this word is "shiyaat شياط", burning, and from it the term "burnt with rage استشاط غضبا" is derived. Rage surely burns! Among what it burns is homes: When a husband is angry with his wife, he goes ahead and divorces her, but rest assured that his divorce in this case is not legitimate at all. Read books of *fiqh* and learn the conditions for one's divorce to be acceptable in Islam.

Shakk شك: doubt, uncertainty, suspicion. In the Holy Qur'an, 49:12, we are told to avoid being too suspicious because sometimes suspicion/doubt can be a sin.

Shari` شارع**: street, road, thoroughfare; **Musharri` مشرع legislator, lawmaker; **Shar` شرع** law, doctrine, canon; **Shir`a شرعه** law, precept, concept; **Musharri` مشرع** legislator, lawmaker, jurist; **Shari`a شريعه** Islamic legislative system; **Shar`i شرعي** legitimate, lawful, legal, rightful, related to the Shari`a

Shari'a شريعة: path, method, way, manner, style, way of life, program; Islamic Shari'a is the legislative system in Islam which is derived from two sources: the Holy Qur'an and the Sunna of the Prophet of Islam (ص). This Sunna, which includes both actions and statements, is reported, narrated, detailed, chronicled and documented by two major groups of followers of Islam: 1) the Sahāba of the Prophet (ص), and 2) the immediate family members of the Prophet (ص) who are referred to the Holy Qur'an as أهل البيت Ahl al-Bayt, people of the house of the Prophet; see Qur'an, 33:33: إِنَّمَا يُرِيدُ اللَّهُ لِيُذْهِبَ عَنكُمُ الرِّجْسَ أَهْلَ الْبَيْتِ وَيُطَهِّرَكُمْ تَطْهِيرًا *Allāh only wishes to remove all abomination from you, you members of the (Prophet's) Fāmily, and to make you pure and spotless.* Followers of the first group like to be called "Sunnis" whereas followers of the other group are referred to as "Shī'ites", "Shī'is", "Shī'ites" or "Shī'as". Unfortunately, some Sunni fanatics, instigated and paid by some politicians for one reason or another, have applied many derogatory names to the followers of Ahl al-Bayt (ع), the Shī'ites, such as "Rafidis" or "Rafidhis" رافضة which means rejectors, perhaps a reference to their rejection of the ascension to power of the first three "righteous caliphs" who saw with their own eyes and heard with their own ears how the Prophet (ص), as ordered by the Almighty, chose Ali (ع) to be his successor rather than this man or that. Anyhow, what is passed is past, and Islam is like one tree stem having two main branches each of which has sub-branches, too. Throughout history, some Muslims, for reasons of their own which may include serious research in Islamic literature and history, have shifted their following from one group to another and this will always take place as is the case with all other religions of the world. An example of such "conversion" from one Islamic sect to another took place in the author's populous tribe, the Jibouris عشيرة الجبور. The author's ancestors, because of an incident that took place about 130 years ago in north-western Baghdad, specifically in the holy city of al-Kādhimiyya where two Imāms, direct descendants of the Prophet (ص), are buried in a magnificent mausoleum visited daily by thousands of the faithful from all over the world, changed their sect from Sunni to Shī'ite. For this reason, his ancestors were subjected to untold persecution, discrimination and suffering which all strengthened their conviction rather than weakening it. The Autobiography of the author of this book details this incident, and it is available for you if you click on this link and search for it: http://www.scribd.com/yasinaljibouri/. Now, dear reader, who do you personally think know the Sunna best: the Prophet's friends or his fāmily members?! May the Almighty keep the Muslim *umma* united and foil the efforts of those who try to divide it, *Allāhomma Aameen* اللهم آمين. The root of this word is "شرع shara'a". Some other derivations of it are: *shar'*, *shir'a* and *tashri'*. Shari'a is the revealed

623

and canonical laws of the Islamic faith. The Holy Qur'an and the sacred Sunna of the Prophet (ص) are the sources of the Shari'a, Islam's legislative code; **Shar`iyya شرعيه** legitimacy, legality. As for the misnomer "Rafidi", please refer to its place in this Glossary.

Sharr شر: evil, mischief; **Shirreer شرير** evildoer, mischief-maker, baneful, pernicious

Shatm شتم: revilement, insulting, calling someone bad names, cursing

Shī'ite or Shi`i شيعي: a Muslim following the Sunna of the Prophet (ص) as reported by the Prophet's immediate family, the Ahl al-Bayt (ع). The number of Shī'ites is estimated to range between 25% and 35% of the entire Muslim population of the world, but little is known about their beliefs for many reasons. Worse is the fact that their beliefs are often misrepresented, distorted, falsified and unjustifiably attacked by some of their ignorant Sunni brethren. This has been going on for centuries. There are many Shī'ite sects which include, among others: الشيعه الجعفريه الاثنا عشريه the Twelvers, that is, the Shi`a Ja`feri Ithna-Asheris (the Twelvers, followers of the fiqh of Imām Ja`fer as-Sādiq (ع) who constitute the majority of Shī'ites of the world), الزيديه the Zaidis who follow Zaid son of Ali son of al-Hussain son of Ali son of Abū Talib (ع) who live mostly in Yemen; الاسماعيليه the Isma`ilis who mostly live in Turkey, العلويه the Alawis or Alawides who live in Syria, and البهره أو البحاريون the Buhris or Biharis who live in India.

Shiqaq شقاق: discord, dissension

Shirk شرك: polytheism, the belief in the existence of partners with Allāh. Shirk can also encompass any object that a person may regard as being higher in status than Allāh. It is the most serious of all sins and can never be forgiven.

Shubha شبهة: (singular) doubt, suspicion, uncertainty; its plural is: shubuhaat

Shura شورى: the principle of mutual consultation, Islam's form of

624

democracy; refer to verse 38, Chapter 42 (Shura or Consultation) of the Holy Qur'an: وَأَمْرُهُمْ شُورَى بَيْنَهُمْ وَمِمَّا رَزَقْنَاهُمْ يُنْفِقُونَ *Those who listen to their Lord and establish regular prayers, who (conduct) their affairs by mutual consultation, who spend out of what sustenance We bestow upon them...* (42:38). Some Muslim governments set up "shura assemblies" to advise top officials and resolve main contentions.

Siddiq or Siddeeq صديق: one who testifies to the truthfulness of a prophet

Sifah سفاح: cohabitation with a woman without a marriage contract, unlawful according to Islam and other divine religions, fornication or adultery.

Sihr صهر: relative by marriage, an in-law

Sin al-Bulugh or al-Boloogh سن البلوغ: This is the age of maturity and puberty. It is the age at which a Muslim is considered to be an adult and, hence, becomes accountable for his/her actions and responsible for the Islamic duties and obligations. There is no fixed age for that in terms of years, and it is decided by three signs: having menstruation or monthly period for girls, and being physically mature, encountering wet dreams growing pubic hair, or reaching the age of fifteen, whichever comes first for boys,.

Sin at-Tamyiz سن التمييز: This is the age of distinguishing. This age is used in *fiqh* to decide the age before which the mother has the right to keep the child after divorce. It varies from one person to another. The age is reached when the child can take care of himself or herself and no longer needs an adult to help him take care of himself/herself. In some Islamic schools of thought, it is seven years for the boy and nine for the girl. The girl is given longer time so that she can learn more about women's habits.

Sinn سن: literally, it means "tooth" or age such as: سن الادراك : age of discretion (or mature realization, of distinguishing between right and wrong, lawful and lawful, etc.), سن البلوغ (الرشد) age of (physical) maturity, adolescence, سن الحداثه age of minors, سن الحضانه age of

625

nurture, of nursing, سن الرشد legal age, full age, سن الرضا age of consent.

Sira or Seera سيره: collective writings of the companions of the Prophet (ص) about him, his personality, his life story, ways of handling different situations…, etc. is called *sira*. Among famous collectors of *sira* are: at-Tabari, Ibn Ishāq and Ibn Hisham.

Sirat صراط: path, highway; same as *sabeel* (*sabil*). As-*Sirat Al-Mustaqeem الصراط المستقيم*: The Straight Path is the one mentioned in Sūrat al-Fātiha and in numerous other verses under different other names, and it is a plea to the Almighty made by the faithful: الْمُسْتَقِيمَ إهدِنَا الصِّرَاطَ Guide us (O Lord!) to the Straight Path" (Qur'an, 1:6), thus praying Allāh Almighty to keep their feet firm as they pass on it so it may lead them to happiness in this life and salvation in the life to come. All souls in the hereafter without any exception have to pass over it, and it is described as a bridge, a path, a passage that stretches from Hell to Paradise; only those who successfully cross it will enter Paradise, the ultimate goal of all believers where they will stay forever. Imām Ja'far as-Sādiq (ع), as recorded on p. 41, Vol. 1, of Tabatabai's *Al-Mizan fi Tafsir al-Qur'an الميزان في تفسير القرآن*, was asked once about the meaning of this verse; so he said, "It means: Guide us to upholding the path that leads to Your pleasure, that ends at Your Paradise, that prohibits us from following our own desires and thus deviate, or follow our own views and thus perish." By the way, Tabatabai's full name is: Muhammed Hussain ibn Sayyid Muhammed ibn Sayyid Hussain ibn Mirza Ali Asgher Tabrizi Tabatabai, the judge. He was born in 1892 in Tabriz and died in Qum in 1981. His 21-Volume exegesis, *Al-Mizan*, is only one of his numerous works. The edition utilized for this book was published in 1991 by Al-A'lami Foundation of Beirut, Lebanon. Hujjatul-Islam Sayyid Saeed Akhtar Rizvi, recognized scholar and founder of the Bilal Muslim Mission of Tanzania, may Allāh fill his resting place with *noor نور*, spent years of his blessed life translating some volumes of this valuable exegesis into English. In his *Tafsir*, al-Ayyashi quotes Imām Ja'far as-Sādiq (ع) as saying that as-Sirat al-Mustaqeem is the Commander of the Faithful Imām Ali (ع). *As-Sirat al-Mustaqeem* is referred to in verse 61 of Sūrat Ya-Sin (Ch. 36), in verse 52 of Sūrat ash-Shura (Ch. 42), in verse 16 of Sūrat al-Ma'ida

(Ch. 5), in verses 126 and 161 of Sūrat al-An'am (Ch. 6), in verses 70 and 174 of Sūrat an-Nisaa (Ch. 4), in verse 42 of Sūrat al-Hijr (Ch. 15), and in other verses where it is described as the *Sabeel*, another word for path, leading to the Almighty.

Abdul-Rahman ibn Muhammed al-Hassam quotes Ahmed ibn 'Eisa ibn Abū Maryam quoting Muhammed ibn Ahmed al-'Arjami quoting Ali ibn Hatim al-Minqari quoting al-Mufaddal ibn Omer as saying, "I asked Abū Abdullāh (Imām as-Sādiq (ع)) about the Sirat, and he said, 'It is the Path to knowing Allāh, the most Exalted, the most Great, and there are two such paths: one in the life of this world, and one in the life hereafter. The Sirat in this life is the Imām whose obedience is incumbent; whoever knows him in this life and follows his guidance will be able to pass on the (other) Sirat which is a path over hell in the hereafter, and whoever does not know him in this life, his feet will slip away from the Sirat in the hereafter, causing him to fall into the fire of hell.'" This is recorded on pp. 13-14 of *Ma'ani al Akhbar* معاني الأخبار and also on p. 66, Vol. 8, of *Bihar al Anwar* بحار الأنوار. It is when you come to this Sirat, and you most certainly will, that you will find out how well you performed your prayers, fast and other religious obligations in the life of this world, how you dealt with your Maker, fāmily, relatives and other members of the society. As-Sirat al-Mustaqeem is the straight path over hell, a fire more intense in heat than boiling molten brass, and it has seven bridges over it: Each is three thousand years in length: one thousand to vertically ascend, one thousand to horizontally cross, and one thousand to descend. It is thinner than a human hair, sharper than the sharpest sword and darker than the darkest night inside a tunnel. Each bridge has seven branches, and each branch is like a long lance with sharp teeth: each servant of Allāh will be confined on each and every one of them and be asked about all the injunctions the Almighty had required him to perform during his lifetime on this planet. In the first of such stops he will be asked about belief and conviction, *shirk* شرك (polytheism) and hypocrisy. In the second he will be asked about prayers, what they entail, how to perform, and whether he performed them properly and on time. In the third he will be asked about *zakat*, its types, and whether he paid it or not. And it is in the fourth that he will be asked about the fast... It is there and then that he will realize whether he upheld this important obligation or not, whether he offered charity or not, and whether he regretted and repented his sins during the month of Ramadan or not. In the fifth he will be asked about the *hajj*, pilgrimage, and *'umra*, why he did not perform them, or why he failed to perform them properly, and how they must be performed. In the sixth he will be asked about *wudu* (ablution) and *ghusul*, how he performed them, which one is compulsory and which is optional. Finally, in the seventh, he will be asked about how kind he was to his parents and kin, and whether he did injustice to any human being. In the absence of sufficient optional good deeds such as offering charity, helping a needy Muslim, performing optional prayers or fasts..., etc., if one gives the wrong answer to any question in any of these stops, he will be prone to fall into the pit of hell underneath..., as Abdel-Jabbar ar-Rubay'i tells us in his book *Al- Tathkira fi ahwal almawt wal akhira* التذكرة في أحوال الموت و الآخرة, having collected such details from various books of *hadīth* and Sunna. He adds saying, on p. 130, that the bridges will be shaken by the weight of crossing people who will climb on top of each other, causing these bridges to move like a ship tossed by a wind storm in the midst of the sea.

As-Sirat separates Paradise from hell. With reference to those who will fall into hell, the Almighty says the following: أَلَمْ تَرَ إِلَى الَّذِينَ بَدَّلُواْ نِعْمَةَ اللّهِ كُفْرًا وَأَحَلُّواْ قَوْمَهُمْ دَارَ الْبَوَارِ؟ "Have you not considered those who have changed Allāh's favor into blasphemy and caused their people to fall into the abode of perdition?" (Holy Qur'an, 14:28) where the "abode of perdition" connotes Hell; "... وَمَن يَحْلِلْ عَلَيْهِ غَضَبِي فَقَدْ هَوَى upon whomsoever My wrath descends shall fall therein" (Holy Qur'an 20:81) where the "fall" here means falling into Hell; فَمَنِ اتَّبَعَ هُدَايَ فَلا يَضِلُّ وَلا يَشْقَى "Whoever follows My guidance will not lose his way nor fall into perdition" (Holy Qur'an, 20:123); وَمَا يُغْنِي عَنْهُ مَالُهُ إِذَا تَرَدَّى "... Nor will his wealth benefit him when he falls headlong (into the pit of fire)" (Holy Qur'an, 92:11). So, if one is found as having been derelict in performing any of his obligations, the angels questioning him will try to find out whether he somehow made up for it with optional good deeds. Once he is cleared, he will be escorted into Paradise. It is to such stopping and questioning that the Almighty refers when He addresses His angels to وَقِفُوهُمْ إِنَّهُم مَّسْئُولُونَ "Stop them, for they must be questioned" (Holy Qur'an, 37:24).

On p. 133, Vol. 17, of his book titled *Al-Mizan*, `allama Tabatabai quotes various views regarding what the questions on this Sirat will be. He says that some scholars are of the opinion that they will be asked about the Unity of Allāh, while others believe it will be about the *wilayat* ولاية of Imām Ali (ع), but he also concedes that such stopping and questioning will take place on the Sirat over hell. On p. 107 of as-Sadūq's *Al-Amali* الأمالي, and also on pp. 64-65, Vol. 8, of al-Majlisi's *Bihār al-Anwār* بحار الأنوار, al-Waleed quotes as-Saffar quoting Ibn 'Eisa quoting Muhammed al-Barqi quoting al-Qasim ibn Muhammed al-Jawhari quoting Ali ibn Abū Hamzah quoting Au Busayr quoting Abū Abdullāh Imām Ja'far as-Sādiq (ع) as saying, "People will pass on different levels on the Sirat, and it is thinner than hair and sharper than the sword. Some will pass as swiftly as lightning, while others will pass as fast as a horse, while some of them will crawl on it, some will walk on it, while some others will pass hanging, so the fire will consume some of their body parts and leave others." Imām Abū Ja'far al-Bāqir (ع) is quoted on p. 65, Vol. 8, of al-Majlisi's *Bihār al-Anwār* as saying, "When the verse saying 'And hell is brought that Day' was revealed, the Messenger of Allāh (ص) was asked about what it meant, so he (ص) said, 'The trusted Spirit (Gabriel) has informed me that when Allāh, the One and only God, resurrects all people and gathers their early generations and the last, hell will be brought by a hundred thousand angels, very stern and mighty angels, and it will be coming roaring, inhaling and exhaling. The force of its exhalation is such that had Allāh not delayed them for the reckoning, it would have caused everyone to perish. Then a flame will come out of it and encircle all humans, the good and the bad, so much so that any servant of Allāh, be he an angel or a prophet, will call out: `Save me, O Lord, save me,' except you, O Prophet of Allāh, for you will call out: Save my nation, O Lord, save my nation!'" Muqatil, `Ataa and Ibn Abbas are among the greatest traditionists in the history of Islam without any contention. They are the ones who transmitted the *ahadīth* أحاديث of the Messenger of Allāh (ص) for all posterity. All three of them, as stated on p. 67, Vol. 8, of *Bihar al Anwar*, have interpreted the verse saying:

يَا أَيُّهَا الَّذِينَ آمَنُوا تُوبُوا إِلَى اللهِ تَوْبَةً نَصُوحًا عَسَى رَبُّكُمْ أَن يُكَفِّرَ عَنكُمْ سَيِّئَاتِكُمْ وَيُدْخِلَكُمْ جَنَّاتٍ تَجْرِي مِن تَحْتِهَا الأَنْهَارُ يَوْمَ لا يُخْزِي اللهُ النَّبِيَّ وَالَّذِينَ آمَنُوا مَعَهُ نُورُهُمْ يَسْعَى

بَيْنَ أَيْدِيهِمْ وَبِأَيْمَانِهِمْ يَقُولُونَ رَبَّنَا أَتْمِمْ لَنَا نُورَنَا وَاغْفِرْ لَنَا إِنَّكَ عَلَى كُلِّ شَيْءٍ قَدِيرٌ

"O you who believe! Turn to Allāh with sincere repentance: In the hope that your Lord will remove your ills and admit you into gardens beneath which rivers flow, the Day that Allāh will not permit the Prophet and the believers with him to be humiliated. Their light (*noor* نُورُهُمْ) will shine before them and on their right hands, while they say, 'Lord! Perfect our light for us, and grant us forgiveness, for You have power over all things'" (Qur'an, 66:8) to mean: "Allāh will not torment the Prophet (that Day, the Day of Judgment)," and the phrase "and those who believed with him" to mean that He will not torment Ali ibn Abū Talib, Fatima, al-Hassan, al-Hussain, peace be with them, al-Hamza, and Ja'far, Allāh be pleased with them, that "their light runs before them" means "Their light shall illuminate the Sirat for Ali and Fatima seventy times more so than light in the life of this world." Their light will then be before them as they continue to cross. The intensity of their light will be indicative of their *iman* بِأَيْمَانِهِمْ, conviction. Others will follow. "Members of the Ahl al-Bayt (ع) of Muhammed (ص) will pass over the Sirat like swift lightning. Then they will be followed by those who will pass like a speedy wind. Then there will be those who will pass as fast as a racing horse. Then another group of people will pass in a walking pace followed by those who will crawl on their hands and bellies, and finally by those who will crawl on their bellies (with extreme difficulty). Allāh will make it wide for the believers and very narrow for the sinners." Then these narrators interpret the verse saying: رَبَّنَا أَتْمِمْ لَنَا نُورَنَا "Lord! Complete our light for us" to mean "complete it for us so that we may be able to pass on the Sirat."

Ibn Shahr Ashub, in his *Manaqib Ali ibn Abi Talib* مناقب علي بن أبي طالب, comments, as quoted by al-Majlisi on the same page, saying, "'The Commander of the Faithful (ع) will pass in a howdah of green emeralds accompanied by Fatima on a conveyance of red rubies, and she will be surrounded by seventy thousand *huris*, as fast as lightning." On p. 182 of his *Amali*, at-Tusi quotes al-Fahham quoting Muhammed ibn al-Hashim al-Hashimi quoting Abū Hashim ibn al-Qasim quoting Muhammed ibn Zakariyya ibn Abdullāh quoting Abdullāh ibn al-Muthanna quoting Tumamah ibn Abdullāh ibn Anas ibn Malik quoting his father quoting his grandfather quoting the

630

Prophet (ص) saying, "On the Day of Judgement, the Sirat will be spread over hell. None can pass over it except one who carries a permit admitting the *wilaya* (mastership) of Ali ibn Abū Talib (ع)." Also with reference to the Sirat, Abū Tharr al-Ghifāri, may Allāh be pleased with him, is quoted by both al-Majlisi on p. 67, Vol. 8, of his book *Bihar al Anwar*, and by al-Kulayni on p. 152, Vol. 2, of his *Al-Kafi*, as saying, "I have heard the Messenger of Allāh (ص) say, 'The edges of our Sirat on the Day of Judgment will be kindness to the kin and the returning of the trust. When one who is kind to his kin and faithful to his trust passes (over the Sirat), he will make his way to Paradise, but when one who is unfaithful to the trust and severs his ties with his kin passes, none of his good deeds will avail him, and the Sirat will hurl him into hell." There are so many references to *noor* نور, divine celestial light, throughout the Holy Qur'an, in the *hadīth*, and in *du'a*, supplication. It is the light of guidance whereby the Almighty guides whomsoever He pleases both in the life of this fleeting world and in the hereafter. Such light will be most sorely needed especially in the life hereafter. The reader is reminded that the intensity of his light, be it during the period of the *barzakh* برزخ, when most graves will be almost as dark as hell, during the time when people are judged on the Day of Judgment, or as one passes over the Sirat..., all depends on the depth and sincerity of his conviction, on his *iman* ايمان. No good deeds, no matter how great, will avail him as will his sincere and deep conviction regarding the Unity (توحيد *tawhid*) and Justice (عدل *'Adl*) of the Almighty, the truth which He revealed to His prophets (نبوة *Nubuwwah*), and that we will most certainly be resurrected and judged (*Ma'ad* معاد), so that one will be either rewarded or punished.

There will be no sun in the life hereafter as we know it, nor will there be electricity; so, one's own light will be his guiding star. Everything in the life hereafter will have a light of its own; there will be no reflection, nor can one walk in the beam of another's light, nor can one be benevolent and give of his light to another; it is non-transferable! There will be no giving. The time of giving is right here, in this life, folks; so, it is now your golden opportunity to give your all to your Maker, to worship Him and obey Him as He ought to be worshipped and obeyed—or at least try; pay Him His dues, and be aware of your responsibilities towards His servants, the believing

631

men and women, and to all mankind, your extended family, regardless of their creeds, for they are your brothers and sisters in humanity Give others of what Allāh has given you; pray for your believing brethren; be kind to everyone; do not hurt the feelings of anyone. Think well of others so that they may think well of you, too. Observe the fast in months other than the month of Ramadan in order to remind yourself of the hunger from which others, especially indigent Muslims, suffer, and give by way of charity; otherwise, keep everything to yourself, hoard, treasure, and be forever damned. Hell is characterized by its darkness, yet its residents will still be able to see things, and whatever they will see will not please them at all. May Allāh Subhanahu wa Ta'ala keep us all away from it and keep it away from us, *Allāhomma Ameen* اللهم آمين.

Nobody in the entire lengthy history of Arabia has ever been known to be more courageous and daring, when confronting his foes on the battlefield, than Imām Ali ibn Abū Talib (ع) who was the right hand of the Messenger of Allāh (ص). Ali was the man who single-handedly uprooted the main gate of the fort of Khaybar of Medīna's Jews of the time, that is, in the year 628 A.D., a gate so heavy it required forty men to close or open. Ali (ع) once was suffering acutely from an inflammation of the eye, and he was in extreme pain, screaming, the hero that he was. The Messenger of Allāh (ص) visited him and saw him scream, so he asked him whether he was suffering from an acute pain or whether it was due to his frustration and agony. The Imām (ع) said, "How intense my pain is! I have never felt such pain...," whereupon the Prophet (ص) said to him, "When the angel of death comes to take away the soul of a disbeliever, he brings with him a rod of fire whereby he takes his soul away. It is then that hell itself will scream because of the intensity of his pain and suffering." Having heard him say so, the Imām (ع) stood up then sat and said, "O Messenger of Allāh! Please repeat what you have just said, for it has made me forget my own pain." Then the Imām (ع) asked the Messenger of Allāh, "Will the soul of any member of your nation be taken away as you have described?" The Prophet (ص) answered, "Yes! The soul of an unjust ruler, or of one who consumes the wealth of an orphan, or of one who falsely testifies [will be thus taken away]." The disbeliever referred to in this tradition is one who is unfair to Allāh, Glory to

Him and Exaltation, regarding one of the commandments which He has required him to uphold, one who does not recognize the Prophethood of Muhammed (ص) and his sacred Sunna السنة النبوية الشريفة or anything required by Islam; such is the disbeliever.

You can reduce the agony of your death, or that of your loved one, by offering charity, fasting, or praying *nafl* (optional) prayers. Among such prayers is one performed in two *rek'ats* ركعات; in each *rek'a*, you should recite Sūrat al-Fātiha once and al-Ikhlas thrice. The intention for that prayer is to pray it seeking nearness to Allāh. Once you complete it, you supplicate to the Almighty thus: "O Allāh! Send blessings to Muhammed and the Progeny of Muhammed and send the rewards for these two *rek'ats* ركعات to so-and-so", naming the dead person, be he/she one of your parents, or both of them, or anyone else. How about you send it as a gift to all Muslims, alive and dead? Imagine how many rewards you will then get, if your imagination can really grasp it! Never underestimate the extent of kindness and mercy of the Almighty; they are unlimited, infinite, and His doors of mercy are always open; how Great He is! If you fast either a few days or all of the months of Rajab and Sha'ban, according to your ability, the Almighty will reduce the agony of your death and the pain of loneliness in the grave. If you are truly concerned about these matters, and you most definitely should be, the month of Ramadan is your golden opportunity to earn as many blessings as Allāh enables you to. It is an opportunity that may not recur, for nobody knows when his/her turn comes to die. We pray the Almighty to enable us to cross over His Sirat with hardship only in the life of this world, and without any hardship in the life hereafter, to forgive our sins, and to accept our fast and repentance, *Allāhomma Ameen* اللهم آمين.

Sirwal سروال: long under garment worn by the Arabs

Siwak سواك: a piece of tree branch or root used as a toothbrush, also called *miswak*

Siyam صيام **(or Sawm):** Islamic fast, abstention from eating, drinking, smoking, intercourse or just speaking; in my book titled *Fast of the Month of Ramadan: Philosophy and Ahkam*, you can read about the 40 (forty) types of fast in Islam.

Subhanahu wa ta'ala سبحانه و تعالى: This is an expression used by Muslims use whenever the name of Allāh is pronounced or written. It means: "Praise to Allāh above having any partners, the most Exalted One above having a son". Muslims believe that Allāh has neither partners nor offspring. Sometimes Muslims use or articulate other expressions when the name of Allāh is written or pronounced. Some of these expressions are: "'Azza Wa Jall", that is, He is the Mighty and the Majestic; "Jalla Jalaluh", His Greatness is Great.

Suffa صفه: a raised platform that was used by the Prophet as a welcoming point for newcomers or destitute people rows of rooms accommodating poor and indigent Muslims who had no houses of their own. They were adjacent to and formed part of the Prophet's *masjid*, mosque, at the time.

Sufi صوفي: an ascetic, a mystic; it is derived from suf or soof, wool, because early Sufis used to wear coarse wool clothes; if we discuss Sufis and Sufism, we will need to write an entire book!

Suhoor or Suhūr سحور: time or meal taken before daybreak in preparation for fasting during the day

Suhuf صحف: pages, manuscripts, tablets

Sujood or Sujūd سجود: The root of those word is *sajada*, prostration to Allāh, usually done during one's daily prayers. When in the position of *sujūd*, a Muslim praises Allāh Almighty and glorifies Him.

Sultān سلطان: ruler who rules in the name of Islam, a Muslim monarch

Sunan سنن: plural of *sunna*, a highly commended or obligatory act of worship or way whereby a Muslim seeks nearness to Allāh

Sunna or Sunnah سنة: In general, the word Sunna means: way of life, habit, practice, customary procedure, action, norm and tradition followed by tradition. Usually, the word Sunna refers to what Prophet Muhammed (ص) had said and done or approved of when said or done by someone else. It includes the Prophet's sayings, practices, living habits, etc. The *hadīth* reports on the Sunna. The two major legal sources of jurisprudence in Islam are the Qur'an and the Sunna.

Sunni or Sunnite سني: a follower of the Islamic faith as reported, narrated and recorded by the Prophet's *sahāba* صحابة, companions, and *tabi'in* تابعين, those who learned from the *sahāba*, may the Almighty be pleased with the good ones among them. Shī'ite Muslims differ from their Sunni brothers when it comes to these sahāba: The Sunnis believe that they all were great, like stars in the heaven shining on earth, and whoever follows any of them, he is rightly guided. Sunnis believe that if a scholar from amongst them acts on his *ijtihad*, and if his *ijtihad* is sound, he will be rewarded twice. But if he errs, he will be rewarded only once, something with which the Shī'ites totally disagree. Shī'ites differ: They say that not all of those *sahāba* were good folks, that many of them were interest seekers who did not hesitate to sacrifice Islam to achieve their objectives. Shī'is say that if a *mujtahid* errs, he will have to bear the burden not only of his own error but that of all those who follow him as well. The Sunni branch of the Islamic faith is comprised mostly of 4 sects: 1) Hanafi, after "Abū Haneefah" Nu'man ibn Thabit ibn Zuta ibn Maah ibn Marzuban, who was born in 80 A.H. and died in 150 A.H. (699 – 767 A.D.); 2) Hanbali, after its founder, namely Ahmed ibn Muhammed ibn Hanbal ibn Hilal ibn As'ad ibn Idrees ibn Abdullāh ibn Hayyan ibn Abdullāh ibn Anas; he was born in 164 A.H. and died in 241 A.H. (781 – 856 A.D.); 3) Shafi'i after its founder, "Abū Abdullāh" Muhammed ibn Idris ibn Abbas ibn Othman ibn Shafi'i ibn Saa'ib ibn Ubayd ibn Abd Yazeed ibn Hashim ibn Muttalib ibn Abd Munaf, of a Quraishi Muttalibi Hashimi lineage; he was born in 150 A.H. and died in 204 A.H. (767 – 820 A.D.); and 4) Maliki after Malik ibn Anas ibn Malik ibn Abi Aamir, "Abū Abdullāh," who was born in 95 A.H. (some say 93 A.H.) and died in 179 A.H. (714 – 795 A.D.).

Sūra or Soorah سوره: The Qur'an is composed of 114 chapters or *suras*. The plural of *sura* is *suwar* سور, chapters.

S.W.T.

These letters are acronyms for "Subhanahu wa Ta'ala". When the name of Almighty Allāh is pronounced, a Muslim is expected to show his veneration to Him. The meaning of this statement is that Allāh is too pure to have partners or sons or any fāmily members or relatives.

T ت، ط، ذ

Ta`atuf تعاطف: sympathy, favour, support

Ta`ayush تعايش: coexistence

Ta`addi تعدي: assault, assailing, attack, invasion, trespassing, encroachment

Ta`ahhud تعهد: pledge, commitment, promise, warrant, warranty

Ta`ammuq تعمق: doing (something such as report, study, research, survey, book, etc.) in depth rather than superficially, the making of a profound (study or inquiry)

Ta`aqqul تعقل: prudence, good judgment

**Tabi`i تابعي:** (sing.:) one who accompanied for a good period of time and learned from a *sahabi* صحابي, a companion of the Holy Prophet Muhammed (ص); its plural is: tabi`in تابعين

Tabthir تبذير: extravagance, profligacy, dissipation, wastefulness

Tadamun تضامن: solidarity, unity, sympathy

Tadarub تضارب: conflict, discordance, clash, discord

Tadarru` تضرع: supplication, imploration, earnest plea, prayer

Tadlis or Tadlees تدليس: deraud or defrauding, deception

Tadnis تدنيس: defilement, desecration, profanation

Tafadi تفادي: Avoidance, evasion, escape from, shunning or eschewing, sidestepping, overlooking

Tafadul تفاضل: Making a preference, preferring (something or someone) over others

Tafarruq تفرق: dispersal, scattering, division

Tafa'ul تفاؤل: optimism, anticipating the best, auguring well, taking a bright view of something

Tafawut تفاوت: variance, disparity, discrepancy, diversity

Tafawwuq تفوق: excellence, superiority

Tafawud تفاوض: negotiate, confer

Tafsir تفسير: interpretation, explanation, elucidation

Tahaffudi تحفظي: precautionary, protective (measure, custody, etc.), preventive, conservative, moderate

Tahajjud تهجد: night devotions. *Mutahajjid* is one who keeps vigilance, spending the night praying; the *tahajjud* prayer is an optional prayer that is supposed to be performed in the middle of the night. It is required that a person sleeps a little before getting up for the *tahajjud* prayers. It can be performed anytime during the period between the *isha* (evening) and the *fajr* (pre-dawn) time.

Tahakkum تهكم: sarcasm, taunting, deriding with irony

Tahara طهاره: purification, the act of removing *najasa*, uncleanness or impurity

Tahattuk تهتك: immorality, debauchery, licentiousness

Tahayyub تهيب: feeling afraid or scared of/about, apprehension, timidity

Tahkim تحكيم: arbitration

Ta'ib تائب: repentant, penitent, regretful, contrite

Tajrid تجريد: divestment, divestiture (of title), despoliation, deprivation or privation

Tajweed تجويد: a saying or an act of reciting the Qur'an in accordance with the established rules of *Nutq*, pronunciation and intonations, such as *tafkheem*, velarization, chanting and *Iqlab*, transposition

Takbir تكبير: the glorifying of Allāh by declaring in an audible voice: الله أكبر! "Allāho Akbar!" Allāh is Great! By the way, the Prophet's flag was green on which this declaration is written in white cloth.

Takfir or Takfeer تكفير: labeling someone as "kafir", apostate, unbeliever, excommunicating from the creed. People who do that are called "Takfiris" or Takfeeri". The terms is applied mostly to the most extremist and fanatical offshoot of the Wahhabi movement الحركه الوهابيه, and the Takfiris (التكفيريون) loosely apply this term to those who do not follow their own line, ideology or version of "Islam". They have so far killed, through acts of terrorism and sabotage, more Muslims than non-Muslims although they claim to be the protectors of the Islamic creed... They are found mostly in Saudi Arabia, the Gulf region, Afghanistan, India, Pakistan and lately Iraq. Al-Qaeda is these days one of the most famous and active Takfiri organizations due to the funding it receives from these Wahhabis and Takfiris. Their ideology is an interpretation of their own of one "Abū Taymiyyah", namely Ahmed ibn (son of) Abdul-Halim ibn Abdul-Salam ibn Abdullāh al-Khidr, also known as "Taqiyy ad-Din" and as "Abul-`Abbas". He was born in 661 A.H./1263 A.D. in Harran, now an area north of Syria, and died inside a Damascus, Syria, prison in 728 A.H./1328 A.D. Abū

Taymiyyah had his own personal radical and un-orthodox way of interpreting *hadīth* and was at the time reputed as a scholar who followed the Hanbali school of Sunni Muslim Law. Since these interpretations differed from those of anyone else, including his own contemporaries as well as classic jurists (*faqihs*), he distinguished himself from all other scholars of jurisprudence. Those who adopt his views are called "Salafis", people who claim to follow in the footsteps of the "pious predecessors" (السلف الصالح). Abū Taymiyyah is on the record as beign the first person to disbelieve in the intercession شفاعه on the Judgment Day although numerous references to intercession exist in the Holy Qur'an such as these (first number corresponds to the Chaper/Sura and the next to the verse): 2:255, 4:85, 7:53, 21:28, 26:100, 74:48, 6:51. 6:70, 10:3, 32:4, 40:18, 7:53, 30:13, 39:43, 6:94, 10:18, 2:48, 2:123, 2:254, 4:85, 19:87, 20:109, 34:23, 39:44, 43:86, 74:48, 36:23 and 53:26. If all these Qur'anic verses do not convince Ibn Taymiyyah and his followers that intercession does exist in this life and will exist in the life to come, nothing else at all will convince him and them. Since they do not believe in intercession, most likely they will never see such intercession; neither the Prophet nor anyone else will intercede on their behalf on the Judgment Day. For more details, read an extensive 463-page book titled *Ibn Taymiyyah* by a great scholar and researcher, namely Sa'ib Abdul-Hamid, but do not let the Salafis or, worse, the Takfiris, catch you reading it! Here in Iraq, al-Qaeda terrorists, who are brainwashed by the philosophy of this man and of Abdul-Wahhab, behead Muslims and say that anyone who severs a certain number of heads (7 or 70) is guaranteed to go to Paradise, so he is exempted for the rest of his life from having to pray, fast, perform the pilgrimage or perform any other Islamic rite...! The Prophet of Islam (ص) continued to pray till the last day of his holy life; does this mean that he had no guarantee to go to Paradise?! We seek refuge with Allāh from the evil, mischief and schemes of such twisted minds.

Takhmin تخمين: surmising, appraisal, assessment, guesswork

Takia or Takya تكية: place where Sufis perform their rituals and practices

Takmili تكميلي: complementary, supplemental

Takwin تكوين: formation, formulation

Talakku' تلكؤ: procrastination, lingering, taking too long to do something

Talaq طلاق: divorce. Divorce in Islam is one of the most complicated teachings, and scholars of jurisprudence differ among themselves regarding its rules and regulations a great deal. According to Grand Ayatollah Sayyid Ali as-Sistani, divorce is of two main types: 1) رجعي, *raj'i,* revocable; and 2) بائن ba'in, irrevocable. Other types of divorce are: 1) خلعي *talaq khal'i*: It is one initiated by the wife. Yes, Islam permits the wife in certain circumstances to divorce her husband. It is a self-redemption divorce initiated by the wife; and 2) طلاق المباراة *talaq al-mubarat*: It is a divorce based on mutual dislike for marriage and the desire to end it. How many conditions are there for a divorce to be valid according to Islam? You are dead wrong if you think that by merely pronouncing the statement "You are divorced أنت طالق" that the divorce becomes valid even if you repeat it not three but three hundred times.

Talawwuth تلوث: pollution, contamination

Talbiyah تلبية: uttering of لبيك! "*Labbayk!*" which means "Here I come, at your service!"

Taleeq طليق: an unconfined (free) man of Mecca who remained a non-believer in Islam till the conquest of Mecca in 630 A.D.

Talih طالح: bad, evil, wicked

Talqeen تلقين: addressing/instructing a dead person during the early stages of his long trip to the Hereafter. It is instructing the deceased person, who then hears the living but cannot respond to them, about the basics of his creed. One who does so is the *mulaqqin* ملقن. Make sure you choose your *mulaqqin* before it is too late. For more details, refer to منزل *Manzil* above in the paragraph dealing with the questioning in the grave by angels Munkir and Nakeer.

Tamadi تمادي: transcending limits, indulgence in excesses, giving free rein (to)

Tamaluk (نفس) تمالك: (self) restraining, self-control

Tamarud تمارض: feigning sickness, pretense of sickness

Tamarrud تمرد: rebellion, mutiny, disobedience

Tamarrus تمرس: acquiring mastership, becoming skilled, acquiring proficiency

Tamawut تماوت: feigning death, pretending to be dead

Tanafur تنافر: conflict, discord, feeling offended with/by, clash, disagreement, disharmony, revulsion

Tanafus تنافس: competition or competing, being in a contest, rivalry

Tanasul تناسل: procreation, propagation, reproduction

Tanasuq تناسق: consistency, coordination, uniformity

Tanjim or Tanjeem تنجيم: astrology, star science, star reading

Tannoor تنور: open oven, tandor. Another meaning is mentioned in the Holy Qur'an in two places when the Almighty narrates to us the great flood of Prophet Noah (ع): و فار التنور... : "... and the *fountains of the earth* gushed forth..." (Qur'an, 11:40 and 23:27), according to one translation of the Holy Qur'an. You can refer to other translations of the Holy Qur'an for both 11:40 and 23:27 if you wish. Is there any similarity between an "open oven" in which people bake their bread or meat and "fountains of the earth"?! In his translation of the Holy Qur'an, S.V. Mir Ahmed Ali uses the word "oven", too. And surely Allāh knows best.

Taqadum تقادم: process of becoming old, obsolete or antiquated

Taqashuf تقشف: austerity measures, extreme economizing, the leading of a very simple life

Tamasuk تماسك: cohesion, adhesion, conglomeration

Taqiyya تقيه: an obligatory measure for one whose life is endangered to exert precaution in order to save his creed or life when either is in jeopardy; a way for a Muslim to try to survive in the presence of sure perils.

Taqleed or Taqlid تقليد: emulation or emulating, following a *mujtahid* or an authority recognized as the *a'lim*, scholar or a most knowledgeable person in Islamic *fiqh*

Taqribi تقريبي: approximate, almost, not equal but close

Taqwa تقوى: love and awe that a Muslim feels for Allāh. A person having *taqwa* in his heart desires to please Allāh, so he stays away from doing things which displease or incur the Wrath of Allāh. He is careful not to go beyond the boundariess and limits set by Allāh.

Taraweeh تراويح: prayers performed in congregation by Sunnis during the nights of the month of Ramadan

Tareeqa طريقة: a Sufi method of conducting rituals, a Sufi code of ritualistic religious conduct

Tarikh or Taareekh تأريخ: history writing, chronicling (of events)

Tarteel ترتيل: chanting the Holy Qur'an and following certain relevant rules of recitation

Tarwiyah ترويه: The Day of Tarwiyah is the 8th of Thul-Hijjah when the pilgrims fill their water bags and prepare to go to Mina.

Tasahul تساهل: toleration, tolerance, indulgence

Tasaluh تصالح: reconciliation, patching up, mending walls, making peace

642

Tasannu` تصنع: pretension, make-belief, simulation

Tashahhud تشهد: the testimony regarding Allāh being the Lord and Muhammad being His Servant and Messenger; it is the uttering of أشـهد أن لا الـه الا الله و أن محمـدا عبده و رسوله *"Ashhadu an la ilaha illa-Allāh, wa anna Muhammed abdoho wa rasooloh"*

Tashreeq تشريق: the cutting and sun-drying of sacrificed meat

Tathir تطهير: purification, disinfection, purgation or expurgation

Tawakkul توكل: reliance or dependence on, trust in

Tawatur تواتر: consecutive reporting (of *hadīth*, incident, etc.), succession of narrators or narratives, sequence, succession, repetition, frequency

Tawaf طواف: the circling of (going around) the Ka'bah seven times, usually during *umra* or *hajj*.

Tawatur تواتر: consecutive reporting, the tracing of one particular *hadīth* to its respective chronological chain of narrators

Tawbikh or Tawbeekh توبيخ: reprimanding, reproofing

Tawhid or Tawheed توحيد: confirming or testifying to the Oneness of Allāh. It is the basis of Islam, the concept of the absolute Unity of God, the belief that God is One and indivisible, One—and Only One—God.

Taw`iya توعيه: raising consciousness or awareness, awakening

Tawwabeen توابين: the penitent ones, reportedly 686 in number, those who repented their reluctance to go to the rescue of Imām Hussain (ع) when he was confronted with Yazid's huge armies. These penitents enlisted under the military command of al-Mukhtar ibn Abū Ubayd ath-Thaqafi(*cir.* 622 – 687 A.D.) and went on hot pursuit of those who massacred Imām Hussain son of Ali ibn Abù T alib, killing them all.

Tayammum تيمم: the method of using clean dust to perform ablution (*wudu*) in the absence of water or for health-related or other justifiable reasons

Tayammun تيمن: optimism, seeing or expecting realization of a good omen

Tayh تيه: willful misleading, perdition or loss, straying, deluding, loss of the right path or guidance

Tazammut تزمت: Zealotry, fanaticism, excessive conservatism

Thakireen ذاكرين: those who quite often mention the Name of the Almighty and Glorify Him

Thabat ثبات: firmness, steadfastness, holding grounds (in battle, etc.), solidity, stability

Thana' ثناء: praise, commendation, compliment

Thaqib ثاقب: piercing, penetrating

Thawab ثواب: reward of blessing

Thayyib ثيب: a widow or divorcee

Thiqal ثقل: weight, burden, pressure

Thiqat ثقاة: plural of thiqah ثقة, a trustworthy authority; this term is often used to testify to the truthfulness of some narrators of *hadīth*.

Thireed ثريد: pieces of bread cut and dipped in stew

Tih or Teeh (ضياع) تيه: dispersion, diaspora, loss, random wandering without sense of direction

Tughyan طغيان: tyranny, despotism, oppression, escessive or abusive exercise of power or authority

Turath تراث: legacy, heritage, patrimony

U أ، ع

`**Ulama or Ulema or** `**Ulema** علماء: plural of `*alim*, scholar-theologian, learned, knowledgeable in Islam

Umma or Ummah أمه: nation, group of people, a community. It is used in reference to the community of Believers

Umm al-Mu'mineen or Um al-Mu'mineen أم المؤمنين: "mother of the Believers" or of the faithful. This was the title of each of the Prophet's wives; (Sura 33 Ayah 6 stipulated that they could not marry after the Prophet's death because all of the believers were their spiritual children).

Umra عمره: minor pilgrimage; pilgrimage to Mecca during any time other than the prescribed (first ten) days of the month of Thul-Hijja

Urf عرف: custom, radition, social usage; عرف سائد : prevailing custom; عرف عام: general custom; عرف متوطد: established custom; عرف مهنه: trade usage

Urwa عروه: tie, link, bond

Usool or Usul أصول: the basics of jurisprudence

Uzza عزى: a chief goddess according to the beliefs of pre-Islamic Arabs, i.e. during the days of *jahiliyya*

W و

Wahi or Wahee وحي: revelation through arch-angel Gabriel or a divine inspiration

Wajib واجب: compulsory, obligatory, binding

Wakil or Wakeel وكيل**:** a person who is an authorized representative or proxy; agent. It can also mean lawyer in Urdu.

Wali or Walee ولي**:** person to whom *wilayat* ولايـه و is obligatory. A *wali* والي, however, is a governor appointed by a Muslim ruler of a higher authority (such as a caliph, sultan, etc.), legal guardian, friend or protector, someone who is supposed to look after your interest

Walima وليمه**:** post-wedding feast, reception.

Wasi وصي**:** successor to a prophet; guardian, protector, custodian

Wilayat ولايـه**:** a binding supreme authority that combines both temporal and religious powers

Wisal وصال**:** fasting the last day of every lunar calendar month

Wudu or Wuzu وضوء**:** a purification (*ablution*) which must be performed before the *salat* or the recitation of the Qur'an

Z ز،ض، ظ

Zakat or Zakat زكاة**:** One of the five pillars of Islam is *zakat* which literally means "purification", an increment of one's wealth. A Muslim who has money beyond a certain quantity is to pay *zakat*. It is also called "alms dues" or "poor dues" except it is not optional. It is to be distributed for specific categories for the welfare of the society. These categories are mentioned in the Qur'an which include: the poor, the needy, the destitutes, the captives, the ones in debt, in the cause of Allāh, the wayfarers and for those who collect it. Literally, it means "purification;" it is a compulsory 2.5% tax on one of three categories of wealth 1) metal coins (gold, silver, etc.), 2) grain crops (barley, wheat, grain, rice, etc.), and 3) animals raised for food consumption. *Zakiat* is somehow a complicated subject. For details, the readers are advised to consult books dealing with *fiqh*. Among its types are: *zakat al-mal* (taxable wealth accumulated during one full year) and *zakat al-fitr* (a tax to be paid by the head of a household at the end of the fast of the month of Ramadan).

Zaman or Dhamaan ضمان: guarantee, security, guaranty, warranty; variations: ضمان لمحكمه recognizance, ضمان إضافي collateral security; ضمان حسن سلوك security for good behavior; ضمان شخصي personal security; ضمان عقاري real estate security; ضمان لياقه warranty of fitness; ضمان مطلق absolute guaranty

Zawaj زواج: marriage, legal, legitimate and permissible cohabitation; spouses are: **Zawj** زوج husband and **Zawja** زوجه wife

Zawal زوال: disappearance, passage, lapse, discontinuance. It also refers to the certain times related to the position of the sun: It may be a sunset غروب or midday, meridian منتصف النهار.

Zendiq or Zindiq or Zindeeq زنديق: heretic, one who believes neither in the Unity of the Creator (*Tawhid*) nor in the Hereafter, one who goes so far into innovated and deviant beliefs and senseless sophistry without sticking to the truth which is already stated in the Qur'an and the Sunna to such an extreme extent that he actually leaves Islam altogether. Accprding to *Lisan al-Arab* lexicon by Ibn Manzour, this word is not originally Arabic; its root is the Persian *zand-kirai* which means one who believes that life is eternal and that there is no life hereafter.

Zihar ظهار: the making of a similitude between the back of one's wife and that of his mother; i.e. saying that his wife's back looks similar to his mother's back, a custom followed during the time of ignorance (*jahiliyya*) which Islam banned; doing so implied that such a wife was divorced.

Ziyara زياره: visit, social get-together. A pilgrimage to a holy site other than Mecca and Medīna is also called Ziyara and the one who performs it is a **Za'ir** زائر.

Zuha ضحى: afternoon; also: title of Chapter 93 of the Holy Qur'an which comprised of 11 verses.

Zuhr or Dhuhr ظهر: the obligatory *salat*, prayer, performed in the afternoon right after the sun moves away from its zenith

Zuhoor or Zuhur ظهور: Its simple meaning is "the appearing", or
the coming out. If you give it the definite article "the" and make it
الظهور, you will be referring to the time when the Awaited One, the
Mahdi, the Living 12th Imām (عج) comes out of his occultation,
concealment, and starts working on filling the earth with justice and
ease after being filled with injustice, oppression and depression, and
there will be so much prosperity that nobody will be needy. Any
research about this reappearance of al-Mahdi (عج) cannot be covered
fully and fairly except by a voluminous book. But let me give you
few thoughts to consider about this momentous event: Just as there
is One God, call Him Allāh, Khuda, Diu, Jehovah, or whatever, for
He is One and the same, there is also one single family that
descended from Adam and Eve, our extended human family. And
there is only one truth: It is revealed to nations each according to its
history, culture, traditions, ways of life and levels of sophistication.
Likewise, there is one and only one Awaited Savior: The Christians
believe he will be Christ re-incarnated, the Jews believe he will be
one of the descendants of Prophet David, peace be with him, while
other religions refer to a savior of some sort. Just as the Creator has
many names, so does this savior. In Islam, he is al-Mahdi (عج), the
guided one, the guide. Let us tell you a little about this great
personality: Imām al-Mahdi (عج) was born to the 11th Imām,
Muhammed son of Hassan al-`Askari, who is buried in Samarra,
Iraq, in what is now known world-wide as the "Askari Shrine" which
was bombed by Wahhabi Takfiri terrorists on Wednesday, February
22, 2006, an event which almost hurled the Iraqis into the inferno of
civil war. This shrine, which is now being rebuilt, has always been
visited by the faithful from various parts of the world, so much so
that plans are now plans underway to build an intenational airport in
Samarra to cater to the influx of these pilgrims. His mother is Lady
Nerjis Khatun, granddaughter of the Imām al-Askari's contemporary
Byzantine king who was a descendant of prophet Sham`un or
Simon, trustee of Jesus Christ. Imām al-Mahdi (عج) was born on the
15th of Sha`ban of 255 A.H./July 29, 869 A.D. and became the Imām
following the martyrdom of his revered father in 260 A.H./874 A.D.
when he was only five. Do not be surprised and ask: How can a boy
who is only five years old be an Imām?! Let me remind you that

Prophet Yahya (John the Baptist) was a prophet even when he was a child with neither a beard nor a moustache. The Almighty can do anything at all. His period of Imāmate lasted till the year 260 A.H./874 A.D. He went into the "minor occultation", that is, not appearing in public so he would not be a target of the enemies of the Prophet's family from among those who ruled the Muslims in the name of "Islam" (and there are some of such people living even in our time), during the period which extended from 260 to 329 A.H. (874 – 941 A.D.). During this period, he had deputies or representatives who acted as liaisons between him and the public and their names and biographies are available for review in books which discuss the Imām (ع). After 329 A.H./874 A.D., it was too dangerous for anyone to represent the Imām (ع) even to his followers, so he went into the period of the "major occultation" which extended from 329 A.H./941 A.D. to our time and will continue till his re-appearance which many Islamic scholars now stress will be very soon especially since the signs marking his re-appearance, as recorded in Sunna books, have already materialized, and there is no room to detail them here. Where will the Imām (ع) reappear? His reappearance will be in Mecca, Saudi Arabia, and it will be seen on television screens all over the world. He will lead a campaign to purge the Islamic world of all those who do not deserve to live on our planet then establish alliances with non-Muslim countries based on mutual respect and brotherhood, and these non-Muslims will for the first time feel fully secure. We believe that he will reappear accompanied by prophet Jesus Christ so the whole world will see how close these two religions are to each other, and Christ will dissociate himself from all those who throughout the centuries played havoc with the pristine divine message which he had brought the world. We must add that there have been many imposters each one of whom claimed to be Imām al-Mahdi (ع) in both Shī'ite and Sunni societies, but their falsehood was bared before the world, and most likely there will be many more in the future as well till the real Imām al-Mahdi (ع) appears to start his global revolution in defense of the poor, rightousness, justice, equality and toleration.

A lengthy tradition (*hadīth* حديث) quoted in the classic reference *Thawab al-A`mal* ثواب الأعمـا ل cites Imām Ja'far as-Sādiq (ع) quoting the Messenger of Allāh (ص) saying, "Time will come to my nation during which their inwardly intentions are bad while they display good attitudes only because they covet this life and they do not desire what Allāh, the most Exalted, the most Great, has. They will have pretension without fear, so much so that they will be blinded by Allāh with penalty from Him, whereupon they will plead to him like one about to drown, but He will not respond to their plea."

Another tradition in the same source quotes the Messenger of Allāh (ص) as having said, "Time will come upon my nation (Muslims) during which nothing remains of the Qur'an except its form, nor of Islam except its name. They are called Muslims while they are the furthermost of people from it: Their mosques are crowded, yet they lack guidance. The *faqihs* فقهاء (jurists) of that time will be the worst under the sky; from them did فتنه strife begin, and to them it shall return."

In the classic reference *Ikmal ad-Deen* إكمال الدين, we read the following tradition quoted from Imām Muhammed al-Bāqir (ع), father of Imām Ja'far as-Sādiq (ع), saying, "Al-Qā'im القائم (one of the titles of Imām al-Mahdi (عج)) will be supported with fear (in the hearts of his opponents), backed by victory; distances in the earth will be shortened for him; treasures will appear for him, and his authority will reach the east and the west. Allāh, the most Exalted, the most Great, will let His creed (Islam) be the uppermost through him though the infidels abhor it. There will be no ruin on earth without being repaired. And Ruhullah روح الله Jesus Christ will descend and pray behind him. This will happen when men will look like women and women will imitate men, when a man is satisfied [sexually] by a man and a woman by a woman, when females ride and false witnesses are accepted by courts while those of just men will be rejected, when people take bloodletting lightly, when adultery is committed and usury is consumed, when evildoers are avoided for fear of what they would say, when the Sufyani comes out of Syria and the Yemani out of Yemen, when the desert gapes outMuhammed and a young man from among the descendants of (ص) is killed between the Rukn and the Maqam (in Holy Ka'ba) named Muhammed son of al-Hassan, a man of a pure soul, and when a cry comes out of the sky that he is a man of the truth and so are his followers; it is then when our Qā'im القائم comes out (of his occulation). So, when he comes out, he will recline his back on the Ka`ba, and 313 men will join him. The first that he will articulate is this verse: 'That which is left by Allāh for you is good for you, if you are believers' (Qur'an, 11:86). He will then say, 'I am what is left by Allāh for you in His land.' When the full number of his supporters is complete, which is 10,000 men, anything worshipped on earth other than Allāh, the most Exalted One, the most Great, such as idols and other things, is set on fire and is burnt. This will take place after a long period of occulation so Allāh may ascertain who obeys Him in the unseen and who believes in Him."

There are numerous theories surrounding this reappearance of al-Mahdi (عج); some of them make some sense whereas others make some sense to some people and none to others, depending on people's level of understanding. One of these theories says that there will be major sites where vital roles will be played, all related to this reappearance. These include: Yemen, Hijaz (Saudi Arabia), Iran, Iraq, Syria, Palestine, Egypt and Europe. Apparently, very significant events will take place in all these countries. This theory goes on to state that allies in Yemen will stage a revolution only a couple of months before the reappearance, which is commonly referred to as the Zuhoor ظهور. These Yemenites will fill up the political vacuum in Hijaz (Saudi Arabia) and will also assist the Imām (عج) in his sweeping revolution. The reason for this vacuum will be the death of King Abdullāh who is currently the ruler of Saudi Arabia. This Abdullāh is supposed to be the last monarch to rule Hijaz and Nejd (the two main parts of Saudi Arabia, the only country in the world named after its ruling Wahhabi minority clan). After him, there will be a huge fight for the inheritance of the throne. The fight for the throne will go on till the advent of our Imām (عج). The monarchist system that has been ruling Saudi Arabia since 1932 will be reduced to few months. There shall be constant clashes among the tribes in Hijaz after the death of King Abdullāh, and one person amongst these rulers will ruthlessly murder 15 important leaders or famous `ulema, scholars, and their sons who belong to his opponent's tribe.

More details about al-Mahdi (عج) are provided above under the item

"Mahdi, al-" to which you may refer if you wish.

We pray the Almighty to hasten the reappearance of our Hidden Imām, al-Hujja, al-Mahdi (عج), and to count us among his soldiers who defend his message and to bless the humble effort exerted in putting this book together, *Ameen*.

APPENDIX

ARABIC POEMS EULOGIZING IMĀM HUSSAIN'S MARTYRDOM

These poems are too beautiful to be translated in any language at all. This is why we leave them as they are, hoping the faithful will recite them during Muharram and other somber occasions:

هذه مختارات من قصائد في مديح أبي الشهداء الحسين (ع) و أهل بيته الطيبين الطاهرين آثر المؤلف أن يدرجها في كتابه هذا للناطقين بالضاد لقراءتها في المحرم و مآتم أهل البيت (ع).

أبو البحر صفوان بن إدريس بن إبراهيم النجيبي المرسي (561 - 598ه):

على منزلة الهدى يتعلم	سلام كأزهار الربى يتنسم
لا وجههم فيه بدور وأنجم	على مصرع للفاطميين غيبت
لعاينت أعضاء النبي تقسم	على مشهد لو كنت حاضر أهله
وإلا فأن الدمع أندى وأكرم	على كربلاء لا أخلف الغيث كربلا
وناح عليهن الحطيم وزمزم	مصارع ضجت يثرب لمصابها
وموقف حج والمقام المعظم	ومكة والأستار والركن والصفا
رأى ابن زياد أمه كيف تعقم	لو أن رسول الله يحيى بعيدهم
تنادي اباها والمدامع تسجم	وأقبلت الزهراء قدس تربها
كما صاغة قيس ومامج أرقم	تقول: أبي هم غادروا أبني نهبة
كأنهم قد أحسنوا حين أجرموا	وهم قطعوا رأس الحسين بكربلا
وأجفان عين تستطير وتسجم	فخذ منهم ثأري وسكن جوانحاً
وغلته والنهر ريان مفعم	أبي وأنتصر للسبط وأذكر مصابه
لبنت رسول الله أين تيمم؟	فيا أيها المغرور والله غاضب
ألا أدمع تجري ألا قلب يضرم	ألا طرب يقلى ألا حزن يصطفى

653

لتصغر في حق الحسين ويعظم	قفوا ساعدونا بالدموع فأنها
تعبــر عن محض الأسى وتترجم	ومهما سمعتم في الحسين مراثياً
وصلوا على جد الحسين وسلموا	فمدوا أكفاً مسعدين بدعوة

دعبل : أنقل لكم أخوتي في الأسطر القليله الآتيه بعض القصائد العظيمه لشاعر أهل بيت العصمه (ص) دعبل الخزاعي رضوان الله تعالى عليه ولنشاركه جميعاً بالدمعة والعبره فطالما بكى وأبكى رضوان الله عليه

لَم تَترُكـي منّي ولم تُبْقي	يا نكبةً جاءتْ مِنَ الشَّرقِ
مِن سَخَطِ الله على الخَلْقِ	مَوْتُ عليِّ بن موسى الرضا
وباتت الأحشاء في الخَفْقِ	وبات طَرْفي مانعاً للكَرى
لثُلمَـة بـاينـة الرَّتـقِ	وأصبحَ الإسلام مُستَعبراً
بأرضِ طُوسٍ ، سبل الوَدقِ	سَقى الغريب المُنتَني قبرهُ

ألا أيها القبر الغريب:

بطوس ، عليك السَّارياتُ هُتـونُ	ألا أيها القبـرُ الغريبُ مَحَلَّــة
بك الدّيـن والدّنيـا ، وأنت ضمينُ	بك العلمُ والتّقوى ، بك الحُلمُ والحِجى
ولكنني فيمـا دهاكَ ظنينُ	جرى الموتُ على خَيرِ النّبيين فارتقى
فأمسى يُعاني السَّمَ وهوسَجينُ	ومن قَبلُ موسى كم بَدَت منهُ آية
بها السَّـمِّ ، والمَكرُ الخَفيُّ يبينُ	فيا لَقتيلَيْ غَـدرة قدْ سُقيتما
ومَنْ كـان أوحى ، والحديثُ شُجونُ	سأبكيكما عمـري وألعن غـادراً

نذكر هناك في الأسطر القادمه قصيدتان لدعبل الخزاعي رضوان الله تعالى عليه في رثاء سيدنا ومولانا قتيلُ العَبره سيد الشهداء أبي عبدالله الحسين عليه أفضل الصلاة والسلام

جاؤوا من الشّام:

بالشّـؤمِ يَقـدُمُ جندهـم إبليـسُ	جاؤوا مِنَ الشّام المَشومة أهلها
تركـوه وهو مُبَضّعٌ مَحموسُ	لُعنوا ، وقد لُعنوا بقتـل إمامهـم
عَبْرى حَواسِرَ ما لهنّ لَبوسُ	و سَبَوْا – فواحَزنـي- بنات محمّدٍ
بالنـار ؟ ذَلَّ هنالك المَحبوسُ	تبـاً لكـم ، يا وَيْلكـم ، أرضيتـم
عِزُّ الحيـاة ، و إنّـهُ لَنفيسُ	بعتّـم لدنيا غيركـم ، جَهـلاً لكـم
لُعنَت ، و حَظُّ البايعين خسيسُ	أخسِـرْ بها مِن بيعة أمَويةٍ
بإمامكـم وَسْطَ الجحيم حبيسُ	بؤساً لمـن بايعتـم ، وكأنّني
مِن عُصبـة هم في القِياس مجوسُ ؟	يـا آل أحمدَ ما لقيتـم بعـدهُ
يـوم الطّفوفِ على الحُسَينِ نفوسُ	كـم عبرةٍ فاضت لكـم وتقطّعت
فيـها ، وفَـوْقَ الذّابـلاتِ روؤسُ	واحَسـرتاهُ !! لكم جسومٌ بالعرا

صبراً موالينا ، فسوف يُديلُكم	يومٌ على آل اللعين عبوسُ
ما زلتُ متّبعاً لكم ولأمركـم	وعليه نفسي ما حييت أسوسُ

رأس ابن بنت محمد:

رأس ابن بنت محمدٍ و وَصيّـه	يـا للرجال، على قناةٍ يُرْفعُ
والمسلمون بمنظرٍ وبمسمع	لا جازعٍ مـن ذا ، و لا تَخشَّعُ!!
أيُـقظْت أجفاناً وكنتَ لها كرىً	و أنمْتَ عَيْناً لم تكُن بك تهْجعُ
كُـحِلَتْ بمنظركَ العيونُ عمايةً	و أصمَّ نَعْيُك كـلَّ أذنٍ تسمعُ
مـا روضةٌ إلّا تمنّت أنّهـا	لك مضجعٌ ، و لَخَطَ قبرك مَوْضعُ

قصيدة جداً رائعة من أجمل قصائد نزار قباني:

سـأل المخالف حين انهكه العجب	هل للحسين مع الروافض من نسب
لا ينقضي ذكر الحسين بثغرهم	وعلـى امتداد الدهـر يُوقـِد كاللَّهب
وكـأنَّ لا أكَـلَ الزمانُ علـى دم	كدم الحسين بكربلاء ولا شرب
أوَلَم يَحنْ كفُ البكاء فما عسى	يُبدي ويُجدي والحسين قد احتسب
فأجبته مـا للحسين وما لـكم	يـا رائدي نـدوات آليـة الطرب
إن لـم يكن بين الحسين وبيننـا	نسبٌ فيكفينا الرثاء له نسب
والحر لا ينسـى الجميل وردّه	ولأنْ نسى فلقد أساء إلى الأدب
يـالائمي حب الحسـين أجنـننا	واجتاح أودية الضمائر واشرأبُّ
فلقد تشـرّب في النخاع ولم يزل	سـريانه حتى تسلَّط في الرُكب
مـن مثله أحيى الكرامة حينما	ماتت على أيدي جبابـرة العرب
وأفاق دنيـاً طـأطأت لولاتـها	فـرقى لذاك ونال عـالية الرتب
و غدى الصمود بإثره متحفـزاً	والـذل عن وهج الحياة قد احتجب
أما البكاء فـذاك مصدر عزنـا	وبه نواسيهم ليـوم المنقلب
نبكي على الـرأس المـرتل آية	والرمح منبره وذاك هو العجب
نبكي على الثغر المكسر سنه	نبكي على الجسد السليب المُنتهب
نبكي على خدر الفواطم حسرة	وعلى الشبيبة قطعوا إرباً إرب
دع عنك ذكر الخالدين وغبطهم	كي لا تكون لنار بارئهم حطب

قصيدة الجواهري في رثاء الحسين ع:

فِـداءً لمثواكَ من مَضجَع	تَنَـوَّر بالأبلَـجِ الأروَع
بـأعبقَ من نفحات الجِنانِ	رُوْحـاً ومن مِسـكِها أضوَع
وَرَعْياً ليومِكَ يوم "الطُفوف"	وسَقْياً لأرضِكَ مـن مَصرَع
وحُـزناً عليك بِحَبْس النفوس	على نَهْجِكَ النَّيِّر المَهْيَع
وصَوْنـاً لمجدِكَ مِـنْ أنْ يُذال	بما أنتَ تأبـاهُ مِـنْ مُبْدَع
فيا أيُّها الوثَـرُ في الخالدينَ	فَـذاً ، إلى الآن لم يُشْفَع

ويـا عظَّةَ الطامحيـنَ العظـامَ   للاهيـنَ عـن غَدِهِم قُنَّعِ

تعاليتَ مـن مُفزِعٍ للخُتوفِ   وبُورِكَ قبرُكَ مـن مَفزَعِ

تلوذُ الدُّهورُ فَمَن سُجَّدٍ   على جانبيـته ومـن رُكَّعِ

شَمَمتُ ثَراكَ فهبَّ النَّسيمُ   نَسيمُ الكَرامَـةِ مِـن بَلْقَعِ

وعَفَّرتُ خَدّي بحيثُ استراحَ   خَدٍّ تَفَترَّى و لـم يَضْرَعِ

وحيثُ سنابكُ خيلِ الطُّغاةِ   جالثْ عليـهِ و لـم يَخْشَعِ

وخِلتُ وقد طارتِ الذكرياتُ   بـروحي إلى عَالمٍ أرْفَعِ

وطُفتُ بقبرِكَ طَوفَ الخَيالِ   بصومعةِ المُلْهَمِ المُبْدِعِ

كأنَّ يَداً مِن وَراءِ الضَّريحِ   حمراءَ "مَبْثُـورَةَ الإصْبَعِ"

تَمُدُّ إلى عالمٍ بالخُنوعِ   والـضَّيمُ ذي شرَقٍ مُشرَعِ

تَخَبَّطَ فـي غابةٍ أطْبَقَتْ   على مُذْنِبٍ منـه أو مُسبِعِ

لتُبدِّل منـه جَديبَ الضَّميرِ   بـآخـرَ مُعشَوشِبٍ مُمرَعِ

وتدفعَ هذي النفوسَ الصغارَ   خوفاً إلـى حَـرَمٍ أمْنَعِ

تعاليتَ مـن صاعقٍ يلتظى   فـإن تَـدْجُ داجِيـةٌ يَلْمَعِ

تأرَّم حقداً على الصاعقاتِ   لـم تُـنْءِ ضَيْراً ولم تَنْفَعِ

ولـم تَبذُرِ الحبَّ إثـرَ الهشيمِ   و قـد حَرَّقَتْهُ و لـم تَـزْرَعِ

ولـم تُخْلِ أبراجَها في السماءِ   ولم تـأتْ أرضاً ولم تُدْقِعِ

ولـم تَقطَعِ الشَّرَّ من جِذمِه   وغِـلَّ الضمائرِ لـم تَـنْزِعِ

ولـم تَصْدِمِ الناسَ فيما هُمُ   عليـهِ مِـنَ الخُلقِ الأوْضَعِ

تعاليتَ مـن "فَلَكٍ" قُطْرُهُ   يَـدُورُ على المِحْوَرِ الأوْسَعِ

فيابنَ البتولِ وحسْبي بها   ضَمَاناً عـى كُـلِّ مـا أدَّعي

ويابنَ التي لـم يَضَعْ مِثلُها   كمِثْلِكَ حَمْـلاً ولـم تُرْضِعِ

ويابنَ البَطينِ بـلا بِطْنةٍ   ويـابنَ الفتى الحاسِـرِ الأنْـزَعِ

ويا غُصنَ "هاشمَ" لـم يَنْفَتِحْ   بـأزْهَـرَ منكَ ولـم يُفرَعِ

ويا واصلاً من نشيدِ الخُلودِ   خِتـامَ القصيدةِ بالمَطْلَعِ

يَسيـرُ الوَرى بركابِ الزمانِ   مِـن مُسْتَقيمٍ ومِـن أظْلَعِ

وأنتَ تُسَيِّرُ رَكْبَ الخلودِ   مـا تَـسْتَجِدُّ لـهُ يَتْبَعِ

تَمَثَّلْتُ يومَكَ فـي خاطِري   ورَدَّدْتُ صوتَكَ فـي مَسْمَعي

ومَحَّصْتُ أمْرَكَ لـم أرْتَهِبْ   بِنَـقْلِ "الـرُّواةِ " ولـم أُخْدَعِ

وقُلْتُ: لعلَّ دَويَّ السنينِ   بـأصـداء حادثِكَ المُفْجِعِ

وَمَا رتَّلَ المُخْلِصونَ الدُّعاةُ   مِـن "مُرْسِلينَ" ومِـنْ "سُجَّعِ"

ومِـن "ناثِراتٍ" عليكَ المساءَ   والصُّبْحَ بالشَّـعْرِ والأدْمَعِ

لعلَّ السياسةَ فيما جَنَتْ   على لاصِـقٍ بِـكَ أو مُدَّعِ

وتشـريدَها كـلَّ مَن يَدَّلي   بِحَبْـلِ لأهْلِيـكَ أو مَقْطَعِ

لعلَّ لـذاكَ و"كَـوْنٍ" الشَّجيَ   ولُـوعاً بِكُلِّ شَـجٍ مُوْلَعِ

يداً في اصطباغِ حديثِ الحُسَينِ   بلـونٍ أُريـدَ لَـهُ مُمْتَنِعِ

وكانَتْ ولَمَّا تَـزَلْ بَـرْزَةً   يـدُ الواثِـقِ المُلْجَأِ الألْمَعِ

صَناعاً متى ما تُـرِد خُطَّةً   وكيـفَ ومهمـا ثـرِد تَـصْنَعِ

ولمَّا أزَخَّتْ طِـلاءَ القرونِ   وسِـتَّرَ الخِـداعَ عَـنِ المُخْدَعِ

أريدُ "الحقيقةَ" في ذاتِهـا | بغيـر الطبيعـة لــم تُطبَـع
وجَدْتُكَ فـي صورةٍ لـم أُرَعْ | بِـأَعظَـمَ منهـا ولا أُروَعْ
وماذا! أَأَروَعُ مِنْ أَنْ يَكُون | لَحْمُـكَ وُقُـفَ عَلى المِبْضَع
وأنْ تَتَّقِـي - دونَ مـا تَرْتَئِي- | ضميـرَكَ بالأسَـلِ الشُّــرَّع
وأنْ تُطعِـمَ المـوتَ خيرَ البنينَ | مِـنَ "الأكُهَليِنَ" إلى الرُّضَّع
وخيـرَ بني " الأبِ " مِـنْ تُبَّع | كَانُـوا وُقَـاءَكَ ، و الأُدرَعْ
وخيرَ الصِّحاب بـخيرِ الصُّدُورِ | ثِيَابَ التُّقَـاةِ و لَـم أَدَعْ
وقَـدَّسْتُ ذكرَاك لَــمْ انتحلْ | يضِـجُّ بجُذرَانِـه الأَربَـع
تَفَحَّمْتَ صَدْرِي ورَيْبُ الشُّكُوك | عَلَـيَّ مِـنَ القَلَـقِ المُفْزِع
وران سَحَابٌ صَفيِقُ الحجاب | و" الطَّيِّبيِـنَ " ولـم يُقْشَـع
وهَبَّتْ ريـاحٌ مـن الطَّيِّبَـات | تَأَبَّـى و عـادَ إلـى مَوضِع
إذا مـا تَزَحْزَحَ عَـنْ مَوْضِع | "الجدُودِ" إلى الشَّكِّ فيما مَعِي
وجازَ بِي الشَّكُّ فيما مَـعَ | مِـنْ " مِبدأ " بِـدَمٍ مُشبَـع
إلـى أن أَقَمْتُ عَلَيـه الدَّليلَ | وأَعْطَـاكَ إذْعَانَـةَ المُهطِع
فأَسْلَـمَ طَوْعـاً إليكَ القِيَادَ | وقَوَّمْـتَ مـا اعوَجَّ مِن أضْلَعِي
فَنَوَّرْتَ مـا اظْلَمَّ مِـنْ فِكْرَتِي | سِـوَالعَقْل في الشَّكِّ مِـنْ مَرْجِع
وآمنْتُ إيمانَ مَـنْ لا يَـرَى | وفَـيْضَ النُّبُـوَّةِ ، مِـنْ مَنْبَـع
بأنَّ (الإبـاءَ) ووحيَ السَّماء | تَنَـزَّهَ عـن (عَـرَضٍ) المَطْمَع
تَجَمَّعَ فـي (جوهـرٍ) خالصٍ |

قصيدة لآبي الحسن علي بن أحمد الجرجاني في رثاء الحسين عليه السلآم

زادوا عليه بحبس المـاء غلتـه | تبا لـرأي فـريق فيه مغبـون
نالـوا أزمة دنياهم ببغيهـم | فليتهم سمحوا منها بماعـون
حتى يصيح بقنسرين راهبها يـا | فرقـة الغي يا حزب الشياطين
أتهـزؤن برأس بات منتصبـا | على القناة بدين الله يوصيني
آمنت ويحكـم بالله مهتديـا | و بالنبي و حب المرتضى ديني
فجدلـوه صريعا فوق جبهتـه | وقسموه بـأطراف اسـاكين
وأوقـروا صهوات الخيل من | إحـن على اساراهم فعل الفراعين
مصفدين علـى أقتـاب أرحلهم | محمولـة بـين مضروب ومطعون
أطفـال فاطمة الزهراء قد فط | مـوا مـن الثدي بأنياب الثعابين
يا أمة ولـي الشيطان رايتها | ومكن الغي منهـا كـل تمكين
مـا المرتضى وبنوه من معاوية | ولا الفـواطم مـن هند وميسون ؟
آل الرسول عبابيد السيوف فمن | هـام علـى وجهـه خوفـا ومسجون
يـا عين لا تدعي شينا لغادية | تهمي ولا تـدعي دمعـا لمحزون
قومي علـى جدث بالطف فانتق | ضي بكل لؤلؤ دمـع فيك مكنون
يـا آل أحمد إن الجوهري لكم | سـيف يقطع عنكم كل موصون

قال علي بن الحسين علاء الدين الحلي في قصيدته السادسة في رثاء الحسين عليه

657

السّلام:

تؤديه إن عزَّ الرسول قبول	عسـى موعد إن صح منك قبول
و صبَّ لها دمع عليه همـول	قتيـل بكت حزنا عليه سماءها
و خيل العدى بغيا عليه تجول	ءأنسـى حسينا للسـهام رمية
و من أحمد عند الخطابة قيـل	له من علي في الخطوب شجاعة
لأحمـد و الطهر البتول سليل	كفـاه علـوا في البرية أنـه
و لاكـل أم في النسـاء بتول	فمـا كل جد في الرجال محمـد
لدا الطف من آل الرسول قبيل	بنفسي و أهلى عافر الخط حولـه
شرار الورى عن ورده و نغول	قضى ظاميا و المـاء طام تصدّه
و قـد ملأ البيداء منه صهيل	وآب جواد السـبط يهتف ناعيا
لراكبـه و السرج منه يميل	فلما سـمعن الطـاهرات نعيه
لهن علـى الندب الكريم عويل	بـرزن سليبات الحلي نوادبـا
و نـارا لها بين الضلوع دخيل	فيا لك عينـا لا تجف دموعها
إلى الناس من رب العباد رسول	أيقتل ظمانـا حسـين وجده
يقـوم عليها في الكتاب دليل	بها مـن علي في علاك مناقب
فمـاذا عسـى فيما أقول أقول	إذا لظقت آي الكتـاب بفظلكم
لساني على التقصير في شرح وصفكم قصير و شـرح الاعتذار طويل	

للصنوبري :

مـن جميـع الأنبيـاء	يـا خير مـن لبس النبـوة
ليس يـؤذن بانقضـاء	وجدي على سـبطيك وجد
و ذا قتيـل الأدعيـاء	هـذا قتيـل الأشـقياء
الأرض بـل دمـع السماء	يـوم الحسـين هرقت دمع
العز مهجـورى الفناء	يـوم الحسـين تركت باب
كـرب علـي و مـن بـلاء	يـا كربـلاء خلقت مـن
ماؤه مـاء البهـاء	كـم فيك مـن وجـه تشـرب
نـار الوغـى أي اصطلاء	نفسي فـداء المصطلي
كالكـواكب فـي السماء	حيث الأسـنة في الجواشن
الصبر مـن لبس السناء	فاختـار درع الصبـر حيث
الأسـد صادقـة الإبـاء	و أبى إبـاء الأسـد إن
ظمآن فـي نفـر ظمـاء	و قضى كريمـا إذ قضى
وجدوا لمـاء طعم مـاء	منعـوه طعـم المـاء لا
ممـال أعـواد الخباء	مـن ذا لمعفـور الجـواد
يانـا مخلـى بـالعراء	مـن للطريـح الشل وعر
للمغسـل بالدماء	مـن للمحنط بـالتراب و
عـن عيـون الأوليـاء	مـن لابن فـاطمة المغيب

658

للامام الشافعي :

و أرق نومي فالسهاد عجيب	تأوه قلبي و الفؤاد كئيب
و إن كرهتها أنفس و قلوب	فمن مبلغ عني الحسين رسالة
صبيغ بماء الأرجوان خضيب	ذبيح بلا جرم كأن قميصه
و للخيل من بعد الصهيل نحيب	فللسيف إعوال و للرمح رنة
و كادت لهم صم الجبال تذوب	تزلزلت الدنيا آل محمد
و هتك أستار و شق جيوب	و غارت نجوم و اقشعرت كواكب
و يغزى بنوه إن ذا لعجيب	يصلى على المبعوث من آل هاشم
فذلك ذنب لست عنه أتوب	لئن كان ذنبي حب آل محمد
إذا ما بدت للناظرين خطوب	هم شفعائي يوم حشري و موقفي

للجوهري :

خذوا حدادكم يا آل ياسين	عاشورنا ذا ألا لهفي على الدين
بنات أحمد نهب الروم و الصين	اليوم شقق جيب الدين و انتهبت
يقول من ليتيم أو لمسكين	اليوم قام بأعلى الطف نادبهم
أمسى عبير بخور الحور و العين	اليوم خضب جيب المصطفى بدم
على مناخر تذليل و توهين	اليوم خرت نجوم الفخر من مضر
و جررت لهم التقوى على الطين	اليوم أطفئ نور الله متقدا
و برقعت غرة الإسلام بالهون	اليوم هتك أسباب الهدى مزقا
و طاح بالخيل ساحات الميادين	اليوم زعزع قدس من جوانبه
مما صلوه ببدر ثم صفين	اليوم نال بنو حرب طوائلها
من نفسه بنجيع غير مسنون	اليوم جدل سبط المصطفى شرقا

نقل الكنجي في الكفاية في رثاء الحسين عليه السّلام قصيدة منها:

لآل النبي المصطفى و عظام	و أبكت جفوني بالفرات مصارع
من كريم قد علاه حسام	فكم حرّة مسبية فاطمية و كم
فشبّت و إني صادق لغلام	أفاطمة أشجاني بنوك ذو و العلا

المصادر: كفاية الطالب: ص 297.

قال الحافظ البرسي في قصيدته في رثاء الإمام السبط الشهيد عليه السّلام:

و لا السلام على سلمى بذي سلم	ما هاجني ذكر ذات البان و العلم
أصخى بكرب البلاء في كربلاء ظمي	لكن تذكرت مولاي الحسين و قد
قبلي و لم استطع مع ذلك منع دمي	و هام إذ همت العبرات من عدم
أجل اجالنا بين تلك الهضب و الأكم	بكربلاء هذه تدعى فقال:
و أجسادها تروي بفيض دم	فهاهنا تصبح الأكباد من ظمأ حرى

659

و راح ثـــم جـواد السبط يندبه
عالـي الصهيل خليا طالب الخيم

فمذ رأته النسـاء الطاهرات بدا
يكـادم الأرض في خد له و فم

فجئن و السبط ملقى بالنصال أبت
من كف مسـتلم أو ثغر ملتثم

و الشمر ينحر منه النحر مـن حنق
و الأرض ترجف خوفا من فعالهم

فتستـر الوجه في كم عقيلته
و تنحني فـوق قلب والـه كلم

هذي سكينة قد عزّت سكينتها
و هـذه فاطم تبكـي بفيض دم

يـا جد لو نظرت عيناك من حزن
للعترة الغر بعد الصون و الحشم

أيـن النبي و ثغر السبط يقرعه
يزيد بغضا لـخير الخلق كلهم

يـا ويله حين يأتـي الطهر فاطمة
في الحشر صارخة في موقف الأمم

أيا نبي الوحي و الذكر الحكيم و من
و لا هـم أملي و البرء مـــن ألمي

نجل الحسيـن سليل الطهر فاطمة
و ابن الوصي علـي كاسـر الصنم

يـابن النبي و يابن الطهر حيدرة
يـابـن البتول و يابن الحل و الحرم

متى نـراك فـــلا ظلم و لا ظلم
و الدين فـي رغد و الكفر فـي غمم

أو يختشي الزلة البرسي و هو يرى و لا كم فـوق ذي القربـى و ذي الرحم

المصادر: الغدير: ج 7 ص 62.

قال علاء الدين الحلي في قصيدته في رثاء الحسين عليه السّلام:

أم ابتسـمت عن لؤلؤ من ثغورها
أبرق ترائي عـــن يمين ثغورهـا

جلاآ لعيني درة مـــن درورها
سـلام على الدار التي طالما عدت

بليل عذاري السبط و خط قتيرها
و لولا مصاب السبط بالطف ما بدا

بنفس خلت مـــن خلها و عشيرها
و ما أنس لا أنسـى الحسين مجاهدا

من النصر خلوا ظهره من ظهيرها
بنفسـي مجروح الجوارح آيسـا

حدود شفار أحدقت بشفيرها
يتوق إلـى ماء الفرات و دونه

و عوذر مقتـولا دويـن غديرها
قضى ظاميا و المـــاء يلمع طاميا

لـــه الجن في غيطانها و حفيرها
و أعلنت الأمـــلاك نوحا و أعولت

و تقلع مـن أنفس عن سرورها
على مثل هذا الرزء يستحسن البكاء

و أكـرم خلق الله و ابـن نذيرها
أيقتل خيـــر الخلق أمـا و والدا

و حـوش الفـلا ريانة من نميرها
و يمنع من مـــاء الفرات و تغتدي

سنان ألا شـــلّت يمين مديرها
يدار على رأس السـنان برأسه

ألا روحـي الـفداء لأسيرها
و يؤتى بزين العابدين مكبّلا أسيرا

و يمسي حسين عاريا في حرورها
و يمسـي يزيد رافلا في حريرة

بنشد أغانيـهـا و سكب خمورها
و دار بني صـخر بن حرب أنيسته

شبّرها مولى الورى و شبيرها
و دار علي و البتول و أحمد و

زائرها يبكـي لـفقد مزورها
معالمها تبكي على علمائها و

المشوم و إن طال المدى من دهورها
فيا يوم عاشوراء حسبك إنك

على سـيرة لم يبق غير يسيرها
متى يظهر المهدي من آل هاشم

و يسعد يوما ناظري من نصيرها
و تنظر عيني بهجة علويـة

660

المصادر: الغدير: ج 6 ص 373.

أيضا لعلاء الدين الحلي من قصيدته الخامسة في رثاء السبط الشهيد الحسين عليه السّلام:

و صافحتك أكف الطل يا طلل	حلّت عليك عقود المزن يا حلل
و عهد الغانيات كفيء الظل نسعل	مالت إلى الهجر من بعد الوصال
و قابلوه بعدوان و ما قبلوا	من معشر عدلوا عن عهد حيدرة
و ما عدلوا في الحب بل عدلوا	و بدّلوا قولهم يوم الغدير له غدرا
لهم أمانيهم و الجهل و الأهل	و أجمعوا الأمر فيما بينهم و غوت
له حادث مستصعب جلل	أن يحرقوا منزل الزهراء فاطمة فيا
من غير ما سبب بالنار يشتعل	بيت به خمسة جبريل سادسهم
بين الأراذل محتف بهم و كل	و أخرج المرتضى عن عقر منزله
بين الطغاة و قد ضاقت به السبل	لهفي سبط رسول الله منفردا
بالترب ساجدة من وقعه العلل	ألقى الحسام عليهم راكعا فهوت
حميد الذكر ما راعه ذل و لا فشل	أردمه كالطود عن ظهر الجواد
خبائه و به من أسهم قزل	لهفي و قد راح ينعاه الجواد إلى
قلب تزايد فيه الوجد و الوجل	لهفي لزينب تسعى نحوه و لها
لشمال تستر وجها شأنه الخجل	تدافع الشمر عنه باليمين و با
قتل ابن فاطمة لا يخمد العجل	تقول: يا شمر لا تعجل عليه ففي
بجده ختمت في الأمة الرسل	أ ليس ذا ابن علي و البتول و من
يجدي عتاب لأهل الكفران عذلوا	أبى الشقي لها إلا الخلاف و هل
عليهم بعد رب العرش أتكل	يا آل أحمد يا سفن النجاة و من
فريدة طاب منها المدح و الغزل	فدونكم من علي عبد عبدكم
أرجو بها جنة أنهارها عسل	أعددتها جنة من حر نار لظى

المصادر: الغدير: ج 6 ص 390.

قال جنّي في رثاء الحسين عليه السّلام:

و لقتله زلزلتم و لقتله انكسف القمر	أبكى ابن فاطمة الذي من قتله شاب الشعر
و احمرّ آفاق السماء هن العشية و السحر	
و تغيرت شمس البلاد له و أظلمت الكور	
أورثنا ذلّا به جدع الأنوف مع الغرر	ذاك ابن فاطمة المصاب به الخلائق و البشر

المصادر:. ناسخ التواريخ: ج 3 الإمام الحسين عليه السّلام ص 245.:

قال حكيم بن داود الرقي: إنّ جدي حدثني أنه إذا قتل الحسين عليه السّلام رثاه جنّ بهذه الأشعار:

و ابكي فقد حقّ الخبر	يا عين جودي بالعبر
ورد الفرات و ما صدر	أبكي ابن فاطمة الذي
لما أتى منه الخبر	الجنّ تبكي شجوها
تعثا لذلك من خبر	قتل الحسين و رهطه
العشاء و بالسحر	فلأبكينّك حرقة عند

المصادر: ناسخ التواريخ: ج 3 مجلد الإمام الحسين عليه السّلام ص 240.

قال ابن العودي النيلي في قصيدته:

و قد لجّ في الهجران من ليس يرحم	متى يشتفي من لاعج القلب مغرم
و للنفر البيض الذين هم هم	و أصفيت مدحي للنبي و صنوه
هم شجر الطوبى لمن يتفهّم	هم التين و الزيتون آل محمد
هم اللوح و القف الرفيع المعظم	هم جنة المأوى هم الحوض في غده
هم سبأ و الذاريات و مريم	هم آل عمران هم الحج و النسا
هم النحل و الأنفال إن كنت تعلم	هم آل ياسين و طه و هل أتى
و لا هبطا للنسل حوا و آدم	فلولاهم لم يخلق الله خلقه
فعاد المنادي فيهم و هو ضحم	هم باهلوا نجران من داخل العبا
أبو القاسم الهادي النبي المكرم	أبوهم أمير المؤمنين و جدهم
و عمهم الطيار في الخلد ينعم	و خالهم إبراهيم و الأم فاطم
سراياكم صلبانهم و ظفرتم	كأنهم كانوا من الروم فالتقت
فلم أنتم آباءكم قد ورثتم	منعتم تراثي ابنتي لا أبا لكم
ألأجنبي الإرث فيما زعمتم	و قلتم نبي لا تراث لولده
و يحيى لزكريا فلم ذا منعتم	فهذا سليمان لداود وارث
من الله في العقبى عقاب و مأثم	فحسبهم في ظلم آل محمد
نجوم الهدى للناس و الأفق مظلم	فيا رب بالأشباح آل محمد
و آبائه الهادين و الحق معصم	و بالقائم المهدي من آل أحمد
فأنت إذا استرحمت تعفو و ترحم	تفضل على العودي منك برحمة

المصادر: الغدير: ج 4 ص 372 ح 48.

قال الشريف الرضي في قصيدة يرثي الحسين عليه السّلام يوم عاشوراء:

و اسكب سخي العين بعد جمادها	هذي المنازل بالغميم فنادها

كلا و لا عين جرى لرقادها	لم يبق ذخر للمدامع عنكم
لبكاء فاطمة على أولادها	شغل الدموع عن الديار بكاؤنا
دفع الفرات يزاد عن أورادها	لم يخلفوها في الشهيد و قد رأى
لقنا بني الطرداء عند ولادها	أترى درت أن الحسين طريدة
أموية بالشام من أعيادها	كانت مآتم بالعراق تعدها
تبعت أمية بعد عزّ قيادها	وا لهفتاه لعصبة علوية
و تزحزحي بالبيض عن أغمادها	يا غيرة الله اغضبي لنبيه
و بنيه بين يزيدها و زيادها	من عصبة ضاعت دماء محمد
و أكف آل الله في أصفادها	صفدات مال الله ملئ أكفها
ضرب الغرائب عدن بعد ذيادها	ضربوا بسيف محمد أبناءه

المصادر: 1. الغدير: ج 4 ص 215، عن ديوان الشريف الرضي. 2. ديوان الشريف الرضي، على ما في الغدير. 3. المنتخب للطريحي: ص 110، شطرا منه.

قال مهيار الديلمي في قصيدة في 70 بيتا مستهلها:

و لوى لويا فاستزل مقامها؟	من جب غارب هاشم و سنامها
تلك القبور الطاهرات عظامها	و مضى بيثرب مذعجا ما شاء من
بالطف في أبنائها أبامها	يبكي النبي و يستنيح لفاطم
فاستسلمت أم أنكرت إسلامها	أتناكرت أيدي الرجال سيوفها
قدر أراح على الغدو سوامها	أم غال ذا الحسين حامي ذودها

المصادر: الغدير: ج 4 ص 211،؛ ديوان مهيار الديلمي: ج 3 ص 266.

كلام الصنوبري يرثي فيها أمير المؤمنين عليه السّلام و ولده السبط الشهيد عليه السّلام بقوله:

و الخلق أنهما نعم الشهيدان	نعم الشهيدان رب العرش يشهد لي
من ذا يعزيه من قاص و من دان	من ذا يعز النبي المصطفى بهما
عن بعلها و ابنها أنباء لهفان	من ذا لفاطمة اللهفاء ينبؤها
و قابض النفس في الهيجاء عطشان	من قابض النفس في المحراب منتصبا
نعم و شمسان إما قلت شمسان	نجما في الأرض بل بدران قد أفلا
و في يمينيهما للحرب سيفان	سيفان يغمد سيف الحرب إن برزا

و له يرثي الإمام السبط الشهيد عليه السّلام:

يا خير من لبس النبوة من جميع الأنبياء
و جدي على سبطيك و جد ليس يؤذن بانقضاء
هذا قتيل الأشقياء و ذا قتيل الأدعياء

663

يوم الحسين هرقت دمع الأرض بل دمع السماء

يوم الحسين تركت با ب العزّ مهجور الفناء

يا كربلا خلقت من كرب علىّ و من بلاء

من للطريح الشلوع ريانا فحلى بالعراء

من للمحنط بالتراب و للمغسل بالدماء

من لابن فاطمة المغيب عن عيون الأولياء

المصادر: الغدير: ج 3 ص 371.

كلام الشيخ هادي ابن الشيخ أحمد النحوي في رثاء الإمام السبط عليه السّلام:

يمينا بنا حادي السري إن بدت نجد   يمينا فللعاني العليل بها   نجد

كأني بمولاي الحسين و   رهطه   حيارى و لا عون هناك و لا عضد

يسائلهم هل تعرفوني   مسائلا   وسائل دمع العين سال به الخد

فقالوا نعم أنت الحسين بن فاطم   و جدك خير المرسلين إذا عدوا

كلام للشاعر المذكور في رثاء الإمام السبط الشهيد عليه السّلام:

دمع يبدّده   مقيم   نازح   و دم يبدّده مقيم   نازح

هو سيد الكونين بل هو أشرف   الثقلين حقا   و النذير الناصح

و الأم فاطمة البتول و   بضعة   الهادي الرسول المهيمن مانح

حورية   إنسية   لجلالها   و جمالها الوحي المنزل شارح

حزني لفاطم تلطم الخدين من   عظم المصاب لها جوى و تبارح

يا فاطم الزهراء قومي و انظري   وجه الحسين له الصعيد مصافح

كلام الحافظ البرسي في رثاء الإمام السبط عليه السّلام:

ما هاجني ذكر ذات البان و العلم   و لا السلام على سلمي بذي   سلم

أين النبي و ثغر سبط يقرعه   يزيد بغضا لخير الخلق   كلهم

يا ويله حين تأتي الطهر فاطمة   في الحشر صارخة في موقف الأمم

فليس للدين من حام و منتصر   إلا الإمام الفتى الكشاف للظلم

نجل الحسين سليل الطهر فاطمة   و ابن الوصي على كاسر الصنم

يابن النبي و يابن الطهر حيدرة   يابن البتول و يابن الحل و الحرم

كلام الحسين عليه السّلام لما رأى العباس صريعا على شاطئ الفرات:

تعدّيتم يا شر قوم ببغيكم   و خالفتم دين النبي محمد

أما كانت الزهراء أمي دونكم ؟ أما كان من خير البرية أحمد؟

664

كلام الحسين عليه السّلام لما ركب فرسه و تقدم إلى القتال:

عن ثواب الله رب العالمين	كفر القوم و قدما رغبوا
فأنا ابن العالمين	من له جد كجدي في الورى أو كشيخي
قاسم الكف ببدر و حنين	فاطم الزهراء أمي و أبي

كلام الحسين عليه السّلام حين وقف قبالة القوم و سيفه مصلّت في يده، آيسا من الحياة عازما على الموت:

كفاني بهذا مفخرا حين أفخر	أنا ابن علي الطهر من آل هاشم
و نحن سراج اللّه في الأرض نزهر	وجدي رسول الله أكرم من مضى
و عمي يدعى ذا الجناحين جعفر	و فاطم أمي من سلالة أحمد

كلام سيف بن عميرة في قصيدته:

حلّ المصاب بمن أصبنا فأعذري   يا هذه و عن الملامة فاقصري
رزو الحسين الطهر أكرم من بري   باري الورى من سوقه و مؤمر
و البضعة الزهراء فاطم أمه   حوراء طاهرة و بنت الأطهر
يابن النبي المصطفى خير الورى   و ابن البتولة و الإمام الأطهر
يدعون أمهم البتولة فاطما   دعوى الحزين الواله المتحير
يا أمنا هذا الحسين مجدلا   ملقى عفيرا مثل بدر مزهر
يا أمنا نوحي عليه و عولي   في قبرك المستور بين الأقبر
يا أمنا لو تعلمين بحالنا   لرأيت ذا حال قبيح المنظر
أنا ابن علي الطهر من آل هاشم   كفاني بهذا المفخر حين أفخر
و فاطم أمي ثم جدي محمد   و عمي يدعى ذا الجناحين جعفر

و قال بعد حين:

عن ثواب الله رب الثقلين	كفر القوم و قدما رغبوا
وارث العلم و مولى الثقلين	أمي الزهراء حقا و أبي
أو كأمي في جميع المشرقين	من له جد كجدي في الورى

36. في ج 2 ص 466: في كلام الشاعر المحب في قصيدته:

تقول و دمع العين يهمي و يهمل	و لم أنس من بين النساء سكينة
بقلب حزين بالكآبة مقفل	و تشكو إلى الزهراء بنت محمد

37. ج 2 ص 468: كلام في المدائح و المراثي لأهل البيت عليهم السّلام:

فأهل البيت هم أهل الكتاب	تمسك بالكتاب و من تلاه
نبيي و الوصي أبو تراب	شفيعي في القيامة عند ربي
يخلد في الجنان من الشباب	و فاطمة البتول و سيدا من

38. ج 2 ص 472: كلام محمد بن حماد في رثاء الحسين عليه السّلام:

و لم نحظ بالحظ الذي أنت طامع	لغير مصاب السبط دمعك ضائع
حقير و رزؤ السبط و الله فازع	و كل مصاب دون رزء ابن فاطم
شربة و الذئب و الكلب شارع	و للفاطميات العفاف تلهف على

39. ج 2 ص 475: كلام محب في رثاء الحسين عليه السّلام:

يودّع أهليه و يوصي و يعجل	و لم أنس مولاي الحسين و قد غدا
فأبصرن منه ما يسوء و يذهل	و قمن النساء الفاطميات و لها
و تندب مما نالها و تولول	و تشكو إلى الزهراء فاطم حالها
حبيبك ملقى في الثرى لا يغسل	أيا أم قومي من ثرى القبر و انظري
بأنّا حيارى نستجير و نسأل	و هل أنت يا ست النساء عليمة
أسير عليل في القيود مغلّل	و هل لك علم من علي فإنه

كلام الخليعي في قصيدته:

للقتيل الظامي و أي قتيل	ما لدمعي لم يطف حر غليلي
وا أخي وا مؤملي وا كفيلي	و أتت زينب إليه تنادي
وا سبائي وا ذلتي وا غليلي	يابن أمي يا واحدي يا شقيقي
أدركيني و عجّلي و اندبي لي	ثم تدعو بأمها أم يا أم
دموعي عليك غير بخيل	يابن بنت النبي جفني بتسكاب

42. في ج ص 500: كلام أم كلثوم حين توجّهت إلى المدينة، جعلت تبكي و تقول:

فبالحسرات و الأحزان جئنا	مدينة جدنا لا تقبلينا
بناتك في البلاد مشتّتينا	أفاطم لو نظرت إلى السبايا
و لا قيراط مما لقينا	أفاطم ما لقيت من عداكي

كلام القطان لرثاء الحسين عليه السّلام:

جادك مسحنفر هطول	يا أيها المنزل المحيل
فلا كتال و لا رسول	يا قوم ما بالنا جفينا
لكاتبونا و لم يحولوا	لو وجدوا بعض ما وجدنا
كأنه مرهف صقيل	يسطو علينا بلحظ جفن

666

أراذل ما لهم أصول	كما سطت بالحسين قوم
بنا و لم أنتم نكول	يا أهل كوفان لم غدرتم
عزا أطرفها الذهول	و أم كلثوم قد تنادي و قد
ناغاه في المهد جبرئيل	أين الذي حين أرضعوه
و أمه فاطم البتول	أين الذي حيدر أبوه
اعتقادي ومذهبي عنه لا أحول	ما الرفض ديني و لا

14. ج 2 ص 128: في كلام علي بن أحمد النيشابوري في مدح أهل البيت و أولاد فاطمة عليها السّلام:

محبة أولاد النبي عقيدتي	أيا سائلي عن مذهبي و طريقتي
و فاطمة الزهراء بنت خديجة	هما الحسنان اللؤلؤان تلألنا
محمد المختار هادي الخليفة	سرور فؤاد المصطفى علم الهدى
أبي الحسن الكرار مردي الكتيبة	و قرة عين المرتضى أسد الوغى
بهم مع اثنين ثم امح سواهم أو أثبت	و خذ سبعة من بعدهم و افتخر
لفي من يعاديني شديد الوقيعة	فلا ترمني بالفرض ويلك إنني

كلام الشافعي في حب فاطمة عليها السّلام و ذكر الشيعة:

و سبطيه و فاطمة الزكية	إذا في مجلس ذكروا عليا
سقيم من حديث الرافضية	يقول لما يصح ذووا فهذا
يرون الرفض حب الفاطمية	برئت إلى المهيمن من أناس
أفاضوا بالروايات الوقية	إذا ذكروا عليا أو بنيه

كلام الشريف السيد الرضي في قصيدة له:

لبكاء فاطمة على أولادها	شغل الدموع عن الديار بكاؤها
تبعت أمية بعد عزّ قيادها	وا لهفتاه لعصبة علويه
تزخرجي بالبيض عن أغمادها	يا غيرة الله اغضبي لنبيه و
و بنيه بين يزيدها و زيادها	من عصبة ضاعت دماء محمد

كلام الجوهري الجرجاني في قصيدته:

تهمي عليه ضلوعي قبل أجفان	وجدي بكوفان لا وجدي لكوفان
جهد الصدى فتراه غير صديان	فمن قتيل بأعلى كربلاء على
هذا و ترجون عند الحوض إحسان	قتلتم ولدي أصبر على الظماء
بني البتول و هم روحي و جثماني	سبيتم، ثكلتكم أمهاتكم ،
و الحاكم اللّه للمظلوم و الجاني؟	ماذا تجيبون و الزهراء خصمكم
عليكم الآي من مثنى و وحدان	أهل الكساء صلاة الله ما نزلت

667

20. ج 2 ص 137: كلام المنسوب إلى عبد الله بن عمار البرقي المقتول سنة 245 ه؛ قطع لسانه و خرق ديوانه بسبب شعره في قصيدته الطويلة:

لآل رسول الله انهلّ دمعتي	إذا جاء عاشور تضاعف حسرتي
فلو عقلت شمس النهار لخرّت	أريقت دماء الفاطميين بالفلا
يداها بساق العرش و الدمع أذرت	كأني ببنت المصطفى قد تعلّقت

21. ج 2 ص 139: كلام الصاحب بن عباد في قصيدته الطويلة:

بلغت نفسي مناها بالموالي آل طاها
برسول الله من حاز المعالي و حواها
و ببنت المصطفى من أشبهت فضلا أباها

23. ج 2 ص 145: كلام جعفر بن عفان في قصيدة طويلة:

تبكي العيون لركن الدين حين و هى و للرزايا العظيمات الجليلات
هل لإمرئ عاذر في خزن أدهمه   بعد الحسين و سبي الفاطميات
ينقلن من عند جبار يؤنّبها   لآخر مثله نقل السبيات

24. ج 2 ص 145: كلام الناشئ علي بن وصيف الشاعر المعروف ـ المتوفى 366 ه ـ مما يناح في الماتم:

أما سبحاك يا سكن قتل الحسين و الحسن
ظمأت من فرط الحزن و كل و غدنا هل
يقول يا قوم أبي علي البر الأبي
و فاطم بنت النبي أمي و عني سائلوا
فيا عيوني إسكبي على بني بنت النبي
بفيض دمع و اهضبي كذاك يبكي العاقل

25. ج 2 ص 152: كلام الصاحب بن عباد في قصيدته:

و اتركي الخد كالمحل المحيل	عين جودي على الشهيد القتيل
هراء صرخن حول القتيل	و استباحوا بنات فاطمة الز
الحكم إذا حان محشر التعديل	سوف تأتي الزهراء تلتمس
فخرا أن يقولوا من قيل إسماعيل	قد كفاني في الشرق و الغرب

26. ج 2 ص 156: كلام العوين الشاعر في قصيدة:

أيا بضعة من فؤاد النبي   بالطف أضحت كئيبا مهيلا
و يا حبة من فؤاد البتول   بالطف سلّت فأصحت أكيلا
قتلت فأبكيت عين الرسول و أبكيت من رحمة جبرئيلا

27. ج 2 ص 157: كلام بعض الشعراء فيما يناح به في قصيدة:

يا قتيل ابن زياد	يا حسين بن علي
بدموع كالعهاد	لو رأى جدك يبكي
فيه لا سيف المرادي	لو رأى حيدر أودي
نوح ورقاء بوادي	أو رأت فاطم ناحت
لك تبكي و تنادي	وأقامت وهي ولهى
كبدي حب فؤادي	ولدي قرة عيني
لصعيد و صعاد	أنت روحي قسّموها

و قالوا نحن أشياع الرسول	لقد ذبحوا الحسين بن البتول
أمامك يابن فاطمة البتول	و إن موفّقا إن لم يقاتل
تنقل في الحزون و في السهول	فسوف يصوغ فيك محبرات

قصيدة لـ "معاوية" لشاعر سوريا الكبير الدكتور محمد مجذوب*:

والصافنات وزهوها والسؤددُ	أين القصور أبا يزيد ولهوهـا ***
أعتاب دنيا زهوهـا لا ينفـذ	اين الدهاء نحرت عزته علـى ***
هو لو علمت على الزمـان مخلدُ	آثرت فانيها على الـحـق الـذي ***
وبقيت وحدك عبرة تتجـددُ	تلك البهارج قد مضت لسبيلهـا ***
لا سال مدمعك المصير الأسودُ	هذا ضريحك لو بصرت ببؤسـه ***
سكر الذباب بها فـراح يعربدُ	كتل من الترب المهين بخـربةٍ ***
فكأنها في مجهل لا يقصـدُ	خفيت معالمها على زوارهـا ***
فبكل جزء للفنـاء بهـا يـدُ	والقبة الشماء نكس طرفهـا ***
والريح في جنبـاتها تتـرددُ	تهمي السحائب من خلال شقوقها ***
مـذ كـان لم يجتز به متعبـدُ	وكذا المصلى مظلم فكأنـه ***
تجلى على قلب الحكيم فيرشـدُ	أبا يزيد وتلك حكمـة خـالـق ***
أودى بلبك غـيهـا الترصـدُ	أرأيت عاقبة الجموح ونزوة ***
دين وبغضته الشقاء السرمـدُ	تعدوا بها ظلما على من حبه ***
فيكاد من بريده يـشرق احمـدُ	ورثت شمائله براءة أحمـد ***
ارثـا لكل مدمم لا يحمـدُ	وغلوت حتى قد جعلت زمامها ***
ومضى بغير هواه لا يتقيـدُ	هتك المحارم واستباح خدورهـا ***
جهلاء تلتهم النفوس وتفسـدُ	فأعادها بعد الهدى عصيبـة ***
وكأن أمته لآلك أعبـدُ	فكأنما الأسلام سلعة تاجـر ***
عن تلكم النار التي لا تخمـدُ	فاسأل مـرابض كربلاء ويثـرب ***

669

أرسلت مارجها فماج بحره *** أمس الجدود ولن يجتنبها غد
والزاكيات من الدماء يريقها *** باغ على حرم النبوة مفسد
والطاهرات فديتهن حواسرا *** تنثال من عبراتهن الأكبد
والطيبين من الصغار كأنهم *** بيض الزنابق ذيد عنها المورد
تشكو الظما والظالمون أصمهم *** حقد أناخ على الجوانح موقد
والذائدين تبعثرت اشلاؤهم *** بدوا فثمة معصم وهنا يد
تطأ السنابك بالظعة أديمها *** مثل الكتاب مشى عليه الملحد
فعلى الرمال من الأباة مضرج *** وعلى النياق من الهداة مصفد
وعلى الرماح بقية من عابد *** كالشمس ضاء به الصفا والمسجد
ان يجهش الأثناء موضع قدره *** فلقد دراه الراكعون السجد
أبا يزيد وساء ذلك عثرة *** ماذا أقول وباب سمعك موصد
قم وارمق النجف الشريف بنظرة *** يرتد طرفك وهو باك أرمد
تلك العظام أعز ربك قدرها *** فتكاد لولا خوف ربك تعبد
ابدا تباركها الوفود يحثها *** من كل حدب شوقها المتوقد
نازعتها الدنيا ففزت بوردها *** ثم انقضى كالحلم ذاك المورد
وسعت الى الأخرى فخلد ذكرها *** في الخالدين وعطف ربك أخلد
أبا يزيد لتلك آهة موجع *** أفضى اليك بها فؤاد مقصد
أنا لست بالقالي ولا أنا شامت *** قلب الكريم عن الشتامة أبعد
هي مهجة حرى اذاب شفافها *** حزن على الاسلام لم يك يهمد
ذكرتها الماضي فهاج دفينها *** شمل لشعب المصطفى متبدد
فبعثته عتبا و ان يك قاسيا *** هو في ضلوعي زفرة يتردد
لم أستطع صبرا على غلوائها *** أي الضلوع على اللضى تتجلد

*قال هذه القصيده بعد ان رأى قبر معاويه في سوريا.

و حكى سهيل بن ذبيان بن فضل قال: دخلت على الإمام علي بن موسى الرضا عليه السّلام في بعض الأيام قبل أن يدخل عليه أحد من الناس، فقال لي:

مرحبا بك يابن ذبيان؛ الساعة أراد رسولنا يأتيك لتحضر عندنا. فقلت: لماذا يابن رسول الله؟ فقال: لمنام رأيته البارحة و قد أزعجني و أرقّني. فقلت: خيرا يكون إن شاء الله تعالى. فقال: يابن ذبيان، رأيت كأني نصب لي سلّم فيه مائة مرقاة؛ فصعدت إلى أعلاه.

فقلت: يا مولاي، أهنّئك بطول العمر، ربما تعيش مائة سنة، لكل مرقاة سنة. فقال لي: ما شاء الله كان، ثم قال: يابن ذبيان، فلما صعدت إلى أعلى السلم رأيت كأني دخلت في قبّة خضراء يرى ظاهرها من باطنها، و رأيت جدي رسول الله صلّى الله عليه و آله جالسا فيها، و إلى يمينه و شماله غلامان حسنان يشرق النور من وجوهما، و رأيت إمرأة بهية الخلقة، و رأيت بين يديه شخصا بهي الخلقة جالسا عنده، و رأيت رجلا واقفا بين يديه و هو يقرأ هذه القصيدة: «لأم عمرو باللوي مربع». فلما رآني النبي صلّى الله عليه و آله قال لي: مرحبا بك يا ولدي يا علي بن موسى الرضا؛ سلّم على أبيك علي عليه السّلام،

670

فسلّمت عليه. ثم قال لي: سلّم على أمك فاطمة الزهراء عليها السّلام، فسلّمت عليها. فقال لي: و سلّم على أبويك الحسن و الحسين عليهما السّلام، فسلّمت عليهما. ثم قال لي: و سلّم على شاعرنا و مادحنا في دار الدينا السيد إسماعيل الحميري، فسلّمت عليه و جلست.

فالتفت النبي صلّى الله عليه و آله إلى السيد إسماعيل و قال له: عد إلى ما كنا فيه من إنشاد القصيدة.

فأنشد يقول:

لأم عمرو باللوى مربع طامسة أعلامه بلقع

فبكى النبي صلّى الله عليه و آله. فلما بلغ إلى قوله: «و وجهه كالشمس إذ تطلع»، بكى النبي صلّى الله عليه و آله و فاطمة عليها السّلام معه و من معه، و لما بلغ إلى قوله:

قالوا له لو شئت أعلمتنا إلى من الغاية و المفزع

رفع النبي صلّى الله عليه و آله يديه و قال: إلهي أنت الشاهد عليّ و عليهم إني أعلمتهم إن الغاية و المفزع علي بن أبي طالب عليه السّلام، و أشار بيده إليه و هو جالس بين يديه.

قال علي بن موسى الرضا عليه السّلام: فلما فرغ السيد إسماعيل الحميري من إنشاد القصيدة التفت النبي صلّى الله عليه و آله إليّ و قال لي: يا علي بن موسى الرضا، أحفظ هذه القصيدة و أمر شيعتنا بحفظه و أعلمهم أن من حفظها و أدّ من قراءتها ضمنت له الجنة على الله. قال الرضا عليه السّلام:

و لم يزل يكرّرها عليّ حتى حفظتها منه. القصيدة هذه:

طامسة أعلامه بلقع	لأم عمرو باللوى مربع
و الأسد من خيفته تفزع	تروح عنه الطير وحشية
إلا ظلال في الثرى وقّع	برسم دار ما بها مونس
و السم في أنيابها منقع	رقش يخاف الموت من نفثها
و العين من عرفانه تدمع	لما وقفن العيس من رسمها
فبثّ و القلب شج موجع	ذكرت من قد كنت ألهو به
من حب أروى كبد تلذع	كأن بالنار لما شفنى
بخطبة ليس لها موضع	عجبت من قوم أتوا أحمدا
إلى من الغاية و المفزع	قالوا له: لو شئت أعلمتنا
و فيهم في الملك من يطمع	إذا توفّيت و فارقتنا
ذبا كجرباء إبل شرّع	يذبّ عنها ابن أبي طالب

671

ذاك و قد هبت به زعزع	و العطر و الريحان أنواعه
ذا هبة ليس لها مرجع	ريح من الجنة مأمورة
قال لهم تبا لكم فارجعوا	إذا دنوا منه لكي يشربوا
يرويكم أو مطمع يشبع	دونكم فالتمسوا منهلا
و لم يكن غيرهم يتبع	هذا لمن والى بني أحمد
و الويل و الذل لمن يمنع	فالفوز للشارب من حوضه
خمس فمنها هالك أربع	و الناس يوم الحشر راياتهم
و سامري الأمة المشنع	فراية العجل و فرعونها
عبد لئيم لكع أكوع	و راية يقدمها أذلم
للزور و البهتان قد أبدع	و راية يقدمها حبتر
لا برّد الله له مضجع	و راية يقدمها نعثل
ليس لهم من قعرها مطلع	أربعة في سقر أودعوا
و وجهه كالشمس إذ تطلع	و راية يقدمها حيدر
و راية الحمد له ترفع	غدا يلاقي المصطفى حيدر
و النار من إجلاله تفزع	مولا له الجنة مأمورة
يرووا من الحوض و لم يمنع	إمام صدق و له شيعة
يا شيعة الحق فلا تجزعوا	بذاك جاء الوحي من ربنا
و لو يقطع إصبع إصبع	الحميري مادحكم لم يزل
و صنوه حيدرة الأصلع	و بعدها صلوا على المصطفى
كنتم عسيتم فيه أن تصنعوا	فقال لو أعلمتكم مفزعا
هارون فالترك له أودع	صنيع أهل العجل إذ فارقوا
كان إذا يعقل أو يسمع	و في الذي قال بيان لمن
من ربه ليس لها مدفع	ثم أتته بعد ذا عزمة
و الله منهم عاصم يمنع	أبلغ و إلا لم تكن مبلغا
كان بما يأمره يصدع	فعندها قام النبي الذي
كف علي ظاهرا يلمع	يخطب مأمور و في كفه
يرفع و الكف الذي ترفع	رافعها أكرم بكف الذي
و الله فيهم شاهد يسمع	يقول و الأملاك من حوله
مولى فلم يرضوا و لم يقنع	من كنت مولاه فهذا له
على خلاف الصادق الأضلع	فاتهموه و جنت منهم
كأنما آنافهم تجدع	و طل قوم غاضهم فعله
و انصرفوا عن دفنه ضيع	حتى إذا واروه في قبره
و اشتروا الضرّ بما ينفع	ما قال بالأمس و أوصى به
فسوف يجزون بما قطّع	و قطعوا أرحامه بعده
تبا لما كان به أزمع	و أزمعوا غدرا بمولاهم
غدا و لا هو فيهم يشفع	لا هم عليه يردوا حوضه
أيلة و العرض به أوسع	حوض له ما بين صنعا إلى
و الحوض من ماء له مترع	ينصب فيه علما للهدى
أبيض كالفضة أو أنصع	يفيض من رحمته كوثر

و لؤلؤ لم تجنه أصبع	حصاه ياقوت و مرجانة
يهتزّ منها مونق مربع	بطحاؤه مسك و حافاته
وفاقع أصفر أو أنصع	أخضر ما دون الورى ناضر
يذبّ عنها الرجل الأصلع	فيه أباريق و قد حانه

المصادر: المنتخب للطريحي: ص 315.

قال ابن منير الطرابلسي في قصيدته:

و أذبت قلبي بالفكر	عذبت طرفي بالسهر
من بعد بعدك بالكدر	و مزجت صفو مودتي
الميامين الغرر	و اليت آل أمية الطهر
عدلت عنه إلى عمر	و جحدت بيعة حيدر و
أقول ما صح الخبر	و إذا رووا خبر الغدير
بين قوم و اشتهر	و إذا جرى ذكر الصحابة
ثم صاحبه عمر	قلت المقدم شيخ تيم
عن التراث و لا زجر	كلا و لا صدّ البتول
شرب الخمور و لا فجر	و أقول إن يزيد ما
أبناء فاطمة أمر	و لجيشه بالكف عن
و لا ابن سعد ما غدر	و الشمر ما قتل الحسين
تنصّل و اعتذر	و الله يغفر للمسيء إذا
ولاءه و لمن كفر	إلا لمن جحد الوصي

المصادر: 1. الغدير: ج 4 ص 326 ح 45، عن ثمرات الأوراق. 2. ثمرات الأوراق: ج 2 ص 44. 3. تذكرة ابن العراق، على ما في الغدير. 4. مجالس المؤمنين: ص 457، على ما في الغدير. 5. أنوار الربيع: ص 359، على ما في الغدير. 6. الكشكول لصاحب الحدائق: ص 80، على ما في الغدير. 7. نامه دانشوران: ج 1 ص 85، على ما في الغدير. 8. تزئين الأسواق: ص 174، على ما في الغدير. 9. نسمة السحر فيمن تشيّع و شعر، على ما في الغدير. 10. أمل الآمل، على ما في الغدير، شطرا منها.

معمر بن خلاد و جماعة قالوا: دخلنا على الرضا عليه السّلام، فقال له بعضنا: جعلني الله فداك، ما لي أراك متغير الوجه؟! فقال عليه السّلام: إني بقيت ليلتي ساهرا مفكّرا في قول مروان بن أبي حفصة:

لبني البنات وراثة الأعمام	أنّى يكون و ليس ذاك بكائن

ثم نمت، فإذا أنا بقائل قد أخذ بعضادتي الباب و هو يقول:

للمشركين دعائم الإسلام	أنّى يكون و ليس ذاك بكائن

673

و العم متروك بغير سهام	لبني البنات نصيبهم من جدهم
سجد الطليق مخافة الصمصام	ما للطليق و تراث و إنما
فمضى القضاء به من الحكام	قد كان أخبرك القرآن بفضله
حاز الوراثة عن بني الأعمام	إن ابن فاطمة المنوه باسمه
يرثي و يسعده ذوو الأرحام	و بقى ابن نثلة واقفا مترددا

المصادر: 1. عيون أخبار الرضا عليه السّلام: ج 2 ص 175 ح 2. 2. بحار الأنوار: ج 49 ص 109 ح 3. 3. عوالم العلوم: ج 22 ص 194 ح 5، عن العيون.

قال العوني في رثاء الحسين عليه السّلام:

يا لطف أجرت كثيبا مهيلا	فيا بضعة من فؤاد النبي
يا لطف ثلت فأضحت أكيلا	و يا كبدا في فؤاد البتولة
و أبكيت من رحمة جبرئيلا	قتلت فأبكيت عين الرسول

المصادر: تاريخ الأمم و الملوك للطبري: ج 4 ص 422.

سافر أبو المحاسن إلى مكة و معه كثير من الدراهم و الدنانير و الأموال. فلاقاه جماعة بني داود بن موسى بن عبد الله بن محض بن حسن مثنى بن حسن بن علي بن أبي طالب و هجموا عليه و أخذوا أمواله. فكتب أبو المحاسن حاله و قصته إلى ملك عزيز بن أيوب حاكم يمن، و دفع سادات بني الحسن و حرّضه بهذه الأشعار:

و حزت في الجواد حد الحسن و الحسنا	أعيت صفات نداك المصقع اللسنا
من خلّص الزبد ما أبقى لك اللبنا	و ما تريد بجسم لا حياة له
فما يساوى إذا قايسته عدنا	و لا تقل ساحل الأنج أفتحه
قوم أضاعوا فروض الله ذو السننا	و إن أردت جهادا دون سيفك من
و ما أحاط به من خسة و خنا	طهّر بسيفك بيت الله من دنس
أدركوا آل حرب حاربوا الحسنا	و لا تقل أنهم أولاد فاطمة لو

فإذا أنشد أبو المحاسن هذه القصيدة و أرسل إلى ملك عزيز لقتل أولاد الحسن بن علي عليه السّلام و نهبه، قال: رأيت في المنام إن فاطمة بنت رسول الله عليها السّلام مشغول بطواف بيت الحرام. فسلّمت عليها فأعرضت عني و لم يردّ الجواب. فخرج أبو المحاسن بالذل و الضراعة مما رأى من السيدة. فسئل عنها عن ذنبه، فأجابه فاطمة عليها السّلام بهذه الأشعار:

674

من خسة تعرض أو من خنا	حاشا بني فاطمة كلهم
و فعلها السوء أساءت بنا	و إنما الأيام في عذرها
إثما بنا يأمن ممن حنا	فتب إلى الله فمن يعترف
يجعل كل السبت عمدا لنا	لئن أساء من ولدي واحد
و لا تهن من آله أعينا	فأكرم لعين المصطفى أحمد
به في الحشر منا و منا	فكمل ما نالك منهم غدا تلق

فنهص أبو المحاسن بالوحشة و الرعدة من نومه و لا يرى في بدنه جراحة مما أصابت من بني داود، و أنشد هذه الأشعار للتوبة و المعذرة:

تصفح عن ذنب محب جنا	عذرا إلى بنت نبي الهدى
مقالة توقعه في العنا	و توبة تقبلها من أخي
منهم بسيف البغي أو بالقنا	و الله لو قطعني واحد
بل إنه في الفعل قد أحسنا	لم أر ما يفعله سيئا

المصادر: 1. ناسخ التواريخ: ج 2 من مجلدات الإمام الحسن عليه السّلام ص 389. 2. ديوان أبي المحاسن، على ما في الناسخ. 3. در النظيم في مناقب الأئمة اللهاميم عليهم السّلام، على ما في الناسخ. 4. دار السلام للمحدث النوري: ج 2 ص 5. 5. عمده الطالب، على ما في دار السلام. 6. بيت الأحزان: ص 13، عن عمدة الطالب. 7. جواهر العقدين في فضل الشرفين: ص 355، بتغيير فيه.

قال الجوهري في مراثي ولد فاطمة عليها السّلام: ...

و قسّموه بأطراف السكاكين   فجدّلوه صريعا فوق جبهته

محمولة بين مضروب و مطعون   مصفّدين على أقتاب أرحلهم

من الثدي بأنياب الثعابين   أطفال فاطمة الزهراء قد فطموا

مكّن الغيّ منها كل تمكين   يا أمة ولي الشيطان رأيتها و

و لا الفواطم من هند و ميسون   ما المرتضى و بنوه من معاوية

و قال في ص 222:

فلو عقلت شمس النهار لخرّت   أريقت دماء الفاطميين بالملأ

بأيدي كلاب في الجحيم استقرّت   ألا بأبي تلك الدماء التي جرت

بنفسي جسوم بالعراء تعرّت   بنفسي خدود في التراب تعفّرت

حواسر لم تقذف عليهم بسترة   بنفسي من آل النبي خرائد

المصادر: ناسخ التواريخ: ج 4 من مجلدات سيد الشهداء عليه السّلام ص 222.

في المنتخب من أشعار محمود الطريحي في مراثي ولد فاطمة عليها السّلام:

إذا أهلّ في دور الشهور محرم   هجوعي و تلذاذي على محرم

ولي مدمع هام هام هامول مجسم   أجدّد حزنا لا يزال مجدّدا

هاشم و ما ظفرت أيد أولي البغي منهم   و أبكى على الأطهار من آل

بتول و مولانا علي أبوهم   و جدهم الهادي النبي و أمهم

و فاطمة بالطف زرء معظم   يعزّ على المختار و الطهر حيدر

لكتب من الطاغين بالخدع تقدم   و قد صار بالرهط الحسين بن فاطمة

فلم ينبعث مهر و لم يجر منسم   إلى أن أتى أرض الطفوف بأهله

و توجع ضربا بالسياط و تشتم   و في هذه تبدوا البنات حواسرا

و أضحى فريدا لفّه الترب و الدم   إلى أن فنوا أصحابه و رجاله

فصاحت و نار الحزن في القلب تضرم   و زينب في صدر الحسين مرضفا

المصادر: 1. ناسخ التواريخ: ج 4 من مجلدات سيد الشهداء عليه السّلام ص 195، عن المنتخب. 2. المنتخب للطريحي، على ما في الناسخ.

عن ذي النون المصري، قال: خرجت في بعض سياحتي حتى كنت ببطن السماوة، فأفضى لي المسير إلى تدمر. فرأيت بقربها أبنية عادية قديمة؛ فساورتها فإذا هي من حجارة منقورة فيها بيوت و غرف من حجارة، و أبوابها كذلك بغير ملاط و أرضها كذلك حجارة صلدة. فبينا أجول فيها إذ بصرت بكتابة غريبة على حائط منها. فقرأته فإذا هو:

و مكة و البيت العتيق المعظم   أنا ابن منى و المشعرين و زمزم

ولايته فرض على كل مسلم   و جدي النبي المصطفى و أبي الذي

إذا ما عددناها عديلة مريم   و أمي البتول المستضاء بنورها

676

و أولاده الأطهار تسعة أنجم	و سبطا رسول الله عمي و والدي
تفز يوم يجزي الفائزون و تنعم	متى تعتلق منهم بحبل ولاية
فإن كنت لم تعلم بذلك فاعلم	أئمة هذا الخلق بعد نبيهم
به الخوف و الأيام بالمرء ترتمي	أنا العلوي الفاطمي الذي ارتمى
برحبها و لم استطع نيل السماء بسلم	فضاقت بي الأرض و الفضاء
عليها بشعري فاقرأ إن شئت و المم	فألممت بالدار التي أنا كاتب
فليس أخو الإسلام من لم يسلم	و سلّم لأمر الله في كل حالة

قال ذو النون: فعلمت إنه علوي قد هرب، و ذلك في خلافة هارون، وقع إلى ما هناك.

فسألت من ثم من سكان هذه الدار- و كانوا من بقايا القبط الأول- هل تعرفون من كتب هذا الكتاب؟ قالوا: و الله ما عرفناه إلا يوما واحدا، فإنه نزل فأنزلناه. فلما كان صبيحة ليلة غدا، فكتب هذا الكتاب و مضى. قلت: أي رجل كان؟ قالوا: برجل عليه أطمار رثة، تعلوه هيبة و جلالة و بين عينيه نور شديد؛ لم يزل ليلته قائما و راكعا و ساجدا، إلى أن انبلج له الفجر، فكتب و انصرف.

المصادر: 1. بحار الأنوار: ج 48 ص 182 ح 25، عن المقتضب. 2. مقتضب الأثر: ص 55.

من أشعار ابن الحناط في ذكر بني فاطمة الزهراء عليها السّلام:

و بالسماح غذو و الجود إذ فطموا	أبناء فاطمة رسل العلا رضعوا
خير البرية لم يحنث لهم قسم	قوم إذا حلف الأقوام أنهم
بيت تداعت إليه العرب و العجم	سما لهم من سماء المجد من شرف

كأنما هي في ألف العلا شمم	مناقب سمحت في كل مكرمة

المصادر: تاريخ الأدب العربي: ج 4 ص 486.

قال أبو العلاء السروي في مدح بني الزهراء:

من بعد ما افترقا في الدهر و اختلفا	ضدان جالا على خديك فاتفقا
و ذا بأعلام سود انطوى ففعفا	هذا بأعلام بيض اغتدا فبدا
عن الشعارين في الدنيا و ما وصفا	أعجب بما حكيا في كتب أمرهما
لبس السواد و أبقوه لهم شرفا	هذا ملوك بني العباس قد شرعوا
بيضاء تخفق إما حادث أزفا	و ذا كهول بني السبطين رأيتهم
و بين شيب عليه بالنهى عطفا	كم ظل بين شباب لا بقاء له
سوى صحيح هنالك عن وجه الدجى كشفا	هل المشيب إلى جنب الشباب
سوى كدر أعقبت منه صفا	و هل يوذي شباب قد تعقبه شيب
من شاهد غير هذا في الورى فكفى	لو لم يكن لبني الزهراء فاطمة
سوداء تشهد فيه التيه و السرفا	فراية لبني العباس عابسة
بيضاء لعرف فيه الحق من عرفا	و راية لبني الزهراء زاهرة
فبح بها و انتصف إن كنت منتصفا	شهادة كشفت عن وجه أمرهما

المصادر: 1. المناقب لابن شهر آشوب: ج 3 ص 300. 2. المناقب لابن شهر آشوب: ج 2 ص 72. 3. الغدير: ج 4 ص 119.

قتل المتوكل من أصحاب الرضا عليه السّلام أهل التقى مثل يعقوب بن السكيت الأديب، و سبب قتله أنه كان معلّما للمعين و المؤيد ابني المتوكل، إذ أقبل فقال له: يا يعقوب! أهما أحبّ إليك أم الحسن و الحسين عليهما السّلام؟ فقال: و الله أن قنبرا غلام علي عليه السّلام خير منهما و من أبيها. فقال المتوكل: سلّوا لسانه من قفاه. فسلّوه فمات؛ و مثل دعبل الخزاعي. و انتهت بالمتوكل العداوة لأهل البيت عليهم السّلام إلى أن أمر بهجو علي و فاطمة عليهما السّلام و أولادها. فهجاهم ابن المعتز بن الجهم و ابن سكرة و آل أبي حفصة و نحوهم، لعنهم الله جميعا، و صار من أمر المتوكل إلى أن أمر بهدم البناء على قبر الحسين عليه السّلام و إحراق مقابر قريش، و في ذلك أنشد حيث قال:

بخلاف أمر إلهه في الناس	قام الخليفة من بني العباس
سفها فعال أمية الأرجاس	ضاها بهتك حريم آل محمد
معشار ما فعلوا بنو العباس	و الله ما فعلت أمية فيهم
من حرقهم من بعد في الارماس	ما قتلهم عندي بأعظم مأتما

ثم جرى الظلم على ذلك إلى هدم سبكتكين مشهد الرضا عليه السّلام و أخرج أبوابه و أخرج منه و قرّ ألف جمل مالا و ثيابا و قتل عدة من الشيعه. قيل: و ممن دفن حيا من الطالبيين عبد العظيم الحسني بالري و محمد بن عبد الله بن الحسين.

و لم يبق في بيضة الإسلام بلدة إلا قتل فيها طالبي أو شيعي، حتى ترى الظلمة يسلّمون على من يعرفونه دهريا أو يهوديا أو نصرانيا و يقتلون من عرفوه شيعيا، يسفكون دم من إسمه علي؛ ألا تسمعون بيحيى المحدث كيف قطعوا لسانه و يديه و رجليه و ضربوه ألف سوط ثم صلبوه، و بعلي بن يقطين كيف اتهموه، و زرارة بن أعين كيف جبّهوه، و أبي تراب الرموزي كيف حبسوه، و منصور بن الزبرقان من قبره كيف نبشوه، و لقد لعن بنو أمية عليا عليه السّلام ألف شهر في الجمع و الأعياد و طافوا بأولاده في الأمصار و البلاد

المصادر: المنتخب: ج 1 ص 6.

قال القضاعي: إن سيدة انتقلت من المنزل الذي نزلت به إلى دار أبي جعفر خالد بن هارون السلمي، و هي التي وهبها لها أمير مصر السري بن الحكم في خلافة المأمون. فأقامت بها حينا إلى زمن وفاتها، و حفرت قبرها بيدها في بيتها، و كانت تصلّي فيها كثيرا ...، لا زالت كذلك إلى أول جمعة من شهر رمضان، فزاد بها الألم و هي صائمة. فدخل عليها الأطباء الحذاق و أشاروا عليها بالإفطار لحفظ القوة، فقالت: وا عجبا لي! ثلاثون سنة أسأل الله عزوجل أن يتوفاني و أنا صائمة فأفطر؟! معاذ الله.

ثم أنشدت تقول:

اصرفوا عني طبيبي و دعوني و حبيبي
زاد بي شوقي إليه و غرامي في لهيب

قالت زينب: ثم إنها بقيت كذلك إلى العشر الأواسط من شهر رمضان، فاحتضرت و استفتحت بقراءة سورة الأنعام. فلا زالت تقرأ إلى أن وصلت إلى قوله تعالى: «قُلْ لِلَّهِ كَتَبَ عَلى نَفْسِهِ الرَّحْمَةَ»، ففاضت روحه الكريمة.

و في درر الأصداف عنها: فلما وصلت إلى قوله تعالى: «لَهُمْ دارُ السَّلامِ عِنْدَ رَبِّهِمْ وَ هُوَ وَلِيُّهُمْ بِما كانُوا يَعْمَلُونَ» «1»، غشي عليها. فضممتها لصدري، فتشهدت شهادة الحق و قبضت عليها، و ذلك في سنة ثمان و مائتين، و دفنت بمزار بدرب السباع، و كان يوم دفنها يوما مشهودا، و أتوها من البلاد و النواحي يصلّون عليها بعد دفنها، و أوقدت الشموع تلك الليلة و سمع البكاء من كل دار بمصر و عظم الأسف عليها.

و أقامت بمصر سبع سنين و يزورون قبره بهذه الكلمات عند ضريحها:

السلام و التحية و الإكرام و الرضا من العلي الأعلى الرحمان على السيدة نفيسة سلالة نبي الرحمة و هادي الأمة؛ من أبوها علم العشيرة و هو الإمام حيدرة. السلام عليك يا بنت الحسن المسموم عليه السّلام أخي الإمام الحسين عليه السّلام المظلوم. السلام عليك يا بنت فاطمة الزهراء عليها السّلام بنت خديجة الكبرى ...

قال المقريزي: قبر السيدة نفيسة أحد المواضع المعروفة بإجابة الدعاء بمصر.

المصادر: نور الأبصار: ص 207.

بسم الله الرحمن الرحيم

القصيدة الميمية

فخـذ الحيـاة وخـذ دمـي	لـك يـا حسين أنتمـي(١)
ـون مقطعـاً بالمنسـم	إنّـي عزمـتُ لأن أكــ
سـأجنُّ إنْ لم تُهـشّـم	وضـلوعي مثـل ضـلوعك
ـحق ليت دونـك أعظمي	بحـوافرٍ للخيـل تـسـ
سـأجن إنْ لم يُفطـم	ورضـيعي مثـل رضـيعك
ثيـك ومـن يغلـق فمي	ساضـجّ في الـدنيا وأر
ـود يـا حسين مـأتمي	سـأقيم في كـلّ الوجـ
صـارت كـشهر محـرم	أيـام عمـري كلّهـا
هـي لا تمـرّ بمبسـم	هجـرتْ شـفاهي بـسمتي
ـين لـك المـشاعر تنتمي	نـادت جـوارحي يـا حـس
ـب أتـاك قلـبُ متـيّم	تـدعو جراحـك يـا حبيـ
أتـاك يـسبق مقـدمي	لبّـى ومـن جـني فـرّ

---

(١) الانتماء العقائدي لهذا الإمام الشهيد عليه السلام.

وسبطهُ تناول الرسولُ	لجــده أتــت بـــه البتــولُ
سماه مثل اسم شقيق شبّر [١]	لمــا رآهُ جــده إستبـشرَ
ثم عليه جدهُ أجرى السُنن [٢]	أعني حسينا ذا مصغر الحسن
ثم أقــام جـدهُ في البسرى	فــأذن في أذنــه الــيمنى [٣]
وأعلــن مولــده وأفشى	وعـق بعـد ذاك عنـه كبشا [٤]
جــده عنـه فضة إذ حلقـا	بــوزن شعـره لقـد تصدقـا

وهي أربعة وعشرون شهرا ومن النساء من تلد لسبعة أشهر فيكون مع حولي الرضاع أحدا وثلاثين شهرا وإن المولود لا يعيش لست ولا لتسعان وإن مولد الحسين عليه السلام كان لستة أشهر ورضاعه أربعة وعشرون شهرا (الموسوعة: ٧).

(١) في الإرشاد للمفيد وكذا ورد في تهذيب الكمال في أسماء الرجال للمزي وكذلك تاريخ ابن عساكر وغيره في الموسوعة أنه عن سلمان قال: قال رسول الله صلى الله عليه وآله وسلم: «سمى هارون ابنه شبرا وشبيرا وإني سميت ابني الحسن والحسين بما سمى به هارون ابنيه شبرا وشبيرا». وغير هذا الحديث.

(٢) السنن التي أجراها رسول الله صلى الله عليه وآله وسلم ستأتي في الأبيات التالية كالأذان والإقامة في أذنه والعق عنه.

(٣) ذكر في (تذكرة الخواص) ابن الجوزي الحنفي قائلا عن ابن سعد في الطبقات قال: قال ابن سعد ولما ولد ـ أي الحسين عليه السلام ـ أذن رسول الله صلى الله عليه وآله وسلم في أذنه، راجع (الموسوعة، ج٢، ٥٧٧) وغير هذا الحديث أيضا ورد.

(٤) ذكر أمين الإسلام في إعلام الورى باعلام الهدى أنه (جاءت به فاطمة الزهراء عليهما السلام أمه إلى رسول الله صلى الله عليه وآله وسلم فسماه حسينا وعق عنه كبشا). (الموسوعة: ج٢، ١١٣).

أقول: وأيضا في إعلام الورى ذكر الطبرسي أمين الإسلام رحمه الله هكذا (ثم عق عنه يوم سابعه بكبشين أملحين وحلق رأسه وتصدق بوزن شعره ورقا ـ فضة ـ طلى رأسه بالخلوق وقال: الدم فعل الجاهلية وأعطى القابلة فخذ الكبش). (انتهى الموسوعة، ج٢، ٤١٩).

١٠ـ قب: المناقب لابن شهرآشوب المرتضى.

إن يوم الطف يـوما كان للـدين عصيبا   لم يدع للقلب مني في المـسرات نصيبا

لعن الله رجـالا أترعوا الدنيا غصوبا   سالموا عجزا فلما قـدروا شنوا الحروبا

طلبوا أوتار بدر عندنا ظلما و حوبا

وله:

لقد كـدرت للدين في يـوم كربلاه   كسائر لا تــوسى ولا هـي تسجبر

فـإما سـبي بـالرماح مسوق   وإمــا قـتيل بـالتراب معفر

وجرحى كـما اختارت رماح وأنصل   وصرعى كـما شاءت ضباع وأنسر

بيان: يوم عصيب أي شديد و أترعه أي ملأ و النزع محركة الإسراع إلى الشر و ترع فلان كفرح
اقتحم الأمور مرحا و نشاطا و الحوب بالضم الإثم و الهلاك و البلاء قوله لا توسى من أسوت
الجرح أي داويته الرضي.

كـربلاه لا زلت كـربا و بـلا   مـا لقـي عنـدك آل المصطفى

كم عـلى تـربك لمـا صرعوا   من دم سـال و من دمع جرى

و ضـيوف لفـلاة قـفرة   نزلوا فـيها عـلى غـير قرى

لم يـذوقوا المـاء حتى اجتمعوا   بحدى السيف على ورد الردى

تكسف الشمس شموس منهم   لا تـدانيها عـلوا و ضبا

وتنوش الوحش مـن أجسادهم   أرجل السبق و أيمان النـدا

ووجـوهـا كـالمصابيح فمن   قمر غـاب و من نجم هـوى

غـيرتهن اللـيالي و غـدا   جائر الحكم عليهن البلى

يـا رسـول الله لو عـاينتهم   و هم مـا بـين قتـل و سبا

مـن رميض يـمنع الظل و من   عـاطش يسقي أنابيب القنا

و مسـوق عـاثر يسـعى بـه   خلف محمول على غير وطء

جزروا جـزر الأضاحي نسله   ثـم سـاقوا أهله سوق الإما

قـتلوه بـسعد عـلم منهم   إنـه خـامس أصحاب الكسا

مـيت تـبكي له فـاطمة   و أبـوهـا و عـلي ذو العلا

وله أيضا:

شغل الدموع عن الديار بكاؤها[٣]   لبكـاء فـاطمة عـلى أولادها

لم يخلفوها في الشهيد و قد رأى   دفع القرات يـذاد عـن ورادهـا

أتـرى درت أن الحسين طـريده   لقنا بـني الطرداء عند ولادها

كانت مآتم بـالعراق تـعدها   أموية بـالشام مـن أعيادها

مـا راقبت غضب النبي و قد غدا   زرع النبي مسلطنة لحصادها

جعلت رسول الله مـن خصائها   فليس مـا ادخرت ليـوم معادها

نسل النبي عـلى صعاب مطيها   و دم الحسين على رءوس صعادها

683

را لهـــفتاه لعـــصبة عـــلوية | تــمت أمـــية بــعد ذل قــيادها
جــعلت عــران الذل فــي آنــافها | و غــلاظ وسم الضـيم فـي أجـيادها
و اسـتأثرت بــالأمر عــن غـيابها | و قــضت بـما شـاءت عـلى أشـهادها
طـلبت تـراث الجـاهلية عـندها | و شــفت قـديم الغـل مـن أحـقادها
يـا يـوم عـاشوراء كم لك لوعة | تــترقص الأشـياء مـن إيـقادها

أقول: و لي في بعض الكتب فيه زيادة:

إن قــوضت تـلك القـباب فـإنها | خـرت عـماد الدين قـبل عـمادها
هـي صفوة الله التـي أوحي بـها | و قــضى أوامـــره إلى أمـجادها
يــروي مــناقب فـضلها أعـداؤها | أبــدا فــيعندها إلى أضـدادها
يـا فـرقة ضـاعت دمـاء محمد | و بــسنه بـين بـزيدها و زيـادها
صـفرا بـمال الله مـلء أكـفها | و أكــف آل اللـه فـي أصـفادها
ضـربوا بـسيف مـحمد أبـناءه | ضــرب الغـرائب عـدن بـعد ذيـادها
يـا يـوم عـاشوراء كـم لك لوعة | تــترقص الأحشـاء مـن إيـقادها
مـا عـدت إلا عـاد قـلبي عـلة | حزني و لو بالغت في إيرادها

بيان: قوله بحدى السيف أي حداهم السيف حتى اجتمعوا على نوبة هلاكهم أو على ما يورد عليه من الهلاك و يمكن أن يكون بحد السيف على التخفيف لضرورة الشعر و في بعض النسخ بـعدا السيف أي قبال السيف قوله تكسف الشمس أي هم شموس كل منهم يغلب نوره نور الشمس ويكسفها و النوش التناول قوله جائر الحكم حال عن البلى أي بلى كثير كأنه جار في الحكم و لعل مراده غير المعصوم فإنه لا يتطرق إليه البلى مع أنه في الشعر قد لا يراعى تلك الأمور.

قوله شغل الدموع أي شغل البكاء على تلك المصيبة الدموع عن انصبابها لذكر ديار المـحبوبين ومنازلهم فالضمير في بكاؤها راجع إلى العيون بقرينة المقام و الأصوب شغل العيون أي عن النظر إلى الديار قوله لم يخلفوها أي لم يرعوا حرمة فاطمة في الشهيد و الدفع بضم الدال و فتح الفاء جمع الدفعة أي دفعات الفرات و انصبابها و الدفاع طحمة الموج و السيل.

قوله درت أي علمت فاطمة ﵁ قوله بني الطرداء أي أبناء الذين كانوا مطرودين ملعونين حين تلد فاطمة تلك الأولاد و الزرع الولد و الأخر مرعى و السعدة القناة المستوية تنبت كذلك لا تحتاج إلى تثقيف و الصعاد جمعها و المران العود الذي يجعل في وتره أنف البخني.

١١ـقب: [المناقب لابن شهر آشوب] آخر:

تــبيت النشـاوى من أمية نـوما | و بـالطف قـتلى مـا يـنام حـميمها
و مـا قـتل الإسـلام إلا عـصابة | تـأمر نـوكاها و نـام زعـيمها
فأضحت فناة الدين في كف ظالم | إذا اعوج مـنها جـانب لا يـقيمها

غيره:

را خجلة الإسلام من أضداده | ظفروا له بمعايب و معاير

اللهم صلي على محمد و آل محمد

آل العزيز يعظمون حماره | و يرون فوزا لثمهم للحافر
وسيوفكم بدم ابن بنت نبيكم | مخضوبة لرضى يزيد الفاجر

وفي رواية:

وا خجلة الإسلام من أضداده | ظفروا له بمعايب و معاير
رأس ابن بنت محمد و وصيه | تهدى جهارا للشقي الفاجر

الصنويري :

يا خير من لبس النبوة من جميع الأنبياء | وجدي على سبطيك وجد ليس يؤذن بانقضاء
هذا قتيل الأشقياء و ذا قتيل الأدعياء | يوم الحسين هرقت دمع الأرض بل دمع السماء
يوم الحسين تركت باب العز مهجور الفناء | يا كربلاء خلفت من كرب علي و من بلاء
كم فيك من وجه تشرب ماؤه ماء البهاء | تفسي فداء المصطفى نار الوغى أي اصطلاء
حيث الأسنة في الجواشن كالكواكب في السماء | فاختار درع الصبر حيث الصبر من لبس السناء
وأبا إبا الأسد إن الأسد صادقة الإباء | و قضى كريما إذ قضى ظمآن في نفر ظماء
منعوه طعم الماء، لا وجدوا لما طعم ماء | من ذا لمعفور الجواد ممال أعواد الخباء
من للطريح الشلو عريانا مخلى بالعراء | من للمحنط بالتراب و للمغسل بالدماء

من لابن فاطمة المغيب عن عيون الأولياء

بيان: الشلو بالكسر المضر من أعضاء اللحم و أثلاء الإنسان أعضاؤه بعد التفرق.

١٢ـ قب: [المناقب لابن شهرآشوب] للشافعي

تأره قلبي و الفؤاد كئيب | و أرق نـومـي فـالـسـهاد عجيب
فمن مبلغ عني الحسين رسالة | و إن كـرهتها أنـفـس و قـلـوب
ذبيح بلا جرم كأن قميصه | صبيغ بمـا الأرجـوان خضيب
فللسيف إعوال و للرمح رنة | و للخيل مـن بعد الصهيل نحيب
تزلزلت الدنيا لآل محمد | و كـادت لهم صم الجبال تذوب
و غارت نجوم و اقشعرت كواكب | و هتك أستار و شق جيوب
يصلى على المبعوث من آل هاشم | و يغزى بسنوه إن ذا لعجيب
لئن كان ذنبي حب آل محمد | فذلك ذنب لست عـنـه أتوب
هم شفعائي يـوم حشري و موقفي | إذا ما بـدت للناظرين خطوب

الجوهري :

عاشورنا ذا ألا لهفي على الدين | خذوا حدادكم يا آل ياسين
اليوم شق جيب الدين و انتهبت | بنات أحمد نهب الروم و الصين
اليوم قام بأعلا الطف نادبهم | بـقـول مـن ليتيم أو لمسكين

اللهم صلي على محمد و آل محمد

685

أمسى عبير نحور الحور و العين	اليوم خضب جيب المصطفى بدم
على مناحر تذليل و توهين	اليوم خر نجوم الفخر من مضر
و جزرت لهم التقوى على الضين	اليوم أطفئ نور الله متقدا
و برقعت عزة الإسلام بالهون	اليوم هتك أسباب الهدى مزقا
و طاح بالخيل ساحات الميادين	اليوم زعزع قدس من جوانبه
مما صلوا ببدر ثم صفين	اليوم نال بنو حرب طوائلها
من تشفه بنجيع غير مسنون	اليوم جدك سبط المصطفى شرقا

إيضاح: الحداد بالكسر ثياب المأتم السود و طاح أي هلك و سقط و الطوائل جمع طائلة و هي العداوة و الترة و النجيع من الدم ما كان إلى السواد و قيل هو دم الجوف خاصة و المسنون المتغير المنتن و قوله شرقا فعل و الألف للإشباع أي شرق بسبب مصيبة من هو بمنزلة نفسه بدم طري من الحزن.

١٣ـ القب [المناقب لابن شهرآشوب] شاعر:

كم فيك من ساق ومن جمجمة	يا كربلاء يا كربتي وزفرتي
للفاطميات العظام الحرمة	ومن يمين بالحسام بينت
وغلقت أبوابه و سدت	قد خر أركان العلى وانهدت

تلك الرزايا عظمت و جلت

أخر:

فديته السيد الغريب	كم سيد لي بكربلاء
للموت في صدره وجيب	كم سيد لي بكربلاء
عسكره بالعرا نهيب	كم سيد لي بكربلاء
ليس لما يشتهي طبيب	كم سيد لي بكربلاء
خاتمه و الرداء سليب	كم سيد لي بكربلاء
خضب من نحره المشيب	كم سيد لي بكربلاء
مسلمه و الردا خضيب	كم سيد لي بكربلاء
يسمع صوتي و لا يجيب	كم سيد لي بكربلاء
ينظر في ثغرة القضيب	كم سيد لي بكربلاء

أخر :

للناظرين على قناة يرفع	رأس ابن بنت محمد و وصيه
لا منكر منهم و لا متفجع	والمسلمون بمنظر و بمسمع
و أصم رزءك كل أذن يسمع	كحلت بمنظرك العيون عماية
و أنت عينا لم تكن بك تهجع	أيقظت أجفانا و كنت لها كرى
لك منزل و لخط قبرك مضجع	ما روضة إلا تمنت أنها

اللهم صلي على محمد و آل محمد

686

لآل رسـول اللـه و انـهـل عـبـرتـي	إذا جـاء عـاشـوراء تـضـاعـف حـسـرتـي
وجـومـا عـلـيـهـا و الـسـمـاء الشـعـرت	هـو اليـوم فـيـه اغـبـرت الأرض كـلـهـا
فـلـو عـقـلت شـمـس النـهـار لخـرت	أريـقـت دمـاء الفـاطـمـيـن بـالـمـلا
بـنـفـسـي جـسـوم بـالعـراء تـعـرت	بـنـفـسي خـدود فـي التـراب تـعفـرت
إلى الشـام تـهـدى بـازقات الأسـنـة	بنفسي رءوس معـلـيـات على القنا
و لم تـحـظ مـن مـاء الفـرات بـقطرة	بـنـفـسي شـفـاه ذابـلات مـن الظـمـا
إلى المـــاء مـنـهـا قـطرة	بـنـفـسي عـيـون غـائـرات سـواهـر
حـواسـر لم تعـرف عـليـهم بـسـترة	بعد قطرةبنفسي من آل النـبي خرائـد

إيضاح: قال الجوهري وجم من الأمر وجوما والواجم الذي اشتد حزنه حتى أمسك عن الكلام ويوم وجيم أي شديد الحر وقال الفيروز آبادي الزفت الملء والغيظ والطرد والسوق والدفع والمنع وبالكسر القار والمزفت المطلي به والظاهر بارفات كما سنجي والخريدة من النساء الحية والجمع خرائد قوله لم تعرف من العرف والمعروف بمعنى الإحسان.

١٤ـ قب: (المناقب لابن شهرآشوب) لأبي الفرج بن الجوزي.

قـسـا يـكـون الحـق فـيـه مـسـائلي	أ حسين و المـبعوث جـدك بـالهدى
تـنـفـيس كـربـك جـهـد بـذل البـاذل	لو كنت شـاهـد كـربـلا، لبـذلت فـي
جـلالا و حـد الـسـمـهـري الذابـل	و سـقيت حد الـسـيـف مـن أعدائكم
فـبـلابـلي بـين القـري و بـاسـل	لكـنـتني أخـرت عـنـك لشـقـوتي
فـأقـل مـن حـزن و دمـع سـائل	إذ لم أفـز بـالنصر مـن أعـدائكـم

آخر:

انهد ركني يا أخي و القوا	يا حر صدري يا لهيب الحشـا
ذخـر و لا ركن و لا مـلتجا	كنت أخي ركني و لم يبق لي
مـا كنت أرجـوه فـخاب الرجـا	وكـنت أرجـوك فـقد خـانـني
رأيت مـني مـا يـسر العدا	[٧٦] يـا ابـن أمـي لو تـأملتني
مـن ألم الـسـيـر و ذل السبا	حـل بـأعدائك مـا حـل بـي
يـومـك هـذا و أكـون الفـدا	و يا شـقيقي أنـا أفـديك مـن
مـا عـشت مـن بـعدك أو أدفنـا	و لا هنـأني العـيش يـا سـيدي

آخر:

و الرأس مـنـه عـال فـي ذروة القـناة	يا من رأى حسينا شلوا لدى الفـلاة
يـا جـد لو تـرانـا أسـرى مـهتكات	وزيـنـب تـنـادي قـد قـتلوا حمـاتي

توضيح: الجلل بالتحريك العظيم و السمهري الرمح الصلب و البلابل شدة الهموم و الوساوس.

اللهم صلي على محمد و آل محمد

687

١٥ـ أقول رأيت في بعض مؤلفات المتأخرين أنه قال حكى دعبل الخزاعي قال دخلت على سيدي و مولاي علي بن موسى الرضا﷾ في مثل هذه الأيام رأيته جالسا جالسة الحزين الكئيب و أصحابه من حوله فلما رآني مقبلا قال لي مرحبا بك يا دعبل مرحبا بناصرنا بيده و لسانه ثم إنه وسع لي في مجلسه و أجلسني إلى جانبه ثم قال لي يا دعبل أحب أن تنشدني شعرا فإن هذه الأيام أيام حزن كانت علينا أهل البيت و أيام سرور كانت على أعدائنا خصوصا بني أمية يا دعبل من بكى و أبكى   على مصابنا و لو واحدا كان أجره على الله يا دعبل من ذرفت عيناه على مصابنا و بكى لما أصابنا من أعدائنا حشره الله معنا في زمرتنا يا دعبل من بكى على مصاب جدي الحسين غفر الله له ذنوبه البتة.

ثم إنه﷾ نهض و ضرب سترا بيننا و بين حرمه و أجلس أهل بيته من وراء الستر ليبكوا على مصاب جدهم الحسين﷿ ثم التفت إلي و قال لي يا دعبل ارث الحسين فأنت ناصرنا و مادحنا ما دمت حيا فلا تقصر عن نصرنا ما استطعت قال دعبل فاستعبرت و سالت عبرتي و أنشأت أقول:

و قد مات عطشانا بشط فرات	أفاطم لو خلت الحسين مجدلا
و أجريت دمع العين في الوجنات	إذا للطمت الخد فاطم عنده
نجوم سماوات بأرض فلاة	أفاطم قومي يا ابنة الخير و اندبي
و أخرى بسفح نالها صلواتي	قبور بكوفان و أخرى بطيبة
معرسهم فيها بشط فرات	قبور ببطن النهر من جنب كربلا
توقيت فيهم قبل حين وفاتي	تواقوا عطاشا بالماء فليتني
سقتني بكأس الثكل و الفجعات	إلى الله أشكو لوعة عند ذكرهم
و جبريل و القرآن و السورات	إذا فخروا يوما أتوا بمحمد
و فاطمة الزهراء خير بنات	و عدوا عليا ذا المناقب و العلا
و جعفرها الطيار في الحجبات	وحمزة و العباس ذا الدين و التقى
سمية من نوكى و من قذرات	أولئك مشئومون هندا و حربها
و هم تركوا الأبناء رهن شتات	هم منعوا الأبناء من أخذ حقهم
و ما ناح قمري على الشجرات	سأبكيهم ما حج لله راكب
فقد آن للتسكاب و الهملات	فيا عين بكيهم و جودي بعبرة
و آل رسول الله منهتكات	بنات زياد في القصور مصونة
و آل رسول الله في الفلوات	و آل زياد في الحصون مصونة
و آل زياد تسكن الحجرات	ديار رسول الله أصبحن بلقعا
و آل زياد غلظ القصرات	و آل رسول الله نحف جسومهم
و آل زياد ربة الحجلات	و آل رسول الله تدمى نحورهم
و آل زياد آمنوا السربات	و آل رسول الله تسبى حريمهم
أكفا من الأوتار منقبضات	إذا وتروا مدوا إلى وانسربوا
و نادى منادي الخير للصلوات	سأبكيهم ما ذر في الأرض شارق
و بالليل أبكيهم و الغدوات	و ما طلعت شمس و حان غروبها

١٦ـ و رأيت في بعض مؤلفات بعض ثقات المعاصرين بعض المراثي فأحببت إيرادها للشيخ الخليعي

لم أبك ربعا للأحبة قد خلا   و عفا و غيره الجديد و أمحلا

كلا و لا كلفت صحبي وقفة   في الدار إن لم اشف ضبا عللا

و مطارح النادي و غزلان النقا   و الجزع لم أحفل بها متغزلا

و بواكر الأظعان لم أسكب لها   دمعا و لا خل نأى و ترحلا

لكن بكيت لفاطم و لمنها   فدكا و قد أتت الخئون الأولى

إذ طالبته بميراثها فسروى لها   خبرا ينافي المحكم المنزلا

لهفي لها و جفونها قرحى و قد   حملت من الأحزان عبئا مثقلا

وقد اعتدت منيفة و حييها   مستطيرا ببكائها متقلا

تخفي تفجعها و تخفض صوتها   و تظل نادبة أباها المرسلا

تبكي على تكدير دهر ما صفا   من بعده و قرير عيش ما حلا

لم أنسها إذ أقبلت في نسوة   من قومها تروي مدامعها الصلا

و تنفست صعدا و نادت أيها   الأنصار يا أهل الحماية و الكلا

أترون يا نجب الرجال و أنتم   أنصارنا حماتا أن نخذلا

مالي و ما لدعي تيم ادعى   إرثي و ضل مكذبا مبدلا

أعليه قد نزل الكتاب مبينا   حكم القرائض أم علينا نزلا

أم خصه المبعوث منه بعلم ما   أخفاه عناكي نضل و نجهلا

أم أنزلت آي بسمنعي إرثه   قد كان يخفيها النبي إذا تلا

أم كان في حكم النبي و شرعه   نقص فتممه الغوي و كملا

أم كان ديني غير دين أبي فلا   ميراث لي منه و ليس له و لا

قوموا بنصري إنها لغنمة   لمن اعتدى لي ناصرا متكفلا

و استعطفوه و خوفوه و اشهدوا   ذلي له و جفاه لي بين الملا

إن لج في سخطي فقد عدم الرضي   من ذي الجلال و للعقاب تعجلا

أو دام في طغيانه فقد اقتنى   لعنا على مر الزمان مطولا

أين المودة و القرابة يا ذوي الأ   يمان ما هذا القطيعة و القلا

أفسهل عسيتم إن توليتم بأن   تمضرا على سنن الجبابرة الأولى

و تنكبوا نهج السبيل بقطع ما   أمر الإله عباده أن يرصلا

و لقد أزالكم الهوى و أحدكم   دار البوار من الجحيم و أدخلا

و لسوف يعقب ظلمكم أن تتركوا   ولدي برضاه الطفوف مجللا

في فــتـيـة مـثـل البـدور كـواملا   عـرض الـمحاق بـها فـاضحت آفلا
و أقـوم مـن خـلل اللــحود حـزينة   و القـوم قـد نـزلت بـهم غير البـلا
ويـــروعني نـقط القنـا بـجسومهم   و يسوؤني شكل السيوف على الطلى
فــأقيل النـحر الخـضيب و أمـسـح   الوجه التريب مضمخا و مرملا
ويـقوم سـيدنا النـبي و رهـطه   مسـتلهفا مـتأسفا مسـتقللا
فـيرى الغريب المستضام النازح   الأوطان ملقى في اثرى ما غـلا
وتـقوم آسـية و تـأتي مـريم   يـبكين مـن كـربي بـعرصة كربلا
ويطفن حولي نادبات الجن إشفاقا   عـلي يـغضن دمـعـا مسـبـلا
وتـضج أمــلاك الســماء لعـبرتي   و نـسعى بـالشكوى إلى رب العـلى
وأرى بـنـاتي يشـتكين حـواسـرا   تـهب المـعاجر والهـات ثكـلا
وأرى إمـام العـصر بـعد أبـيه فـي   صفد الحـديد مقللا و مـعللا
وأرى كـريم مـؤملي فـي ذاهـل   كـاليدر فـي ظـلم الدباجي يجتلي
يهدى إلى الرجس اللعين فيشتني   مـنه فـؤاد بـالحقود قـد امتلأ
ويظل يـقرع مـنه ثـغرا طال مـا   قـدما تـرشفه النـبي و قـبلا
ومـضلل أضـحى يـوطن عـذرة   و يـقول و هو مـن البصيرة قد خلا
لو لم يـحرم أحـمد مـيراثـه   لم يـسـمعوه أهـلـه و تـأولا
لأجبته إصـر بـقلبك أم قـذا   في العين منك عدتك نبصرة الجلا
أو ليس أعطاها ابـن خـطاب لحـيد   رة الرضا مسـتعتبا مسـتصلا
أتـراه حـلل مـا رآه مـحرما   أم ذاك حـرم مـا رآه مـحللا
يـا راكـبا تطوي المـهامة عيمه   طـي الردا و تـجوب أجواز الفـلا
عـرج بـأكناف الغري مبلغا   شوقي و نـاد بـها الإمـام الأفضلا
و مـن العـجيب تشـوقي لمزار من   لم يـستخذ إلا فـؤادي مـنزلا
فاحبس و قل يا خير من وطن الثرى   و أعـزهم جـارا و أعـذب مـنهلا
لو شئت قمت بـنصر بضعة أحمد   الهـادي بـعقد عـزيمة لن تحللا
و رمـيت أعـداء الرسـول بـجمرة   مـن حـد سـيفك حرها لا يصطلى
لكن صـبرت لأن تـقام عـليهم   حجج الإله و لن تـرى أن تـعجلا
كـيلا يـقولوا إن عـجلت عـليهم   كنا نـراجع أمـرنا لو أمـهلا
مـولاي يـا جنب الإله و عـينه   يـا ذا المناقب و المـراتب و العلا
إحياؤك العـظم الرمـيم و ردك   الشمس المنيرة و الدجى قد أسبلا
و خضوعها لك في الخطاب و قولها   يـا قـادرا يـا يـا قاهرا يـا أولا
و كـلام أصحاب الرقـيم و ردهـم   منك السلام و ما استنار و ما انجلى
و حـديث سلمان و نـصرته عـلى   أسـد الفرات و علم ما قد أشكلا
لا يستفز ذوي النـهى و يـقل مـن   أن يـرتضى و يـجل مـن أن يـذهلا
أخـذ الإلـه لك العـهود على الورى   فـي الذر لما أن بـرا و بك ابتلى
فـي يـوم قال لهـم ألنتُ بـربّكُمْ   و علي مـولاكم معا فألوا بلى

قسما بوردي من حياض معارفي   و بشربي العذب الرحيق السلسلا

و من استجارك من نبي مرسل   و دعا بحقك ضارعا متوسلا

لو قلت إنك رب كل فضيلة   ما كنت فيما قلته متنحلا

أو بحت بالخطر الذي أعطاك رب   العرش كادوني و قالوا قد غلا

فإليك من تقصير عبدك عذره   فكثير ما أنهي يراه مقللا

بل كيف يبلغ كنه وصفك قائل   و الله في علياك أبلغ مقولا

و نفائس القرآن فيك تنزلت   و بك اغتدى متحليا متجملا

لاستجلها بكرا فأنت مليكها   و على سواك تجل من أن تجتلي

و لئن بقيت لأنضطم قلائد   ينسى تراصعها النظام الأولى

شهد الإله بأنني مستبرئ   من حبتر و من الدلام و نعثلا

و براءة الخلعي من عصب الخنا   تبنى على أن البرا أصل الولا.

قصيدة لابن حماد   رحمه الله:

مصاب شهيد الطف جسمي أنحلا   و كدر من دهري و عيشي ما حلا

فما هل شهر العشر إلا تجددت   بقلبي أحزان توسدتي البلى

أذكر مولاي الحسين و ما جرى   عليه من الأرجاس في طف كربلاء

فر الله لا أنساه بالطف قائلا   لعترته الغر الكرام و من تلا

ألا قاتلوا في هذه الأرض و اعلموا   بأني بها أمسي صريها مجدلا

و أسقي بها كأس المنون على ظما   و يصبح جسمي بالدماء مغسلا

و لهفي له يدعو اللئام تأملرا   مقالي يا شر الأنام و أرذ لا

ألم تعلموا أني ابن بنت محمد   و والدي الكرار للدين كملا

فهل سنة غيرتها أو شريعة   و هل كنت في دين الإله مبدلا

أحللت   ما قد حرم الطهر أحمد   أ حرمت ما قد كان قبل محللا

فقالوا له دع ما تقول فإننا   سنسقيك كأس الموت غصبا معجلا

كفعل أبيك المرتضى بشيوخنا   و تشفي صدورا من ضغائنكم ملا

فأتى إلى نحو النساء جواده   و أحزانه منها الفؤاد قد امتلأ

و نادى ألا يا أهل بيتي تصيروا   على الضر بعدي و الشدائد و البلاء

فإني بهذا اليوم أرحل عنكم   على الرغم مني لا ملال و لا قلا

فقوموا جميعا أهل بيتي و أسرعرا   أودعكم و الدمع في الخد مسبلا

فصبرا جميلا و اتقوا الله إنه   سيجزيكم خير الجزاء و أفضلا

فأتى على أهل العناد مبادرا   يحامي عن دين المهيمن ذي العلا

و صـــال عـلـيهم كـالهزبر مـجاهدا   كـفعل أبـيه لن يـزل و يـخذلا

فمال عـلـيه القـوم مـن كـل جـانب   فـألقوا عـن ظهر الجـواد مـجدلا

و خـر كـريم السـبط يـا لك نكبة   بـها أصبح الديـن القـويم مـطلا

فـارتجت السـبع الشـداد و زلزلت   و ناح عليه الجـن و الوحش في الفلا

و راح جـواد السـبط نـحو نسائه   يـنوح و يـستبي الظـامئ المـترملا

خـرجن بنـات البتـول حواسـرا   فـعاين مهر السبط و السرج قـد خـلا

فـأدمين بـاللطم الخـدود لفقده   و أسكـبن دمـعا حـره ليس يـصطلى

و لم أنس زينـب تستغيث سكينة   أخـي كـنت لي حصنا حصينا و موئلا

أخـي يـا قتيل الأدعـياء كسرتني   و أورثـتني حـزنا مـقيما مطولا

أخـي كـنت أرجـو أن أكـون لك الفدا   فـقد خبت فـيما كـنت فـيه أؤمـلا

أخي ليتني أصبحت عميا و لا أرى   جبينك و الوجـه الجميل مـرملا

و تـدعو إلى الزهـراء بنت مـحمد   أيـا أم ركني قـد وهـى و تـزلزلا

أيـا أم قـد أمسى حبيبك بـالعرا   طريحا ذبـيحا بـالدماء مـفلا

أيـا أم نـوحي فـالكريم عـلى القنا   يـلوح كـالبدر المـنير إذا انجلى

و نوحي على النحـر الخضيب و اسكبي   دمـعا على الخد التـريب المـرملا

و نـوحي على الجسم التـريب تدوسـه   خـيل بـني سـفيان قـي أرض كربلاء

و نوحي على السـجاد في الأسر بـعده   يسـاق إلى الرجس اللـعين مـغللا

فـيا حسـرة مـا تنقضي و مصيبة   إلى أن نـرى المـهدي بـالنصر أقـبلا

إمامه يـقيم الديـن بـعد خفائه   إمـام لـه رب السـماوات فـضلا

أيـا آل طـه يـا رجـائي و عـدتي   و عـوني أيـا أهـل المـفاخر و العلا

يـمينا بـأني مـا ذكـرت مصابكم   أيـا سـادتي إلا أبيـت مـثقلا

فـحزني عـليكم كـل آن مـجدد   مـقيم إلى أن أسكـن التـرب و البـلا

عبيدكم العبـد الحـقير مـحمد   كـئيب و قـد أمسى عـليكم مـعولا

يـؤملكم يـا سـادتي تشفعوا لـه   إذا مـا أتى يـوم الحسـاب ليسألا

فـو الله مـا أرجـو النـجاة بـغيركم   غـدا يـوم أتـي خـائفا مـترجلا

إذا فـر مـني والدي و مـصاحبي   و عاينت مـا قدمت في زمن الخـلا

و مـنوا على الحضار بالعفو قي غد   لأن بكـم قـدري و قـدرهم عـلا

عـليكم سـلام الله يـا آل أحـمد   سـلام على مـر الزمـان مطولا

أيضا لابن حماد:

أهـجرت يـا ذات الجمـال دلالا   و جعلت جسمي للصدود خـبالا

وسـقيتي كـأس الفـراق مـرارة   و منعت عذب رضابك السلسالا

أسفا كـما منع الحسين بكربلاء   مـاء الفـرات و أوسعـوه خـبالا

وسقو، أطراف الأسنة و القنا
لم أنس مولاي الحسين بكربلا
واحسرتى كم يستغيث بسجده
ويقول يا جداه ليتك حاضر
ويقول للشمر اللعين و قد علا
يا شمر تقتلني بغير جناية
واجتز بالعضب المهند رأسه
وعلا به فوق السنان و كبروا
فارتجت السبع الطباق و أظلمت
و بكين أطباق السماء، و أمطرت
يا ويلكم أتكبرون لفقد من
تركوه سلبا في الفلاة و صيروا
و لقد عجبت من الإله و حلمه
كفروا فلم يخسف بهم أرضا يما
و غدا الحصان من الوقيعة عاريا
مسئوجها نحو الخيام مخضبا
و تقول زينب يا سكينة قد أتى
قامت سكينة عايته محمحما
فبكت و قالت وا شمانة حاسدي
يا عمتا جاء الحصان مخضبا
لما سمعن الطاهرات سكينة
أبرزن من وسط الخدور صوارخا
فلطمن منهن الخدود و كشفت
و خمشن منهن الوجوه لفقد من
قتل الإمام ابن الإمام بكربلا
و تقول يا جداه نسل أمية
يا جدنا فعلوا علوج أمية
يا جدنا هذا الحسين بكربلا
ملقى على شاطئ الفرات مجدلا
ثم استباحوا في الطفوف حريمه
و غدوا بزين العابدين مكتفا
يسبى أباء بعبرة مسفوحة

و يزيد يشرب في القصور زلالا
ملقى طريحا بالدماء رمالا
و الشمر منه يقطع الأوصالا
فعساك تمنع دوننا الأنذالا
صدرا تربى في تقى و دلالا
حقا ستجزى في الجحيم نكالا
ظلما و هز برأسه العالا
لله جل جلاله و تعالى
و تزلزلت لمصابه زلزالا
أسفا لمصرعه دما قد سالا
قتلوا به التكبير و التهليلا
للخيل في جسد الحسين مجالا
في الحال جل جلاله و تعالى
فعلوا و أسهلهم به إمهالا
ينمى الحسين و قد مضى إجفالا
بدم الحسين و سرجه قد سالا
فرس الحسين فانظري ذا الحالا
ملقى العنان فأعولت إعوالا
قتلوا الحسين و أيتموا الأطفالا
بدم الشهيد و دمعه قد سالا
تنمى الحسين و تظهر الأعوالا
يندبن سبط محمد المفضالا
منها الوجوه و أعلنت إعوالا
نادى مناد في السماء و قالا
ظلما و قاسى منهم الأهوالا
قتلوا الحسين و ذبحوا الأطفالا
فعلا شنها يدهش الأفعالا
قد بضعوه أسنة و نصالا
في الفاضرية للورى أمثالا
نهبوا السراة و لوضوا الأحمالا
فوق السطية يشتكي الأهوالا
أسروه مضني لا يطيق نزالا

و أتـوا بـه نـحو الخيـام و أمـه — تـبكي و تسـحب خلفه الأذيالا

و تـقول ليت الموت جـاء و لم أر — هـذي الفعـال و أنـظر الأنـذالا

لو كـان والده عـلي المـرتضى — حـيـا لـجـدل دونـه الأبـطالا

و لقـر جـيش المـارقين هـزيمة — مـن سـيفه لا يسـطيع قتـالا

يـا ويـلـكم فستـسحبون أذلة — و سـتحملون بـفعلكم أثـقالا

فـعلي ابن سعد و اللـعين عبيده — لعـن تـجدد لا يـزول زوالا

و عـلى محـمد ثـم آل محمد — روح و ريـحان يـدوم مـقالا

و عليهم صلى المهيمن ما حدا — فـي البـيد ركـبان تسير عجالا

فـمتى تـعود لآل أحـمد دولة — و نـرى لـملك الظـالمين زوالا

يـا آل أحـمد أنـتم سـفن النجاة — و أنـا و حـقكم لكـم أتـوالى

أرجـوكم لي فـي المـعاد ذريعة — و بكـم أفـوز و أبـلغ الآمـالا

فـلأنتم حـجج الإلـه عـلى الورى — مـن لم يـقل ما قلت قال محالا

و الله أنزل هل أتـى فـي مدحكم — و النـمل و الحـجرات و الأنـفالا

و المرتقى من فـوق منكب أحمد — مـنكم و لو رام السـماء لنـالا

و عـليكم نـزل الكـتاب منفصلا — و اللـه أنـزله لكـم إنـزالا

نـص بـإذن اللـه لا مـن نـفسه — ذو العـرش نـص بـه لكم إفضالا

فـتكلم المـختار لمـا جـاء — مـن ربـه جـبريـلهم إرسـالا

إذ قـال هـذا وارثـي و خـليفتي — فـي أمـتي فـتسمعوا   مـا قـالا

أفـديكم آل النـبي و بـمهجتي — و أبـي و أبـذل فـيكم الأمـوالا

و أنـا ابـن حـماد وليكـم الذي — لـم يـرض غـير كـم و لم يـتوالا

أصبحت مـعتصما بـحبل ولاتكم — جـدا و إن قـصر الزمـان و طـالا

و أنـا الذي أهـواكم يـا سـادتي — أرجـو بـذاك عـناية و نـوالا

بـعد الصـلاة علـى النبي محمد — مـا غـرد القـمري و أرخـى البـالا

أقول: لبعض تلامذة والدي الماجد نور الله ضريحه و هو محمد رفيع بن مؤمن الجيلي تجاوز الله عن سيئاتهما و حشرهما مع ساداتهما مراثي مهكية حسنة السبك جزيلة الألفاظ سألني إيرادها   لتكـون لسـان صدق له فـي الآخـرين و هي هذه.

المرثية الأولى

كـم لـريب المـنون مـن وثـبات — زعـزعتني فـي رقـدتي و ثـبائي

كـيف لي و الحـمام أغـرق فـي النـز — ع و لا يسـخطني الذي فـي الحـياة

نـفسي المـقتضى مسـرة نـفي — فـي بـلوغي منـيتي خـطواتي

كـيف يـلتذ عـاقل لحـياة — هـي أسـطى الرحال نـحو المـمات

هل سليم المـذاق يشـهى و يستصفي — أجـاجا فـي وهـدة الكـدرات

هـذا دار رحـلة غب حـل — كـآتي فـي الطـريق وسـط الفـلاة

694

لا مكـان الثـواء و الظعـن و الا   مـن مـن الأخـذ بـغتة و البيـات

بـنـت الدار إذ قـد اجتمعت فيهـا   صـرف الأكـالب الضـاربات

ذل فيها أولو الشرافـة و المجد   و عـزت أرافل الـعـبـلات

دور أهـل الضـلال فـيها استجدت   و رسـوم الهـدى عـفت دائـرات

أف للـدار هـذه ثـم تـبا   لا أرى عنـدها مكـان الثبـات

كـالبغاة الزنـاة آل زيـاد   نـطف العـاهرين و العـاهرات

أنـرى مـن يـقول ذاك الـفـترا   أو رمـى المحصنين و المـحصنات

لا و رب المـقام و البـيت و الحجر   و جـمـع و الخـيـف و العرفات

هـل سـمعت الذي تـواتـر مـعنى   مـن نـبي الورى بـنقل الثـقات

إن مـن كـان مـبغضا لعـلي   فـهـو لا شك خـائن الأمـهات

مـا وجـدنا أشـد بـغضا و حـقدا   مـن عـبد الفريق فـي اللعـنات

كـافر فـاسق دعـسي خـبيث   فـاجر ظـالم شـقي و عـات

نـال آل الرسـول مـن ذلك الرجس   رزايـا قـد هـدت الراسـيات

يـا لها مـن مـصيبة رق فـيها   قـلب كـل الأنـام حـتى العـداة

يـا لهـا مـن مـصيبة صـاح فيها   فـرق الجـن صـيحة الثـاكـلات

يـا لهـا مـن مـصيبة أسـبلت دمـع   الأولى مـا بكـوا لدى النـازلات

لهـف قـلبي لسـادة الخـلق إذ   هـم ذلـلوا فـي إسـار قـوم طـغاة

لهـف قـلبي و لجـة البغي هاجت   فـأنـالت بـاللطم سـفن النـجاة

لهـف قـلبي لغـتة كـبدور   خـسفت مـن تـراكـم الظـلمات

لهـف قـلبي لنسـوة شـبه حـور   أخـرجت مـن حظائر القـادسات

و كـأني بـزينب و هـي تـدعو   أمـهـا بـالنحيب و الزفـرات

آه وا سـرأتـاه يـا أم قـومي   فـبانكـليا مـجامع الثـائحات

هـل تـرينا الحسـين مسـتفر الخـد   و أوداجـه لغـددت شـاخيات

هـل تـرينا الحسـين مـات عليلا   يـابس الحلـق و هـو عنـد الفرات

يـا أبـي يـا أبـا الضـعاف اليتامى   يـا مـغيث اللهيف فـي الطـائحات

لو رأيت الحسـين بـين الأعـادي   كـغـريب فـي الأكـلب العـاويات

طـارده مـا يـصول قـدامـه إذ   عـفه فـي الوراء أخـر عـات

مسـتغيث يـقول هـل مـن مـغيث   أو خـليل مـوئـس و مـوات

ليت فـي القـوم مـن يـدين بديني   ليت فـي القـوم مـن يـصلي صـلاتي

عـلكم أيـهـا العـصابة صـم   صـما نـالكم مـن الأمـهات

أنـتـم جـاحدوا نسـوة جـدي   أنـتـم عـابدوا مـنات و لات

هـل بكـم من مروة العـرـ شـيءـ   أو حـياء النسـاء لا و حـياتي

أهل بيت الرسـول فـي شـرف العـوت   ليـبـس الشـفـاه و اللهـوات

أنـتـم مسـظهرو دهـاء و زهـر   و نشـاط بـحبس مـاء الفرات

أهل بيت الرسـول فـي الطف صـرعى   ذو بـطون خـميصة غـامرات

أنتم فـي تـنعم و رفاء — مـن لذيذ اللحوم و المرقات

أنتم فـي الرحيب مجتمع الشمل — و آل الرسـول رهـن شتات

أيـن ترحيبكم أبيدت قراكم — بـسنزيل دعوتم دعرات

أيـن إيـفاء مـا كنتم إلينا — و وعـدتم لنـا بـه وعدات

ويـلكم مـا جـوابكم إذ دعاكم — يـوم فصل الخصام قاضي القضاة

فـعليكم لعـن الإله وبـيلا — مـا تـلظى السـعير بـاللهبات

ثـم لعـن الرسول فالخلق طـرا — كـل لعـن مستتبع اللعنات

وعـلى مـن بكى لنا أو تباكى — صـلوات مـن ربـنا دائمات

رب هـذا القصيد قد نظم الجيلي — فـانظمه فـي عـداد الرثات

وتـجاوز عـن سـيئات جناها — يـوم يـدعى يا غافر السيئات

المرتبة الثانية له عفي عنه:

أمـا الهموم فـقد حـلت بـوادينا — واستـولت إذ رأت حسن القرى فينا

وهـل تـرى أحـدا أخـرى بصحتها — مـمن حـوى الفضل والآداب والدينا

أنـى يكـون لأهـل الفضل مـن فرح — ومـا يـصفي عيشهم من لوعة حينا

ألا تـرى السـادة النجب الكرام بني — سـليلة المـصطفى الفـر المـيامنا

أصابهم من بني حرب الخبث أذى — له الـسماوات والأرضـون يـبكينا

لهفي على قول مولانا الحسين لصحبه — وأعـداؤه جـاءوا يـناورنا

ألا دعـوني ألا فـامضوا لشأنكم — إن البـغاة إذن إيـاي يـبغونا

لا يشـتفي غـلهم إلا بـسفك دمـي — إن كـان ذا قـسغيري لا يـبالونا

فـقال مـن هـؤلا الرهط طائفة — كـانوا نـفوسهم للخلد شارينا

فـداك آبـاؤنا يـا ابن الرسول لقد — كـنا عـلى مـا لـه صـرنا مصرينا

تـالله لو قـطعت أعضاؤنا قـطعا — لـما عـدلنا بـها دنـيا المفضلينا

هـديتمونا إلى الإسـلام ليس عـلى — وجـه البـسيط فـريق مثلنا دينا

لولاكـم مـا عـرفنا اللـه خـالقنا — و لا صـلاة و تـطهيرا و تـأذينا

أنـتم دلائـلنا أنـتم وسـائلنا — أنـتم إلى الفـوز بـالرضوان هادونا

أليس جـدك غـير المـرسلين ألا — أبـوك مـنه كمـا مـوسى و هـارونا

فكيف نسلمك العـلج الزنيم و قـد — نـرى أخـبث فرعون مضى طينا

نـعوذ بـالله مـن ذا بـل نـقاتلهم — بـالسم و السيف و العسال مسنونا

حـتى يـغيثوا إلى أمـر الإلـه و يـسر — قـعوا بـذ البغي عن خير المصطفى لنا

قـال الحسين أتيتم بـالوفاء إذن — جـزاكـم اللـه عـنا آل يـاسينا

فـأنزلوا يـا جـنود اللـه رحنكم — ثـم استعدوا لبلوى سوف يأتينا

شدوا حيازيمكم للمـوت و اصطبروا — و لا تـخافوا بـأن المـوت لاقينا

و هـل نخاف بـأن الخصـم يـقتلنا — و الحـزن و اللـه فـينا ليس يبعدونا

لا عـار للسـمح لو تـفقأ كربمته — إن كـان مستبصرا قـد أحكم الدينا

القوم من نيل روح الله قد ينبروا — و مـوقف العرض مـن ذا لا يبالونا

القـوم قـد آثـروا الدنـيا و زيـنـتها و يسـعدون مـراهـم و الشـياطنـا

بـغـرا رخـى بـن زيـاد خـاب أمـلهم يـمـرحون أولادنـا يـبـون أهـلنا

يسـقون أفـراسـهم مـاء الـفـرات و يـسـتـادون آل رسـول اللـه ظـامنا

يـا لـت فـاطمـة الطـهـر البتـول تـرى مـا نـاتـنا مـن بـنـي حـرب و نـيـكنا

هـل مـن حـبـير بـبلواتـنا يـمر علـى زقـبـان طـيـبـة يـسـكـنا و يـرتينا

يـقول يـا مـصطفى إنـي خـرجـت و قـد تـركـت ابـنـك منـحـورا و مـطعونا

يـقول آخـر يـا طـهـر البـتول لقـد تـركـت ابـنـك مـحـزونـا و مسـجونا

وا حـسـرتـى لطـريـح بـالـعـراء و لـم يـدفـن و مـاكـان مـغـفـلا و مـكـفنا

وا لهـف قـلـبي لفـتـيان أولـي شـرف قـد نـثـروا و هـم القـرآن تـالونا

وا لهـف قـلـبي لـنـسوان مخـدرة ابـرزن بـالطـف فـي قـوم مـلاعنا

يـا رب عـذب عـذاب الهـون رائسـهم يـزيد ثـم عـبـيدا فـالاعنـيا

و اغـفـر لمسـكـيـنـا الجـبـلي زلتـه آمـيـن آمـين يـا غـفار آمـينا

المـوثـبـة الثـالثـة لـه عفي عنه

ألا لـيس مـن فـقـد الخـليل هـزالي و لا مـن مـزاج الـسـوء سـوأة حـالي

ولا نـابـني ضـيـق المـعـاش فـعابني خـلـيطي و أقـرانـي بـقـلة مـالي

ولكـن خـيول الغـم والكـرب والنـوى ثـوالت عـلى بـالي وأي ثـوالي

لـما حـل مـن أصـنـاف بـلوى ومحنة بـآل رسـول اللـه أكـرم آل

فكـم مشـرب كـأس الحـتوف فـبعضهم يـدس ويـبـعض مـوذنـا بـقـتال

ألم تسـمع الـملعـونة الرجس إذ مضت تـوس للأخـرى بـوعد وصـال

إلى أن قـتلن المـجـنبى احـسـن الذي لـه مـع حسـن الوجـه حسن خصال

فـيا لـت كـبد قـطعـت حـين شـربـه نـسـقـع سـموم خـال كـأس زلال

ويـا لـت شـمس الـيـوم كـالليل سـردت بـما اخـضر وجـه مشـرق كـلتالي

بـنـفـي إذ جـاءتـه زيـنـب أخـتـه وقـد شـاهـدت حـالا وأيـة حـال

فقال تعـالي يـا ابـنـة الخـير فـاعجبي فكـم فـلذة مـني سقـطن حـمالي

تـعالي تـعالي يـا ابـنة الأم فـانظـري أخـاك بـكـبـد قـاء أم بـسطحال

بـنـفـي إذ وصـي أخـاه سـماتـنا بـسـتفـي الإلـه الخـالـق المـتعال

ويـالـصبر والتـسـلـيم للـه والرضـي ويـالـشكر والتـوحـيد أيـة حـال

وقـال تـذكر نـقل مـعراج جـدنا و مـالك مـن قـصر الجـنان و مـالي

فـهـذا اخـضراري قـد تـحقـق حسـبما هـنـاك و فـي عـلم الإلـه جـرى لي

سيدون نـحراكـان فـي غـير مـرة يسـفـبه الجـد الجـليل حـمالي

فـتحـمر وجـهـا حـيث لا يـنـير اللـواذ بـأنـصار و لا بـسـوالي

فـوا حـسـرتى وا سـوأنـا وا مصـينا لمـذبوح أرض الطـف يـوم نـزال

بـزيد بـما استـحلـت هـتك حـريمه و حـرمت شـرب المـاء رد سـوالي

تـدور بـدور الـفخر و العـز و العلى زقـبـا بـلاد الشـام فـوق جـمال

أطـاب بـيض كـالشـمس وجـوهها بـسـفـير شـمـوس فـي مصـير فـلال

فـرارى رسـول اللـه شـد وثـاقـهم كـمـر أسـارى أوثـبـت بـجبال

تـنـزل مـآتـم الحسـين مسـانـدا | و قـد كـان لـلأيـتـام خـيـر ثـمـال
فكـيـف إذا استعدى عـلـيـك مـحمـد | لـدى حـاكـم ذي نـقـمـة و نـكـال
وبـطـش شـديـد و انـتـقـام و سـطوة | و سـلطنة فـي عـزة و جـلال
عـليـك إلى يـوم الجـزاء و بـعده | مـن اللـه لعـن دائـم مـتـال
إلهـي أنـا الجيلي عـيـدك مـذعنا | بـمـا كـان مـني مـن قـبـيـح فـعـال
ولكـنـني رائـي الحسـين و نـاشـر | مـدائـح سـاداتـي بـلحن مـقـال
مـحبة أولاد الـرسـول تـعـرقت | بـيالي فـلا بـالموت بـعد أبـالي
ولم أتـخـذ دون الوصـي وليـجة | و هـذا عـطـاء مـنـك قـبـل سـؤالي
وأنت عـليـم مـن ضـمـيـري بـأنتي | بـبـغـيـض لأعـداء الوصـي وقـال
فـلا تـبـعدني عـنـه حـيا و مـيتا | و عـمم بـهـذا الفضـل كـل مـوال

المرثية الرابعة أيضا له عفي عنه

اطلبوا للضحك دوني وعلى الحزن دعوني | حـرم الـضحك أخـلائـي عـن أهـل الشجون
حـزني ليس لخـل أو أنـيـس أو قـريـن | أو لولد كـنـت أرجـو مـنـهم أن يـخـلفـوني
إنـما حـزني وبـثـي ورنـيـني وأنـيـني | لشهيد الطف سـبط المصطفى الهادي الأمـين
لهف قلبي إذ يـنـادي قـومه هل من معين | مـا لقـومي لا يـجـيـبـون إذ قـد سـمـعوني
ألهـا فـي قـلبهم مـني مـن داء دفـين | أم لهم بـغض علـى الإسـلام أم لم يـعـرفوني
هـا أنـا ابن المصطفى الآتـي بـقـرآن مـبين | هـا أنـا ابن المرتضى الهادي إلى ديـن مـبـين
أمـسـي الزهـراء مـخدومة جـبـريـل الأمـين | مـذهبي التوحيد و التقـديـس و الإسـلام ديـني
هل على الأرض نظيري اليـوم قومي أنصفوني | قـبـما اسـتحللتم هـتك حـريمي أخـبـرونـي
ويـلكم يوم يـنـادي المرء يـا رب ارجعوني | و أنـا أشـكـو إلى جـدي بـالصوت الحـزين
جـد يـا جـد تـرى قومي كيف اسـتضعفوني | ثـم لم يـرضـوا بـالاستضعاف حتى قـتلوني
آه مـن جور عـبـيد الفـاسق العلج الهجين | آه مـن شمـر و شبـث يـظهران الحقد دوني
آه مـن إدمـاء نـحري آه مـن عـثـر جبيني | آه من أجل صبايا هـن من لحمي و طـيـني
آه مـن ذي ثـفنات هـو نـفـي و وتـيـني | آه إذ أبـرزت النسـوان مـن حـصن حـصين
حاسرات ظلامات خـافضات للأنـين | آه مـن جـور يـزيد بـن اللعـين بن اللعـين
رب عـذبهم بـتعذيب ألـيـم و مـهـين | و احشـر الجيلي فـي زمـرة أصحاب اليـمـين

أقول: روي في بعض كتب المناقب القديمة بإسناده عن البيهقي عن علي بن محمد الأديب يذكر بإسناد له
أن رأس الحسين بن علي ﷺ لما صلب بالشام أخفي خالد بن عفران و هو من أفضل التابعين شخصه من أصحابه
فطلبوه شهرا حتى وجدوه فسألوه عن عزته قال أما ترون ما نزل بنا ثم إنشاء يقول:

جاءوا برأسك يا ابن بنت محمد | مـتـرملا بـدمائه تـرمـيلا
وكأنما بك يا ابن بـنت محمد | قتلوا جهارا عـامديـن رسـولا
قـتلوك عطشانا ولم يـترقبوا | في قـتـلك التـنزيل والتـأويلا
ويكبرون بـأن قـتلت وإنـما | قـتـلـوا بك التكبير والتهليلا

أخبرني سيد الحفاظ أبو منصور شهردار بن محبي السنة أبي الفتح الديلمي عن محي السنة أبي الفتح إجازة قال أنشدني أبو
الطيب البابلي أنشدني أبو النجم بدر بن إبراهيم بالدينور للشافعي محمد بن إدريس:

698

تأوب همي و الفؤاد كئيب — و أرق نومي فالرقاد غريب

وما نفى جسمي و شيب لمتي — تصاريف أيام لهن خطوب

فمن مبلغ عني الحسين رسالة — و إن كرهتها أنفس و قلوب

قتلا بلا جرم كأن قميصه — صبغ بما الأرجوان خضيب

وللسيف إعوال و للرمح رنة — و للخيل من بعد الصهيل نحيب

تزلزلت الدنيا لآل محمد — و كادت له صم الجبال تذوب

يصلي على المهدي من آل هاشم — و يغزي بنوه إن ذا لعجيب

لئن كان ذنبي حب آل محمد — فذلك ذنب لست منه أتوب

أخبرني أبو منصور الديلمي عن أحمد بن علي بن عامر الفقيه أنشدني أحمد بن منصور بن علي القطيعي المعروف بالقطان ببغداد لنفسه:

يا أيها المنزل المحيل — غائلك مستخفر هطول

أودى عليك الزمان لما — شجاك من أهله الرحيل

لا تغترر بالزمان و اعلم — أن يد الدهر تستطيل

فإن أجالنا قصار — فيه و آمالنا تطول

تغني الليالي و ليس يغني — شوقي و لا حسرتي تزول

لا صاحب منصف فأسلو — به و لا حافظ وصول

و كيف أبقى بلا صديق — باطنه باطن جميل

يكون في البعد و التداني — يقول مثل الذي أقول

هيهات قل الوفاء فيهم — فلا حميم و لا وصول

يا قوم ما بالنا جنينا — فلا كتاب و لا رسول

لو وجدوا بعض ما وجدنا — لكاتبونا و لم يحولوا

لكن خانوا و لم يجودوا — لنا بوصل و لم ينيلوا

قلبي قريح به كلوم — أفنته طرفك البخيل

أنحل جسمي هواك حتى — كأنه حصرك التحيل

يا قاتلي بالصدود رفقا — بمهجة شفها غليل

غصن من البان حيث مالت — ربع الخزامي به تميل

يسطو علينا بغنج لحظ — كأنه مرهف صقيل

كما سطت بالحسين قوم — أراذل ما لهم أصول

يا أهل كوفان لم غدرتم — بنا و كم أنتم نكول

أنتم كنتم إلي كنا — و في طرياتها ذحول

اللهم صلي على محمد و آل محمد

فـراقـبـوا اللـه فـي خـباي
و أم كـلـثـوم قـد تـنـادي
تـقـول لمـا رأتـه خـلـوا
جـاشت بشـط الفرات تـدعو
أيـن الذي حـين أرضـعـوه
أيـن الذي حـين غـمـدوه
أيـن الذي جـده النـبي
أنـا ابـن مـنصور لي لسـان
ما الرفض ديني و لا اعتقادي

قال و لدعبل الخزاعي رحمه الله:

أأسـبلت دمـع العين بـالعبرات
و تـبكي لأثـار لآل مـحمد
ألا فـابكهم حـقا و بـل عـليهم
و لا تـنس فـي يـوم الطـفوف مـصابهم
سقى الله أجدانا على أرض كربلاء
وصلى على روح الحسين حبيبه
قـتيلا بـلا جـرم فـجيعا بـفقده
أنـا الظامئ العطشان في أرض غربة
و قـد رفعوا رأس الحسين على اقنا
فـقل لابـن سعد عذب الله روحه
سأقنت طول الدهر ما هبت الصبا
على معشر ضلوا جميعا و ضيعا

قال ولدعبل أيضا رحمه الله:

يـا أمـة قـتلت حسـينا عـنوة
قـتلوه يـوم الطـف طـعنا بـالقنا
ولطـال مـا تـادهم بكـلامه
جـدي النـبي أبـي عـلي فـاعلموا
يـا قـوم إن المـاء يشـربه الورى

فـيه لنـا فـتية غـفول
ليس الذي حـل بـي قـليل
قـد خـفت صدره الخيول
مـا فـعل السـيد القتيل
نـاغاه فـي المـهد جبرئيل
قـبله أحمـد الرسـول
و أمــه فـاطم البـتول
على ذوي النـصب يستطيل
و لست عن مذهبي أحول

و بث تـقـاسي شـدة الزفـرات
فـقد ضـاق مـنك الصدر بـالحسرات
عـيونا لريب الدهـر مـنسكبات
و داهـية مـن أعـظم التكبات
مـرابيع أمـطار مـن المـزنات
قـتيلا لدى النـهرين بـالفلوات
فـريدا يـنادي أين أين حمـاتي
قـتيلا و مـطلوبا بـغير تـرات
و سـائرا نسـاء ولهـا خـفرات
مستقي عـذاب النار بـاللعنات
و أقـنت بـالآصال و الغـدوات
مـقال رسـول اللـه بـالشبهات

لم تـرع حـق اللـه فـيه فـتهتدي
ويكـل أبـيض صـارم ومـهند
جدي النبي خصيمكم في المشهد
و الفخـر فـاطمة الزكية مـحتدي
و لقد ظلمـت و قـل مـنه تجلدي

قــد شـقني عطـشي و أقـلقني الذي   ألقاه   مـن ثقل الحـديد المـزيد

قـالوا له هــذا عــليك مـحرم   هـذا حـلال مـن يـبايع للغبي

فــأتاه مــم مـن يـد مشئومة   مـن قـوس ملعون خبيث المـولد

يـا عين جـودي بـالدموع و جـودي   و ابكي الحسين السيد بـن السـيد

قال ولبعضهم :

إن كـنت مـحزونا فـما لك تـرقد   هـلا بكيت لمـن بكـاه محمد

هلا بكيت على الحـسـين و نسله   إن البكـاء لمثلهم قـد يـحمد

لتـضعضع الإسـلام يـوم مصابه   قـالجود يـبكي فـقده و الـسـؤدد

أنسيت إذ سـارت إليـه كتائب   فـيها ابن سعد و الطغاة الجحد

فسقوه من جرع الحتوف بمشهد   كـثر العـداة بـه و قـل المسعد

ثـم استباحوا الصائنات حواسرا   و الشمل من بعد الحسين مبدد

كيف القرار و فـي السبايا زينب   تـدعو العسا يـا جدنا يـا أحمد

هـذا حسين بـالحديد مـقطع   مـتخضب بـدمائه مستشهد

عار بـلا كفن صـريع فـي الثرى   تحت الحوافر و السنابك مقصد

و الطيبون بـنزك قـتلى حـوله   فـوق الـتراب ذبـائح لا تـلحد

يـا جد قد منعوا الفرات و قتلوا   عطشنا فليس لهم هنالك مـورد

يا جد من تكلي و طول مصيبتي   و لسا أعـايـنه أقـوم و أقـعد

وله:

حسب الذي قتل الحسين من الخسارة و الندامةأن الشفيع لدى الإله خصيمه يوم القيامة.

قال و لدعبل أيضا رحمه الله:

مـنازل بـين أكـتاف الغـري   إلى وادي الـسـيماء إلى الطوي

لقد شغل الدموع عن القواني   مصاب الأكـرمين بـني علي

أنى أسغي على هفرات دهـر   تـضائل فـيه أولاد الزكي

ألم تـقف البكـاء عـلى حسين   و ذكـرك مصرع الحـبر التقي

ألم يـحـزنك أن بــني زيـاد   أصابرا بـالتراب بـني النبي

وأن بـني الحصان يمر فيهم   عـلانية سـيوف بـني البغي

قال و للرضي الموسوي نقيب النقباء البغدادي:

سـقى اللـه المـدينة مـن محل   لباب الودق بـالنطف العـذاب

وجاد على البـقيع و سـاكنيه   رخـي البـال ملثان الوطـاب

وأعـلام الغري و مـا أساخت   معـالمها مـن الحسب اللباب

وقـبرا بـالطفوف يـضم شـلوا   قـضى ظـمأ إلى بـرد الـشـراب

ويـغدادا و سـامرا و طـوسا   هـطول الـودق مـنخرق الـعـباب

بكم في الشعر فـخري لا يشـعري   و عنكم طـال بـاعي فـي الخطاب

ومـن أولى بكـم مـني وليـا   و فـي أيـديكم طـرف انتسابي

قال ولأبي الحسن علي بن أحمد الجرجاني من قصيدة طويلة يمدح أهل البيت ﷺ:

وجدي بكوفان مـا وجـدي بكـوفان   تهمي علـيه ضـلوعي قـبل أجـفان

أرض إذا نـفحت ريـح العراق بـها   انت بـنـاشتها أقـصى خـراسـان

ومـن قـتيل بـأعلى كربلاء علي   جـهد الصدى نـتراه غـير صـديان

وذي صـفائح يستسقى البقيع بـه   ري الجوانح من روح و رضوان

هـذا قسيم رسول الله من آدم   لـدا مـعا مـثل مـا قـد الشـراكان

وذاك سـيطا رسول الله جدهما   وجه الهدى و هما في الوجه عيناه

وا خجلنا مـن أبـيهم يـوم يشـهدهم   مـضرجين نشاوى مـن دم قان

يـقول يـا أمـة حـف الضلال بـها   فـاستبدلت لـلعمى كـفرا بـايمان

مـا ذا جـنيت عـليكم إذ أتـيتكم   بـخير مـا جـاء، من آي و فـرقان

ألم أجـركم و أنتم فـي ضـلالتكم   عـلى شـفا حفرة من حـر نيران

ألم أوثق قلوبا منكم مـزق فـرقا   مـتـارة بـين أحـقاد و أضـغان

أمـا تـركت كـتاب اللـه بـينكم   و آيـة الـغر فـي جمع و قـرآن

ألم أكـن فـيكم غـرثا لـمطهد   ألم أكـن فـيكم مـاء لظمآن

قـتلتم ولـدي صـبرا عـلى ظـمإ   هذا و ترجون عند الحوض إحسـاني

سـيـتيم تكـلتكم أمـهـاتكم   بني البتول و هـم لحـمي و جثماني

مـزقتم و نكـثتم عـهد والدهـم   و قـد قـطعتم بـذاك النكث أقرائي

يا رب خذ لي مـنهم إذ هم ظـلموا   كرام رهـطي و رامـوا هـدم بـنياني

مـا ذا تجيبون و الزهراء، خصمكم   و الحاكم اللـه للـمظلوم و الجـاني

أهل الكسـاء، صـلاة الـله مـا نـزلت   عليكم الدهر من متى و وحـدان

أنـتم نجوم بـني حـواء مـا طـلعت   شمس النهار و مـا لاح السماكان

ما زلت منكم عـلى شـوق يـهيجني   و الدهـر يـأمرني فـيه و يـنهاني

حتى أتـيتك و التـوحيد راحـلتي   و العدل زادي و تقوى الله إمكاني

هـذي حـقائل لفـط كلما بـرقت   ردت بـلالاتها أبـصار عـميان

هـي الحـلي لبـني طـه و عـترتهم   هـي الردي لبـني حـرب و مـروان

هـي الجـواهر جـاء الجوهري بـها   مـعبة لكـم مـن أرض جرجان

قال و له أيضا في يوم عاشوراء من قصيدته الطويلة:

يا أهل عاشوراء يا لهفي على الدين

إلى آخر ما مضى في رواية ابن شهرآشوب   و زاد فيه:

زادوا عليه بحبس الماء غلته

نالوا أزمة دنياهم ببغيهم

حتى يصيح بقنسرين راهبها

أتهزءون برأس بات منتصبا

آمنت ويحكم بالله مهتديا

فسجدوا صريعا فوق جبهته

و أوقروا صهوات[٥] الخيل من أحن

مصفدين على أقتاب أرحلهم

أطفال فاطمة الزهراء قد نظموا

يا أمة ولي الشيطان رأيتها

ما المرتضى و بنوه من معاوية

آل الرسول عياديد السيوف فمن

يا عين لا تدعي شيئا لغادية

قومي على جدث بالطف فانتقضي

يا آل أحمد إن الجوهري لكم

قال و لغيره عاشورية طويلة انتخبت منها هذه الأبيات:

إذا جاء عاشوراء تضاعف حسرتي

هو اليوم فيه اغبرت الأرض كلها

مصائب سامت كل من كان مسلما

إذا ذكرت نفسي مصية كربلا

أضاقت فؤادي و استباحت تجارتي

أريقت دماء الفاطميين بالملا

إلا بأبي تلك الدماء التي جرت

توابيت من نار عليهم قد أطبقت

فشتان من في النار قد كان هكذا

بنفسي خدود في التراب تعفرت

بنفسي رءوس معلبات   على القنا

خذوا حدادكم يا آل ياسين:

تسما لرأي فريق فيه مغبون

فليتهم سمحوا منها بماعون

يا فرقة الغي يا حزب الشياطين

على القناة بدين الله يوصيني

و بالنبي و حب المرتضى ديني

و قسموه بأطراف السكاكين

على أساراهم فعل الفراعين

معمولة بين مضروب و مطعون

من الشدي بأنياب التعابين

و مكن الغي منها كل تمكين

و لا الفواطم من هند و ميسون

هام على وجهه خوفا و مسجون

تهمي و لا تدعي دمسا لمحزون

بكل لؤلؤ دمع فيك مكنون

سيف يقطع عنكم كل موصون

لآل رسول الله و انهل عبرتي

وجوما عليهم و السماء اقشعرت

و لكن عيون الفاجرين أقرت

و أشلاء سادات بها قد تعفرت

و عظم كربي ثم عيشي أمرت

فلو عقلت شمس النهار لخرت

بأيدي كلاب في الجحيم استقرت

لهم زفرة في جوفها بعد زفرة

و من هو في الفردوس فوق الأسرة

بنفسي جسوم بالعراء تعفرت

إلى الشام تهدى بارقات الأسنة

بــنفسـي شــفاه ذابــلات مــن الظــما
بــنفسـي عيــون غــائرات ســواهر
بــنفسي مــن آل النــبي خــرائـد
تــفيـض دمــوعا بــالدماء مشــوبة
عــلى خــير قتــلى مــن كهــول و فتية
و سبــي اليتــامى و الأرامــل فــابكها
و أعــلام ديــن المصــطفى و ولاتـه
يــنادون يــا جــداه أيــة مــحنة
طــغا ابــن سميــة بعــد ستيـن أظهــرت
شهــدت بــأن لم تــرض نــفس بهــذه
كــأنـي بــبنت المصــطفى قــد تعلقت
و فــي حجــرها ثــوب الحسيــن مضرجـا
تقـول أيا عـدل اقـض بيني و بيـن مـن
أجــالوا عــليه بــالصوارم و القنــا
عــلى غـير جـرم غـير إنكــار بيــعة
لــمبغضـي عــلى قــوم عــليه تــألبوا
و يســقون مــن مــاء صــديد إذا دنـا
مــودة ذي القــربى رعــوها كمــا تـرى
نكــم عجــرة قــد اتبعــوها بعجــرة
هــم أول العابــدين ظلمـا عــلى الورى
مضــوا و انقضـت أيــامهم و عهــودهم
لآل رســول اللــه ودي خــالصا
و هــا أنــا مــذ أدركـت حـد بلاغـتي
و قــول النـبي المـرء مـع مــن أحبــه
عــلى حــبهم يــا ذا الجــلال تــرقني

و لم تــحظ مــن مــاء الفــرات بــقطرة
إلى المــاء، منهـا نـظرة بعــد نــظرة
حــواسـر لم تــنفذ   عــليهم بستــره
كفطـر الغــوادي   مــن مدافـع سـرة
مصــاليت أنــجاد إذا الخيــل كـرت
مــدارس للقــرآن فـي كـل ســحرة
و أصــحاب قــربان و حــج و عــمرة
تــرى عليــنا مــن أميــة ســرت
و كــانت أجنـت فـي الحشـا و أسـرت
و فــيها مــن الإسـلام مثقــال ذرة
يــداهـا بسـاق العـرش و الدمـع أذرت
و عنــها جمــيع العــالمين بحــيرة
تعــدى عــلى ابـني بعـد قهـر و قسـرة
و كــم جــال فيهم مـن سنـان و شفـرة
لمنســلخ مــن ديـن أحمـد عنـوة
بســوء عــذاب النـار مـن غيـر فـترة
شـوي الوجـه و الأمعـاء، منـه تهـددت
و قــول رســول اللـه أوصـى بعتـرتي
و كــم لغــدرة قـد ألغفـوها بغـدرة
و مــن ســار   فيهم بـالأذى و المضـرة
ســوى لعنــة بــاءوا بهـا مستمـرة
كمـا لمراليهـم ولائـي و نصـرتي
أصــلي عليهـم فـي عشـيي و بكـرتي
يــفري رجـائي فـي إقـالة عـثرتي
و حــرم عـلى النيـران شيـبي و كبـرتي

قال ولعلي بن الحسين الدوادي   من قصيدة طويلة انتخبت منها:

اللهم صلي على محمد و آل محمد

بنو المصطفى المختار أحمد طهروا   و أثنى عليهم محكم السورات

بنو حيدر المخصوص بالدرجات   من الله و الخواض في الغمرات

فروع النبي المصطفى و وصه   و فاطم طابت تلك من شجرات

و سائلة لم تسكب الدمع دائبا   و تقذف نارا منك في الزفرات

نقلت على وجه الحسين و قد ذرت   عليه السوافي ثائر الهبرات

فقد غرقت منه المحاسن في دم   أهدي للشفار فوق قناة

و حلن عن ماء الفرات و قد صفت   موارده للشاء و الحمرات

على أم كلثوم تساق سبية   و زينب و السجاد ذي الشفنات

أصيبوا بأطراف الرماح فأهلكوا   و هم للورى أمن من الهلكات

بهم عن شفير النار قد نجى الورى   فجازوهم بالسيف ذي الشفرات

فيا أقبرا حطت على أنجم هوت   و فرقن في الأطراف مغتربات

و ليس قبورا هن بل هي روضة   منورة مخضرة الجنبات

و ما غفل الرحمن عن عصبة طغت   و ما هتكت ظلما من الحرمات

أمقروعة في كل يوم صفائكم   بأيدي رزايا فتن كل صفات

فحتام أتقى جدكم و هو مطرق   غضيض و ألقى الدهر غير مؤات

فيا رب غير ما تراه معجلا   تعاليت يا ربي عن الغفلات

قال و للصاحب كافي الكفاة إسماعيل بن عباد من قصيدة طويلة انتخبت منها هذه الأبيات:

بلفت نفسي مناها بالموالي آل طاها   برسول الله من حاز المعالي و حواها

و بنت المصطفى من أشيبت فضلا أباها   و بعب الحسن البالغ في العليا مداها

و الحسين المرتضى يوم المساعي إذ حواها   ليس فيهم غير نجم قد تعالى و تناهى

عترة أصبحت الدنيا جميعا في حماها   ما يحدث عصب البغي بأنواع عماها

أردت الأكبر بالسم و ما كان كفاها   و انبرت تبغي حسينا و عرته و عراها

منعت شربه و الطير قد أروت صداها   فأفاتت نفسه يا ليت روحي قد فداها

بنته تدعو أباها أخته تبكي أخاها   لو رأى أحمد ما كان دهاه و دهاها

و رأى زينب إذ شمر أتاها و سباها   لشكا الحال إلى الله و قد كان شكاها

و إلى الله سيأتي و هو أولى من جزاها

وللصاحب أيضا منتخبة من قصيدته:

ما لعلي العلا أشباه   لا و الذي لا إله إلا هو

سبناه سبني النبي تعرفه   و ابناه عند التفاخر ابناه

لو طلب النجم ذات أخمصه   أعلاء و الفرقدان نعلاه

يا بأبي السيد الحسين و قد   جاهد في الدين يوم بلواه

يا بأبي أهله و قد قتلوا   من حوله و العيون ترعاه

يـا قبـح اللـه أمـة خـذلت   سـيدها لا تـريد مـرضاة

يـا لعـن اللـه جيفة نجسا   يـفرع مـن بغضه ثناياه

وللصاحب أيها منتخبة من قصيدته:

سـرت مـن الأرجـاس رهـط أمـة   لمـا سمع عندي من قبح لغذائهم

ولعنهم خـير الوصيـين جهـرة   لكـفرهم المـعدود فـي شـرذاتهم

وقـتلهم السـادات مـن آل هـاشم   و سـبيهم عـن جـرأة لنسـائهم

وذبـحهم خـير الرجـال أرومـة   حسـين العـلا بالكرب فـي كربلائهم

وتشتيتهم شـمل النبـي محـمد   نمـا ورثـوا مـن بغضه فـي فئاتهم

ومـا لحضبت إلا لأحسامها الثني   أديـلت و هـم أنصـارها لشقائهم

أبا رب جنبني المكاره و اعف عن   دنـوبي لمـا أخـلصته مـن ولائهم

أبـا رب أعـدائـي كـثير فـزدهم   بغـيظهم لا يـسظفروا بـاسـتغائهم

أبـا رب مـن كـان النبـي و أهـله   و سـائلك لم يـبخش مـن غـلواتهم

حسـين نـوصل لي إلى الله إنـني   بليت بـهم فـادفع عـظيم بـلاتهم

نكم قـد دعـوني راقـبا لحبكم   فـلم يبتنـي عنكم طويل عـواتهم

وللصاحب أيها من قصيده منتخبة:

يـا أصـول عـترة أحمد لولاك لم   يك أحمد الصبحوت ذا أعقاب

ردت عليك الشمس و هـي فضيلة   بـهرت فـلم تستر بكف نقاب

لم أهك إلا مـا روتـه تـواصب   عـادتك فـهي سماحة الأسلاب

عـوملت يـا تـلو النبي و صنوه   بـأرابـيد جـاءت بكل عـجاب

قـد لضيوك أبـا تـراب بعد مـا   بـساعوا شـربيتهم بكف تـراب

أتنلك فـي لعـني أمية بعد مـا   كـفرت على الأحرار و الأطياب

قـتلوا الحسـين فيا لعولي بعـده   و لطول حزني أو أصير لمـا بي

فسـبيروا بنات محـمد نكأتها   طلبوا دخـول الفـتح و الأحزاب

رفقا لفـي يـوم القيامة غنية   و النـار بـاطشة بصوت عقاب

وللصاحب أيها من قصيدته الطويل:

أجـروا دمـاء أخـي النبي محمد   فـتنجر غـزر دمـوعنا و لنسهل

ولتـسمدر اللـعنات لغـير مـزالة   لعداه من مـاض و من مـستقبل

ونسـجروا لبـنيه تـم بـناته   بعظائم فـاسمع حـديث المـقتل

منعوا الحسين المـاء و هو مجاهد   فـي كربـلا فتح كنزح المعول

منعوه أعـذب منهل و كـذا غدا   يـردون فـي النيران أوخم منهل

أبيز رأي ابن النبي و فـي الورى   حـبي أمـام ركـابه لم يـقتل

وبنو السفاح تحكموا فـي أهل حي   على الفـلاح يفرضة و تـسعجل

نكت الدعي بن البغي ضواحكا   هـي للنبي الخير خـير منقبل

تـمضي بـنو هند سيوف الهند   لـي أرداج أولاد النبـي و تـستلي

ناحت ملائكة السماء لقتلهم
فأرى البكاء على الزمان محللا
كم قلت للأحزان دومي عكذا

و بكوا فقد سغرا كنوس الذبل
و الضحك بعد الطف غير محلل
و نزلي في القلب لا ترحل

ولزينب بنت فاطمة البتول من قصيدة انتخبت منها هذه:

تمسك بالكتاب و من تلا
بهم نزل الكتاب و هم تلوه
إمامي وحد الرحمن طفلا
علي كان مصدق البرايا
شفيعي في القيامة عند ربي
و فاطمة البتول و سيدا من
علي الطف السلام و ساكنيه
نفوسا قدمت في الأرض قدما
فضاجع فئة عبدوا فناموا
علتهم في مضاجعهم كعاب
و صيرت القبور لهم قصورا
لئن وارتهم أطباق أرض
كأقمار إذا جاسوا رواض
لقد كانوا البحار لمن أتاهم
فقد نقلوا إلى جنات عدن
بنات محمد أضحت سبايا
مغيرة الذيول مكشفات
ثن أبرزن كرها من حجاب
أيخل في الفرات على حسين
قلي قلب عليه ذو التهاب

فنأهل البيت هم أهل الكتاب
و هم كانوا الهداة إلى الصواب
و آمن قبل تشديد الخطاب
علي كان فاروق العذاب
نبيي و الوصي أبو تراب
يخلد في الجنان مع الشباب
و روح الله في تلك القباب
و قد خلصت من النطف العذاب
هجردا في القفائد و الشعاب
بأوراق منعمة رطاب
مناخا ذات أقنية رحاب
كما أغمدت سيفا في قراب
و أساد إذا ركبوا غضاب
من العاقين و الهلكى السغاب
و قد عيضوا النعيم من العقاب
يسقن مع الأسارى و النهاب
كسبي الروم دامية الكعاب
فهن من التعفف في حجاب
و لقد أضحى مباحا للكلاب
لي جفن عليه ذو انسكاب

ولدعبل الخزاعي من قصيدته الطوبلة:

جاءوا من الشام المشومة أهلها
لعنوا و قد لعنوا بقتل إمامهم
و سبوا فوا حزني بنات محمد
تبا لكم يا ويلكم أرضيتم
يعتم بدنيا غيركم جهلا بكم

للشوم يقدم جندهم إبليس
تركوه و هم مبضع مخموس
عبري حواسر ما لهن لبوس
بسائار ذل هنالك المحبوس
عز الحياة و إنه لنفيس

اللهم صلي على محمد و آل محمد

707

أحـسر بـها مـن بـيعة أمـوية

بـؤنا لمـن بـايعتم و كـأنـي

يـا آل أحـمد مـا لقـيتم بـعده

كم عبرة فاضت لكـم و تـفطمت

صـبرا مـوالينا فـسوف نـديلكم

مـا زلت مـشتعا لكـم و لأمركم

ومن قصيدة لجعفر بن عفان الطائي رحمه الله:

لبيك على الإسلام من كان باكيا

غـداة حسـين للـرماح دريـة

و غـودر فـي الصحراء لحمـا مبددا

لمـا نصرتـه أمة السوء إذ دعا

ألا بل سـحبوا أنوارهـم بـأكفهم

و نـاداهـم جهدا بـحق محمد

فما حفظوا قرب الرسول و لا رعوا

أذاقتـه حـر القتل أمة جده

فـلا قدس الرحمـن أمة جده

كما فجعت بنت الرسول بنسلها

ومن قصيدة طويلة انتخيت منها أبياتا:

بكى الحسين لركن الدين حين وهى

هل لامرئ عاقل في حزن دمعه

أم هـل لمكتسب حران فـقده

مثل النجوم الدراري في مرائبها

بـا أمة السوء، هاتوا ما حجاجكم

و أحمد خصمكم و الله منصفه

ألم أبيـن لكـم مـا فيـه رشدكم

فـما صنعتم أهـل الله سعيكم

أمـا بنـي فـمقتول و مكبول

و قـد أخفتم بناتي بين أظهركم

بـتفلن مـن عند جبار يعاهده

لعنت و حظ البائعين خسيس

بـأمامكم وسط الجحيم حسيس

من عصبة هم في القياس مجوس

يوم الطفوف على الحسين نفوس

يـوما على آل اللعين عيوس

و عليه نفسي ما حيت أسوس

فـقد ضيعت أحكامه و استحلت

و قـد نهلت منه السيوف و علت

عـليه عنـاق الطير بـاتت و ظلت

لقد طاشت الأحلام منها و ضلت

فـلا سلمت تلك الأكف و شلت

قـإن ابنه مـن نفسه حيث حلت

و زلت بـهم أقدامـهم و استزلت

هفت نعلها في كربلا و زلت

و إن هـي صامتا للإله و صلت

و كانوا حماة الحرب حين استغلت

و للأمـور العطيمات الجليلات

بـعد الحسين و مسبى الفاطميات

لذاذة العـيش نكـرار الفـجيعات

إن غاب نجم بدا نجم لسبقات

إذا بـرزتم لجبـار السمـارات

بالحق و العدل منه لا المحابات

مـن الحلال و من ترك الخبيئات

فيما عهدت إليكم في وصايات

و هـارب فـي رؤوس المشمخرات

مـا ذا أرؤتم شفيتم من بـنياتي

إلى حبـابر أمثـال السبـيات

708

أكـان هـذا جـزائـي لا أبـا لكـم   فـي أقـربائي و فـي أهـل الحـرمـات
ردوا الجـحـيم فـحـلوها بـسعيكم   ثـم أخـلـدوا فـي عـقـوبـات أليـمـات

قال ومن مرثية زينب بنت فاطمة   أخت الحسين ﷺ حين أدخلوا دمشق:

أمـا شجـاك يا سكـن قتـل الحسـين و الحـن   قمآن مـن طـول الحـزن و كـل وفـد نـاهل
يـقـول يـا قـوم أبـي عـلي النـر الوصـي   و نـاطم أمـي النبي نهـا النفـر و الثـائل
سـوا على ابـن المصطفى بشربة يحيـا بـها   أطفـنـا مـن الظمـا، حيـث الفـرات سـائل
قـائرا له لا مـد، لا إلا السـيوف و القـنـا   فـنـازل بـحكم الأدعـي فقـال بـل أنـاضـل
حتى أنـاء، متـنـفص رمـاه، وقـد أبـرص   مـن سـفر لا يـخلص رجـس دعـي واغـل
فـهللوا بـختله و اعـمـصوصبوا لقـتله   و مـوته فـي نفـله قـد أقحـم المنـاضـل
وعـفـروا جـبينه و خـضبوا عثـنونه   بـالـدم يـا مـحينة مـا أنـت عـنه غـافـل
وهـتكـوا حـريمـه و ذهـبوا فـطيمـه   و آثـروا كـظلومـه و سـليت الحـلائل
يسـقـن بـالتـاليف بـفجـعة الهـواتـف   و أدمـع ذوارف عـقـولها زوائـل
يقـلن يـا مـحمد يا جـدنـا يـا أحمد   قـد أسـرتـا الأعـبد و كـنـا تـواكل
تهـدى سـبايا كربـلاء، إلى الشـئام و البـلاء   قـد انـثعلـن بـالدمـاء ليـس لهـن نـاهل
إلى يـزيـد الطـاغـية مـعـدن كـل داهـبة   مـن نـحو بـاب الجـابهة بجـاهد و خـالل
حتى دنا بـدر الدجى رأس الإمـام المـرتجى   بسين يـهدي شـر الورى ذاك اللعـين القـاتل
يـطـل فـي بـنـاته قـضـيب خـيـزرانـه   يـنـكت فـي أنـثـانه قـطعت الأنـامـل
أنـامـل بجـاهد و حـاقد مـراصد   مكـابه صـمائد فـي صـدره غـوائل
طـوائـل سـدرة لغـوائـل كـفرية   شـروها، جـاهلية ذلت لهـا الأفـاضـل
فـا عيوني اسكـبي على بـني بـنت النبي   يـفيض دمع نـاضب كذاك يبكي العـاقل

روى أن أبا يوسف عبد السلام بن محمد القزويني ثم اليغدادي قال لأبي العلاء المعري هل لك شعر في أهل بيت
رسول الله فإن بعض شعراء، قزوين يقول فيهم ما لا يقول شعراء، تتوخ فقال له المعري و ما ذا تقول شعراؤهم فقال
يقولون:

رأس ابن بنت محمد و وصيه   للمسلمين على قـناة بـرفع
والمسلمون بـمنظر و بـمسمع   لا جـازع منهم و لا مـتوجع
أيقظت أجفانا و كنت لهـا كرى   و أنـت عنهـا لم تكن بك تهجع
كحلت بمنظرك العيون عمـاية   و أصـم نـعيك كـل أذن تسـمع
مـا روضـة إلا تمنت أنـها   لك مضجع و لخط قبر موضع

فقال المعري و أنا أقول:

مسح الرسول جبينه فله بـريق في اتخدود   أبواء من علبا قريش جده خـبر الجدوه
ولبعض الثامين:

يـا حسين بـن عـلي يـا قتيل بن زياد   يا حسين بن علي يا صريعا في البـوادي

709

لو رأت فاطم بكت بدموع كالعهاد   لو رأت فاطم ناحت نوح ورقاء بوادي

و لقامت و هي ولهاء و تبكي و تنادي   ولدي سبط نبي قد بالسمر الشداد

أ من شمر بغي كافر و ابن زياد   لعن الله يزيدا و ابن حرب لعن عاد

هم أعادي لرسول الله أنثاء أعادي   و لهم عاجل خزي و عذاب في النـاد

و مهاد في الجحيم إنها شر مهاد

ولبعض الشيعة

متى يشفيك دمعك من هـمول   و يبرد ما بقلبك مـن غـليل

قتيل ما قتيل بني زياد   إلا بأبي و نفسي مـن قتيل

أريق دم الحسين فلم يراعوا   و في الأحياء. أمـوات العقول

فدت نفسي جبينك من جبين   جرى دمه على خد نبيـل

أيخلو قلب ذي ورع تقي   من الأحزان و الألم الطـويل

و قد شرقت رماح بني زياد   بري من دماء بني الرسول

فؤادك و السلو فإن قلبي   سيأبى أن يعود إلى ذهـول

فيا طول الأسى من بعد قوم   أديـر عليهم كأس الأفـول

تعاورهم أسنة آل حرب   و أسياف قليلات الفلول

بتربة كربلاء لهـم ديـار   بسنام الأهـل دارسـة السلول

تسحبات و مغفرة و روح   على تلك المحنة و الحلول

و أوصال الحسين ببطن قاع   صلاعب للـدبور و للـغيول

بشرتنا يا رسول الله ممن   أصابك بالأذاء، و بالذحـول

ولمنصور بن النمري

يقتل ذرية النبي و يرجون   جنان الخـلـود للقاتل

ما الشك عندي في كفر قائله   لكني قد أشك في الخاذل

وللصاحب رحمه الله:

لا يشتفي إلا بسبي بناته   وجدتها التخويف و الإبعاد

إن لم أكن حربا لحرب كلها   فسفاني الأبـاء و الأجـداد

إن لم أفضل أحمدا و وصيه   لهدمت مجدا شأوء عباد

يا كربلاء تحدثي بلايا   و بكربلا أن الحـديث يعاد

أسد نسماه أحمد و وصيه   أرداه كلـب قـد نماه زياد

فالدين يبكي و الملائك تشتكي   و الجو أكلف و السنون جماد

ولسليمان بن فتة:

مررت على أبيات آل محمد   فلم أرها أمثالها حين حلت

فلا يبعد الله الديار و أهلها   و إن أصبحت منهم بزعمي تخلت

710

ألا ابن قتلى الطف من آل هاشم   أذلت رقاب المسلمين فذلت

وكانوا غيانا ثم أضحوا رزية   ألا عظمت تلك الرزايا و جلت

وأنشدني الإمام الأجل ركن الإسلام أبو الفضل الكرماني رحمه الله أنشدني الإمام الأجل الأستاذ فخر القضاة
محمد بن الحسين الأرسابندي لواحد من الشعراء:

عين جودي بعبرة و عويل   و اندبي ابن بكت آل الرسول

وأندبي تسعة لصلب علي   قد أصيبوا و خمسة لعقيل

وأندبي كلهم فليس إذا ما   ضن بالخير كلهم بالخيل

وأندبي ابن ندبت عونا أخاهم   نبي فيها بنوبهم يخذول

وسمي النبي غودر فيهم   قد علوه بصارم مسلول

قال فخر القضاة وأنشدني القاضي الإمام محمد بن عبد الجبار السمعاني من قيله:

بمحمد سلوا سيوف محمد   رضخوا بها هامات آل محمد

ولغيره:

محن الزمان سحائب مترادفة   هي بالفوادح و الفواجع ساجمة

وإذا الهموم تجاورتك فسلها   بمصاب أولاد البتولة فاطمة

وللصاحب كافي الكفاة إسماعيل بن عباد رحمه الله

عين جودي على الشهيد القتيل   و اتركا الخد كالمحيل المسيل

كيف يشفي البكاء في قتل مولاي   إمام التنزيل و التأويل

و لو أن البحار صارت دموعي   ما كفتني لمسلم بن عقيل

قائلا لله و النبي و مولاهم   علها إذ قاتلوا ابن الرسول

صرعوا حوله كواكب دجن   قتلوا حوله ضراغم خيل

إخوة كل واحد منهم ليث   عزين و حد سيف صقيل

أرسعوهم ضربا و طعنا و نحرا   و انتهابها يا ضلة من سبيل

و الحسين الممنوع شربة ماء   بين حر الظبي و حر الغليل

مستكلا بأبنه و قد ضمه و هو   غريق من الدماء الهمول

فجعوه من بعده بمرضع   هل سمعتم بمرضع مقتول

ثم لم ينصفهم سوى قتل نفس   هي نفس الكبير و التهليل

هي نفس الحسين نفس رسول الله   نفس الوصي نفس البتول

ذبحوه ذبح الأضاحي في قلب   تصدع على العزيز الذليل

وطئوا جسمه و قد قطعوه   ويلهم من عقاب يوم وبيل

أخذوا رأسه و قد بضعوه   إن سعي الكفار في تضليل

نصبوه على القنا قدمائي   لا دموعي تسيل كل مسيل

و استباحوا بنات فاطمة الزهراء   لما صرخن حول القتيل

حملوهن قد كشفن على الأقتاب   سبيا بالعنف و التهويل

يـا لكـرب بكـربـلاء عـظيم | و لرزء عـلـى الـنـبـي ثــقيل
كـم بكـى جـبـريل مـذ دهـاء | فـي بـيتـه صـارا عـلى جـبـريل
سـوف نـأتـي الـزهـراء تـنتـصـر | الـحـكـم إذ حـان محـشر الـتـعـديـل
و أسـوهـا و يسـلهـا و بـنـوهـا | حـولهـا و الـخـصـام غـير قـليل
و تـنـادي يـا رب ذبـح أولادي | لمـا ذا و أنـت خـبـر مـدبـل
فـينـادي بـمـالـك ألهب الـنـار | و أجـج و خـذ بـأهل الـغـلـول
يا بني الـمصطفى بكـيت و أبكـيت | و نـغـنـي لم تـأت بـعـد بـحـزل
ليت روحـي ذابـت دمـوعـا فـأبكي | للـذي نـالكـم مـن الـتـنـزيـل
فـولائـي لكـم عـتـادي و زادي | يـوم ألـقـاكـم عـلـى سـلسـل
لي فـيكـم مـدائـح و مـراثـي | حـفظت حفـظ محـكم الـتـنزيل
قـد كفـاهـا فـي الشـرق و الـغـرب فخـرا | أن يـقـولـوا هـي مـن قـبل إسمـاعـيل
و مـتـى كـدانـي الـنـواصـب فـيكـم | حسـبي اللـه و هـو خـبـر وكـيل

وللصاحب أيضا رحمه الله من قصيدة طويلة:

هـم وكـدوا أمـر الـدعي بـيزيد مـلفـوظ الـسـفـاح | فطـا على روح الـحسين و أهـله هم الـجمـاح
صـرعوهم تـنـحرهم نـحرومو نـحر الأضـاحـي | يا دمـع هي على انسجـام ثـم حـي على انـسفـاح
فـي أهل حي على الـصلاة و أهل حـي على الـفلاح | بـحـمـي يـزيد نسـاء بـين الشـفـائـد و الوشـاح
وبـنات أحمد قـد كشـف على حـريم مـتـباح | ليت الـنوائح مـا سكـنن عن الـنـاحة و الـمـصبـاح
يا سـادني لكم ودادي و هو داعـية امتـداحـي | و ذكـر فضلكم اغتـنـائي كل يـوم و اصطبـاحـي

قزه ابن عبـاد ولاءكم الصريح بلا بـراح

أقول: و قال ابن نـاس رحمه الله رويت إلى ابن عائشة قال مر سليمان بن قنة العدوي مولى بني تيم بكـربلاء بعد قتل الحسين (ع) ثلاث فنظر إلى مصارعهم فانكأ على فرس له عربية و أنشأ:

مـررت عـلـى أبـيـات آل محـمد | فـلـم أرهـا أمـثـالها يـوم حـلت
ألم تـر أن الـشمـس أضحـت مـريضة | لفـقد حسـين و الـبـلاد اقشـعرت
وكـانـوا رجـاء ثـم أضحـوا رزيـة | لقـد عظمت تـلك الـرزايـا و جلت
وتـسـألنـا قـيس نـنمـطي نـقبرهـا | و نسـقـتنا قـيس إذا الـسـعل زلت
وعـند غـنـي نـطرة مـن دمـائنا | سـنطلبهم يـومـا بـهـا حيث حـلت
فـلا يـبـعد اللـه الـديـار و أهلهـا | و إن أصبحت منهم بـزعمـي تخـلت
وإن قـتل الـطف مـن آل هـاشـم | أذل رقـاب الـمسـلمـين فـذلت
وقـد أصولت تـبكـي الـسمـا لفقـده | و أنـجمهـا نـاحت عليه و صلت

وقيل الأبيات لأبي الرمح الخزاعي حدث المرزباني قال دخل أبو الرمح إلى فاطمة بنت الحسين بن علي (ع) فأنشدها مرثية في الحسين (ع)

اللهم صلي على محمد و آل محمد

فلم تصح بعد الدمع حتى ارمعلت	أجالت على عيني سحائب عبرة
و ما أكثرت في الدمع لا بل أقلت	تبكي على آل النبي محمد
و قد نكأت أعداؤهم حين سلت	أولئك قوم لم يشيموا سيوفهم
أذل رقابا من قريش فذلت	و إن قتيل الطف من آل هاشم

فقالت فاطمة يا أبا رمح هكذا نقول قال فكيف أقول جعلني الله فداك قالت قل أذل رقاب المسلمين فذلت. قال لا أنشدها بعد اليوم إلا هكذا.

أقول ما قيل من المراثي في مصيبته صلوات الله عليه جمة لا تحصى و لا يناسب إيرادها ما نحن بصدده في هذا الكتاب و إنما أوردنا قليلا منها رجاء أن يشركني الله تعالى مع من يبكي و يفرح بها في ترابه و لذلك عدونا ما التزمناه في صدر الكتاب بذكر بعض القصص عن التواريخ و الكتب التي لم تكن في درجة ما أوردته في الفهرست في الوثوق و الاعتماد و تأسينا بذلك علماءنا الماضين رضوان الله عليهم فإنهم في إيراد تلك القصص الهائلة اعتمدوا على التواريخ لقلة ورود خصوصياتها في الأخبار على أن أكثرها مؤيدة بالأخبار المعتبرة التي أوردناها و الله الموفق و عليه التكلان.

العلة التي من أجلها أخر الله العذاب عن قتلته صلوات الله عليه و العلة التي من أجلها يقتل أولاد قتلته ۞ و إن الله ينتقم له في زمن القائم ۞

١ ـ ع: [علل الشرائع] إن: [عيون أخبار الرضا ۷] الهمداني عن علي عن أبيه عن الهروي قال قلت لأبي الحسن الرضا ۷ يا ابن رسول الله ما تقول في حديث روي عن الصادق ۷ أنه قال إذا خرج القائم قتل ذراري قتلة الحسين ۷ بفعال آبائها فقال ۷ هو كذلك فقلت و قول الله عز و جل «وَلَا تَزِرُ وَازِرَةٌ وِزْرَ أُخْرَى» ما معناه قال صدق الله في جميع أقواله و لكن ذراري قتلة الحسين يرضون بفعال آبائهم و يفتخرون بها و من رضي شيئا كان كمن أتاه و لو أن رجلا قتل بالمشرق فرضي بقتله رجل بالمغرب لكان الراضي عند الله عز و جل شريك القاتل و إنما يقتلهم القائم ۷ إذا خرج لرضاهم بفعل آبائهم فإن قلت له بأي شيء يبدأ القائم منكم إذا قام قال يبدأ ببني شيبة فيقطع أيديهم لأنهم سراق بيت الله عزوجل

٢ ـ م: [تفسير الإمام ۷] ج: [الإحتجاج] بالإسناد إلى أبي محمد العسكري عن آبائه ۷ أن علي بن الحسين ۷ كان يذكر حال من مسخهم الله قردة من بني إسرائيل و يحكي قصتهم فلما بلغ آخرها قال إن الله تعالى مسخ أولئك القوم لاصطيادا السمك فكيف ترى عند الله يكون حال من قتل أولاد رسول الله ۷ و هتك حريمه إن الله تعالى و إن لم يمسخهم في الدنيا فإن المعد لهم من عذاب الآخرة أضعاف أضعاف عذاب المسخ فقيل له يا ابن رسول الله فإنا قد سمعنا منك هذا الحديث فقال لنا بعض النصاب فإن كان قتل الحسين باطلا فهو أعظم من صيد السمك أفما كان يغضب على قاتليه كما غضب على صيادي السمك قال علي بن الحسين قل لهؤلاء النصاب فإن كان إبليس معاصيه أعظم من معاصي من كفر بإغوائه فأهلك الله من شاء منهم كقوم نوح و قرعون

اللهم تقبل منا انك أنت السميع العليم

سورة العلق

بِسْمِ اللَّهِ الرَّحْمَنِ الرَّحِيمِ

اقْرَأْ بِاسْمِ رَبِّكَ الَّذِي خَلَقَ ۝ خَلَقَ الْإِنْسَانَ مِنْ عَلَقٍ ۝ اقْرَأْ وَرَبُّكَ الْأَكْرَمُ ۝ الَّذِي عَلَّمَ بِالْقَلَمِ ۝ عَلَّمَ الْإِنْسَانَ مَا لَمْ يَعْلَمْ ۝ كَلَّا إِنَّ الْإِنْسَانَ لَيَطْغَى ۝ أَنْ رَآهُ اسْتَغْنَى ۝ إِنَّ إِلَى رَبِّكَ الرُّجْعَى ۝ أَرَأَيْتَ الَّذِي يَنْهَى ۝ عَبْدًا إِذَا صَلَّى ۝ أَرَأَيْتَ إِنْ كَانَ عَلَى الْهُدَى ۝ أَوْ أَمَرَ بِالتَّقْوَى ۝ أَرَأَيْتَ إِنْ كَذَّبَ وَتَوَلَّى ۝ أَلَمْ يَعْلَمْ بِأَنَّ اللَّهَ يَرَى ۝ كَلَّا لَئِنْ لَمْ يَنْتَهِ لَنَسْفَعًا بِالنَّاصِيَةِ ۝ نَاصِيَةٍ كَاذِبَةٍ خَاطِئَةٍ ۝ فَلْيَدْعُ نَادِيَهُ ۝ سَنَدْعُ الزَّبَانِيَةَ ۝ كَلَّا لَا تُطِعْهُ وَاسْجُدْ وَاقْتَرِبْ ۩

و آخر دعوانا ان الحمد لله رب العالمين

و الصلاة و السلام على أشرف الأنبياء و المرسلين محمد و آله الطيبين الطاهرين

اللهم صلي على محمد و آل محمد